EAGLE MOON OF CHANGE

Medium: Acrylic and mixed on paper

As First Nations People, we are in a time of rebirth. For many moons we have felt the pains of change, much of it through no fault of our own. History reveals many events which have not been kind to our people, but we will forgive and for the rest we will take our time to heal.

This painting Speaks of that healing, a healing that will take us all back to where we were meant to be in the great lodges of the creator. It will be the creator that will direct us all to our pathway. Once on this path, we can once more fly high like the great winged-one being, the eagle. We will look over this land, care for it, love it and protect it. For this land is knowledge and knowledge is the creator's greatest gift to all beings.

Dale Auger
1997

First Nations in Canada

Perspectives on Opportunity, Empowerment, and Self-Determination

First Nations in Canada

Perspectives on Opportunity, Empowerment, and Self-Determination

J. Rick Ponting
University of Calgary

McGraw-Hill Ryerson Limited
Toronto Montreal New York Auckland Bogotá Caracas Lisbon London Madrid
Mexico Milan New Delhi San Juan Singapore Sydney Tokyo

McGraw-Hill
Ryerson Limited

A Subsidiary of The McGraw-Hill Companies

FIRST NATIONS IN CANADA
Perspectives on Opportunity, Empowerment, and Self-Determination

ISBN: 0-07-552847-9

1 2 3 4 5 6 7 8 9 10   W   5 4 3 2 1 0 9 8 7 6

Printed and bound in Canada

Care has been taken to trace ownership of copyright material contained in this text. The publishers will gladly take any information that will enable them to rectify any reference or credit in subsequent editions.

Sponsoring Editor: Gord Muschett
Associate Editor: Margaret Henderson
Developmental Editor: Marianne Minaker
Production Co-ordinator: Nicla Dattolico
Cover Designer: Dianna Little
Cover Illustration: Dale Auger
Typesetter: Bookman Typesetting Co.
Printer: Webcom

Canadian Cataloguing in Publication Data

Ponting, J. Rick
    First Nations in Canada : perspectives on opportunity, empowerment, and self-determination

Includes bibliographical references.
ISBN 0-07-552847-9

1. Indians of North America–Canada.   2. Indians of North America–Canada–Social conditions.   I. Title.

E78.C2P655 1997   971'.00497   C97-931214-0

CONTENTS

ABOUT THE CONTRIBUTORS

Auger, Dale F.

Dale Auger is a Sakaw (bush) Cree from the Bigstone Cree reserve in northern Alberta. He has a strong grounding in traditional Cree spiritualism. He also holds a Master's degree in Education from the University of Calgary. An accomplished visual artist, singer, playwright, musician, and photographer, he is also a gifted story-teller and theatrical director. He uses a variety of media to break down cultural barriers and explain First Nation traditions and history to non-Natives. He has produced Native theatre in a variety of settings ranging from the conventional stage to a 500-metre-wide natural amphitheatre. His vivid acrylic paintings portray Native spirituality at its deepest and most powerful levels.

Brown, Rosemary

Since 1990, Rosemary Brown has been a staff member at Arusha, a centre which offers alternative resources and programming on social justice issues. She works in the area of anti-racism education and the global economy. She is a founding member of the Committee Against Racism, which has worked in solidarity with the Lubicon Nation's land claim struggle since the mid-1980s. A long-time activist in the feminist movement, she is currently a member of the Women's Committee of the Calgary & District Labour Council. She holds an Honours B.A. (1971) in African History from the School of Oriental and African Studies, London, England; an M.A. (1973) in African History from the University of Toronto; and an M.A. (1990) in Social Anthropology from the University of Calgary. She lives in Calgary with her husband, three children, and two cats.

Calliou, George

George D. Calliou is the Director of The Native Centre at The University of Calgary. A Treaty 8 Cree, he has extensive experience in a variety of roles where he has built bridges between aboriginal and non-aboriginal society. He is a member of the Calgary Police Commission, a founding member of the Calgary Chamber of Commerce's Aboriginal Opportunities Committee, and the City of Calgary's Aboriginal Urban Affairs Committee. He has served as Director of Native Affairs for a large oil company, as a community development worker, and as a private consultant. He and his wife and three children live in a residential development owned by the T'suu Tina Nation west of Calgary. They also own and operate a group home for aboriginal youth in the Calgary area.

Cockerill, Jodi

Jodi Cockerill is from Saskatoon, Saskatchewan. Even as a schoolchild in Masset, B.C., she came to appreciate various aspects of the culture of her Haida classmates. She subsequently obtained an M.A. degree in Political Science at the University of Calgary and is now a Ph.D. student in Political Science at Notre Dame University in Indiana. She specializes in classical western political philosophy and finds a certain compatibility between the ancient Greeks' conception of nature and the cosmos, on the one hand, and that of First Nations, on the other.

Crowfoot, Strater

Strater Crowfoot is Associate Executive Director of Indian Oil and Gas Canada, a division of the Department of Indian Affairs and Northern Development. He served eight years as elected Chief of the Siksika Nation in southern Alberta. Before that, he was economic development officer of the Siksika Nation. In the early 1990s he was a member of advisory panels to the Minister of Indian Affairs and Northern Development on such issues as the Lands and Trusts Review and *Indian Act* revisions to facilitate economic development on reserves. He currently sits on various boards, including the Indian Taxation Advisory Board. He represents the Indians of North America on the L.D.S. Church Social Services Board. With his wife Ellen, he is parent to six children. From Brigham Young University he achieved an undergraduate degree in Managerial Science (Accounting and Spanish) and a Master of Business Administration degree. He is the great-great-grandson of the famous Siksika Chief Crowfoot who signed Treaty Seven with the representatives of the Crown in 1877.

Dion Stout, Madeleine

Madeleine Dion Stout is a Cree from the Kehewin First Nation community northeast of Edmonton, Alberta. She earned her RN designation from the Edmonton General Hospital and later earned a Baccalaureate degree in Nursing from the University of Lethbridge and an M.A. in International Affairs at the Norman Paterson School of International Affairs at Carleton University. She is presently an Assistant Professor in the School of Canadian Studies at Carleton. She has been involved in a number of health organizations, including a term as President of the Aboriginal Nurses Association of Canada. In 1992 she was appointed Director of the Centre for Aboriginal Education, Research, and Culture at Carleton University. She has served on various equality-seeking boards, including the Legal Education and Action Fund (LEAF). She was also an appointee to the National Forum on Health.

Gibbins, Roger

Roger Gibbins (Ph.D., Stanford, 1974) is Professor of Political Science and former head of the Department of Political Science at the University of Calgary. He is the author of numerous books and journal articles on western alienation, political values, and First Nation matters. He is the co-author of *Out of Irrelevance: A Socio-political introduction to Indian Affairs in Canada* and co-director of the first comprehensive national survey of public opinion on First Nation issues. He is in high demand as a media commentator on political affairs. As a consultant to the Privy Council Office of the Government of Canada, he was intimately involved in the constitutional reform initiatives of 1990–91.

Kiely, Jerilynn

Jerilynn Kiely has a varied background. She attended The Alberta College of Art and, in an earlier career, held supervisory positions as a graphic artist in the business world. She is an experienced designer and facilitator of workshops on self-development. She has been extensively involved in immigration issues, including as a board member of the Calgary Immigrant Women's Association. She has also served on the executive of the board of Interfaith Youth Services in Calgary.

Presently she is in the Sociology M.A. programme at the University of Calgary in pursuit of an academic career as a professor of Sociology.

Légaré, André

André Légaré is a Research Associate and a Ph.D. candidate in the Department of Geography at Queen's University in Kingston, Ontario. He holds Master's degrees in both Geography and Political Science from Laval University. For the past ten years he has travelled widely in Canada's North and has written several articles on Nunavut in both English and French. He recently authored a monograph on the political and constitutional development of the Northwest Territories under the title *The Evolution of the Government of the Northwest Territories (1967–1995)*. He is a member of the GÉTIC (Inuit and Circumpolar Studies Group) of Laval University.

Ponting, J. Rick

J. Rick Ponting (Ph.D., Ohio State, 1973) is a Professor of Sociology at The University of Calgary. He has authored or edited two books and various articles on First Nations people, including *Out of Irrelevance* (1980, with Roger Gibbins) and *Arduous Journey* (1986). He has directed or co-directed two pioneering national surveys of non-Native public opinion toward Native people and Native issues. He has served as a consultant to government and First Nations. In 1996 he won the Rev. Dr. John Snow Award for outstanding service and dedication to Native students at the University of Calgary.

Symons, Gladys

Gladys Symons (Ph.D., York, 1976) is a Professor at the École national d'administration publique in Montréal. Her research and publications are in the areas of the sociology of Québec society, race and ethnic relations, gender relations, organization studies, and emotions. An affiliated professor at the University of Montréal, she is a member of the Group de recherche, Ethnicité et Société at that university's Centre for Ethnic Studies. Her recent work deals with policing and the social construction of the "Other" and she is currently working on a project studying police work and emotions. As a former president of The Association for Canadian Studies and the Regroupement québecois des sciences sociales, she has been active both nationally and internationally in interpreting Canadian society to others.

PREFACE

A NOTE ON TERMINOLOGY

When social relations in some sector of society are in a state of flux, the related language similarly exhibits change and instability. Gender relations provide a good case in point. The aboriginal peoples of Canada provide another.

The title of this book refers to "First Nations". That designation for those indigenous peoples who fall under the jurisdiction of the *Indian Act* of Canada has come into popular usage among political leaders and was endorsed by the Royal Commission on Aboriginal Peoples.[1] It is especially suited to aboriginal leaders who are pursuing a nationalist political agenda that focuses on wrestling jurisdictional responsibility away from other governments. Whether it would have come into widespread political use if the political agenda had been set by other actors with a greater concern for such issues as child neglect and personal healing is an open question.

Fashion in language use does change with changing sensitivities, ideological environment, and political threats and opportunities. Thus, in the era shortly after the release of the federal government's 1969 policy paper advocating an assimilationist approach, sensitivities to assimilation were particularly acute and the term "Native" was resisted by the leaders of those who fell under the jurisdiction of the *Indian Act*. They feared that its use was part of a larger government plan to strip them of their special rights and privileges under the treaties and the *Indian Act*, and to leave them in a similar situation to "non-status Indians" — that is, with the government having no fiduciary ("trustee-like") obligations to them. Hence, they preferred to be called "Indians". Yet, at the same time, others with identical legal standing rejected the term "Indians" as a grating reminder of the colonizers' ignorance and insensitivity in treating the highly diverse aboriginal peoples of "Turtle Island" ("the Americas") the same. Leaders of these peoples preferred such names as "Haida", "Kainai", "Dene", etc.

Among the laws of the dominant Canadian society is the *Indian Act*. This federal statute has been applied to one category of peoples — the descendants of most of those who have inhabited this land since time immemorial — known as "Indians" — but not to the Inuit — whose ancestors have also inhabited this land since time immemorial.[2] The federal government keeps a register of those who fall under the jurisdiction of (have status under) the *Indian Act*. Hence, they have been called "Registered Indians" or "status Indians". This book is about them — the First Nations people. Because they have been set aside for separate treatment under the law, their situation has come to differ markedly from those of both of the other types of people whom Canada's constitution recognizes as "aboriginal people" — namely, the Inuit and Métis. It is for that reason that the focus of most of this book is confined to Registered Indians. A notable exception is one chapter on the future government of Nunavut, the eastern arctic territory where the Inuit form a large majority.

At the level of social psychology or culture or experience with racism and discrimination, there is often very little difference between a "Registered Indian" (a "First Nation person") and many other indigenous people in Canada. Therefore, occasionally contributors to this book will refer to all three categories of aboriginal people in Canada, in general, using the term "Native" or "aboriginal". It is also because of similarities of culture and social psychology among the different indigenous peoples of Canada that authors will make the simple distinction between "Native" and "non-Native". Variations in use of terminology in this book largely reflect the predispositions of contributing authors. No attempt has been made by the editor to impose uniformity in this regard. I, myself, tend to use the terms "First Nation" (adjective) and "First Nations" (noun), but to avoid cumbersome terms like "non-First Nation", I usually use "non-Native" instead.

The demography chapter calls for a certain precision of usage that is not necessary in most other chapters. Reliant as much of it is on census data, demographic analysis must cope with potential confusion between national origin (e.g., an "Indian" as someone born in India or descended from someone who was), ethnic identification (whereby "North American Indian" would include persons who are not included in the federal government's Indian Register, plus those who are so-registered), and legal status ("Registered Indian"). To avoid ambiguity, the text of the demographic chapter will usually refer to "Registered Indian" or "status Indian" to signify that the data base from which a particular finding comes includes only those persons who fall under the jurisdiction of the *Indian Act*.

The closely intertwined themes of empowerment, self-determination, and opportunity are threads that wind their way through most of the chapters. These three terms are used here in a manner that is consistent with their usage by The Royal Commission on Aboriginal Peoples (RCAP). RCAP makes a conceptual distinction between self-determination and self-government wherein *self-determination* refers to the collective power of choice and *self-government* refers to one possible result of that choice.[3] This book deviates slightly from the Royal Commission by allowing for self-determination at the level of both the individual and the collectivity, and by assuming a close link in practice between collective self-determination and self-government. *Empowerment* can occur in a number of different realms of life, such as the economic, political, legal-constitutional, cultural, and spiritual. *Opportunity* refers to the availability of choices to enhance one's quality of life. Sociologists are especially interested in opportunity in terms of the probabilities of access both to occupational fulfillment and the attainment of satisfactory levels of physical, emotional, cognitive, and spiritual health. Sociologists are especially interested in self-determination in terms of "agency" — the power to be the proactive agent shaping one's own destiny rather than an "acted-upon object" who is victim of circumstance and subordination.

While editor and authors of this book might be inclined to imbue all three of the above themes with positive value judgements, we must bear in mind that non-Natives have no monopoly on corruption, tyranny, and other human vices and pathologies. While choice is implicit in opportunity, empowerment, and self-determination, one should not expect First Nation people to make the best choices one hundred percent of the time. Nor should observers be surprised when empowerment sometimes results in abuse of power or the pursuit of narrow self-interest. We know better than to hold unrealistically lofty expectations (as opposed to hopes and ideals) for non-Natives; neither should we hold them for Natives. To say that is not to condone corruption and greed; it is merely to warn against appying a double standard.

A NOTE ON COVERAGE

This book was conceived with the intention of making some of my published and unpublished work more readily accessible in the public realm than has heretofore been the case. However, that original purpose was transformed into one of providing an updated general introduction to the sociology of First Nations. In the process, I invited contributions from several First Nation individuals, three of whom are of Cree cultural background. Two of the chapters by non-Natives also focus on Crees (Lubicons and James Bay). By no means, though, is the resultant product, taken as a whole, applicable mainly just to Crees. On the contrary, with the possible exception of Auger's chapter on a Sakaw Cree philosophy of education, the vast majority of the book has applicability or major relevance to most First Nations; some has applicability beyond First Nations to the Métis and/or Inuit. Racism, public opinion, Supreme Court of Canada decisions, the *Indian Act*, claims-making, demographic change, leadership, self-determination, and many other phenomena studied in this volume are as relevant to Blackfoot (Siksika), Mohawk, Dene, Haida, and Innu, as to Mi'kmaq, Ojibwa, Slavey, and Algonquin, as to Cree. Furthermore, the theories and models used (e.g., Marx's theory of the articulation of modes of production, Spector and Kitsuse's theory of claims-making, Goffman's ideal-type model of the total institution) are usually of such a level of abstraction as to transcend the cultural boundaries between First Nations. Finally, even the contributions of Cree authors George Calliou and Madeleine Dion Stout draw heavily upon the experiences of non-Crees.

ACKNOWLEDGEMENTS

In addition to the many kind persons who are acknowledged at the beginning of certain chapters, I wish to take this opportunity to express my sincere appreciation to certain other individuals for their valuable contributions to this book.

Within The University of Calgary Department of Sociology, Margaret Duddy's logistical assistance and Lana Westergaard's technical assistance in preparing part of an earlier draft were much appreciated, as was Carol Lacey's role in making important resources available to facilitate the completion of the project. Dr. Thomas Huang, diagnostician and problem-solver extraordinaire, worked his incomparable computer magic on various file management, word processing, and statistical problems. Jerilynn Kiely was a dedicated and conscientious research assistant with whom it was a distinct pleasure to associate.

This manuscript was scrutinized by a mini-army of anonymous external reviewers who have since agreed to relinquish their anonymity that I might acknowledge them here. From universities across Canada and a spectrum of disciplines, they are: William Asikinack, Saskatchewan Indian Federated College; Kurt Bowen, Acadia University; Sheldon Cardinal, University of Saskatchewan; Ed Hedican, University of Guelph; Warren Kalbach, University of Calgary; Nahum Kanhai, University of Sudbury; Charles Menzies, University of British Columbia; Virginia Miller, Dalhousie University; Antonia Mills, University of Northern British Columbia; David Newhouse, Trent University; Robert Robson, Lakehead University; Victor Satzewich, McMaster University; Fred Shore, University of Manitoba; John Sorenson, Brock University; Roger Spielmann, University of Sudbury; and Linda Sutherland, Saskatchewan Indian Federated College. Their input is greatly appreciated.

At McGraw-Hill Ryerson, Sponsoring Editor Gord Muschett and his colleagues proved that large, multinational corporations can have a human face. This project owes much to Gord's personal commitment to making First Nation matters a priority field for McGraw-Hill Ryerson. To its credit, McGraw-Hill Ryerson backed this project with a generous allocation of resources that greatly facilitated its completion and effective distribution.

Also in the private sector, The Angus Reid Group Ltd. very kindly provided 1992 and 1994 public opinion data for Chapter Six. To Messrs Angus Reid, Darrel Bricker, and Glen Radewich, and their colleagues who prepared the data tapes for my use, I am indebted.

Numerous people in the Government of Canada were extremely helpful in various ways. Tony Reynolds at The Royal Commission on Aboriginal Peoples (RCAP), Andy Siggner at RCAP and Statistics Canada, Ellen Bobet at Health Canada, Jacques Desrochers and France Bernard at Indian Affairs, and Tina Hussein and Strater Crowfoot at Indian Oil and Gas Canada all stood out in this regard. Marlene Brant Castellano, formerly of the Royal Commission, was also extremely helpful.

I also owe a debt of gratitude to the contributors of various chapters in this volume. They graciously endured the rigours of producing their respective chapters so as to add their insight, knowledge, and experience to round out a volume that, if it had had to rely on my knowledge and contributions alone, would have been seriously deficient. Their patience with me is also much appreciated. Especially noteworthy in this regard is Dale Auger, whose enthusiasm for the spiritual revival among First Nation peoples has started me on another learning journey of my own.

The many students, Native and non-Native alike, whom I have taught in the Sociology 307 course at The University of Calgary have been a source of information and inspiration for me. It was they (especially Janice Soltysiak and the rest of the crew in Spring term 1995) who, by their reactions to the course, convinced me of the importance of completing this long-delayed project.

Dr. Beth Blachford was a source not only of more energy and support than she will ever know, but also of important insights into First Nation community functioning.

On the family front, Susan and Mike Ponting were very tolerant, understanding, and helpful vis-a-vis the disruptions and impositions associated with this undertaking. It is co-dedicated to them.

JRP
Calgary
December 1996

NOTES

[1] In each volume of the Royal Commission's final report a prefatory note on terminology states "… the term *First Nation* replaces the term *Indian*."

[2] Section 4 of the *Indian Act* explicitly excludes its *application* to the Inuit peoples.

[3] Royal Commission on Aboriginal Peoples, *Final Report: Restructuring the Relationship* (Vol. 2, Part One), Ottawa: Minister of Supply and Services Canada, 1996, p. 175.

First Nations in Canada

Perspectives on Opportunity, Empowerment, and Self-Determination

Introduction

CHAPTER 1

EDITOR'S INTRODUCTION

MODELS AND THEORETICAL PERSPECTIVES

The sociological realities lived by First Nation people in contemporary Canada are extremely complex and diverse. Some First Nations are large; some are small. Some have great resource wealth; some live in Third World conditions. Some have a large land base; others have "postage stamp" reserves. Some communities are remote; some are urban; some are in between. Some are said to be ruled by tyrants, others by democrats. Some have been physically relocated; most have not. Most First Nation individuals live on-reserve; almost as many (42%) do not. Some have lost their Indian status; some have regained it; some have never had to deal with the intricacies of the register provisions of the *Indian Act*. Some First Nations have private land tenure (certificates of possession); some do not. Some First Nation individuals have experienced the residential school first-hand; others only indirectly. The list of dimensions of variability could be elaborated at length to include employment status, educational attainment, degree of traditionalism, cultural origin, and others. No single model or theoretical perspective could possibly hope to adequately take into account even the broad contours of that diversity and complexity. Hence, this book is unabashedly eclectic in its theoretical approaches.

The book is by no means intended as a theory testing project. While models and middle range theories are invoked at various points as organizing devices to guide the choice of observations for inclusion in the text, much description is offered without theoretical road signs along the way. The sociology of First Nations is still a relatively young field of study which lacks theoretical cohesion and still stands in need of base line description, of which one useful form is "analytic description". Among other things, analytic description is description which employs the concepts, propositions, and empirical generalizations of a body of theory as the basic guides in analysis and reporting (McCall and Simmons, 1969: 3). In this volume, three of the concepts used are the themes in the subtitle: opportunity, empowerment, and self-determination. Analytic description is the approach taken at various points in the book, especially in the chapters dealing with demography and leadership.

Notwithstanding the above, this section provides a general orientation both to the types of theoretical foundations on which certain chapters of this volume have been built and to the theoretical context that surrounds a chapter. The chapter by Ponting and Symons on the conflict between the James Bay Crees and Hydro-Québec provides one of the more fully developed examples of the use of theory in this volume. The chapter itself uses claims-making theory and frame alignment theory to organize the descriptive data which depict the interactions in which these two actors are engaged. The concluding part of the chapter examines how "the new world order" can affect claims-making activities. In this introductory chapter the theoretical context is set by linking that "new world order" to world systems theory. Broader theoretical considerations also impinge on that chapter, for it stands as an object lesson in resistance to domination ("two-way flow of power") — a phenomenon which contemporary theorists (e.g., Parkin, 1979) urge sociologists to study.

The eclecticism of the collection of papers in this volume is evident in the fact that contributors focus not merely on *conflict theory's* "four Cs" — social class, conflict, contradiction, and control — but also on the meanings and interpretations which *symbolic interactionist theory* and *existential sociology* emphasize. Contributors draw upon not only macrosociological perspectives, but also microsociological perspectives. We turn now to these theories. At the end of the chapter we shall consider the issue of appropriation of voice.

A. Micro Approaches

Most micro approaches focus upon features of the setting of social interaction and upon meanings and interpretations of human interactions. As part of the latter we can include a focus on efforts at legitimating or de-legitimating a particular definition of the situation, as I do below in my consideration of claims-making.

i. The "Looking Glass" Self   Concern with the identity and sense of self-worth of First Nation individuals is found at various points in this volume. If not paramount, considerations of identity and self-worth are at least very important to any consideration of such topics as the legacy of the residential schools (editor's introduction to Part 2), stereotyping (Ponting and Kiely), family violence (Dion Stout), coping in the institutions of the larger society (Calliou), relating to the land and the larger cosmos (Calliou; Auger), healing and "getting on with life" (Dion Stout; Ponting), and even status politics (e.g., the quest for sovereign authority discussed by Cockerill and Gibbins). Fundamental to sociologists' understanding of the self is the notion that *the self is a social product*, an outcome of social interaction (Cooley, 1922). That is, we tend to form our self-image on the basis of feedback which we receive from others. When those others have seemingly absolute power over us and when they aggressively claim moral and spiritual authority for what they tell us and discredit our other sources of input about our selves, we are highly likely to accept their views of us. Just such an imbalance of power and style of discourse characterized the relationship between residential school children and the teachers and clergy at residential schools.

Similarly, when others repeatedly treat us as mere objects (e.g., sex objects or impersonal objects to be processed by a bureaucracy) or with abuse in the form of violence, ridicule, teasing, disdain, or condescension, we are prone to call into question our own worth, precisely because we are social animals. Labelling theory (Lemert, 1951) in sociology leads the social analyst to look for reactions to the stigma which others attach to us. Those negative labels (e.g., "irresponsible", "bad", "lazy", "promiscuous", etc.) can become *self-fulfilling prophecies,* for one result of the label being attached to us is that others begin to treat us differently, especially by closing opportunities to us. Once those opportunities begin to close, our options for coping are reduced.

These processes of formation of self, labelling, and reacting to labelling are very germane to the disempowerment of First Nation individuals. As Chapter Five notes, the sense of self-worth of residential school students and their children has been a common casualty of the residential school experience. As Dion Stout discusses, the problem can spiral into abuse in successive generations as low self-esteem increases the risk of individuals being both victims and perpetrators of abuse. The larger society's racism and stereotyping, discussed in the chapters by Calliou and by Ponting and Kiely, also contribute to First Nation individuals holding negative self-images. As Dion Stout asserts and the suicide data in the demography chapter attest, the anger and aggression which racism and stereotyping engender are sometimes displaced onto self or other members of the First Nation community. This displacement probably also helps to explain the "pettiness" which Crowfoot's chapter identifies as one of the obstacles with which First Nation leaders must cope in their communities.

ii. The "Total Institution"   A useful model for understanding the functioning of the residential school is Erving Goffman's (1962) model of the total institution which he developed on the basis of his covert participant observation at a mental hospital. Although Goffman did not formally define a "total institution", the following definition can be inferred from his work:

> A total institution is a confining formal organization usually intended to forcibly change people's behaviour and self-concept by means of the rigid structuring of daily routines and assault upon personal dignity and autonomy.

The authoritarian orientation that staff members of a total institution take toward the clients/inmates is made possible by: (i) the large power differential between the two strata of individuals within the organization, and (ii) the fact that the organization is so encompassing of the lives of the less powerful members as to break down the normal barriers between their spheres of sleep, work, and play, and organize almost all of their daily needs. This can be readily seen when we look at other examples of total institutions, such as prisons, armies, convents, orphanages, concentration camps, work camps, and boarding schools.

Goffman identified a pattern of similar experiences shared by the inmates of total institutions. The first of these he called *mortification of self*. Commonly inflicted upon inmates at the time of admission to the institution, this involved a "series of abasements, degradations, humiliations, and profanations of self" and was achieved through such processes as loss of name, role dispossession (e.g., loss of role as son or daughter), confiscation of personal possessions, treating the person as an object, removal of clues as to social status in the outside world, enforced deference, violation of one's informational preserve about oneself, loss of some civil rights, physical nakedness, imposition of the requirement of confessions, and degradation ceremonies.

A second common feature of the inmate experience is that inmates experience anxiety over their own safety, for both staff and other inmates pose dangers to their safety.

Thirdly, inmates in the total institution tend to be manipulated by a privilege system. In the total institution, privileges or rewards, often in the form of things previously taken for granted, are available in exchange for obedience to staff in both action and attitude, but are withdrawn for disobedience.

The fourth and fifth features of the inmate experience are loss of privacy and participation in activities which are incompatible with the inmate's self-conception. The inmate is never fully alone; instead (s)he is always under some form of surveillance or is with other inmates. That is just one contributing factor to the sixth feature — namely, acute stress.

Regimentation and forced compliance with petty rules for inmate conduct together constitute the seventh feature of the inmate experience in Goffman's ideal type. The final feature, secondary adjustments, refers to coping strategies and other practices that allow inmates to obtain forbidden satisfactions or obtain permitted satisfactions by forbidden means. These provide the inmates with a modicum of self-determination and, psychologically, enable the inmates to reject their rejectors (the staff). Inmates tend to develop a stratification hierarchy based on success at these adjustments.

In the editor's introduction to Part 2 of this volume I shall use this model to describe the residential school experience of First Nation children. From the foregoing, though, it is already apparent that to the extent that the model is applicable, the impact on the sense of self-worth of the children would be devastating.

iii. Discourse of Claims-Making   The basic premise of the *social constructionist* perspective (Spector and Kitsuse, 1987) in sociology is that issues do not exist intrinsically as problems or controversies waiting to be discovered. Rather, social problems are constructed by social actors. Sociologists using this perspective do not deny the gravity of many situations which come to be labelled as social problems. Rather, they believe that, as sociologists, their main contribution is to be made in furthering our understanding of the interaction dynamics that lead to societal acceptance (or rejection) of a definition of some situation as a social problem. Consider, for instance, the release of the final report of the Royal Commission on Aboriginal Peoples in 1996. The Commissioners engaged in concerted efforts to get the mass public and the federal government to accept the Commission's definition of the situation as one of great urgency. Readers who observed the futility of those efforts will appreciate the value of understanding the dynamics of the process whereby a particular definition of a situation comes to be accepted or rejected.

Social constructionist theorists contend that by crafting their discourse to appeal to prevailing societal values, social actors attempt to impose a particular meaning on a situation and try to make that definition of the situation normative.[1] From this perspective, then, social problems are conceptualized not as a condition, but as a kind of *activity* known as "claims-making". As Spector and Kitsuse (1987:72) note, "It is definitions that are socially processed. In this sense, we can say that definitions have careers".

Claims-making activity can take many forms, such as petitions, demonstrations, publicity "stunts ", blockades, boycotts, advertisements, presentation of briefs to regulatory agencies, manifestos, and acts of "terrorism". Responses to claims can define the claims as reasonable, or conversely, as rebellion, mental illness, criminal activity, or some other kind of deviance. Claims-making is couched in a vocabulary of discomfort (e.g., claims to being victimized) which seeks to resonate with the *values* held by a target population. Values are a resource, and the choice of values on which to base a claim is a strategic one. So, too, is the choice of forums for claims presentation. Some agencies selectively encourage or discourage certain kinds of claims, and sometimes the substantive nature of the claim is altered as it is rejected by one agency and taken on by another.

Claims-making is fundamentally an *interactive* process between contestants or between claimants and their targets. It often involves exchange of insults, imputation of motives and/or solicitation of experts whose legitimacy or credentials are used to refute the other's arguments. (The experts themselves, however, can acquire vested interests in a certain definition of the situation.)

The *frame alignment* approach to social movements (Snow et al., 1986) complements the social constructionist model discussed above. A "frame" is an interpretative scheme enabling individuals to perceive, identify, and label objects and events (Goffman, 1974). It is a set of categories through which we perceive and give meaning to the world. Frames organize experience and provide guides for action. "Frame alignment" is the process whereby an individual's interpretive orientations (frames) are linked with the interpretive orientations offered by "claims-makers".[2] Some set of interests, values, and beliefs is made to fit with the activities, goals, and ideology of the claims-makers.

There are various types of frame alignment processes, such as frame amplification, frame extension and frame transformation. They are discussed by Ponting and Symons in Chapter Eight, where we also identify some of the values to which claims-makers in the realm of First Nation affairs appeal. Elsewhere (Ponting, 1990), I provide a similar analysis of the discourse used by aboriginal peoples and the Government of Canada in their attempts to get a visiting delegation from the European Parliament to accept their respective definitions of the situation surrounding the "Oka crisis" of 1990.

iv. Existentialism   Existential sociology exists on the periphery of the discipline (Ritzer, 1988: 360–364). It is committed to the naturalistic study of social actors and their thoughts, feelings, and actions. Another central concern of existential sociology is the individual's sense of self — "the individual's total experience of being" (Kotarba and Fontana, 1984, cited in Ritzer, 1988: 364) — and incessant sense of becoming. This is of considerable relevance to Auger's chapter in this volume, but that is *not* to say that Auger is an existential sociologist.

Auger's chapter takes as its point of departure the dictum of the elders: "Go inside. Go and talk to your spirit, your soul". He calls this "exploring the Core". His exploration provides us with an insightful picture of traditional Sakaw Cree epistemology (ways of knowing). His ethnographic account is generous in sharing with the reader the feelings which Auger experienced while acquiring knowledge and acting upon his world. For instance, he articulates the feeling that came over him while weaving a basket under the tutelage of the Birch Woman, as follows: "I could feel the crossing of knowledge working through my fingers as I created the basket. The making of the basket and its result was not what this was all about. It was something greater: the pleasurable feeling you get when you can see the spiritual beings working together as one. Oh, how I felt so pure as one who creates. For the next several days I could feel the Spirit Beings with me, so clearly". Later in the chapter, he describes the Land as "the central core of their [Native peoples'] existence" and the Spirit Beings as crucial to expanding human consciousness into other realms ("crossing over to access knowledge from many sources", like the animals, birds, and trees) to make the knowledge acquired part of themselves. He laments the dominant society's emphasis, in its schools, on humans as only body and mind, for to a Sakaw Cree traditionalist that diminishes humans as also spirit and divorces the spirit from teaching and learning.

To go beyond this in trying to force Auger's chapter into the mould of existential sociology would do violence to his intentions in contributing the chapter and would accentuate the tenuousness of my own grasp of existential sociology. Suffice it to say, therefore, that there is at least a certain affinity between Auger's approach and existential sociology. Those who regard his chapter as out of place in a sociology book would do well to consider both that affinity and the fact that, in addition to the scientific method, there exists a multiplicity of ways of knowing. Sakaw Cree ways have served the Sakaw Cree well since time immemorial. We, as readers, are richer for our exposure to those ways.

B. Macro (Structural) Approaches

i. Colonialism Blauner (1969) and Frideres (1993: 3–8) identify the basic components of internal colonialism as:

- incursion of a foreign population into a geographic area already inhabited by an indigenous population and the subsequent forced integration of the indigenous people into the dominant society;
- constraint, transformation, or destruction of the culture and social structure of the indigenous people by policy of the colonizers;
- emergence of racism as a system of domination (including colour-based barriers to social mobility and to intergroup relations) and as a justifying ideology;
- administration of members of the colonized group by members of the dominant group, especially in such a way that the colonized are managed and manipulated in terms of their ethnic status;
- indirect rule (external political control through the use of "puppet" chiefs under the control of government);
- economic dependence of the indigenous people and exploitation of them for their labour; and
- provision of low quality social services.

After surveying the literature, Wotherspoon and Satzewich (1993: 8–12) offer a useful critique of this model. Four of their arguments are particularly relevant for our purposes. First, they note that the model contributes little to our understanding of off-reserve aboriginal people. Secondly, they point out that in treating the aboriginal population as homogeneous, the internal colonialism model fails to take into account significant divisions, such as those based on class, gender, ideology, and politics. Thirdly, the model treats the role of the state too glibly by failing to address other social, political, and economic relations that have a bearing on the state's policies toward aboriginal people. Finally, the model tends to portray aboriginal people as passive victims and fails to recognize their various forms of resistance. Despite these criticisms, Wotherspoon and Satzewich (1993: 11) conclude:

> [W]e do not question whether internal colonialism actually occurred. Clearly, a colonial relationship has characterized aboriginal and non-aboriginal relations in Canada.

However, we do question the ability of these models to understand these processes and grasp the wider social and economic sources of oppression of aboriginal peoples.

In Part 2 of the present volume, an effort is made to consider some of those wider social and economic sources of oppression. For instance, Brown's chapter on the Lubicon Lake Crees addresses the Marxian notion of clashing modes of production, while Ponting and Kiely's chapter addresses such forces as cultural racism, systemic racism, and non-Native public opinion. Also, world systems theory, while not explicitly incorporated into any of the chapters, is described below, for it does help us to take into account some of those wider social and economic sources of oppression to which Satzewich and Wotherspoon refer.

ii. World Systems Theory   The chapter by Brown on the Lubicons' struggle with governments and multinational oil and paper corporations and the chapter by Ponting and Symons on the struggle between the James Bay Crees and Hydro-Québec both cry out to be set in a larger theoretical context. Here world systems theory, originally developed by Immanuel Wallerstein (1974), is offered to that end.

Wallerstein's theory focuses, in the first instance, on international economic relationships. He sees three broad types of society in the modern world: industrialized, dominant, "core" societies, and economically weaker "peripheral" and "semi-peripheral" societies. Core societies, like the U.S.A., and now Japan and Germany, invest in peripheral and semi-peripheral societies because the core societies "need" the markets, resources, and labour of the peripheral and semi-peripheral societies. Canada is a semi-peripheral society. American corporations and consumers "need" northern Alberta's oil and natural gas and the James Bay project's power. Japanese paper companies, like Daishawa, and their customers "need" the fibre from northern Alberta forests. The Alberta government "needs" not only the royalty revenues derivable from the extraction of the oil and gas, but also the political credit derivable from the job creation in the forestry and oil and gas industries. Hydro-Québec, a state-owned corporation, "needed" both the export (U.S.A.) markets for the power that was to be generated by the James Bay II project and the financial support of foreign investors for that multi-billion dollar project. Hydro-Québec's political masters, the Québec government, needed the political credit derivable from job creation in the construction of the project. Such a constellation of vested interests on the part of specific players in the world economic system created near genocidal conditions for the Lubicons as the other players barged ahead with dogged determination in pursuit of their own interests. The Lubicons resisted, but to little avail. The James Bay Crees, starting from a better-financed base, more numerous in population, and with better access to national and international media close to home, were more successful in their resistance when they took that resistance abroad.

The world economic system posited by Wallerstein is also characterized by a penetration of technology, modes of organization, and other aspects of culture from core societies into peripheral and semi-peripheral societies. These facets of "globalization" are extremely important. For instance, they take the form of television and satellite receivers in even remote First Nation communities, such that the materialistic and sensationalistic (e.g., violence saturated) culture of the core society infiltrates First Nation communities and undermines allegiance to traditional values and norms. Dion Stout's chapter identifies assimilation, in the form of loss of respect for traditional values, as a factor contributing to family violence in aboriginal communities. Ponting's and Symons' chapter underscores the importance of a technologically advanced, globalized mass media for pressing First Nation claims.

Neo-Marxists would argue that most First Nation communities and individuals throughout Canada experience the direct or indirect impact of globalization on a daily basis. Corporate downsizing as a response to global competition diminishes employment opportunities for workers, including First Nation individuals. In addition, the fiscal "crisis" of the Canadian state in the 1990s was partly induced by tax concessions and other benefits bestowed upon corporations to attract them to, or retain them in, Canada. This results in less money being made available for addressing First Nations' needs. A similar outcome — insufficient money being made available to First Nations — arises out of the federal government's expenditures to open foreign markets for Canadian manufacturers. This was driven home forcefully when, within days of the Minister of Indian Affairs declaring that it would be difficult to get the Finance Minister to release the additional $1.5 billion per year that the Royal Commission on Aboriginal Peoples had just recommended be spent on ameliorating aboriginal conditions, the federal government announced that it would loan the Peoples' Republic of China over $1 billion to purchase a CANDU nuclear reactor from Atomic Energy of Canada Limited. Other instances of global economic forces impinging on First Nations would include the Innu of Labrador having to contend with multinational corporate giants like Inco Ltd. at Voisey's Bay (not to mention low-level N.A.T.O. training flights over Innu lands), and First Nations in northern Ontario and in British Columbia having to contend with multinational paper companies who seek to despoil their land. Yet other First Nations seek to sell into international markets or to place their labour (e.g., Mohawk iron workers) there. Clearly, then, the global economic forces identified in world systems theory and other neo-Marxian literature are an highly germane factor in understanding the situation and responses of First Nations as we embark upon the new millennium.

iii. Marxian Articulation of Modes of Production[3]   Modes of production is a Marxist concept crucial to Marx's theory of social change. According to Marx, a mode of production consists of the forces of production — for example, technology and resources — and the relations of production — the way people are related to each other, and to the resources and technology in the course of production. Further, the mode of production conditions social, political, and intellectual life. Marx explained the course of European history leading up to the development of capitalism as shifts from one mode of production to another. He stated that shifts occurred when changes in technology and resources outstripped the ways people related to each other. The ensuing contradictions led to changes in consciousness and subsequent transformations in political, legal, and social structures, which resulted in a new mode of production (Marx and Engels, 1846: 31, 42 and Marx, 1859: 503–504).

In the 1970s, some French anthropologists (Rey, 1973, 1975, 1979; Meillassoux, 1972, 1975) expanded upon the concept of modes of production in their analyses of colonial societies experiencing the introduction of capitalist relations of production. Known as French structural Marxists, these scholars considered these colonial societies to be composed of more than one mode of production. These modes did not exist side by side, but were articulated or interconnected and were in contradiction with each other. The points of articulation and contradiction were among and between the relatively autonomous but interconnected structures they saw as comprising each mode of production: the economic base (elements and relations of production), the juridical/political superstructure (legal and government systems), and the ideological superstructure (belief systems).

Brown uses this theoretical framework to examine changes in the roles and relationships of Lubicon Lake Cree women as their society, based on an hunting, trapping, and gathering mode of production, clashed with the larger Alberta society and its industrial mode of production. Her field observations of the Lubicon society grappling with the rupturing of its ties to the land led her to a partial reformulation of mode of production theory in a manner which better recognizes the centrality of women's reproductive roles and the social values associated with them.

iv. Structures of Accommodation   From a sociological perspective, treaties and comprehensive land claim settlements can be viewed as examples of what Grimshaw (1970) calls "structures of accommodation". Structures of accommodation are arrangements put in place to keep within manageable limits the conflict (actual or potential) that exists between two sectors of the population which stand in a relationship of subordination-superordination. Examples from outside the realm of First Nation affairs would include the system of equalization payments in Canadian confederation, the federal *Official Languages Act*, and the practice of regional representation in the federal Cabinet. Inevitably, Grimshaw's theory posits, conflict regulating mechanisms break down. That is, accommodative structures are fundamentally unstable and eventually lose their viability. This can occur in a number of different ways, many of which are related to real or perceived changes in the distribution of power. For instance, the subordinate group might gain in relative power through demographic change, internal organization, or outside assistance. Alternatively, subordinate group members might come to realize the latent power that they already possess. The dominant group or even the arrangements themselves might lose legitimacy due to corruption or abuse of power or the introduction of new perspectives on legitimacy (e.g., from anti-colonial movements elsewhere). To cite one final example from among others given by Grimshaw (1970: 19), a reversal after a period of rising hopes and expectations by the subordinate group could also precipitate a breakdown in the accommodative structures.

When accommodative structures break down, the relationship between the two parties becomes *contested terrain* on which a new accommodation is sought by the subordinate group and usually resisted or minimized by the dominant group. The contest for a realignment or at least a readjustment of the power relations between the two groups can be fought in a variety of arenas, some institutional (e.g., educational institutions, the press, the courts, the government bureaucracies, legislatures and legislative committees, constitutional negotiations, external tribunals) but some outside the institutions imposed and controlled by the dominant group (e.g., the armed resistance at Gustafsen Lake, Ipperwash, Oka, and elsewhere).

Grimshaw's theory can be applied to various aspects of First Nations' relations with the larger Canadian society. The treaty negotiation process launched in British Columbia in the mid-1990s and the earlier treaty renovation process in Saskatchewan are examples of the negotiation of new accommodative structures. Another example, on a grander scale, is found in the recommendations of the Royal Commission on Aboriginal Peoples for a new *relationship* between aboriginal people and the government of Canada based on a new Royal Proclamation that recognizes the *nation-to-nation* character of that relationship (RCAP, 1996a: 675–696; 1996b: 68). Indeed, the very title of the second volume of the Commission's final report — *Restructuring the Relationship* — and the commissioners' warning of the dire consequences of ignoring their advice, attest to the breakdown of the earlier accommodations and the need to replace them.

C. Theoretical Potential

The field of aboriginal affairs in general, and First Nation affairs in particular, offers fertile ground for theoretical development that can cast light upon many issues that have emerged as focal concerns of the great theorists of our times.[4] Just as aboriginal cultures have much of value to teach the larger Canadian society (e.g., about the natural environment, criminal justice, respect for the elders, individual autonomy, holism) so, too, do First Nation and other aboriginal communities have much to teach sociologists. That is, those communities are a strategic research site for a variety of pivotal issues in sociological theory. A few examples are provided to illustrate this point and to suggest possible directions for the future development of the field. There is a great potential here for exciting insights into Native society and the larger society, especially as the corps of Native sociologists increases over time.

Sociology in the 1980s devoted much attention to the matter of the linkage between macrolevel and microlevel social phenomena. In First Nation communities and individuals, macro- and microsocial forces are brought into bold relief. The system of colonial hegemony, with its legislation, its ideological structures (e.g., Christianity), its supporting administrative apparatus in the Department of Indian Affairs and Northern Development (DIAND), and its accompanying systemic racism, is ubiquitous in the daily lives of First Nation people in their families (or lack thereof), work places (or lack thereof), personal health, spirituality, and other realms. In one sense, the most macro of macrolevel analysis must be at the level of the cosmos. Auger's chapter in this volume shows one way in which First Nation traditionalists place themselves in interaction with the dynamic forces of the cosmos. At the microlevel that placement and interaction shapes their self-conception and their interpersonal relations within the community, while at the macrolevel it can shape institutions. For instance, the educational system advocated by Auger is a far cry from the bureaucratized school system of the larger society, just as aboriginal religion is a far cry from the bureaucratized Christian churches.

The marginality experienced by many aboriginal individuals, such as Bill C-31 reinstatees denied membership in the First Nation to which they previously belonged, is another point where the institutions of the larger society and the lived daily experience of the individual intersect and the institutional contradictions are embossed upon the psyche of the individual.

First Nations also offer potential insight into the dynamics involved in the larger society in the exercise of power and the persistence of domination. Anthony Giddens (e.g., 1984: 258, as cited in Grabb, 1997: 167–168) and others have conceived of power and domination as dynamic phenomena that are *regenerated* over time. Implicitly, Crowfoot's chapter entices us to explore the regenerative persistence of domination. The obvious measures, like the Department of Indian Affairs' obstructionism, bureaucratic games playing, and manipulation of resources, are highly germane to our understanding of the contemporary situation of First Nations. However, I submit that some particularly promising leads for future research on the regenerative persistence of domination are to be found in Crowfoot's attention to such normative phenomena as "authenticity tests"; nepotism and diffuse obligations; and informal social control designed to curb upward social mobility. Also beckoning the theorist in this regard is Crowfoot's discussion of ideology at the grassroots level of First Nation communities. That ideology emphasizes risk aversion and is preoccupied with allocative fairness. Important also to our understanding of domination is his discussion of social psychological factors such as the dependency, entitlement, and grievance mindsets; economic and cultural insecurity; and, especially, generalized distrust. Research which would focus on these and other factors in order to identify that which is unique to First Nation communities and that which can be generalized to other social settings of domination (e.g., gender domination) would be valuable in refining existing theories of social stratification such as Giddens' theory of "structuration".

To cite, but not develop, two last examples, Jurgen Habermas' theory of distorted communication as arising out of systematically distorted social structures and his notion of communicative interaction (Pusey, 1987) might be fruitfully explored in the context of the aftermath of the residential school experience and the consensual decision-making style which is very common in aboriginal society, respectively.[5]

APPROPRIATION OF VOICE

If this book were being written and compiled by a First Nation individual educated as a professional sociologist, what would be the main differences in content and approach from what the reader will encounter here? Should a book which professes to offer a general sociological introduction to this field of study be undertaken only by a First Nation person? These questions raise the issue of "appropriation of voice". It is best to confront it head-on.

Let us begin with my biases. I am not a First Nation person by birth, upbringing, tutelage, or formal education. Some broad precepts of aboriginal cultures I have come to appreciate and adopt, but that constitutes a very limited degree of assimilation on my part. My eclectic professional training within the discipline of sociology leads me to focus on cause-and-effect relations and conditions under which a relationship occurs; meanings of social phenomena for social actors; structures and processes; and power, conflicts, classes, and contradictions. Such emphases are very different from the emphasis of many aboriginal cultures on fate, spirits, and the cosmos. Yet, my socialization also taught me the evils of ethnocentrism and my upbringing in the Anglican Church has made me a spiritual person intent on being open-minded and cognizant of the severe limitations of knowledge gained through the scientific method in the physical and social sciences. In addition, my personal experiences have left me convinced of the validity of the Biblical adage "The Lord works in mysterious ways". Hence, I have no difficulty in accepting as true such stories as the one which Dale Auger relates in his chapter in this volume, wherein birds led a frustrated Cree hunter to the wounded moose that had earlier escaped the hunter's *coup de grace*. The intelligence of the birds and animals and the unity of all creation are not intimidating concepts.

The issue of appropriation of voice is a multi-faceted one. At one level it is about epistemology, the method or grounds of knowledge. As a means of knowing, sociologists value empirical research that can be replicated. The scientific method is sometimes held up as an ideal in this regard, but sociology as a discipline is sufficiently diverse to allow also for more subjective ways of knowing. Academics of any stripe, not just sociologists, also value book knowledge. A First Nation individual with a sociological education could, presumably, offer any of these types of knowledge, plus knowledge based on personal observation and experience as a First Nation person. Such an individual might also have been exposed to information and experiences, such as certain spiritual experiences and elders' stories, which would not be open to a non-Native. That would certainly give him/her an advantage and a claim to greater authenticity. This limitation of the present work must be recognized. However, as learners, we are particularly fortunate that First Nation authors have agreed to contribute to this volume.

Let us consider further this matter of authenticity or legitimacy. Bearing in mind that there is no one First Nation voice, we can ask: "Who is a legitimate authority on our subject? What constitutes being 'qualified' to write or teach on the topic?" The matter is not as straightforward as one might anticipate. For instance, might a First Nation person who has been born and raised on-reserve justifiably challenge the qualifications of a lifelong urban First Nation individual to write about reserve life? Also, let us not overlook the fact that a person who is "authentically Indian" for a non-Native might not be considered so by some other First Nation individuals. For instance, consider Strater Crowfoot, a former chief of a First Nation and heir of the legendary Chief Crowfoot who signed Treaty Seven. With credentials like that, a non-Native might consider him well qualified to write on the topic of First Nation communities. Yet, Crowfoot writes that his authenticity as an Indian was called into question by his political opponents.

At another level, the issue of appropriation of voice evokes concerns about values and differences in emphasis that a First Nation editor and a non-Native editor might exhibit when selecting chapters for inclusion herein. For instance, it is quite possible that a First Nation editor would dwell longer than I on the treaties, history, resistance, and the achievements of First Nation peoples. It is undeniably true that a person's values necessarily intrude on the practice of his/her profession. As learners, we are the richer for that. No claim to having a monopoly on knowledge about First Nations is made in this volume, and we can safely assume that readers of this volume know how to access other sources (books, films, world wide web sites, etc.) created by First Nations individuals.

To raise issues of the appropriation of voice is also to question the existing power structure. That is, not everyone is given the opportunity of having a platform such as this book to present his/her perspectives on the topic under consideration. In large measure, I have that opportunity now because I have had it in the past. That is, my record of having been involved in the field and having produced work that was acceptable to colleagues and editors, in combination with my experience teaching in this area, led the publisher to enter into the publishing contract with me for this book. That, in turn, raises the question as to who is being denied the opportunity, not only to publish, but even to amass a "track record" in the field? Of related concern is the question as to whose standards are the ones that a publisher or journal editor uses in choosing who will be asked to review a manuscript for publication consideration? Then, what standards will those reviewers apply?

Concerns about the appropriation of voice are, in part, also concerns that the sacred will be profaned unknowingly by those who have not been initiated into the spiritual mysteries. Consider, for instance, the fact that there will be persons who take issue with Dale Auger's sharing of some of the details of Sakaw Cree spirituality with the non-Native readers of this volume, for to them such sacred matters are not to be openly discussed. From the vantage point of his rich spiritual background, Dale Auger deliberated at length on his decision to make his chapter available. Conversely, my own spirituality did not equip me with the same sensitivities in my editorial role. Had a First Nation individual been serving as editor instead of me, out of respect for the sacred (s)he might never have approached Dale Auger about contributing his chapter.

To a large degree, concerns about the appropriation of voice are also concerns about bias in the form of distortion, one-sidedness, blindness, imposition of values, imposition of perspective, and the like. On these counts I am vulnerable as both author and editor in this volume. The filters which I bring to my work are the filters of the dominant culture and of a person educated as a sociologist. Examples of the relevance of this can be found in my treatment of community conflict and dysfunction. As a sociologist, I regard conflict as entirely natural and community dysfunction as an entirely understandable consequence of the dominant group's imposition of a colonial regime. Accordingly, in my capacity as editor I chose to make room for the inclusion of those topics, such as in Strater Crowfoot's chapter. A First Nation individual serving as editor might not only have considered that to be an inappropriately public airing of "dirty laundry", but might also have been concerned that its inclusion would give added life to non-Natives' stereotypes of dysfunctionality within First Nations. Accordingly, (s)he might have made the editorial decision to economize on production costs of this volume by excluding that same material.

From the above it is obvious that First Nation authors and editors face certain implicit pressures against which the non-Native is much more insulated. Examples of other topics for which public discussion has been taboo in many First Nation communities are child neglect, sex abuse, spousal violence, social class stratification, and the treatment of Bill C-31 reinstatees. Such taboos raise the question of whose interests are served if non-Native authors and editors, out of concern about appropriation of voice, refrain from publishing on these topics. It is ironic that some dominant group scholars who exhibit the utmost sensitivity to concerns about domination when viewed from the perspective of dominant group relations with a subordinated group, are blind to the same issues of exploitation that arise out of stratification and abuse of power within the subordinate group itself. In my opinion, to refrain from commenting on such issues out of concern with issues of appropriation of voice would be to take sides implicitly with the powerful within the subordinated group against the powerless members of that group.

Another issue in the consideration of appropriation of voice is that of language. Languages, of course, are not merely interchangeable sets of symbols for conveying common meanings. Instead, language shapes the very categories through which we perceive the world and therefore influences even our sensitivities. Hence, a speaker of only western languages would be oblivious to certain phenomena that his/her own language is incapable of conceptualizing. Related to that is the fact that some phenomena are simply not translatable from one language to another. Finally, whether consciously wielded as such or not, language is sometimes an instrument of power, particularly as utilized by an editor. For instance, if there were not close consultation between author and editor, the editor's efforts to push an author into greater analytic precision through the selection of particular vocabulary would run a high risk of distorting the intended meaning of the author who experiences the world in a more intuitive, holistic manner. Similarly, compared to me, an author/editor whose mother tongue is an aboriginal language would undoubtedly bring different insights to understanding the impact of the residential school or the significance of a political speech.

Of course, non-Natives should hear aboriginal perspectives on aboriginal people's situations. I have compiled certain perspectives; the reader is free to seek out others and juxtapose them with those presented here. Increasingly, aboriginal authors are making their voices heard in the print mode. However, the fact that aboriginal perspectives do exist on some matter does not necessarily invalidate non-aboriginal perspectives on that same matter. Rather, the two kinds of knowledge complement each other; neither is complete on its own. The fact that Native students in my course on the sociology of First Nations report having learned much in the course leads me to believe that there will long be a place for non-Natives to write and teach about First Nations.

NOTES

[1] A definition of a situation becomes normative when it is widely shared and violations of it are met with at least mild negative sanctions, such as ridicule or teasing.

[2] Snow et al. focus on social movement organizations as claims-makers.

[3] Most of this sub-section on modes of production theory was written by Rosemary Brown.

[4] See Grabb (1997), Ritzer (1988), and Tavistock Publications' *Key Sociologists* series (e.g., Pusey, 1987) for convenient summaries of these focal concerns and how they have been addressed.

[5] I am grateful to Bruce McGuigan for drawing this to my attention.

REFERENCES

Cooley, Charles Horton
1922   *Human Nature and the Social Order.* New York: Scribner's.
Frideres, James S.
1993   *Native Peoples in Canada.* Scarborough, Ont.

Giddens, Anthony
1984 *The Constitution of Society.* Berkeley: University of California Press.
Goffman, Erving
1962 *Asylums: Essays on the Social Situation of Mental Patients and Other Inmates.* Chicago: Aldine.

1974 *Frame Analysis: An Essay on the Organization of Experience.* Cambridge, Mass: Harvard University Press.
Grabb, Edward G.
1997 *Theories of Social Inequality: Classical and Contemporary Perspectives.* Third Edition. Toronto: Harcourt Brace.
Grimshaw, Allen D.
1970 "Interpreting Collective Violence: An Argument for the Importance of Social Structure", *Annals of the American Academy of Political and Social Science* Vol. 391: 9-20.
Kotarba, Joseph A. and Andrea Fontana (eds.)
1984 *The Existential Self in Society.* Chicago: University of Chicago Press.
Lemert, Edwin M.
1951 *Social Pathology.* New York: McGraw-Hill.
Marx, Karl
1859 "Preface To A Critique of Political Economy", pp. 502–506 in *Marx and Engels: Selected Works.* Moscow: Progress Publishers (1969).
Marx, Karl and Frederick Engels
1846 "Chapter 1 of *The German Ideology*", pp. 16–47 in *Marx and Engels: Selected Works.* Moscow: Progress Publishers (1969).
McCall, George and J.L. Simmons
1969 *Issues in Participant Observation.* Don Mills, Ont.: Addison-Wesley.
Meillassoux, Claude
1972 "From Reproduction to Production: A Marxist Approach to Economic Anthropology." *Economy and Society 1*, no. 1: 93–105.

1975 *Maidens, Meal and Money: Capitalism and the Domestic Community.* Cambridge: Cambridge University Press.
Parkin, Frank
1979 Marxism and Class Theory: A Bourgeois Critique. London: Tavistock.
Ponting, J. Rick
1990 "Internationalization: Perspectives on an Emerging Direction in Aboriginal Affairs", *Canadian Ethnic Studies*, XXII, 3: 85–109.
Pusey, Michael
1987 *Jurgen Habermas.* London: Tavistock.
Rey, Pierre-Philippe.
1973 *Les Alliances des Classes.* Paris: Francois Maspero.

1975 "Les formes de la decomposition des sociétés précapitalistes au nord Togo..." In Samir Amin (ed.), *L'Agriculture Africaine et le capitalisme*, Paris: Editions Anthroposidep.

1979 "Class Contradictions in Lineage Societies". *Critique of Anthropology* IV, nos. 13 and 14: 41-60.

Ritzer, George
1988   *Contemporary Sociological Theory*. Second Edition. New York: Knopf.
Royal Commission on Aboriginal Peoples
1996a   *Report of the Royal Commission on Aboriginal Peoples: Vol. 1 — Looking Forward, Looking Back*. Ottawa: Minister of Supply and Services Canada.

1996b   *Report of the Royal Commission on Aboriginal Peoples: Vol. 2 — Restructuring the Relationship*. Ottawa: Minister of Supply and Services Canada.
Snow, David A. et al.
1986   "Frame Alignment Processes, Micromobilization, and Movement Participation", *American Sociological Review*, Vol. 51: 464–481.
Spector, Malcolm and John I. Kitsuse
1987   *Constructing Social Problems*. Hawthorne, New York.: Walter de Gruyter.
Wallerstein, Immanuel
1974   *The Modern World System*. New York: Academic Press.
Wotherspoon, Terry and Vic Satzewich
1993   *First Nations: Race, Class, and Gender Relations*. Scarborough, Ont.: Nelson Canada.

CHAPTER 2

HISTORICAL OVERVIEW AND BACKGROUND: PART I[1]

Roger Gibbins

A proper understanding of the contemporary situation of First Nations in Canada is impossible without some understanding of the diversity of the aboriginal population, and some flavour of the history of relations between First Nations and the rest of Canada since at least the mid-nineteenth century. This chapter provides that contextual information.

From the outset, the difference between status ("registered") Indians and nonstatus Indians must be noted. Status Indians, who are the focal concern of this book and of whom there were about 611,000 in 1996, are persons who fall under the legal jurisdiction of the federal *Indian Act* and therefore have their names included on a register kept by the Department of Indian Affairs and Northern Development (DIAND). Nonstatus Indians are either (i) former registered Indians who have lost their registered status by marriage to a non-Indian or by a process (discussed later) known as enfranchisement, or (ii) the offspring of such persons. Métis are the offspring of a mixed (Indian and non-Indian) marriage. Métis are sometimes known as "half-breeds" and sometimes identify themselves as nonstatus Indians. However, as Sealey and Lussier (1975) have demonstrated, many Métis have a distinct Métis self-identity which contrasts sharply with a First Nation identity, and is sometimes based in part upon the larger society's denial to Métis of rights and privileges which are held by status Indians.

In addition to Métis, status Indians, and nonstatus Indians, the aboriginal or "Native" peoples include the Inuit population in Canada who, in 1996, numbered about 42,500, including over 8,200 in northern Québec who have been served by the Indian and Inuit Affairs Programme of DIAND rather than by DIAND's Northern Development Programme or by the governments of the Northwest Territories and Yukon.

The vast majority of First Nation individuals ("status Indians") are members of a band, which is a political-administrative unit created by the federal government. Notable exceptions are individuals who have been reinstated as Registered Indians under Bill C-31 (see footnote #3) but who have been denied membership in their former band under its formal membership code. Contrary, to the frequent usage of the term "treaty Indian" in the popular media, not all Registered Indians are treaty Indians. Indeed, in many parts of Canada, treaties were never signed (nor offered) such that today only about 57% of all status Indians are also treaty Indians. Map 1 shows those parts of the country which are covered by treaty.

MAP 1 Treaty Areas of Canada

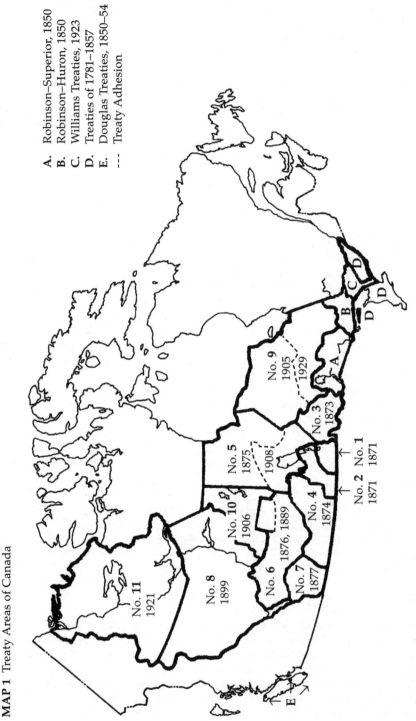

A. Robinson–Superior, 1850
B. Robinson–Huron, 1850
C. Williams Treaties, 1923
D. Treaties of 1781–1857
E. Douglas Treaties, 1850–54
--- Treaty Adhesion

No. 9 1905 1929
No. 3 1873
No. 5 1875 1908
No. 1 1871
No. 2 1871
No. 4 1874
No. 10 1906
No. 6 1876, 1889
No. 7 1877
No. 8 1899
No. 11 1921

Source: Adapted from Map 15-6 Canada: Indian Treaties. Copyright © 1991 Department of Energy, Mines and Resources Canada.

The First Nation population is extremely diverse ethnically. Indeed, different peoples whom Canadians of European ancestry group together under the term "Native Indian", have long thought of themselves as quite separate (e.g., Cree, Mi'kmaq, Haudenosaunee, Haida, Dogrib). This self-definition of separateness is reinforced by different ecological adaptations to quite different physical environments, with resultant major variation in symbolic and material culture and in economies in earlier times. Geographical and linguistic barriers once reinforced these contrasts. Thus, it is not very realistic for other Canadians to expect "Indians" to be able to develop unity and sustain it for a lengthy period of time. However, notwithstanding the ethnic diversity within the First Nation population, there is one thing which all First Nations in Canada have held in common, at least since the middle of the nineteenth century. This factor, one of the central features in the daily lives of First Nation individuals, is First Nations' relationship with the Government of Canada, especially as that relationship has been mediated through the *Indian Act* and its predecessor statutes. It is to a consideration of these that we now turn.

THE INDIAN ACT OF 1876 AND ITS EVOLUTION [2]

The *Indian Act* is of great importance because it touches, and not lightly, virtually every aspect of First Nation individuals' lives. As Dr. Munro, former assistant deputy minister of the Indian Affairs Branch, describes it:

> The *Indian Act* is a Lands Act. It is a Municipal Act, and Education Act and a Societies Act. It is primarily social legislation, but it has a very broad scope: there are provisions about liquor, agriculture and mining as well as Indian lands, band membership and so forth. It has elements that are embodied in perhaps two dozen different acts of any of the provinces and overrides some federal legislation in some respects. ... It has the force of the Criminal Code and the impact of a constitution on those people and communities that come within its purview."

(Cited in Doerr, 1974: 40)

Thus, in the scope of its impact upon the lives of individuals, the *Indian Act* approximates what sociologists call a "total institution". Furthermore, it is in many respects the *Indian Act*, and not the treaties, that defines the relationship between First Nations and the broader Canadian society. Yet, it is the treaties and not the *Act* that protect land, hunting, fishing, and trapping rights, to the extent that this is done at all. The treaties and the *Act* are not two sides of the same coin — while the former provide a limited form of protection, the latter provides a comprehensive mechanism of social control.

Definition of "Indian"

Under the *Indian Act* of 1876, an "Indian" became any male person of Indian blood reputed to belong to a particular band, any child of such person, and any woman who is or was lawfully married to such a person. Excluded from Indian status were persons living continuously five years or more in another country, Indian women marrying non-Indian men and, in some cases, illegitimate children. Through this definitional exercise the *Indian Act* fragmented the aboriginal population in Canada into legally and legislatively distinct blocs experiencing quite different rights, restrictions and obligations. The contemporary conflicts among status Indians, nonstatus Indians, and Bill C-31 reinstatees are today's legacy of this definitional approach. However, readers should bear in mind that while the *Indian Act* applies only to Indians as defined by the *Act*, the responsibilities and legislative prerogatives of the federal government are not so limited. In contrast to usage in this book, the term "Indian" has been more broadly interpreted with respect to the *British North America Act* (now known as the *Constitution Act, 1867*) than it has been within the *Indian Act*. Thus, while Parliament has the power to legislate for all Natives, under the *Indian Act* Parliament chooses to make laws only for some.

The *Indian Act* set forth a process of enfranchisement whereby registered Indians could acquire full Canadian citizenship by severing their ties to the Native community. The *Act* also laid down the framework for a limited form of local government and for the election of chiefs and councils: "the Government no doubt assumed that substitution of limited local administration for existing tribal organizations would accelerate the assimilation process" (Miller et al., 1978: 66).

First Nation Lands

Clause 25 of the *Act* retained the government's guardianship of First Nation lands. Land surrender procedures were put in place by the *Act* to protect First Nation interests in the conveyance process. In this and related sections, the *Act* establishes what might be termed "boundary-maintenance" mechanisms for the First Nation societies, mechanisms that First Nations were unable to provide internally (Weaver, 1973: 5). These mechanisms protected First Nation societies by inhibiting assimilation.

First Nation land was also protected in part through clauses which "... excluded Indian people from taxes, liens, mortgages or other charges on their lands and from loss of possessions through debt or through pawns for intoxicants" (Miller et al., 1978: 66). However, while protecting First Nation land, these provisions often made it almost impossible for First Nations to raise outside investment capital, for potentially valuable First Nation land cannot be mortgaged. Thus, First Nations usually have had to rely on the federal government for the capital needed to promote economic development. These provisions of the *Act*, necessary as they once might have been, now serve as a shackle on First Nation self-reliance. Amendments such as the so-called Kamloops Amendment in the 1980s have attempted to circumvent these provisions of the *Act*.

Concentration of Authority

Over the long run the most contentious aspect of the *Indian Act* was the sweeping power that it gave to administrators and to the federal government. The *Indian Act* extended the regulatory reach of the government into virtually every nook and cranny of First Nation life. Unlike other Canadians, First Nations were not faced with a plurality of governments and government departments but with a single government and single department. Although the *Act* presented a veneer of self-government and of First Nation individuals' participation in the control of their lives, even the veneer was an illusion.

The *Indian Act* was administered in the First Nation communities by the Indian agent. In the words of Manuel and Posluns (1974: 54), "it was the job of these new white chiefs to displace our traditional leaders in their care over our day-to-day lives in order to bring our way of life into line with the policies that had been decreed in Ottawa". To assist him in this task the agent, like the head of other total institutions (e.g., the prison warden), had an extraordinary range of administrative and discretionary powers; he was an instrument of social control par excellence. Because of his sweeping powers, the agent inevitably generated a state of dependency among his First Nation clientele. Also, because the agent personified the *Indian Act* and the character of the relationship between First Nations and the government, he became the focal point for First Nation hostility and anger, no matter how repressed. Despite the admirable personal qualities of some agents, few First Nation leaders today would contest Manuel's and Posluns' description of the Indian agent as a destructive force within First Nation communities.

In large part it has been the social control features of the *Indian Act* that have placed First Nations in the position of a colonized people. In this respect Harold Cardinal (1969: 43–44) asserts that "...instead of implementing the treaties and offering much-needed protection to Indian rights, [the *Indian Act*] subjugated to colonial rule the very people whose rights it was supposed to protect". He goes on to argue (1969: 45) that the *Indian Act* "...enslaved and bound the Indian to a life under a tyranny often as cruel and harsh as that of any totalitarian state". Paradoxically, however, the *Act* is also perceived by some First Nations today as one of the major protections for First Nation rights (as discussed later in this chapter), and plans for its abolition in 1969 met with vociferous First Nation opposition.

Amendments to the Act

The *Indian Act* has been subjected to frequent legislative fine-tuning and amendment. However, prior to the amendments introduced into Parliament in 1996, very few of its basic features have ever been altered,[3] such that the legislation governing First Nation affairs in the 1990s bears a close resemblance to the *Act* passed in 1876.

The passage of amendments to the *Indian Act* in 1889 demonstrated a move to greater government control over First Nation education, morality, local government and land. For example, the government was given the power to override a band's reluctance to lease reserve land. In 1920 the Conservative government, led by Arthur Meighen and displaying his same insensitivity to minority views that had already won the lasting antipathy of French Canadians, passed legislation empowering the government to order the enfranchisement of qualified First Nation individuals without any such request from the individuals concerned. The *Indian Act* was also amended in 1924 to give the Superintendent-General of Indian Affairs responsibility for Canada's Inuit population (then known as "Eskimos"). Interestingly, though, the *Indian Act* itself is not applied to the Inuit, in part due to the feeling that the Act was doing little to help First Nations and that the problem should not be compounded by extending its coverage to other groups. (See note #2 in Preface.)

The 1951 *Indian Act*, like its predecessors, was framed to promote the integration and assimilation of First Nation individuals into Canadian society. The main features of the 1876 legislation had not been altered, although the revised *Act* reduced the degree of government intrusion into the cultural affairs of First

Nations. The prohibition on the potlatch was repealed, First Nation individuals were now allowed to consume liquor in public places, and the provision that allowed a First Nation person to be enfranchised without his/her consent was dropped, as was a 1927 ban on political organizing and collection of funds for land claims. In general the powers of the Minister were curtailed, although they remained formidable.

A change of at least major symbolic significance occurred in 1960 when legislation prohibiting residents of reserves from voting in federal elections was repealed. Enfranchisement ceased to be held out as an enticement for assimilation. Citizenship and assimilation were no longer equated; one could be both a First Nation person and a full-fledged Canadian citizen. That had been largely prevented by previous federal legislation.

In the 1960s the *Indian Act* still dominated First Nation affairs in Canada. However, it should be noted that with the general expansion of government activity after the Second World War, First Nations came to be affected by an array of federal and provincial legislation from which the *Indian Act* and the treaties offered little shelter. As Cardinal (1973: 97) has written, "it is difficult for Indian people to understand that many decisions that vitally affect them are made for reasons totally unrelated to the Indian scene and without regard to their effect on the [First Nations]". Thus, as First Nations today try to redefine their relationship with the government and with the larger Canadian society, more than the *Indian Act* and the constitution is at issue. To mention but a few illustrations, the Fisheries Act, the Migratory Birds Convention Act, and provincial fish and game regulations all come into play.[4]

THE EVOLUTION OF FIRST NATION POLICY

The confinement of legislative activity in Indian affairs to the national government and the legislative dominance of the *Indian Act* — compared to over 4,000 separate and unsystemized statutory enactments in the United States — make the evolution of First Nation policy relatively easy to follow (Harper, 1946: 298). There are, of course, some complications. For example, the policies of the national government, particularly in the early decades after Confederation, were often different in eastern Canada than they were in the west. Prime Minister Macdonald, for instance, in discussing 1880 legislation that restricted the sale of agricultural products by the First Nations of western Canada, commented that the "wild nomads of the North-West" could not be judged on the same basis as the First Nations of Ontario. Nevertheless, the major threads of public policy can be readily followed. Several major goals or policy motifs can be isolated and these will now be discussed in turn.

Protection

The officials who forged Canadian First Nation policy were not imbued with an overly noble view of white society. While they might have believed that European civilization was unsurpassed in the advantages it had to offer, they were acutely aware of the evils of drink, greed, dishonesty and prostitution that flourished in great abundance, particularly on the edge of the frontier. Thus, one of the earliest and most humanitarian goals of First Nation policy was the protection of First Nations from the manifest evils of the white society. This goal led to laws prohibiting: the private sale of First Nation land, First Nation consumption of alcohol, and the prostitution of First Nation women. The reserve system itself was in part a device to isolate and protect First Nations, while at the same time becoming "...the cradle of the Indian civilizing effort and the means of securing the white man's freedom to exploit the vast riches of a growing dominion" (Harper, 1945: 132). The prominence of protection as a policy goal, faded over time, although as late as 1930 there was an amendment to the *Indian Act* restricting the use of poolrooms by Registered Indians, and it was not until the 1960s that all prohibitions on Registered Indians' use of liquor were removed.

The policy of protection, guardianship, or wardship fostered in the administration of Indian affairs an air of paternalism that has been difficult to dispell. The development of paternalistic attitudes was understandable given the early history of contact in North America. First Nations had not been successful in defending themselves or their land in the face of advancing settlement and the government had become a buffer between the First Nations and the crush of settlers. However, rather than acting as an impregnable wall, the government pursued the more limited goal of temporarily protecting First Nations until they could be assimilated into the white society. This protective stance led in turn to the attitude that First Nation people's views on their own welfare were not to be given much weight, that the government knew the best interest of the First Nation people in the long run. This outlook, coupled with the sweeping powers of the *Indian Act* and the high proportion of former military men and clergymen in the Indian Affairs bureaucracy, entrenched paternalism within the Department.

Assimilation

If there has been a central pillar to the Government of Canada's policy toward First Nation people, it has been the goal of assimilation. While the terminology has varied among "assimilation," "integration," "civilization," and "moving into the mainstream," the policy remained virtually unaltered for generations after the first *Indian Act*: First Nation individuals were to be prepared for absorption into the broader Canadian society. It was expected that eventually First Nation individuals would shed their Native languages, customs and religious beliefs, and would become self-sufficient members of the modern Canadian society and labour force. In 1880 Sir John A. Macdonald, speaking as Minister of Indian Affairs, stated that government policy towards First Nations was:

> ...to wean them by slow degrees, from their nomadic habits, which have become almost an instinct, and by slow degrees absorb them on the land. Meantime, they must be fairly protected.

> (Cited in Miller et al., 1978: 191)

In 1950 the then-Minister, Walter E. Harris, announced a new First Nation policy that echoed the words of Macdonald seventy years earlier:

> The ultimate goal of our Indian policy is the integration of the Indians into the general life and economy of the country. It is recognized, however, that during a temporary transition period ... special treatment and legislation are necessary.

> (Cited in Miller et al., 1978: 191)

In the intervening years, interpretations of First Nation policy followed the same theme. In 1920, for instance, the Deputy Superintendent-General of Indian Affairs spoke as follows to a Special Committee of the House of Commons on proposed changes in the enfranchisement provisions of the *Indian Act*:

>...our object is to continue until there is not a single Indian in Canada that has not been absorbed into the body politic and there is no question, and no Indian Department; that is the whole object of this Bill.

(Cited in Miller et al., 1978: 114)

After the end of the Second World War, when the period of settlement and treaty-making was long past and when the process of assimilation was well underway, the complete assimilation of First Nations into the Canadian mainstream became a less pressing concern. In the postwar years there was an increased acceptance of cultural pluralism, and the positive aspects of First Nation traditions began to be entertained. Nevertheless, the principle of assimilation that had guided First Nation policy over the past hundred years was neither abandoned nor fundamentally modified. Some First Nation leaders in the 1990s contend that it still has not been abandoned to this date.

The goal of assimilation raises the very sensitive issue of cultural genocide. The word "genocide", one of the most emotionally charged in the English language, must be used with caution. Nevertheless, the primacy of assimilation as a policy goal gives credence to First Nation claims that cultural genocide has been at least an implicit goal in the administration of Indian affairs. When an outside observer (Harper, 1945: 127) concludes that "the extinction of Indians as Indians" is the ultimate end of Canadian public policy, the charge of genocide cannot be lightly brushed aside. In addition, Patterson (1972: 63, 74) notes that not only were bounties placed on the heads of the Beothuk indigenous people in Newfoundland, but the British General Jeffrey Amherst waged biological warfare against the First Nations. He distributed to First Nation people blankets known to be infected with smallpox, when it was also known that the disease was often fatal to First Nation individuals due to their lack of natural immunity to it.[5]

Despite the zeal with which assimilation was pursued, the policy largely failed. Due to First Nation people's isolation on reserves, racial and linguistic distinctiveness, marginality to the labour force, and the gulf between Native and European cultural patterns, First Nation individuals proved to be difficult people to assimilate. A large part of the responsibility for the failure of assimilation must be laid at the feet of the broader Canadian society, for the obstacles posed by societal discrimination and prejudice were immense. Government policy tried to induce First Nation individuals into a mainstream that was unwilling to receive them.

Christianity

The policy of assimilation was buttressed by a number of supporting policies, one of which was the spread of Christianity to the First Nation population. As Harper (1946: 122) observed:

>In Canada the civilization of the Indian is made synonymous with his Christianization. Indian missions, in fact, enjoy government favour; the aboriginal religious and ceremonial practices are officially discouraged. Next to

the attainment of the goal of self-support, the Indian's conversion from pagan belief to Christianity is the most important criterion for judging his fitness to assume an equal place in the white man's society.

It must be remembered here that the entwinement of the Christian church with the administration of First Nation affairs was virtually inevitable. In many cases missionaries spearheaded the first white contact with First Nations in the interior of the continent and the missionaries were frequently the most successful in learning First Nation languages and mores. Many missionaries worked vigorously to protect First Nations and often found themselves serving as intermediaries between government officials and the First Nations. It must also be borne in mind that the early church and missionary work in North America attracted some individuals of outstanding character and drive who were bound to leave their stamp on the policies of their times.

The church came to play a very important role in the education of First Nation people. In the early years, education was viewed, as it still is in some quarters, as an essential tool of assimilation. The responsibility for First Nation education, however, was largely delegated by the government to the churches. In the long run this strategy was to prove unsatisfactory. Because the religious residential schools isolated First Nation children from other students, assimilation was impaired. Because their curricula served as much as a vehicle for Christianization as for secular education, the secular education of First Nation students suffered in comparison to that received by others. Finally, as will be discussed later in this book, the residential schools were a source of great disruption, pain, and antagonism within the First Nation communities and did little to enhance the value of education in the eyes of Native students.

By the 1960s the traditional role of the church in First Nation affairs was drawing to a close. As a result of the increased secularization of the Canadian society and the almost total separation of church and state, Christianization flagged as a policy goal. The education of First Nation children passed into secular hands and by the mid-sixties the denominational residential school system was being abandoned. Although education remained a vehicle for assimilation, it was no longer a vehicle driven by the churches.

Reserves and Self-Sufficiency

An important means of assimilation was the settlement of First Nation people into agriculturally-based communities. Settlement allowed other instruments of assimilation, such as churches, schools and limited local government, to be more readily brought into effect. Moreover, to the extent that settlement proceeded, large tracts of land formerly held by First Nations could be appropriated by the state and freed for settlement by others. Indeed, the immigration boom of the early twentieth century increased pressure even on the newly-founded First Nation reserves and the government began to actively encourage First Nation land surrenders and moved to make "excess" First Nation reserve land available for settlement by others. In 1911 the *Indian Act* was amended to allow for the expropriation of reserve lands for public works. Speaking to the amendment, Minister of the Interior Oliver "... claimed that the whim of a band would no longer obstruct a provincially-chartered railroad company from developing a certain part of the country" (Miller et al., 1978: 108). In the clash between non-Native settlement and the protection of First Nation interests, public policy clearly came down on the side of the former, although First Nation interests were by no means totally abandoned. Boldt (1993: 77-79) asserts that "the national interest" takes precedence over First Nation interests at every crucial juncture to this day.

In the pursuit of assimilation the government tried to make First Nation people as self-supporting as possible. This policy was not motivated solely by the desire to limit public expenditures in support of First Nations; the desire to promote the integration of First Nation individuals into the Canadian economy was also an important motivation. Yet, here again, the policy was frustrated by the legislative restrictions of the *Indian Act*. The prohibition of mortgages on First Nation land and restrictions on the ability of outside creditors to collect debts from reserve residents curtailed the infusion of outside capital into the First Nation economy. Self-support and fiscal self-management were also frustrated by the paternalism of the Department of Indian Affairs. Not only were band funds under the control of the Department, but even the most straightforward financial and entrepreneurial enterprises by First Nation individuals required departmental approval if they involved contact with the larger society.

An interesting step toward greater self-sufficiency was taken by the community development program launched by Indian Affairs in the early 1960s. This program sought to mobilize the First Nation population, to create conditions of economic and social progress for the whole community by encouraging the maximum amount of community participation, initiative, and self-reliance. The program called for a change in emphasis from people administration to people development. To this end sixty-two community development officers were hired by Indian Affairs to work as resource persons and co-ordinators in the First Nation communities. However, despite — or because of — its early successes, the program quickly disintegrated in a welter of bureaucratic infighting and conflicts among the community development staff, Indian agents, senior bureaucrats, and factions in the First Nation communities. The community development staff, torn between loyalty to their employer and to the First Nation people, frequently found themselves as partisans on the side of the First Nations against the government, and as such their support and effectiveness within the Indian Affairs bureaucracy rapidly dissipated. Concluding that the community development program threw sand in the gears of efficient administration, Indian Affairs moved to emasculate the program.

Enfranchisement

The principal reward held out to First Nation individuals contemplating assimilation was enfranchisement. The equation of assimilation with enfranchisement and full citizenship was not an unexpected policy in a young country faced with the absorption of a large and polyglot immigrant population; in this sense, First Nation policy reflected a more general policy perspective of Anglo-conformity within the society. However, the costs to be paid by a First Nation individual seeking enfranchisement far surpassed those paid by immigrants to Canada.

The enfranchisement provisions of the *Indian Act* equated citizenship with cultural characteristics; only First Nation individuals who fit the dominant cultural mode could be full citizens. First Nation individuals who clung to Native traditions or to reserve land clearly did not fall into this category. We can assume that in the eyes of policy makers, "rights" (as we know them today) were associated with enfranchisement. Here we include such things as the right to vote, freedom of speech, the right to organize, and so forth. The "rights" imbedded in the *Indian Act* and the treaties, on the other hand, were seen more as transitory means of protection than as inalienable rights as we perceive such today. According to that line of thought, these lesser rights could be justifiably trimmed away when they were no longer needed as a means of protection. For example, reserve land that was not needed to support the First Nation population could be made available for non-Native settlement or farming; the First Nation's right to the land in this case was not equated with the more basic property rights associated with enfranchisement and citizenship. In effect, the types of First Nation rights recognized today were probably not recognized as rights, per se, in the nineteenth century thinking that prevailed well into the twentieth century.

As a lure for assimilation, enfranchisement clearly failed, for the rate of assimilation remained extremely low. However, in 1960 all First Nation individuals were granted the vote in federal elections. The law recognized, at last, that full citizenship in Canada need not be conditional upon complete assimilation into the Canadian society. The legitimacy of cultural pluralism and cultural distinctiveness for Canada's aboriginal inhabitants had been recognized, or so it seemed.

The Treaties

The first treaty between First Nations and colonial officials in North America was signed in 1670. Prior to the comprehensive land claim agreements of the modern era, the last Canadian treaty (by such name) was signed in 1921.[6] During the intervening years a multitude of treaties of varying format and complexity was concluded. These generally included many or most of the following provisions: an agreement of peace and amity, the cession of land, initial payments to First Nations, small annual payments in cash and/or goods, the designation of chiefs and councillors to negotiate and administer the treaty, guarantee of land reserved for First Nations and/or the right to use unoccupied territory in its natural state, and promises of government services such as education.

The major treaties in Canada were the numbered treaties on the prairies. Starting with Treaty One in 1871 and ending with Treaty Ten in 1906, they opened the western territories for settlement and the construction of the Canadian Pacific Railway. Modern treaties (comprehensive land claim settlements) of the late twentieth century far surpass those earlier treaties in length, complexity, and fairness to the First Nations.

Reflected in the numbered treaties are some policy perspectives that should be mentioned. For example, as the treaties were signed to extinguish First Nation title to the land, they carried with them the explicit recognition of First Nation ownership rights. Treaty Seven (see Appendix A), to cite but one illustration, calls for First Nations to "cede, release, surrender, and yield up to the Government of Canada" traditional lands in the then NorthWest Territories. Lands not so released remained as Indian reserves, legal title to which was held in trust for First Nation people by the Crown.

Readers should bear in mind that even the various numbered treaties are by no means identical in content and that no land cession treaties were signed with First Nations in Québec, the Maritimes, and most of British Columbia prior to the late twentieth century. For the many thousands of registered Indians not under treaty, the only claim to their original lands is that based on aboriginal rights, that is, the rights of first occupancy of the land where those rights have never been officially yielded to the Canadian government.

There is also room for confusion about the conception of "rights" that was brought to the treaty-making process by First Nations and whites. As Smith points out, it can never be assumed that the treaties truly reflect the agreement and understanding of First Nations (Cited in Miller et al., 1978: xxviii). The First Nation perspective is set out by Cardinal (1969: 29). To First Nations, the treaties were:

> ...the beginning of a contractual relationship whereby the representatives of the Queen would have lasting responsibilities to the First Nation people in return for valuable lands that were ceded to them.

In this respect, First Nation organizations argue that First Nations have paid for free First Nation education in perpetuity by the lands released by treaty. The government perspective at the time of the signings was quite different, although this conclusion is deduced from the First Nation policies of the time rather than from the letter of the treaties themselves. To government officials, the critical feature of the treaties was that they ceded First Nation ownership of the land; the treaties were more important for what First Nations gave up than for the "concessions" given to First Nations. Government officials also viewed the treaties as a means of providing transitional protection of an indigenous people who were faced with eventual assimilation or extinction. It is unlikely that officials at the time read into the treaties the scope and duration of responsibilities that First Nations are claiming and courts came to recognize in the 1980s and 1990s.

It is likely that the process of making the numbered treaties often lacked the bilateral quality that is sometimes assumed or asserted today. Most of the numbered treaties were approached by the government less as a matter of negotiation than as a "take-it-or-leave-it" proposition, although variations in the content of the treaties do, to a certain extent, reflect the differential bargaining power of different First Nation signatories. Finally, it should also be noted that the conditions surrounding the signing of the treaties were often less than equitable and were not such as to ensure that First Nation interests were fairly protected (Cardinal, 1969: 36).

The policy interpretations applied to the numbered treaties came to take on a moral character that went beyond the narrow legal phraseology of the treaties. For example, the Chiefs of Alberta argued in *Citizens Plus* that treaty clauses promising machinery and livestock symbolized a lasting government commitment to economic development. The medicine chest clause in Treaty Six, signed in 1876, provides another example of expansive interpretation. It states that "a medicine chest shall be kept at the house of each Indian agent for the use and benefit of the Indians at the direction of such agent." The scope of this and broadly similar clauses (e.g., concerning education) in other treaties has come under considerable debate. In 1935 the Treaty Six clause was interpreted by the Exchequer Court of Britain (*Draver vs the King*) to mean that all drugs or medical supplies required by First Nation individuals should be supplied to them free of charge. However, in this decision testimony from First Nation persons who were actually present at the signing of the treaty and at related discussions was critical; the letter of the treaty alone did not form the basis of the court decision (Macdonald, 1970: 177). Subsequently, Supreme Court of Canada decisions in the Simon (1985) and Sioui (1990) cases reaffirmed the expansive interpretation of the treaties. Recognizing that the honour of the Crown is at stake in the interpretation of the treaties, the country's highest court ruled both that treaties must be interpreted in a flexible manner that takes into account changes in technology and practice and that the treaties must be construed in a liberal manner such that ambiguities are resolved in favour of the First Nation peoples.

The evolution of First Nation policy in Canada has been shaped by changes in the larger society which have exerted very significant pressure on First Nations, on the administration of Indian Affairs, and on the direction of this policy. A striking example of the impingement of external societal developments on the evolution of First Nation policy is provided by the 1969 white paper, a document renowned for renewing the assimilationist orientation of the earlier era.

The 1969 White Paper[7]

The 1960s witnessed the initial stirrings of Native activism both in Canada and the United States. The American civil rights movement indirectly called into question the legal segregation of Canadian First Nations through the *Indian Act*, and civil rights advocates in Canada began to pay increased attention to the plight of First Nations. Many Canadians felt that advances in civil rights, such as the provisions of the 1960 Bill of Rights outlawing discrimination on the basis of race, colour, or creed, should apply equally to First Nations as to other Canadians. Politically, a new Liberal government led by Pierre Trudeau, with his promise of a "just society," was elected in 1968 and Canadians within and outside the government tried to reconcile the promise of the "just society" with the conditions faced by Canadian First Nations. These various forces were not to leave First Nation affairs untouched.

The new government was imbued with a strong liberal ideology that stressed individualism and the protection of individual rights. It adopted a new approach to First Nation affairs that reflected a combination of North American ideological tenets that can be traced back to the American Revolution, Trudeau's personal ideological beliefs, and his deep antagonism to ethnic nationalism in Québec. The new approach emphasized individual equality and de-emphasized collective ethnic survival. First Nation individuals were to be helped at the expense of First Nations as a collectivity. On June 25, 1969, Jean Chrétien, then-Minister of Indian Affairs and Northern Development, tabled in the House of Commons "A Statement of the Government of Canada on Indian Policy".

That "white paper" proposed that the legislative and constitutional bases of discrimination be removed; the *Indian Act* was to be repealed. Rather than being legislatively set apart, First Nation individuals were to receive the same services as other Canadians and these were to be delivered to First Nation individuals through the same channels and from the same government agencies as serviced other Canadians. The unique federal government responsibility for First Nations was to end. The Indian and Inuit Affairs Programme within DIAND was to be abolished and any residual responsibilities that were not transferred to provincial governments or to bands were to be transferred to other departments within the federal government. The white paper also recognized that any lawful obligations that the government had incurred through the signing of the treaties must be recognized, although here the government expressed the very limited interpretation of treaty rights discussed above.

The white paper was also a response to values within the policy-making arena of the national government. It was designed more to protect the government from external criticism than to meet the aspirations of Canadian First Nations as these were articulated by First Nation leaders. In its emphasis upon achieving contemporary equality for First Nation individuals, the white paper paid scant attention to the liabilities that had been accumulating for First Nations from the inequalities of the past. Nor did the white paper acknowledge that discrimination "in fact" (*de facto*) may exist even when discrimination "in law" (*de jure*) has been abolished, and that as a consequence, special legal protection of minority rights might be necessary. As Weaver (1973: 3) points out, the problem of reconciling demands for special status with the principle of equality is an old and enduring one for democratic societies; the white paper solution was to come down on the side of equality-as-uniformity. The rights of the individual were placed above the collective survival of the group.

First Nation hostility to the white paper was crystallized in a number of documents, one of which was Harold Cardinal's book *The Unjust Society*. Cardinal charged that the new First Nation policy was "… a thinly disguised programme of extermination through assimilation", that the white paper postulated that "the only good Indian is a nonIndian". Cardinal was particularly opposed to the proposal to turn over the responsibility for First Nations to the provincial governments. A second document, *Citizens Plus*, was presented by the Chiefs of Alberta to Prime Minister Trudeau in June, 1970. *Citizens Plus* was introduced by the following excerpt from the Hawthorn report:[8]

> Indians should be regarded as "Citizens Plus"; in addition to the normal rights and duties of citizenship, Indians possess certain additional rights as charter members of the Canadian community.

Through these and other similar documents, as well as through statements to the press, First Nation organizations registered their unequivocal opposition to the white paper.

The 1969 white paper was the capstone of a policy of assimilation that can be traced back to the pre-Confederation years. Its rejection by First Nations and its eventual retraction by the government in March of 1971 thus marks a watershed in the evolution of First Nation affairs in Canada. Assimilation was at least officially placed aside as an explicit policy goal, although it continues as a socio-economic and cultural process and, First Nation leaders allege, as an hidden agenda behind federal government action. Formally, at least, the page was being turned on what had been the central theme of First Nation policy over the previous one hundred and thirty years. The rejection of the white paper, therefore, opened up a new and confused policy era; the direction of First Nation policy in the 1970s was suddenly "up for grabs". The development of alternative policies was to prove to be an incredibly complex process, though, in part due to a basic change in the composition of the policy making bodies. Through to the publication of the white paper, First Nation policy had been formulated with very little First Nation input and frequently in opposition to First Nation goals and interests. After the 1969 white paper, First Nation leaders or their appointees would sometimes be deeply involved (e.g., in the 1970s and in the 1992 Charlottetown Accord); yet, sometimes they would not. Indeed, the criticisms of lack of consultation and going against First Nation goals and interests were levelled at the proposed amendments to the *Indian Act* tabled in Parliament in 1996, just as they had been levelled at the white paper more than a quarter century earlier.

The next chapter discusses the stages through which First Nation policy and practice evolved during the period after the 1969 white paper, and other major developments of the late twentieth century.

NOTES

[1] This chapter is excerpted and slightly revised from J. Rick Ponting (ed.), *Arduous Journey: Canadian Indians and Decolonization*, Toronto: McClelland and Stewart, 1986, pages 18-34. It is produced here with the permission of Oxford University Press Canada. Many of the citations in the original have been omitted here.

[2] Editor's Note: A "plain language" version of the controversial proposed amendments to the *Indian Act*, which were made public by the Minister in September 1996 and tabled in Parliament in December 1996, was posted on the world wide web at the following address: http://www.inac.gc.ca/news/sept96/9638pl.html The Assembly of First Nations' concerns were posted at http://www.afn.ca/indact_analysis.htm

[3] One noteworthy exception is the set of amendments introduced in 1927 and removed in 1951, as described below. Another important set of changes took the form of Bill C-31 (1985), in which enfranchisement was abolished, bands were given control over their own membership codes, and sex discrimination was removed (from the present generations) such that persons who had lost their Registered Indian status (notably Indian women who had married non-Indian men, and their children) were entitled to be reinstated as Registered Indians. Other proposed amendments, tabled in Parliament in December 1996 against the strong opposition of The Assembly of First Nations, also contained some significant changes, such as those concerning lands.

[4] The final report of the Royal Commission on Aboriginal Peoples (1996a: 259) stated: "[M]ost still agree that progress in self-government, in economic development and in eradicating the social ills afflicting many Indian communities cannot be accomplished within the confines of the *Indian Act*." The Commission recommended several new statutes, including an Aboriginal Nations Recognition and Government Act (Rec. #2.3.27).

[5] Historian Olive Dickason (1992: 183) supports Patterson here, with her reference to Amherst's "notorious directive about distributing smallpox-infected blankets in their encampments."

[6] Comprehensive land claim agreements, such as the 1975 James Bay and Northern Québec Agreement, are essentially modern-day treaties and are recognized as such under *The Constitution Act, 1982*. The 1996 Agreement-in-Principle between the Nisga'a Tribal Council and the governments of Canada and British Columbia is formally called a treaty.

[7] For an excellent and detailed discussion of the formulation of the policy contained in the 1969 white paper, see Weaver (1980).

[8] The Hawthorn Report was a two-volume report of a study team commissioned by the federal government to survey First Nation conditions in the mid-1960s. It was virtually a royal commission. See Hawthorn (1967: 13).

REFERENCES

Boldt, Menno
1993   *Surviving as Indians*. Toronto: University of Toronto Press.
Cardinal, Harold
1969   *The Unjust Society: The Tragedy of Canada's Indians*. Edmonton: Hurtig.

_____
1973   *The Rebirth of Canada's Indians*. Edmonton: Hurtig.
Dickason, Olive P.
1992   *Canada's First Nations: A History of Founding Peoples From Earliest Times*. Toronto: McClelland & Stewart.
Doerr, Audrey D.
1974   "Indian Policy." pp. 36–54 in G. Bruce Doern and V. Seymour Wilson (eds.), *Issues in Canadian Public Policy*. Toronto: MacMillan.
Harper, Allan G.
1945   "Canada's First Nation Administration: Basic Concepts and Objectives." *American Indigena* IV, 2: 119-132.
Hawthorn, Harry B. (ed.)
1967   *A Survey of the Contemporary Indians of Canada: A Report on Economic, Political, Educational Needs and Policies*. Part I. Ottawa: DIAND.
Macdonald, R. St. J.
1970   *Native Rights in Canada*. Toronto: Indian-Eskimo Association.
Manuel, George and Michael Posluns
1974   *The Fourth World: An Indian Reality*. Toronto: Collier MacMillan.
Miller, Kahn-Tineta et al.
1978   *Historical Development of The Indian Act*. Ottawa: DIAND.
Patterson, E. Palmer I
1972   *The Canadian Indian: A History Since 1500*. Don Mills, Ont.: Collier MacMillan.
Royal Commission on Aboriginal People
1996a *Final Report of The Royal Commission on Aboriginal People; Vol. 1: Looking Forward, Looking Back*. Ottawa: Minister of Supply and Services Canada.
Sealey, Bruce and Antoine S. Lussier
1975   The Métis: Canada's Forgotten People. Winnipeg: Manitoba Métis Federation Press.
Weaver, Sally M.
1973   "Segregation and The *Indian Act*: The Dialogue of Equality vs 'Special Status'", Paper presented to the Canadian Ethnic Studies Association National Conference on Canadian Culture and Ethnic Groups, Toronto.

_____
1980   *The Making of Indian Policy, 1968–70: The Hidden Agenda*. Toronto: University of Toronto Press.

CHAPTER 3

HISTORICAL OVERVIEW AND BACKGROUND: PART II 1970–96[1]

J. Rick Ponting

OVERVIEW

The approximately one-quarter century from the beginning of the 1970s to the time of writing in the mid-1990s saw First Nations experience numerous social changes which were reminiscent of those of the so-called "quiet revolution" which transformed Québec society in the 1960s. Although the Québec changes were more profound and more rapid-paced and started from a very different base level of "development", the broad direction (decolonization), causes, and accompanying phenomena are highly similar.

Both populations have gone through a secularization of their educational system and in both populations the average level of educational attainment has increased significantly. In step with urbanization and educational change there has emerged a new First Nation middle class, proportionately smaller than that in Québec but in attitudes, skills and aspirations not unlike the new Québec middle class that was such a driving force for social and political change. Both populations have experienced a blossoming of institutions which are under their control and are staffed by that new middle class.

Like the Québécois, First Nations have been exposed to movements of national liberation throughout the world, and those nationalist examples have exerted an influence on the political thought, demands, and rhetoric of leaders of both populations. As Québécois nationalists stressed and defended the territorial sovereignty of Québec, so, too, have First Nations repeatedly emphasized the importance of First Nation land, and of First Nation control of First Nation land. In addition, First Nations, like the Québécois, stress their nationhood and unique cultural identity. Indeed, they have vied with each other for the important symbolic designation of "distinct society" in Canada's constitution. In addition, leaders of both populations have challenged the value of a pan-Canadian nationality. Finally, demands for First Nation government, or the transfer of the political authority of the federal government to First Nation hands, parallel, in many respects, the early Parti Québécois' proposals for sovereignty-association. In fact, Assembly of First Nations (AFN) Grand Chief Ovide Mercredi succeeded in getting chiefs to adopt a sovereignty-association platform for First Nations in a 1996 AFN general assembly.[2] He urged chiefs to go forth and unilaterally assert their sovereignty.

Although the term "quiet revolution" is a convenient label for summarizing the social transformation taking place among First Nations, it glosses over important phases and variations which occurred during that period. This chapter outlines the main developments of that era. Developments within the federal state and within the First Nation population will be treated separately, because during that period the federal government and First Nation organizations were often out of step, if not actually working at cross-purposes.

CHANGES IN THE FEDERAL STATE

Coping with the rejection of the 1969 white paper and with the numerous changes which occurred in the First Nation population in the decades thereafter proved to be an enormous challenge for the federal government and its policy makers. By no means were they always up to the task. At times they stumbled badly or figuratively stuck their head in the sand. At times they showed flashes of boldness. At times they retraced ground already covered. At times they seemed immobilized by the gravity and enormity of the need and the complexity of the situation. Box 1 identifies several phases through which the federal state can be said to have passed as it reacted to, and attempted to shape, events in "Indian country" during approximately the last third of the twentieth century.

Phase I: Policy Retreat

The first phase encompassed the period from shortly after the release of the 1969 white paper until its withdrawal in 1971. Although the policy was eloquently defended by Prime Minister Pierre Trudeau using the language of the liberal ideology (Ponting and Gibbins, 1980: 27–28 and 327–331), it came under vehement attack from First Nation organizations and was officially abandoned. During the interim, it overshadowed all other federal initiatives in the field and made progress almost impossible on other issues such as First Nation health and housing. The policy also stoked the glowing embers of First Nation distrust of the federal government; the resultant fire consumed most of whatever good will had been created prior to the release of the white paper. That distrust flared up again periodically over the subsequent decades, most notably during the fifth phase described below.

Phase II: Turmoil and Floundering

Clearly a new policy approach was needed. Yet the time from the withdrawal of the white paper until perhaps the late 1970s was a period of turmoil and floundering as the Department of Indian Affairs and Northern Development

---

BOX 1 Phases in the Federal Government's Reaction to the First Nation "Quiet Revolution"

• Policy Retreat	1969–71
• Turmoil and Floundering	1971–80
• Quest for Self-Government and Constitutional Reform	1980–87
• Localization and Fiscal Restraint	1985–90
• Rude Awakening and Bold Initiatives	1990–92
• Reversion to Localization and Restraint	1993–

(DIAND) experienced a rapid succession of ministers and senior bureaucrats (deputy-ministers and assistant deputy ministers), underwent significant organizational re-structuring, offered a series of policy initiatives which were usually denounced by First Nation organizations, and witnessed a variety of other federal government departments encroach on its domain (e.g., Secretary of State) or become more active in a "regulatory" manner (e.g., Treasury Board, Auditor General). This was also a period of considerable conflict within the department itself, as tensions between the "old guard" (veteran DIAND employees) and "new guard" (younger, innovative, more client-oriented employees) broke into open bureaucratic warfare.

In the wake of the withdrawal of the 1969 white paper, DIAND groped for new policy thrusts. The first of these new policies involved the reversal, as a result of the 1973 Supreme Court of Canada ruling on the Nisga'a land claim, of the government's refusal to recognize aboriginal rights. Less popular with First Nations was the policy contained in a 1976 cabinet-endorsed document entitled "The Nature of Government First Nation Relations". Since this document is critiqued elsewhere (Ponting and Gibbins, 1980: 176–177), suffice it to say here that it not only fell short of First Nations' demands, but actually ran counter to several of those demands. Another policy prepared for Cabinet that same year encompassed all Native people and was vehemently rejected by status Indians for a variety of reasons among which one of the most important was that it suggested curtailing of funding for status Indians (Ponting and Gibbins, 1980: 177–178). A fourth new policy involved a process for the recognition and settlement of two distinct forms of First Nation claims — namely, comprehensive claims (involving unextinguished aboriginal rights to large tracts of land) and specific claims (e.g., involving unfulfilled provisions in treaties; compensation for small parcels of land illegally expropriated from, or sold on behalf of, First Nation bands; etc.). Although most First Nation organizations to this day reject the policy's principle of extinguishing aboriginal title to land in exchange for compensation, some (e.g., the James Bay Cree, the Nisga'a) have submitted claims which have been processed under this policy. Finally, the fifth policy proposal (1978-79), which signalled a transition into the third phase, was for a "charter system of First Nation government" whereby First Nation bands would negotiate a charter or constitution with the federal government so as to remove certain aspects of local government from the jurisdiction of the *Indian Act* and the arbitrary powers of the minister therein (Ponting and Gibbins, 1980: 189–190). This, too, was rejected by The National Indian Brotherhood (the predecessor to The Assembly of First Nations); NIB criticized it as mere "sandbox politics" in which First Nations are expected to play at governing themselves while the minister retains the important powers.

Phase III: Quest for Self-Government and Constitutional Reform

Modest steps in the direction of self-government were made in the late 1970s with the implementation of memoranda of agreement calling for individual bands to take over from DIAND the administration (and in some cases the designing) of various DIAND programmes on their reserve. However, it was perhaps not until the recognition of aboriginal rights in the final constitutional package of 1981 or even the creation of the Special Parliamentary Committee on

Indian Self-Government (Keith Penner, M.P., Chairman) in 1982 that the federal government entered this phase in earnest. This phase witnessed yet another major change in the key policy actors, as DIAND lost its lead role to the newly-created Office of Aboriginal Constitutional Affairs (OACA), to the Privy Council Office, and to the Department of Justice. In addition, the provincial premiers and their advisers and officials now also became central participants, as did various Native organizations representing the aboriginal interests of Inuit, Métis, and non-status Indians.

During this third phase, the federal government and *some* First Nation organizations finally came to follow more or less the same trajectory. This was largely as a result of the recommendations of the Penner committee, which, in the thinking of non-Native politicians, gave a major boost of legitimacy to First Nation leaders' aspirations for self-government. A fundamental act of convergence occurred when The Assembly of First Nations (AFN) dropped its demands for sovereign authority and indicated its conditional willingness to accept authority delegated from the federal government as the basis of First Nation self-government.[3] However, not all provincial premiers were on this "track", as some of them (particularly in western Canada) were of the opinion that administrative, fiscal, or legislative reform, rather than the constitutional entrenchment of aboriginal rights to self-government, were the preferable courses to follow. Added to the premiers' "go slowly" approach was an increased factionalism among aboriginal peoples (including between treaty and non-treaty sectors of the status Indian population). All these factors and others combined to militate against a major constitutional breakthrough.

The main concrete accomplishments of this third phase consisted of the entrenchment of constitutional recognition and partial protection of aboriginal rights in *The Constitution Act, 1982*, and a constitutional amendment guaranteeing constitutional conferences on aboriginal rights until the year 1987. These conferences included delegations led by the Prime Minister, the provincial premiers, leaders of the main aboriginal organizations (excluding the Prairie Treaty Nations Alliance), and the government leaders of Yukon and Northwest Territories. Although these proved to be valuable educational forums for the politicians and others, and although the very fact that they were held must be seen as a major symbolic gain for aboriginal peoples, deliberations reached an impasse with the failure to attain an agreement at the final conference in 1987[4]. That conference broke up in bitterness which featured what surely must be some of the most undiplomatic and ad hominem attacks ever found in Canadian political discourse, as reported in Box 2.

Phase IV: Localization and Fiscal Restraint

The failure of the 1987 constitutional conference occurred early in what can be seen now as a fourth phase. The June 1985 imposition of Bill C-31 (an *Act* amending the *Indian Act*. See note #3 in Chapter Two of this volume) against the wishes of many status Indian leaders, the leaked report of the Deputy Prime Minister's task force on Native programmes (Study Team, 1985), and the introduction of the *Sechelt Indian Band Act* bore the hallmarks of that fourth phase: fiscal restraint and/or a more piecemeal (less global) approach targetted at First Nation communities and individuals. That approach, which involved more modest challenges of consensus-building, was the central thrust

BOX 2 Excerpts from the Remarks of Native Leader Jim Sinclair at the First Ministers' and Aboriginal Leaders' Conference on Aboriginal Rights in the Constitution, March 1987

"We feel that the conference has been a failure....We don't really know if the good will was ever there to make a deal....I'm disappointed that some of the premiers made a stand ... against us for reasons that I consider were invalid. Premier Vander Zalm, you pointed out to us that you came from Holland in 1949 and you said that you met Indian and Native troops from Canada who went into your country and died for your country and for your people. We have them buried all over Europe and Asia. And they went out to die for this country, even though they weren't even recognized when they stepped off the train to come home to this country. And its a shame when you can come here and in a few years become the premier of one of the largest provinces in Canada, and that you will not recognize the rights of our people here in this country — the originals. [applause in conference hall]....

Quebec, I'm very disappointed at you. We had hopes that you would come to our aid when we needed you, as Riel fought for your rights in western Canada and Indians fought and died for your rights in western Canada. They were hanged along with the Métis, for their position and their fight for land.... You came here and advanced your own cause. And we're not going to go away with any hard feelings. We wish you the best of luck, that you will acquire your rights and your place in the constitution of Canada, and I'm sure you will, because this government and the provinces around here will accommodate you because they can't leave out their own.

Mr. Devine, I have a few words to say to you.... You talked about Saskatchewan and about the one million dollars a day that you spend on aboriginal people in Saskatchewan. That's three hundred and sixty-five million dollars a year. You are saying that the provinces are going to earn ... half that amount next year. But at the same time you came to the Prime Minister here and he bought an election for you for one billion dollars. [applause and cheers] You've spent money on jails in Laloche where the unemployment was so heavy and so bad that people fought for the jobs to build that million dollar jail. And then the day after the job was completed, they were in it. Now, that's your kind of justice. [applause]

You made a deal with Weyerhauser, the pulp company in Saskatchewan, not too long ago. You asked us for definitions when we talk about self-government. You gave them an open-ended agreement that gave them more land than all the reserves put together in Canada. And you didn't ask them for a definition. You gave them one year where an eight hundred page document came out with not one definition, but three hundred definitions. Now that's what you got from a big company that you gave a blank cheque to ....

And I think it's unfair of you to accuse all of Saskatchewan of racism when you're advancing it at this table....

We pay twice as much in northern Saskatchewan for food as you would in the south. Yet, for every bottle of wine and every bottle of whiskey that you send north of P.A. [Prince Albert] you put a subsidy on that so the price of that wine is the same price in Laloche as it is in Regina. [applause] At the same time, there is no subsidy for the price of milk for our children ....

I think by leaving here today without an agreement we have signed a blank cheque for those who want to oppress us.... Your attitude at this conference, from Alberta and from Saskatchewan, from British Columbia, is not going to bring five thousand members to the Ku Klux [Klan] meeting next July in Calgary or Edmonton. It's going to bring 50,000, because there's an open market on racism and white supremacy in this Canada ...!"

of the Community-Based Self-Government policy announced in 1986.[5] Under that policy, individual First Nations could apply to enter an elaborate and protracted procedure for negotiating with the federal government various provisions for self-government. As in the Sechelt model, agreements would be tailored to the circumstances of the individual First Nation (or group of First Nations) and, upon being cast in legislation, would bring the First Nation out from under the jurisdiction of certain parts of the *Indian Act*. Many of the First Nations which entered this process put considerable time and energy into this generously funded initiative, for it was widely believed that the federal government would use the process to develop a few basic models of self-government and then give all other First Nations the option of choosing one of those models or remaining under the full *Indian Act*. This "localization" approach was the approach to which the federal government returned after the cul-de-sac detour of the Charlottetown Accord.

The relatively generous funding of the community-based self-government initiative stood in contrast to a more general trend of fiscal restraint during this period. Particularly noteworthy were the funding cuts imposed upon First Nation cultural, political, and communications organizations, the capping of post-secondary education funding at levels that provoked a student hunger strike in Ottawa in 1989, and a housing budget that failed to meaningfully address the housing crisis of the burgeoning First Nation population.[6] The Mulroney Conservative government was ideologically predisposed to favour the notion that First Nation entrepreneurs, rather than the federal government, would be the long-term answer to First Nation communities' economic development needs. To that end the government engaged in various initiatives to facilitate and promote aboriginal businesses during this period.

Phase V: Rude Awakening and Bold Initiatives

The so-called "Meech Lake Crisis" and "Oka Crisis" of summer 1990 clearly signalled a new phase in the federal government's relations with First Nations. This phase might be called the period of "rude awakening" — a period, as in 1970 in Québec's "quiet revolution", when the "quiet revolution" was definitely not quiet. Early in this phase the Supreme Court of Canada issued landmark decisions (e.g., the Sparrow decision and the Sioui decision released in the Spring of 1990) reinforcing the 1985 ruling in the Simon case. Together, these three rulings reflected an expansive interpretation of aboriginal rights in the constitution, a liberal (pro-First Nation) interpretation of the treaties,[7] and a conceptualization of the treaties as "sui generis" (that is, "of a kind of their own", not subject to the principles and tests developed in other forms of law such as contract law and international law). These decisions included judicial discourse which seemed to signal a new era, such as when the government was told that it must act so as to preserve the honour of the Crown and must construe treaties liberally and resolve ambiguities in favour of the First Nations.

Mere weeks after the Supreme Court's Sparrow decision, First Nations flexed their political muscle in a manner which proved devastating to then Prime Minister Mulroney's cherished Meech Lake Accord. Manitoba Cree M.L.A. Elijah Harper, acting on the basis of aboriginal people's grievances over having been ignored in and insulted by the Accord, succeeded in vetoing even consideration of the Accord by the Manitoba legislature. In combination with the actions of Premier Clyde Wells of Newfoundland, Harper's actions caused the death of the Accord.[8] Aboriginal people signalled thereby that they could no longer be ignored, dismissed, or otherwise taken for granted in future constitutional reform efforts. For the Mulroney government this was, indeed, a rude awakening; the top priority item on the Prime Minister's political agenda had been subverted by aboriginal politicians.

If there were any doubt as to whether a new era was upon us, that doubt was removed by the shock of armed confrontation, loss of life, and violent white backlash at Kanehsatake (adjacent to Oka, Québec) and Kahnawake (across the St. Lawrence River from Montréal) in the summer of 1990.[9] Sympathy blockades elsewhere around the country by other Natives and the widespread support expressed for the Mohawk "warriors" whom the government sought to dismiss as terrorists and criminals, drove home to government the gravity of the situation.[10] Also alarming was the demonstrated ability of those supporters to seriously disrupt the daily life of large numbers of non-Natives. Suddenly, not only were government's relations with First Nations seen as being in crisis, but around the world Canada was receiving large amounts of extremely negative publicity over its aboriginal policies. Canada's international credibility as a human rights advocate was in grave jeopardy[11] and with it our foreign policy initiatives in such places as South Africa and the United Nations.

The "Oka crisis" produced a flurry of government activity related to the settling of land claims. For instance, the government established a Land Claims Commission, the members of which formally resigned in frustration five years later during the Chrétien regime. With the end of the Oka crisis, though, aboriginal issues plummetted overnight on the list of priorities of the Canadian mass public and non-Native elected leaders.[12] Eventually (August 1991), the Mulroney government appointed a Royal Commission on Aboriginal Peoples, with a sweepingly broad mandate not restricted to land matters. By the end of 1991, the government announced policy changes wherein it would no longer require the extinguishment of aboriginal title as a precondition to settling comprehensive land claims[13] and would accelerate the processing of land claims.

The renewed atmosphere of crisis on the national unity front led to the inclusion of First Nation and other aboriginal leaders in the constitutional summitry which produced the Charlottetown Accord of August 1992. In fact, several factors combined to produce an extraordinary surge in the political will of the First Ministers to see justice done for aboriginal people. Among those factors were the demonstrated power of aboriginal people to disrupt[14] and embarrass, the desperation of the federal and provincial governments to stem the flow of support for Québec separation which had increased dramatically during the Meech crisis, the decisions of the Supreme Court of Canada on various aboriginal matters, and the glare of international publicity. Out of those constitutional negotiations came the Charlottetown Accord with its truly remarkable provisions for aboriginal self-government, including such clauses as the recognition of aboriginal peoples' inherent right to self government and a guarantee that the treaties would be interpreted in a liberal manner with ambiguities to be resolved in favour of the First Nations. (See World Wide Web.)

The defeat of the Charlottetown Accord in the national referendum of 1992 and the failure of then leader of the Assembly of First Nations, Ovide Mercredi, to deliver majority support for the Accord from his constituents can be said to mark the end of the "rude awakening" phase. Even the Davis Inlet near-tragedy in early 1993 did not galvanize the government into any bold new policy or programmatic ventures. The Davis Inlet crisis was precipitated by release to the news media of a video tape from the Innu[15] community of Davis Inlet. The tape's appalling footage captured the rescue of several suicidal children from an unheated shack where they were sniffing gasoline. Carried around the world by news media, the footage jolted stereotypical illusions of Canada held abroad. However, Canadian governments and many Canadian citizens had long been aware of the desperate poverty and dysfunctionality of some First Nation communities. Perhaps that, and the lack of political pressure emanating from that awareness, was what enabled the governments of Canada and Newfoundland and Labrador to contain the crisis to the realm of public relations rather than allowing it to prolong or revive the "rude awakening" phase with its political imperatives for meaningful Canada-wide action.[16]

By Fall of 1992 the Canadian electorate was clearly unsympathetic to any policy initiative that granted "special status" to any sector of the population. "Distinct society" status for Québec, multiculturalism, and aboriginal rights all came under popular attack, "constitutional fatigue" set in, concern with governments' huge debts and deficits mounted, and interest in social justice for aboriginal people returned to traditionally modest to low levels. Clearly, the political climate after the defeat of the Charlottetown Accord (even during the height of the Davis Inlet news coverage) was not conducive to further grandiose initiatives in the First Nation policy field. Indeed, it might never again be conducive. Instead, the Mulroney government made modest amendments to the *Indian Act* and concluded protracted negotiations which produced comprehensive land claims agreements in Yukon and the Northwest Territories. The federal Liberal government, elected in 1993, reverted to the Mulroney government's earlier policies of localization and restraint.

Phase VI: Reversion to Localization and Restraint

During the sixth phase the federal government actively circumvented The Assembly of First Nations, which had been effectively emasculated by the results of the Charlottetown Accord and the related debacle at Squamish (see below and Aubrey, 1992). As in the fourth phase, the government sought to increase its impact at the regional (tribal council) and grassroots level of First Nation communities. Examples are the redeployment of funds from other parts of the DIAND budget into on-reserve housing, as announced in a new housing policy in 1996, and a 1995 policy proposal for a much more limited form of local self-government than the Charlottetown Accord envisaged (Delacourt, 1995). It also entered into a 1994 agreement with The Assembly of Manitoba Chiefs to dismantle the Department of Indian Affairs and Northern Development there and to restore jurisdictions to the governments of the Manitoba First Nations.[17] This re-emphasis on the reserve level perhaps offers the greatest potential for concrete achievements over the short term. At that level consensus is easier to build, objectives are usually more attainable, and a pool of leadership and expertise is building.

The government was criticized (e.g., Miller, 1996: 340–341, 433–434) during this period for not showing a greater awareness of the importance of individual and community healing, especially in light of the traumatic and long-lived impacts of the residential school experience. Even in response to the recommendations of the Royal Commission on Aboriginal Peoples (RCAP, 1996c: 201–364), the federal government avoided making a more concerted policy thrust to address the widespread and profound need for healing.

In fact, displaying a moral, fiscal, and political myopia that left this observer incredulous, the Chrétien government totally "stonewalled" both the Royal Commission and First Nations' National Day of Protest (April 17, 1997) against government inaction on the Commission's recommendations. The government claimed that the Commission's report showed that the government was already on the right track. The minister said that the government could not afford to implement the Commission's recommendations, while the Prime Minister, displaying total ignorance of the holistic premises and long-term orientation of the Commission's report, said that there could be "no quick fixes" and that the government would continue with its "one solution at a time" approach. The Prime Minister refused to meet with Ovide Mercredi, the National Chief of The Assembly of First Nations.[18] One could say that with that intransigence, the Prime Minister practically invited increased militancy among First Nation people. In my estimation, the probability of violent confrontation escalated markedly with the federal government's response to the Royal Commission.

The restraint which characterized the sixth phase was not merely financial. It was exhibited also in the realm of social control. That is, as armed stand-offs occurred around the country, such as at Gustafsen Lake, Douglas Lake, and Camp Ipperwash, the federal government actively sought to avoid provoking another Oka-type clash. Patience and forbearance appeared to be the order of the day for the R.C.M.P and/or the Canadian military, even when those orientations were apparently not shared by the provincial government involved, or in the case of Gustafsen Lake, by the First Nation demonstrators.[19] A similar restraint characterized the federal government's orientation toward the smuggling of cigarettes across the Canada–U.S.A. border, even when such trade turned violent. The federal government's approach was to lower the federal taxes on cigarettes, so as to reduce the incentive to smuggling, rather than confront the armed smugglers more forcefully than an inter-governmental co-ordinated enforcement task force already was. In fact, Insp. Wayne Blackburn, an RCMP officer responsible for seizing assets acquired through criminal activity, was publicly quoted as saying that no smuggled goods had been seized on-reserve and refused to answer when asked why. Earlier he had referred to the political ramifications which arise from "questionable" police activities vis-à-vis Natives (Burke and Nielsen, 1996).

CHANGES AMONG FIRST NATIONS

First Nation organizations, communities, and individuals were going through a quite different transformation between 1970 and 1996. That development was galvanized by the release in 1969 of the federal government's white paper, a document which had the effect of uniting First Nations and focusing their action to an unprecedented degree. In this regard, it is important to realize that throughout most of the first half of the twentieth century, numerous factors militated against the establishment of First Nation organizations at any level above that of the band (Hawthorn, 1967: 364–365; Frideres, 1974: 112; Tennant, 1990). Those factors included First Nation poverty and adult illiteracy, interference by the Indian agent or the RCMP, a requirement of the Indian Affairs Branch that all grievances be routed through the local Indian agent, and a section in the *Indian Act* (1927) prohibiting political organizing. Other factors included the lack of the federal franchise; the geographic dispersal and, in many cases, isolation of the First Nation communities; the linguistic diversity of First Nations and lack of a shared second language; parochial identifications with a particular tribe or treaty; and the lack of explicitly articulated common objectives.[20]

Phase I: Reactive Mobilization and Consolidation

Many of those obstacles no longer remained when the white paper was issued. In 1968 the National Indian Council (encompassing status and non-status Indians, and Métis) split into two organizations — the National Indian Brotherhood and the Canadian Métis Society. With that split status Indians, now represented by the National Indian Brotherhood (NIB), embarked upon a period of *consolidation*. This involved the securing of resources (especially funding) and the building of a consensus among the provincial and territorial member organizations such as the Indian Association of Alberta and the Indians of Québec Association. Another front on which consolidation was pursued was that of First Nation communities on reserves. Under the leadership of NIB President George Manuel, bands were exhorted to tackle their social and economic problems by following the principles of collective endeavour (community development) as enunciated by Manuel's model, President Julius Nyerere of Tanzania. Finally, the period of internal consolidation was also characterized by a quest for legitimacy not only at the level of reserves and the level of the federal government, but also within the international community.

Phase II: Protest and Engagement

The mid-1970s was a period of contrasting behaviours. At the community level vigorous *protest* against, and *confrontation* with, DIAND was rampant and a new generation of young and determined political leaders rose to prominence in band politics. Yet, while DIAND was virtually under siege in the regions, at Ottawa headquarters an era of *engagement* or co-operation, and some would say co-optation, was underway. NIB became heavily involved in federal government committees and task forces and in developing programs which could be implemented under the existing *Indian Act*. One particularly noteworthy example of such program development and engagement is found in NIB's development of a policy and program of First Nation control of First Nation education.

BOX 3 Phases in the First Nation "Quiet Revolution"

• Reactive Mobilization and Consolidation	1969–73
• Protest and Engagement	1973–78
• Disengagement and Confrontation	1978–80
• Re-engagement and Constitutional Striving	1981–87
• Eclipse and Revival	1987–92
• Marginalization and Desperation Politics	1992–

Another is the revival of the treaty-making phenomenon, as manifested in the James Bay and Northern Québec Agreement. In return for compensation and for the creation of various governing institutions on which the Cree First Nations would have representation or control, the latter Agreement permitted construction of Québec's massive James Bay hydroelectric power project which flooded large tracts of First Nation land in the region.

Another particularly noteworthy example of engagement was NIB's lobbying for, and participation in, a joint committee with the federal cabinet. This committee was born out of a September 1974 physical clash between demonstrators and RCMP guards on Parliament Hill. Its three and a half year existence was marked by modest progress at best, infrequent meetings, and a high level of mutual frustration. It came to an abrupt end in April 1978 when NIB announced its surprise withdrawal and denounced the government (Ponting and Gibbins, 1980: 257–269; Weaver, 1982).

Phase III: Disengagement and Confrontation

Better than any other event, NIB's withdrawal from the joint committee with Cabinet signalled an end to the era of national-level co-operation and the beginning of the period of *disengagement and confrontation* at the national level. This new period was marked by a heightening of mutual distrust between NIB and DIAND and by a mutual challenging of the legitimacy of the other. DIAND's attempts to interest NIB in amending the *Indian Act* fell on deaf ears as NIB channelled most of its efforts into responding to the window of opportunity opened by Prime Minister Trudeau's constitutional initiative. Local protests and confrontations (e.g., involving conservationists, sportfishing groups and the federal Department of Fisheries and Oceans over First Nation fishing rights in New Brunswick, British Columbia and elsewhere), along with warnings and threats of racial violence, formed the backdrop to the early months of this stage. Such events could only have strengthened national First Nation leaders' determination to entrench aboriginal rights in the new Canadian constitution.

Confrontation continued during the short-lived Clark government as First Nations felt they were being shut out of the constitutional renewal process. For instance, a delegation of 300 First Nation Chiefs visited Britain to press their point but were denied an audience with the Queen as a result of instructions from the Clark government.

Phase IV: Re-engagement and Constitutional Striving

With the 1980 re-election of a Liberal government determined to patriate and revise the constitution, First Nations combined with other Natives to press on the federal and provincial governments their case for the recognition and elaboration of aboriginal rights. The strategy of *engagement* was revived and over the next several years First Nations and other Natives bounced back and forth between strategies of engagement and confrontation as they were buffeted by stronger political winds emanating from other political storms. Suffice it to say here that the first half of the 1980s saw aboriginal peoples (or their rights) excluded from the proposed constitution; then re-included amidst literal tears of joy in parliamentary committee; excluded again in the November 5, 1981, constitutional "accord"; re-included weeks later; fighting the new constitution in the British Parliament and courts; enmeshed in negotiations and discussions with the provinces and the federal government; and finally locked in an impasse with the provincial and federal governments at the 1985 constitutional conference on the issue of First Nation self-government. That impasse persisted at the 1987 constitutional conference.

Not surprisingly, such a roller coaster ride took its toll not only on unity between status Indians and other Natives, but also on unity among status Indians themselves, where strains between those in western Canada who had signed land cession treaties and those elsewhere who had not were never far below the surface. For instance, prairie treaty organizations balked at constitutional proposals which would give provincial governments (with whom they have no treaty or legal relationship) veto power over constitutional changes in First Nations' relationship with the federal government. Indeed, prairie treaty organizations at one time balked at even proceeding down the path of constitutional reform, for they felt their professed status as sovereign nations to be irreparably compromised by having First Nations included in another nation's (Canada's) constitution. Consequently, in the 1980s The Assembly of First Nations (AFN), as the restructured[21] NIB is known, came to be essentially a shifting coalition into and out of which some western provincial-level First Nation associations seemed to move on almost an issue-by-issue basis.

Of course, such instability undermined the AFN's leadership. This was particularly so in 1985 when prairie associations withdrew from AFN in response to George Erasmus' defeat of Saskatchewan politician David Ahenakew in the AFN presidential election. The instability of the national-level First Nation organization, set in the context of a constitutional stalemate and explicit assertions from various other First Nation organizations that "AFN does not represent us", reinforced the predisposition of new DIAND minister David Crombie (former mayor of Toronto) to work most closely with local rather than national level political leaders. This pattern was to be repeated after Erasmus' successor, Ovide Mercredi, was rebuffed by First Nation chiefs (lack of a quorum at the ratification vote) when, at a notorious meeting at Squamish, B.C., he sought ratification of provisions he had negotiated for First Nations in the Charlottetown Accord of 1992. He was similarly undermined by low attendance of chiefs at an AFN national assembly in 1996 when his motion in favour of adopting sovereignty-association as the goal of First Nations came to a vote. Mercredi's inability to demonstrate that his people are behind him reinforced the federal minister in his strategy of circumventing the AFN except when the AFN was needed to confer legitimacy or to resolve escalated conflicts such as those at Ipperwash and Gustafsen Lake in 1995.[22]

Phase V: Eclipse and Revival

The stalemate at the 1987 constitutional negotiating table and the release of the Meech Lake Accord less than three months later are among the low points in First Nations' political history. For instance, the original Meech Lake Accord not only was formulated without aboriginal input, but also did not mention aboriginal people, contained a pronounced dualistic (English-French) bias rooted in the "two founding peoples" paradigm which aboriginal leaders reject as insulting and racist, and granted to Québec the "distinct society" status which aboriginal leaders had unsuccessfully sought for aboriginal people. Formal constitutional recognition of sociological distinctiveness had become contested terrain and First Nations lost the contest. Furthermore, First Nations and other aboriginal peoples had clearly been displaced from the political agenda and from the political game after having enjoyed access to the inner circles of power during the constitutional negotiations earlier in the 1980s.

The opportunity for reviving their political influence was not to present itself until the crisis over the ratification of the Meech Lake Accord in June 1990. Riding a wave of populist anti-elitism in the Canadian mass public and indignation among aboriginal people, Manitoba M.L.A. Elijah Harper took on an instrumental role in defeating the Meech Lake Accord. In so doing, he served notice that aboriginal people were a force with which Canadian political leaders would have to reckon.

The "Oka crisis", which vaulted to international prominence the next month, reaffirmed that message. Across the country it was a period of enormous pride and solidarity among First Nation peoples, for someone was standing up and forcefully driving home the clear message "Enough is enough! Aboriginal people will not be pushed around on land issues any longer!" The prospect of additional crisis-ridden, highly expensive, "long hot summers" of First Nation protest did much to motivate federal and provincial officials to seriously entertain aboriginal grievances.

First Nation and other aboriginal (male) leaders were intimately involved in negotiating the Charlottetown Accord. If an earlier generation of national First Nation leaders had sought the "Holy Grail", Ovide Mercredi had found it. Mercredi interacted at the pinnacle of Canadian politics with the political elite of the larger society, achieved spectacular success[23] in terms of the content of the Charlottetown Accord, and then plummetted to the depths of virtual irrelevance to the federal political process as the Accord failed to win the approval of either the chiefs or, in the referendum, even on-reserve voters.[24]

Although it might appear harsh to suggest that political manoeuvering undermined visionary leadership, the conclusion seems inescapable, for it was supporters of Mercredi's rival, Phil Fontaine, who succeeded in denying Mercredi the quorum of chiefs which he needed to bring the Accord to a ratification vote at the aforementioned chiefs' assembly in Squamish prior to the national referendum. Ratification was also impeded, though, by the long-standing distrust which grassroots First Nation individuals feel for non-Native governments, and perhaps even by the reluctance to take on responsibility about which Strater Crowfoot writes in his chapter in this volume.

Phase VI: Marginalization and Desperation Politics

The Assembly of First Nations itself emerged as perhaps the largest immediate loser from the Charlottetown Accord fiasco, for its power base disintegrated beneath it. As Weaver (1985) has found in both Canada and Australia, the federal government confers and withdraws legitimacy from organizations like AFN as it suits the best interests of the government to do so. After 1992, it suited the Government of Canada to largely ignore the AFN until armed confrontations broke out at such places as Gustafsen Lake, B.C., and Camp Ipperwash, Ontario, in 1995. Mercredi's unsuccessful attempts to mediate in those conflicts seemed to confirm AFN's marginality, especially when First Nation militants accused him of being part of the problem as one who had "sold-out" to the federal government and had not pushed First Nation interests with sufficient vigour. Significantly, it was First Nation spiritual leaders, like Arvol Looking Horse,[25] and particularly Spotted Bird (John Stevens),[26] who commanded sufficient moral authority to influence the Gustafsen Lake occupiers to end their standoff with police.

The Assembly of First Nations and many other First Nation organizations faced the 1995 Québec referendum in a weakened position. Dreams of prodding Québec and Canada into a competitive bidding "war" for aboriginal support faded as the outcome of the pending Québec referendum began to take on a greater air of uncertainty and the discourse of the campaign came to focus increasingly (albeit by no means exclusively) on the issue of the fate of the aboriginal inhabitants of Québec if Québec were to separate from Canada. In particular, the issue of whether an independent Québec could itself be partitioned so as to enable First Nations to remain part of Canada took on great prominence. The Mohawks had already engendered great antipathy among French Québécois for their stance during and after the "Oka crisis" and for their involvement in cross-border smuggling, and the James Bay Crees had thwarted the high-profile James Bay II project which was of great symbolic importance to Québec nationalists. Now the First Nations appeared to be standing in the way of Québec nationalists' "rendezvous with destiny" by opposing Québec sovereignty and threatening the territorial integrity of an independent Québec. Tensions were heightened by rhetoric like "If Canada is divisible, so is an independent Québec", Cree contentions that the James Bay Agreement was null and void, and then-Premier Parizeau's bitter comment on referendum night "We have been defeated by money and the ethnic vote". To be a conspicuous campaign issue without having the votes or other resources to shape the outcome of an emotionally laden, high-stakes campaign is, I submit, not to be in a position of power, but rather to be a pawn in a position of vulnerability.

The Assembly of First Nations' response to its predicament came two months later. Shortly after a December 1995 international Sacred Assembly called by Elijah Harper, Mercredi pursued a long-standing interest (Mercredi and Turpel, 1993: 53–55) in Mahatma Gandhi's teachings and politics by visiting India. He returned to declare Gandhian non-violent direct action, including civil disobedience, to be the new course which AFN would chart. Strategically, this course offered a constructive outlet for the energy and spirituality of First Nation youths and young adults frustrated by the slow and unspectacular changes in the structure of opportunities which they faced. It was also a strategically appropriate course for a people who lacked the political resources to win at conventional politics but who were experiencing a spiritual revival, could claim the moral high ground, could attract intense international media attention, and could expect significant and effective international support for their cause. Nevertheless, to this outside observer, there were no indications that it ever got off the ground.

A few months later, after being denied participation in a First Ministers' conference on the future of Canada, Mercredi asked the AFN's assembly of chiefs to endorse a goal of sovereignty-association for First Nations throughout Canada. The wheel had come full circle. Once again, though, a lukewarm response from the chiefs[27] left AFN in a position where it could be easily dismissed by federal government politicians, and it was. On its world wide web home page, AFN's appeal[28] for support from other Canadians bore further testimony to just how far AFN had fallen politically.

As Gibbins (1986: 308) observed concerning the events leading to the recognition and affirmation of aboriginal and treaty rights in *The Constitution Act, 1982*, First Nations at that time seemed to be riding a roller coaster without having any control over its direction or speed. At the national level, the same appeared to be the case in the mid-1990s for AFN, and making matters worse, the roller coaster train was on a decidedly uphill stretch of track. That is, AFN at that time was operating in a political climate which had deteriorated significantly over the previous ten years, as egalitarian norms in opposition to "special status" came to be championed in the populist discourse of such opinion leaders as Reform Party of Canada leader Preston Manning. As noted elsewhere in this book, most Canadians had come to view equality in terms of an uniformity model (no "special status" or "special privileges" for any sector of society) rather than an equity model which would recognize the need for different arrangements for differentially situated sectors of society. Furthermore, as we shall see, public opinion polls revealed Canadians to have very little sympathy for even mildly coercive protest tactics. Seen in this light, Mercredi's endorsement of non-violent direct action, which usually is quite coercive even though non-violent, in pursuit of a goal of sovereignty-association, took on a certain appearance of desperation politics.

OTHER THEMES

The Assembly of First Nations provides a convenient vantage point on changes in Indian country, but by no means is it the only useful vantage point. Various other themes can be discerned by shifting our gaze. Particularly noteworthy among them are the following:

- healing and revitalization
- awakening of the women and reclaiming of voice
- internationalization
- commodification of culture
- assertiveness
- new institutional "accommodations" (including land claims)

We consider each in turn, although some only in passing.

Healing and Revitalization

One of the ironies of First Nations' history is that one man, Manitoba leader Phil Fontaine, played both a pivotally destructive and a pivotally constructive role. His role in marginalizing AFN politically was noted above. His constructive contribution was a sociological and psychological one which came in his 1990 public announcement that he had been sexually abused as a schoolboy by Oblate clergy at the Fort Alexander school (Miller, 1996: 328). This breaking down of the wall of silence by such a prominent public figure served as a signal to other First Nation individuals who had survived the sexual or physical abuse of the residential schools and/or of their family situations. The message was that it is not only appropriate to talk about such abuse, but that disclosure is necessary if healing is to begin.

Healing has been identified as one of the greatest needs and "basic challenge" of First Nation communities (Ponting, 1993; Mercredi and Turpel, 1993: 163). Such an assessment would be difficult to challenge, given the existing documentation (e.g., Haig-Brown, 1988; AFN Health Commission, 1994) of the debilitating direct and indirect impacts of the physical, emotional, and sexual abuse that occurred in various residential schools and that have been endemic[29] in many First Nation communities. Those impacts produce dysfunctional individuals, families, and communities. Indeed, for some former students, it is entirely appropriate to speak of the residential school experience as akin to an holocaust.

Abundant resources could be put at the disposal of First Nation individuals and communities, but if substantial healing has not already occurred the results will usually be highly disappointing, as the rapid deterioration of a significant portion of the on-reserve new housing stock attests. Much of the healing will be spiritually based. So important is that spiritual basis of healing that it is doubtful that healing will lead to lasting personal empowerment if the spiritual foundation is not reasonably firm. Otherwise stated, individuals probably need to be spiritually healthy to make the most constructive (as defined by First Nations' standards) use of the power they are acquiring.

Phil Fontaine's courageous disclosure has empowered others to come forth with painful, heart-rending disclosures of their own. This has resulted not only in a small number of criminal prosecutions (Miller, 1996: Chapter 11) and convictions, but more importantly, in public apologies and very modest restitution. That restitution has come from government (Canadian Press, 1996d) and from the various religious denominations which operated residential schools where sexual abuse of students (and sometimes of Native staff) occurred. Such apologies are crucial to the validation of victims' experience, which in turn is an important step in many victims' healing. Public disclosures have also been instrumental in enabling the Royal Commission on Aboriginal Peoples (1996a: 333–410) to assemble a compelling case on the malignant effects of the residential schools and in favour of healing programmes, activities, and facilities receiving the funding priority which they need.

Thus, one of the consequences of Fontaine's disclosure has been that a start has been made on the retrieval of a huge amount of lost human potential. In First Nation terms, the lost and wandering spirit of many First Nation individuals has begun the journey back to its rightful home in those individuals (AFN Health Commission, 1994: 108). Because of that, there is now realistic hope for a sustainable revitalization of First Nation families and communities in various locales across Canada. Rupert Ross' book, *Returning to the Teachings (1996)* offers various uplifting community examples of this healing and the Royal Commission on Aboriginal Peoples (1996c: 201–364) provided a national strategy.

Awakening of the Women and Reclaiming of Voice

The awakening of First Nation women was another major development of the late twentieth century. As noted above, the long struggle for equality within the *Indian Act* and the constitution was rewarded with an amendment to Sec. 35 of *The Constitution Act, 1982*, to guarantee aboriginal and treaty rights equally to aboriginal men and women, and with Bill C-31, an act to amend the *Indian Act* (Jamieson, 1986). Bill C-31 terminated sections of the *Indian Act* which discriminated against Indian women. For instance, Indian women, but not Indian men, had lost their status as Registered Indians when they married a non-Indian. Bill C-31 ended that phenomenon for the present generation of adults and also provided the opportunity for persons (primarily women and their children) who had lost their legal status as Registered Indians to regain it. However, acceptance of the new statute was uneven across the country. Resistance was particularly strong in Alberta, where the wealthy Sawridge Band helped launch a court challenge against the amendment. Some First Nations in Alberta and elsewhere adopted membership codes which made it very difficult for persons reinstated as Registered Indians to regain membership in their particular First Nation. That, and the fact that in Bill C-31 the sex discrimination was merely displaced onto the grandchildren's generation, mean that the battle on this issue is far from over.

The awakening of First Nation women has also occurred in the political arena. Particularly noteworthy have been the efforts of the Native Women's Association of Canada (N.W.A.C.) on two fronts. One front is the constitutional one, where N.W.A.C. fought unsuccessfully (Nagle, 1992; Green, 1993) in the political and legal arenas to obtain a seat at the constitutional bargaining table with the First Ministers and male aboriginal leaders in the 1990s. Distrustful of the male biases of AFN's leaders, N.W.A.C. actively sought to put First Nation women's concerns forward in their own voice. The other particularly noteworthy front on which N.W.A.C. took action is the area of self-government and criminal justice reform. N.W.A.C. and other First Nation women's organizations, of which there are now many, have gone to great lengths to impress upon policy makers their concerns that First Nation governments must not be exempted from the Canadian *Charter of Rights and Freedoms* (Canadian Press, 1992a; Nagle, 1992). They fear what Cockerill and Gibbins in this volume call "the tyranny of the majority in small societies". In particular, First Nation women have expressed doubts that justice as they conceive of it will be meted out by what they see as patriarchal, male-dominated First Nation government institutions such as courts, councils, and child-welfare agencies (Nagle, 1992). To substantiate their concerns, they point to attempts to cover up wife abuse and child sexual abuse in certain communities where the alleged perpetrators are relatives of powerful males in the community (e.g., Canadian Press, 1992a).

Another indicator of the awakening of First Nation women can be found in the growth of numerous Native women's organizations at the national, provincial, and local levels. Many of them submitted briefs to the Royal Commission on Aboriginal Peoples (RCAP) as part of its Intervenor Participation Programme and many others participated in the public hearings by making an oral presentation to the commissioners. One of the most commonly expressed concerns of these and other First Nation women's organizations in the 1980s and 1990s has been family violence. A landmark document on that topic was produced by The Ontario Native Women's Association under the title *Breaking Free*. It showed the alarming extent of violence within aboriginal communities and highlighted the pressing need for the issue to be addressed before such dangerous behaviour becomes any more firmly established as normal for aboriginal communities than it already is. RCAP took up the issue and commissioned some powerful research in this area, such as that by Madeleine Dion Stout (1996) and that by Danielle Descant et al. (1993).

Women's awakening at the local level includes a variety of activities. Among these are mobilizing politically to share in scarce resources (e.g., Fiske, 1990), exercising leadership in community revitalization and healing activities (e.g., Evans, 1990; Descant et al., 1993), actively defending their culture and land claim through civil disobedience and other measures (see Brown in this volume), teaching the aboriginal language and passing on other forms of traditional knowledge and practice, participating as students in post-secondary education and as graduates in the professional careers arising therefrom, building and operating shelters for the victims of family violence, and engaging in the arts and in entrepreneurial business activities.

In the opinion of this author, women in many, perhaps most, First Nation communities are the pivotal actors on whom the community's prospects for healing, survival, and development depend. Brown reaches a similar conclusion à propos Lubicon women in her chapter in this volume. Cree (male) artist Dale Auger captures the same notion in his painting: women, he observes, have been the stable influence, a sustaining force which has carried First Nation men. Now that First Nation women are moving and the power is passing from the politicians to the community, First Nation men will have to move also, he submits.

First Nation women are also reclaiming their voice on issues such as stereotyping. The derogatory stereotype of "the squaw" and the seemingly flattering but also disempowering stereotype of "the Indian princess" were forcefully challenged during the era under examination. No longer would First Nation women remain silent about stereotyping. Their voices were heard in the daily press and broadcast media on the Pocahontas myth (e.g., Stevenson, 1995), in a documentary on stereotypes of Indians (Matthews, 1992) on the Canadian Broadcasting Corporation's *Ideas* radio program, in books (e.g., Acoose, 1995; Cuthand, 1989; Fife, 1993; Miller and Chuchryk, 1996; and Silman, 1987), in Native Studies classes at universities and colleges, in television docudramas, and elsewhere in the arts and performing arts (e.g., the CBC television show *North of 60*).

Part of First Nation women's awakening can be traced to their increased rate of participation in post-secondary education (Voyageur, 1993: 109). Wotherspoon and Satzewich (1993: 144) also note that "some of the strongest advocates of aboriginal rights ... have [been] women attending or recently graduated from post-secondary institutions." Furthermore, they point out that First Nation women have potentially greater access to expanded educational services and support.[30] Accordingly, we should anticipate First Nation women's voice becoming more forceful and more frequently activated.

The large amount of attention devoted to aboriginal women in the final report of the Royal Commission on Aboriginal Peoples (e.g., RCAP, 1996d: 7–106) will buttress the legitimacy of First Nation women's voices among the predominantly male decision-makers in the governments and media of the larger society. Within First Nation communities, though, Voyageur's (1993: 106) assertion that "Indian leaders — that is Indian men — must loosen their grasp on the power given to them by the government", should not be interpreted to mean that such an opening of power structures to women will be automatic or easy. Like most phenomena in "Indian country", such empowerment will proceed very unevenly from one First Nation to another. Power, especially when it is in as scarce supply as it is among a colonized people, will not be given up voluntarily. The period of transition into the new millennium could well exhibit some very intense power struggles between entrenched male power brokers and emerging female challengers at the local and national levels. Where female challengers succeed, a modification of political priorities should be expected (e.g., family violence and child care given prioritiy over the constitution) along with a reallocation of opportunities in such areas as local employment, occupational training and post-secondary education funding, and housing allocation.

Internationalization

Aboriginal peoples are taking an increasingly prominent place on the stage of international politics (van de Fliert, 1994). The phenomenon of First Nations using foreign arenas to pursue objectives in relationships with governments and corporations in Canada is a prominent form of "internationalization". In an article entitled "Internationalization: Perspectives on an Emerging Direction in Aboriginal Affairs" (Ponting, 1990), I identify other aspects of internationalization and provide a case study and cursory historical overview of the phenomenon. In the present volume, Symons' and my chapter, entitled "Environmental Geo-Politics and the New World Order", also provides a case study in international relations related to First Nation issues. Limitations of space preclude an extended discussion of the internationalization phenomenon here. Suffice it to say that the interest of the world's mass media in Canadian aboriginal affairs continued unabated during the first half of the 1990s (e.g., the worldwide coverage given to the Davis Inlet situation) and that the United Nations and other international forums (e.g., the Rio Summit on the Environment) continued to provide a stage on which some scenes of the Canadian aboriginal drama were played out. To the extent that certain conditions obtain — namely, progress on First Nation issues in Canada is blocked, First Nation people hold little political power in Canada, and international actors become implicated in Canadian aboriginal affairs — we should expect First Nation leaders and activists to play more to the international audience in the hope of applying some leverage to Canadian governments. That is precisely what they did, for instance, with the Assembly of First Nations' European tour just prior to the National Day of Protest in 1997.

Commodification of Culture

In Europe there is a widespread fascination with aboriginal peoples and cultures. In Canada, the earliest modern manifestations of any similar interest are found in the realm of art (e.g., Inuit sculptures) and artifacts (e.g., totems and masks). Aided by the ideology of multiculturalism, by business development loans and other forms of government facilitation, and by the healing and cultural revival that is occurring in numerous First Nations, First Nation artists and entrepreneurs have ventured forth into the marketplace with a variety of forms of cultural expression. This might be done with a mixture of motives which can span a broad range. One imputes motives for any given undertaking at one's peril.

The forms which the commercialized cultural blossoming takes vary from the sublime to the possibly ridiculous. Among the former are the magnificent works of such gifted artists as Dale Auger, Jackson Beardy, Benjamin Chee Chee, ioyanmani (Maxine Noel), Norval Morrisseau, Daphne Odjig, Susan Point, Bill Reid, Roy Vickers, Clem Wescoupe, and architect Douglas Cardinal. Among the ridiculous, in the uneducated opinion of this observer, would be aboriginal pin-up calendars (Redekop, 1995) marketed in Manitoba. Examples of other forms in which Native culture can be found commercially are Native dinner theatre, commercial cultivation of wild rice, commercial "pow-wows" intended for the non-Native market, recordings of Native drummers and/or vocalists, craft shops, dream catchers for use in automobiles(!), Native clothing, the proposed Natives of the Americas theme park in Alberta, museums intended to bring in tourists, and "coffee table" books of Native art.[31] Considerable commercial success has been experienced by some of these ventures, such as the musical group Kashtin.

There are, of course, numerous other commercial ventures on-reserve where the commercial availability of First Nation culture is non-existent, incidental, or merely implicit.

Assertiveness

As I first wrote this section, the morning news carried a story of First Nations people blowing up a logging bridge in the Temagami wilderness of Ontario (Canadian Press, 1996c). The previous year saw the occupation and take-over of Canadian Forces Base Ipperwash by members of the Kettle and Stoney Point Chippewas,[32] the shooting at police by First Nation protesters during the armed confrontation at Gustafsen Lake, and First Nation leaders' assertions that if Canada is divisible, so is a separate Québec. These were just a few of many incidents that year. Earlier in the decade sensationalistic instances of the new assertiveness of First Nation people were plentiful. Just a few examples are:

- Chief Katie Rich's expulsion of the RCMP from the Innu community of Davis Inlet
- crashing of fences at C.F.B. Goose Bay by Labrador Innu to hold a demonstration on the air strip in protest against low-level N.A.T.O. warplane flights
- near Pemberton, B.C., the bombing of a forestry bridge leading to a construction site for a logging road which the Lil'Wat Peoples Movement vowed to stop because it would go through Lil'Wat (Lillooet) ancestral burial grounds
- armed resistance by Milton Born-With-a-Tooth against the building of the Oldman River dam in southern Alberta and the Lonefighters Society's attempted diversion of the river around the dam
- the unilateral assertion of sovereignty by armed Mohawk warriors at Oka/Kanehsatake, by Mohawk cigarette and liquor smugglers, and by First Nations (e.g., White Bear in Saskatchewan) opening gambling casinos in defiance of provincial government laws.

Less sensationalistic examples of First Nation assertiveness can be found in a court challenge by The Native Women's Association of Canada to gain standing in constitutional reform negotiations, and by road or rail line blockades by, among others, the Upper Nicola Band at the Douglas Lake cattle ranch in B.C., the Lac Barrière Algonquins in Québec, the Penticton First Nation in B.C., and various First Nations (e.g., the Mount Currie band in B.C. and the Pays Plat band in Ontario) in support of the Mohawks during the Oka conflict of 1990.

Clearly, for many First Nation individuals and communities, patience has run out. The subtitle — *Anger and Renewal in Indian Country* — of a book authored by Boyce Richardson (1989) and co-published by The Assembly of First Nations is indicative of that. The government's intransigence in response to the recommendations of the Royal Commission on Aboriginal Peoples could prove to be "the last straw". Moderate First Nation leaders warned governments that if they decline to negotiate meaningfully and productively with them, then those governments would have to deal with more radical leaders (Caragata, 1991). By the mid-1990s that prediction was coming true. For instance, Ovide Mercredi lamented publicly that First Nation people are starting to turn on their local chiefs who do not have enough money to deal with the housing, education, and welfare crises on reserve.[33] Of particular concern, in light of the disproportionately young age structure of the First Nation population, should be the potential radicalization of First Nation youth. If they conclude that conventional means of pressing grievances are ineffective and that their future is so bleak as to leave them little to lose, a significant escalation in protest tactics can be expected.

New "Accommodations"

As Calliou's chapter in this volume notes, the institutions of "mainstream" Canadian society have a long way to go in adjusting to the presence of aboriginal people. In particular, aboriginal people seek reforms which require fundamental structural changes, rather than mere "tinkering" at the margins of existing institutions, if obstacles to equality, opportunity, and empowerment are to be removed. However, there has been some noteworthy progress on a variety of fronts. That progress should not go unnoticed, for it holds considerable potential for the future. This section provides a glimpse of "accommodations" in various institutional sectors. The word "accommodations" is placed in quotation marks initially to signify that it is used here in the narrow sociological sense to refer to adjustments made to a relationship, and to the institutions in which that relationship occurs, in order to mitigate conflict by reducing its likelihood, frequency, severity, or consequences. No connotations of condescension or of "noblesse oblige" on the part of the more powerful actor in the relationship are intended. Hence, the term can be used, without giving offence (I hope), even to describe the recognition of pre-existing aboriginal rights.

The state plays a pervasive role in the lives of First Nation people. Accordingly, we should expect it to have exhibited some leadership in accommodating the needs and preferences of First Nation people and in seeking to expand opportunity structures for First Nation people. Compared to the private sector, the federal government has taken the lead, although an undetermined number of federal innovations undoubtedly came from First Nation initiatives. Among the innovations funded by the federal government to accommodate First Nation people (and in some cases, other Natives) through special programs or parallel structures, have been those identified in Box 4.[34] The vast majority of programs funded entirely by DIAND are not included, but some that are included are jointly funded with the provincial/territorial governments.

Lest the reader be swept away with visions of the magnanimity of the federal government, it is useful to remember that many of the programmes cited in Box 4 are poorly funded, fund mainly "dead-end" pilot projects, are subject

BOX 4 Selected Program and Structural Changes Introduced by the Federal Government to Accommodate Native People

Canada Employment Insurance Commission
- Affirmative Action Program and Federal Contracts Program to promote affirmative action measures among public and private sector employers and private sector contractors. Aboriginal people are one of four target groups.
- Options North program to provide special support for individuals in NWT who are adjusting to wage employment

Canada Mortgage and Housing Corporation
- on- and off-reserve housing loans to individuals and band councils at current or reduced interest rates

Corrections Canada (Solicitor-General)
- permitting Native inmates to have Native healing circles and to practice Native spirituality

Fisheries and Oceans
- creation of an aboriginal fishery on the Fraser River and precedence given to it over the non-Native commercial fishery
- Salmonid Enhancement Program
- Community Economic Development Program to increase fish production in British Columbia through low-technology, community-oriented techniques

Health Canada
- National Native Alcohol and Drug Abuse Program for treatment and rehabilitation services
- Hospital Services
- Capital Construction of hospitals, nursing stations, health centres, etc. both on- and off-reserve
- Non-Insured Health Benefits, including payment of health care premiums, drugs, glasses, health transportation, etc.
- Community Health Services, including communicable disease control, nursing services, mental health, nutrition and health education

Heritage Canada
- Native Communications Program to enable Native people to develop and control modern communications networks
- Northern Broadcast Access Program to assist Native communications companies to produce regional Native language radio and television programming in the North
- CBC Northern Service radio programming
- creation of "Studio I" (aboriginal projects) within the National Film Board
- introduction of programs about First Nation people (e.g., North of 60)
- Native Representative Organizations Program to provide "core" operating funds to organizations representing aboriginal people
- Native Friendship Centres Program to help migrating and resident Native peoples adjust to the urban environment
- Aboriginal Women's Program to support projects and activities for the participation of Native women in Canadian society
- Native Social and Cultural Development Program in support of language retention projects, elders' conferences, Native awareness weeks, pow-wows, etc.

Justice
- Charlottetown Accord
- Recognition of aboriginal rights in the Constitution

BOX 4 *(continued)*

- Native Court Worker Program offering para-legal court services to Native accused persons in order to bridge the cultural gap between Native and non-Native justice systems.
- use of sentencing circles under some circumstances, at discretion of presiding trial judge
- Native Law Students Program to assist aboriginal people to enter the legal profession

Privy Council Office / Constitutional Affairs
- participation of aboriginal leaders in constitutional negotiations with the First Ministers

Public Service Commission
- National Indigenous Development Program to improve the representation of indigenous people at middle and senior levels in federal public service

RCMP and DIAND-funded Policing
- On-Reserve Special Constables Program
- Band Constable Program for funding constables who are appointed by the RCMP, but employed by, and report to, the band council
- "Option 3B" program for funding provision of peace officers to First Nations
- Quebec Amerindian Police initiative to provide Indian-controlled police service supervised and managed by the Amerindian Police Council

Regional Industrial Expansion
- Native Economic Development Program
- Special ARDA (Agricultural and Rural Development Act) programs to improve income and employment opportunities of disadvantaged people, particularly of Indian ancestry, in rural areas.

Other: procurement
- adoption of a preference for aboriginal suppliers in DIAND purchasing

---

Source: Primarily taken from Study Team on Indian and Native Programs (1985: passim).

---

to bureaucratic meddling and interference by the government, had their funding drastically reduced as part of larger federal budgetary restraint policies, or address symptoms rather than root causes. Driben and Trudeau (1983) provide other examples of how well-intentioned programs can go awry.

Box 4 does not identify one of the most significant accommodations made by governments — namely, the institutional arrangements contained in various land claim settlements. Some highlights of the 1996 Agreement-in-Principle for the Nisga'a land claim in the Nass River region of northwestern British Columbia are shown in Box 5.

Provincial and municipal governments have been less active in developing special accommodations for First Nations. In fact, because constitutional jurisdiction for First Nations lies with the federal government, most provinces have actively refused to get involved in providing support to on-reserve First Nation populations and often even to off-reserve First Nation populations. However, among provincial accommodations that have occurred, some of the most noteworthy have been:

- child welfare agreements with individual First Nations or tribal councils

BOX 5 Selected Provisions of the Nisga'a Land Claim Agreement-in Principle, 1996

Land, Compensation, and Fiscal Transfers
- recognition of Nisga'a title (rather than Crown title) to about 1,900 square kilometres of land in the lower Nass Valley of British Columbia
- a "capital transfer" (financial compensation) in the amount of $190 million, paid in instalments, plus on-going funding (where feasible, to be reduced over time) to the Nisga'a Central Government in order to enable it to provide the public services and programs agreed-upon in the Agreement-in-Principle
- the right to have Nisga'a cultural values taken into account in establishing the size of fiscal transfers to the Nisga'a Central government
- funding in the amount of $11.5 million to enable the Nisga'a Central Government to increase its capacity (vessels and licences) to participate in the coast-wide commercial fishery
- exemption of Nisga'a Government corporations, operating solely on Nisga'a lands, from federal and provincial income taxes

Natural Resources, Marine Species, and Wildlife
- Nisga'a ownership of all mineral resources on or under Nisga'a lands
- Nisga'a entitlement to a guaranteed share of the harvest of salmon and other marine and wildlife (e.g., moose, grizzly bear, mountain goat) species, subject to conservation measures
- the right of Nisga'a citizens to harvest migratory birds and their eggs for domestic purposes, subject to measures necessary for conservation and the protection of public health and safety; and the right of the Nisga'a Central Government to be consulted on Canada's position in relation to international agreements which might significantly affect migratory birds or their habitat within the Nass area
- a commitment by the Government of British Columbia to approve the acquisition by Nisga'a Central Government of a forest tenure (e.g., a tree farm licence for logging purposes)
- guarantees of a specified volume of flow from the Nass River for Nisga'a uses and the right to be consulted by the provincial government on the granting of all water licences pertaining to streams within Nisga'a lands
- representation equal to that of Canada and British Columbia, respectively, on the committee that advises the responsible federal, provincial, and Nisga'a ministers on fisheries management
- representation equal to that of British Columbia on the committee that advises the provincial minister responsible for the management of wildlife

Jurisdiction and Powers of Nisga'a Central Government
- the Final Agreement to prevail over federal and provincial laws to the extent that there is any inconsistency or conflict between the Final Agreement and those laws
- the right of the Nisga'a Central Government to make laws governing the adoption of Nisga'a children, including Nisga'a children residing off Nisga'a lands if the parent or guardian having lawful custody consents
- the right of the Nisga'a Central Government to tax Nisga'a citizens on Nisga'a lands
- the right of the Nisga'a Central Government to make various other laws

Environmental Protection
- the right of the Nisga'a Central Government to participate in any environmental assessment related to any proposed project which will be located outside Nisga'a lands but which can be reasonably expected to have adverse environmental effects on residents of Nisga'a lands

---

BOX 5 *(continued)*

Administration of Justice
- the establishment of a Nisga'a Court with the right to issue summons, subpoenas, and warrants and the right to impose penalties and remedies on Nisga'a citizens in accordance with generally accepted principles of sentencing recognized in law, although accused persons may elect to be tried in provincial court if the alleged offence is punishable by imprisonment under Nisga'a law

Other Cultural
- the right of legal ownership and repatriation to Nisga'a Central Government of each item in a list of Nisga'a artifacts held by The Canadian Museum of Civilization and by the Royal British Columbia Museum, and of others so held and later identified as Nisga'a artifacts
- the substitution of thirty-one Nisga'a place names on gazetted maps in place of presently existing (usually English language) place names on those maps
- the protection of certain Nisga'a sites under the provincial Heritage and Conservation Act

Source: Canada, British Columbia, and Nisga'a Tribal Council (1996).

- policies attempting to keep First Nation adoptees and foster children in their home community with First Nation families
- negotiated arrangements to permit the operation of gambling casinos by First Nations
- northern social or employment development initiatives
- joint participation with the federal government in the funding of various programmes listed in Box 4 (e.g., the Native Court Worker Program)
- various Native-oriented programmes in universities and community colleges, such as Native Studies programmes, outreach teaching programmes, and pre-entrance preparation programmes.

At the municipal level, legal distinctions as between different types of aboriginal people tend to be less salient than they are for federal and provincial governments. Nevertheless, special accommodations for Native people tend to be few and far between, although highly variable from one community to another in accordance with the size of the aboriginal population in the community. Perhaps among the more common adjustments are the rather limited ones of including Native representatives on certain municipal government committees, sub-committees, and advisory committees, and seeking to hire some token aboriginal police officers. Some municipal programs, though, especially in the social services, do have a disproportionately large Native clientele.

In the private sector, special accommodative arrangements tend to be rare. Perhaps most visible are programmes developed by natural resource exploration and pipeline companies and by banks. In the natural resources field, various companies have special hiring and training programmes for Natives, special Native community liaison officials, Native scholarships, and Native internship programmes. Banks have moved to capitalize on lucrative land claim settlements and, because as a federally regulated industry banks fall under the jurisdiction of the federal *Employment Equity Act*, have instituted aboriginal hiring policies. Other initiatives by banks include opening branches on a small number of reserves,[35] offering small business loans, establishing advisory committees of elders, and a pilot project offering mortgages for on-reserve homes with no form of guarantee from the band council.[36] Joint ventures between First Nation firms and non-Native firms is another form of private sector involvement with aboriginal people.

Calliou's chapter in this volume alludes to another type of private sector accommodation for Native people — namely, special aboriginal affairs committees in chambers of commerce. Considering all institutional spheres, Calliou's comments on the limitations of programmatic accommodations in the absence of more deeply rooted policy, procedural, and structural accommodations are well worth the attention of organizational officials throughout Canadian society.

CONCLUSION

In the approximately one-third century since the 1969 white paper, First Nations have experienced enormous changes of a magnitude that were utterly inconceivable even in the late 1960s. The legitimacy of the paternalistic and ethnocentric policies and forms of administration which characterized the two hundred years surrounding confederation has been shattered. Once treated as second class citizens by arrogant Indian agents and junior bureaucrats in government, First Nation leaders at the local level now command audiences with cabinet ministers while their national leaders negotiate with prime ministers and premiers and meet with popes and monarchs. Once shunted to the political, economic, and geographic periphery of Canadian society, First Nations now have aboriginal rights recognized in the very constitution of the country, undertake multi-million dollar economic development projects on reserves, and lay claim to immensely valuable real estate scattered throughout the country.

Notwithstanding the linearity exhibited in some of the above changes, along some dimensions the wheel has come full circle. For instance, the national-level political organization in the mid-1990s — as in the late 1960s, early 1970s, and mid-1980s — finds itself in the midst of a crisis of legitimacy and unity and the Department of Indian Affairs again finds itself in the midst of a major re-structuring and a threatened dissolution. Reserve-level community development and devolution of authority from DIAND to bands once again appear to be "where the action is". The fiscal problems of the debt-ridden federal government raise again the spectre of federal government attempts to transfer federal responsibilities for First Nations to the provinces.

While significant progress has been made, some of that progress has been undermined by demographic change within First Nation society and ideological change within the larger Canadian society. At time of writing, among non-Native leaders there was scant evidence of the political will to undertake the paradigm shift that is necessary. In this observer's opinion, the clock counting down the time before Canada's day of reckoning with First Nations raced ahead during the 1990s after the failure of the Charlottetown Accord. First Nation leaders have largely exhausted their strategic options: access to the Minister, access to key bureaucrats, a special Cabinet committee (Weaver, 1982), access to Treasury Board, constitutional reform and access to First Ministers, affirmative action, Supreme Court of Canada, entrepreneurialism, international pressure, royal commission, and alarmist rhetoric. In one very real sense, all of these strategies have failed. That is, First Nations remain grossly over-represented at the bottom of the social stratification hierarchy in Canada, structurally subordinated and largely lacking in self-determination. If non-Native political leaders continue to marginalize First Nation people, First Nations will assert themselves. The day of reckoning for Canada will be ugly, shocking, tragic, and suffused with racism. If it does not come before the turn of the century, that would be a miracle.

NOTES

[1] The portion of this chapter dealing with events between 1970 and 1985 is excerpted from J. Rick Ponting *Arduous Journey: Canadian Indians and Decolonization*, Toronto: McClelland & Stewart, 1986, pp. 34–41 and is reprinted here with the kind permission of Oxford University Press Canada.

[2] For a more detailed discussion of similarities and differences in the situation of First Nations and French Québécois see Ponting and Gibbins (1980: 321–323).

[3] Personal conversation with a First Nation leader who wishes to remain anonymous, February 1985.

[4] Earlier conferences produced meagre concrete results. The most noteworthy accomplishments were the amending of *The Constitution Act, 1982* to recognize: (1) aboriginal rights as pertaining equally to aboriginal men and aboriginal women; and (2) comprehensive land claims settlements as having treaty status under the constitution.

[5] See Ponting (1991) for a more detailed discussion of this policy.

[6] Of approximately 76,000 houses on-reserve in the mid-1990s, more than half were considered to be substandard. Approximately 8,000 households on reserve live in overcrowded or multiple-family situations. These data are from DIAND (1996).

[7] Boldt (1993: 32-39) offers a forceful critique of the notion that the Sparrow decision favours First Nations.

[8] The Meech Lake Accord was deemed to require ratification by all provincial legislatures within the three year period after it was finalized in June of 1987.

[9] See Campbell and Pal (1991) for a very detailed account of this crisis. Pal's concluding comments about trust are of particular interest to sociologists.

[10] Similarly, during the FLQ crisis of 1970, governments sought to dismiss the FLQ as terrorists and criminals and were surprised to find a high level of support for them in the population (of French Québécois).

[11] In an action that some might well see as tantamount to an admission that human rights in Canada are on a par with those in some "banana republic", and that others might view in opposite terms, the Mulroney government agreed to the presence of international human rights observers in conjunction with "the Oka crisis". See Campbell and Pal (1991).

[12] Immediately after the end of the standoff at Oka, the Liberal Senators engaged in their much-publicized "shenanigans" in the Senate on the issue of the introduction of the Mulroney government's Goods and Services Tax (GST). Media interest in aboriginal issues, and any accompanying sense of urgency for government to address them, promptly evaporated.

[13] Despite that policy, provisions of recently negotiated comprehensive land claim settlements with the Nisga'a and in Yukon have been tantamount to the extinguishment of aboriginal title.

[14] The disruption was multi-dimensional. One dimension was financial. Poirier (1991) reports the cost of the Mohawk crisis of summer 1990 to have been $112 million to the Québec government alone, including a $72 million bill for more than two million hours of Québec provincial police overtime. In addition, the federal Department of National Defence reported spending $83 million on the crisis.

[15] The Innu people are Registered Indians, not Inuit.

[16] It was to take over three years before the two governments and the people of Davis Inlet reached an agreement to relocate the poverty-stricken island community nearby at Sango Bay on the Labrador mainland. See Canadian Press (1996a).

[17] The agreement is entitled "The Dismantling of the Department of Indian Affairs and Northern Development, The Restoration of Jurisdictions to First Nations Peoples in Manitoba and Recognition of First Nations Governments in Manitoba: Framework Agreement, Workplan, Memorandum of Understanding (December 7, 1994)".

[18] CBC-TV, The National, April 17 and 18, 1997.

[19] News reports of the day identify two instances when police came under gunfire from the Gustafsen Lake occupiers.

[20] For a more detailed discussion of the founding of the National Indian Brotherhood and the history of its precursors, see Ponting and Gibbins (1980, Chapter 7).

[21] The NIB was re-structured such that all of the country's chiefs became the voting members, in place of delegates from the various provincial/territorial member organizations.

[22] In February 1997, Mercredi announced that he would not seek another term as AFN leader.

[23] Some observers would disagree with this assessment of the content of the Charlottetown Accord. For instance, in western Canada the Accord was portrayed as a threat to treaty rights. In my judgement, it would be impossible to find words in the English language to protect treaty rights more fully than did the words of the legal text of the Charlottetown Accord, given the other political constraints operating at the time. Readers can judge for themselves how revolutionary the Accord was through reading the actual legal text or the synopsis and commentary on it on my web page at http://www.ucalgary.ca/~ponting

[24] Incomplete returns (based on about 750 on-reserve polling stations) reported to Dudley (1992) by a source at The Assembly of First Nations indicated that between sixty and seventy percent of persons voting on-reserve rejected the Charlottetown Accord.

[25] At time of writing, the world wide web home page address of a site about Arvol Looking Horse was http://indy4.fdl.cc.mn.us/~isk/arvol/arv_menu.html

[26] See Windspeaker (1995: 1).

[27] News reports estimated that only about fifteen percent of the chiefs of Canada were present for the vote on Mercredi's proposal to adopt sovereignty-association as First Nations' goal. The resolution passed in diluted form. See Canadian Press (1996b).

[28] The AFN national appeal was located at http://www.unity96.com/support.htm

[29] Canadian Press (1992b) quoted then Assembly of First Nations Vice-President Bill Wilson as saying: "Sexual abuse is rampant in Indian communities... If Indian leaders aren't admitting that, then they are gutless, cowardly people". Canadian Press (1993a, 1993b) reports on one such community — Sandy Bay, Manitoba — where sexual abuse apparently was rampant. There it was alleged that at least 50

children and young adults were sexually abused by a number of persons charged by RCMP and by a number of minors not charged. Even more alarming is Canadian Press' (1993c) report quoting Dr. Sally Longstaff, co-author of a study entitled *A New Justice for Indian Children*, as saying that her research team found sexual abuse of children to be widespread among Manitoba reserves, not merely confined to Sandy Bay. Longstaff accuses the federal and provincial governments of turning their backs on the victims due to fears of a backlash from First Nation leaders. Bagnall (1992) reports on sex charges laid against over thirty men in the Algonquin community of Grand Lac Victoria in Québec.

[30] Reference here is to the higher proportion of females than males among the Bill C-31 reinstatees and among the off-reserve First Nation population in general.

[31] Some observers might add to this list Native Studies courses in universities.

[32] In the shooting death of Ipperwash Native protestor Dudley George, Ontario Provincial Police sergeant Kenneth Deane was convicted of criminal negligence causing death when Judge Hugh Fraser rejected as "concocted" testimony by Deane and OPP constable Chris Cossit to the effect that Dudley George was armed and had fired first. Deane's union president said that Deane will appeal the conviction. See Grange (1997).

[33] CBC Radio News, The World at Six, February 25, 1997.

[34] For further details and additional examples, see Study Team on Indian and Native Programs (1985). Not all of the programs listed in Box 4 are necessarily still in existence and most others introduced since the Study Team's report are not included in Box 4. Also excluded are initiatives, such as the division of the Northwest Territories to create Nunavut, which primarily benefit aboriginal people other than status Indians.

[35] Maclean (1996) reports a speech by the Bank of Montreal's vice-president responsible for aboriginal banking in which the official stated that the Bank of Montreal has fourteen branches on-reserve in Canada and about five hundred aboriginal employees.

[36] The *Indian Act* exempts Indians from the seizure of on-reserve property upon defaulting on a loan. Hence, banks have been understandably reluctant to provide mortgages for on-reserve housing.

REFERENCES

Acoose, Janice (Misko-Kisikawihkwe)
1995   *Iskwewak: Neither Indian Princesses nor Easy Squaws*. Toronto: Women's Press.
AFN Health Commission
1994   *Breaking the Silence*. Ottawa: Assembly of First Nations.
Aubrey, Jack
1992   "Mercredi Loses Ground", *Ottawa Citizen*, Oct. 19.
_____
1994   "New Policy May Benefit Aboriginal Firms", *Calgary Herald*, October 12, A11.
Bagnall, Janet
1992   "30 Charged With Abuse of Women, Children", *Montreal Gazette*, June 18.
Boldt, Menno
1993   *Surviving as Indians: The Challenge of Self-Government*. Toronto: University of Toronto Press.

Burke, Martyn and Richard Nielsen (Exec. Producers)
1996   *The Dark Side of Native Sovereignty*. A film by Norflicks Productions Ltd., broadcast on CBC-TV's Witness, August 20.
Campbell, Robert M. and Leslie Pal
1991   *The Real Worlds of Canadian Politics: Cases in Policy and Process.* (Second Edition) Peterborough, Ont.: Broadview Press.
Canada, Government of, Government of British Columbia, and Nisga'a Tribal Council
1996   *Nisga'a Treaty Negotiations Agreement in Principle.* Victoria: Office of Aboriginal Affairs.
Canadian Press
1992a   "Native Women Fear Autonomy Will Hide Sex Abuse", *Calgary Herald*, July 29, A9.

1992b   "Native Women Urged to Ignore 'White Feminists'", *Calgary Herald*, July 31, A10.

1993a   "30 Face Sex Assault Charges", *Calgary Herald*, February 8, A2.

1993b   "Manitoba Reserve Demands Assistance", *Calgary Herald*, February 15, A9.

1993c   "Child Abuse Charges Laid in Manitoba", *Calgary Herald*, July 25, A7.

1996a   "$85 million Relocation: Davis Inlet Innu Moving", *Calgary Herald*, July 10, p. B8.

1996b   "Poor Attendance: Native Chiefs Water Down Proposal for Autonomy", *Calgary Herald*, July 11, p. B9.

1996c   "Logging Bridge Blasted: Native Band Claims Responsibility", *Calgary Herald*, August 28, A7.

1996d   "Sex-Abuse Victims Get Compensation", *Calgary Herald*, December 7: All.
Caragata, Warren
1991   "Indian Leader Issues Clear Warning", *Calgary Herald*, June 8, A5.
Cuthand, Beth
1989   *Voices in the Waterfall*. Vancouver: Lazara Press.
Delacourt, Susan
1995   "Natives Offered Limited Powers: Aboriginal Groups Unhappy as Ottawa Lays Out Terms for Self-Government", *The Globe and Mail*, August 11, A1.
Descant, Danielle et al.
1993   *Violence and Healing: Data on Family Violence and Healing Among the Innuat of Uashat mak Mani-Utenam*. Ottawa: Royal Commission on Aboriginal Peoples. Draft report.
DIAND (Department of Indian Affairs and Northern Development)
1996   "Backgrounder: On-Reserve Housing". Press Release, July 27.
Dickason, Olive P.
1992   *Canada's First Nations: A History of Founding Peoples From Earliest Times.* Toronto: McClelland & Stewart.
Dion Stout, Madeleine
1996   *Family Violence in Aboriginal Communities: The Missing Peace*. Ottawa: Royal Commission on Aboriginal Peoples. Draft report.

Driben, Paul and Robert S. Trudeau
1983   *When Freedom Is Lost: The Dark Side of the Relationship Between the Government and the Fort Hope Band*. Toronto: University of Toronto Press.

Dudley, Wendy
1992   "Aftermath: Mercredi Blasts Voters for Bias", *Calgary Herald*, October 28, A1.

Evans, Heather Anne
1990   *A Native Model of Community Based Sobriety*. Calgary, Alta.: The University of Calgary, M.A. Thesis .

Fife, Connie (ed.)
1993   *The Colour of Resistance: A Contemporary Collection of Writing by Aboriginal Women*. Toronto: Sister Vision Press.

Frideres, James
1974   *Canada's Indians: Contemporary Conflicts*. Scarborough, Ont.: Prentice-Hall.

Fiske, Jo-Anne
1990   "Native Women in Reserve Politics: Strategies and Struggles", pp. 131–146 in Roxana Ng et al., *Community Organization and the Canadian State*. Toronto: Garamond Press.

Grange, Michael
1977   "Officer Guilty in Ipperwash Killing", *The Globe and Mail*, April 29: A1.

Green, Joyce
1993   "Constitutionalizing the Patriarchy: Aboriginal Women and Aboriginal Government", *Constitutional Forum* IV, 4: 110–119.

Haig-Brown, Celia
1988   *Resistance and Renewal: Surviving the Indian Residential School*. Vancouver: Tillacum.

Hawthorn, Harry B. (ed.)
1967   *A Survey of the Contemporary Indians of Canada*. Ottawa: DIAND.

Jamieson, Kathleen
1986   "Sex Discrimination and the Indian Act", pp. 112–136 in J. Rick Ponting (ed.), *Arduous Journey*. Toronto: McClelland & Stewart.

Krosenbrink-Gelissen, L.
1991   *Sexual Equality as An Aboriginal Right*. Saarbrucken, Germany: Verlagbreitenbach.

Maclean, Mairi
1996   "Native Communities Attract Better Service," *Calgary Herald*, May 9, D8.

Matthews, Maureen
1992   *Isinamowin: The White Man's Indian*. Toronto: Canadian Broadcasting Corporation. (Transcript)

Mercredi, Ovide and Mary Ellen Turpel
1993   *In the Rapids: Navigating the Future of First Nations*. Toronto: Viking.

Miller, Christine and Patricia Chuchryk
1996   *Women of the First Nations: Power, Wisdom, and Strength*. Winnipeg: The University of Manitoba Press.

Miller, J.R.
1996   *Shingwauk's Vision: A History of Native Residential Schools*. Toronto: University of Toronto Press.

Nagle, Patrick
1992   "Male Domination Heightens Fears of Self-Rule", *Calgary Herald*, April 1, B8.

Platiel, Rudy
1992   "Native Women to Challenge Proposal on Aboriginal Rights", *The Globe and Mail*, January 17, A6.
Ponting, J. Rick and Roger Gibbins
1980   *Out of Irrelevance: A Socio-political Introduction to Indian Affairs in Canada.* Scarborough, Ont.: Butterworth.
Ponting, J. Rick (ed.)
1986   *Arduous Journey: Canadian Indians and Decolonization.* Toronto: McClelland and Stewart / Oxford University Press.

_____
1990   "Internationalization: Perspectives on an Emerging Direction in Aboriginal Affairs", *Canadian Ethnic Studies* XXII, 3: 85–109.

_____
1991   "An Indian Policy for Canada in The Twenty-first Century", pp. 431–446 in C.H.W. Remie and J.-M. Lacroix (eds.), *Canada on the Threshold of the 21st Century: European Reflections Upon the Future of Canada.* Amsterdam: John Benjamins Publishing.

_____
1993   "Crisis and Response: Challenges of the 1990s in Alberta Indian Affairs", pp. 89–104 in James S. Frideres and Roger Gibbins (eds.), *Alberta into the Twenty-first Century.* Calgary: The University of Calgary Faculty of Social Sciences.
RCAP (Royal Commission on Aboriginal Peoples)
1996a   *Report of the Royal Commission on Aboriginal Peoples; Vol. 1: Looking Forward, Looking Back.* Ottawa: Ministry of Supply and Services Canada.

_____
1996c   *Report of the Royal Commission on Aboriginal Peoples; Vol. 3: Gathering Strength.* Ottawa: Ministry of Supply and Services Canada.

_____
1996d   *Report of the Royal Commission on Aboriginal Peoples; Vol. 4: Perspectives and Realities.* Ottawa: Ministry of Supply and Services Canada.
Redekop, Bill
1995   "Aboriginal Cheesecake: Entrepreneur Publishes Calendars to Promote Native Modelling Agency", *Winnipeg Free Press*, December 10, D1.
Richardson, Boyce
1989   *Drumbeat: Anger and Renewal in Indian Country.* Ottawa and Toronto: Assembly of First Nations and Summerhill Press.
Ross, Rupert
1996   *Returning to the Teachings: Exploring Aboriginal Justice.* Toronto: Penguin.
Silman, Janet
1987   *Enough is Enough: Aboriginal Women Speak Out.* Toronto: Women's Press.
Stacey-Moore, Gail
1993   "In Our Own Voice", *Herizons: Women's News and Feminist Views* VI, 4: 21–23.
Stevenson, Winona
1995   "The Cowboys Have Won Again", *Calgary Herald*, July 2, A4.
Study Team on Indian and Native Programs
1985   *Improved Program Delivery — Indians and Natives: Report to the Task Force on Program Review.* Ottawa: Supply and Services Canada.
Tennant, Paul
1990   *Aboriginal Peoples and Politics: The Indian Land Question in British Columbia, 1849–1989.* Vancouver: University of British Columbia Press.

van de Fliert, Lydia (ed.)

1994   *Indigenous Peoples and International Organizations.* Nottingham: Spokesman.

Voyageur, Cora J.

1996   "Contemporary Indian Women", pp. 93–115 in David Alan Long and Olive P. Dickason (eds.), *Visions of the Heart: Canadian Aboriginal Issues.* Toronto: Harcourt Brace Canada.

Weaver, Sally M.

1982   "The Joint Cabinet/National First Nation Brotherhood Committee: A Unique Experiment in Pressure Group Relations". *Canadian Public Administration* XXV, 2: 211–239.

———

1985   "Political Representivity and Indigenous Minorities in Canada and Australia", pp. 113–150 in Noel Dyck (ed.), *Indigenous Peoples and The Nation State.* St. John's: Nfld., Institute of Social and Economic Research, Memorial University of Newfoundland.

Windspeaker

1995   "Spiritual Healer Helps to End Standoff", *Windspeaker*, Vol. 13, No. 6 (October): 1.

Wotherspoon, Terry and Vic Satzewich

1993   *First Nations: Race, Class, and Gender Relations.* Scarborough, Ont.: Nelson Canada.

CHAPTER 4

THE SOCIO-DEMOGRAPHIC PICTURE[1]

J. Rick Ponting

POPULATION SIZE AND DISTRIBUTION

Demographers' and historians' estimates of the size of the aboriginal population prior to European contact vary greatly. Kroeber estimates that prior to the arrival of Europeans, the total Indian population of North America was about 900,000 people, of whom about 220,000 were in what is now Canada (Kroeber, 1939, cited in Siggner, 1986). This estimate has been criticized as too conservative in that it does not adequately account for the devastating impact of European diseases that spread in advance of extensive contact. Some estimates of the Indian population in the territory that is now Canada place it at two million, but the Royal Commission on Aboriginal Peoples (1996a: 13) cites 500,000 as the most widely accepted figure for the time of initial, sustained contact in what is now Canada.

Warfare, famine, and diseases against which Indians had no immunity depleted those numbers to an alarming extent. Such diseases as smallpox sometimes nearly decimated communities. Accordingly, shortly after Confederation the Aboriginal population of what is now Canada is estimated to have been about 102,000. Not until 1941 did that population begin to show a pattern of sustained growth which, in 1966, finally again took its Registered Indian component to and beyond what the number of Indians probably was just prior to European contact (Siggner, 1986). As of the end of 1996, the total Registered Indian population was slightly under 611,000.[2] In comparison, the population identifying as Métis was projected by Statistics Canada to be about 153,000 persons in 1996, while the Inuit population that year was projected to be about 42,500 (RCAP, 1996a: 16).[3] In all of Canada as of 1996, the total population *identifying* as a member of one of the *aboriginal* groups is estimated by the Royal Commission to be about 811,400 or 2.7% of an estimated Canadian population of 29,963,700.[4]

About 104,000 persons are included in the total Registered Indian population of 1996 as a result of legislative changes contained in Bill C-31 which was proclaimed into law in 1985. Yet, even without considering Bill C-31 (re)instatees added to the Indian Register in any given year, the Indian population in the early 1990s was exhibiting a growth rate of over 3.5%, which had slowed to about 3% by the mid-1990s (DIAND,1993a: 7 and 1997b: 7). At such rates, the Registered Indian population would double about every twenty-two years. The Registered Indian population exhibits a rate of natural increase (excess of live births over deaths) of about 24 per 1000 population, which is more than three times the rate of about 7 per 1000 in the population of Canada as a whole (Muir, 1991: 10).

Bill C-31 contains a set of controversial amendments to the *Indian Act* of Canada.[5] A response to both domestic and international political pressure, and to the fact that the gender equality provisions of *The Canadian Charter of Rights and Freedoms* were about to render some of the membership provisions of the *Indian Act* unconstitutional (Jamieson, 1986), Bill C-31 granted membership to those persons who had lost their legal status as Registered Indians. Foremost among these were Indian women who had married non-Indians, and the off-spring of such marriages. As of the end of August 1996, almost 190,000 (non-duplicate) applicants for legal status as Registered Indians had come forward. Of them, some 103,800 (fifty-five percent, or fifty-nine percent of the com-pletely-processed applicants) had been approved.[6] Norris (1996: 215) estimates that a total of some 143,000 persons will have become Registered Indians under Bill C-31 by the year 2016.

It is now apparent that this legislative intervention by the Department of Indian Affairs and Northern Development (DIAND) has had an enormous and wide-ranging impact on First Nations (Jamieson, 1986; DIAND, 1990; RCAP, 1996d: 33–53). One demographic impact has been an increase in the size of the Registered Indian population, as of the mid-1990s, by over one fifth of what it otherwise would have been.[7] Another impact has been on the age and sex com-position of the Registered Indian population, for the Bill C-31 population is older than the rest of the Indian population and is disproportionately female. Another demographic impact has been a significant increase in the proportion of the Registered Indian population living off-reserve, as about ninety percent of Bill C-31 (re-)instatees live off-reserve. Some of the other impacts of the legis-lation arise from such factors as the federal government failing to make available various additional resources — notably land and sufficient funding under cer-tain programs — commensurate with this very significant population increase.

As we observe in Graph 1, Nault et al. (1993) project that, under assump-tions of a medium growth rate (and taking into account Bill C-31), the total Registered Indian population will increase to about 670,000 persons by the turn of the century and to about 890,000 by the end of the year 2015, which is dou-ble what it was in 1988.[8] That many people cannot be ignored: sheer force of numbers will create opportunity, both in terms of markets and in terms of gov-ernment programs.

In the mid-1990s Registered Indians comprised almost exactly 2% of the total Canadian population. This was up from about 1.3% a decade earlier. However, these proportions vary considerably from one region to another. For instance, as Table 1 shows, in Saskatchewan and Manitoba the 1996 figure was about 9% and in the Northwest Territories and Yukon it was around 22%. Of course, the larger the proportion, and the more geographically concentrated the First Nation population is, the greater the opportunity for using the larger society's political system to address the needs and constricted opportunities of First Nation people. Thus, for instance, in the Northwest Territories the demo-graphic "clout" of the aboriginal peoples has made the territorial government more responsive to aboriginal peoples' needs than any provincial government in Canada. Indeed, the territorial government itself is officially multilingual in various aboriginal languages. Sociologists (e.g., Breton, 1986: 31) emphasize that it is important that peoples be able to recognize themselves in such sym-bolic output of government, for in the absence of such recognition, individuals become alienated, which in turn contributes to disempowerment.

GRAPH 1 Projections of the Registered Indian Population, On- and Off-Reserve, 1991–2015

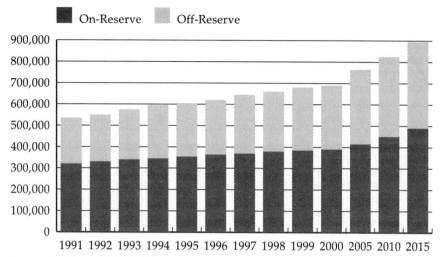

Source: Nault et al. (1993: 83)

The Registered Indian population is divided into 609 bands, which are political-administrative units created for the convenience of DIAND. The Minister can create or abolish bands, so the number can fluctuate slightly from one year to another. Table 1 shows the distribution of bands across Canada, while Table 2 shows their land holdings. British Columbia, with about one-sixth of the First Nation population, has about one-third of the bands. This fragmentation of the First Nation population in B.C. among almost two hundred bands yields the smallest average band membership size among the regions outside Yukon. The 518 members of the average B.C. band amount to only about half the 1,000 members of the average band across Canada. Such fragmentation is practically a recipe for disempowerment and is, by definition, antithetical to economies of scale among First Nation governments in B.C.

Table 1 reveals that, after B.C., the prairie provinces have the largest single geographic block of bands (174 bands, which contain 44% of the First Nation population). In fact, both Saskatchewan and Manitoba, taken separately, have a greater First Nation population than Québec and Atlantic Canada combined. This demographic weight of the prairie provinces is significant because it gave First Nation chiefs in those provinces considerable political power within The Assembly of First Nations (and its predecessor The National Indian Brotherhood) when its elections were organized on the basis of one vote for every band chief. Furthermore, the vast majority of *treaty* Indians is also located in the prairie provinces. Thus, within the Assembly of First Nations the regional cleavage is reinforced by the cleavage between treaty and non-treaty First Nations. Ontario, at 126 bands and 23% of the Registered Indian population, is the only other demographic power block. (Its northwestern section also falls under treaty.) Yukon and the Northwest Territories have a tiny proportion of the total First Nation population, although First Nation people in the territories constitute a larger proportion of the jurisdiction's population than do First

Nation people in any of the provinces. Indeed, when we add the Métis and Inuit, aboriginal peoples comprise a majority of the NWT population.

Band Size

The prospects for successful self-government, and for the expansion in the local opportunity structure which accompanies self-government, are also dependent upon the presence of a critical mass of population which permits **economies of scale** in the delivery of services. For instance, a small population will be unable to support specialized professional staff in its institutions of self-government, such as a speech therapist employed by the school board of a small First Nation. Unfortunately, most First Nations lack a critical mass of population, as we observe in Table 1. Indeed, almost half (45%) of all bands,[9] containing 13% of all band members, had a 1993 population of fewer than 500 Registered Indian members[10] (about 6% of bands had fewer than 100 persons). As in any band, many of their members presently do not live on-reserve. As of the mid-1990s, only about one-third of all bands had one thousand or more members, which itself is below the critical mass needed for the cost-efficient delivery of most government services. Almost two thirds of the Registered Indian population is affiliated with bands of fewer than two thousand persons.

Average band size is largest in Alberta (N=1777 members), which is home to such large bands as the Bloods (1996 population = 8,338), Saddle Lake (6,948), Samson (5,113), and Siksika (4,706). However, the largest First Nations in Canada are the Six Nations of the Grand River (19,084 scattered over southern Ontario), the Mohawks of Kahnawake (8,441 across the St. Lawrence River from Montréal) and the Mohawks of Akwesasne (8,601 near Cornwall, Ontario). In Québec, Manitoba, and Alberta a majority or near majority of the Registered Indian population belongs to large bands (bands having a population of 2,000 or more). Notwithstanding the above, by outside standards even the largest First Nations are comparatively small in population.

On- and Off-Reserve Distribution

The shortage of housing and job opportunities on-reserve has been a major factor impelling many First Nation individuals to leave the reserve in search of opportunities off-reserve. Given the marginal economic potential of numerous reserves and the federal government's fiscal constraints, this off-reserve migration is likely to continue into the future. Furthermore, as noted above, the ranks of the off-reserve First Nation population have been swelled by Bill C-31 reinstatees, about 90% of whom live off-reserve (Nault et al., 1993: 30). The net result of these phenomena, plus fertility factors, is captured by Graph 1. There we observe that almost half of the First Nation population will live off-reserve by the year 2015. What the graph does not show, though, are the large interprovincial and sex differences in the proportion of the population residing on-reserve (DIAND, 1997a: xvii–xxxvi). For instance, at the end of 1996, slightly more men than women lived on-reserve, but that proportion ranged from a low of 53% of Registered Indian males in British Columbia to a high of 73% for Québec. For Registered Indian women the proportion ranged from 48% in British Columbia to 69% in Québec.[11] The national totals were 61% for men and 56% for women. The off-reserve figures show corresponding variation. In

TABLE 1 Distribution of the Registered Indian Population

	Canada	Atlantc	Quebec	Ont.	Man.	Sask.	Alta.	B.C.	NWT	Yukon
Total Registered. Indian Population as of Dec. 31, 1996	610,874	23,959	58,640	138,518	95,113	94,953	76,419	102,075	13,998	7,199
% of Total Registered Indian Pop.	100.0	3.9	9.6	22.7	15.6	15.5	12.5	16.7	2.3	1.2
Population as % of Total 1996 Provincial/Territorial Pop.	2.1	1.03	0.8	1.2	8.5	9.6	2.8	2.7	21.7	23.4
% Off-reserve, Dec. 31, 1996	42.0	34.3	29.3	49.2	36.2	48.2	33.5	49.0	26.8	48.0
Number of Indian Bands, 1996	609	31	39	126	61	70	43	197	26	16
% of Indian Bands, 1996	100	5	6	21	10	11	7	32	4	3
Average Band Membership, 1996	1003	773	1504	1099	1559	1356	1777	518	538	450
DISTRIBUTION OF POPULATION BY SIZE OF BAND OR REGISTRY GROUP, 1993										
a. Number of Bands										
Band Size < 100 persons	36	2	0	5	1	1	0	22	4	0
Band Size 100–249 persons	101	5	2	20	5	3	3	58	2	4
Band Size 250–499 persons	145	8	8	42	5	9	7	51	7	8
Band Size 500–999 persons	153	10	10	31	23	21	9	39	7	3
Band Size 1000–1999 pers.	125	4	10	27	15	26	18	22	2	1
Band Size >2000 persons	59	2	10	13	12	10	8	4	1	0
b. Percent of Bands										
Band Size < 100 persons	6	6	0	4	2	1	0	11	17	0
Band Size 100–249 persons	16	16	5	16	8	4	7	30	9	25
Band Size 250–499 persons	23	26	21	33	8	13	16	26	30	50
Band Size 500–999 persons	25	32	26	25	38	30	20	20	30	19
Band Size 1000–1999 pers.	20	13	26	21	25	37	40	11	9	6
Band Size >2000 persons	10	6	26	10	20	14	18	2	4	0

continued

TABLE 1 (*continued*)

	Canada	Atlantc	Quebec	Ont.	Man.	Sask.	Alta.	B.C.	NWT	Yukon
c. Band Population										
Band Size <100 persons	1948	147	0	260	75	77	0	1107	282	0
Band Size 100–249 persons	17628	880	387	3437	888	614	529	10026	352	515
Band Size 250–499 persons	53279	3030	2997	15464	2147	3105	2590	17807	2829	3310
Band Size 500–999 persons	106816	6982	6364	20982	17612	17087	5670	25230	5024	1865
Band Size 1000–1999 persons	174004	5611	13948	38508	22503	35709	24563	29851	2194	1117
Band Size >2000 persons	198585	4845	30329	46971	40787	28814	34665	9964	2210	0
Total:	552260	21495	54025	125622	84012	85406	68017	93985	12891	6807
d. Percent of Band Population										
Band Size <100 persons	0	1	0	0	0	0	0	1	2	0
Band Size 100–249 persons	3	4	1	3	1	1	1	11	3	8
Band Size 250–499 persons	10	14	6	12	3	4	4	19	22	49
Band Size 500–999 persons	19	32	12	17	21	20	8	27	39	27
Band Size 1000–1999 persons	32	26	26	31	27	42	36	32	17	16
Band Size >2000 persons	36	23	56	37	49	34	51	11	17	0
Total:	100	100	100	100	100	100	100	100	100	100

Sources: DIAND (1994a, 1997a); Statistics Canada (1994a: 10; Cat. #91-002); DIAND (1993a: 19); Nault et al. (1993:19) and Statistics Canada Cat. #93-357-XPB at http://www.statcan.ca/english/census96/table1.htm

Table 1 we note that about 42% (256,500 individuals) of the Registered Indian population lived off-reserve by the end of 1996, but among the provinces that ranged from a low of 29% in Quebec to highs of about 49% in Ontario, Saskatchewan, and British Columbia. These latter three provinces are on the verge of reaching the "tipping point" where the majority of the First Nation population lives off-reserve. That could have significant negative implications for the federal government's willingness to provide services and for economies of scale on-reserve.

The off-reserve population is not homogeneous in social class terms. First, there is an educated middle class which is able to take advantage of opportunities created in such areas as the intergovernmental relations sector, the service sector, and land claim settlements, and in such affirmative action programs as those mandated by the federal government's *Employment Equity Act* and its federal Contract Compliance Program.[12] Secondly, the off-reserve First Nation population also includes an undereducated, low-skilled (at least for the urban economy) reserve army of cheap labour which tends to be in and out of paid employment as the last hired and first fired. Thirdly, there is a similarly-equipped proletariat holding paid employment in working class jobs. Finally, there is a skid row "lumpenproletariat" (Wotherspoon and Satzewich, 1993: 52–64). Prospects for the opening of opportunities for all but the existing middle class are bleak and deteriorating, as they are being joined by an increasing number of similarly low-skilled, relatively undereducated non-Natives who are deemed surplus to the needs of modern corporations engaged in intense competition with a narrow focus on short-term profitability.

In Graph 1 the off-reserve First Nation population (the grey part of the bars) is projected by Nault et al. (1993: 89) to almost double from about 215,000 in 1991 to about 406,000 in the year 2015 (based on the set of medium growth assumptions). That growth (89% over 25 years) is faster than what is projected for the on-reserve population, which is expected to increase from about 314,000 in 1991 to about 484,000 (54% over 25 years; Nault et al., 1993: 86).[13]

The **impact** of this population distribution on reserve life could be considerable. For instance, at almost half a million persons in the year 2015, the on-reserve population will be almost as large as the combined on- and off-reserve population a quarter century earlier. A population that large constitutes a significant market for First Nation entrepreneurs, but its fragmentation across about 2,400 reserves militates against successful commercial enterprises oriented toward capturing an on-reserve consumer market. However, the increased on-reserve population could come to be regarded by enterprising First Nation government bureaucrats as a significant source of revenues to be collected through user fees and per capita levies. Furthermore, with almost as many First Nation individuals living off-reserve (46%) as on-reserve (54%) by the year 2015, pressures might emerge for First Nation governments to extend both the reach of their services (directly or on a contracting-out basis) and voting rights to off-reserve locations, where that is not already done. This would significantly alter First Nation politics and could significantly increase the overhead and service delivery costs of First Nation governments. Finally, it is likely that the increased population pressure on the land will not only generate more land claims and greater militancy in their pursuit, but will also heighten the salience of land tenure issues in on-reserve politics.[14]

Distribution Among Cities

Not all First Nation individuals living off-reserve dwell in an urban area. Also, some reserves are part of, or adjacent to cities, such that they are included in the census metropolitan areas designated by Statistics Canada. Thus, that part of Graph 2 which shows the distribution of individuals self-identifying as Indians cannot be construed as representing the distribution of the off-reserve First Nation population. Nevertheless, the data are very useful. The black bars in the graph represent persons who *self-identified* as "North American Indian" (Registered and non-status) in the 1991 census. The grey bars represent those same individuals, plus persons who self-identified as Métis or Inuit. Both sets of data are included because non-Natives who observe an aboriginal person in an urban area will often form impressions without knowing whether the individual is Indian, Métis, or Inuit.

From Graph 2 we observe that aboriginal people constitute an highly visible presence in Vancouver, Edmonton, and especially Winnipeg, for there were 25,000 to 35,000 *aboriginal-identifiers* tallied by the census in these respective cities, while an unknown number of other aboriginal persons living a more transient lifestyle in these cities was missed by the census. These three census metropolitan areas, plus Toronto, all had more than ten thousand persons who identified themselves as *"North American Indian"*. By now, Calgary will have joined their ranks. Regina and Saskatoon exhibit surprisingly low absolute numbers; however, as a percentage of the total population, aboriginal identifiers are more prevalent there than in the aforementioned much larger cities. In addition, the under-counting problem also exists in Regina and Saskatoon.

GRAPH 2 Self-Identifying Aboriginal and Indian Populations in Selected Urban Areas, 1991 Census

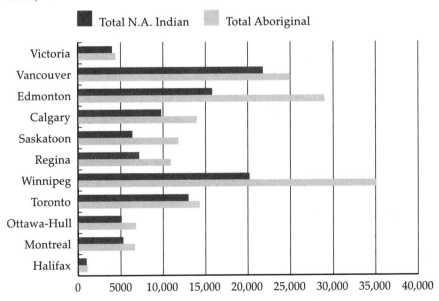

If we focus on persons whose *ancestry* (single or multiple ethnic origins), rather than self-identification, is *aboriginal*, the numbers in cities increase significantly (not shown in graph). For instance, the Royal Commission on Aboriginal Peoples (1996d: 607) reports five cities with more than forty thousand persons of aboriginal ancestry in 1991: Winnipeg (45,000), Montréal (44,600), Vancouver (42,800), Edmonton (42,700), and Toronto (40,000). Other cities with more than twenty thousand persons of aboriginal ancestry are Ottawa-Hull (30,900) and Calgary (24,400). Saskatoon had only 14,200 such persons, while the count in Regina and Halifax was 12,800 and 6,700, respectively.

Distribution by Other Geographic Area

Table 2 provides data on Indian lands and the distribution of the Registered Indian population on those lands. As of 1992, about 38% of the Registered Indian on-reserve population lived in, or within 50 kilometres of, an urban area and another 42% lived in rural areas that are between 50 and 350 kilometres from the nearest "service centre" with year-round road access.[15] In most cases the economic opportunities for individuals on these reserves are probably much better than they are for the remainder of the on-reserve population. That remainder comprises the 2% of on-reserve persons who resided in remote areas (over 350 kilometres from the nearest service centre with year-round road access) and the 18% who reside in what we might call "extremely remote" (and DIAND calls "special access") areas (DIAND, 1993a: 124) that have no year-round road access to the nearest service centre. Most individuals in these remote and "extremely remote" areas will be marginal to the mainstream economy, although some will be active participants in the traditional and resource extraction economies. On most such remote and "extremely remote" reserves the prospects are not encouraging for successful, multifacetted, self-government and for diverse occupational opportunities.

Reserve lands[16] are a site of opportunity for First Nations, insofar as those lands are close to markets or contain valuable renewable or non-renewable resources. The total area of reserve lands is shown in Table 2 as 3.1 million hectares (about 7.75 million acres). Not shown there are lands which do not fall under the *Indian Act*, such as lands in the James Bay and Northern Québec Agreement. Four-fifths of reserve lands are less than five hundred hectares in area (RCAP, 1996b: 810).

Perhaps most striking in Table 2 is that British Columbia has two thirds of the total number of reserves, although they amounted to only about 12% of all First Nation lands in Canada in 1996. Also, recall from Table 1 that B.C. has almost one third of all Indian bands in Canada and about one sixth of the total Registered Indian population of Canada. The administrative fragmentation of the B.C. First Nation population is exacerbated by geographic fragmentation: at an average size of about 220 hectares (less than a square mile), B.C.'s almost 1700 reserves are the smallest of any province's.

It is also worth noting that about three quarters of First Nation land is held in just three provinces — Ontario, Alberta, and Saskatchewan — which contain about half the total Registered Indian population. Furthermore, we must bear in mind that many reserves are uninhabited by people; some are merely cemeteries or a tiny island, and the like. It would be a mistake to think of all reserves as communities, for only about one third are inhabited (RCAP, 1996b: 807).

TABLE 2 First Nation Lands and Population, By Region

	Cda	Atl.	Que.	Ont.	Man.	Sask.	Alta.	B.C.	NWT	Yuk.
Total Registered Indian Pop. × 1000[1]	610.9	24.0	58.6	138.5	95.1	95.0	76.4	102.1	14.0	7.2
Number of Indian Bands, 1996	609	31	39	126	61	70	43	197	26	16
Number of Reserves,1996[2]	2483	77	34	228	135	177	108	1687	3	34
% of Indian Bands, 1996	100	5	6	21	10	11	7	32	4	3
% of Reserves, 1996	100	3.1	1.4	9.1	5.4	7.1	4.3	67.9	0.1	1.4
% of On-Reserve Pop. By Location Type[3]										
i. Special Access, 1995	18	0	17	27	32	6	7	15	35	6
ii. Remote, 1995	2	0	0	0	0	2	0	6	9	32
iii. Urban and Rural, 1995	80	100	83	73	68	93	93	79	56	62
Approx. Total Area of Reserves, 1996 (× 1,000 hectares)[4]	3100	33	100	978	265	645	682	376	17	4
Average Area of Reserve or Settlement, 1996 (× 1000 hectares)	1.25	0.42	2.04	4.29	1.96	3.64	6.32	0.22	5.76	0.12
Percent of all Reserve Area, 1996	99.9	1.0	3.2	31.6	8.5	20.8	22.0	12.1	0.6	0.1
Number of Reserves and Settlements for which no data	239	20	17	38	20	20	20	68	31	5

Notes:

[1] Population data on this line are as of 96-12-31.

[2] Total obtained from adding across columns. Column numbers do not sum to total cited elsewhere by DIAND.

[3] Quebec excludes 15 Cree and Naskapi bands for this dimension.

[4] 1 Hectare = 2.5 acres; 1000 hectares = 2500 acres = 3.91 sq. mi.

Sources: DIAND (1994a); DIAND (1993a:19); DIAND (1997b: 19) and personal communication with M. Jacques Desrochers.

FERTILITY

Birth rates are an important influence on structures of opportunity, for they are an important determinant of such things as the level of competition for scarce resources and services, the magnitude of the economic dependency "burden" which the young pose for a society or sub-society, and the size of certain markets. Birth rates also have an effect on female labour force participation rates, and vice versa.

The First Nation population has experienced what demographers call the **demographic transition**. That is, like developing countries elsewhere around the world, the population has experienced three phases of demographic performance: (i) a prolonged era (prior to the 1950s) of high birth rates and high death rates, followed by (ii) a brief period (the 1950s and 1960s) of rapidly declining death rates accompanied by continuing relatively high birth rates, followed by (iii) a contemporary period of comparatively low fertility and low mortality. First Nation fertility rates are now converging on First Nation mortality rates and on the fertility rates of the larger Canadian population. However, a significant fertility gap remains between the two populations. For instance, for Registered Indians the total fertility rate ("TFR")[17] declined from 6.1 births per woman in 1968 (Norris, 1996: 201) to 4.15 in 1975 to 2.72 in 1990, while the total fertility rate of the total Canadian population declined from 1.85 to 1.83 between 1975 and 1990. Thus, a difference of 2.30 children per woman was narrowed to slightly less than one child per woman over just a fifteen year period (Nault et al., 1993: 15). The First Nation data are plotted in Graph 3, with projections after 1990 based on assumptions of a slow decline in First Nation fertility rates.

GRAPH 3 Total Fertility Rate, Indian Women, 1975–90 and Projected to 2015, and All Canadian Women, 1975–90

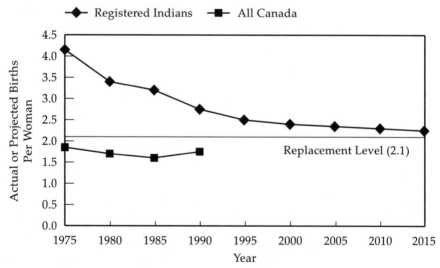

Sources: Nault et al. (1993: 19) and Statcan Cat. 84-210 (1995).

That decline in First Nation fertility has occurred in all age ranges except the 15–19 age group.[18] From the perspective of our interest in opportunity, it could be argued that teenage motherhood is a major constraint upon the future economic and career opportunities of at least the mother. However, its meaning to teenage girls is, of course, often quite different.

The First Nation population experienced a **"baby boom"**, although several years later than the rest of the Canadian population. In 1966, just one year after the peak of the First Nations' baby boom, there were 222 births per 1000 First Nation women in the childbearing age range (age 15–44). By 1976 that figure, known as the "general fertility ratio", had declined to 132 (Siggner, 1980: 39). When considering such phenomena as the population's housing needs, educational enrolments, job creation needs, social assistance needs, aging, and structures of opportunity in general, we should bear in mind the passage of the baby boom cohort and its "echo" effect (the children of the boomers) through the First Nation population.

First Nation fertility rates vary considerably from one region of Canada to another and Nault et al. (1993: 16) report no clear evidence of any narrowing of these regional fertility differentials over time. Thus, to take the extremes, First Nation women in Saskatchewan had, on average, about one and one-quarter more children than First Nation women in British Columbia (TFRs of 3.49 and 2.24, respectively).[19] First Nation fertility rates also tend to be significantly lower off-reserve than on-reserve.[20]

Fertility rates are influenced by such factors as declining infant mortality and increases in urbanization, education, income, and female labour force participation. The probable continuing convergence of First Nation rates with rates of the total Canadian population on these dimensions provides an argument for expecting a continuing **convergence** in fertility rates. Yet, there is no guarantee of this. Thus, Nault and his colleagues have considered it entirely plausible that, by the year 2015, the First Nation total fertility rate (TFR) could be anywhere between the present 2.7 children per woman and 2.0, the latter of which is slightly below the replacement level (2.1).

MORTALITY AND MORBIDITY[21]

Mortality

First Nation mortality rates exhibited a pronounced decline over the last half of the twentieth century. The **crude death rate** (CDR) is the number of deaths per 1,000 population. The annual number of deaths among Registered Indians in the mid-1990s was around 2500, which yields a crude death rate of about 5.6 deaths per 1000 population (down from 8.4/1000 in 1967). The First Nation CDR is now actually lower than the CDR for the overall Canadian population, but the comparison is misleading because it is affected by the very different age structures of the two populations. Therefore, a more accurate comparative measure is the **age-standardized mortality rate** of the two populations. For the Registered Indian population it is the equivalent of the crude death rate which the Registered Indian population would have if it had the same age structure as the overall Canadian population. The most recently available data (1993) yield an age-standardized Registered Indian mortality rate of 10.8 (10.0 for females and 11.5 for males), which is over one and one-half times as high as for the overall Canadian population.[22] The rate varies markedly from one region of the country to another (Muir, 1991: 13), although some of that variability is attributable to under-reporting and other limitations of coverage of the data.

One measure of life chances and a widely used indicator of a population's mortality experiences is **life expectancy at birth**. Historically, First Nation people have had a significantly lower life expectancy at birth than the overall Canadian population. For instance, Indian males born in 1975 could expect to live 11.8 years less than their counterparts in the overall Canadian population (59.2 years vs. 70.0 years) and Indian females born that year could expect to live 11.4 years less (65.9 vs. 77.3).[23] Norris (1996: 203) reports that, as of 1991, this gap had narrowed to 7.7 years among males (66.9 vs. 74.6) and 6.9 years among females (74.0 vs. 80.9). Nault et al. (1991: 23) project the Indian-nonIndian gap in life expectancy to decrease to less than five years for each sex by the year 2015.[24] Although these are by no means Third World levels, the discrepancies with non-Indian life expectancies do reflect the lower socio-economic status and health status experienced by First Nation people, especially on-reserve.

A major contributing factor to the increase in life expectancy has been the dramatic decline in the **infant mortality rate**, which is the number of deaths before age one, per one thousand live births in any given year. This measure, which is used internationally as an indicator of the overall standard of living of a society, has declined precipitously to the point where it has almost converged with that of the larger Canadian society. This is shown in Graph 4. There we observe that during the thirty year period beginning in 1960, infant mortality rates of First Nations plummeted from a scandalously high 82 infant deaths per 1000 live births to around 11.[25] The corresponding rates for the total Canadian population were 27 and 7.

Lest these numbers become mere abstractions, we should bear in mind that the increase of 0.7 infant deaths per 1000 live births between 1991 and 1992 means that in 1992 the tragedy of losing a baby to death afflicted thirteen more families (for a total of 152 families) than the 139 families who were so afflicted in 1991.[26]

Muir's (1991: 14) brief synopsis of some pertinent medical research illustrates how First Nation people's generally low socio-economic status adversely affects life chances in the case of infant mortality. She emphasizes that low birth weight is a powerful determinant of infant mortality and that pregnant women in poverty have a higher probability of giving birth to a baby of low birth weight than do other women. That is because birth weight itself is affected by poor nutrition, small stature, increased stress, and obstetric complications, all of which are more common among poor women. In addition, she notes, "poor women may have inferior health status both before and during their childbearing years, which can influence birth outcome". Behaviours which are detrimental to the foetus, such as smoking, alcohol use[27] and drug use during pregnancy, are also associated with poverty.

Turning from low birth weight to Sudden Infant Death Syndrome (S.I.D.S.), Muir (1991: 17) again calls upon social factors to help explain why Indian rates for S.I.D.S. are three times as high as the overall Canadian rate (3.1 vs 1.0 per 1000 live births in the late 1980s). For instance, a Manitoba study by Moffat et al. found that social risk factors predominated in Indian cases for which descriptive information was available, as "many of the mothers [of S.I.D.S. victims] were less than 20 years of age, had delayed prenatal care, and had no more than elementary school education".[28]

GRAPH 4 Infant Mortality Rates for Canada and On-Reserve Registered Indians, 1960–1993

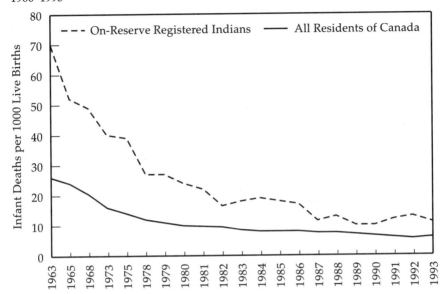

Note: Indian rates for 1985 to 1990 exclude B.C. Indian rates since 1987 exclude N.W.T.
Sources: DIAND (1996: 29); Wadhera and Strachan (1993: 22–23) and http://www.statcan.ca/Documents/English/Pgdb/People/Health/health21.htm

Striking differences emerge when we compare **causes of death** for First Nation people and other Canadians. Most shocking are the rates for deaths by poisoning or injury (especially motor vehicle accidents), which is the leading cause of death among First Nation people and accounts for more than one-quarter of all First Nation deaths (DIAND, 1993a: 31; Health Canada special tabulation, 1996; and Muir, 1991: 47). For the Registered Indian population, death by injury and poisoning occurred at a rate which fluctuated between 107 and 154 per 100,000 population during the late 1980s and early 1990s. For the total Canadian population the rates were roughly one-half to one-third of that.[29] The most recently available data (1993) for "Injury and Poisoning" reveal that registered Indians' are dying by this cause at a rate about 3.2 times as high as that of persons in the total Canadian population (148.7 vs 46.9 per 100,000 population).

For all ages combined, the next most common cause of death among First Nation people is diseases of the circulatory system (e.g., heart attack). Comparisons with the non-Native population on this dimension are unstable from one year to another. Cancer is the third most common cause of death, but First Nation males are much less likely to die of cancer than are non-Native males (Bobet, 1994: 59–60).[30] Together, these three causes account for about two-thirds of the deaths among Registered Indians (Health Canada special tabulation, 1996).

Significantly, the rate of mothers' death due to complications of pregnancy or childbirth is extremely low among First Nation persons. For instance, the most recently available data show only one such death in 1993. That stands in marked contrast to the very high rates in Third World countries.

Graph 5 shows recent trends in the mortality rates for these three leading causes of death among Registered Indians. A five-year "rolling" average is used to diminish anomalies created by short-term idiosyncratic factors operating in this relatively small population. The graph reveals that the trend is downward for injuries and poisonings, but slightly upward for cancers. In part, the upward trend for cancers could be a reflection of the increased longevity of individuals in the First Nation population. That is, in living longer, individuals are more likely to die from late-onset diseases.[31]

The leading cause of death for First Nation people varies from one region to another. For instance, in the west it is injury and poisoning, while east of Manitoba it is diseases of the circulatory system (Muir, 1991: 18).

Also very noteworthy is the comparatively high rate of **stillborn deliveries** by First Nations women.[32] Muir (1991: 15) reports that during the period 1985–88, the rate for Indian women was 10.2 stillbirths per 1000 total births, while that for all of Canada was 6.2. Alberta rates available to the author suggest that Indian rates remained high into the 1990s, as did the differential with rates for non-Indians in Canada as a whole.[33] Still births are caused by such factors as gestational diabetes, cigarette smoking by the mother,[34] and alcohol and drug abuse by the mother.[35] As such, the high First Nation rates reported here are both understandable and partially amenable to amelioration through health education.

GRAPH 5 Five-Year Rolling Mortality Rates For Selected Causes of Death, Registered Indians, 1982 to 1993

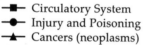

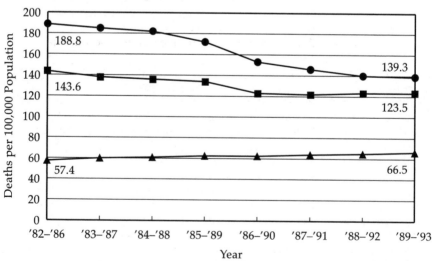

Source: Special tabulation, Native Health Statistical Analysis System, Medical Services Branch, Health Canada, May 1996.

Turning to First Nation **suicide rates**, we again use five year averages as the basis of analysis[36] and again must rely on Health Canada data, with all its limitations.[37] Those rates, which smooth out random or idiosyncratic fluctuations somewhat, reach alarmingly high levels which speak volumes about First Nation individuals' perceptions of the structure of opportunity available to them. Consider, for instance, the 1987–91 period. Federal government data show the suicide rate among Registered Indians during that period to have averaged 33 per 100,000 population, while for all of Canada the average was only 13 per 100,000 population.[38] Suicide rates for First Nation males are typically three or four times higher than for First Nation females, although more First Nation women than men *attempt* suicide. As depicted in Graphs 6A and 6B, the aforementioned federal government data set shows that for Registered Indian males in the age 15–24 group, the suicide rate was an astonishing 114 per 100,000, which was more than *four times* the rate (26 per 100,000 population) for their age counterparts in the larger Canadian population.[39] However, among those aged 65 and over, rates for First Nation men and women are both actually lower than those of persons the same age in the larger Canadian population. Regional variation, not shown in the graphs, is pronounced.[40]

Muir (1991: 41), drawing from an American study, summarizes some of the social factors contributing to the high suicide rates in the First Nation population:

> Parents, frustrated by the overwhelmingly rapid culture change, involved in alcohol abuse, and suffering from frequent family disasters, have little time or emotional resources to give to their children. Frequent experience of bereavement and exposure to pain through neglect, hunger, physical abuse, and disease cause many ... children to grow up scared and depressed. They lack the feeling of basic trust and possess few inner resources to deal with stress. Few of the parents' generation have the resources to help youth in crisis. Non-indigenous health and social services staff, who often lack knowledge of the socio-cultural situation, have great difficulty comprehending the psycho-social problems of young indigenous people. ... To Amerindian youth this life is devoid of meaning and worth little, whereas death is a way of finding peace and reunion with glorified ancestors. Suicide is often viewed as a brave, heroic act. ... Self-destructive behaviour becomes a learned and rewarded pattern. Those who die by suicide become the idols of their peer group.

Under those circumstances, suicide epidemics are more readily understandable.

The gravity of the suicide problem led the Royal Commission on Aboriginal Peoples to publish a separate report on it. Said the Commissison:

> The Commissioners believe it is a matter of utmost urgency that the people and governments of Canada, Aboriginal and non-Aboriginal alike, join in a concerted effort to bring high rates of Aboriginal suicide and self-injury to a rapid end.

(RCAP, 1995: 89)

and

> We have concluded that suicide is one of a group of symptoms, ranging from truancy and law breaking to alcohol and drug abuse and family violence, that are in large part interchangeable as expressions of the burden of loss, grief, and anger experienced by Aboriginal people in Canadian society.

(RCAP, 1995: 90)

GRAPH 6A Age-Specific Male Suicide Rates (1987–91 average) per 100,000 population, Registered Indians and Total Canada

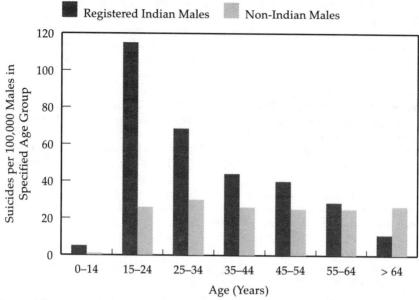

Source: Planning & Informatics Co-ordination, Medical Services Branch, Health Canada, Ottawa.

GRAPH 6B Age-Specific Female Suicide Rates (1987–91 average) per 100,000 population, Registered Indians and Total Canada

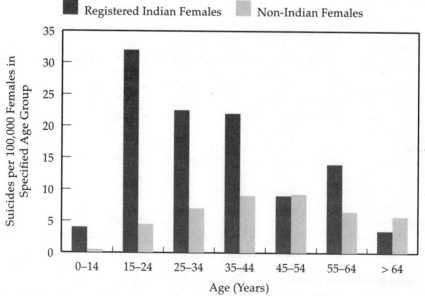

Source: Planning & Informatics Co-ordination, Medical Services Branch, Health Canada, Ottawa.

Morbidity

We turn now from mortality to sickness and health.

Only 13% of the First Nation adult population responding to the Aboriginal Peoples Survey (APS) in 1991 reported themselves as being in "poor" or only "fair" health, while 57% reported themselves as being in "excellent" or "very good" health. The corresponding figures for the total Canadian population in a 1994 national survey were 11% and 62%, respectively (Statistics Canada Daily, Sept. 25, 1995), which is a surprisingly small difference that underscores the subjectivity of the measure. On-reserve respondents reported slightly worse health than other aboriginal respondents. However, only 4% of on-reserve residents, but fully 11% of off-reserve residents (compared to over one-fifth of Métis) said that their special medical needs were not being met by the medicare system (Statistics Canada, 1993c: Tables 4.3, 4.5, and 4.7).

About 8% of First Nation respondents (on- or off-reserve) reported in the 1991 APS that the availability of food was a problem at some time over the past year, including 1% on-reserve and 2% off-reserve for whom that was the case more than two days per month. This, however, is by no means a proxy indicator of the extent to which *nutritional* needs are being met.

The comparatively high incidence of **tuberculosis** among the First Nation population stands out, although the most recently available data reveal the rate to be declining significantly. For instance, DIAND (1997b: 29) reports that the rate dropped from 85 cases per 100,000 population in 1980 to 47 per 100,000 population in 1994. However, conspicuous by its absence in DIAND's report is the fact that this is about seven times higher than the rate of about 7.2 per 100,000 population for the total Canadian population (*Statistics Canada Daily*, May 26, 1994).

Diabetes is another disease which affects a disproportionately high number of First Nation individuals and is of particular concern to health officials. It is the most prevalent chronic health problem for First Nations (Muir, 1991: 23) and is very significant because it causes a number of serious side effects, including heart and circulatory disease, blindness, kidney malfunction, and nerve damage (McDougall, 1994; Warden, 1995). The type of diabetes which is most common among First Nation people is non-insulin-dependent diabetes mellitus (NIDDM or "type 2" diabetes), which mainly, but not only, affects people in older age groups (Muir, 1991: 35). An idea of its prevalence can be obtained from the 1991 Aboriginal Peoples Survey (APS), where 6.6 % of persons identifying as Indian (8.6% on-reserve and 5.5% off-reserve) reported having diabetes (Statistics Canada, 1993c).[41] In comparison, Statistics Canada's 1991 General Social Survey found only 4% of the total Canadian adult population reported having diabetes (Statistics Canada, 1993d: 165). A significant increase in prevalence rates within the First Nation population is found from remote to rural to urban areas. In general, rates also increase from north to south and from west to east, which patterns might be a reflection both of genetic differences within the First Nation population and of the degree of isolation (Muir, 1991: 35; Warden, 1995).

Diabetes mellitus is associated with **obesity**, which can be measured using the Body Mass Index (BMI). The BMI is calculated as a person's body weight (in kilograms) divided by the square of his or her height (in metres). The desirable range for scores on this index is between 20 and 25. Muir (1991: 37) summarizes findings of an obesity study conducted by Young and Sevenhuysen using a sample of 704 individuals living in six remote Cree and Ojibway communities in northwestern Ontario and northeastern Manitoba. The researchers found that a large proportion of individuals in all age-sex groups was "obese" (BMI ≥ 26), including almost 90% of the women between the ages of 45 and 54 years. Compared to data from the overall Canadian population studied in the 1981 Canada Fitness Survey, the proportion of the Indian population with a BMI ≥ 26 was higher in all age groups for both men and women. Interestingly, employment was positively associated with BMI among First Nation males, but negatively associated with BMI for First Nation females.

Smoking of tobacco poses, of course, a serious risk to the health of both the smoker and non-smokers exposed to the smoke. Findings on smoking are mixed (Statistics Canada, 1993c). For instance, off-reserve First Nation individuals responding to the questions on smoking on the 1991 APS questionnaire are less likely than on-reserve individuals to be even occasional smokers. Forty-six percent of off-reserve Indians and 40% of on-reserve residents are non-smokers. In comparison, a large survey of the total Canadian adult population conducted in 1991 and 1994 by Statistics Canada found that a substantial majority (69%) of non-aboriginal Canadians comprises non-smokers.[42]

Alcohol consumption, when taken to excess, is another phenomenon which, obviously, has a pronounced effect upon both health, risk of death, and broader life chances of oneself and one's family members. For instance, a Saskatchewan study cited by Muir (1991: 42) found alcohol to be involved in 46% of suicides in the 15–34 year old population, 92% of fatal motor vehicle accidents where the deceased was the driver, over 38% of the homicides, and over half of the deaths by fire and drowning. Table 3 provides some interesting quantitative data which compare self-reports from the 1991 APS with self-reports from a 1989 survey of the entire Canadian population. Before examining the data, two caveats should be mentioned. First, the data bear on frequency, rather than amount, of consumption. Thus, some of those reporting drinking only once per week would, nevertheless, be abusing alcohol as binge drinkers.

TABLE 3 Self-Reported Frequency of Alcohol Consumption

	Total Canada Non-Aboriginal	Total Indian	On-Reserve	Off-Reserve
	(percent)			
Have Never Consumed an Alcoholic Beverage	7	16	22	13
Former Drinkers (Abstained Last 12 Months)	16	15	18	14
Currently a Drinker	78	69	60	73
a) Less than once per month	20	20	16	21
b i) Once or twice per month		21	21	22
ii) One to Three times per month	20			
c) One to Three times per week	30	21	16	24
d) Four or More times per week	9	3	2	4
e) Dont' Know Frequency		4	6	2
TOTAL	101	100	100	100

Sources: For total Canada: Eliany et al. *(1992: 17–18).* For Indians: Statcan (1993c), Cat. # 89-533 Table 4.3, pp. 130, 138, 150.

Secondly, in light of the stigma attached to alcoholism, it is reasonable to assume some under-reporting of consumption, especially among those who report that they do not know the frequency with which they consume.

Be that as it may, the data show that a significantly larger proportion of the First Nation population than of the overall Canadian population reports itself to be complete abstainers (16% vs. 7%) while a virtually identical percentage (15% and 16%, respectively) reports having abstained during at least the twelve months prior to the survey. Among current drinkers, non-Native Canadians report the most frequent consumption. Other noteworthy findings in the table are that off-reserve Indians emerge both as more frequent consumers than on-reserve residents and as more similar in this respect to the non-Native population than to the on-reserve population. Finally, in contrast to the stereotype, less than a quarter of the Indian population (18% on-reserve and 28% off-reserve), as compared to almost four in ten persons in the non-Native population, reports drinking one or more times per week. The higher frequency reported by off-reserve residents might well be indicative of a higher level of daily stress faced by off-reserve First Nation individuals who, often, are removed from networks of social and spiritual support and must cope with the racism and alien culture of the larger society.

Despite the above statistics, 73% of on-reserve residents interviewed for the 1991 Aboriginal Peoples Survey held the opinion that alcohol abuse is a problem in their community, while only 56% of off-reserve First Nations individuals shared that view. To place that in a comparative context, we note that unemployment is cited as a problem in the community by 78% of on-reserve residents and by 60% of off-reserve First Nation individuals (Statistics Canada, 1993c: 144 and 154).

In the same survey, ten percent of on-reserve First Nation adults who reported having seen someone about their health during the previous twelve months, and half as many off-reserve, reported that they saw a **traditional healer** (Statistics Canada, 1993c: pp. 138, 206, 148, and 208). While fair remuneration is necessary for traditional healers, a boosting of the rate of utilization of traditional healers for certain health services could lighten the financial costs of health services delivery for First Nation governments in the future.

Severe **disability** of one type or another is reported by 3.9% of the First Nation persons age 15 and over who responded to the questions on disability on the 1991 APS (Statistics Canada, 1994b: 14, 20, and 26). The rate is slightly higher on-reserve than off-reserve (4.5% vs 3.5%). Another 7%, both on- and off-reserve, reported a moderate degree of disability. Both on- and off-reserve the most commonly reported type of disability (for all degrees of severity combined) among adults was mobility-related, as 14% of adult respondents cited this as a disability. In contrast, only 4% of the overall Canadian adult population surveyed in the 1991 General Social Survey reported a mobility-related disability (Statistics Canada, 1993d: 55).

In 1988 the federal Cabinet gave approval to Health Canada to transfer federal resources for Indian health programs south of the sixtieth parallel to First Nations' control. This has been a controversial move which has been fuelled by First Nations' concerns over jurisdiction, funding, and aboriginal and treaty rights relating to health care (Muir, 1991: 9). Whether this will eventually prove to be as successful as the policy transferring control of elementary and secondary education to First Nations remains to be seen.

AGE STRUCTURE

The First Nation population is a remarkably young population. For instance, in 1995, 31% of the Registered Indian population was under age 15 and virtually half (49.8%) was under age 25. The corresponding figures for all Canadians were only 20% under age 15 and one third (33.8%) under age 25. The **median age** — the age at which half of the population is younger and half is older — for the Registered Indian population was 25 in 1995, but that for Canada as a whole was 35. While the median age of both populations is increasing, a set of medium growth projections for both predicts that the large gap will persist.[43] Later in this section we shall consider the constraints which this age structure places upon the First Nation population.

The First Nation population has been noteworthy for its high birth rates and correspondingly high proportion of the population who are children. For instance, in the midst of the First Nations baby boom in 1966, almost half (48%) of the First Nations population was under age 15 (Siggner, 1986: 66)! However, as a comparison of Graph 7A with Graph 7B shows, a **"rectangularization"** of the First Nation population structure is underway. The proportion of the First Nation population under age 15 is projected to decrease over the coming years to about one quarter (26.2%) by the year 2015, but the corresponding figure for Canada as a whole is much lower at about one-sixth (16.8%).[44] The shape of the population pyramid for Registered Indians in 1995 resembled a silhouette of the "Stanley Cup", which stood in marked contrast to the "midriff bulge" ("Michelin Man") shape of the 1995 pyramid for Canada as a whole (Graph 7C). By the year 2015 or 2016, the differences between the Registered Indian and overall Canadian pyramids (Graphs 7B and 7D) are not nearly as pronounced. Even then, though, the inverted pyramid shape of the overall Canadian population pyramid will not be exhibited by the Registered Indian pyramid with its still reasonably wide base.

For the Registered Indian population, the **youth dependency ratio** — the ratio of children under age 15 to persons in the more "economically productive" age range of 15 to 64 — has declined precipitously from a remarkably high 1.04 (48%/46%) in 1966 to 0.49 (31.3%/64.2%) in 1995 and is projected to drop much further to 0.39 (26.2%/67.3%) by the year 2015.[45] That this is an enormous demographic shift over just half of a century can be appreciated by re-stating the above numbers: *in 1966, the First Nation population contained over ten children for every ten adults in the labour force age range, but 50 years later there will be only about four children for every ten First Nation adults of labour force age.*

In contrast to the overall Canadian population, where the proportion of **senior citizens** in the population is increasing markedly, in the First Nation population the easing of the youth dependency economic "burden" is *not* counteracted by a significant increase in the proportion of persons in that "retirement" age range of 65 years and older. Their proportion of the First Nation population stood at 6% in 1966, 4.6% in 1995, and is projected to return to about 6.5% in the year 2015 (as compared to about 17% for the overall Canadian population in 2015). However, the absolute numbers of First Nation seniors will more than double from about 27,000 in 1995 to about 58,000 in 2015.

The **overall dependency ratio** is the ratio of children (under age 15) and seniors (age 65 and over) to those in the 15–64 age group. In the First Nation population it dropped from 1.17 in 1966 to 0.56 in 1995 and is projected to decrease further to 0.49 by 2015. This represents a potentially significant increase

GRAPH 7A Registered Indian Population, by Age and Sex, 1995

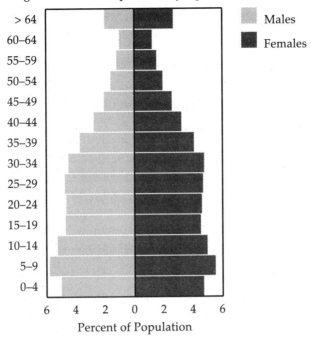

Percent of Population

Source: DIAND (1997b: 21)

GRAPH 7B Registered Indian Population, by Age and Sex, 2015

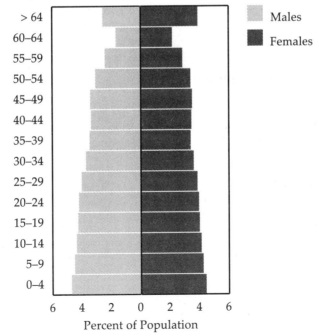

Percent of Population

Source: Nault et al. (1993).

GRAPH 7C   Canadian Population, by Age and Sex, 1995

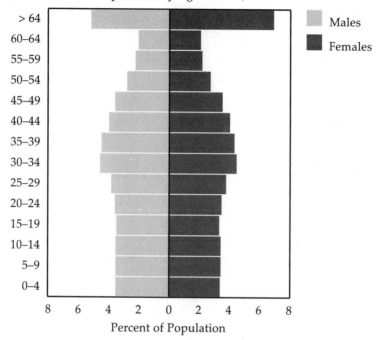

GRAPH 7D   Canadian Population, by Age and Sex, 2016

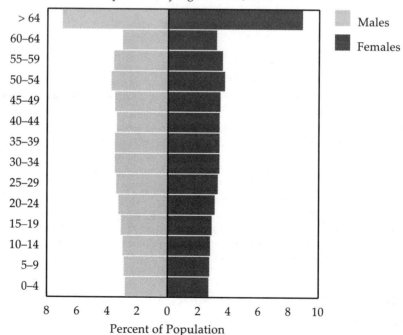

Source: Source: Statistics Canada. CANSIM matrix 6900

in economic well-being for First Nation families and individuals. However, that potential will be realized only if there is an expansion in other structures of opportunity such that First Nation individuals are better able to find gainful employment in either the traditional or modern sector of the economy. The medium growth scenario projects an increase of about 270,000 individuals in the 15–64 year old age group over the twenty-five years ending in 2015, or about 11,000 persons per year (combined on- and off-reserve). That is a lot of people entering the labour force. One way of visualizing this is by relating it to the on-reserve population's contribution to that increase. That is, even if only about half of those persons were to enter the paid labour force, for that on-reserve population growth (Nault et al., 1993: 86) to be absorbed on-reserve without increasing the already very high levels of unemployment, at least four new, permanent jobs would have to be created each year for each of the over six hundred First Nation "bands" in Canada. The unlikelihood of that many jobs being created in most "bands" suggests that off-reserve migration will continue apace. Individuals will leave the reserves not only because of the pull of employment prospects off-reserve, but also because of the deterioration of social conditions on-reserve as a consequence of that more widespread unemployment on their reserve.

A further note of caution is in order à propos the age structure of the First Nation population. Reference here is to the young adults in the **"family forming" age group** (ages 15 to 29). They will constitute a diminishing proportion of the First Nation population over the next two decades, as they shrink from about 28% to about 24% of the population over the 1995 to 2015 period. However, the fact that their absolute numbers will increase from about 166,000 to about 214,000 over that period underscores the fact that the First Nation housing crisis cannot be solved by demographic means alone. Indeed, because of that large increase in absolute numbers, the housing situation will be exacerbated by demographics. We shall return to housing later in this chapter.

R. M. Jiobu (1990) has argued that every ethnic group has a demographic potential or demographic capacity, that tends to elevate or lower the group's socio-economic status. For First Nations, the age structure of the population is crucial in this regard, as is the small population size of First Nation communities. Both of these factors operate to constrict economic opportunity and depress levels of socio-economic attainment. The broad base of the First Nation population pyramid not only depresses female labour force participation rates and generates a need for major expenditures (e.g., new school construction). It also implies a large population competing for labour-force openings. That, in turn, depresses wages and undermines hope among young adults. Young adults who are short on hope are more likely to come into conflict with the law, which diminishes their mobility opportunities and diverts community expenditures into social control and away from the generating of opportunities. A broad base on a population pyramid also suggests that public expenditures will rise at a rate that is likely to alarm some politicians and lead them to call for expenditure reductions which could curtail opportunities even more.

MIGRATION AND MOBILITY[46]

In the study of population movement, we can break down the population of "movers" (people who change residence) into "migrants" — namely, persons who relocate to a different community or geographic area outside their community — and "non-migrant movers" — namely, persons who change residences within the *same* community or narrowly defined geographic area. The push and pull factors which influence migrants are probably a better indicator of macro-level opportunity structures than are the push and pull factors which influence non-migrant movers.

Reserves and Large Cities as Origins and Destinations

The constricted opportunity structure on reserves, especially in terms of the availability of housing and employment, led to a substantial migration of First Nation people from reserves to urban (and other) areas during the 1960s and 1970s (Siggner, 1980: 44–47; Norris, 1996: 212–213). The 1991 Census and 1991 Aboriginal Population Survey reveal that the Registered Indian population flow to the large cities continued over the 1986–91 period. Over one-third (35%) of all Registered Indian migrants during that period went to the large cities. Norris (1996: 212) shows that to be a 5% increase over the previous five-year period. Yet, this amounted to the large cities' net gain in population of only 3,855 Registered Indians through migration (Clatworthy, 1995: 62, 64) — a net gain of only 67 migrants per 1000 Registered Indian residents in those large cities. (Only about 58,000 people in the off-reserve Registered Indian population are in large cities.) The majority of individuals within the stream to the large cities comes from the rural off-reserve areas and small cities, rather than from reserves.

Equally important to note, is the **reversal** of the earlier population drain from the reserves.[47] Although there had always been some return flow of migrants back to reserves, there is now *a net in-flow of Registered Indian migrants to the reserves* from the large cities, from the small cities, and from the rural off-reserve areas, respectively (Clatworthy, 1995: 64). This is probably indicative of both some disillusionment with opportunities off-reserve, and some enhancement of housing and employment opportunities on-reserve.

In addition, the return of **Bill C-31 (re)instatees** to the reserves accounted for about 21% (2,005) of the net gain of 9,230 Registered Indians which reserve populations experienced from a total of 20,630 aboriginal persons migrating to or from reserves between 1986 and 1991 (Clatworthy, 1995: 70, 64, 58–59).[48] Membership codes are, obviously, an important part of the entire set of opportunities, or lack thereof, on-reserve.[49] That is to say, a restrictive membership code, such as that of Alberta's wealthy Sawridge band, effectively denies potential returnees' access to those opportunities which do exist on the reserve.

Relative Flux or Stability?

Several types of data provide perspectives on the relative state of flux or stability of the Registered Indian population.

- Persons living on-reserve in 1991, of whom about 95% were Registered Indians, had a 56% probability of *not* having moved during the previous five years (Clatworthy, 1995: 18, 28, 55) or a 44% five-year mobility rate (including within the same community). As we note below, this is almost identical to the rate for the total Canadian population. However, off-reserve Registered Indians boost the overall Registered Indian rate substantially; among off-reserve Registered Indians the ratio of movers to non-movers is 2:1.[50] Overall, 57% of all Registered Indians, including those living off-reserve, changed residence during the period 1986–91. This was significantly lower than the rate for other aboriginal people, but significantly higher than the 43%[51] rate which Norris (1996: 208) cites for the total Canadian population. Thus, on-reserve Registered Indians are only about as mobile as the overall Canadian population, but by those same overall Canadian standards, off-reserve Registered Indians and other aboriginal people are highly "transient", although some of that 'transience' merely involves changing residence within the same community.

- During the *most recent* year (1990–91) prior to the 1991 census, only 9% of the Registered Indian population had changed residences (Clatworthy, 1995: 183) as either migrants or non-migrant movers.
- An *annual* average of only about 4% of the entire Registered Indian population would be classified as *migrants* (as opposed to non-migrant movers) during the five-year period 1986–91 (Clatworthy 1995: 76). Accordingly, over that five-year period a total of about 20% of the entire Registered Indian population was a *migrant*, which was about a 2% increase from the 18% exhibited in the 1981–86 period (Norris: 1996: 213). The 1986–91 Registered Indian rate was almost identical to the rate for the total Canadian population (Clatworthy, 1995: 30; Norris, 1996: 208).[52]
- Only about 2% of the Registered Indian population reported more than one change of residence in the twelve months prior to the 1991 Aboriginal Peoples Survey (Clatworthy, 1995: 188).
- Inter-provincial migration flows of Registered Indians tend to be small, as only about 4,400 Registered Indians per year migrated across provincial or territorial borders during the five-year period (Clatworthy, 1995: 41–42). *Net* inter-provincial flows are particularly low, as only British Columbia, at plus 1125 persons, gained or lost as many as 700 Registered Indian persons from/to inter-provincial migration over the full five-year period.

Considering the above points, we conclude that the Registered Indian population on-reserve cannot be described accurately as a population in a high state of flux, although the off-reserve Registered Indian population can be.

Factors Associated With Out-Migration From Reserves

What are the factors which influence out-migration from Indian reserves? The availability of housing and employment has already been identified as one such factor. Gerber's work (summarized in Clatworthy, 1995: 8) has identified several main factors. For instance, the greater a reserve's distance from a major urban centre and the greater the institutional completeness[53] of the reserve, the less the likelihood that a person in that community would leave that community. Conversely, the greater a person's "human capital" (education and occupational skills), the greater the likelihood of migration. In addition, migration tends to be higher from communities with an individualistic, rather than a communal, orientation.

Who are the Registered Indian migrants and non-migrant movers? The data reveal them to be especially likely to be young adults (the highest mobility rate is in the 25–34 year old age group) and especially *un*likely to be age 55 or older. Females are over-represented in the mobile population (Clatworthy, 1996: 86), and are far more likely than men to be among those migrating away from reserves.[54] Norris (1996) points out that this tendency is "similar to, but much more pronounced than, the higher out-migration of women than men from rural areas among the general [total Canadian] population". However, the push-pull factors experienced by aboriginal women on reserves are different than for non-aboriginal women.

When interviewed in 1991, Registered Indian migrants were found (Clatworthy, 1996) to have the following additional characteristics, as compared to Registered Indian non-migrants:

- be changing residence with their family
- graduation from secondary school or have some post-secondary education[55]
- attending school
  Among Registered Indians, migrants were almost twice as likely as non-migrants to be attending school (18% vs 10%, respectively; Clatworthy, 1996: 99)
- high labour force participation rates
  Registered Indian migrants had higher labour force participation rates (78% for males; 55% for females) than Registered Indian non-migrants (66% for males; 49% for females).
- a higher unemployment rate
  Registered Indian migrants had higher unemployment rates (33% for males; 29% for females) than Registered Indian non-migrants (32% for males; 21% for females).[56] However, taking both sexes combined, there was little difference between migrants and non-migrants in the number of weeks worked in the year before the census. A slight majority of both (51% for migrants and 54% for non-migrants) had worked forty or more weeks.[57]
- a higher employment income
  Registered Indian migrants had an employment income in 1990 that was about 10% higher than Registered Indian non-migrants ($16,980 vs $15,469, respectively). This was true regardless of the number of weeks worked.[58]

HOUSING

As Siggner (1986: 71) notes, the deplorable state of on-reserve housing has improved significantly since a major housing study was done in 1977. For instance, there has been a significant increase in the number of housing units such that the number of persons per unit has decreased from six to slightly over four in 1991 (as compared to less than three for non-Native Canadians); the number of units considered to be unsalvageable has decreased dramatically; and far more houses now have basic amenities.

Nevertheless, part of the persistent stereotyped view of First Nations as an economically impoverished people is the image of **substandard** housing. Data in Table 4 enable us to discover just how accurate the stereotype is in this case. There we find that on virtually every indicator available, the on-reserve population stands out as having inferior housing to that of both non-Natives and other Natives (except the Inuit on some indicators).

First Nation persons' houses are smaller than those of non-Native Canadians; yet, more people occupy each First Nation house. On-reserve there are twice as many people per room as there are among non-aboriginal Canadians and almost one-quarter of on-reserve houses are deemed to be inadequate by virtue of needing more bedroom(s).

TABLE 4 Housing Comparisons: Overall Canadian Population and Population Reporting Aboriginal Identity

	Total Cdn Non-aborig. Population	Total Aboriginal Identifiers	Total N. Amer. Indian	On-Reserve Indian	Off-Reserve Indian	Métis	Inuit
Number of Private Dwellings*	10,018,265	239,240	177,450	39,870	137,580	65,005	9,655
Size and Density of Occupancy							
Average # of Persons per Dwelling	2.7	3.5	3.5	4.3	3.3	3.3	4.3
Average # of Rooms per Dwelling	6.1	5.8	5.8	5.5	5.9	5.9	5.4
Average # of Persons per Room	0.4	0.6	0.6	0.8	0.6	0.6	0.8
Average # of Bedrooms per Dwelling	2.6	2.7	2.7	2.9	2.6	2.7	2.7
% of dwellings needing more bedroom(s)	n.a.	11	12	24	8	8	19
Age of Dwellings							
% constructed on or before 1945	18	14	14	2	18	14	3
% constructed 1971 to 1980	25	29	26	27	25	30	29
% constructed 1981 to 1991	22	27	28	52	21	22	40
State of Repair							
% needing major repairs	8	20	21	39	15	17	18
% needing minor repairs	24	29	29	29	30	30	24
% needing only regular maintenance	68	51	50	33	55	53	57
	100%	100%	100%	100%	100%	100%	100%

continued

TABLE 4 (*continued*)

	Total Aboriginal Identifiers	Total N. Amer. Indian	On-Reserve Indian	Off-Reserve Indian	Métis	Inuit
Amenities and Safety Features						
% with electricity	93	93	94	93	94	95
% with a flush toilet	88	87	75	91	92	91
% with hot running water bathtub or shower in working order	87	86	73	90	90	90
% where main source of heat is wood stove, cooking stove, or fireplace	23	24	48	17	19	14
% with smoke detector in working order	70	68	53	72	74	83
% with fire extinguisher in working order	39	38	31	40	38	69
Source of Drinking Water						
% of dwelling units obtaining water from:						
• municipal system	71	69	36	79	76	68
• community well or cistern	10	11	35	4	6	6
• household well	9	9	14	8	10	3
• surface water (lake, river, stream) or rain, snow, or dugout	5	4	11	2	3	26
• bottled water	3	3	4	3	3	2

Note: A dwelling unit is included in the aboriginal data if it was occupied by *at least one* person who identifies as a North American Indian, Métis, or Inuit, or who is classified as a Registered Indian under the *Indian Act* of Canada

Source: Excerpted from Statistics Canada (1994b, Cat. #89-535) Highlights and Tables 2.1, 2.3, 2.5, 2.7, and from Statistics Canada (1993b, Cat. #93-314).

First Nations and the federal Department of Indian Affairs and Northern Development (DIAND) have allocated considerable resources to on-reserve housing,[59] especially in response to the baby boom children of the 1960s entering the family formation stage themselves. For instance, slightly more than half of the houses now occupied on-reserve were built between 1981 and 1991, which makes the on-reserve housing stock much newer than that of any of the other comparison groups shown in the table. Yet, proportionately speaking, compared to houses occupied by any of the other groups, from two to almost five times as many on-reserve houses stand in need of major repair (e.g., 39% on-reserve, 15% off-reserve, and 8% among non-aboriginals). One might speculate that this discrepancy reflects both the high levels of alienation and the low levels of income that exist on many reserves.

Electricity is almost universal (93%) among First Nation dwellings, but a flush toilet and functioning bath or shower with hot running water are absent in about one in ten off-reserve First Nation homes and one in four on-reserve homes. Almost half of on-reserve dwellings rely on a wood stove, cooking stove, or fireplace as their main source of heat, while for drinking water one in nine on-reserve homes (as compared to 2% of off-reserve Indian dwellings and 26% of Inuit dwellings) relies on surface water (lake, river, or stream) or on rain, snow, or a dugout. Not shown in the table is the fact that in 11% of on-reserve homes the drinking water must be treated by a resident in order to make it safe to drink (Statistics Canada, 1994b: 96).

Unfortunately, the tragedy of death by fire is no stranger to on-reserve residents. Although First Nation councils have pressed for government funding for better fire-fighting equipment on-reserve, the table shows that, at the level of individuals' own responsibility, only slightly more than half of on-reserve homes have a smoke-detector in working order and fewer than one-third have a fire extinguisher in working order.[60]

In summary, First Nation housing conditions overall are significantly above what one might visualize when contemplating third world countries, due in large part to the contribution made by off-reserve First Nation homes and to recent ameliorative efforts by governments. Nevertheless, even that off-reserve housing compares unfavourably with the housing stock of non-Native Canadians. Indeed, the data show the First Nation housing situation to be deplorable in several respects, particularly on-reserve. Notable here is the overcrowding, the widespread state of major disrepair, the widespread reliance on stoves or fireplaces for heating, and the low level of basic infrastructure for piped "municipal" running water. Furthermore, hot running water for bathing or showering is unavailable in a surprisingly large proportion of on-reserve homes and potable water is lacking in a small but significant proportion of on-reserve dwellings.

These housing conditions have an adverse **impact on the life chances** of First Nation individuals, especially insofar as health is concerned. For instance, over-crowding and inadequate heating promote the spread of respiratory infection and other communicable diseases. In addition, overcrowding constitutes a significant interference with a student's ability to concentrate on his/her studies, which in turn can produce poor academic performance and either dropping out of school or not being admitted to the post-secondary institution of choice. Clearly, poor housing is a major contributor to the "vicious cycle" of poverty.

EDUCATION

In contemporary Canadian society the attainment of an advanced level of formal education is clearly one of the major factors shaping an individual's life chances, especially the chances of breaking out of the grip of internal colonialism and multi-generational welfare dependency. As society moves further into the "information age", that truism will become even more important. However, First Nation education has an inglorious history marred by both a genocidal and then an alienating curriculum and abuse of students in the residential schools. Consequently, education is a phenomenon that some First Nation parents still do not trust, and that distrust is manifested in the high absenteeism rates of their children and, in some communities, in their own lack of support for their children's schooling.

Those patterns, and the associated very high drop-out/push-out rates, have begun to change, though, as the 1974 **policy of "Indian control of Indian education"** has gradually taken root. DIAND data show that band-operated schools increased in number from 53 in academic year 1975–76 to 429 in 1995–96 (DIAND, 1997b: 39). At that later date, a majority (57%) of First Nation elementary and secondary students was enrolled in band-operated schools. With the hiring of qualified Indian teachers and teachers' aides, and with the incorporation of elders in the teaching of traditional languages and ways, the dropout/pushout rates have fallen. For instance, DIAND (1997b: 35) data on **participation rates** show that the proportion of on-reserve students remaining in school until Grade 12 (or 13) for consecutive years of schooling increased from 3% to 75% over the thirty-three year period ending in the 1995–96 academic year. Although this still bespeaks a large pool of untapped human potential, it also has resulted in a huge increase in the number of First Nation individuals going on to post-secondary education. That number more than doubled, from about 11,200 to 26,300 between Fall 1985 and Fall 1995 and First Nations' post-secondary enrolment rate of 6.5% of persons aged 17–34 is closing in on the rate of 10.4% for all of Canadian society (DIAND, 1997b: 36-7). Even more dramatically, the number of Registered Indians enrolled in university, per se, increased from sixty in Fall 1960 to over seven thousand by Fall 1993 (DIAND, 1996: 43), but had fallen somewhat to 6636 by 1995. In 1995 over 1700 First Nation individuals graduated from universities (including over 200 with post-baccalaureate degrees). It is probably safe to assume that those who graduate from university will be instrumental in creating employment opportunities for other First Nation persons.

The above changes in participation are reflected in the 1991 Census data on formal education **attainment** in Table 5. Admittedly, we observe there that First Nations still lag considerably behind the total Canadian population. On-reserve First Nation individuals (and Inuit) stand out as being particularly over-represented among those with less than a high school education. Similarly, in both groups only about one-quarter of the population (aged 15–49) has any post-secondary education, as compared to about half of the total Canadian population in the same age range. However, off-reserve First Nation individuals have significantly more education than their on-reserve counterparts, and over 900 on-reserve Indians and about 6600 off-reserve Indians were identified in the Census as holding *university degrees*. Taking into account those First Nations which did not participate in the 1991 Census, the total would probably have

TABLE 5 Formal Education Attainment of Persons Aged 15–49 in 1991

	Total Canada	Total Aboriginal	Total N.A. Indian	On-Reserve	Off-Reserve	Métis	Inuit
			(Percentage)				
No Formal Schooling		0.9	0.8	1.3	0.5	0.4	4.3
1 to 8 years		15.9	15.7	26.8	10.1	12.0	33.3
Sub-total	6	16.8	16.5	28.1	10.6	12.3	37.6
Secondary	37	49.6	49.5	46.1	51.2	53.1	35.8
Cumulative Sub-total	43	66.4	66.0	74.2	61.8	65.5	73.4
Some Post-Secondary		13.9	14.2	11.1	15.8	13.7	11.3
Certificate or Diploma		16.5	16.6	12.9	18.5	17.3	14.1
University Degree		2.7	2.7	1.0	3.6	3.1	0.6
Sub-total: Any Post Sec	51	33.1	33.5	24.9	37.9	34.1	26.0
Not specified		0.5	0.5	0.9	0.3	0.4	0.5
Total Pop. age 15–49	100	100	100	100	100	100	100

Source: Statistics Canada (1993a, Cat. #89-534), Tables 1.1, 1.3, 1.5, and 1.7.
Note: Among adults aged 50–64 a university degree was held by 130 of the 13,130 on-reserve Indians, by 885 of the 19,560 off-reserve Indians, and by 335 of the 9,710 Métis. Inuit figures were too small to be considered reliable. (Source: as above)

swollen to well over ten-thousand individuals by the mid-1990s, as compared to about 2600 identified in the Census fifteen years earlier (Siggner, 1986: 76).

While we must be on guard against an ethnocentric bias in favour of university education, the fact remains that most of these university graduates could offer valuable skills to First Nation communities, should they turn there for employment. Some will be barred from returning to reserve communities, despite the acute needs there. Others will find the structure of opportunities on-reserve to be very constraining. Probably most will be structurally integrated into the labour force of the larger Canadian society off-reserve, where their performance could help to undermine present stereotypes.

The federal *Employment Equity Act* threatens post-secondary institutions with loss of eligibility for government contracts and research grants if satisfactory affirmative action programs are not undertaken for aboriginals (and women, people of colour, and the disabled). As a result of that and other factors, **post-secondary institutions** are becoming increasingly aware of the special needs of First Nation students. Hence, despite the fact that racism on campus remains no small problem (see Calliou's chapter in this volume), post-secondary institutions are becoming somewhat more hospitable to aboriginal students and aboriginal students are now enrolling in a wider range of programs than the education and social work programs which predominated among them in the 1970s and 1980s.[61] Among the other changes occurring are such things as the introduction of special transition programs for Native students, special tutors, more courses and programs of Native Studies, involvement of elders, separate First Nation colleges (e.g., Saskatchewan Indian Federated College) and separate facilities where Native students can gather together in comfortable, less alienating surroundings. However, hiring of aboriginal instructors lags far behind these other changes.

The **federal government's policy** of capping post-secondary education funds at a time of increasing demand, resulted in a waiting list of qualified First Nation students seeking post-secondary education. The short-sightedness of that policy decision was lamentable and, in the minds of many observers, called into question DIAND's commitment to fostering First Nations' development. Indeed, it is not surprising that the policy provoked a hunger strike among First Nation youths in 1989, for among treaty First Nations, education at all levels is widely regarded as a treaty right, while members of other First Nations regard it as a fiduciary obligation of the federal government. Conversely, the federal government, points to the fact that education is not mentioned in most treaties; therefore, it treats the provision of post-secondary education funding as merely a policy rather than a treaty obligation. Such an orientation seriously under-mines First Nations' ability to develop the human capital necessary to make self-government successful.

LABOUR FORCE, UNEMPLOYMENT, AND WELFARE DEPENDENCY

A person is considered to be a participant in the labour force if, in the week prior to being surveyed, the person was either employed or unemployed but actively seeking work. Of the Registered Indian on-reserve population aged 15 and over, not quite half (47%) were participating in the labour force around the time of the Aboriginal Population Survey in 1991, whereas two-thirds (68%) of Registered Indians off-reserve were in the labour force.[62] The on-reserve male labour force **participation rate** (55%) was much higher than the on-reserve female partici-pation rate (38%) and both exhibited significant increases over the previous decade. However, these rates are well below the rates for non-aboriginal Canadians and reflect differences in the employment opportunity structure. Official **unemployment rates** tend to show First Nations as having an unem-ployment rate which is two and one half to three times higher than the rate for Canada as a whole.[63] This is misleading, though, since some communities expe-rience near-universal unemployment.

Business ownership is an avenue of opportunity which some First First Nation people have pursued in the absence of other employment opportunities. RCAP (1996d: 213) reports that 3.3% of on-reserve Indians over age 15 in 1991 currently own their own business. The figure for the corresponding total Canadian population is 9.9%.

The Royal Commission on Aboriginal Peoples (RCAP, 1996b: 802) provides interesting census data on the distribution of the Registered Indian employed labour force by **industrial sector** in 1991. Only 8%, compared to 6% in the total non-aboriginal population, was found in primary industries like natural resource extraction, agriculture, and fishing, and trapping. Not surprisingly, government services was also heavily represented, at 29% (vs. 8% for the total non-aboriginal population). Eighteen percent was found in health and educa-tion services and 8% in manufacturing (vs 15% and 14%, respectively, for non-aboriginals). The Registered Indian population was heavily under-represented in other tertiary industries (37% vs 56% for non-aboriginals).

Table 6, taken from the 1991 APS, identifies some of the **obstacles** which First Nation and other aboriginal people face in seeking employment. Cell

TABLE 6 Barriers Faced by Aboriginal People in Seeking Employment

	Total Aboriginal	Total N.A. Indian	On-Reserve	Off-Reserve	Métis	Inuit
Percent of Adults (age 15+) Reporting Problems in Finding a Job Because:						
• few or no jobs in the area where they live	66	66	**75**	61	62	71
• their education or work experience did not match jobs available	41	41	41	41	43	38
• child care unavailable	8	8	8	8	8	9
• not enough information about available jobs	26	27	**32**	25	22	24
• they are aboriginal	16	18	**22**	16	12	12
• other reasons	10	11	7	13	9	8
Total number of persons reporting looking for work in 1990 or 1991	127,685	93,630	31,790	61,840	28,215	7,255

Note: Column totals sum to more than 100% because multiple responses were allowed.
Source: Statistics Canada. (1993a, Cat. #89-534), Tables 3.1, 3.3, 3.5, and 3.7.

entries are percentages of adults (age 15 and over) who reported problems in finding a job. Column totals exceed one hundred percent because any given respondent could cite more than one type of problem. From the table we observe that the scarcity of available jobs, of jobs commensurate with the applicants' skills, and of job information are, far and away, the factors most frequently cited by respondents. The constricted structure of employment opportunity is especially evident on-reserve, in that 75% of on-reserve respondents who reported problems in finding a job attributed those problems to the scarcity of jobs in the area where they live. Note, though, that "racial" discrimination is reported as a problem encountered by more than one-fifth of those surveyed on-reserve.

In addition to high levels of unemployment, the rate of **dependency on social assistance** payments is high. In fiscal year 1995–96 the monthly average number of social assistance recipients (70,000) and their dependants (83,500) amounted to an estimated 153,500 persons, which is 25% of the First Nation population (DIAND, 1997b: 53). Almost all First Nations (95%) now administer their own social assistance programs.

The significance of income data must be treated with caution, especially to the extent that a people rely on the traditional hunting, fishing, and trapping economy for subsistence. (One-third of on-reserve adults who eat meat, fish, or poultry reported in the 1991 APS that they obtain at least half of their meat, fish, or poultry from hunting and fishing.)[64] Special tabulations done for RCAP from the 1991 APS reveal major disparities between Registered Indians and the total Canadian population on various crude measures of income. For instance, whereas one-fifth of all Canadian males (aged 15+) earned less than ten thousand dollars in 1990, over half (52%) of First Nation males fell in that category. For females, the figures are 36% and 63%, respectively.[65] Similarly, the average total annual income for all Canadian males (aged 15+), at $30,200, is more than double the $15,000 of their First Nation counterparts. The disparity among females is less ($17,600 vs $11,100), but very pronounced, nevertheless (RCAP, 1994d: 14).

SUMMARY AND CONCLUSION

In the face of such a barrage of data as we have encountered in this chapter, it would be easy to lose sight of "the big picture". In an attempt to avoid that, the findings of the chapter are summarized below under headings derived from the sub-title of this volume. Some classification of observations under one or another of the themes is arbitrary. For instance, empowerment usually increases opportunities.

Opportunity

- Bill C-31 opened to re-instatees the opportunities and privileges which status as Registered Indians entails but which would otherwise have been denied to them. One result has been slightly diminished opportunity for existing on-reserve persons, due to inadequate resourcing by DIAND.
- Rapid on-reserve population growth and return migration from off-reserves creates a larger market for First Nation entrepreneurs.
- The housing crisis and shortage of job opportunities on-reserve will continue to generate a migratory stream of persons seeking opportunity elsewhere, but the reversal of the net outflow from reserves suggests either that opportunities on-reserve are expanding or opportunities off-reserve are constricting, or both.
- The marked reduction in the youth dependency ratio of the First Nation population as the First Nation "baby-boomers" have entered the age of labour force participation supposedly represents an opportunity in the sense that resources can be reallocated from education to areas of greater need. However, the First Nation population is still quite youthful and that age structure alone limits the potential for improving the socio-economic status of the First Nation population.
- The sharp reduction in First Nation fertility rates and infant mortality rates means that First Nation women are less constrained by child-rearing obligations and are more available to enter the paid labour force.
- The dramatic decline in First Nation mortality rates and increase in life expectancy provide one of the most obvious examples of improved opportunities. However, for some infants opportunity is truncated or snuffed out entirely even before leaving the womb or shortly thereafter, due to stillbirth or fetal alcohol syndrome or sudden infant death syndrome. Rates for all three are higher among First Nation people than in Canada as a whole. Predisposing factors for these causes of death are correlated with poverty. Notwithstanding the declines in mortality rates, First Nation individuals still have a markedly shorter life-expectancy than the rest of the Canadian population.
- The astonishingly elevated rates of suicide in the First Nation population attest to the victims' assessment that the opportunities facing them are woefully lacking.

- First Nation individuals are particularly prone to some potentially debilitating diseases which diminish opportunity for the sufferer. Among the diseases are diabetes and tuberculosis.
- Job creation initiatives lag far behind the demand for jobs created by the entry of the First Nation baby-boomers into the labour force. Employment opportunities remain highly constricted.
- Migration is associated with an opening of opportunity structures. That is, migrants, on average, experience significantly more remunerative employment that non-migrants.
- The very poor housing conditions (over-crowding, lack of amenities like hot running water or a central heating system), as found in a minority of First Nation homes, have deleterious "ripple" effects on opportunities in other spheres.
- Numerous barriers to employment have been identified by First Nation people. Among the most frequently cited are the scarcity of jobs, scarcity of information about jobs, inadequate skills; and discrimination by non-Natives. Inadequate child care is an obstacle to a significant minority of First Nation women.

Empowerment

- The substantial growth in size of the First Nation population increases its "clout" in the political system of the larger society, but the geographic dispersal of the First Nation population sets a relatively low upper limit on its electoral power.
- With off-reserve First Nation individuals accounting for an increased proportion of the total Registered Indian population, some shifting of power from reserves to off-reserve band members might occur.
- Highly restrictive membership codes adopted by some First Nations are seemingly designed to disempower Bill C-31 re-instatees and foreclose opportunity structures to them.
- Welfare dependency is widespread in First Nation communities, in the sense that about one quarter of the population is dependent upon social assistance in any given month. This dependency is disempowering to those who are caught in "the welfare trap".

Self-Determination

- The large proportion of Bill C-31 re-instatees living off-reserve, combined with other growth of the off-reserve population, accentuates challenges of legitimacy and service delivery faced by reserve-based First Nation governments.
- The geographic fragmentation of the First Nation population and small population size of the average band make it very difficult for First Nation governments to achieve economies of scale.
- The substantial increase in educational attainment and attendance at university and other post-secondary education institutions means that when such graduates work for First Nation organizations, the negotiating strength of those organizations is increased substantially, as is their ability to design the programs and policies needed by First Nation governments. This is an

important part of the capacity-building which figures so prominently in the development strategy advocated by sociologists (e.g., Ponting, 1991: 439) and the Royal Commission on Aboriginal Peoples (1996b: 326–353).

- The fact that First Nations have taken control of education has greatly enhanced educational outcomes, including the proportion of students staying in school until the end of grade 12 or 13. Similarly, enhancement of health outcomes could occur with First Nations' takeover of the delivery of health services.
- High rates of welfare dependency militate against the members of the First Nation community supporting self-government initiatives, for fear of the unknown (especially fear of losing one's support from DIAND) leads welfare dependent persons to adhere to the status quo.

Considering all of the above, one could conclude that the socio-demographic situation of First Nations has evolved to the point that *there has been a significant opening of opportunity structures, but that they are still much more constricted than those enjoyed by other Canadians.* Empowerment has occurred, mainly in the form of greater educational attainment. Self-determination has been augmented somewhat by demographics, but for the most part, demographics have been augmented by self-determination. In the next chapter we consider the constraints which three additional factors place on self-determination, empowerment, and opportunity. Those factors are the criminal justice system, racism, and public opinion.

NOTES

[1] Readers unaccustomed to demographic detail might find it helpful to read the concluding section of this chapter first. The author gratefully acknowledges the generous assistance, in compiling the data for this chapter, of France Bernard, Ellen Bobet, Stewart Clatworthy, Jacques Desrochers, Pierre Gauvin, and especially long-standing family friend Andrew J. Siggner. This chapter has also benefitted greatly from the critical comments of Professor Warren Kalbach, whose assistance is also gratefully acknowledged.

[2] Note that not all Registered Indians identify as Indians, especially non-Native women who acquired Indian status as a result of marrying an Indian man before 1985. Using RCAP (1996a: 15) and DIAND (1997b: 7) figures for 1991, we can say that about 14% of the Registered Indian population does not identify as Indian.

[3] The 1991 census also identified about 112,600 so-called "non-status Indians". These are persons who identified themselves as being of Native Indian *ancestry*, but did not self-identify as Métis and were not registered under the *Indian Act* (RCAP, 1996a: 17).

[4] As RCAP (1996a: 15) notes, some unknown portion of the additional approximately 375,000 persons who have aboriginal *ancestry* but who do not presently *identify* as aboriginals might come to identify with their aboriginal ancestry at some time in the future.

[5] For a non-demographic discussion of Bill C-31 and its effects see RCAP (1996d 33–52).

[6] Of those applicants granted Registered Indian status to the end of August 1996, 75,844 were adults and 35,901 were minors. (Unlike the totals cited elsewhere in this section, these totals include 7,921 persons who have legal status as Indians

under section 6.1.a of the *Indian Act*. DIAND's reporting system excludes them from the Bill C-31 applicants registered. They include Indian women who married a non-Indian — and the offspring of that marriage — and who, prior to Bill C-31 coming into effect, would have lost their status as Registered Indians.) Only 19% of completely-processed, non-duplicate applicants were disallowed. Among the reasons for an applicant not being approved are duplicate applications and applications rendered dormant by applicants not responding to DIAND mail (wrong address, etc.). Data on Bill C-31 (re)instatements are taken from internal DIAND printouts entitled "Reinstatement of Status Information System: Report S4 — Entitlement Status, 96-Sept.- 04" and "Reinstatement of Status Information System: Report S3 — Individual Entitlements, 96-Sept.-04". The author gratefully acknowledges the assistance of DIAND's Indian Registration and Band Lists Directorate, especially Jacqui Powless and Mireille Leroux, who provided this information.

[7] However, Bill C-31, over the longer term, will also diminish the size of the Registered Indian population. Norris (1996: 215–216) explains that, if current trends in fertility and out-marriage persist, close to 43,000 births to status Indians would be transferred to the non-status Indian population over the period 1991–2016. These births occur under the following scenario: a Bill C-31 reinstatee marries a person who is not a Registered Indian; any child of that marriage acquires status as a Registered Indian him/herself; however, if that child marries someone who is not a Registered Indian, then the offspring of that union are not entitled to Registered Indian status and would be categorized as part of the non-status Indian population instead. This is an example of the so-called "blood quantum" approach to designating Registered Indian status.

[8] Even Nault et al.'s (1993) slow growth model (not shown) foresees a population of almost 825,000 by the year 2015, while their rapid growth model (not shown) projects a population of about 934,000 by the end of the year 2015.

[9] In 1994 there were 605 bands, but 619 "registry groups". The figures used here are based on registry groups, but because the numbers are almost identical, the "band" terminology is retained for the sake of simplicity. The discrepancy between "registry groups" and "bands" is entirely due to the Stoneys of Alberta (comprising three registry groups — Chiniki, Goodstoney, and Bearspaw) and the Six Nations of the Grand River (comprising 13 registry groups — Bay of Quinte Mohawks, Lower Cayuga, Oneida, etc.).

[10] For purposes of this discussion only and for the sake of simplicity, the term "members" will be used below in this section to designate Registered Indian members. In actual practice, bands can admit to membership individuals who are not Registered Indians, but such individuals do not enjoy the rights, privileges, and constraints extended to (or imposed upon) Registered Indians by the Government of Canada.

[11] The high figures for Québec reflect the language barriers faced off-reserve by First Nations people in Québec, few of whom speak French.

[12] See Wotherspoon and Satzewich (1993: 64–72) for a discussion of the aboriginal bourgeoisie and petite bourgeoisie.

[13] Annual off-reserve growth rates under this (medium growth) scenario average 4.0% during the 1990s and will not drop below 2% until the year 2010. The on-reserve population in this scenario averages about 2.3% annual growth during the 1990s, will drop below 2% in 1999, and will reach 1.6% by 2015 (compared to 1.7% for the off-reserve population that year).

[14] See Boldt (1993: 122–125) for general background on such land tenure conflict.

[15] DIAND (1993a: 124) defines a "service centre" as a community where the following are available: (a) supplies, material, and equipment; (b) a pool of skilled or semi-skilled labour; (c) at least one financial institution; and (d) provincial and federal services. Because new roads are constantly being built, the classification of some bands changes each year. Data for "remote" and "special access" were unchanged by 1995, but those 1995 data no longer separated the "rural" from the "urban" category (DIAND, 1997b: 19).

[16] Under the *Indian Act* (Sec. 2.1), a reserve is a "tract of land, the legal title to which is vested in her Majesty, that has been set apart by Her Majesty for the use and benefit of a band".

[17] The Total Fertility Rate (TFR) is the sum of single-year age-specific fertility rates during a given year. It indicates the average number of births per woman if the current age-specific fertility rates prevail over her reproductive period.

[18] There is a trend whereby First Nation women over age 30 account for a smaller proportion of births than previously, whereas the contribution of women under age 25 has gradually increased (Nault et al., 1993: 15). The maximum contribution to fertility has consistently come from the 20–24 age group.

[19] The other rates, also for 1990, are: Atlantic, 2.82; Quebec, 2.56; Ontario, 2.33; Manitoba, 3.01; NWT, 2.88; Yukon, 2.37; and total Canada (Registered Indian), 2.72.

[20] Norris (1996: 202) cites 1991 Registered Indian Total Fertility Rates of 3.3 for women on-reserve, but only 2.5 for women in rural areas and 2.2 for women in urban areas.

[21] The author gratefully acknowledges the assistance of Ms. Ellen Bobet, Health Data Analyst, Medical Services Branch, Health Canada in providing data for this section, including special computer tabulations for age-standardized and cause-specific death rates. See the methodological appendix for important information on the limitations of this data.

[22] Data here are from a special tabulation provided courtesy of Medical Services Branch, Health Canada. The rates are calculated on the basis of age-specific and sex-specific mortality rates for the Registered Indian population, as applied to the age and sex structure of the Canadian population in 1991. For the total Canadian population the rate per 1000 population was 6.9 (6.3 for females and 7.4 for males).

[23] See Norris (1996: 203) for comparisons in life expectancy at birth for various years as far back as 1900. For 1995, DIAND (1997b: 24) identifies Registered Indians' life expectancies as being 76.2 years for females and 69.1 years for males.

[24] The gap in life expectancy at birth is projected to decrease to as little as 4.9 years for males (life expectancy at birth of 72.9 for Indian males) and the female gap to decrease to as little as 4.4 years (life expectancy at birth of 80.1 years for Indian females) by the year 2015.

[25] Nault et al. (1993) cite the 1990 Registered Indian infant mortality rate as 12.2 (adjusted for the late-reporting and under-reporting of births and deaths), whereas DIAND (1993a: 29) reports a 1990 rate of 10.2 and a 1991 rate of 11.9 (with no mention of adjustments being made for late-reporting or under-reporting). Since 1987 the Indian data do not include N.W.T. Indians due to the transfer of health services to the Government of the Northwest Territories. See DIAND (1997b: 82–83) for 1994 and earlier data on infant mortality in Yukon and NWT.

[26] The data reported here are subject to important limitations. See methodological appendix.

[27] For a discussion of foetal alcohol syndrome (FAS) and foetal alcohol effects (FAE) as they relate to the aboriginal population, see RCAP (1996c:132–134).

[28] A Winnipeg study cited by Muir (1991) found "a strong relationship between S.I.D.S. and income level, irrespective of ethnicity".

[29] Bobet (1994: 58) reports that for one specific age group, males age 15 and over, the Registered Indian rate of deaths by accident in the mid-1980s was *four* times that for non-Native men (378 vs 95 per 100,000 population). For Indian females in that same age range, deaths by accident occurred more than *three* times as frequently as among non-Native women.

[30] In 1993 Registered Indians died of cancer at a rate of 73.3 per 100,000 population, while the rate for the total Canadian population was 197.5. In both populations, women were much more likely than men to die of this cause (e.g., rates of 81.9 vs 64.9 for Registered Indian women and men, respectively).

[31] However, when we examine a larger data set (not shown) for the individual years from which the averages in the graph were compiled, we find that between 1990 and 1993 mortality rates in eight of seventeen major reporting categories (International Classification of Diseases) were actually increasing. DIAND (1996: 30) suggests that this change might be an artifact produced by improvements in the collection of mortality data.

[32] These are foetal deaths which occur before birth but after twenty-two weeks of gestation or, if before twenty-two weeks of gestation, where the foetus weighs five hundred grams or more.

[33] The Alberta 1991 and 1992 Indian rates were both 14 per 1000 total births, while the rates for all residents of Alberta hovered around 7. (Source: Medical Services Branch, Alberta Region, Health Canada, in-house data.)

[34] A 1988 national survey of 3,543 births in seven regions served by Health Canada's Medical Services Branch found that 54% of the Indian women smoked cigarettes before pregnancy and almost as many smoked cigarettes during (49%) and after (49%) the pregnancy. For non-aboriginal women the comparable rates were 29%, 27%, and 26%.

[35] The author gratefully acknowledges the input of Dr. Richard Musto, community health physician, formerly with the Treaty 7 office of Health Canada's Medical Services Branch. He notes that still birth rates are highly variable, even as between northern and southern Alberta. For instance, the 1990 rate among Treaty 8 First Nations (northern Alberta) was 13.4 per 1000 total births, whereas among Treaty 7 First Nations (southern Alberta) the rate was 8.5 and among Treaty 6 (central Alberta) First Nations the rate was 6.3 (Communication of 94-07-18).

[36] Mass media coverage in the 1990s has shown that Indian suicides often occur in clusters that are like an epidemic within one community over the course of a few months. For example, see the discussion of the 1992–93 epidemic (eight suicides) on the Big Cove reserve in Canadian Press (October 18, 1993), the discussion of the epidemic of seventeen deaths by accident and suicide on the Stoney reserve near Calgary in the first half of 1991, or Brazao's (1994) coverage of the five suicides and 47 attempted suicides among Pikangikum youths during several months of 1993–94. The use of five year averages disguises clustering and "imitation" effects.

[37] Data for the First Nation population do not include the Northwest Territories since 1987 and British Columbia during the period 1985–90 and are not age-standardized (that is, there has been no statistical adjustment to compensate for the larger proportion of young people in the First Nation population). Data from east-

ern Canada cover only the on-reserve population. Data for Manitoba westward cover all Registered Indian people in the province.

[38] Data supplied by Medical Services Branch, Health Canada. For similar data for the mid-1980s, see Bobet (1994: 58–59). Muir (1991: 40) reports that applying Indian age-specific suicide rates to the Canadian population for 1986 yields an age-standardized suicide death rate for Registered Indians of 34.6 per 100,000 population, which is 2.4 times the Canadian rate for 1986.

[39] This Indian male youth suicide rate can be put in perspective by realizing that if the university where the author works had the same suicide rate in its population of about 18,100 undergraduate students, it would have about *twenty* suicides *per year*!

[40] Alberta has particularly high rates of Indian (and non-Indian) suicides, whereas Indian rates in Manitoba and Québec tend to be much closer to the lower rates of the non-Indian population.

[41] Because diabetes is more prevalent in older age groups than among the young, an age-standardized rate is the most appropriate measure of prevalence. Muir (1991: 35) reports that a 1986–87 national survey of diabetes in the aboriginal population served by Health Canada's Medical Services Branch found that the age-adjusted prevalence rate for the Indian *and Inuit* population in most regions was two or three times the Canadian rate of 2.4% reported in the 1985 General Social Survey of the overall Canadian population. There is, however, wide regional variation in the prevalence of known diabetes within the aboriginal population.

[42] In the total Canadian population, 69% of adults reported themselves to be non-smokers, while 25% are daily smokers and 6% smoke less than one cigarette per day (*Statistics Canada Daily*, August 18, 1994). Among the APS respondents, off-reserve residents who smoke daily are somewhat more likely (30% vs 25%) than their on-reserve counterparts to be heavy smokers (more than ten cigarettes per day).

[43] The median age for the First Nation population in 2015 is predicted to rise to 30, while that of the overall Canadian population is projected to rise to 41 over the same period (Nault et al., 1993: 42)

[44] Statistics Canada, CANSIM, Matrix #6900.

[45] The youth dependency ratio for the total Canadian population in the year 2015 is projected to be much lower at 0.25 (16.8%/67.2%).

[46] This part of the chapter draws almost exclusively from Norris (1996) and from Stewart Clatworthy's (1995) comprehensive report to the Royal Commission on Aboriginal Peoples. The kind co-operation of Mr. Tony Reynolds, Executive Director of the Royal Commission, in making the latter report available in advance of publication, is gratefully acknowledged. Notwithstanding Clatworthy's thoroughness, we must bear in mind the limitations of the 1991 Census and Aboriginal Population Survey (APS 1991) on which his report is based. That is, seventy-eight Indian reserves and settlements, comprising about 38,000 persons, refused to participate in the Census. An additional 181 reserves or settlements, comprising approximately an additional 20,000 persons, were not included in the 1991 APS. Also excluded from the mobility data are the unknown number of international emigrants from Canada and the approximately 2,220 individuals of any aboriginal origin (not just Registered Indians) who immigrated to Canada (Clatworthy, 1995: 18, 29; and personal communication from A. Siggner, June 19, 1996).

[47] One must be careful to avoid misrepresenting the mobility of the earlier period. For instance, the migration from reserves to large cities constituted only 3% of all

Registered Indian *mobility* between 1966 and 1971, as captured by the 1971 census (Siggner, 1980: 45). Of the Registered Indians who changed residence during that period, 26% went to large cities (population of 100,000 or more), including 10% who came from other large cities, 6% who came from smaller urban areas, 3% who came from reserves, and 7% who came from rural, non-reserve areas.

[48] This figure of 20,630, like all other absolute numbers drawn from the Census or the 1991 Aboriginal Peoples Survey, understates the actual numbers due to the non-participation of some First Nation communities in these two data collection undertakings. Note, however, that both the Census and the Aboriginal Peoples Survey probably did capture most of the out-migrants from non-participating reserves.

[49] The proportion of Bill C-31 re-instatees in the net gain from aboriginal migration experienced by reserves varied widely from region to region, due mainly to the differential strictness of the membership codes of First Nations in different provinces.

[50] Comparisons of the mobility and migration rates for women aged 15 to 24 illustrate well the rate differentials as between on- and off-reserve Registered Indians and the total Canadian population. The data below are from Norris (1996: 209–210). Cell entries are the 5-year (1986–91) rates per 1,000 women aged 15 to 24.

	Population		
	On-Reserve	Off-Reserve	All Canadians
Mobility (incl. within same community)	475	750	540
Migration (to different community)	150	380	240

[51] If external migrants from outside Canada are included, the migration rate for all Canadians would be 47%, according to Norris (1996: 208).

[52] The figures for migrants as a percentage of the population (aged 5 years and over) are: for Registered Indians, 20%; for non-status Indians, 28%, for Metis, 24%; and for Inuit, 13%.

[53] The "institutional completeness" of a community or an ethnic group refers to the extent to which members of the community or ethnic group can meet their daily needs for goods and services within the confines of the community or ethnic group.

[54] Using 1991 census data, Norris (1996: 210) points out that among youths aged 15–24, the five year rates of migration away from reserves were 50 per 1000 for males but 86 per 1000 for females.

[55] Over half (51%) of Registered Indian migrants, but only about one third (35%) of Registered Indian non-migrants, had a secondary school graduation certificate or some post-secondary education.

[56] Data are from Clatworthy (1996: 117 and 118) and exclude full-time students.

[57] Data are from Clatworthy (1996: 123) and exclude persons attending school full-time in 1990.

[58] Among those who worked forty or more weeks, the average employment incomes were about $25,200 for migrants and $22,350 for non-migrants, which is a 13% difference. Data are from Clatworthy (1996: 128) and are for persons aged 15 and over who were not attending school full-time in 1990.

[59] For instance, in fiscal year 1992–93, DIAND provided capital subsidies for the construction of slightly under 4300 new houses and for the renovation of about 2600 others (DIAND, 1993a: 69). However, by fiscal year 1995–96 those numbers were only about 2400 and 3300, respectively (DIAND, 1997b: 58). In 1996 DIAND announced a new housing policy under which $140 million over five years would

be reallocated from other parts of the DIAND budget to bring DIAND's annual on-reserve housing budget to $223 milliion. (See Platiel, 1996 and the DIAND News Releases page on the World Wide Web.) The Canada Mortgage and Housing Corporation also contributes substantially to First Nation housing.

[60] See Ross (1992: 50–58) for a discussion of fate in First Nations' world views.

[61] The Royal Commission on Aboriginal Peoples reports the distribution of post-secondary students by major field of study (RCAP, 1996c: 549). The most heavily subscribed fields of study are shown below for Registered Indians. Figures in parentheses are the percent of the entire post-secondary Registered Indian student population of each respective sex, with males shown first and then females: Engineering, applied science technology, and trades (54%; 6%); Commerce, management and administration (11%; 30%); Health Science and Technology (3%; 19%); Education, recreaton, and counselling (7%; 17%); Social Sciences (11%; 14%); all other fields (14%; 14%).

[62] Drawing from the same data source (Statcan, 1995a: 18), RCAP (1996d: 14) identifies the overall participation rates for Registered Indians as 68% for males and 49% for females. For off-reserve Registered Indian males and females, the participation rates are 76% and 61%, respectively.

[63] For the out-of-school First Nation population aged 15 and over, RCAP (1996d: 14) reports a 1991 unemployment rate of 32% for males and 23% for females. Elsewhere, RCAP (1996d: 211) reports a 1991 "North American Indian" unemployment rate of 31% on-reserve and 23% off-reserve. "North American Indians" includes persons who identify as Indians but are not Registered Indians.

[64] The data are from Statistics Canada (1993c), Cat. # 89-533, Tables 4.3, 4.5, and 4.7. Forty-six percent of on-reserve adult respondents who eat meat, fish, or poultry reported that they obtained "some" of their meat, fish, or poultry from hunting and fishing. Only 14% said that none was obtained from that source. Not surprisingly, off-reserve Registered Indian respondents reported much lower levels of reliance on hunting and fishing.

[65] See RCAP (1996d: 211) for data on the income of on-reserve and off-reserve persons who *identify* as North American Indians.

REFERENCES

Bobet, Ellen
1994 "Indian Mortality", pp. 57–60 in *Canadian Social Trends*. Toronto: Thompson Educational Publishing.

Boldt, Menno
1993 *Surviving as Indians*. Toronto: University of Toronto Press.

Brazao, Dale
1994 "Months Later, Teen Suicides Still Plague Reserve: 47 Attempts Made Since Aid Promised", *Toronto Star*, August 9: A1.

Breton, Raymond
1983 "Multiculturalism and Canadian Nation-Building", pp. 27–66 in Alan Cairns and Cynthia Williams (eds.), *The Politics of Gender, Ethnicity and Language in Canada*. Research Report #34 of The Royal Commission on The Economic Union and Development Prospects for Canada. Toronto: University of Toronto Press.

Canadian Press
1993   "Despite the Odds ... Micmac Teen Survives Life on the Reserve", *Calgary Herald*, October 18: C5.

Clatworthy, Stewart
1995   *The Migration and Mobility Patterns of Canada's Aboriginal Population.* (Report prepared for the Royal Commission on Aboriginal People.) Winnipeg: Four Directions Consulting Group.

DIAND
1990   *Impacts of the 1985 Amendments to the Indian Act (Bill C-31) — Summary Report.* Cat. #R32-104/5-1990. Ottawa: Minister of Supply & Services.

———
1991a   *Annual Report.* Ottawa: Minister of Supply and Services.

———
1993a   *Basic Departmental Data, 1993.* Ottawa: Departmental Statistics, Management Information and Analysis, Corporate Services.

———
1993b   *Schedule of Indian Bands, Reserves and Settlements Including Membership and Population, Location, and Area in Hectares, December 1992.* Ottawa: Minister of Government Services Canada.

———
1996   *Basic Departmental Data, 1995.* Ottawa: Departmental Statistics Section, Information Quality and Research Directorate, Information Management Branch.

———
1997a   *Indian Register Population by Sex and Residence, 1996.* Ottawa: Minister of Public Works and Government Services Canada.

———
1997b   *Basic Departmental Data, 1996.* Ottawa: Departmental Statistics Section, Information Quality and Research Directorate, Information Management Branch.

Eliany, Marc et al.
1992   *Alcohol and Other Drug Use By Canadians: A National Alcohol and Other Drugs Survey (1989) Technical Report.* Health and Welfare Canada, Cat. #H39-251/1992E, Ottawa: Minister of Supply and Services Canada.

Gerber, Linda
1977   "Community Characteristics and Out-Migration from Indian Communities: Regional Trends". Paper presented at Department of Indian Affairs and Northern Development, Ottawa, November 9.

Jamieson, Kathleen
1986   "Sex Discrimination and the *Indian Act*", pp. 112–136 in J. Rick Ponting (ed.), *Arduous Journey: Canadian Indians and Decolonization.* Toronto: McClelland & Stewart.

Jiobu, R.M.
1990   *Ethnicity and Inequality.* Buffalo, N.Y.: SUNY Press.

Kroeber, Alfred L.
1939   *Cultural and Natural Areas of Native North America.* Berkeley: University of California Publications in American Archaeology and Ethnology, #38, University of California Press.

Mate, Susan
1991   "Suicide: Poverty, Despair Destroying Stoney's Young", *Calgary Herald*, June 13: A1.

McDougall, Tom
1994   "Type 2 Diabetes 'Epidemic' in Fact Better Detection", *Calgary Herald*, July 20: B4

Muir, Bernice L.
1991   *Health Status of Canadian Indians and Inuit, 1990*. Ottawa: Health and Welfare Canada.

Nault, Francois, Jiajian Chen, M.V. George, and Mary Jane Norris
1993   *Population Projections of Registered Indians, 1991–2015*. Ottawa: Indian and Northern Affairs Canada.

Norris, Mary Jane
1990   "The Demography of Aboriginal People in Canada", pp. 33–59 in Shiva S. Halli, Frank Trovato, and Leo Dreidger (eds.) *Ethnic Demography: Canadian, Immigrant, Racial and Cultural Variations*. Ottawa: Carleton University Press.

1996   "Contemporary Demography of Aboriginal Peoples in Canada", pp. 179–237 in David A. Long and Olive P. Dickason (eds.), *Visions of the Heart: Canadian Aboriginal Issues*. Toronto: Harcourt Brace Canada.

Platiel, Rudy
1996   "Native Reserves Get $140-million For Housing", *Globe and Mail*, July 26: A3.

Ponting, J. Rick
1991   "An Indian Policy for Canada in the Twenty-first Century", pp. 431–446 in Corneleus H.W. Remie and J.-M. Lacroix (eds.), *Canada on the Threshold of the 21st Century: European Reflections Upon the Future of Canada*. Amsterdam and Philadelphia: John Benjamins Publishing.

RCAP (Royal Commission on Aboriginal Peoples)
1995   *Choosing Life: Special Report on Suicide Among Aboriginal People*. Ottawa: Minister of Supply and Services Canada.

1996a   *Report of the Royal Commission on Aboriginal Peoples; Vol. 1: Looking Forward, Looking Back*. Ottawa: Minister of Supply and Services Canada.

1996b   *Report of the Royal Commission on Aboriginal Peoples; Vol. 2: Restructuring the Relationship*. Ottawa: Minister of Supply and Services Canada.

1996c   *Report of the Royal Commission on Aboriginal Peoples; Vol. 3: Gathering Strength*. Ottawa: Minister of Supply and Services Canada.

1996d   *Report of the Royal Commission on Aboriginal Peoples; Vol. 4: Perspectives and Realities*. Ottawa: Minister of Supply and Services Canada.

Research Directorate
1994   *Customized Data from the 1991 Aboriginal Peoples Survey*. Ottawa: Royal Commission on Aboriginal Peoples.

Ross, Rupert
1992   *Dancing With a Ghost: Exploring Indian Reality*. Markham, Ont.: Octopus Publishing.

Siggner, Andrew J.
1980   "A Socio-demographic Profile of Indians in Canada", pp. 31–65 in J. Rick Ponting and Roger Gibbins, *Out of Irrelevance: A Socio-political Introduction to Indian affairs in Canada*. Scarborough, Ont.: Butterworth.

1986   "The Socio-Demographic Conditions of Registered Indians", pp. 57–83 in J. Rick Ponting (ed.), *Arduous Journey: Canadian Indians and Decolonization.* Toronto: McClelland & Stewart / Oxford.

Statistics Canada

1993a   *Schooling, Work and Related Activities, Income, Expenses, and Mobility — 1991 Aboriginal Peoples Survey.* Cat. # 89-534. Ottawa: Minister of Industry, Science and Technology.

1993b   *Occupied Private Dwellings: The Nation.* Cat. #93-314. Ottawa: Minister of Industry, Science, and Technology.

1993c   *Language, Tradition, Health, Lifestyle, and Social Issues: 1991 Aboriginal Peoples Survey.* Cat. # 89-533. Ottawa: Minister of Industry, Science, and Technology.

1993d   *General Social Survey 1991.* Cat. #11-612E, No. 8. Ottawa: Minister of Industry, Science, and Technology.

1994a   *Quarterly Demographic Statistics, October-December 1993*, Vol. 7, No. 4 (Cat. #91-002).

1994b   *1-Disability 2-Housing — 1991 Aboriginal Peoples Survey.* Cat. #89-535. Ottawa: Minister of Industry, Science and Technology.

1995   *Births: 1992.* Cat. #84-210. Ottawa: Ministry of Industry, Science, and Technology.

1995a   *Profile of Canada's Aboriginal Population.* Cat. #94-325. Ottawa: Ministry of Industry, Science, and Technology.

Wadhera, Surinder and Jill Strachan

1993   *Selected Infant Mortality and Related Statistics, Canada, 1921–1990.* Ottawa: Statistics Canada, Minister of Industry, Science and Technology.

Warden, Kathryn

1995   "Native Community Assaulted by Diabetes", *Saskatoon Star Phoenix*, June 3.

Wotherspoon, Terry and Vic Satzewich

1993   *First Nations: Race, Class, and Gender Relations.* Scarborough, Ont.: Nelson Canada.

FURTHER READING

Waldrum, James B. et al.

1995   *Aboriginal Health in Canada: Historical, Cultural, and Epidemiological Perspectives.* Toronto: University of Toronto Press.

METHODOLOGICAL APPENDIX

Much of the data in this chapter is drawn from the 1991 Census of Canada and a 1991 follow-up survey known as the Aboriginal Peoples Survey (APS). The APS consisted of a sample of 20% of those persons who met the following conditions: (i) on the Census question on *ancestry*, indicated at least one aboriginal origin and/or, answered "yes" when asked on the census if they are a Registered Indian under the *Indian Act* of Canada; AND (ii) on the APS screening question on *identity*, indicated that they identify with at least one aboriginal group or report being registered under the *Indian Act* of Canada. Ninety-nine percent of individuals thus recorded as aboriginal identified with only one aboriginal group (North American Indian, Métis, or Inuit). Our focus is on those who are Registered Indians.

These data are subject to particular limitations as a result of the refusal of some First Nations to participate in the 1991 Census. In the census there were 78 incompletely enumerated Indian reserves and settlements containing approximately 38,000 individuals. The APS lacks those participants *plus* another 181 reserves and settlements representing approximately 20,000 additional individuals. This represents an estimated total population of 58,000 persons or approximately 26% of the total on-reserve North American Indian population of Canada (Research Directorate, 1994: 38). Nevertheless, these are the best data available. For many variables, the under-enumeration of the First Nations will not introduce any systematic bias if percentages, rather than raw numbers, are considered. Statistics Canada does not have the data to publish a profile of non-participating First Nations, so the preceding statement is, in part, a matter of speculation.

Population counts shown in APS publications are based on persons' usual place of residence, regardless of where they happened to be on census day.

Other data in this chapter are based on the Indian Register. Indian Register data are characterized by a small amount of late reporting and by underreporting of both births and deaths, but for population counts they offer much more complete coverage than data from the census or the APS. Where possible and practical, demographers at DIAND adjust Register data for late reporting and under-reporting. Nault et al. (1993: 12) report that for 1990 (the then most recent year) the adjusted figures *increase* the Registered Indian population by 4.3% from 490,178 to 511,382. Note that this refutes political accusations made by the Reform Party of Canada in 1994 to the effect that inaccuracies in the Indian Register *inflate* counts of the Registered Indian population. The criticism appears unwarranted and seems to be based on the lower counts obtained in the 1991 Census which, as noted, had incomplete coverage due to a variety of reasons, particularly the refusal of many First Nations to participate.

Data from Health Canada, used in the section entitled "Mortality and Morbidity", are subject to other limitations, as Muir (1991:7) reports. That is, for the Atlantic region, data do not include the off-reserve population. In Quebec, only about half of the Registered Indian population is covered, as data exclude individuals covered by the James Bay and Northern Quebec Agreement, individuals living off-reserve, and individuals living in communities where Health Canada's Medical Services Branch has no field personnel. Ontario data exclude the off-reserve population and the population of twelve small communities. In all remaining regions the data come from provincial/territorial data systems which collect data for the entire registered Indian population in the region rather than just the population served by the Medical Services Branch. Since 1985, difficulties have existed in obtaining data from provincial government sources in British Columbia, such that statistics for British Columbia Indians are incomplete. Overall, reports Muir, Medical Services Branch data cover approximately 64% of the Registered Indian population.

PART 2

Empowerment and Disempowerment in Relations with the Larger Society

CHAPTER 5

AN OVERVIEW OF FIRST NATIONS' EMPOWERMENT AND DISEMPOWERMENT
EDITOR'S INTRODUCTION TO PART 2

J. Rick Ponting

The subtitle to this volume refers to empowerment. Lack of power has been a hallmark of First Nations' existence for well over a century now. Dispossessed of their lands, pushed to the geographic, economic, and political margins of Canadian society, denied the vote (prior to 1960 in federal elections), and made the object of a campaign of cultural genocide, First Nation people must have thought that they had reached their nadir. Then, in the 1960s, the Canadian welfare state reached out its tentacles and swept them into its grasp, sometimes figuratively, but sometimes literally as in the apprehension of First Nation children by social workers during the infamous "scoop of the sixties".[1]

Discussing empowerment necessarily involves discussing disempowerment, for an actor's existing situation in power relations provides an obvious reference point for describing future empowerment. In the case of First Nations, there have been multiple sources of disempowerment. The literature suggests that the most important are colonialism, the residential schools, racism and other forms of extremism, capitalism, systemic discrimination, and social control.

COLONIALISM

European intentions in Canada were originally mercantilist, but became colonial with the arrival of the settlers and the decision of some of the traders to stay on in this "newly discovered" land. Once Canada usurped First Nations' sovereignty and imposed the *Indian Act*, we moved clearly into what Blauner (1969) called **internal colonialism**. An ethnocentric, colonial philosophy governed the administration of First Nations' affairs from at least the middle of the nineteenth century, as was discussed in Chapter Two of this volume.

From the features of colonialism identified in Chapter One flow certain others. For instance, the fact that the dominant group administers the colonized people implies the creation of a government bureaucracy. The very act of organizing creates power, and large, complex bureaucracies, such as the federal Department of Indian Affairs and Northern Development (DIAND) create large amounts of power. Ponting (1986) has identified various ways in which that bureaucratic power could be used at the micro level in a manner indicative of internal colonialism. These are shown in Box 1. For instance, in interviewing a small sample of First Nation chiefs and administrators, he found that even though DIAND is essentially a "money-moving" department,[2] it woefully underfunds economic development in absolute dollars and in comparison to other spending categories like social assistance. In the official spending estimates which the government brought to Parliament for fiscal year 1995–96, DIAND allocated to economic development only 1.4% ($53 million) of its $3.854 billion budget for Indian and Inuit Affairs (RCAP, 1996e: 35). The Solicitor General's Department allocated almost as much ($50 million) to aboriginal policing. DIAND allocated $1.108 billion for social assistance and social services.

Overall, though, Ponting's findings were mixed, such that he concluded that there is a need for more sophisticated explanatory models to complement the colonialism model. Significantly, he suggested that those explanations are to be found at the macrolevel in terms of such phenomena as the latent function of *containment* which DIAND performs vis-à-vis First Nations and contradictions in the roles that the state plays in society (facilitating the accumulation of wealth by the capitalist class and legitimating the existing class system to those who are not its primary beneficiaries, while at the same time protecting the state's own interests). At the microlevel, Ponting pointed to bureaucrats' coping strategies in a siege environment and to staff composition (especially the presence of an "old guard"). It is noteworthy that these explanations revolve around factors that can have just as disempowering an effect as does internal colonialism itself.

The *Indian Act* is a colonial instrument par excellence. Gibbins' discussion of it in Chapter Two points out that it touches every aspect of the life of a First Nation person. Conceived in an ethos of social control, rather than in a spirit of generating opportunity, it was a consolidation of various statutes from the pre-1876 colonial era. It gives sweeping powers to administrators and thereby creates power-dependency relations. Although some recent amendments, like the so-called "Kamloops amendments" of the late 1980s, have been motivated by a desire to create economic opportunity, the present day *Act* retains many features of social control, such as the Minister's power of disallowance over band by-laws.[3]

Appendix C provides examples of some of the provisions of the *Act*. Not shown there is the **fiduciary obligation**. In the so-called Musqueam case (Guerin vs. The Queen) of 1985, the Supreme Court of Canada ruled that a fiduciary obligation, on the part of the federal government, characterizes the government's relationship with First Nations under the *Indian Act*. As a relationship somewhat akin to that between a trustee and his/her "ward", the fiduciary relationship is inherently paternalistic, inherently colonial, and inherently unbalanced in power. The desire of some First Nation persons to retain the Crown's fiduciary obligations toward First Nations is an irony that speaks volumes about the insecurity that First Nation people feel in the larger Canadian society. This is a point to which Crowfoot alludes in this volume in his discussion of the reluctance of some First Nation people to take responsibility for their own destiny.

The *Indian Act* and the way in which it has been implemented have contributed greatly to a dependency mindset among some indeterminable number of First Nation people. Among some others, the predominant psychological orientation is despair; among some of the remainder, alienation. These are not ori-

---

BOX 1 Empirical, Microlevel Indicators of Internal Colonialism

---

1. Preparation of bands for administering their own affairs
   e.g., inadequate funds for training in modern skills of administration
2. Economic underdevelopment
   e.g., making available only woefully inadequate economic development funds; refusing to relinquish control over economic development
3. Intemperate orientation toward risk
   e.g., excessive risk aversion to the point of over-protectiveness; or irresponsible exposure of bands to excessive risk
4. Flow of information
   e.g., manipulation of information as a form of social control; excessive secrecy; overly rigid or overly frequent accountability required; inadequate consultation
5. Decision-making and control over allocation of scarce resources
   e.g., excluding First Nations from decision-making; depriving bands of control over allocation of resources
6. Obstructionism
   e.g., insistence on "bureaucratic red tape", rather than taking a facilitative role
7. Socio-fiscal control
   e.g., manipulation of discretionary funds; withholding of funds
8. Divide and rule tactics

Source: (Ponting: 1986: 86)

---

entations which are conducive to activist, effective resistance designed to rectify the power imbalance. Instead, they are disempowering. By contributing to withdrawal and escapism, they exacerbate the power imbalance.

Another feature of the colonial orientation adopted by the federal government toward the First Nations is the geographic fragmentation and dispersal of the First Nation population. Such a distribution of any population militates against it ever acquiring the requisite number of members in any given constituency (of the larger society's political system) to be able to effectively engage in bloc voting for electoral gain. However well intentioned, the placement of First Nation children in non-Native adoptive homes also had the effect of dispersing the population and reducing the likelihood that the adoptees would be politically mobilized by First Nation leaders. A common pattern among the adoptees was acute adolescent identity crisis manifested in rebellious and dysfunctional behaviour.

The colonizers' assault on First Nation lands, languages, cultures, and social structures was also highly disempowering. In confiscating First Nation lands, the colonizers struck at the very soul of First Nations' existence. That is, historically, for an aboriginal person, one's identity and understanding of one's place in the cosmos was intimately tied to his/her relation to the land and the spirits which inhabit it. The government's assimilative policies, particularly as implemented in the residential schools, also scarred and distorted First Nation people's identities. Other colonial policies interfered with First Nations' basic adaptations to the physical and social environment in ways that were inimical to a healthy, functioning, social and economic order. The overall destructive impact was like that of a lethal computer virus with which some malicious hacker infects an elegantly designed computer. It was as if the system crashed and many of the basic operating commands of the system were corrupted, such that thereafter the computer could operate only at partial capacity in a highly degraded mode. Such are the grotesque distortions which the colonizers inflicted upon First Nation institutions, including the family, the polity, the economy, religion and dispute resolution. Taken together, their impact was almost crippling.

THE RESIDENTIAL SCHOOLS

The Indian residential schools were operated by the Christian churches — especially Roman Catholic and Anglican, but also some other denominations such as United, Methodist, and Presbyterian — from the mid-nineteenth century until as recently as the 1970s, by which time almost all had been closed. By 1880 eleven were in operation and by 1909 their number had increased to seventy-seven. However, only a fraction of Indian school-aged children attended. For instance, only about 15% attended during the early twentieth century and only an estimated half attended during the 1940s (Assembly of First Nations, 1994: 1, citing Barman, Hébert, and McCaskill, 1986: 7). Miller's (1996) very useful maps show them to have been scattered throughout the provinces and territories, except that there was only one in the four Atlantic provinces.

Although not all First Nation children attended the residential schools, it is said that no First Nation person has escaped the direct and indirect effects of the residential schools. To First Nations, the residential school phenomenon was a **primordial event** — an occurrence of such fundamental importance as to indelibly stamp its imprint on the unfolding of the peoples' history thereafter. Said the Royal Commission on Aboriginal Peoples (1996a: 337):

> [O]f course, the memory [of the residential school experience] did not and has not faded. It has persisted, festered and become a sorrowful monument, still casting a deep shadow over the lives of many Aboriginal people and communities and over the possibility of a new relationship between Aboriginal and non-Aboriginal Canadians.

In some respects, among French Canadians the analogy would be the conquest of the French by the British on the Plains of Abraham; among Jews, the Holocaust. The residential school was like a sociological earthquake whose aftershocks still rumble today. Yet, the analogies are only approximate, for as traumatic as the residential school experience was for many of the students who came through it, there are others who speak positively of their experience in those schools. Furthermore, as debilitating as the effects of the residential schools have been on First Nation cultures and families, we must also credit them with a pivotal act of empowerment. That is, it was through the residential schools that numerous First Nation individuals learned the English language. It subsequently served as a lingua franca that permitted co-operative political organization among First Nation peoples who had previously been fragmented by fifty different languages.

Our focus in this section will be on the disempowering impact of the residential schools. In fairness, though, it must be emphasized that not all residential schools abused the children and even those that did sometimes did so only during the tenure of a certain administrator or staff member(s). It would be very inaccurate to tar all and sundry with the same brush.

The Indian residential school in Canada was patterned after the industrial schools in Britain. A significant difference, though, is that cultural genocide was not the objective of the British schools.

Goffman's model of the total institution outlined in Chapter One is an ideal type. That is, no single real-life example will exhibit all of the characteristics specified in the model. Nevertheless, the model has a remarkable ability to capture the worst experiences of First Nation students at the residential schools, as described in the growing literature on residential schools (e.g., King, 1967; Haig-Brown, 1988; Knockwood, 1992; Assembly of First Nations, 1994; Miller, 1996). Below we see how strikingly applicable Goffman's model is for the residential schools.

The *mortification of self* occurred not only upon admission, but intermittently thereafter. Calliou's chapter in this volume cites one example. The literature is replete with other accounts of what anthropologists would call "degradation ceremonies". Those accounts invoke our horror or disgust: children forced to eat their own vomit and a spectacle being made of a girl upon her first menstruation,[4] humiliation and horrible beatings for wetting the bed (Knockwood, 1992: 30), and head-shaving as a punishment for boys (Knockwood, 1992: 80). Sometimes the humiliation was inadvertent. For instance, Haig-Brown (1988: 54) writes of an incident at the Kamloops school where a nun asked a little girl to help a bigger girl who was new to the school: "Although intended to be helpful, the sister's action violated a social rule. To be helped by someone obviously smaller and younger in front of other people was public humiliation. To this day, losing face publicly is seen by many Shuswap people as a terrible insult; to that child on that day so long ago, the action was devastating".

Unfortunately, most of Goffman's other generic ways in which mortification of self is inflicted are found in former students' accounts of life in the residential schools. For instance, Knockwood (1992: 28) writes about her arrival at the Shubenacadie Residential School:

> ... we were put in the tub. When we got out we were given new clothes with wide black and white vertical stripes. Much later I discovered that this was almost identical to the prison garb of the time. We were also given numbers. I was 58 and Rosie was 57. ... Next came the hair cut. Rosie lost her ringlets and we both had hair cut short over our ears and almost straight across the top with bangs.

Knockwood (1992: 34) also quotes Shubenacadie R. S. student Peter Julian on the loss of civil rights:

> ... all our mail was censored. If there was any mention about the school, you were taken in front of Father Mackey and given a beating. And also [you] were forced to tear up the letter and write another one. ... All the incoming mail was either read by Father or the nuns.

Anxiety over physical safety is the second feature of the inmates' experience which Goffman identified. Many accounts (e.g., A.F.N., 1994: 49–53; Miller, 1996: 317–342) describe the intense fear which students felt due to bullying by the older students, sadistic corporal punishment,[5] and rape, molestation and other forms of sexual abuse by staff and older students. Witnesses have also come forward with allegations that some murders did occur, particularly as students succumbed to strappings.[6] One allegation (Canadian Press, 1995) is that a reported suicide of a student two weeks before his graduation in the 1960s was actually a murder motivated by a desire to silence the student who told staff that he planned to disclose abuse at the school once he graduated.

That the students were *manipulated by a system of privileges, rewards, and punishments* was one of the hallmarks of the residential school experience. The cruel arbitrariness, capriciousness, and/or viciousness of the rewards and punishments stands out. Knockwood (1992: 82–85) reports:

> Such rewards as were meted out depended on the nuns' whims. Even if you won something by chance it could be snatched away from you. ...
>
> I lived in perpetual fear of saying and doing anything, even if it was good, for if my work was too good, I knew that it would bring the response, "Who do you think you are? You think you're such a big shot!" And I was always afraid to do my best.
>
> There always seemed to be something arbitrary about the way any treats were handed out.

Knockwood (1992: 90) also reports student Rita Howe's account of a priest repeatedly punching a girl in the face in 1949 as punishment for saying the word "sow" when she accidentally dropped a wash rag from atop a ladder while washing walls:

> Father Mackey came into the classroom looking for Barbara and when she went to the front of the class, he asked her if she had said the word "sow", and she answered, "Yes". She explained that it was an accident and that she was sorry and promised not to say it again. Then he hauled off and smashed her in the face, not with an open hand, but with a fist. She fell down and he told her to get up. She got up again and he smashed her again with both fists this time. She went down again and he ordered her up again. He even pushed some of the desks back to get at her. I think she tried to crawl away, but her nose and mouth were bleeding and he smashed her again and she went down again but didn't get up. ... And it frightened every kid in the school... The classroom was grade five and every kid was screaming and crying while the Sister just stood there with her arms folded. ...

Father Mackey was a boxer. Small wonder that the students feared for their physical safety and experienced *acute stress*.

At the residential schools, Goffman's notion of *forced participation in activities which are incompatible with the inmate's self-conception* was manifested in the requirements that the students confess their "sins" (whereas most had no conception of sin, per se), deny their own spiritual beliefs, and denounce as "pagan" the parents and grandparents whom they loved.

Loss of privacy in the residential schools took various forms, including the staff reading and censoring students' mail, communal showers (sometimes in the presence of a staff member of the opposite sex), monitoring of visits from loved ones, and even the regular inspection of students' underwear and sheets for personal hygiene.

Regimentation was another prominent feature of the residential school experience reported in inmates' accounts. Typical of the form which this regimentation and routine would take was wake-up at the same time each day, enforced silence, attendance at religious services, enforced segregation of the sexes, classroom desks aligned in neat rows, afternoon chores, mealtimes and scant variation in diet, evening prayers, and "lights out". Concerning meals, Haig-Brown (1988: 61) writes:

The dominant impression of mealtime is a sense of regimentation. Individuality here and at other times was not a concern. The numbers of children who had to be fed were seen as objects to be processed as cheaply and efficiently as possible, then passed along to the next station.

Let us turn to the impact of the residential schools. It is patently obvious from the foregoing that one fundamental feature of total institutions was the large *power differential* between staff and inmates. The experience that flowed from that power differential and from the assimilationist goal of the schools was such as to leave the children in a situation of dependency with feelings of fear and vulnerability, powerlessness, marginality, disconnectedness, and inferiority or low self-esteem. These feelings, to the extent that they endure, render very difficult the task of those who subsequently undertake community development or political organizing work. This is one sense, then, in which the legacy of the residential schools was disempowering. Unfortunately, it was not the only sense in which that was the case.

Various psychological reactions to the distress, and in some cases, trauma, of the residential school experience were also inimical to the healthy functioning of families or other community institutions and as such could be said to be disempowering. Among these reactions were rage, acute distrust, alienation, moral confusion, guilt, escapism, and fear of intimacy due to fear of rejection or abandonment. Some of these reactions were transmitted to successive generations of family. Cognitive processes were also disrupted in that children were left with a victim mentality, intellectual confusion, a confused identity, little experience at problem-solving, suppressed creativity, and undeveloped critical thinking skills. In addition, in the absence of parental role models, many of the students who came through the residential school exhibited few parenting skills later in life. As a result of this, too, dysfunctionality was sometimes passed on to the next generation.

Faced with authoritarian role models, some of the students later in life experienced difficulty knowing how to exercise power. Crowfoot's chapter in Part 3 discusses abuse of power by First Nation leaders of the past and relates it back to the experience of colonialism.

Finally, the impact of the residential schools on the spiritual plane must also be recognized. The schools, with their emphasis on Christian doctrine and attack on aboriginal spirituality, left the children feeling guilt, shame, and confusion over their aboriginal spirituality. The children also were confused by the hypocrisy of some of the religious staff of the schools. In addition, some students left the school feeling quite unconnected not only to the world of the spirits, but also to the larger cosmos. As one former student explained, the residential school experience made the students feel like their own spirit was lost and wandering. For many individuals and their descendants, that lack of stable spiritual anchorage militates against effective coping and seizing of opportunity when opportunity knocks.

Although in important ways the residential school experience worked at cross-purposes with the empowerment of First Nation people, it would be a mistake to regard the students as totally powerless. Parkin (1979) and others emphasize the *two-way flow of power* in relations of subordination-dominance. Indeed, most of the literature on residential schools (e.g., Haig-Brown, 1988; Miller, 1996: 343–374) emphasizes the *resistance* put up by the students, especially in the form of escape attempts, but also in the form of the *secondary adjust-ments* of which Goffman wrote. Miller (1996: 345) writes:

> [Various] factors sometimes created circumstances in which protests from parents could have limited effect. ... What emerges from a survey of the inter-action of both schoolchildren and their adult communities is a picture not simply of authority and submission, but of a subtle and shifting interplay of forces. Influence and power could, in some instances, flow in favour of the Aboriginal constituency, in spite of the apparent dominance of government and church. Although too much should not be made of this phenomenon, ... it is important to understand that protest and resistance could and did have some effect.[7]

The rekindling of that sense of resistance to colonial forces is one of the tasks faced by contemporary First Nation leaders whose communities have been scarred by the residential school and its trans-generational aftermath.

RACISM AND EXTREMISM

Because Chapter Six addresses racism in some detail, no attempt will be made to do so here. Ponting's research (1987c: 20) found that less than 5% of non-Native adult Canadians expressed consistently anti-aboriginal extremist views to his interviewers. Nevertheless, encounters with racists in the normal routine of daily life can be hurtful, vexing, and even frightening, and are not to be dis-missed. It is important to bear in mind, though, that insofar as *public policy* is concerned, racist or other extremist attitudes are consequential only when acted upon in some manner. For instance, if they are registered with a pollster, a politi-cian, or appear in a public medium such as a call-in show, a website home page, or a letters-to-the editor page of a newspaper, they can begin to affect the polit-ical will of politicians concerning the adoption of public policies that bear on opportunities for First Nations.[8] Only a tiny fraction of the small minority of Canadians holding extreme anti-aboriginal *attitudes* has been mobilized into backlash *behaviours* such as joining in the anti-Mohawk violence surrounding the Oka-Kahnawake events or joining social movement organizations like B.C. F.I.R.E. (British Columbia Foundation for Individual Rights and Equality) and On F.I.R.E. (Ontario F.I.R.E.). Other organized backlash behaviours have occurred, such as by property owners near Oka, loggers in British Columbia and Temagami, realtors in B.C., and salmon fishers like the B.C. Fisheries Survival Coalition in B.C.; they appear to be motivated primarily by economic self-inter-est rather than by prejudice or racism.

Organized actors with vested economic or political interests pose a greater danger to the interests and aspirations of First Nation peoples than do individ-ual racists in the mass public. Examples include opinion leaders and other "right-wing" ideologues with regular access to the mass media such as is enjoyed by the leader of the Reform Party of Canada, the director of the Fraser Institute, and the editor and columnists of such magazines as *Alberta Report* and *B.C. Report*.

Let us consider the Reform Party here. It advocates policy which, in impor-tant ways, is diametrically opposed to First Nations' interests, although para-doxically, in other ways, such as its accountability provisions, it is sensitive to the interests of the grassroots members of First Nation communities. Box 2 critically examines excerpts from the 1995 report of the Reform Party's Aboriginal Affairs Task Force. Together, the points there constitute a programme which is very similar to the assimilationist termination policy which F.I.R.E. advocates. With minor changes, the points in Box 2 were adopted as policy by the Reform Party at its 1996 Assembly (Reform Party, 1996: 24–25).

The party task force report also includes the following statement which appears to be tantamount to recommending a termination policy involving the abolition of aboriginal rights: "However, it is clear from the courts that Aboriginal Canadians do possess certain rights — not including sovereignty — that cannot and should not be abolished without compensation". The Party's individualistic bias against collective rights, its longstanding concern with the financial health of government treasuries, and its distrust of "special-interest groups" are also reflected in the following comment by the task force:

> In short, many Aboriginal people would like to decide which organizations they will support, and to what length this support should go. This can only be done if the grassroots are financially empowered. Empowerment could be achieved by having moneys paid directly to the individual or the band, and by allowing the individuals to determine the level of funding to these political organizations.

Hence, First Nation political organizations would be reduced to competing with the many thousands of other charities in Canada, although it is unclear whether they would have charitable organization status under the *Income Tax Act* such that their financial contributors could obtain a tax deduction for their contribution. Finally, it is noteworthy that the Reform Party's aboriginal affairs policy no longer includes the principle "that Aboriginal individuals or groups are free to preserve their cultural heritage using their own resources". Presumably, that meant that existing cultural development funding from government would be terminated. However, in the 1997 federal election campaign, Reform's platform included a one billion dollar cut to the DIAND budget.

CAPITALISM

Capitalism, First Nations, and the "Criminal Justice" System

In Chapter Six Ponting and Kiely document the heavy over-representation of First Nation individuals as clients in the "criminal justice" system. That over-representation is related to our capitalist form of economic organization. For instance, a large proportion of First Nation individuals in custody is there for an alcohol-related offence, such as impaired driving, public drunkenness, causing a disturbance, breaking and entering (to obtain alcohol), and assault (after consuming alcohol). The consumption of alcohol is a well-known response to the marginality and despair felt by many First Nations people who, as part of the reserve army of cheap labour, have been relegated to the periphery of our anorexic capitalist economy. Secondly, many First Nation individuals are in custody because they could not afford to buy their way out; that is, they could not afford expensive legal counsel (and therefore had to rely on a legal aid lawyer)[9] or were unable to pay a fine.

The political economy school of thought (Panich, 1977: 3–27) contends that one of the functions of the state is to facilitate the accumulation of wealth by the capitalist class — that is, to reproduce the existing capitalist social order.

BOX 2 Selected Provisions of the Report of the Task Force on Aboriginal Affairs, Reform Party of Canada, 1995, And Critical Interpretations

Statement	A Critical Interpretation
1. Indian treaties will be fully honoured according to their original intent and in keeping with Court interpretation.	The reference to "original intent" appears to be a preference for a minimalist, rather than an expansive, interpretation of the treaties, but this is qualified by a recognition of the ultimate authority of the Supreme Court of Canada.
3. Indian self-government will be a delegated form of government and not a recognition of inherent Aboriginal sovereignty: – the laws of Canada (and the Provinces and Territories), including the Canadian Constitution and the Charter of Rights and Freedoms, will apply.	This is a large step back from what was contained in the Charlottetown Accord. Even after the defeat of the Accord, the Liberal government adopted a policy formally recognizing the inherency of the aboriginal right to self-government. The application of the Charter of Rights and Freedoms, with its individualistic bias, remains controversial among First Nations, as some sectors (e.g., some women's organizations) favour this provision while others (e.g., A.F.N.) oppose it as an imposition of non-Native values.
4. Land claim agreements and self-government agreements will be negotiated under the principle of equality for and among all persons: – settlement of land claims will be negotiated publicly. All settlements will outline specific terms, be final, and conclude within a specific time frame; – final settlements will be affordable to Canada and / or the Provinces;	Should non-Natives living on-reserve have the same voting rights as band members? This seems to suggest so. Calling for public negotiation of agreements is like calling for public negotiation of corporations' contracts with the federal government. Insistence on finality in land claims settlements goes directly contrary to the recommendations in the report (*Living Treaties, Lasting Agreements*) of the 1985 Coolican committee and will increase the reluctance of Native communities to ratify negotiated agreements. The "sunset clause" recommendation for a termination date to these new treaties is subject to the same criticism. The "affordability" recommendation is tantamount to saying that instead of justice being determined by principles of fairness and morality and restitution, justice must take its place amidst the transient political priorities of the day.
5. Individuals residing on settlement lands will have the freedom to opt for private ownership of their entitlements.	This is an assimilationist formula guaranteed to alienate First Nation land from First Nation collectivities and First

BOX 2 *(continued)*

Statement	A Critical Interpretation
	Nation individuals. It would fragment the reserves into a checkerboard mix of non-contiguous First Nation lands interspersed among non-Native owners, as has happened in the U.S.A. Alienation of Indian lands and intensification of intergroup tensions has been the outcome there. Even if non-Natives were prohibited from owning reserve land, the existing social class divisions on-reserve would be exacerbated.
6. Property owners forced to defend their property rights as a result of Aboriginal land claims will be compensated for defence of the claim.	An interesting violation of the tenet of "let the buyer beware", this provision will drive up land claim settlement costs and timetables beyond the present levels that are a source of major concern to the Reform Party.
7. Individuals may decide whether they wish to contribute financially to Indian political organizations such as the Assembly of First Nations. This will replace direct federal funding of these organizations.	This would emasculate First Nation advocacy organizations and would not be viable in the long term, for in situations of conflict governments need organized opponents to aggregate and articulate the demands of the aggrieved group and to lend legitimacy to government policy. Governments move to create such organizations where they do not exist.
8. Individuals who live on reserves and who are eligible to receive benefits such as social assistance may receive those benefits either from the federal government or through Indian self-government.	By reducing the size of the serviced population, this provision would create inefficiencies (loss of economies of scale). It would also drive up the cost of First Nation government by creating unnecessary duplication.
9. The Auditor General of Canada will have full authority to review the Indian management of federal funds.	Such authority does not exist for funds transferred from the federal government to the provinces. This is essentially meddling in First Nations' internal affairs and blurs the lines of accountability. It is a form of socio-fiscal control.
10. The Chief Electoral Officer of Elections Canada will have the same authority to examine Indian election procedures as he/she would have in any other federal jurisdiction.	This provision is also a form of meddling in First Nations' internal affairs. It would replace a paternalistic power of the DIAND minister under the *Indian Act* with a paternalistic power of the Chief Electoral Officer of Elections Canada.

BOX 2 *(continued)*

Statement	A Critical Interpretation
11. As the economic climate within Indian-governed communities improves and money is transferred from senior governments to individuals, Indian governments will fund their operations by taxing the members of these communities.	Although even some First Nation leaders see this as the way of the future, it will be staunchly resisted by First Nation individuals, for it removes one of the few rights (exemption from taxation of income, wealth, and property on reserve) contained in the *Indian Act*. See #12 below.
12. Since equality of all citizens is the ultimate goal, Indian persons and corporations will be subject to the same taxation provisions as other Canadians. As Indian economic conditions improve, the taxation exemption under Section 87 of the *Indian Act* will be eliminated.	Fierce opposition would come from the grass roots of First Nation communities, as noted in #11 above. A belief of many First Nation persons is that the value of the resources extracted from the lands ceded by First Nations to the Crown amounts (past, present, and future) to so many trillions of dollars as to have effectively prepaid First Nation individuals' taxes in perpetuity.
13. The *Indian Act of Canada* will be repealed and replaced by legislation respecting the above principles.	First Nation individuals tend to be very ambivalent about repeal of the *Indian Act*. It is erroneously regarded by many as the source of many rights, whereas it actually confers very few rights.
14. A new relationship with Aboriginal peoples shall begin with a convention of Indian representatives from across Canada (elected by Aboriginal people) who will meet with senior government leaders to discuss how to apply these principles.	All of the above is so opposed to the agenda of most First Nation leaders that it is questionable whether any leader would attend such a convention and whether they could deliver the consent and compliance of their putative constituents. A major cleavage would open in First Nation communities and those who attend the convention would be disparaged as "sell-outs" by their political opponents.

Source: Reform Party of Canada website: http://www.reform.ca/english/tskfrce/aborig/index.html. No longer posted.

Another function of the state, as viewed from the political economy perspective, is the exercise of social control. Aboriginal people are sometimes considered to pose problems in both these regards and that can bring them into contact with the criminal justice system. As Samuelson (1991, quoted in Wotherspoon and Satzewich (1993: 207)) reminds us:

> The criminal justice system has commonly been employed as a method for containment and control of problem populations such as transients, the chronically unemployed, the dispossessed, and alcoholics, drug addicts, and prostitutes.

Owners and managers of retail businesses sometimes regard the presence of lower class First Nation persons as a deterrent to business and activate the criminal justice system by enlisting police help in removing them from the business premises or the neighbourhood.

Chapter Six discusses the imposition of a western legal system of control upon First Nations for whom it was entirely foreign. While that discussion is couched in terms of the criminal law, we should not lose sight of the fact that the scope of the dominant society's social control over First Nation people is much broader than merely the criminal law. We shall take up this point later in this introduction.

Leverage and Vulnerability in The New World Order: Corporate Interests versus First Nation Interests

Chapters Seven and Eight, by Brown and by Ponting and Symons, respectively, are case studies which focus upon instances where First Nation interests clash with the economic interests of powerful corporations in the dominant capitalistic society. The Cree in Chapter Eight fought aggressively against Hydro-Québec.[10] They were trying to avoid any more of precisely those wrenching social disruptions which left the Lubicon of Chapter Seven a disempowered and largely defeated people after their hunting and trapping mode of economic production collided with the advanced capitalist mode of production of the oil industry.

Chapter Eight is set in the context of the "new world order" of capitalist economic relations. In that chapter the new world order is defined in terms of the heightened importance of international economic relations (including extreme mobility of investment capital), the predominance of multinational corporations, and increased international awareness of events in distant lands due to information-sharing technology and global mass media (which are themselves often corporate conglomerates). These and other features of the new world order create new points of vulnerability for political regimes, their state-controlled companies and the transnational corporations upon which they have come to depend. Lacking in conventional political resources, like money and force of numbers, First Nations are increasingly resorting to strategies which seek to exploit those points of state and corporate vulnerability, as we observe in Chapter Eight.

Both the James Bay Cree and the Lubicon have waged spirited warfare at home and abroad against huge resource exploitation corporations. The Cree have achieved much greater success, despite the generally similar strategies. The different outcome is probably attributable to the much greater **leverage** that the Cree enjoy. That is, although both the Cree and the Lubicon attacked their corporate enemy with powerful symbols and economic strategies directed at the enemy's commercial markets, the Cree had two "trump cards". That is, they had the added ability to derail or sabotage both the James Bay II project itself (important to then-Premier Bourassa both as a symbol and as a creator of jobs for Quebecers) and the separatist project which was the highest priority of the Parti Québécois government when it was re-elected in 1994. That leverage resulted in the Parti Québécois government announcing the suspension of the project, for the government was anxious to avoid another potentially disruptive Cree offensive in the middle of the 1995 sovereignty referendum campaign.

Conversely, the Lubicon threats of sabotaging the oil development on their lands were not taken seriously by government and their attempts to obstruct the industry were met with overpowering police force. They did protest against the Daishawa corporation's plans to log land claimed by the Lubicon, and against the Unocal corporation's locating of a gas processing plant near their land. However, those protests were not backed by effective actions on the ground to establish themselves as being a sufficiently powerful and credible threat as to jeopardize the corporations' objectives.

Leverage is an important resource precisely because, as noted above, First Nations rarely control sufficient other resources to make their will predominate over the wishes of non-Native individuals, governments, or corporations in a contest of raw power. Consider, for instance, the Innu of Labrador. In the absence of both leverage and conventional political resources, their land claim negotiations with government dragged on for seven years. With the discovery of rich mineral resources (nickel, copper, and cobalt) at Voisey's Bay in Labrador, they finally gained some leverage — namely, the prospect of them filing lawsuits that could seriously encumber the profitability of the operations of giant nickel company Inco Limited. That led to the negotiations being "kick-started". Just weeks after Inco's acquisition of a major economic interest in the area in 1996, a "fast-track" schedule of negotiations was announced.

A marked contrast is to be found in the loss of the leverage that the Lubicon and various other First Nations in northern Alberta had in the 1970s. Part of their leverage came from a favourable legal precedent in the Northwest Territories, in which Mr. Justice Morrow permitted the aboriginal claimants to file a *caveat* on lands slated for mineral development. The *caveat* would have registered an aboriginal interest in any revenues which corporations derived from that mineral development. The other part of the Alberta First Nations' leverage was based on government and corporate eagerness to develop the oil sands and other lucrative oil plays in northern Alberta. That leverage left members of those First Nations optimistic that they would finally attain the land claim settlement that had eluded them since they were missed by the treaty commissioners generations earlier. However, in an act of naked power designed to protect the fiscal interests of the already corpulent provincial treasury and the multinational oil companies, then-Premier Peter Lougheed's government passed *retroactive* legislation (*Bill 29*, tabled in the provincial legislature on April 27, 1977) that prohibited the filing of a caveat. With the stroke of a pen, the leverage of the First Nations was vaporized.

The northern Alberta example is just one instance of what Boldt (1993: 67–79) describes as the tendency for justice for aboriginal people to be sacrificed to **"the national interest"**. Boldt regards the concept of "the national interest" as "an artificial construct, a device of the reigning Canadian 'establishment' for asserting its political, economic, and social hegemony over the Canadian nation". One of the most contentious assertions of "the national interest" has come in comprehensive land claim settlements (involving lands where treaties had not been signed). There the federal government has insisted on extinguishing aboriginal title to most of the land being claimed. In that insistence we see the state acting to clear the path for the reaping of corporate profits by big business at the expense of the original occupants of the land. Of course, the state is not a disinterested party to land claim negotiations, for the state receives taxation revenues from non-Indian corporations, but not from First Nation corporate entities operating on First Nation lands. The upshot is that although comprehensive claim settlements open the doors of opportunity for aboriginal entrepreneurs and the managers of new aboriginal government corporations,[11] the balance of opportunity is usually in favour of third party corporate interests. That occurs because the tracts of claimed land over which First Nations are required to cede their rights are always much larger than the tracts over which they are allowed to retain full rights.

Another extremely important manifestation of Boldt's point is to be found in governments' responses to the neo-conservative assertions of The Business Council on National Issues (B.C.N.I.) that, "in the national interest", governments must eliminate their fiscal deficits before we "hit the wall".[12] B.C.N.I.'s and the Reform Party's call for massive slashing of government spending has succeeded in changing the terms of policy debate in Canada. Deficit reduction and its cousin "affordability" have displaced social justice as criteria for judging how "sound" a public policy is, as we observed above in the Reform Party task force report. Displaying a distinct lack of political courage, many governments have made large, relatively uniform "across-the-board" cuts to the budgets of all departments, rather than making the value judgements that would protect through exemption those least able to absorb the cuts and the increase in user fees. First Nation people are over-represented in the ranks of the poor; as such, their capacity for absorbing the cuts and user fees is very low. As a result, the door of opportunity often slams in their face.

The clash of economic interests between First Nations and non-Natives can also occur in other realms of micro-economics. Political economists point to the limitation of First Nation economic opportunity by an inherent contradiction within the state. That is, the federal state's role of advancing the economic interests of First Nations is constrained by the fact that if First Nation economic development programs were to be successful, that would put First Nation peoples in a position of potential conflict with non-aboriginal businesses which are seeking the same markets. Discussing the Saskatchewan government's Indian Economic Development Program, which assigns low priority for funding to aboriginal business proposals which "obviously displace or create unfair competition for existing businesses and employees", Wotherspoon and Satzewich (1993: 257–258) conclude:

> [T]he task that aboriginal businesses will face in the future is finding profitable niches in markets that are not already filled, or dominated, by white-owned businesses. The difficulty, of course, is that given the nature of capitalism, which contains a tendency towards monopoly and centralization, it is extremely difficult to find new niches in the economy that are profitable, and which will remain profitable in the long run.

In light of those low profit margins, the short-term prospects for the economic empowerment of some First Nations are not bright.

Social Control and Globalization

An important role of the state is to exert control over the First Nation population. That is achieved in part through the imposition of a legal system which favours individual rights over collective rights and which goes to great lengths to protect the property rights of individuals and corporations.[13] The northern Alberta case described above is a good case in point. Social control is also the script underlying various government policies, such as the 1996 proposed revisions to the *Indian Act* which retained the Minister's power of disallowance of band by-laws. As a DIAND policy director once told the author concerning the department's 1978 proposals to amend the *Indian Act*,

> I don't see that we can make much more extensive changes than what we are now proposing. We have to take the middle of the road approach between what Indians want and what our masters — Parliament and the public — will accept.

> (Ponting and Gibbins, 1980: 104)

An especially disempowering form of social control is what Ponting and Gibbins (1980: 124–127) have called **socio-fiscal control**. This takes various forms, only some of which are related to broader influences of globalization. Among those which are not is the simple power of the purse strings. The belief that (s)he who pays the piper gets to call the tune is often construed to mean that the provision of money carries with it the right to demand proof that the funds have been spent in accordance with certain stipulations and the right to arbitrarily reduce or terminate funding. Examples of socio-fiscal control are not difficult to find and include:

- excessive financial accountability reporting requirements;
- DIAND's attempts to curb political deviance through the suspension of funding (for examples see Ponting and Gibbins, 1980: 125);
- DIAND's attempts to control certain factions on reserves through the dispensing of patronage;
- DIAND's attempts to sow disunity among First Nations by telling one First Nation organization that there are insufficient funds available for it because another has a disproportionately large share;
- the government's withholding of adequate funding for basic community infrastructure (e.g., housing, water and sewage systems) on reserves in the knowledge that that will impel migration to off-reserve locations where DIAND disclaims jurisdiction; and
- the perpetuation of welfare dependency, which drains individuals of the initiative and sense of self-esteem that are necessary for launching effective challenges to the status quo.

In the contemporary era, another form which socio-fiscal control takes is the slashing of budgets as part of a larger government austerity program to achieve deficit reduction. This is very much related to globalization, in that some corporate actors have convinced governments that if our accumulated debt grows too large, international investors will come to doubt our ability to repay the loans and will invest their highly mobile money elsewhere.

Social control and globalization of an entirely different genre came to the fore in the armed stand-offs at Oka/Kanehsatake and at Kahnawake (across the St. Lawrence River from Montréal) in the summer of 1990. For centuries First Nation land has been coveted by Euro-canadians for their economic gain, but "the Oka crisis" involved Euro-canadian attempts to develop for leisure (golfing) purposes land claimed by the Mohawks of Kanehsatake. When the Mohawks resisted, with the help of heavily armed warriors from the nearby Akwesasne reserve, the Québec government deployed a provincial police tactical squad in an attempt to forcibly remove the First Nation occupiers of the disputed land. That proved disastrous, as police Cpl. Marcel LeMay was killed in an exchange of gunfire during the assault. Soon the army was mobilized to take control of an out-of-control situation. Notwithstanding the restraint exhibited by the military in the face of provocation and political pressure, the episode now ranks as one of the foremost examples of the state's use of force against First Nation people in Canada.

The "Oka crisis" was also the occasion for First Nations to score a major diplomatic coup with Canada's allies in Europe. Specifically, First Nation diplomats succeeded in getting the European Parliament to adopt a motion which was generally supportive of the Mohawks.[14] (See Ponting (1990) for an analysis of the discourse surrounding the "Oka crisis".) In that incident we saw First Nations attempt to co-opt the political power of foreign powers as part of a leveraging strategy. That is consistent with the increasing role that foreign actors play in various domestic policy fields, including First Nation matters. That has become possible as the global village of telecommunications has become a reality and as the trend toward global interdependence and awareness has been accentuated. While it was precisely those global interdependencies which the Lubicon and the James Bay Cree used for their purposes, the Mohawks of Kahnawake and Kanehsatake utilized global awareness. Like governments' financial books, governments' human rights performances have also become subject to international scrutiny and action; Canada's record is no exception and First Nations will ensure that that continues to be so.

SYSTEMIC DISCRIMINATION

Employment equity legislation and the affirmative action programs issuing from it are designed to combat systemic discrimination. Systemic discrimination often occurs without being fuelled by any racist beliefs or discriminatory intent when the state or other organizations adopt an egalitarian operating philosophy based on uniformity of treatment for all persons. "One law for all" and "no special status" are the *leitmotif* of this philosophy of blind or radical egalitarianism. Such a philosophy fails to take into account history and such contemporary complexities as cultural differences and the institutionalized disadvantages of some sectors of society. Although appealing in its simplicity, this philosophy produces very inequitable outcomes. The Reform Party task force report discussed above suffers from this blindness, as do many of the critics of employment equity legislation and affirmative action programmes. Seemingly oblivious to Canada's history of failed efforts at assimilation — to wit, Hutterites, French Québécois, the Indian residential schools, the *Indian Act*, and the 1969 White Paper — and blind to the deficiencies of "human capital" (e.g., formal education) in many First Nation populations, the Reform Party task force report erroneously assumes that all First Nation individuals want to be like other Canadians and will be able to do so on their own.

Aboriginal people are one of the four beneficiary groups[15] targeted by the federal government's *Employment Equity Act* and the associated contract compliance program. The implementation of Reform's recommendations and the rescinding of employment equity legislation would further entrench First Nation disadvantage. Such policies would also contribute to the perpetuation of the culture of poverty which acts as a barrier to participation in Canadian society for large numbers of First Nation individuals. Under this approach, systemic discrimination would run rampant and equality of opportunity would be a slogan with an even more hollow ring than it now has for many aboriginal people.

Affirmative action programs are no panacea. The Royal Canadian Mounted Police's 1996 survey of 525 "Regular Members" of all ranks (Mofina, 1996a and 1996b) and follow-up evaluations of the federal *Employment Equity Act* attest to the fact that even after employment equity initiatives are implemented, racism and systemic discrimination can be slow to diminish.[16] Mofina reports that twenty years after the RCMP began hiring women, the force is still rife with sexual harassment. Women, aboriginals, and "visible minorities" all leave the RCMP at a higher rate than do white males. Of particular relevance to our interests is the survey's finding that almost half of the aboriginal Mountie respondents report having seen what they deem to be racist material (e.g., posters, notes, and calendars) in RCMP offices. This finding underscores a more general point long recognized by public policy analysts. That is, the street-level bureaucrats (e.g., police officers on the street and in the detachment office, teachers, social workers, low-level supervisors) shape a given public policy by the way they implement it. If they have not been consulted in the formulation of the policy, or are otherwise disinclined toward it, or are driven by stereotypes, they can subvert it not only in their relations with their colleagues, but particularly in exercising their discretionary authority in their capacity as agents of social control or of service delivery.

Chapter Nine, by Calliou, reveals the hardships faced by First Nation persons inside and outside Native communities when they attempt to participate in the institutions of Canadian society on such an individualized basis as the Reform Party favours. The chapter also illustrates the aforementioned organizational deviance and depicts in rich detail how affirmative action policies can fail if organizational procedures, processes, and philosophies are not also transformed. Calliou's parable of the elephant and the giraffe drives home the point that *honourable intentions, when accompanied by sociological naiveté, will be ineffective in opening opportunity structures to First Nation people.*

EMPOWERMENT

My first book in this field was published in 1980 under the title *Out of Irrelevance.* That title signified that First Nation collectivities and individuals had begun to move from the geographic, economic, social, and political margins of Canadian society to a position closer to centre stage. That is, First Nations had started to become "a power to be reckoned with", a factor that could no longer consistently be ignored. That is not to say that First Nation interests would always prevail, as we observed in Chapters Two and Three of the present volume. Instead, they became more likely to be taken into account by other societal actors and would sometimes prevail or be partially accommodated, but sometimes be totally over-ridden. In this section we consider empowerment to be a multifacetted phenomenon involving change along an economic dimension, a cultural-symbolic-spiritual dimension, and a political-legal dimension. Each is addressed in turn below.

Economic Power

A thorough analysis of First Nations' growing economic power is beyond the purview of this volume and the expertise of the author. However, some indicators are obvious and can be readily catalogued, which is our task here.

The stereotype of First Nation peoples as mired in a state of welfare dependency is overdrawn. While unemployment and welfare dependency are indisputably high, there are also sources of large scale capital flows that must be taken into account. Indeed, the very magnitude of the social assistance incomes and of First Nation organizations' contracts and payrolls is now recognized as an important part of an economic development strategy on many reserves.

In important respects, DIAND is now a "money-moving" department. DIAND (1997: 67) reports that in the 1995–96 fiscal year (FY), 83% (or $3.066 billion) of the Indian and Inuit Affairs Program's total expenditures of $3.688 billion was made through band councils, tribal councils, or other First Nation organizations. If more of that money is spent within First Nation communities rather than outside, it will have a significant job-creating multiplier effect. By the same token, some First Nations, whose members spend considerable sums in neighbouring off-reserve communities, are awakening to the opportunity to use that purchasing power and the implicit or explicit threat of economic boycott to bring about change in merchandising behaviour (e.g., removal of substances amenable to abuse), in customer relations, or in civic policy in those neighbouring communities.

Land claim settlement moneys are one of the largest sources of economic "clout" enjoyed by First Nations and other aboriginal peoples. Box 3 provides some particulars on the economic dimension of selected comprehensive land claim settlements. The substantial amounts involved, and First Nations' need to invest those funds, have aroused the keen interest of various banks. In addition, as one Mohawk banker from Six Nations in Ontario observed, aboriginal people will control a large proportion of Canada's land mass by the year 2000 (Maclean, 1996). Economic development provisions are crucial components of contemporary comprehensive land claims agreements.

Also arousing the interests of banks are potentially lucrative gambling operations operated by First Nations. For instance, the $44 million casino on the Rama reserve near Orillia in Ontario's cottage country is described by Platiel (1996) as having an "anticipated $84 million economic impact", and annual gross revenues of $200–$300 million. Off-site, Platiel reports, the 18,000 square metre casino "is expected to generate $24 million in food sales and $13.5 million in retail sales". Not surprisingly, area businesses and politicians are reported to be enthusiastic about the project, which opened in August 1996 and could dominate the local economy.

Another development in the realm of banking is the creation of the First Nations Bank of Canada as a partnership between the Saskatchewan Indian Equity Foundation and the Toronto Dominion Bank. The business plan is for the bank to be fully owned by aboriginal people within ten years. Chief of the Federation of Saskatchewan Indian Nations, Blaine Favel, described the creation of the bank as "a breakthrough moment, a watershed moment in the growth of the Indian economy and the establishment of our self-sufficiency and pride". He added: "It will put our people in control of a major financial institution, which will exercise its business clout and its political influence as all other

---

BOX 3 Dollar Payments* of Selected Aboriginal Comprehensive
Land Claim Settlements (Final or Proposed)

James Bay and Northern Québec Agreement, 1975 and N.E. Québec Agreement
• $230 million over 20 years

Inuvialuit Final Agreement, 1984
• $45 million over 13 years
• $10 million economic enhancement fund
• $7.5 million social development fund

Yukon Umbrella Final Agreement, 1990
• $243 million over 15 years
• unspecified annual operating budgets of certain agencies, such as the Yukon
  Development Assessment Board, Yukon Land Use Planning Council
• $6.5 million to a Training Trust
• $4 million operating capital for the Yukon First Nation Implementation Fund
  and $0.5 million for the development of implementation plans
• $1 million contribution to the Yukon Fish and Wildlife Enhancement Trust, over
  4 years

Gwich'in Agreement, N.W.T., 1992
• $75 million over 15 years

Nunavut Land Claims Agreement, 1993
• $1.17 billion over 14 years

Nisga'a Agreement-in-Principle, 1996
• $190 million basic capital transfer (to be adjusted once for inflation for the latest
  quarter prior to the signing of the Final Agreement)
• $10 million contribution to a fisheries conservation trust
• $11.5 million contribution to enable the Nisga'a Central Government to increase
  its capacity (in the form of licences and/or vessels) to participate in the coast-
  wide commercial fishery
• less repayment of loan used to fund Nisga'a negotiating team

---

*Figures cited are those stated in the agreements and are not adjusted to take into account inflation.
Source: DIAND (http://www.inac.gc.ca/pubs/information/treaty.html)

---

banks do" (Canadian Press, 1996). Not to be left out, The Canadian Imperial
Bank of Commerce (CIBC) made a commitment in 1996 to be a permanent sup-
porter of aboriginal programs at the Banff Centre for Management in Banff,
Alberta, and made its first annual donation of $50,000. Echoing the general sen-
timents expressed by other banking spokespersons, a CIBC vice-president said
the support responds to a combination of economic and political trends that
"make aboriginal Canada one of the single greatest market opportunities in this
country" (Jaremko, 1996).

   Natural resources are another major revenue source. Of the $1.1 billion of
band revenues held in trust for bands by DIAND (DIAND, 1997: 94), natural
resources revenues would account for the vast majority. A small number of First
Nations, mainly in northeastern British Columbia and Alberta (e.g., Sawridge,
Enoch, and the four nations of Hobbema), enjoy prodigious oil and gas revenues which they have used to diversify their holdings by moving into fields
such as commercial banking (Peace Hills Trust) and tourism (e.g., the Samson

Mall at Lake Louise, Alberta). In lawsuits before the courts in 1992, the Samson Cree First Nation at Hobbema sued the federal government for $575 million for alleged mismanagement of Samson oil and gas revenues (the government agreed to hand over $400 million), while in a similar breach of trust case the Enoch First Nation west of Edmonton sued for $400 million in damages and transfer of oil and gas revenues still held in trust by the government (Canadian Press, 1992).

Another example of windfall natural resources is the highly controversial "liquidation logging" conducted by members of the Stoney tribe in the foothills of the Rocky Mountains west of Calgary. By the calculations (of unknown reliability) of one environmentalist who had flown over the reserve and counted logging trucks leaving the reserve, a "conservative" estimate of the Stoneys' income from timber harvesting over a two-month period in 1994 was $18 to $25 million. (Barnett, 1995).

Some First Nations enjoy a strategic geographic location vis-à-vis large population centres and are able to convert that into economic development opportunities. The Rama casino is one example and the Tsuu T'ina reserve adjacent to Calgary is another. Saskatchewan First Nations are able to use treaty entitlement settlement moneys to purchase new lands, including lots and buildings in existing urban areas.

First Nation entrepreneurship is also blossoming. Over eighteen thousand aboriginal businesses were in existence by the mid-1990s in a wide range of industries. Various industry associations (e.g., the National Aboriginal Forestry Association, the Native Investment and Trade Association, and the Canadian National Aboriginal Tourism Association) had also emerged, some with government assistance, to play a facilitative role. First Nations' use of the internet for commercial purposes was quite evident as early as 1996. There one could find web pages not only for the above-named associations, but also for The Native Business Network (to advise potential buyers of aboriginal services and products), for various First Nation artists, and for the Directory of B.C. Aboriginal Exporters, among others.

Another form of First Nation business of enormous dollar volume is smuggling. One 1994 media report (Moon, 1994) quoted an estimate of $1 billion per year in lost tax revenues for the federal and provincial governments from the surreptitious importation of cigarettes and alcohol into Canada. Near the Akwesasne Mohawk territory on the Ontario-Québec-New York border, this form of economic empowerment flourished, but at great cost to public safety on the St. Lawrence River and on land. Gunfire and hijackings were not uncommon, and one murder was reported in conjunction with the trade. (The trade eventually expanded into the lucrative business of smuggling human cargo entering the USA).

The foregoing demonstrates that some First Nations are acquiring considerable economic power. Although generous sharing is sometimes manifested by the First Nations holding such wealth, we should not lose sight of the fact that it is a relatively small proportion of all First Nations that becomes wealthy. The hard facts of the matter are that a large proportion of First Nations is located a great distance from markets and has a land base that is too small to hold much natural resources wealth. Similarly, at the individual level, although incomes are rising, they continue to lag considerably behind incomes of the larger Canadian population. Economic empowerment is underway, and great strides have been taken in some cases, but of course, on the economic plane no First Nation is a match for a corporate giant or for the provincial or federal state.

As the economic revival of First Nation communities unfolds, two things merit our close attention. The first is the extent to which First Nation business ventures produce a greater polarization of the social classes than already exists in First Nation communities. Part of that issue involves the question of whether the aboriginal managers of First Nation corporate entities will align their decisions with the interests of the corporation or of the members of the community. The other key issue revolves around the allocation (within the First Nation, including its off-reserve members) and between First Nations, of the surplus revenues from these economic forays. It is entirely conceivable that even greater disparities than presently exist could become institutionalized in Canadian society within the First Nation population.

For the multi-facetted economic development strategy proposed by The Royal Commission on Aboriginal Peoples, see RCAP (1996b: 825–1014).

Cultural, Spiritual, and Symbolic Power [17]

In contrast to the thesis of First Nation cultural empowerment found in this volume, sociologist Menno Boldt (1993: 167ff), writing in the early 1990s, contended that First Nation cultures in Canada are in a state of crisis. Indians, he wrote, will not survive *as Indians* unless they take immediate and intensive measures to revitalize traditional First Nation cultural philosophies, principles, languages, and social and normative systems. Traditional values, norms, customs, and social systems have lost their relevance and their legitimacy, and therefore their ability to maintain social order in their communities, he maintained. Shkilnyk's (1985) account of the social disorganization of an Ojibwa community, and especially of the breakdown of traditional sexual taboos against incest, is a graphic but exaggerated portrayal of what Boldt saw.

Boldt (1993: 176) further asserted that "a culture reduced to its expressive-ritualistic function is inadequate as a design for surviving and living". Traditional cultural precepts, he argued, had been displaced by a culture of poverty and a culture of dependence, the products of which are individuals' loss of self-esteem, feelings of hopelessness and disempowerment, and resultant apathy and alienation. These are atomizing or individuating responses. That is, they are inimical to the formation of a collective will or a collective sense of self-determination.

The final part of Boldt's thesis is that Indian leaders must take a more proactive role as "cultural maximizers" — persons who maintain and push further the greatness and integration of the culture. "Unless Indian leaders undertake this challenge", he writes, "it is doubtful that Indians can survive and live *as Indians*. If they choose to allow cultural change to occur spontaneously in the 'spirit of the times', that is if they continue to let cultural change occur as a series of unplanned, ad hoc deletions and additions — whatever is convenient — then the extinction of Indian cultures will occur as a legacy of contemporary Indian leaders' neglect" (Boldt, 1993: 182). He sees First Nation leaders as doing a poor job as cultural maximizers. They are, he contends, more concerned with politics than with cultural adaptation and development. One result is culturally bifurcated First Nation communities, in which the elite is largely acculturated to the larger society and the masses are trapped in a culture of dependence.

Boldt's self-confessed (1993: xiv) rhetorical style is forceful and thought-provoking. While I agree with the central thrust of much of his argument, I believe that he has given insufficient weight to the positive cultural developments of the last two decades of the twentieth century. Furthermore, those developments have proceeded apace since Boldt wrote, which also weakens his case.

Boldt writes off most of the First Nation cultural revival as merely "expressive-ritualistic" — that is, ceremonies, songs, dance, art, traditional legends, and the like. In contrast, I believe that such "expressive-ritualistic" cultural manifestations are rooted in rich **meaning** and impart some of that meaning to their First Nation practitioners and First Nation audiences, even when those cultural practices are severed from the mode of economic production (e.g., hunting, fishing, trapping, gathering) with which they were once associated. If suicide, substance abuse, and other forms of escapism (e.g., bingo) are rampant in a First Nation community, is it not in large part because life has become painful and lost most of its meaning to many of the people in that community?

Boldt (1993: 179) asserts that a culture is inseparable from the day's work and to a degree he is correct. However, meaning can be found elsewhere than in work: Boldt's close linkage of work and culture perhaps reflects the bias of Marxian materialism (ideas as mere epiphenomena derivable from material conditions) or of the Protestant work ethic. A different perspective allows that human beings are capable of more compartmentalization of our daily lives than Boldt seems to assume. From that perspective I submit that many individuals, Native and non-Native alike, function in the larger society in jobs that they merely tolerate as a means to other ends. Those other ends sometimes include participation in rich, largely "expressive ritualistic" cultural traditions which shape those persons' identity, cognitions, interaction networks, sense of allegiance, and sense of moral obligations (Isajiw, 1990). That is no small part of their life and to them is a source of great meaning in life.

Further points on which Boldt can be challenged concern cultural pride and cultural serenity. The "expressive-ritualistic" culture can serve as a source of great pride for those who practice it or observe and identify with it. That pride combats the alienation, hopelessness and the low self-esteem which Boldt sees as part of the cultural crisis of dependency. In short, the causal arrows can flow both ways. That is, while the elimination of the objective conditions (e.g., unemployment, paternalistic administration of the *Indian Act*) of dependency can contribute to a culture adapting and becoming revitalized, so too can the revival of the expressive-ritualistic culture instill a pride, hope, and determination that can mobilize the individual to take action to end those objective conditions of dependency. It is, perhaps, less than fair for Boldt to attack First Nation leaders who focus resolutely on that inherently political task of removing the objective conditions of dependency. Furthermore, as an inside observer once pointed out to me, many of those politically-focused leaders derive their sustenance from their practice of, and commitment to, their culture. The image of Elijah Harper, holding an eagle feather while blocking the Meech Lake Accord, comes readily to mind.

I believe that "expressive-ritualistic" manifestations of culture also have an important role to play in the healing which is desperately needed in many First Nation communities in response to the residential school experience, family violence, neglect, escapism, and disempowerment. Traditional songs, dance, and ceremonies, and sometimes even contemporary art, do not exist in isolation from aboriginal spirituality; rather, they are expressions of it. For many First Nation individuals, that spirituality will be the pivotal component of any healing (a form of personal empowerment) which they experience. At the psychological level, surely the essence of healing is the formulation of new "designs for surviving and living", which is precisely what Boldt (1993: 176) contends culture should be.

The above makes a case for the value of "expressive-ritualistic" culture and in doing so implicitly calls into question the validity of the distinction between such aspects of culture and other more functionally adaptive (instrumental?) aspects of culture. Let us turn, therefore, to a consideration of the cultural empowerment or revival.

The major revival of First Nations' cultures in the late twentieth century occurred in response to, and in turn contributed to, a resurgence of First Nation nationalism and cultural pride. In Statistics Canada's 1991 Aboriginal Population Survey (APS), two thirds of on-reserve adults reported participating in traditional aboriginal activities, while almost half (45%) of off-reserve First Nation individuals did. The cultural revival took many forms, one of the most important of which was language preservation and language training[18] and another of which was the repatriation of artifacts from museums around the world. These developments enabled First Nation individuals to reconnect in several ways: (i) with their past; (ii) with the aboriginal spirituality from which many had been alienated by their exposure to Christianity; and (iii) with the nuances of meaning and experience that are obscured by the English or French language. These are all stable anchorages that help ground the individual in the reality that he or she experiences. If a lack of stable anchorages contributes to alienation, disorientation, and a sense of one's spirit being lost or wandering, then the presence of these stable anchorages is a source of empowerment.

By 1991, over one-third (37%) of on-reserve children was speaking the aboriginal language at school and 43% were speaking it at home. By the 1995–96 school year, some 429 band operated schools existed and the majority of First Nation children were enrolled in band-operated schools. The "Indian control of Indian education" policy was firmly established and new school construction was commonplace. In marked contrast to the residential schools era, the schools had emerged as a secure platform for teaching Indian culture.

The period also saw a flourishing of First Nation artists working in various media. As noted in Chapter Three, many of these artists have achieved international stature. Their work gives a new vitality to aboriginal world views, while at the same time providing concrete representations of the spirits and other forces that are recognized in aboriginal culture as shaping daily existence. It is striking to see the forceful expressions of power, assertiveness, and reclaimed spirituality in the imagery of some First Nation artists. Furthermore, the recognition bestowed upon some First Nation artists by the larger society, such as when Roy Vickers is commissioned by government to do the painting that will be presented to commonwealth leaders attending a summit in British Columbia or when Bill Reid's work is chosen as a feature display at the national Museum of Civilization in Ottawa/Hull, evokes a sense of pride in First Nation individuals who are aware of it.

The elders, of course, play a pivotal role in this revival, in the schools, in the extended family, in the prisons, in the healing circles and sweat lodges, in the polity, and even in reaching out to non-Natives such as through museums operated by First Nations. (In Part 3 of this volume, Dale Auger recounts in rich detail one such learning session with a Cree elder.) Respect for the elders is being revived in communities across the country. There is resistance in some quarters, though, such as among teens whose seduction by the materialistic culture of the dominant society renders them highly sceptical of what the elders have to offer.

Another aspect of the cultural revival involves the reclamation of traditional songs, dances, and drumming by performing artists. Be it at feasts, pow-wows, ceremonies, or other occasions, these physical and aural components of the occasion contribute substantially to involving participants psychologically and holistically.

Even to an outsider like this author, it is clear that a deep spiritual re-discovery is occurring in First Nation communities. It is especially evident in the psychological healing programs (e.g., Women in Wellness) which are taking root in numerous communities across Canada, but also appears in other places, such as on the university campuses, in art, and in the use of traditional medicines. Among on-reserve adults, ten percent of those who reported having seen someone about their health in the year before the 1991 APS reported having gone to a traditional healer. Off-reserve the figure was only 5%. Although my observations are merely impressionistic, I do sense that a growing proportion of the First Nation population is coming to feel more in harmony with the total environment, including people, spirits, and nature. In its clash with the materialism of the dominant society's advertising, entertainment, and manufacturing industries, this spiritual revival faces a formidable opponent.

Significantly, though, the aboriginal cultural revival is starting to make inroads into the larger society's popular culture. Some aspects of this were identified in the discussion of the commodification of culture in Chapter Three. Among the more positive aspects of this cultural penetration are such phenomena as the telecasting of the National Aboriginal Achievement Awards presentation ceremonies, the television series *North of 60* about life in a First Nation community, and the proliferation of world wide web sites controlled by First Nation or other aboriginal people. Indeed, the speed with which the web caught on among First Nation organizations is remarkable.

It is important to note that First Nation people now control a substantial number of media outlets, albeit few that reach a broad audience in the non-Native community. In addition to the aforementioned web sites, there are various newspapers (e.g., *Windspeaker*) where First Nation people can learn about First Nation cultural events, political events, business opportunities, women's issues, land claim settlements, etc., or where First Nation people can reach out to one another to build solidarity in Canada or abroad.

As part of the treatment of political empowerment below we shall return to a consideration of symbolic power when we consider an important focus of Part 2 — namely, political discourse.

Political-Legal Empowerment

Much attention was devoted to the political empowerment of First Nations in Chapter Three. There, for instance, we observed the mercurial rise and fall of the Assembly of First Nations. Another surge in the AFN's political capital is by no means out of the question, especially if the federal government comes to the conclusion that under a new set of political circumstances it needs the AFN or needs to co-opt the AFN as a means of damage control.

In the absence of substantial power in Canada, the AFN and other First Nation political organizations will turn to the international political arena, as noted earlier. The essence of that political activity is the **political discourse** which they employ in those arenas. Attention is devoted to discourse in Part 2 of this volume because, in a limited but very real sense, language and other symbols *are* power, or at least are potent power resources. If this were not so, Canadian governments (and corporations) would not spend so much money for the services of diplomats and so-called "spin doctors".

Sometimes earning more from a client government than a cabinet minister in that government, a political spin doctor's stock-in-trade is metaphor, symbol, image, and just the right turn of phrase to justify particular actions and inaction of the government. That legitimation is sought by means of projecting a **definition of the situation** which makes government behaviour resonate with the beliefs, values, interests, and anxieties of the audience (e.g., newspaper editors, the undecided voters in the electorate or in a swing constituency, foreign governments). Although government and large corporate coffers dwarf the financial resources which First Nations can devote to advertising, language and other symbols can be a great "leveller". That is, one politically attuned, articulate, creative, and "media-wise" employee of a First Nation political organization operating on a shoestring budget can coin a single phrase (e.g., "environmental racist") or set of phrases of such potency that it effectively off-sets (temporarily) the otherwise substantial power differences between the government and First Nations. Such a creation can derail a government agenda, cast a government as a villain, or otherwise put the government squarely on the defensive, much to the consternation of policy makers and their battery of highly paid media consultants.

Radha Jhappan (1990), writing further to her dissertation entitled "The Language of Empowerment: Symbolic Politics and Indian Political Discourse in Canada" identifies *publicity-seeking* as one of six strategies involving the **manipulation of symbols** which First Nations have used for the internal political development of the First Nation population and for the presentation of First Nation political goals to the Canadian state and society.[19] Her assessment is that some First Nations have succeeded in using publicity-seeking quite effectively to wring concessions from governments under some circumstances. Had she been writing with the benefit of seeing the incorporation of aboriginal leaders into the Charlottetown Accord negotiations, she might have been less reserved in this assessment.

Jhappan's work is an important piece of scholarship on First Nations' political empowerment and it is significant that it is cast in the mould of the broader academic literature (e.g., Edelman, 1964 and 1971) on symbolic politics and political theatre. In Chapter Eight, Ponting and Symons attempt to build upon that by relating Cree protest to the sociological literature on "claims-making", professional social movements, "frame alignment" and federalism. Some aboriginal people resist subsuming aboriginal issues and phenomena under such larger, more abstract analytical frameworks. One senses that the use of those abstract perspectives is felt by them as an appropriation of aboriginal grievances or as a denigration of aboriginal concerns. That is most definitely not the intent nor, we hope, the effect, of our use of the broader theoretical literature.

As an academic, I believe that the use of such abstract analytical frameworks not only serves to advance theoretical insights (admittedly not a priority of most aboriginal people), but also permits a greater understanding of the aboriginal situation through the identification of points of commonality and points of difference with similar situations (e.g., situations in which a people is subordinated and marginalized). In turn, that understanding can provide aboriginal people with valuable insight into potential pitfalls encountered elsewhere and potentially effective strategies and tactics that have been successful elsewhere. To cite but one example from Jhappan's (1990: 21) use of Edelman's more abstract work, *condensation symbols* are symbols which are malleable, allow for a multiplicity of definitions, tend to induce emotional responses and provoke value judgements, and by their imprecision give the appearance of commonality while masking significant differences in interpretation between various users. As First Nations engage in "positional politics" — that is, as First Nations attempt to redefine their status and rights in Canadian society — the choice of the right symbols under which to advance their position becomes crucial. An awareness of the abstract theoretical term "condensation symbol" not only can guide the First Nation strategist in the selection or creation of symbols to use in the struggle, but can also alert him/her to expect later strains toward disunity among allies as they eventually come to appreciate the different meaning that they had been attaching to the symbols.

Political unity is one of the key issues facing First Nation leaders. In Chapter Three we observed that disunity, in the form of the Mercredi-Fontaine rivalry, had a major disempowering impact on the AFN at the time of the Charlottetown Accord. At time of writing, four years after the fiasco, AFN had still not recovered and Mercredi was still complaining of being circumvented by the Minister of Indian Affairs. Not even the controversial proposed amendments to the *Indian Act* in 1996 were able to unite the Mercredi and Fontaine factions. Without unity, though, the limits to AFN's empowerment will be very low, for disunity signals to the federal government that the AFN leader would still be unable to deliver the support of his constituents if the government were to enter another deal with him. That gulf between leader and constituents is ammunition to political enemies such as the Reform Party and gets reflected in the party's position, as seen in Point 7 in Box 2 earlier in this chapter.

The **Reform Party's** electoral prospects at time of writing looked highly uncertain. However, its influence should not be discounted, for it has a track record of being able to set the terms of the political debate[20] and its ideas are often incorporated, in whole or in part, into government policy. The 1996 *Indian Act* amendment proposals bear witness to that, as do numerous examples (e.g., fiscal policy, immigration policy, funding for the CBC, corrections policy) outside the realm of aboriginal affairs. If I am correct in my assessment of the Reform Party as nothing short of an enemy of the empowerment of First Nation peoples, and I fail to see how the party's positions can be interpreted in any other way, then First Nation leaders' strategy of "benign neglect" of the Reform Party should be seriously reconsidered.

Leadership is a fundamental aspect of political empowerment. At the community level, the pool of leadership talent is becoming broader and deeper through the acquisition of higher levels of formal education, the reinstatement of persons under Bill C-31, the reaching of maturity by the baby boomers, the reclaiming of talent previously unavailable due to escapism or abuse, and the acquisition of experience in degrees of self-government. As we look to the future, there are grounds for encouragement in this. However, a reading of Brown's Chapter Seven and of Crowfoot's chapter in Part 3 of this volume should caution us against unrestrained optimism, for the obstacles and constraints faced by First Nation chiefs (and by non-politicians) are also formidable.

Political empowerment is possible through the building of **strategic alliances**. At the national level, aboriginal organizations have seemed reluctant to form coalitions with anyone other than other aboriginal organizations. Distrust and a realistic assessment of the underlying contours of vested interests are probably important in explaining the paucity of aboriginal coalitions with non-aboriginal organizations. Even coalitions with other aboriginal organizations tend to come under enormous strain and are not always sustainable. At the level of communities, though, coalitions with non-Native organizations are more in evidence. Notable examples would include: the Nuu-chah-nulth Tribal Council with environmentalists on the issue of logging in Clayoquot Sound, B.C.; the Lubicon with the Christian churches; the Mohawks with European support groups; and the James Bay Cree with a wide variety of organizations such as American environmentalists and multinational lobby groups like Greenpeace International, Probe International, the National Audubon Society, and the Sierra Club. Notwithstanding these examples, the sensitivity which colonized people exhibit to any potential increase in dominance by the colonizing people, will perhaps always cause their leaders to approach coalitions with caution.

Closely related to political-legal power is **administrative power.** First Nations have made some clear gains here, as the DIAND bureaucracy has undergone a massive reduction in personnel and a considerable amount of money and decision-making authority has been transferred to bands and tribal councils. Many of these gains will persist, due to DIAND's desire to reduce its exposure to legal liability by diluting its fiduciary (trustee-like) responsibilities to First Nations.

In this, the information age, **information *is* power**. Crawford and Crawford (1995) maintain that swiftly evolving information and communication technologies and networking infrastructures are already playing an expanding role supporting the self-determination of peoples and emergent nations, such as in the Chiapas rebellion in Mexico. They write:

> Internally, access to information and facilitation of communication provides new and enhanced opportunities for participation in the process of self-determination, with the potential to accelerate political, economic, social, educational and cultural advancement beyond the scope of traditional institutions and forms of governance. Externally, regional and global information networks expand the voice of emergent nations and peoples with electronic forums to focus international attention and support toward specific self-determination issues and efforts.

As Ronfeldt (1992) notes, the distribution of power is increasingly a function of the differing abilities of governments and political organizations to use the new technologies, including informational technologies. He continues:

> Recognition is spreading in governments around the world that the new technologies may profoundly alter the nature of political power, sovereignty, and governance.

Near the outset of this chapter, manipulation of information was identified as one indicator of colonialism. First Nation leaders in Canada have long complained about what they consider to be DIAND's manipulation of information. In the information age, a closely related concern is that there will develop among the First Nations the informational "haves" and the informational "have-nots". Thus, access to the modern, computer-based communications technology becomes critical. In that regard, it is significant that Industry Canada, an arm of the federal government, has undertaken through its Aboriginal Community Internet Access Project to link four hundred First Nation schools to the information highway. Such linkage can be utilized by students and adults for such political purposes as sharing political intelligence and other information (e.g., on human rights, self-determination, sustainable development, mutual aid), building First Nation pride, and creating solidarity. The famous "moccasin telegraph", a long-standing informal communication network of aboriginal persons, moved into the electronic age with the telephone and the fax. E-mail followed and world-wide web sites and ftp file exchanges have also taken a place. Thus, the marriage of computers and telecommunications technology offers an important resource in combating the disempowering effects of the geographic dispersion of First Nations in Canada.

Eventually, many of the same points raised above as pertaining to the political relationship between First Nations and the larger Canadian state, will also be relevant at the level of internal relations within a given First Nation.

In concluding, it is important to mention **the law** as a source of empowerment. Chapter Six's treatment of the legal system focuses on the criminal law, but **constitutional law** is also of major importance. For instance, the Supreme Court of Canada's rulings on Sec. 35 of *The Constitution Act, 1982*,[21] as it applies to aboriginal fishing rights, was instrumental in shaping the conservation policy of the federal Department of Fisheries and Oceans for Fraser River salmon. Those same rulings are also key to understanding the ability of the Nisga'a to negotiate salmon entitlements for themselves in their 1996 comprehensive land claim settlement (Agreement-in-Principle) with the federal and British Columbia governments.

An authoritative analysis of constitutional developments, even since 1982, is beyond the scope of this book and the expertise of the author. Often, appearances in this realm are deceiving. For instance, the inclusion of the word "existing" in the above Section 35 of *The Constitution Act, 1982* was initially interpreted as a defeat by First Nation leaders, for the word was viewed as limiting those rights. However, that pessimism evaporated when the Supreme Court of Canada subsequently gave an expansive interpretation to those rights. Similarly, the Supreme Court of Canada's decision in the Sparrow fishing rights case was widely hailed as a victory for proponents of aboriginal rights, but Menno Boldt's (1993: 32–38) dissection of the decision is a trenchant critique of it. Boldt dismisses the Sparrow decision as a trivialization of aboriginal rights. Hence, it is too soon to determine whether the 1996 trilogy of Supreme Court of Canada decisions on the Van der Peet, Smokehouse, and Gladstone cases will be the major setback for First Nations' empowerment that they (especially van der Peet) initially appeared to be.

CONCLUSION

As if to underscore the previous sentence's point about indeterminacy, less than two minutes after it was written, the radio news carried a story of the Supreme

Court of Canada's October 1996 decision in two Québec aboriginal fishing rights cases — the Algonquins of Manawaki and the Mohawks of Akwesasne. In that news story the decision was hailed by respected law professor Douglas Sanders as a victory for aboriginal rights. Hence, the point is worth making that the *empowerment or disempowerment of aboriginal people is a phenomenon that can ebb and flow*. In most forms, aboriginal power is somewhat precarious, in part, one could hypothesize, because that power is of relatively recent origin and not yet institutionalized. For most forms of aboriginal power other than the power to embarrass others through publicity, there is no web of other actors with vested interests that have grown up around aboriginal interests in a symbiotic relationship.

Therefore, no gain in power is unassailable and some gains will prove paradoxical, as indeed is often the case with public policy outcomes in other fields. For instance, the gain in administrative power comes only at the cost of a reduction in the umbrella of protection offered by DIAND's fiduciary obligation. The transitory nature of empowerment is illustrated by the fact of the Lubicon victory with Alberta Premier Don Getty being subverted by bureaucrats within Getty's own government and then dashed when taken to the federal government. The James Bay Cree victory over Hydro-Québec could be reversed if the Québec government decides it needs the power or the revenues from its export. Natural resource revenue windfalls can be squandered, as happened with Natives in Alaska, or they could produce social disorientation (and a suicide epidemic) in a community, as happened with the Hobbema First Nations. Similarly, a community can make a commitment to sobriety, but a child's suicide could cause it to come entirely unravelled. It is even conceivable that the inherent right to aboriginal self-government could be entrenched in the constitution, but that the implementation of it could be a colossal failure. To take a final example, the gains in informational power made through the internet could be lost if the internet were to come crashing down under its own weight, as some computer experts predict will happen.

The corollary to the above hypothesis, though, is that precisely because power relationships involving aboriginals are in *a state of flux*, few defeats are irreversible either. The aboriginal defeat at the 1987 First Ministers' conference was reversed in the Charlottetown Accord. Just as Ovide Mercredi's astonishing victory at the Charlottetown bargaining table was rendered hollow (and Mercredi politically impotent) by Phil Fontaine's political manoeuvers at Squamish, so, too, could events, such as another referendum in Québec, propel him or his successor back to the centre of the political stage. Overwhelming opposition to special status in a public opinion poll in 1986 was found to have softened by the time a similarly comprehensive poll was taken in 1994, as we shall observe in the next chapter. It is even conceivable that prevailing conceptions of "the national interest" could change, such that the powerful actors who now define that "national interest" could, like corporate giant Inco at Voisey's Bay, come to regard it as being in their best interest to have a resolution of aboriginal claims and grievances.

In closing, one implication of the high degree of fluidity and indeterminacy of First Nation power relations should be noted. That is, just as it is unwise for First Nation people and their supporters to become too euphoric over any given instance of empowerment, so, too, is it unwise to allow oneself to become despondent over setbacks. While there is such a phenomenon as a momentum to social change, over the short-term future many forms of aboriginal empowerment, with the probable exception of cultural empowerment, might well follow either the pendulum model of social change or the "two steps forward, one step back" model.

NOTES

[1] Data published by the Royal Commission on Aboriginal Peoples (1996c: 126) suggest that a more accurate term would be "scoop of the seventies", for rates of Registered Indian children in care climbed throughout the 1970s to a peak of 6.5% of on-reserve children in 1976–77 and 1978–79. The highest rate reported there for the total Canadian population was 1.3% in 1971–72. By the late 1980s the curve for Registered Indians had descended and levelled off at about 4.0%.

[2] "Money-moving" departments, of which there are many in the federal government, are departments which have as one of their main roles the allocation and transfer of money to recipient organizations.

[3] The proposed amendments to the *Indian Act*, issued September 18, 1996, were posted on the world wide web at http://www.inca.gc.ca/news/sept96/9638pl. html. They did not contain any provisions for eliminating or curtailing the Minister's power of disallowance over band bylaws, although they did propose the repeal of some other provisions that were highly paternalistic (e.g., the Sec. 32 requirement of ministerial permission for prairie First Nations, or their individual members, to sell their agricultural produce and livestock off-reserve). The proposed amendments were not well received by The Assembly of First Nations. A detailed reply to the proposals appeared on the AFN home page at http://www.afn.ca/ The gist of the critique was that the proposed amendments and other aspects of federal policy were an attempt to implement the assimilation and termination policy of the reviled 1969 white paper. Elsewhere (*First Perspective On-line Newspaper*, October 1996 issue at website http://portal.mbnet.mb.ca/firstper/index.html), AFN Grand Chief Ovide Mercredi labelled the proposals little more than a veiled attempt by Ottawa to help the business community increase its commercial opportunities with Indian communities. The changes, he pointed out, could ultimately result in Indian people losing their land in business deals. When the Minister introduced the amendments in the House of Commons on December 12, 1996, he was booed from the public gallery by First Nation leaders.

[4] These two incidents are described by Ann Anderson in the film *The Learning Path*. The Assembly of First Nations (1994: 41) recounts similar incidents. In First Nation cultures, first menstruation was treated as a rite of passage into womanhood and the girl would be taken aside by the female elders for special teaching and social support. The contrast with the degradation of the girl described by Anderson could scarcely be more stark.

[5] Examples include having one's tongue pricked with a pin for speaking one's Native language, receiving a strapping thirty times on each hand, isolation for days without food or water, being forced to kneel for hours on the floor,

[6] Canadian Press (1995) reports three such incidents in British Columbia alone.

[7] Miller (1996: 345–358) documents cases of parental resistance including withholding students from the school, petitions to authorities in the church or government, defecting to a competing denomination's school, litigation and threatened criminal charges, and against the brutal Father Mackey at Shubenacadie, even a planned assassination.

[8] Of course, political parties sometimes attract such extremists or seek to foment extremism for the parties' political gain. According to Denike (1995) there is significant Reform Party representation among the leaders of B.C. F.I.R.E. and On F.I.R.E. The website address for B.C. F.I.R.E. is http://www.vip.net/~bcfire/

[9] This is not intended as a criticism of legal aid lawyers. Rather, legal aid lawyers tend to be poorly paid by the provincial government; therefore, they are not likely to be able to devote a great deal of time to any given legal aid case.

[10] Hydro-Québec is a government corporation, not privately owned. However, its raison d'être and that of the James Bay II project are intimately linked to capitalism (e.g., the provision of electricity at cheap rates to attract industrial investment to Québec; the export of power to meet the needs of industry and residential consumers in the U.S. northeast).

[11] Wotherspoon and Satzewich (1993: 260) cite the sharpening of class divisions within the aboriginal community as a danger associated with some aboriginal economic development strategies. The same argument might apply to some of the economic development provisions of comprehensive claims settlements.

[12] The reduction of government deficits is consistent with corporate interests in several ways. For instance, lower government deficits can clear the way for lower corporate and personal income taxes. In addition, lower government deficits tend to depress interest rates, which makes it less expensive for corporations to borrow money to finance expansion.

[13] Indeed, various statutes define a person as "any individual or corporation".

[14] The second clause of the resolution's preamble reads: "[The European Parliament,] concerned about the unjustified seizure of land by the Canadian authorities in order to make an extension for a golf course...".

[15] The other beneficiary groups are women, the disabled, and "visible minorities".

[16] Another criticism, empirically substantiatable, is that affirmative action programs tend to help disproportionately the middle class of the target groups and, among the target groups, white women. See Fine (1992).

[17] Data in this section from the 1991 Aboriginal Peoples Survey are taken from Statistics Canada (1993: *passim*).

[18] Among on-reserve First Nation persons who had never learned how to speak their aboriginal language, an overwhelming majority (87%) expressed an interest in learning.

[19] The other strategies are: community-building, symbolic reversal, symbolic competition, "using the system", and routinization of conflict.

[20] By injecting its extremist position into the political debate, the party sometimes has the effect of shifting government agendas by shifting what policy makers consider to be middle ground.

[21] Section 35. (1) reads: "The existing aboriginal and treaty rights of the aboriginal peoples of Canada are hereby recognized and affirmed". See also Appendix B.

REFERENCES

Assembly of First Nations
1994   *Breaking the Silence: An Interpretive Study of Residential School Impact and Healing as Illustrated by the Stories of First Nations Individuals.* Ottawa: First Nations Health Commission.
Barman, Jean, Yvonne Hébert, and Don McCaskill
1987   *The Challenge of Indian Education in Canada.* Vancouver: University of British Columbia Press.

Barnett, Vicki
1995 "Special Report: Stoney Logging Practices Slammed", *Calgary Herald*, January 29, A1 and A9.
Blauner, Robert
1969 "Internal Colonialism and Ghetto Revolt", *Social Problems* XVI: 393–408.
Boldt, Menno
1993 *Surviving as Indians.* Toronto: University of Toronto Press.
Canadian Press
1992 "Samsom (sic) Band Will Get $400 million", *Calgary Herald*, January 18, A9.

——— 1995 "Native Residential Schools: Child-killing Claims Surface in Police Probe — Native Elder Recalls Boy Fatally Strapped for Theft of a Prune", *Calgary Herald*, December 21, B12.

——— 1996 "Banking: New Bank Geared Toward Natives", *Calgary Herald*, Sept. 17: F5.
Coolican, Murray
1985 *Living Treaties, Lasting Agreements: Report of the Task Force to Review Comprehensive Land Claims Policy.* Ottawa: Department of Indian Affairs and Northern Development.
Crawford, Mark and Kekula Crawford
1995 "Self-Determination in the Information Age." Posted at the Hawaii Nation website at http://info.isoc.org/HMP/PAPER/230/html/paper.html
Denike, Brian (producer)
1995 "Playing with Fire", CBC (television) News Magazine documentary, November 15.
DIAND
1996 *Basic Departmental Data — 1995.* Ottawa: Departmental Statistics Section, Information Management Branch (DIAND).

——— 1997 *Basic Departmental Data — 1996.* Ottawa: Departmental Statistics Section, Information Management Branch.
Edelman, Murray
1964 *The Symbolic Uses of Politics.* Urbana, Illinois: University of Illinois Press.

——— 1971 *Politics as Symbolic Action.* Chicago: Markham Publishing.
Fine, Sean
1992 "Equity Law's First Report Card", *Globe and Mail*, Dec. 30, A1.
Frideres, James
1993 *Native Peoples in Canada: Contemporary Conflicts.* Scarborough, Ont.: Prentice-Hall.
Goffman, Erving
1962 *Asylums: Essays on the Social Situation of Mental Patients and Other Inmates.* Chicago: Aldine.
Haig-Brown, Celia
1988 *Resistance and Renewal: Surviving the Indian Residential School.* Vancouver: Tillacum.
Isajiw, Wsevolod W.
1990 "Ethnic-Identity Retention", pp. 34–91 in Raymond Breton et al., *Ethnic Identity and Equality: Varieties of Experience in a Canadian City.* Toronto: University of Toronto Press.
Jaremko, Gordon
1996 "CIBC Backs Native Programs at Banff Centre", *Calgary Herald*, October 16, D2.

Jhappan, C. Radha
1990   "Indian Symbolic Politics: The Double-Edged Sword of Publicity", *Canadian Ethnic Studies* XXII, 3: 19–39.
King, A. Richard
1967   *The School at Mopass*. Toronto: Holt, Rinehart, and Winston.
Knockwood, Isabelle
1992   *Out of the Depths: The Experiences of Mi'kmaw Children at the Indian Residential School at Shubenacadie, Nova Scotia*. Lockeport, N.S.: Roseway Publishing.
Maclean, Mairi
1996   "Banking: Native Communities Attract Better Service", *Edmonton Journal*, reprinted in *Calgary Herald*, May 9, D8.
Miller, J. R.
1996   *Shingwauk's Vision: A History of Native Residential Schools*. Toronto: University of Toronto Press.
Mofina, Rick
1996a "Survey Finds RCMP Rife with Harassment", *Calgary Herald*, Sept. 26, A1–A2.

1996b "Force Fights Racism: Survey Reveals Problems", *Calgary Herald*, Sept. 27, A1–A2.
Moon, Peter
1994   "Mohawk Smuggling Continues to Boom: Can't Stop It, Officer Says", *Globe and Mail*, June 29, A1, A6.
Parkin, Frank
1979   *Marxism and Class Theory: A Bourgeois Critique*. London: Tavistock.
Panich, Leo
1977   *The Canadian State: Political Economy and Political Power*. Toronto: University of Toronto Press.
Platiel, Rudy
1996   "Gambling With the Future: Casino Jackpot for Chippewa is Jobs", *Globe and Mail*, July 26, A6.
Ponting, J. Rick and Roger Gibbins
1980   *Out of Irrelevance*. Scarborough: Butterworth.
Ponting, J. Rick
1986   "Relations between Bands and the Department of Indian Affairs: A Case of Internal Colonialism?", pp. 84–111 in J. Rick Ponting (ed.), *Arduous Journey: Canadian Indians and Decolonization*. Toronto: McClelland and Stewart/Oxford.

1987   *Profiles of Public Opinion on Canadian Natives and Native Issues, Module 3*. Calgary: The University of Calgary.

1990   "Internationalization: Perspectives on An Emerging Direction in Aboriginal Affairs", *Canadian Ethnic Studies*, XXII, 3: 85–109.
Reform Party of Canada
1996   *Blue Book, 1996–97*. Calgary: Reform Party of Canada.
Ronfeldt, David.
1992   "Cyberocracy is Coming," Copyright Taylor & Francis. Posted on the web at http://gopher.well.sf.ca.us:70/0/whole_systems/cyberocracy
Royal Commission on Aboriginal People (RCAP)
1996a *Final Report of The Royal Commission on Aboriginal People; Vol. 1: Looking Forward, Looking Back*. Ottawa: Minister of Supply and Services Canada.

1996b *Final Report of The Royal Commission on Aboriginal People; Vol. 2: Restructuring the Relationship.* Ottawa: Minister of Supply and Services Canada.

1996c *Final Report of The Royal Commission on Aboriginal People; Vol. 3: Gathering Strength.* Ottawa: Minister of Supply and Services Canada.

1996e *Final Report of The Royal Commission on Aboriginal People; Vol. 5: Renewal: A Twenty-Year Commitment.* Ottawa: Minister of Supply and Services Canada.
Shkilnyk, Anastasia M.
1985 *A Poison Stronger Than Love: The Destruction of an Ojibwa Community.* New Haven, Conn.: Yale University Press.
Statistics Canada
1993 *Language, Tradition, Health, Lifestyle, and Social Issues — 1991 Aboriginal Peoples Survey.* Cat. # 89-533. Ottawa: Minister of Industry, Science, and Technology.
Wotherspoon, Terry and Vic Satzewick
1993 *First Nations: Race, Class, and Gender Relations.* Scarborough, Ont.: Nelson Canada.

FURTHER READING

Rotman, Leonard I.
1996 *Parallel Paths: Fiduciary Doctrine and the Crown-Native Relationship in Canada.* Toronto: University of Toronto Press.

CHAPTER 6

DISEMPOWERMENT: "JUSTICE", RACISM, AND PUBLIC OPINION[1]

J. Rick Ponting and Jerilynn Kiely

"JUSTICE"

Ostensibly, the Canadian justice system is designed to protect private property and uphold the individual rights and freedoms of Canadian citizens. However, for First Nations people, to encounter Canada's criminal justice system is to enter an adversarial world of bureaucracy, intimidation, coercion, confrontation, and punishment. Not surprisingly, First Nation individuals and other aboriginal people tend to view Canada's justice system as one that is designed to perpetuate alienation and powerlessness.

Since words describing many of the occidental legal concepts are non-existent in most aboriginal languages, it follows that aboriginal world views of justice tend to differ from those of non-aboriginal Canadians.[2] The Assembly of First Nations (1993: 65, cited in RCAP, 1996: 3) describes an holistic conception of justice which is based on a traditional, communal lifestyle and permeates every aspect of aboriginal daily life:

> A justice system from the perspective of First Nations is more than a set of rules or institutions to regulate individual conduct or to prescribe procedures to achieve justice in the abstract. "Justice" refers instead to an aspect of the natural order in which everyone and everything stands in relation to each other. Actions of individuals reflect the natural harmony of the community and of the world itself. Justice must be a felt experience, not merely a thought. It must, therefore, be an internal experience, not an intrusive state of order, imposed from the outside, and separate from one's experience of reality... Justice has traditionally been the daily, shared experience of citizens of the community ... part of the sense of responsibility felt by every community member for the other and for the creatures and forces that sustain all human life.

Thus, among First Nation peoples, justice, harmony and social life are inseparable. When an offence occurs, communities guided by this **restitutive model** of justice seek to heal the entire community in order to restore and maintain social harmony. Box 1 provides the Cawsey commission's[3] summary comparison of these conflicting models of justice. That comparison attests to the high potential for conflict when First Nation people encounter the system of justice imposed by the dominant Canadian society.

BOX 1 Two Models of Justice and Dispute Resolution: Retribution vs. Restoration

Non-Aboriginal Retributive Model	Aboriginal Restitutive Model
Crime is a violation of the state	Crime is a violation of one person by another.
Focus on establishing blame or guilt	Focus on problem solving and restoration of harmony
Truth is found through an adversarial relationship between the offender and the state	Dialogue and negotiation are normative
Punishment deters and prevents and is used to make offender accountable	Restitution and reconciliation are used as a means of restoration
Justice is defined by intent and process (right rules)	Justice is harmony and right relationship
Community does not play a leading role	Community acts as a facilitator in the restorative process
Action revolves around the offender	Offender is impressed with the impact of his action on the total order
Offences are strictly legal and devoid of moral, social, political and economic considerations	The holistic context of an offence is taken into consideration, including moral, socio-economic, political, and religious and cosmic considerations
Social stigma of criminal behaviour is almost indelible	Stigma of offences is removable through conformity
Remorse, restitution, and forgiveness are not important factors	Remorse, repentance and forgiveness are important factors
Offenders play a passive role and are dependent on proxy professionals	Offenders take an active role in the restorative process

Source: Cawsey (1991, Vol. I, Ch. 9: 6).

Aboriginal Over-Representation in the Criminal Justice System

Most Canadians take pride in the belief that ours is a just society, governed by rule of law, with one law applying equally to everyone. Actually, though, that is largely a myth. Not only do different sectors of Canadian society experience differential treatment in law,[4] but aboriginal people are disproportionately represented among those charged, convicted, and incarcerated.

Since the 1967 publication of the Canadian Corrections Association report, *Indians and the Law*, policy makers have been inundated with documented examples of how Canada's criminal justice system has failed First Nation peoples and, in spite of over fifteen hundred recommendations, continues to do so (RCAP, 1996). For instance, the report of The Aboriginal Justice Inquiry of Manitoba opens with this blunt condemnation of the system's inability to deliver justice to aboriginal people:

The justice system has failed Manitoba's Aboriginal people on a massive scale. It has been insensitive and inaccessible, and has arrested and imprisoned Aboriginal people in grossly disproportionate numbers. Aboriginal people who are arrested are more likely than non-Aboriginal people to be denied bail, spend more time in pre-trial detention and spend less time with their lawyers, and, if convicted, are more likely to be incarcerated. It is not merely that the justice system has failed Aboriginal people; justice also has been denied them. For more than a century the rights of Aboriginal people have been ignored and eroded.

(Hamilton and Sinclair, 1991: 16)

The rule of law works to disempower aboriginal people by stripping them of their liberty and dignity. Historically, colonialists have used the culturally-specific western conception of justice and dispute resolution to dismiss all aboriginal world views of justice. This was done without considering that, prior to colonization, the holistic approach of Canada's indigenous people functioned for millennia to maintain harmony and balance in society. The colonizers' euro-centric bias denigrated all aboriginal systems of governance on the basis of being merely "primitive customs", or "savage" and "uncivilized" practices. Accordingly, aboriginal people were stereotyped as "pagans", "savages" and "heathens". These misperceptions have had serious repercussions for aboriginal societies because they "[have] provided a moral justification for imposing western concepts of law and justice in ever-widening geographical and conceptual arcs" (RCAP, 1996: 12–14).

Although the fact that Native people are disproportionately represented in Canada's criminal justice system is well documented, this disconcerting social problem is largely unmitigated and is intensifying. This observation alone provides the most dramatic and overwhelming evidence for the justice system's failure to protect and serve aboriginal peoples (RCAP, 1996: 28–29). What this means is that without wholesale transformation of the criminal justice system, the harshest punishments will continue to be meted out to Native people (Jackson, 1988: 1). Box 2 shows that this imbalance is not simply one of too many aboriginal people being sent to jail; it occurs at every juncture of the judicial process.[5]

Scope and Magnitude of Aboriginal Over-representation

The Canadian Bar Association describes the statistics on Native people in the criminal justice system as "so stark and appalling that the magnitude of the problem can be neither misunderstood nor interpreted away" (Jackson, 1988: 2).

LaPrairie et al. (1996) document the contemporary extent of over-representation of aboriginal people in detention. Most of their statistics deal with all aboriginal people, rather than only Registered Indians. As of 1996, aboriginal people constitute roughly 3% of the total Canadian population of thirty million. Hence, LaPrairie et al.'s (1996: 47) report of the Canadian Centre for Justice Statistics' data showing aboriginal people to account for 12% of federal admissions (1989–94 average) and 20% of provincial admissions, is jarring. These data are reproduced in Table 1. Even more shocking is the provincial breakdown of those figures, which shows aboriginals to account for 55% of federal admissions and 69% of provincial admissions in Saskatchewan. Indeed, for all of the prairie provinces the figures are extremely high.

BOX 2 Systemic Discrimination within the Criminal Justice System

Each stage of the judicial process is punctuated with a disproportionate number of aboriginal people. Statistics summarized below suggest that aboriginal people are victims of a discriminatory criminal justice system.

- Lawyers spend less time with their aboriginal clients than with non-aboriginal clients
- Aboriginal accused are more likely to be denied bail
- Aboriginal people spend more time in pre-trial detention than do non-aboriginal people
- Aboriginal accused are more likely to be charged with multiple offences than are non-aboriginal accused
- Aboriginal offenders are more than twice as likely as non-aboriginal clients to be incarcerated
- More than half of the inmates of Manitoba's jails are aboriginal

Source: Sincair and Hamilton (1991: 86)

Using data from the early 1990s for provinces from Ontario westward, LaPrairie et al. (1996: 49) also report sentencing data in the form of sentenced admissions of aboriginal and non-aboriginal people, per 10,000 people in their respective aboriginal or non-aboriginal populations. The aboriginal rates range from a low of 115 (Ontario) to a high of 681 (Alberta) and average 323. Non-aboriginal rates range from 20 to 94 and average 39 per 10,000 population. Aboriginal sentenced admission rates are almost 25 times higher than non-aboriginal rates in Saskatchewan, about 10 times higher in Manitoba, over 7 times higher in Alberta, over 4 times as high in British Columbia, and over 3 times as

TABLE 1 Aboriginal Admissions to Federal and Provincial Institutions, and Probation Intakes, by Province, 1989–1994 (averaged)

Province or Territory	Aboriginal Admissions as % of Total Federal Admissions	Aboriginal Admissions as % of Total Provincial Admissions	Aboriginal Probation Intake as % of Total Intake
British Columbia	16.2	17.0	15.9
Alberta	23.6	33.4	22.9
Saskatchewan	54.8	69.2	58.5
Manitoba	42.2	48.8	45.6
Ontario	3.8	7.4	4.6
Quebec	2.6	2.0	4.3
New Brunswick	3.6	5.7	—
Nova Scotia	3.2	3.7	3.9
Prince Edward Is.	6.5	3.3	—
Newfoundland	6.6	4.0	5.1
NWT	89.0	90.3	92.5
Yukon	32.4	62.1	73.5
Total	**11.8**	**19.9**	**15.3**

Source: LaPrairie et al. (1996: 47) and Canadian Centre for Justice Statistics (1993).

high in Ontario. On average, across the five provinces, aboriginal rates are 8.28 times higher than non-aboriginal rates

Explanations of Over-Representation

If the needed radical change of Canada's criminal justice system is to occur, it is not enough to simply be aware of the scope and magnitude of the problem. Discovering *why* this troubling phenomenon occurs is essential. Accordingly, the search for the root cause of aboriginal "criminality" has occupied social researchers and government departments for almost thirty years. From this extensive body of research, the Royal Commission on Aboriginal People (RCAP) has identified three main strands of attempted explanation for this tragic social problem: cultural conflict, socio-economic deprivation, and systemic discrimination.

Now, central to understanding the root cause of aboriginal social problems is acknowledgment of the devastating effect of colonialism[6] on aboriginal societies. Hence, every explanation must always be understood in the light of the influence of this imposed world view and moral code and its complete dismissal of other peoples, cultures, and experiences that have existed for thousands of years (RCAP, 1996: 40–47). The ruthless impact of this historical process on the lives of First Nation people cannot be overstated. Indeed, Monture-Angus (1996) argues that until Canada acknowledges the fundamental role played by colonialism, the ongoing problem of aboriginal subjugation is immutable.

Aboriginal "criminality" is a complex issue. In seeking to understand it, we must bear in mind that one theory alone is unlikely to provide all the desired insights and answers. In addition, although different First Nations share some common ground, like other Canadians, aboriginal individuals and peoples are unique in various other respects.

A. Cultural Conflict Explanations

Cultural clash between First Nations peoples and other Canadians is one of the most pervasive explanations for the crisis of aboriginal over-representation in the justice system. This explanation has several variants, the worst of which holds that aboriginal people should assimilate into Canadian society but have not done so due to limitations of aboriginal cultures. This ethnocentric bias favours the Euro-Canadian legal culture over aboriginal values, beliefs, and traditions. Because it points to the inability of aboriginal peoples to adapt to Canadian culture, this view has been a primary source of alienation and disempowerment among First Nation people. Its underlying assumption of aboriginal inferiority leads to the characterization of individual Native people as deviants who are incapable of integrating into Canadian society. Hence, the source of the problem is seen as the personal failure of aboriginal people to adapt to the Canadian judicial system. Other variants of cultural conflict theory are more value-neutral and have some use in advancing our understanding of both policing and the courts.

(i) Differential Policing   From the beginning, the relationship between aboriginal people and Canadian police forces has been paternalistic. In the early

years of Confederation, the Royal Canadian Mounted Police (RCMP) functioned both as law enforcers and as benefactors to Indians starving in harsh winter climes. This contrary relationship set the stage for contemporary extremes of over-policing and under-policing of aboriginal people. Over-policing occurs when police patrol areas where they expect to see Native people gathering together. Based on the stereotypical notion of the "drunken Indian", police search for Native people in bars and back alleys. Because they sometimes find what they expect to see, Native people are arrested and detained more often than non-Native Canadians. The Rolf (1991) commission's inquiry into *Policing in Relation to the Blood Tribe* (in Alberta) concluded that cultural conflict was at the root of aboriginal people's allegation of over-policing during a blockade at Cardston, Alberta. In this instance, the RCMP maintained that the use of force was required to make arrests and to take people to jail. The Blood tribe, on the other hand, perceived these actions as abusive. Because the Blood tribe traditionally resolved incidents by cleansing the perpetrator and compensating the aggrieved (in order to restore equanimity in the community), the Bloods argued that the role of the RCMP was to simply remove the cause of disruption. Conflict arose, Rolf concluded, because the police were not sensitive to these cultural differences (Alberta, February 1991: 185–186).

In the case of under-policing, Brodeur's study for the Grand Council of the Crees of Québec found that "aboriginal communities received proportionately greater law enforcement attention and proportionately less peace-keeping and other services" (Brodeur, 1991: 16–17, cited in RCAP, 1996: 37–39). Brodeur concludes that aboriginal people are more likely than non-aboriginal people, to be arrested and charged for minor or petty offences and less likely to receive police protection in the event of serious crimes. Under-policing can be tantamount to blaming the victim, for it is sometimes rooted in the stereotypical view that criminality is normative in aboriginal culture and that it therefore is not noteworthy and does not warrant serious police response. Unfortunately, under-policing places women and children involved in domestic disputes in particularly vulnerable positions.

(ii) Cultural Conflict in the Courts   Research has shown that, compared to other Canadians, aboriginal people are less likely to plea bargain or to have the benefit of a negotiated plea (RCAP, 1996: 41). Moreover, aboriginal people are also more likely to plead guilty. People will often plead guilty, simply because they are arrested, even when they know they are innocent. The Elizabeth Fry Society of Calgary (1990: 4, cited in Cawsey, 1991, Ch. 4: 28–29) offers this distressing explanation:

> Even more tragic is the consistent statement of these people to us: "I pled guilty and got a $100.00 fine. If I didn't, I'd have to stay in jail for weeks, I'd probably be found guilty anyways and still have to pay the fine." The reality for people in this plight is that they are deliberately pleading guilty to offences, irrespective of their real guilt or lack of guilt, in order to get out of jail.

Some observers suggest that as aboriginal people proceed through the courts, at each step of the way to the sentencing or trial stage, they are less likely than non-aboriginals to understand either what has occurred, or the reason for the occurrence. The debilitating humiliation brought on by this inability to understand proceedings further alienates Native people trapped in the judicial process. Regrettably, the following comment by a young Native person is not uncommon:

> The Judge said something to me. He used many big words. Then he asked me if I understood. I said no. He asked me again if I understood. This made me feel stupid. Though I did not understand I said yes. I knew I would never understand.[7]

Defendants are not the only ones to experience alienation in the courtroom. In his account of his experiences among the Cree and Ojibway of northern Ontario, Crown Prosecutor Rupert Ross (1992) tells of witnesses who, in spite of having provided articulate pre-trial testimonies, virtually hide under their jackets in a cloak of seemingly intimidated silence when they take the witness stand.

(iii) Deterrence and the Norm of Non-Interference   As Sinclair (1994: 29, cited in RCAP, 1996: 41) notes, non-aboriginal Canadians sometimes ask themselves: "What is it about aboriginal people that causes them to behave like that?" This individualizes the problem by situating the responsibility within the character of the Native person. Asked from the point of view of the dominant culture, the question fails to take into consideration that every society's world view brings with it a unique range of attitudes and behaviours. Ross found that, in his experience, ancient norms are applied even to aspects of contemporary Native life. For instance, he discovered that many of his clients complied with what Mohawk psychiatrist, Clare Brant, calls "the ethic of non-interference". A principle tenet of many aboriginal cultures, this norm of non-interference is easily misinterpreted by other Canadians. Brant explains:

> This principle essentially means that an Indian will never interfere in any way with the rights, privileges and activities of another person ... [it] is all-pervasive throughout our culture. We are very loathe to confront people. We are very loathe to give advice to anyone if the person is not specifically asking for advice. To interfere or even comment on their behaviour is considered rude.

> (Ross, 1992: 12–13).

Knowing about this principle helps us to understand why many aboriginal people have difficulty testifying in Canada's confrontational courts of law. Every facet of the adversarial, blame-seeking courtroom drama violates this ethic. Box 3 gives Ross' account of how one First Nation father put this principle into practice in an attempt to prevent his son from engaging in further unlawful behaviour.

(iv) Indigenization Initiatives   Governments have attempted to reduce the impact of cultural clash through "indigenization" initiatives such as the use of aboriginal court workers who are fluent in an aboriginal language. Ostensibly, the goal of these programs is to demystify the criminal justice system for aboriginal people in order to facilitate the judicial process. Overall, the initiatives often do succeed in reducing alienation; however, they do nothing to change the way Native people are treated within the larger system. Designed to make a particular part of the existing system more responsive to aboriginal people, the programs tend to focus on changing and educating individual offenders (RCAP, 1996). Singling out the individual offender reinforces the belief that over-repre-

---

BOX 3 The Norm of Non-Interference

[M]any things … seemed to make sense only if viewed from within such a rule. In particular, there was one court case which had stayed as a puzzle in the minds of many people. A young Indian lad had pleaded guilty to breaking into a reserve school at four in the morning with a group of friends, and trashing the teachers' lounge. The judge asked him what his parents had done when they found out about such outrageous behaviour. He replied that they had done nothing. The judge asked if his parents had said anything. Again, the response was a flat no. Angered by this apparent absence of parental concern, the judge turned directly to the boy's father. He asked him if he'd responded in *any* way to his son's intolerable conduct. The father answered that he had hidden the boy's shoes at night.

Hidden the boy's shoes at night? No punishment? No lecturing? No taking him to the teachers for an apology? No offer to have him clean up the mess? To many people in the courtroom, that was as feeble a demonstration of care and concern as could be imagined … some people chuckled when they heard it; it seemed almost as if the father was afraid of his boy, as if he wanted to keep him at home without ever letting him know that's what he was doing.

That, of course, was precisely what he was attempting to do, but not out of fear of the boy. Rather, it was out of obedience to the rule against interference in the lives of others, even children, and even for their own good. In his own mind, the father had gone even farther than he should have gone in trying to control his son's behaviour. In our minds, however, he had done virtually nothing.

Source: Ross (1992: 17–8).

---

sentation and feelings of alienation are problems attributable to the personal failure of aboriginal people (Monture-Angus, 1996). Politicians, reformers, and the Canadian public in general are absolved from having to consider whether it is something about the "justice" system itself that has failed Native people.

Other indigenization initiatives include: aboriginal paralegal programs; information kits, instructional audio and video tapes in aboriginal languages; aboriginal law school programs; and the recruitment or appointment of aboriginal justices of the peace and aboriginal judges. The idea behind having aboriginal judges in the courtroom is to put the offenders at ease by showing them that this is not simply "white man's justice".

An interesting dilemma arises in the area of language. In most of the provinces, only English and French are allowed in the courtroom.[8] Consequently, those who cannot speak these languages must use an interpreter even if both the Justice of the Peace and the accused speak the same language. The fact that the fundamental legal concept of "guilty/not guilty" is not part of many aboriginal languages, presents problems for the interpreter. The Dene Tha´ Band of Assumption (1990: 12) points out that in the Dene Tha´ language, the word for "police" ("Dene Kuelehi") means "those people who put people in jail". Meanwhile "judge" ("Dene Kuelehiti") is "the big boss of those who put people in jail". Clearly, language creates problems for how the concept of justice is understood by these people in the courtroom.

Employing aboriginal court workers has been somewhat successful because of its compatibility with the Native concept of justice. The role of these workers is to "help aboriginal accused persons understand their rights in the criminal justice process and to explain the process as it unfolds" (RCAP, 1996: 96). Because court workers are not in positions of authority, they are received more as friends and counsellors who facilitate understanding and healing within an alien judicial system. This is particularly important for aboriginal women and children from violent homes (RCAP, 1996: 97–98).

Indigenization is popular with governments. In the province of Ontario alone, almost 90% of the nearly four million dollars spent on aboriginal justice initiatives goes toward indigenization programs. While aboriginal people can receive some benefit from these programs, it could be argued that the real winners are governments. That is, implementing indigenization programs almost precludes politicians from looking at changing the larger social system to be more responsive to First Nation peoples. LaPrairie (1988: 3) elaborates:

> What indigenization fails to do, however, is to address in any fundamental way the criminal justice problems which result from the *socio-economic marginality*. The real danger of an exclusively indigenized approach is that the problems may appear to be "solved"; little more will be attempted, partly because indigenization is a very visible activity. (Emphasis not in original.)

The correlation between poverty and criminality is well established. This has led to the practice of locating the root cause of aboriginal over-representation in Native peoples' state of socio-economic deprivation. While there is no doubt that Native people are disproportionately impoverished, correlations (no matter how strong) do not imply causality. However, RCAP (1996: 42) argues that economic and social marginality is a primary contributor to disproportionate aboriginal "criminality". The rationale behind this explanation cannot be discounted. We turn to it below.

B. Socio-Economic Deprivation Explanations

This approach arises out of the limitations of explanations and ameliorative approaches based on the notion of cultural deficiency. The demography chapter of this volume and other research findings (RCAP, 1996: 42) show that on every index of socio-economic well-being, aboriginal people are the most bereft peoples in Canada. Alberta's Cawsey commission (1991) noted that the reality of everyday life for many First Nation individuals living on reserves is one of abject poverty coupled with rampant unemployment that soars as high as 90%. Is it any wonder that many young Native adults cannot attend post-secondary institutions? For many of these young people, prison terms have replaced college semesters (Jackson, 1988: 3).[9] In addition to coping with these humiliating, debilitating circumstances, many First Nation individuals must contend with the residual effects of the residential school experience. Turpel (1993: 166–167) elaborates on the extensive web of interdependencies involved:

> From economic and social disempowerment to problems in the criminal justice system, aboriginal peoples' issues are seemingly indivisible — one crosses over to another in an interconnected and almost continuous fashion. Alcoholism in aboriginal communities is connected to unemployment. Unemployment is connected to the denial of hunting, trapping and gathering economic practices. Dispossession of land is in turn connected to loss of cultural and spiritual identity and is a manifestation of bureaucratic control over all aspects of life. *This oppressive web can be seen as one of disempowerment of communities and individual aboriginal citizens.* (Emphasis not in original.)

The Royal Commission on Aboriginal Peoples concluded that two of the most damaging consequences of this oppressive social and economic deprivation are a high incidence of aboriginal crime and the grossly disproportionate number of aboriginal men, women and young people in Canada's criminal "justice" system (RCAP, 1996: 42).

A well-documented example of how poverty penalizes aboriginal people in the justice system is in the area of non-payment of fines. Shocking numbers of aboriginal people are in Canadian jails for this infraction. For example, Quigley (1994: 270) found that in Saskatchewan in 1992-1993, almost three quarters of the people in jail for fine default were of aboriginal descent. Thus, "aboriginal people go to prison for being poor" (RCAP, 1996: 43). Of course, many of these people live in communities where unemployment rates are so staggering that most people in the community lack the means to independently provide for their families. Their indignation over then receiving a jail sentence for fine default is difficult for most non-Native Canadians to fathom. As a further assault on their dignity, those charged with a second offence usually receive an automatic sentence. The Cawsey report explains:

> [S]ome Judges keep a "black book" on offenders. ... By means of [this] system, a Judge keeps a tally on those who have failed to meet time limits on previous occasions. When appearing in court again, accused persons do not get time to pay if their names have been entered in the "black book" previously... For a person who is not part of the wage economy and receives welfare, *this sentencing is discriminatory*. It should not continue. (Emphasis not in original.)

Despite the introduction of fine option programs, the Manitoba Aboriginal Justice Inquiry found that aboriginal people are still more likely than non-aboriginal Canadians to be imprisoned for fine defaults (Hamilton and Sinclair, 1991: 420). Other factors come into play here. For example, single mothers face obstacles relating to childcare and transportation which sometimes preclude their participation in community work programs that are established as alternatives to fines (Hamilton and Sinclair, 1991: 424).

Like cultural conflict explanations, socio-economic marginality situates the problem outside the criminal justice system. Once again, aboriginal people are sometimes seen as the source of the problem. Why does this happen? Manitoba Associate Chief Judge Murray Sinclair (1994: 175) argues:

> [N]on-aboriginal people who control the system have not seen the problem as lying within "the system". It is time to question whether at least some of the problem lies in the way we do business within the justice system. Perhaps the question should be ... what is wrong with our justice system ... ?

C. Systemic Discrimination

The magnitude of aboriginal over-representation is either due to aboriginal people committing disproportionately more crimes than do other Canadians, or to the Canadian justice system discriminating against aboriginal people. Which explanation is true? Commissioners Hamilton and Sinclair of Manitoba's Aboriginal Justice Inquiry argue that both explanations are partly correct. They point out that the incidence of aboriginal crime *is* higher than non-aboriginal crime. However, there is no evidence to support the notion that, compared to non-aboriginal Canadians, aboriginal people and cultures are inherently inclined to commit more crimes. Thus, we must look at how Canada's criminal "justice" system has contributed to the situation.

That systemic discrimination exists in the criminal justice system is irrefutable. The Cawsey task force (1991, Ch. 2: 46) defines the concept as follows:

> Systemic discrimination involves the concept that the application of uniform standards, common rules, and treatment of people who are not the same constitutes a form of discrimination. It means that in treating people alike, adverse consequences, hardship or injustice may result.

Both the Aboriginal Justice Inquiry of Manitoba and the Cawsey Report in Alberta identified over-policing as a primary source of systemic discrimination (RCAP, 1996: 35).

Alberta policing agencies argued that because they applied uniform operational policies and practices, aboriginal Albertans were not treated differentially on the basis of race. Indeed, many police officers did not hold prejudiced attitudes toward aboriginal people. However, it was this application of seemingly neutral rules and practices that resulted in the unintended discriminatory consequences. This points to the key to understanding systemic discrimination: it is unintended and it permeates every aspect of the formal structures and rules of social institutions, including the criminal "justice" system. Examples of systemic discrimination are legion. Aboriginal people suffer greatly from it, especially when it is joined with racism and prejudice.

Uniform application of police rules and procedures may create undeserved and undue hardship for Native people. For example, many reserves are in remote areas with poor road access. Because police services tend to be situated in urban areas, arrested individuals who live on reserves face arduous commutes upon release. This problem is not an issue for urban residents.

The lack of means to pay for fines and return court appearances stigmatizes Native people. As a result, warrants are issued for the arrest of many aboriginal accused. They are then detained in remand centres (sometimes for more than a month) until their trial date (Cawsey, 1991).

The decision to impose pre-trial detention is usually based on socio-economic factors such as employment status, educational commitments, homelessness, and prior criminal record. For those Native individuals who are unemployed or repeat offenders of no fixed address, pre-trial detention is virtually a given. Again, judges do not intentionally discriminate against these people. Rather, the system's uniform application of rules produces this result.

Once in remand, the pressure to plead guilty is enormous. The passage below paraphrases Quigly's (1994: 275–276) useful elaboration on the snowball effect of systemic discrimination:

> Add legally relevant criteria to the greater likelihood of being denied bail (which increases the chances of being jailed if convicted), the greater likelihood of fine default, and the diminished likelihood of receiving probation, and there is a greater probability of imprisonment being imposed. Every succeeding conviction is much more apt to be punished by imprisonment; thus creating a snowball effect. Socio-economic factors appear on the surface as neutral criteria, yet they can conceal an extremely strong bias in the sentencing process. The unemployed, transients, the poorly educated are all better candidates for imprisonment. When the social, political and economic aspects

of our society place people disproportionately within these ranks, our society literally sentences more of them to jail. This is systemic discrimination.

That aboriginal people suffer unduly at the hands of our purportedly neutral "justice" system cannot be ignored. This legally authorized oppression perpetuates the downward spiral of poverty and missed opportunity among aboriginal peoples. Clearly, the problem is not simply a result of cultural differences and socio-economic deprivation. Excess aboriginal "criminality" emanates from within the oppressive institutional framework of our criminal "justice" system. Add prejudice and racism to this publicly sanctioned application of power and the outcome is worthy of national shame. Sadly, it is not uncommon for aboriginal people to suffer humiliation, exploitation, persecution, wrongful incarceration, and even death at the hands of "justice".

RACISM AND STEREOTYPING [10]

Racism

Mention the word "racism" today and certain images come quickly to mind: angry mobs burning Indians in effigy during the Oka crisis of 1990 and the equally appalling images of other non-Natives throwing rocks and stones at Mohawk women, children, and elders fleeing Kahnawake across the Mercier bridge during that same crisis. Contrary to what the myth-makers would have us believe, these are not isolated incidents, for racism is pervasive in Canadian society.

We Canadians have prided ourselves on our "tolerance" of diversity, since at least the middle of the twentieth century when American racial conflicts were boiling over in brutal violence perpetrated by the state, and perhaps as far back as the mid-nineteenth century when Canadians gave refuge to fugitive slaves. At times we have adopted an "holier than thou" orientation towards the United States. However, such smugness is quite ill-founded, for racism has been a long-standing feature of Canadian society. For instance, slavery was not abolished in Canada until the passing of the *Emancipation Act* by the British Parliament in 1833. Indeed, slavery was legal and practiced by Europeans in Canada since almost the first European settlement in New France.[11]

Racism in Canada has sometimes been expressed blatantly, such as in our immigration policy and practice prior to 1978. At other times, racism has often been covert and aversive, rather than overt and confrontational. That, however, is of no comfort to its victims, as illustrated by Blacks who say that they would prefer to live in the racism of the U.S. south rather than in Canada, because in the U.S. south a Black person at least knows where (s)he stands.

Adapting the definition of sociologist Pierre van den Berghe (1967: 11), we can say that, strictly speaking, racism is a set of beliefs about the alleged inferiority of individuals who are socially-defined as members of a certain group (a "race") which is distinguished by its physical characteristics. This set of beliefs is usually accompanied by an ideology, often religious, which involves values, assumptions, historical interpretations, and other claims which "justify" the treatment of individuals from that group as inferior. In particular, it is used to justify allocating those individuals to particular economic positions and excluding them from receiving certain economic rewards and political rights (Miles, 1989: 3). Thus, the racial ideology rationalizes, legitimizes, and sustains patterns of inequality (Barrett, 1987: 7).

Physical attributes are used to define social groups ("races") only insofar as those attributes are socially recognized as important because they are believed to be associated with other intellectual, moral, or behavioural characteristics (Li, 1990: 5–6). Thus, "races" are social constructs, not objectively identifiable physical realities, for there is much genetic variation within so-called races that are superficially similar in physical appearance. Sociologically, the *racialization* process, whereby a category of such superficially similar people comes to be socially defined as a "race", is very important. The state often plays a pivotal role in this process, as it did with aboriginal people through the *Indian Act* definitions of who is to be considered an Indian in law, and who is not.

Since the advent of the Black Power movement in the United States in the late 1960s, the term "racism" has come to take on a broader meaning than indicated above. Now, the term is also used to describe outcomes of the operation of institutions when those outcomes differ systematically for people of different "races", regardless of the intentions of the individuals staffing those institutions. This is known as "institutional racism" or "systemic racism", as discussed above. Even though the term "discrimination" would suffice, the term "racism" has also been used to describe the behaviour of individuals who consciously engage in discrimination against members of other "races".

Thus, there is no consensus on the proper use of the terms "race" and "racism". Indeed, some social scientists, like Miles (1989: 72), feel strongly that these terms should be "confined to the dustbin of analytically useless terms". Given the prominence of the terms in popular parlance, that is unlikely to happen. Furthermore, it is important that readers understand the essentially social nature of "races", the historical roots of racial discrimination in Canadian society, and the mechanisms by which discriminatory outcomes are perpetuated despite the intentions of the actors in the system. Only with such an understanding can realistic policy options be formulated.

Like the tap root of the common dandelion, racism's roots extend deep below the surface of Canadian society. They extend far back into our history, where they are intertwined with a very pronounced ethnocentrism (belief in the superiority of the culture of one's own group). In fact, since the time of first British contact with the aboriginal people, Canadian legal traditions have assumed that Indians were too primitive to have a legal system that could be considered "civilized" and "worthy" of recognition by the British-based courts. The non-Christian aboriginals were considered to be "pagans". It was assumed that they had no law, and English law was imposed. To this day, a similarly arrogant orientation can be found in court decisions on comprehensive land claims, as seen in the remarks of Mr. Justice McEachern of the British Columbia Supreme Court in his 1991 ruling on the Gitksan-Wet'suwet'en land claim:

> It is the law that aboriginal rights exist at the pleasure of the Crown, and they may be extinguished whenever the intention of the Crown to do so is clear and plain.

First Nation lawyer and academic Leroy Little Bear (1986: 257) describes the Canadian government's orientation down through history as a "Grundnorm approach", which is to say that the government takes actions which are inconsistent with aboriginal, British, and international law, in the hope that it can "get away with it" in the courts and that the government's actions will, in the future, come to be held to be legal.

Contemporary racism in the employment market and the housing market, while prevalent, receives much less attention in the mass media than certain other, more sensationalistic manifestations of racism, such as police behaviour toward aboriginal people and other racial minorities.

Box 4 outlines the findings of Manitoba's Aboriginal Justice Inquiry which examined two cases where racism on the part of the police was directed toward aboriginal people. Other examples are legion and include the case of Donald Marshall Jr., a Mi'kmaw from Nova Scotia who spent eleven years in jail for a murder he did not commit, and Wilson Nepoose, a Cree from Alberta who was convicted of murder after police withheld from the Crown Prosecutor evidence which further weakened what the Prosecutor described as "one of the weakest cases" he had ever taken to trial.

Racist organizations and others promoting intergroup intolerance have a long history in Canada. In the late twentieth century there emerged numerous small extremist organizations such as The Ku Klux Klan in British Columbia (see Sher, 1983), The Western Guard in Toronto, The Aryan Nation in Alberta, The Canadian Nazi Party, Campus AlterNative, and The White Canada Council. In his landmark study of the right wing in Canada, entitled *Is God a Racist?*, Barrett (1987: 357-360) lists sixty such organizations of the "radical right" — which he defines (p. 9) as "those individuals who define themselves as racists, Fascists, and anti-Semites, and who are prepared to use violence to realize their objectives" — and another seventy less extremist organizations of the "fringe right", all of which have emerged just since the second world war. He identified only 586 members of radical right organizations in Canada, but is "confident" that thousands more like-minded individuals exist here.

Barrett (1987: 327) concludes that there is an overarching dimension which knits together all of the issues on which the radical right focuses — namely, the presumed decay of Western Christian civilization. This is a concern that is reinforced in the writing of some avowedly right-wing columnists in the mainstream print media. For instance, in criticizing certain children's movies produced by the Disney studios, including *Pocahontas*,[12] one such columnist[13] took particular exception to what he saw as the movie's denial of human beings' place atop the created order (see Genesis I: 28). To him, such denial is clearly anti-Western.

Sociologists use the term "ethnocentrism" to refer to a belief in the superiority of one's own culture. Such highly ethnocentric ideologues as certain right-wing columnists, whose opinions can be fully compatible with the underlying angst of white supremacists, do have the ability to achieve widespread dissemination of their views through the increasingly right-leaning popular media of late twentieth-century Canada. That dissemination, backed and defended by the considerable financial muscle of corporate media giants, operates subtly and cumulatively over time to undermine respect for diversity in Canadian society.

BOX 4 Findings and Recommendations of The Manitoba Aboriginal Justice Inquiry

"The justice system has failed Manitoba's aboriginal people on a massive scale.... [However,] it is not merely that the justice system has failed aboriginal people; justice has also been denied to them. For more than a century the rights of aboriginal people have been ignored and eroded. The result of this denial has been injustice of the most profound kind.... A significant part of the problem is the inherent biases of those with decision-making or discretionary authority in the justice system ... [and] even the well-intentioned exercise of discretion can lead to inappropriate results because of cultural or value differences.... However one understands discrimination, it is clear that aboriginal people have been subject to it. They clearly have been the victims of the openly hostile bigot and they also have been victims of discrimination that is unintended, but is rooted in policy and law...."

So said Associate Chief Justice A. C. Hamilton of Manitoba's Court of Queen's Bench (Family Division) and Associate Chief Judge Murray Sinclair of the Manitoba Provincial Court in the report of The Manitoba Aboriginal Justice Inquiry which they led. The Inquiry was established in 1988 after the shooting death of Indian leader J. J. Harper in a scuffle with a Winnipeg policeman and after allegations were made that The Pas residents had known for years the identity of the non-Indian murderers of an Indian teenager by the name of Betty Osborne, but had maintained a conspiracy of silence, and that the RCMP had been less than conscientious in their handling of the case because the victim was aboriginal.

The judges concluded: "It is clear that Betty Osborne would not have been killed if she had not been aboriginal". They asserted: "The murder of Betty Osborne clearly was motivated by racism.... It is not difficult to identify individual acts of racism associated with the Osborne case". While they noted that "[c]ertain specific acts that occurred during the course of the investigation happened because of the discriminatory attitudes or prejudices of some of the police officers...", they expressed their satisfaction that the over ten year delay in building the prosecution's case and the RCMP role in contributing to the delay "were not attributable to racism on the part of the force or any individual within the force...." However, they did comment critically on the segregation of the white and aboriginal populations in The Pas, and did condemn the justice system for systematically excluding aboriginal people from juries in northern Manitoba.

The Inquiry's investigation into the J. J. Harper incident found racism from start to finish. Harper was stopped by Winnipeg Police Constable Robert Cross while Harper was walking down the street. The judges concluded that the original decision by Constable Cross to approach Mr. Harper, ostensibly in connection with a car theft, was unnecessary and racially motivated. "He stopped the first aboriginal person he saw, even though that person was a poor match for the description in other respects and a suspect had already been caught," the judges said.

Hamilton and Sinclair found that racism and negligence were central factors in the killing of Harper and in the hasty exoneration of Cross. They added: "We can say, with some assurance, that the confrontation did not occur in the manner which was accepted as fact by the Firearms Board of Inquiry, the police chief, and Judge Enns at the Inquest.... [T]he effort to protect Cross and to shift the blame to Harper took precedence. This effort precluded any objective determination of the facts.... We have been left with the impression that an 'official version' of what happened was developed. We are satisfied that version is inaccurate.... It is our conclusion that the City of Winnipeg Police Department did not search actively or aggressively for the truth about the death of J. J. Harper. Their investigation was, at best inadequate. At worst, its primary objective seems to have been to exonerate Const. Robert Cross and to vindicate the

---

BOX 4 *(continued)*

Winnipeg Police Department.... We conclude that racism exists within the Winnipeg Police Department and that it was expressed openly the night that Harper was killed".

The judges found that police "collaborated in preparing their notes" and that a number of police officers were "less than truthful" in their notetaking and their testimony about Harper's death.

The judges label Canada's treatment of aboriginal people an "international disgrace". After offering the legal opinion that the existence of aboriginal rights in the *Constitution Act, 1982* includes the right to self-government, they recommended the establishment within Canada of a separate Native justice system with its own criminal, civil, and family laws and its own courts which would have "clear and paramount" authority. Among other things, they also recommended that the courts, the National Parole Board, jails, and police departments vigorously pursue affirmative action plans for the hiring of more Natives.

Source: The Globe and Mail, August 30, 1991

Systemic Racism

Systemic, or institutionalized, racism was defined above. It involves the situation which exists when the norms of an institution are predicated upon assumptions of racial equality that are not met in the society. As Anderson and Frideres (1981) note, systemic racism emerges initially from individuals' racist beliefs, but once created it survives independently of individual racism by virtue of being entrenched in the laws, customs, and practices of the society or organization.

Crucial to an understanding of systemic racism is the notion of **the web of institutional interdependencies**. The quotation from Turpel in the Justice section of this chapter gave us some insight into the concept. We shall elaborate only briefly here. The web of institutional interdependencies involves racial controls and differentiation in one institutional sector, such as the real estate market, fitting together to feed into or reinforce distinctions in other institutional sectors, such as schools and the labour market (Baron, 1969). Thus, it is highly significant that, in a survey done by their own trade association, 92% of all personnel officers surveyed admitted to racial discrimination in hiring or promotion.[14] Significantly, a 1992 survey of persons who graduated from universities and community colleges in 1990 found that aboriginal graduates from community colleges had a significantly higher unemployment rate than the total community college graduating class (22% vs 13%).[15] When racism is so pronounced in such a pivotal institution as the labour market, its effects will be felt across a broad range of other spheres of daily life. For instance, a First Nation individual refused a job that is appropriate to his/her level of training and education will be excluded thereby from certain urban real estate markets. That, in turn, will probably determine the school which his/her children attend and the probability that they will graduate from university, which, of course, affects their job prospects. Thus, Canadians will often be relieved of having to make an explicitly racist choice (e.g., against those children) because it is made for them earlier in a chain of institutional linkages.

Cultural Racism

On a daily basis in society, the hegemony (dominance) of the dominant group's culture is expressed through various acts of omission or commission that redound to the detriment of those of other cultures. When that dominant group is relatively homogeneous in terms of "race", the imposition of its cultural norms and standards on people of other "races", to their systematic detriment, can be called cultural racism. Perhaps the most unmitigated form of cultural racism in Canadian society was the effort by governments and missionaries to "civilize" the aboriginal people, especially in the infamous church-run residential schools.

Schools are a particularly important forum where cultural racism is manifested. For example, requiring excessive qualifications, such as a Ph.D., for the position of director of a Native Studies program in a university, might preclude most of the very candidates (Natives) who can best relate to Native students. Furthermore, the officially prescribed school curriculum regularly gives short shrift to the vital economic, social, and cultural contributions which racial minorities have made to Canadian nation-building. Hence, the educational experience for students from those minorities is often quite alienating and their rate of dropping out or of transferring to vocational streams can become quite high.

The mass media are another central institution which imposes a culturally racist model of Canadian society. This is noteworthy in news, advertising, programming, commentary, and other content. Henry and Tator (1985: 327) submit that "the media create a distorted image of society in which only those with white skin are seen as participating in mainstream activities." Consider, for instance, the absence of an aboriginal reporter from the CBC television news programme "The National", such that aboriginal issues are routinely reported from non-aboriginal perspectives.

Assessment of Canadian Racism

We Canadians can no longer afford to indulge ourselves in the myth that Canadian society is relatively free of racism. We have seen that racism is structured into the major institutions of society, and that aboriginals and members of some other visible minorities, subordinated because of their physical appearance, are reaching the limits of their patience with the larger society. Inter-racial violence is becoming more common and racial tensions are mounting to alarmingly high levels, especially in the cities and among First Nation peoples. People are getting killed because of racism in Canada. Moderate aboriginal leaders, like Georges Erasmus, warn that more violence will come if Canadian authorities do not deal sincerely and productively with existing moderate aboriginal leaders.

The tragedies of Oka, of Betty Osborne, of J. J. Harper and others are profound. Yet, there are other facets of racism that, together, are also taking an alarming toll on Canadian society. First, racism hinders economic competitiveness, because the most qualified workers are often being denied the job, simply because they are not white. Secondly, the legitimacy of the existing political institutions (the political regime) is being called into question due to the inability of those institutions to make much tangible progress toward eradicating racism. A new and growing problem of national unity is emerging as First Nations withdraw whatever legitimacy they had attached to the political community itself. That is, their experience with having been excluded from the mainstream of Canadian society for racial reasons has left many aboriginal people to think of themselves first and foremost as aboriginal people, rather than as Canadians. With that orientation, they see themselves as having little stake in the status quo in Canada. As a result, they feel little compunction about engaging in obstructionist strategies and tactics, even on matters of the utmost importance to the power elite in Canadian society, as illustrated by Elijah Harper's obstruction of the Meech Lake Accord and the James Bay Crees' obstruction of the James Bay II project. Furthermore, issues of racism in Canada are increasingly being drawn into the international arena where the impact is to seriously embarass Canada and to undermine Canada's influence abroad.

Stereotypes Held by Individuals in the Dominant Society

Discussions of negative stereotypes can be unpleasant both for authors and for members of the stereotyped group. While not wishing to give offence, we also do not wish to stick our head in the sand and pretend that there is no stereotyping problem in Canadian society. Hence, we tackle this problem below and include in our treatment a consideration of the effects of stereotypes (including positive ones) upon members of the stereotyped group.

Perhaps because of social desirability bias and the relatively low salience of First Nations to non-Native Canadians, studies of stereotyping of "Indians" yield different results when different methodologies or different phraseologies are employed.[16] Therefore, one must be cautious in making generalizations.

Mackie's (1974) study, conducted during the period 1968-70 in Edmonton, found that respondents' views of "Indians" emphasized laziness (30%), poverty (29%), lack of education (29%), oppression by others (20%), lack of cleanliness (28%), excessive consumption of alcohol (21%), and lack of ambition (15%).

In a 1976 national survey of 1832 residents of Canada, Ponting and Gibbins (1980: 72–75) found Canadians to have very low levels of knowledge about "Indians" and related matters. To questions about the "main differences between Indians and non-Indians" and "the main problems facing Canadian Indians today", only a minority (smaller than in Mackie's sample) responded in ways that clearly indicated that they held very negative views of Indians. Indians were seen as lacking motivation (21%), overly dependent on government handouts (18%), facing serious problems with the use of alcohol (12%), and being factionalized (2%). A larger proportion of the Canadian mass public gave responses indicative of a view of Indians as facing problems that are not of Indians' own creation, such as discrimination and prejudice (39%), lack of economic opportunities (26%), and an obstructionist government (12%). Significantly, regional variation in stereotyping was pronounced. For instance, only 12% of respondents from Atlantic Canada, but 32% from the Prairies, perceived Indians to be characterized by what might be called "personality deficiencies", such as lack of motivation. The prevalence of the "alcoholism" stereotype varied from a high of 28% on the Prairies, to a low of 1% in Quebec.

The "Indian-as-victim" stereotype continued to have currency into the 1980s, although it was still not prominent in the minds of Canadians. For instance, a 1983 "law and justice" national survey found that among the 40% of respondents who felt that "the police in Canada are unfair to some individuals or groups in society", 29% (or only about 9% of the entire sample) cited Natives when asked "Which particular groups of Canadians do you feel the police do not treat fairly?" (Ponting, 1986: 51–52). Such views probably became slightly more widespread as a result of the public inquiries into such sensationalistic cases as the above-mentioned ones of Donald Marshall Jr., Betty Osborne, and J. J. Harper. Yet, it is reasonable to hypothesize that the greater degree of Indian political and tactical assertiveness during the late 1980s and the 1990s would work in the opposite direction, so as to reduce the proportion of the population holding the victim stereotype. In Ponting's 1986 national survey of 1834 Canadian residents, the fact that the notion of Indians as "a bunch of complainers" was rejected overwhelmingly (57% to 23%) by respondents, could be interpreted as suggesting that most Canadians regard Indian protest as justifiable action to step out of the victim role. However, in our thinking we should not exaggerate the effects of mass media coverage, for research shows that a surprisingly large proportion of Canadians simply pays no attention to such media coverage unless the events are sensationalized or affect them personally, as in the Oka and Kahnawake confrontations.

The 1986 survey offers other insight into how widespread the stereotype of Indians as victims or powerless people is. Early in the questionnaire, respondents were asked how much power and influence aboriginal people tend to have on the federal government. The response options and percent choosing each one were: "none" (14%), "a little" (59%), "much" (13%), and "very much" (8%).[17] The data suggest that the stereotype of Indian powerlessness does exist, but is by no means dominant, and is multi-facetted.

The survey also found evidence of the stereotype of Indians as "helpless". Again, though, this was a minority view held by only 18% of respondents,[18] if we take as our indicator a question which asked whether the federal government or adequately-funded Native governments would perform more capably in meeting Natives' needs. However, Canadians in every region exhibit a widespread lack of confidence in Indians' competence in handling money. By an overwhelming margin (57% vs 10%) respondents expressed the opinion that the federal government can do a better job of managing natural resources revenues than can Indian bands.[19] Similarly, evidence of the "incompetent Indian" stereotype can be found perhaps in responses to a 1988 national survey in which a near majority (48%) of respondents preferred to have the federal department of fisheries manage the fishery in rivers that pass through Indian reserves, while only 39% favoured Indian management (Ponting, 1988b: 96–97, 102).

Thomas Dunk conducted participant observation research which yielded important insights that go beyond what survey research is likely to detect. In the male working class culture of Thunder Bay, Ontario, where he conducted his research during the mid-1980s, various stereotypes of Indians prevailed. Among his subjects ("the Boys"), "the Indian" was both the object of derision and the object of envy. Included among the stereotypical images of Indians were: the noble savage; the victim; the backward simpleton; the uncivilized, immoral, lawless, degenerate; the promiscuous "squaw"; and the pampered, dependent welfare bum who exploits taxpayers' generosity without reciprocating (Dunk, 1991: 113–14). Although some of these elements have a positive tinge at the margins — for instance, the "Indian-as-victim" stereotype confers a measure of social equality with Dunk's subjects — most cast "the Indian" as a social inferior.

The negative stereotypes were employed as a symbol through which Dunk's subjects not only *established their own moral worth*, but also their difference from the perceived dominant power bloc of southern Ontario, city-dwelling, liberal, gullible intellectuals (Dunk, 1991: 102-3, 118). That is, the stereotypical "Indian" is perceived by Dunk's subjects not merely as an inferior "other" against whom local whites define themselves (a symbol of what whites are not). As recipient of state largesse in the form of "special privilege" believed to be conferred by the dominant power wielders in southern Ontario, "the Indian", for Dunk's subjects, is also a symbol of the domination of local whites by that external white power bloc. As Dunk (1991: 103) notes, "The least powerful segment (that is, Indians) of local society has come to represent local white powerlessness." Furthermore, Dunk (1991: 131) notes, "For the Boys, what one thinks about Indians is a sign of what side one is on in the struggle to assert one's own moral and intellectual worth".

The Impact of Stereotypes on First Nation Individuals

Stereotypes about "Indians" were once prominent in school textbooks (McDermid and Pratt, 1971) and in Hollywood movies. Although school boards and Hollywood directors are more enlightened about stereotypes and their detrimental impact upon the stereotyped group and have changed somewhat the content of the material they disseminate, old stereotypes die slowly. Change is particularly slow when inter-group contact which provides discomfirming evidence of the stereotype is not frequent and on-going. In Canada, the geographical segregation of Indian reserves militates against such contact. So does the situation of some highly visible urban First Nation individuals — namely, job discrimination and other forms of racism; culture shock, alienation, and escapist behaviour; jurisdictional disputes between different levels of government which leave many desperately needy persons without the services which they require; etc. Hence, stereotypes persist, although any given stereotype will not necessarily be held by a majority of the dominant population.

Even though stereotypes are often false or contain only a kernel of truth, where they persist great harm is done to Native people, especially to their identity. Furthermore, even stereotypes which are no longer part of popular culture still exert a debilitating influence on subsequent generations of Native people. This occurs both through remarks in which dominant group members unwittingly incorporate stereotypical phrases in the presence of Natives and through the negative self-concepts which Native parents have come to hold. For instance, First Nation parents going through childhood in the 1950s were exposed to numerous "cowboy and Indian" movies which portrayed "Indians" in terms of various negative stereotypes, such as that of "the blood-thirsty, wagon-burning, scalping, uncivilized, wild Indian savage". Not only did First Nation viewers fail to recognize themselves in that portrayal, but many actually came to feel ashamed of who they are (Matthews, 1991: 2)[20]. Some who lack a positive self-identity engage in behaviour which embarasses, abuses, or endangers their children, thereby depriving the children of positive parental role models and diminishing their children's own sense of self-worth.

The stereotype of "the drunken Indian" is particularly problematic. As Matthews (1991: 7) and one of her interviewees observe:

> MATTHEWS: Lots of Indians have no problem with booze [but] all Indians have to face the drunken Indian stereotype. Lyle Longclaws knows the double standard it sets up.

LONGCLAWS: If you were a Caucasian and in that kind of state, you were having a great time. But, if you were an Indian in that kind of state, then you were dirty, drunk, and lazy, possibly violent, and then of course they bring in the police and the police as a third-party institution has a certain image towards you as well, and the next thing you know you could spend some time in jail and have this stigma attached to you, etc.

Matthews goes on to point out that stereotypes can become self-fulfilling prophecies. That is, some First Nation individuals, feeling that they have a certain degree of licence to imbibe to excess because it is expected of them by non-Natives, give themselves permission to conform to the stereotype. Misko-Kisikawihkwe (Janice Acoose/Red Sky Woman) makes the point in another way. In a critique of stereotypical images of First Nation people in contemporary literature, she points out (Acoose, 1995: 75) that in W. P. Kinsella's 1977 novel *Dance Me Outside*, Little Margaret Wolfchild's brutal murder and its aftermath presage the real-life case of Helen Betty Osborne a few years later.

In addition, some First Nation students, especially in non-Native schools, have succumbed to the "dumb Indian" stereotype and dropped out of school. Among the many reasons for the high drop-out/push-out rates of First Nation students is that teachers and non-Native students, themselves influenced by the "dumb Indian" stereotype, sometimes make First Nation students feel that they do not belong in school. As Matthews (1991: 10) says:

Belonging is so important in high school and if the thing you belong to, Indianness, is skewed by the dumb Indian stereotype, you haven't much left to hang on to.

Unfortunately, this "buying into" the notion that aboriginal people should not be in school is a destructive, disempowering behaviour. Not only does it deprive Natives of the positive identity that can come from academic achievement and the employment rewards which that can bring; it also can leave Natives feeling dependent and feeling that one's well-being is someone else's responsibility (D. Doxtator in Matthews, 1991: 10). However, as Matthews notes, the more non-Natives intervene to "help", the more powerless Natives become. The stereotypes of "Indians" as helpless and as victim are thereby reinforced. Matthews (1991: 10) poignantly summarizes the effects of these stereotypes:

Lyle Longclaws told me about his Indian classmates at high school. There were thirteen of them, really bright, tough kids. Every one of those kids tried to kill themselves at some point during high school. Four of them succeeded. Of the nine who survived, six are drunks, living pathetic lives on skid row. We place an almost unbearable burden on Indian people when we look at them and see the dumb Indian stereotype instead.

Conversely, the "noble Indian" stereotype allows non-Natives to think about pretend "Indians" whom non-Natives have conjured up in their imagination and entertainment media. Some First Nation people strenuously object to this image as being just as racist as the "helpless Indian" image, for they see it as implying that First Nation people acquiesce in their plight with dignity. Insofar as First Nation individuals believe that First Nation people are *supposed* to acquiesce, this image is disempowering and, ironically, can thereby contribute to a negative self-image. Similarly, even the seemingly positive "Indian princess" image is disempowering, for as Cherokee ethnologist Rayna Green notes (in Matthews, 1991: 19):

> Once you put on the princess costume, once you become their darling, then it's difficult to be the warrior that you need to be. ... You can't ever take off the princess outfit.

Thus, the stereotype of "the Indian princess" contributes to the exclusion of most First Nation women from front-line positions in politics, the modern-day battlefield.

Also devastating in its impact on First Nation individuals is the stereotype of "the squaw", with its strong connotations of promiscuity. Matthews' (1991: 20–21) interviewees capture vividly the experience of living in the face of this stereotype. Excerpts from their accounts follow:

KATHY MALLET: Squaw? I remember being called that word and I just kind of froze. You know, it's like somebody shot you; that's how I felt — like a bullet went right through me.

WOMAN 2: A lot of Native men think ... that Native women are easy ... and they think they're easier than the white woman, you know?"

CONNIE FYFE: [T]he image that ... I deal with constantly is, I'm either a very erotic and exotic little animal [the Indian princess], or I'm not ... I either have this little pedestal that non-Native people put me on or I'm being kicked off of it.

WINOWNA STEVENSON: So what you have happening from the first contact is this stereotypical notion that Native women have fewer sexual morals, for example, than European women. It's an unspoken stereotype, but every Native woman I know who's ever walked on a street alone has suffered from that kind of stereotyping. I'll give you an example. My daughter was eleven. Her and I went into Woolworth's one day, and some middle-aged non-Native man came along and offered us fifty bucks for five minutes of our time. And I am a mother and I have my kid with me and it's really humiliating and it's really hurtful, and it causes a lot of anger. So that kind of stereotype ... follows every Native woman around that I know. And that's one of the big uglies.

The damage to one's sense of self esteem can be profound. For instance, simply because they look aboriginal, these women felt ugly. They reported great difficulty expunging such thoughts from their minds. The difficulty is compounded by the fact that many First Nation men internalize the standards and stereotypes of the non-Native culture, such that in their eyes, marrying a Caucasian woman marks a First Nation man as being more successful than does marrying a Native woman. Thus, First Nation women are denigrated by both cultures and many come to feel frustrated in their attempts at being whole persons. That feeling of being truncated, of not being fully developed, can be especially serious for those who have been taught the holistic aboriginal world view.

Even positive stereotypes can have negative consequences. The examples of "the noble Indian" and "the Indian princess" have already been cited in this regard. Other examples are the stereotype of First Nation people as being highly spiritual and as being good environmental stewards. Those First Nation individuals who cannot measure up to these stereotypes are left feeling inadequate and perhaps guilty about being "not Indian enough".

Thus, as Matthews (1992: 11, 17) notes, non-Natives' stereotypes of First Nation people change the way the latter think about themselves. First Nation individuals are now compelled to rebuild their identity in response to stereotypes and shame, instead of memory and legend.

Stereotypes have other consequences beyond those for a person's identity. For instance, as already discussed, police stereotypes of First Nation people as prone to criminality lead to police harassment of innocent citizens, occasionally with fatal results that also perpetuate the "Indian-as-victim" image. Another example is to be found in the extremely complex Oka crisis of 1990 where media personnel's stereotypes, combined with television's penchant for simplification, led to the framing of the events in the simplistic terms of "the Indian warrior" image (Matthews, 1991: 4).

We must not lose sight of the fact that First Nation individuals' adoption of whites' stereotyped views is processed through certain filters. As Braroe (1975, quoted in Dunk, 1991: 130) observed in a small prairie town, "[E]ach group acts in ways that project this image of inferiority onto the other, though largely ignorant of the result of their actions. There is a sort of negative division of symbolic labour: the attainment of a morally defensible self for both Indian and white occurs at the expense of the other...".

The reader will recall that Dunk found that stereotypes of First Nation people, as held by working class men in northwestern Ontario, came to symbolize for those men both regional alienation and what they, as whites, are not. These are heavy symbolic burdens for First Nation people to bear. One consequence is that they get blamed for a wide variety of deviant behaviour (e.g., vandalism) that occurs in or near the city (Dunk, 1991: 107–109). It also results in whites avoiding First Nation individuals and places where the latter are to be found. Furthermore, negative sanctions are brought to bear against those whites who violate these norms. Out of all this can come segregation, discriminatory behaviour against First Nation people, mutual alienation, and low feelings of self-esteem among First Nation individuals.

PUBLIC OPINION [21]

Sometimes aboriginal leaders are quite prepared to disregard Canadian public opinion, but at other times they are quite attentive to it. Regardless of Native leaders' orientation, non-Native politicians are concerned about, and in their creation of opportunities for First Nations, are somewhat constrained by, public opinion in the Canadian mass public. Indeed, the federal government commissions expensive polling to keep its finger on the pulse of non-aboriginal public opinion on aboriginal issues. The mass media have also taken up the interest and commission polls on the topic themselves.

The first national survey on aboriginal issues was conducted by Ponting and Gibbins in 1976. With few exceptions, such as significant deterioration of support for First Nations in Québec and British Columbia, the findings from that comprehensive survey still hold true today, as evidenced by the findings from Ponting's detailed, ten year follow-up national study and an even more detailed 1994 national survey kindly provided to the authors by The Angus Reid Group. In this part of the chapter we shall discuss the main themes which emerge from those studies. In order to retain focus on the "big picture" and to avoid getting bogged down in detail, we usually report percentages only parenthetically, if at all. Similarly, readers are referred elsewhere (Ponting and Gibbins, 1980: 71–72; Ponting, 1987a: A1–A7) for the methodological details of the surveys. Suffice it to say here that in all three surveys the samples were large (over 1800) and the

1976 and 1986 surveys were conducted using face-to-face interviews in respondents' homes in the official language of the respondent's choice, while the 1994 survey differed by using telephone interviews. All three surveys were conducted by reputable polling firms.

Little Knowledge, Low Priority

Canadians know very little about aboriginal affairs. In part, that is because we tend to pay little attention to most aboriginal matters in the mass media and attach a low priority to aboriginal issues, except when aboriginal issues touch close to home by involving personal inconvenience or threat to our livelihood. The evidence of this widespread ignorance is overwhelming, as measured by such indicators as not knowing the meaning of the term "aboriginal people", not being aware of the existence of the *Indian Act*, not being aware of the existence of aboriginal rights in the constitution, and over-estimating by a factor of at least two the proportion which Native people constitute in the total Canadian population. By means of a complicated analysis, it was concluded that around 15% of Canadians are almost totally oblivious to aboriginal matters in this country.

Opposition to Special Status

With the exception of a select few situations, such as First Nations' special relationship with the land, Canadians manifest a pronounced tendency to reject what they view as "special status" for Natives. Later in this chapter this is shown in the curve in Figure 1, which plots the distribution of the sample on two indexes, one of which is the Index of Support for Special Status for Natives, in the 1986 survey. A respondent's score on this index is his or her average score on four items dealing with special institutional arrangements for Natives. As with most of the indexes reported in this chapter, this one comprises statements with which respondents are asked to indicate their degree of agreement or disagreement, on a scale ranging from "strongly agree" to "strongly disagree".[22]

In Figure 1 we shall observe that most respondents fall at the unsupportive end of the scale measuring support for special status for Natives. In 1986 even stronger opposition to special status was found in most questions which explicitly use the word "special". For instance, in 1986 when respondents were given two statements — one of which described special institutional arrangements for Natives and one of which did not — and were asked to choose the one that comes closer to their views, it was repeatedly found that almost two-thirds of respondents opted for the statement that denied special status to Natives. One concrete example of this involved the two statements: "For crimes committed by Indians on Indian reserves, there should be special courts with Indian judges" (only 27% chose this); and "Crimes committed by Indians on Indian reserves should be handled in the same way as crimes committed elsewhere" (65% chose this). By 1994, there was some softening of this antagonism to special status[23] and the issue had become less clearcut. Some ambivalence had entered Canadians' minds. On some questions, Canadians were still more antagonistic than supportive.[24] On other questions, though, there was more support than antagonism.[25] Our interpretation of this discrepancy is that it is an indication of Canadians' opinions on aboriginal issues being rather **inchoate**. Although opinions on aboriginal issues are not exactly formless, because aboriginal issues are so peripheral to most Canadians we should expect a less consistently structured set of opinions on aboriginal issues than on some other issues such as the environment or national unity.

Such opposition to "special status" as does exist is probably rooted both in the longstanding opposition of many Canadians outside Québec to special status in Confederation for Québec, and in a norm of equality which is widely held among Canadians.

Obviously, Canadians' orientation to "special status" for First Nations could have important implications for the degree of self-determination which is attainable under the federal government's "self-government" legislation. The division of public opinion on this is captured nicely by a 1994 question (L1) pertaining to "self-government for Canada's aboriginal peoples — that is, both status and non-status Indians, the Métis and the Inuit". The remainder of the question and the equal division of respondents across the three response options, is shown below:

> Which of the following three broad statements best describes how you feel about aboriginal self-government, or the right of aboriginals to govern themselves?
>
> • Aboriginal peoples in Canada have an historic, existing, inherent right to self-government. (29%)
> • The federal and provincial governments should allow aboriginal peoples to govern themselves. (27%)
> • Aboriginal peoples have no more right to self-government than other ethnic groups in Canada. (28%)

We pursue these issues of rights and self-government in more detail below.

Support for Self-Government and Aboriginal Rights

Paradoxically, antagonism toward special status co-exists with a support for Native self-government and even for recognition of the inherent right to self-government as an existing aboriginal or treaty right. For many Canadians self-government is less a manifestation of special status than a basic democratic right of self-determination. This interpretation is suggested by the fact that in Figure 1 the curve representing the distribution of the sample on an Index of Support for Native Self-government[26] exhibits a markedly different shape than the curve for the Index of Support for Special Status for Natives. The curve depicting support for Native self-government is akin to the famous bell-shaped curve and the average score is slightly to the supportive side of the mid-point of the scale. The curve for support for special status is highly skewed.

Surprisingly, even when the notion of the inherent right to self-government was linked with the Charlottetown Accord defeated in the 1992 nation-wide referendum, a small majority of the 1994 sample favoured its recognition as an aboriginal and treaty right.

The degree of autonomy of First Nation governments from provincial governments is of pivotal importance in defining the fundamental character of First Nation governments. Replacing non-Native bureaucrats with brown-faced bureaucrats who administer essentially the same provincial policies is not self-determination, by any stretch of the imagination. Yet, that is precisely what a substantial majority (akin to the 1986 survey's two-thirds disapproving of spe-

FIGURE 1 Distribution of the Sample on the Index of Support for Special Status and on the Index of Support for Native Self-Government

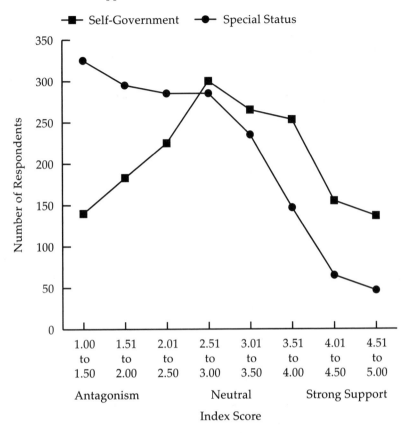

cial status) of the 1994 respondents preferred when given the option between two statements, as follows:

> Aboriginals could develop and run their own programs in [such areas as health, education and child welfare] without the province having any authority. (19%)

versus

> Aboriginals could manage the programs in these areas but they would still be subject to provincial laws and standards. (65%)

Canadians' views of the capability of aboriginal governments are improving.[27] When asked in 1994 "how much confidence you have … in terms of the role they might play in working towards some solutions to aboriginal peoples' concerns", the chiefs of large bands garnered majority support, as did national aboriginal organizations.[28] Also, there is plurality support for the eventual dismantling of the Department of Indian Affairs and strong majority support for the Manitoba approach of transferring DIAND responsibilities to aboriginal control as "a model for moving towards aboriginal self-government across the country". However, indications are that on the matter of the representivity of aboriginal leaders, by 1994 the skeptics had closed the gap on the believers, such that the population had come to be evenly divided.[29]

General Sympathy

To some extent, the above support for Native self-government and Native rights is a reflection of a more general positive orientation toward, or attitudinal support for, Natives. This might be called "sympathy", if that word can be stripped of connotations of condescension. Overall, the Canadian population in both 1976 and 1986 tended to be more sympathetic than antagonistic toward Natives. This observation is based on respondents' scores on composite indexes of several questions in each survey.[30] In 1986 two separate indexes were used. Only about 10–15% of Canadians were *consistently* antagonistic (strongly or mildly) toward Natives across both scales. Twice as many were *consistently* supportive. On both indexes, as on the 1976 index, the average score for the sample was well above the mid-point of the scale. Further evidence of a generalized sympathy comes from other questions not included in any of the indexes. For instance, in 1986 a majority (57%) disagreed with the statement, "Indians are a bunch of complainers" (only 23% agreed), and a large majority (71%) disagreed with the statement, "The more I hear and see about Indians in the news media, the less respect I have for them" (only 13% agreed).

However, there has been a deterioration in support for Native people over the almost two decades covered by the surveys. For instance, in 1976 an overwhelming majority (72%) agreed with the statement "Indians deserve to be a lot better off economically than they are now". By 1986, only a plurality agreed (48% vs 29% disagreeing). The question was not asked on the 1994 survey, but it was a smaller plurality that took the pro-aboriginal stance in response to the following somewhat similar statement: "Most of the problems of aboriginal people are brought on by themselves" (40% disagreed; 31% agreed). Yet, on another question that might carry moral overtones to respondents who adhere to the Protestant work ethic, a solid majority of the 1994 sample agreed (57%, vs 15% who disagreed) with the statement "aboriginal people are hard-working and industrious, and capable of earning their way if given a chance."

The deterioration in support for Native people can be seen in Table 2 below. There we observe that in Canada as a whole, the victimization stereotype of Indians/aboriginals lost about half of its adherents (as a percentage of the total population) between 1976 and 1994, while the alcohol and drug-abuse stereotype almost doubled in prevalence during that period, to the point of reaching parity with the victimization view. Note that in 1976, British Columbia was right at the national average level of sympathy for Natives, but a decade later it was well below the national average. Québec offers another example. For instance, whereas a majority of Quebecers, perhaps expressing a shared sense of deprivation as an ethnic minority in Canada, viewed Indians as victims of racism or discrimination in 1976, by 1994 only one-fifth did. The view that alcohol or drugs was the main problem facing Indians was scarcely detectable in Québec in 1976, but eighteen years later it was not only held by a large minority of Quebecers, but was notably more prevalent in Québec than the view of aboriginal people as victims of racism and discrimination.

TABLE 2 Regional Variation in Public Opinion on Aboriginal Issues

Item or Statement	Cda.	Atl.	Montreal	Rest of Qué.	Tor.	Rest of Ont.	Man.	Sask.	Alta.	Vanc.	Rest of B.C.
Mean Score on Index of:											
Sympathy for Natives, 1976*	3.31	3.10		3.56		3.25	3.15	2.90	3.00		3.30
Sympathy for Natives, 1986*	3.22	3.12	3.17	3.31	3.47	3.30	3.13	2.96	3.13	3.09	2.97
Sympathy for Indians, 1986*	3.29	3.09	3.42	3.45	3.48	3.38	3.39	2.91	3.08	3.04	3.04
Support for Special Status for Native People, 1986*	2.56	2.38	2.15	2.96	2.34	2.45	2.44	2.14	2.07	2.11	2.07
1994 Statement											
It just isn't right for Natives to have special rights that other Canadians don't have.											
% agreeing	41	47		57		24	53	55	47		41
% disagreeing	34	36		32		30	37	34	36		46
1994 Question											
Generally speaking, do you think Canada's aboriginal people are being reasonable or unreasonable in terms of their current land claims?											
Reasonable (%)	38	34		30		32	55	53	50		49
Unreasonable (%)	41	45		66		21	41	43	38		46
Main (1976) / Most Serious (1994) Problem Facing Indians (1976) / Canada's Aboriginal People (1994) Today?											
% citing racism or discrimination											
1976	39	27		51		36		31			44
1994	21	20		20		18	23	28	22		24
% citing alcohol or drugs											
1976	12	7		1		13		28			12
1994	23	25		30		17	29	21	29		13

*Denotes possible range is 1.0 to 5.0, where 5.0 is most sympathetic.

Sensitivity to Natives' Special Relationship to the Land

Respondents exhibited a generally supportive opinion for Natives on matters related to land and land-use conflicts. Two examples, from among several available in the 1986 survey, are:

- a (slight) majority of Canadians agreed (versus one-third who disagreed) with the statement: "Where Natives' use of land conflicts with natural resource development, Native use should be given priority".
- a near majority disagreed (48%, vs 37% agreeing) that giving Native people special hunting rights "just isn't fair".[31]

On a 1994 question a plurality agreed (44%, vs 29% disagreeing) with the statement: "Aboriginals have a special relationship to the land and can be trusted as better caretakers of the environment".

Inconsistency of Opinion

No person's ideology is totally consistent in its internal logic. On matters of such low salience to the mass public as aboriginal issues, we expect to find significant inconsistencies. The survey results conform to our expectations. Box 5 presents several examples from 1994 survey questions which address some key issues. The phraseology in Box 5 remains as true as possible to that in the interview questionnaire. The inconsistencies in Box 5, if inconsistencies is what they are, stand as important qualifiers on some of the observations above concerning support for aboriginal rights and self-government.

Opposition to Tactical Assertiveness

Canadians tend not to be accepting of any escalation of First Nations' protest tactics beyond a rather tame level. Protest was a major focus of the 1976 survey (Ponting and Gibbins, 1981) and the 1994 survey also included several questions on the topic. The results are broadly similar over the two decades. In 1976, the use of the courts and of protest marches received majority approval, as did "requesting that a royal commission be formed to study Indians' problems". The majority disapproved of the more assertive tactics of barricading roads or railroads crossing Indian reserves, and threatening violence. Even boycotting private businesses elicited strong disapproval ratings.

In 1994, among five tactics listed, the only one for which approvers outnumbered disapprovers was the blockading of natural resource extraction on land claimed by aboriginals.[32] A "peaceful blockade of a major highway to press for speedier action on land claims" met with resounding disapproval as did the strategy of unilaterally asserting sovereignty.[33] Even making a formal complaint to the United Nations was approved by only a little more than a third of the sample (37%, vs 45% disapproving). Similarly, only one third approved of delaying completion of a resource maga-project.

Regional Variation

To this point, discussion of public opinion has been couched in terms of Canada as a whole. That, however, obscures important variations from one region of the

BOX 5 Inconsistencies in Public Opinion on Aboriginal Issues, 1994

Pro-Aboriginal Opinion	*Anti-Aboriginal Opinion*
Aboriginal Rights	
• A majority supports the federal government acting as though the inherent right of self-government is an existing aboriginal and treaty right; and • A plurality is of the opinion that aboriginal Canadians should have formally recognized rights such as exemption from certain taxes or special hunting and fishing rights	• A majority agrees that aboriginal people's special status and rights should cease when they eventually have self-government on their own land base. • A plurality opposes, as unfair, special Native rights that other Canadians do not have.
Health, Education and Child Welfare	
• Concerning jurisdiction on aboriginal lands, for each of these three areas at least a plurality was of the opinion that aboriginal peoples should have either significant powers like a province or full independence or sovereignty, rather than mere municipal-type powers or "very little authority".	• For the same three areas, a majority of respondents opted for aboriginals merely managing their own programs while being subject to provincial laws and standards, rather than running their own programs without the province having any authority.
Land and Resources	
• A majority agreed that having a land base with resource rights is essential if aboriginals are to improve their situation.	• A plurality was of the opinion that aboriginal Canadians should have only minority control or no control over oil and gas on Native reserve lands, rather than 100% control or majority control • A majority favoured extinguishing aboriginal ownership of land when land claim settlements provide financial compensation for loss of use of the land in the past, rather than aboriginals receiving compensation and retaining ownership of the land.
Policing	
• Concerning jurisdiction on aboriginal lands, for policing/law enforcement a plurality was of the opinion that aboriginal peoples should have either significant powers like a province or full independence or sovereignty, rather than mere municipal-type powers or "very little authority".	• Responding to an hypothetical situation wherein the leaders on a particular reserve insisted that the members of the reserve would handle law enforcement and that the RCMP should stay off the reserve, a majority of respondents was of the opinion that the RCMP has a responsibility to enforce the law on "aboriginal land reserves" regardless of what the band leaders might want, rather than thinking that the RCMP should respect the wishes of the band leaders and leave law enforcement up to the members of the reserve.

Data Source: Angus Reid Group Ltd.

country to another. Those regional variations take on considerable practical significance when one remembers that many of the reforms sought by First Nations require the approval of provincial governments.

In some provinces, notably Saskatchewan and now Québec, support for aboriginal people is clearly rather low, while in Ontario support is comparatively high. Table 2 provides examples from the three surveys. Note how Quebecers stand out as thinking aboriginal people are being unreasonable in their land claims and how a high proportion of them, along with Manitobans and Albertans view alcohol or drugs as the most serious problem or issue facing aboriginal people in Canada. Conversely, alcohol and drugs rank as only the seventh most serious aboriginal problem in British Columbians' world view. All four western provinces also stand apart from the rest of Canada in thinking that aboriginal people are being reasonable in their land claims.

Table 3 depicts regional variation in answers to the open-ended question asking respondents to name the aboriginal issue or problem which they think is most serious. In numerous ways, this table reveals that Canadians in different regions have a very different picture of aboriginal matters. For instance, "Integration into society" is most commonly identified by Quebecers as the most serious aboriginal issue or problem, whereas, at the other extreme, it ranks ninth in importance in Saskatchewan. Ontarioans and British Columbians rank education as the most serious aboriginal issue or problem, whereas in Québec it ranks seventh. Prairie residents stand apart as being more likely to see self-government as a more serious issue than do residents of other provinces. Regional subcultures are reflected in other ways, too. For instance, Alberta, with its frontier ideology's emphasis on self-reliance and "rugged individualism", has a notably higher proportion of respondents citing "lack of initiative or motivation" than do the Atlantic provinces and Québec, where structural barriers to personal success are more widely recognized and acknowledged.

Regional variation is also pronounced on other measures not shown in Table 2 or 3. For instance, the proportion of the public which is oblivious to Native issues is much larger in Québec than in the other provinces. In addition, familiarity with Native matters tends to be regionally-specific. To the extent that Canadians are familiar with Native matters at all, that familiarity is usually confined to matters in their own region. The 1986 survey found that even on issues that are clearly of national applicability, such as aboriginal rights in the constitution or the 1985 amendments to the *Indian Act* to remove sex discrimination, regional variation emerges in respondents' degree of familiarity.

Causes of Hostility

The 1986 national survey offers some important insights into the causes of hostility toward government policies designed to help aboriginal people. Using advanced statistical techniques, Langford and Ponting (1992) determined that ethnocentrism is a minor to negligible determinant of hostility. Instead, economic conservatism (the "free enterprise" belief that government should minimize its role in economic relations), prejudice, and perceptions of conflicting group interests[34] as between aboriginals and themselves are key determinants of respondents' policy preferences. Furthermore, there is an important *interaction effect* between prejudice and perceived group conflict. That is, to take an hypothetical example, if a British Columbia logger has a low level of prejudice toward Natives, her perception that Native land claims threaten her livelihood

TABLE 3 Most Serious Aboriginal Issue or Problem, by Province, 1994

Problem	Canada		Atlantic		Quebec		Ontario		Manitoba		Saskat.		Alberta		Br. Col.	
	Rank	%	Rank	%	Rank	%	Rank	%	Rank	%	Rank	%	Rank	%	Rank	%
Alcohol/Drugs	1	23.2	2	24.8	2	29.9	5	17.4	2	28.6	5	20.6	1	28.6	7	13.4
Integration in Society	2	22.4	6	14.4	1	38.2	6	16.6	6	14.2	9	8.3	5	18.0	6	15.6
Racism/Discrimination	3	20.8	3	20.4	3	19.6	3	18.4	3	23.3	2	27.7	2.5	21.8	1.5	24.0
Unemployment/Jobs	4	20.2	1	31.2	5	13.7	2	20.4	1	29.4	1	30.5	4	21.3	4	19.8
Education	5	18.9	5	15.1	7	12.6	1	24.6	5	16.3	3	24.1	6	17.7	1.5	24.1
Land Claims	6	16.3	10	10.0	4	16.9	4	17.6	8	10.5	8	8.8	7	13.4	3	23.1
Self-Government	7	14.8	7	14.1	8.3	10.8	7	14.0	4	20.5	4	21.0	2.5	21.7	5	16.3
Culture/Traditions	8	12.7	4	15.3	6	13.2	8	13.8	10.5	9.8	10	8.0	8	10.6	8	12.0
Poverty	9	10.1	8	11.6	8.3	10.8	9	8.4	10.5	9.9	6	12.6	9	9.3	9.5	11.1
Dependency on gov't/want everything for nothing/too much gov't funding/handouts	10	8.6	9	10.3	8.3	10.8	12	4.7	7	11.4	12	3.7	11	7.8	9.5	11.1
People Don't Understand Them	11	5.5	11	8.9	11	4.9	10	7.5	13	4.2	13	2.8	13	2.6	12	4.3
Lack of Initiative or Motivation	12.5	4.3	—	0.0	12	2.3	11	5.4	12	7.1	7	11.1	10	8.9	13	2.6
Low self-esteem/self-worth/self-respect	12.5	4.3	12	3.7	13	1.2	13	3.3	9	10.2	11	7.2	12	7.4	11	8.2
Valid cases	1493		139		451		395		66		66		160		209	

Source: Angus Reid Group Ltd.

from logging would have little impact on her support for Native self-govern-ment or on her support for special status for Natives. However, for another log-ger in whom the level of prejudice against Natives is high, that same perception that his livelihood is threatened by Native land claims will produce a dramati-cally lower level of support for both Native self-government and special status for Natives.

It is also possible to analyze these relationships from the opposite side. In doing so, we found that prejudice has very little impact on the dependent vari-ables (support for Native self-government; support for special status for Natives) when the level of perceived group conflict is low. However, when per-ceived group conflict is high, prejudice again becomes an important determi-nant of Canadians' policy preferences toward aboriginal people.

Our findings suggests the utility of distinguishing between two types of prejudice: dormant and activated. Prejudice against a group is dormant when it is unattached to any sense of conflict with that outgroup. Dormant prejudice has minimal effects on policy preferences vis-à-vis that outgroup. On the other hand, prejudice against a group is activated when it is linked to a perception of contemporary conflict with the outgroup. Such activated prejudice has impor-tant effects on policy preferences.

Regardless of whether prejudice is dormant, activated, or absent, economic conservatism was found statistically to produce antagonism toward aboriginals and their preferred policies. Aboriginal people and their supporters might despair at that finding, in light of the contemporary influence of economic con-servatism and in light of the fact that substantial state financial participation will be necessary to overcome the effects of past and present racism, as the final report of the Royal Commission on Aboriginal Peoples asserted.

CONCLUSION

The forces of disempowerment of First Nation people in Canadian society are formidable. Chapter Five enumerated them and provided relevant background information. In this chapter we have seen the racism of Canadian society come to the fore. It takes especially potent forms in the so-called "criminal justice" sys-tem — a system in which the basic precepts (e.g., deterrence, retribution, guilt, police, adversarial justice) are foreign to many aboriginal cultures and have failed aboriginal people profoundly. First Nation persons' experiences with the "justice" system tend to be highly unsatisfactory and detrimental, marred as they are by systemic discrimination, cultural racism, and sometimes the per-sonal prejudices of agents of that system. To date, indigenization efforts have, in effect, tinkered at the margins. The results, as measured by incarceration statis-tics, remain appalling. This constellation of factors led the Royal Commission on Aboriginal Peoples to recommend urgently the creation of a separate system of Native justice. However, because public opinion in the Canadian mass public is not conducive to such reforms, it is highly questionable whether the spirit of those recommendations will ever be implemented in institutional reforms to create a more pluralistic and more effective Canadian justice system.

Although public opinion has softened slightly over the years on the issue of "special status" for First Nations, debilitating stereotypes remain alive in a sig-nificant minority of the non-Native population. In its broader contours, public opinion is no longer the ally that it was when social scientists first began monitoring it over two decades ago. Canadians have a low tolerance for precisely the kinds of protest strategies and tactics that create leverage for otherwise disempowered peoples. Aboriginal peoples have had to resort to those strategies and tactics and have paid the price in a deteriorating level of support from non-Natives. Furthermore, the very assertiveness that aboriginal peoples are finding necessary to attain concrete results is likely to bring aboriginals into competition with private and commercial interests in the larger society. Non-Natives' perception of such competition as a threat is associated with opposition to government policies favoured by aboriginal leaders.

Non-Native politicians might seek to discount non-Native public opinion on aboriginal issues as uninformed, uninterested, and inconsistent. It is all three of those things. However, there are limits to how far politicians in office are willing to go when, as was the case in Canada in the mid-1990s, the courts are waivering, political opponents are seeking to reap political gain from government's policies toward Natives, financial costs increase relentlessly, and the recommended reforms veer off at a one hundred and eighty degree angle from the increased level of accountability that the mass public seeks from the state.

Violence-prone right-wing extremist organizations do exist in Canada, but they have little influence and, Carnie Nerland notwithstanding,[35] their main focus has not been on aboriginal people. Of more concern should be the more influential right-wing ideologues. Their ethnocentric, anti-statist, pro-individual rights, radical egalitarian, fiscal retrenchment philosophy is profoundly antithetical to First Nations' needs. The probability is that they will inject partisan politics into aboriginal issues such that aboriginal people, lacking electoral clout, will again be buffetted by political forces that are largely beyond their ability to control. A real danger is that the political atmosphere created by right-wing ideologues will lead the state to offer either mere incremental, tokenistic change, which would exacerbate the problems of distrust of government, or conversely, to offer in desperation some drastic "solution" of radical equality. Neither approach offers true justice in the sense of arrangements that permit the survival and well-being of Indians as Indians (Boldt, 1993: 57).

NOTES

[1] The authors gratefully acknowledge the assistance of Carol LaPrairie in providing data for use in this chapter.

[2] National Aboriginal Communications Society, Brief submitted to the Task Force on the Criminal Justice System and its Impact on the Indian and Métis People of Alberta (1990: 5), cited in Cawsey (1991, Ch. 4: 14).

[3] The formal name of the Cawsey commission was Task Force on the Criminal Justice System and its Impact on the Indian and Métis People of Alberta.

[4] Examples of differential treatment in law include: different unemployment insurance regulations in different parts of the country; differential sentencing by judges in different regions when confronted with essentially similar crimes; the existence of aboriginal rights and of protections for official language minorities; and the *Indian Act.*

[5] These findings summarize statistics generated from a Manitoba court study, conducted by the Manitoba Justice Department in 1986. The study used a random sample of aboriginal and non-aboriginal respondents in Winnipeg, Thompson, The Pas and nine reserves in northern Manitoba.

[6] McCaskill (1983: 289) conceptualizes colonialism as "a relationship which leaves one side dependent on the other to define the world. ... [O]ne individual is forced to relate to another on terms unilaterally defined by the other. The justice system becomes a central institution with which to impose the way of life of the dominant society".

[7] Boyle Street Community Services Co-op, "Submission to the Task Force on the Criminal Justice System and its Impact on the Indian and Métis People of Alberta," (1990: 8–9 cited in *Justice on Trial* (Vol. I, 1991, Ch. 4: 5).

[8] *Criminal Code of Canada*, sections 530 and 530.1.

[9] Jackson notes that in 1976 by the age of 25, a 16-year-old Saskatchewan male treaty Indian had a 70% chance of at least one prison term. This figure drops to just 8% for non-Native Saskatchewan males.

[10] In this section, the term "Indian" will usually be used, both because that is in more widespread use among the non-Native population whose views are being discussed here, and because at the time of most of the empirical studies cited herein the term "Indian" was used by researchers addressing respondents in the field.

[11] Dickason (1992) also notes the practice of slavery by some First Nations during the early contact era.

[12] For First Nation persons' critical views on the Disney movie *Pocahontas*, see the following website: http://indy4.fdl.cc.mn.us/~isk/poca/pocahont.html.

[13] For legal reasons, greater specificity is not possible here.

[14] CBC news, March 30, 1988.

[15] Aboriginal graduates earned virtually the same as other graduates in 1992 and among university graduates their employment situation was about the same as for the university graduating class as a whole. See Wannell and Caron (1994).

[16] For instance, using the approach of giving half her sample an open-ended question format and the other half a different format (the so-called "semantic differential"), Mackie obtained quite different results. Another example is from the 1976 national survey. There, alcoholism was cited by only 4% of respondents on a question asking about the main differences between Indians and non-Indians in Canada, but by 12% on that survey's next question which asked about "the main problems faced by Canadian Indians today" (1976).

[17] The distribution on a corresponding question pertaining to power and influence on the respondent's own provincial government was virtually identical (Ponting, 1987c: 31). With regard to the federal government, aboriginal people are widely perceived to have much less power and influence than the French, much more power and influence than Ukrainians, and roughly as much as, or even slightly more than, Jewish people.

[18] However, over a third of the sample straddled the fence on this question and another sixth of the sample was classified as "don't know". Twenty-nine percent responded that adequately funded Native governments would perform more capably than the federal government. (Ponting, 1988a: 18).

[19] A further fifth of the sample expressed the view that the best job could be done by bands and the federal government working jointly to manage the resource revenues. The distribution of respondents in Saskatchewan (75% vs 6%), Alberta (63% vs 7%), and Vancouver (77% vs 13%) was particularly skewed in favour of the federal government's money managing abilities over Indians'. (Ponting, 1988a: 19, 65) In contrast, in 1987 another national survey done by Decima

Research Ltd. found Canadians to be about evenly divided on the following statement: "Aboriginal peoples have been dependent upon the federal government for so long, they aren't competent to run their own affairs" (Decima Research Ltd., 1987: 47).

[20] The remarks referenced under the rubric "(Matthews, 1991)" are actually from a variety of aboriginal speakers featured on this two-hour radio programme prepared by Maureen Matthews and produced by Bernie Lucht.

[21] The 1986 national survey reported in this section was conducted with the aid of a Sabbatical Leave Fellowship from the Social Sciences and Humanities Research Council of Canada (SSHRCC) and with funding from SSHRCC (Research Grants Division), the Multiculturalism Directorate of the federal Department of the Secretary of State (Canadian Ethnic Studies Research Programme), The University of Calgary, and the sale of reports issuing from the study. Data for the 1976 study reported in this section were collected under a generous grant from the Donner Canadian Foundation. The Angus Reid Group conducted the 1994 study reported here. The authors express their sincere appreciation to these supporters of the projects and to the respondents, research assistants, and other support staff members without whose assistance the projects would not have been possible. Data collection in 1976 and 1986 was done under contract by Complan Research Associates Ltd. and Decima Research Ltd., respectively. Percentages cited in this section do not sum to 100% because "Don't Know; No Response" is usually not reported here. In the 1994 survey, the "Don't Know; No Response" category was remarkably constant at about 15% of the sample.

[22] The statements in the 1986 Index of Support for Special Status for Natives are shown below, and are followed by the percent of the sample agreeing (strongly or moderately) and then the percent disagreeing (strongly or moderately) with each one:

> If Parliament and the elected leaders of the Native people agreed that some Canadian laws would not apply in Native communities, it would be all right with me (38% vs 44%);
>
> Native schools should not have to follow provincial guidelines on what is taught (22% vs 67%);
>
> Native governments should have powers equivalent to those of provincial governments (31% vs 51%); and
>
> Native governments should be responsible to elected Native politicians, rather than to Parliament, for the federal government money they receive (28% vs 44%).

[23] Given a choice of the RCMP having the "responsibility to enforce the law on aboriginal land reserves regardless of what the band leaders might want" and the RCMP "respect[ing] the wishes of the band leaders and leaving law enforcement up to the members of the reserve", a majority (56% of the 1994 sample) chose the former and only 25% chose the latter option.

[24] For instance, given the statement "It just isn't right for Natives to have special rights that other Canadians don't have", 41% of the 1994 sample agreed and 34% disagreed. (QI1G) Similarly, in that same survey 51% agreed with the statement (QI1o) "Aboriginal Canadians who eventually have self-government on their own land base should no longer have any special status or rights", while only half as many (26%) disagreed.

²⁵ For instance, almost half (46%) of the 1994 sample agreed that "Aboriginals should have certain formally recognized rights such as these [exemption from certain taxes, special hunting and fishing rights]," while only 37% disagreed (QG1B).

²⁶ The Index of Support for Native Self-government is made up of four items. A respondent's index score is his or her average score across the four items. The items are listed below, and are followed by the percentage of the sample agreeing (strongly or moderately) and then the percentage of the sample disagreeing (strongly or moderately):

   It is important to the future well-being of Canadian society that the aspirations of Native people for self-government be met (42% vs 33%);

   Those provincial premiers who oppose putting the right to Native self-government in the Constitution are harming Native people (38% vs 34%);

   Most Native leaders who call for self-government for Native people are more interested in promoting their own personal career than in helping Native people (30% vs 41%); and

   The constitution of Canada should specifically recognize the right of Indians to self-government (41% vs 40%).

²⁷ In 1986, 30% of respondents thought that, if Native governments were adequately funded, they would be more capable than the federal government in meeting Natives' needs, while 18% thought the federal government would be more capable, and 37% thought that they would be equally capable. In 1994, a large plurality (46%) was of the opinion that "if aboriginal self-government becomes a reality ... the overall standard of living and living conditions of Canada's aboriginal peoples, let's say 10 years down the road" will improve, whereas 19% thought it would stay the same and 18% thought it would get worse. Eighteen percent did not express an opinion. The stability of the "anti-aboriginal" opinion (at 18%) over the eight years is noteworthy.

²⁸ The question also asked 1994 respondents how much confidence they have in each of several other players. The full results are as follows, with the numbers in parentheses representing "a lot of confidence", "a fair amount of confidence", "not much confidence", and "no confidence at all", respectively: Chiefs of large Indian bands (9%, 45%, 19%, and 9%); Your provincial government (6%, 43%, 24%, and 10%) ; the federal government (8%, 45%, 23%, and 8%); Canada's justice system (10%, 43%, 23%, and 8%); the federal Department of Indian and Northern Affairs (5%, 42%, 26%, and 7%); Ovide Mercredi, leader of the Assembly of First Nations (15%, 40%, 14%, and 8%); Ron Irwin, the federal Minister of Indian and Northern Affairs (4%, 36%, 18%, and 7%); The Royal Commission on Aboriginal Peoples (7%, 40%, 19%, and 7%); and National Aboriginal Organizations (9%, 50%, 15%, and 5%).

²⁹ In 1986, in response to the statement "Most Native leaders who call for self-government for Native people are more interested in promoting their own personal career than in helping Native people", 30% agreed (anti-Native) and 41% disagreed (pro-Native). The 1994 survey asked: "Now, thinking about Canada's aboriginal leadership as a whole, based on your own impressions, do you think they represent the views and concerns of: all, most, some, or only a few of the aboriginal people in this country?" The responses were: 4% for "all"; 38% for "most"; 29% for "some"; and 13% for "only a few".

³⁰ See Ponting and Gibbins (1980: 84-85) and Ponting (1987c: B11–B12) for the items comprising these indexes and for the distribution of the samples on those items.

³¹ In a 1988 national follow-up study, when the question was reworded to deal with special fishing rights, rather than special hunting rights, the results were virtually identical.

[32] The item was phrased as follows: "blocking resource companies from taking natural resources such as timber and minerals from lands claimed by aboriginals". Approval was given by 41.6% of the 1994 respondents, while 41.2% disapproved.

[33] The item read: "Indian bands establishing gaming houses and other gambling facilities on their reserve lands without the approval of other governments"; 70% disapproved; 15% approved.

[34] Perceptions of conflicting group interests were measured in terms of such dimensions as the belief that Natives already receive excessive financial assistance from government, and the belief that Natives already exercise considerable power and influence with the federal or provincial government.

[35] A member of The Aryan Nation in Saskatchewan, Nerland was convicted of manslaughter for shooting a Native man (Leo LaChance) who had mistakenly wandered into Nerland's gunshop.

REFERENCES

Acoose, Janice (Misko-Kisikawihkwe [Red Sky Woman])
1995   *Iskwewak — Kah' Ki Yaw Ni Wahkomakanak: Neither Indian Princess nor Easy Squaws*. Toronto: Women's Press.

Anderson, Allan B. and James S. Frideres
1981   *Ethnicity in Canada: Theoretical Perspectives*. Scarborough, Ont.: Butterworth.

Assembly of First Nations
1993   "Reclaiming Our Nationhood, Strengthening our Heritage". Brief to the Royal Commission on Aboriginal Peoples prepared under the Intervenor Participation Program, Ottawa.

Baron, Harold M.
1969   "The Web of Urban Racism", pp. 134–176 in Louis L. Knowles and Kenneth Prewitt (eds.) *Institutional Racism in America*. Englewood Cliffs, N.J.: Prentice-Hall.

Barrett, Stanley R.
1987   *Is God A Racist? The Right Wing in Canada*. Toronto: University of Toronto Press.

Boldt, Menno
1993   *Surviving as Indians. The Challenge of Self-Government*. Toronto: University of Toronto Press.

Braroe, Niels W.
1975   *Indian and White: Self Image and Interaction in a Canadian Community*. Stanford Calif.: Stanford University Press.

Brodeur, Jean-Paul
1991   *Justice for the Cree: Policing and Alternative Dispute Resolution*. Grand Council of the Crees of Quebec.

Canadian Centre for Justice Statistics
1993   *Adult Correctional Services in Canada*. Ottawa: Statistics Canada.

Cawsey, Hon. Mr. Justice Robert A.
1991   *Justice on Trial: Report of the Task Force on the Criminal Justice System and Its Impact on the Indian and Métis People of Alberta*. Edmonton: Queen's Printer.

Decima Research Limited
1987   *A Study of Canadian Attitudes Toward Aboriginal Self-Government*. Toronto.

Dene Tha'Band of Assumption
1990   "Submission to the Task Force on the Criminal Justice System and its Impact on the Indian and Métis People of Alberta". June 12.

Dickason, Olive P.
1992 *Canada's First Nations: A History of Founding Peoples from Earliest Times.* Toronto: McClelland and Stewart.
Dunk, Thomas
1991 *It's A Working Man's Town: Male Working Class Culture in Northwestern Ontario.* Montreal and Kingston: McGill-Queen's University Press.
Elizabeth Fry Society of Calgary
1990 "Submissions of the Elizabeth Fry Society of Calgary Regarding the Task Force on the Criminal Justice System and its Impact on the Indian and Métis People of Alberta". Calgary.
Getty, Ian A.L. and Antoine S. Lussier (eds.)
1983 *As Long as the Sun Shines and Water Flows: A Reader in Canadian Native Studies.* Vancouver: University of British Columbia Press.
Hamilton, Mr. Justice A.C. and Judge Murray Sinclair
1991 *Report of the Aboriginal Justice Inquiry of Manitoba.* Winnipeg: Queen's Printer.
Henry, Frances and Carl Tator
1985 "Racism in Canada: Social Myths and Strategies for Change", in Rita Bienvenue and Jay Goldstein (eds.), *Ethnicity and Ethnic Relations in Canada,* Second Edition. Scarborough, Ont.: Butterworth.
Jackson, Michael
1988 *Locking Up Natives in Canada.* Report of the Canadian Bar Association Committee on Imprisonment and Release. Reprinted in *U.B.C. Law Review* XXIII (1989)
Langford, Tom and J. Rick Ponting
1992 "Canadians' Responses to Aboriginal Issues: The Role of Prejudice, Perceived Group Conflict, and Economic Conservatism." *Canadian Review of Sociology and Anthropology* XXIX, 2: 140–166.
LaPrairie, Carol
1988 "Native Criminal Justice Programs, An Overview." Unpublished.
LaPrairie, Carol et al.
1996 *Examining Aboriginal Corrections in Canada.* Ottawa: Solicitor General of Canada (Supply and Services Canada Cat. No. JS5-1/14-1996E).
Li, Peter S. (ed.)
1990 *Race and Ethnic Relations in Canada.* Don Mills, Ont.: Oxford University Press.
Little Bear, Leroy
1986 "Aboriginal Rights and the Canadian 'Grundnorm'", pp. 243–259 in J. Rick Ponting (ed.) *Arduous Journey: Canadian Indians and Decolonization.* Toronto: McClelland and Stewart / Oxford.
Long, David Alan and Olive P. Dickason
1996 *Visions of the Heart: Canadian Aboriginal Issues.* Toronto: Harcourt Brace.
Matthews, Maureen
1991 "Isinamowin: The White Man's Indian", CBC IDEAS Transcripts #9237, Toronto: Canadian Broadcasting Corporation.
McCaskill, Don
1983 "Native People and the Justice System," pp. 288–298 in Ian A.L. Getty and Antoine S. Lussier (eds.), *As Long as the Sun Shines and Water Flows.* Vancouver: University of British Columbia Press.
McDiarmid, Garnet and David Pratt
1971 *Teaching Prejudice: A Content Analysis of Social Studies Textbooks Authorized for Use in Ontario.* Toronto: Ontario Institute for Studies in Education.

Miles, Robert
1989   *Racism*. London: Routledge.
Misko-Kisikawihkwe (Acoose, Janice [Red Sky Woman])
1995   *Iskwewak — Kah' Ki Yaw Ni Wahkomakanak: Neither Indian Princess nor Easy Squaws*. Toronto: Women's Press.
Monture-Angus, Patricia
1996   "Lessons in Decolonization: Aboriginal Overrepresentation in Canadian Criminal Justice", pp. 335–354 in David A. Long and Olive P. Dickason (eds.), *Visions of the Heart*. Toronto: Harcourt Brace.
Ponting, J. Rick and Roger Gibbins
1980   *Out of Irrelevance: A Socio-Political Introduction to Indian affairs In Canada*. Scarborough, Ont.: Butterworth.

1981   "The Reactions of English Canadians and French Québécois to Native Indian Protest", *Canadian Review of Sociology and Anthropology* XVIII, 2: 222-238.
Ponting, J. Rick
1986   *Arduous Journey*. Toronto: McClelland and Stewart.

1987a   *Profiles of Public Opinion on Canadian Natives and Native Issues. Module 1: Constitutional Issues*. Calgary, Alberta: Research Report #87-01, Research Unit for Public Policy Studies, The University of Calgary.

1987b   *Profiles of Public Opinion on Canadian Natives and Native Issues. Module 2: Special Status and Self-government*. Calgary, Alberta: Research Report #87-02, Research Unit for Public Policy Studies, The University of Calgary.

1987c   *Profiles of Public Opinion on Canadian Natives and Native Issues. Module 3: Knowledge, Perceptions, and Sympathy*. Calgary, Alberta: Research Report #87-03, Research Unit for Public Policy Studies, The University of Calgary.

1988a   *Profiles of Public Opinion on Canadian Natives and Native Issues. Module 4: Native People, Finances, and Services*. Calgary, Alberta: Research Report #88-01, Research Unit for Public Policy Studies, The University of Calgary.

1988b   *Profiles of Public Opinion on Canadian Natives and Native Issues. Module 5: Land, Land Claims, and Treaties*. Calgary, Alberta: Research Report #88-02, Research Unit for Public Policy Studies, The University of Calgary.
Quigley, Tom
1994   "Some Issues in Sentencing of Aboriginal Offenders", pp. 269–300 in R. Gosse, J. Youngblood Henderson and R. Carter (comps.), *Continuing Poundmaker and Riel's Quest: Presentations Made at a Conference on Aboriginal Peoples and Justice*. Saskatoon: Purich Publishing.
Rolf, Mr. Justice C. H.
1991   *Policing in Relation to the Blood Tribe*. Lethbridge, Alberta.: Commission of Inquiry.
Ross, Rupert
1992   *Dancing with a Ghost: Exploring Indian Reality*. Markham, Ont.: Octopus Publishing.
Royal Commission on Aboriginal People (RCAP)
1996   *Bridging the Cultural Divide: A Report on Aboriginal People and Criminal Justice in Canada*. Ottawa: Supply and Services Canada.

Sher, Julian
1983   *White Hoods: Canada's Ku Klux Klan.* Vancouver: New Star Books.
Sinclair, Mr. Justice Murray
1994   "Aboriginal Peoples, Justice, and the Law", pp. 173–184 in R. Gosse, J. Youngblood Henderson and R. Carter (comps.), *Continuing Poundmaker and Riel's Quest: Presentations Made at a Conference on Aboriginal Peoples and Justice.* Saskatoon: Purich Publishing.
Turpel, Mary Ellen
1993   "On The Question of Adapting the Canadian Criminal Justice System for Aboriginal Peoples: Don't Fence Me In", in Royal Commission on Aboriginal Peoples, *Aboriginal People and the Justice System: Report of the National Round Table on Aboriginal Justice Issues.* Ottawa: Supply and Services Canada.
van den Berghe, Pierre
1967   *Race and Racism: A Comparative Perspective.* New York: Wiley & Sons.
Wannell, Ted and Nathalie Caron
1994   "The Class of 1990: Visible Minorities, Aboriginal Peoples, and Persons With Activity Limitations". *Statistics Canada Daily,* October 4.

FURTHER READING

Lovrich, Nicholas P. et al.
1995   "Native Claims and Public Attitudes: The Politics of Context and Culture in British Columbia and Washington State", *International Journal of Canadian Studies (Special Issue on Aboriginal Peoples and Canada)* XII (Fall): 235–260.

CHAPTER 7

EXPLOITATION OF THE OIL AND GAS FRONTIER: IMPACT ON LUBICON LAKE CREE WOMEN[1]

Rosemary Brown

> The greatest strength of the community is in the traditions from the old peo-
> ple...[and] respect for each other, ... but this is breaking down. The Bible
> camps help.

This observation was made during the summer of 1987[2] by a Lubicon Lake Cree
woman in her forties. Her statement reflects the complex, inter-related changes
wrought within Lubicon Lake Cree society when their hunting, trapping, and
gathering mode was transformed into one based upon wage labour and transfer payments. This transformation was brought about by the exploitation of the
oil and gas frontier on traditional Lubicon lands, beginning in the late 1970s.
These changes can best be understood by using an articulation of modes of production framework, as described in Chapter One. Traditional Lubicon Lake
Cree society was a web of economic, social, political, and religious structures
(roles and relationships) shaped by ties to the land. When ties to the land were
ruptured by oil and gas activity, the traditional economic base was destroyed.
As a result, interrelated changes in economic, social, political, and religious
structures occurred. Some of these initial changes triggered others as the
Lubicon created strategies, such as the land-claim struggle, to protect their families and community from the ravages of imposed "development". Underlying
many of these strategies was the persistence of traditional ideological structures
related to stewardship of the land and to the maintenance of the social fabric of
Lubicon society.

   In this chapter I present a brief historical overview of Lubicon Lake Cree
society and a discussion of the aforementioned economic, social, political, and
spiritual changes experienced and perceived by Lubicon women since the late
1970s. I argue that the exploitation of the oil and gas frontier was a negative and
stressful experience for Lubicon women and that as roles and relationships
changed, so did the bases of egalitarian relations between Lubicon women and
men. Furthermore, I argue that however useful an articulation of modes of production framework is in understanding the changes experienced by Lubicon
women, it cannot adequately explain women's perceptions of, and responses to,
change. This is because women's reproductive roles are usually subsumed
under productive roles in modes theory. Their perceptions and actions, specifically their focus upon the impact of alcohol abuse upon the community and

their increasing participation in Pentecostal Bible camps, can be understood only when the centrality of women's roles in both biological and social reproduction is taken into account.

Background: Tradition and Change

In 1988, the Lubicon Lake Cree Nation consisted of 457 members, most of whom lived at Little Buffalo Lake, about ninety-five kilometres northeast of Peace River in northern Alberta.[3] Until the early 1980s, the Lubicon Lake Cree were a traditional hunting, trapping, and gathering society of the boreal forest. They engaged in a complex web of interlocking social, political, and economic roles and relationships shaped by their dependence on the land and its resources. Within this traditional society, Lubicon women held many important roles in the production of use and exchange values, in ritual ceremonies, and in decision making. They controlled the distribution of the products of their labour and game meat brought into the camp or home, and their productive and reproductive roles were compatible. These factors can be interpreted to indicate that gender relations within traditional Lubicon society were generally egalitarian (Sanday 1974, 198; Rosaldo and Lamphere 1974, 12; Sacks 1974, 190; Leacock 1980, 9–10).

With the advent of imposed and intensive exploitation of oil and gas resources on traditional Lubicon land in the late 1970s, the Lubicon Lake Cree began experiencing the latest in what Brody (1981, 1987) calls a series of "cumulative" frontiers: economic (fur, timber, energy resources); political (administration of the *Indian Act*); and ideological (churches and schools). These frontiers have served as points of contact between the Lubicon and the capitalist mode of production. For example, during World War II, several parallel, and at times related, processes began to cause some structural modifications in Lubicon society. The Lubicon had been by-passed during Treaty Eight negotiations in 1899 because of their isolation from major waterways; hence, they had never signed a treaty with the federal government. In 1939 they were officially recognized as an Indian band and promised a reserve, which they never received. A chief was elected, emergency transfer payments became available to band members, and some children were sent off to residential school for their education. Some band members began working for farmers who moved into the area and helped them to clear their lands and harvest their crops.

A more sedentary lifestyle evolved when the Lubicon moved to Little Buffalo in order to send their children to the Baptist school built in the 1950s. Once they were there, the women remained in Little Buffalo with their children for most of the year, while their husbands continued to trap in the bush. Some minor oil and gas activity occurred and jobs became available at the school and on the roads in the 1970s.

These changes occurred slowly and left intact the traditional relationship of the Lubicon to their land, including the hunting, trapping, and gathering mode of economic production. Kenneth Bodden, a scientist working with the Boreal Institute, wrote in a court affidavit (1982: 21):

> It is evident from the large amount of meat harvested ... and from the value of the fur sales ... that traditional lifestyles, based on trapping, hunting, fishing and gathering, provide the residents of Little Buffalo Lake with cultural, economic and social benefits that make subsistence activities attractive despite encroachment of alternative lifestyles.

Despite increased opportunities to engage in wage employment, community [members have] maintained a close and economically viable contact with their natural environment and its resource base.

On the other hand, intensive exploitation of the oil and gas frontier placed the oil companies and the provincial government in direct competition with the Lubicon for their land. Between 1973 and 1978, the province built an all-weather road connecting the community of Little Buffalo to the town of Peace River. The province then issued licenses to multi-national oil companies to explore and develop oil and gas resources on traditional Lubicon lands. A resource "boom" ensued, as between 1979 and 1986 over 400 oil wells were drilled within a twenty-four kilometre radius of the community and between 1980 and 1984 thousands of kilometers of seismic lines were cleared (Ryan 1986).

The overall impact of such development was to rupture the ties between the Lubicon and their traditional lands. Large areas of land were removed from Lubicon control for drilling and storage sites and camps. Access to "private" roads was regulated. Haying fields, berry patches, and traplines were destroyed. Fishing streams were blocked and more traplines and cabins were destroyed by fire. Fur bearing animals were driven from the area, as were moose and smaller game animals.

As a result, wildlife and the habitat required to sustain it dropped to a critical level by the end of 1982 (Factum of Appellants 1982: 32). The number of moose killed for food dropped from 219 in 1979 to 19 by 1983. Average income from trapping during the same period dropped from over $5,000 per trapper to less than $400 (Lubicon Lake Cree Nation, 1989b: 11). In sum, the traditional hunting, trapping, and gathering mode of the Lubicon Lake Cree had been virtually destroyed.

Changing Economic Structures: Dissolution of Traditional Production Relations

The destruction of their traditional hunting, trapping, and gathering economy meant that Lubicon families no longer served as units of production in which men and women filled complementary roles to produce food and other products for their families' use, and sufficient furs, hides, and leather goods for the market. Instead, families became units of consumption. Family income to purchase goods was limited to transfer payments (e.g., social assistance) and the proceeds of the few paid jobs that were created in the community. Ninety-five percent of the community became dependent on transfer payments by the mid-1980s. The corresponding figure in the early 1980s was a mere 10% (Ominayak, 1987).

During this transitional period, women experienced a decline in the practice of many traditional productive skills, a shift to paid labour or welfare, changes in housing and household technology, changing diets and methods of food preparation, and growing incompatibility between their productive and reproductive roles. Very few women, and virtually no women under the age of thirty, continued to snare small game, tan hides, dry meat, manufacture leather items, or do beadwork for their family's use or for exchange. Those women who did, continued to control the distribution of items made or the income from items sold, but in general they had less to distribute because there was less game meat and hide available. However, one activity in which many women did continue to participate, often collectively with other female family members and children, was the gathering and processing of berries.

Meanwhile, many of the men continued to hunt on a part-time basis and many women said that their brothers and sons were still taken into the bush to learn how to hunt and trap with fathers, uncles, and grandfathers. In other words, many boys were still being socialized to be hunters, but it was within a context where hunting provided game meat merely as a dietary supplement, not as a mainstay. In addition, trapping could no longer provide a future for families growing up in Little Buffalo.

Women developed a variety of strategies in response to the destruction of their traditional hunting, trapping, and gathering economy. These included engaging in paid labour, obtaining education and job training, and gaining control over welfare income. Some of the women on welfare who had husbands who abused alcohol asked for the family's welfare cheque to be made out to them, a strategy sometimes suggested by the band office. Several people in the community used the food bank in Peace River and bought clothes and other items second-hand.

All of the women who worked outside the home were employed within the community, except for one woman who, in 1987, had worked cooking and cleaning at a nearby camp for oil-industry workers. Jobs within the community were found in the school, the health centre, the band office and the band store. Women worked as secretaries, cooks, bookkeepers, cleaners, social workers, teaching and counselling aides, and store clerks. A few babysat in their own homes, and a few sold crafts. Although a few women worked as construction workers on band housing in the early eighties, no women worked on housing in 1987 and 1988.

Of those women who were not working, several were continuing their education or hoping to do so, either at the high school in their own community of Little Buffalo or at the Cadotte Vocational Centre, twenty kilometers away.

Women, whether or not they worked outside the home, continued to be responsible for a wide variety of tasks associated with the household. These included food preparation, cooking, cleaning, laundry, and childcare. These tasks were strongly affected by changes taking place in housing and household technology associated with the introduction of provincial and federal housing programs in the 1970s and 1980s, and the installation of power lines after the road was completed in 1978. Electric lights replaced candles and lanterns, electric ovens and stoves replaced wood-burning ones, electric wringer washers replaced scrub boards, electric radios took the place of those operated by battery, freezers were used instead of the muskeg for preserving meat, and televisions, VCRs, and telephones came into the community.

While these new appliances made some tasks easier for Lubicon women, it must be noted that improvements in household technology often increase expectations as to how much work women can do and so, in effect, place more demands upon women. Lubicon women now had larger homes to clean and, because they did not have running water, still had to haul water for housecleaning, cooking, laundry, and bathing. Furthermore, the introduction of electricity and the building of the road created demand for a wide variety of electrically operated consumer items, automobiles, and four-wheel-drive trucks. As a result, Lubicon women and their families were further integrated into the cash economy as they purchased these goods and became responsible for power and telephone bills, and monthly car payments.

The existence of the new road made it easier to go into Peace River to purchase not only general consumer items but also food supplies. Easier access to a shopping centre, as well as the decline of opportunities for hunting, trapping, and gathering, led, in the late 1970s and early 1980s, to a significant decrease in the ratio of "bush" food to store-bought food in the diet of the Lubicon. Before the late 1970s, most diets consisted of game meat, bannock, berries, garden vegetables, and a few store-bought items such as flour, tea, oatmeal, and some tinned goods. After the early 1980s, as less game meat became available, most Lubicon diets consisted of a much larger percentage of store-bought foods such as cold cereals, eggs, bacon, sausages, bread, packaged macaroni and cheese, hot dogs, baloney, candy, soft drinks, potato chips, and a wide range of tinned foods. A small band-operated store carrying these goods was established in Little Buffalo in the mid-1980s. While convenience foods were easier for women to prepare, they were usually less nutritious and not as easy to share as traditional foods. Furthermore, the task of shopping was now added to women's responsibilities, along with the challenge to supply the family with sufficient food from what was often a very limited income.

Although women continued to be responsible for child care, this responsibility was no longer compatible with the jobs women held (except for babysitting) or the educational upgrading in which some women were engaged. Women had always relied upon other women for child-care assistance, but this assistance had always been rendered on the basis of reciprocity. Now, however, women had to pay others, including relatives, for looking after children. The fact that other women were also working or upgrading cut down on the number of women available for babysitting. So did alcohol abuse among some women. The tension that had arisen between productive and reproductive roles was revealed in the replies that twenty-eight women made to a question about who was better off in the community today — men or women. A quarter of the women replied that the men were better off because they were not responsible for the children and therefore were more free to do what they wanted to do. One woman stated: "I have said to my husband `I wish I was you so that I didn't have to look after the children.' Men think women are supposed to stay in and look after the kids and think that women don't work". Another said: "When a woman separates she can't find work to support the kids because there is no babysitter. If a man leaves, he can find work because he has no one to look after".

Some of these changes in economic roles and relationships undermined the basis upon which egalitarian relations between men and women had existed in the past. Sanday (1974: 198), for example, argues that one crucial factor to assess in determining the status of women is the balance between male and female contributions to production. With the destruction of the traditional Lubicon hunting, trapping, and gathering mode of production, families and hunting groups ceased to be units of production within which women's economic roles were complementary to those of men. The husband-wife economic relationship took one of three forms: (i) both husband and wife dependent upon the state for welfare payments; (ii) both employed at paid jobs that bore no relationship to each other; or (iii) one at home while the other worked outside the home. In addition, while hunting remained important as a supplement to family incomes, the tanning of hides did not. Most men who worked at paid jobs still tried to hunt, but no women who engaged in paid work also tanned hides.

Furthermore, the jobs women held as teaching aides, cooks, health-care workers, office workers, bookkeepers, store clerks, or social workers, all fell within the purview of what in the rest of Canada has been traditionally known as "women's work".

Rosaldo and Lamphere (1974: 12) point out that women's status is affected not only by the tasks associated with their roles in production, but also by their degree of control over the product of their labour. Lubicon women still controlled their own incomes, whether from wages or transfer payments. Yet, as always, control was conditioned by family needs. In the past, the significance of Lubicon women being able to control the product of their labour had been related to their ability to distribute that product and the meat that husbands brought into the camp. It was through this act of distribution that social ties had been built and that women had ensured a reciprocal exchange of goods and services. Several women stated that, while it was easy to share when moose meat formed the basis of their diet, it was much more difficult to share tinned goods when the amount of store-bought food one could purchase was limited by one's income. In other words, *store-bought food could not be used to cement social and ritual ties in the same way that moose and other game meat had.* The very fact that, ultimately, women and their families were now dependent upon the state, rather than on each other, undermined the basis for mutual co-operation and sharing.

Another factor to consider when determining the status of women in a society is the relation between their productive and reproductive work (Sacks 1974: 190). All of the paid jobs held by Lubicon women, except for babysitting, were performed outside the home, which increased the gap between the private familial domain and the public one. As a result, women could no longer combine child care with productive work; nor could they assume that relatives were available to look after the children. If they could find sitters, they were now expected to pay.

Changing Social Structures: Weakening of Traditional Ties and Bonds

Related to the changes in economic structures arising from imposed oil and gas activity were changes in social roles and relationships between families and between wives and husbands, parents and children, and elders and youth. The 1980s witnessed an increase in marital conflict and marital breakdown among all age groups, except in marriages where the wife was over fifty. The reasons cited most often for marital breakdown were the increase in alcohol and wife abuse, which in turn were attributed to the fact that men did not have productive work. Some women felt that there "would be less [drinking] if the men had jobs and more self-respect."

Changing patterns of socialization of, and expectations for, children were also related to the shift in productive activity. It was now the school that was to prepare children for the future on the basis of a curriculum designed to integrate children into the wage-labour economy. This increasing reliance upon the school for the education of children was parallelled by the decline in bush skills learned from their parents by girls and younger women, and to a lesser extent by boys and younger men. Play among children also reflected the shift in the mode of production and related changes. Although girls still played with dolls, children otherwise were no longer socialized through play to take on traditional economic activities. Meanwhile, new agents of socialization — television and VCRs — were introduced into the community. While television and movies provide hours of entertainment, they also expose children (and adults) to the sex-role sterotyping and "consumerist" attitudes that dominate the larger Canadian and American societies.

As for the relationship between elders and youths, when seventeen women in their twenties and younger were asked about the values they learned from their parents, only six mentioned respect for the elders. However, fourteen out of eighteen women over the age of thirty who were asked the same question mentioned respect for elders. Several women commented: "The young don't listen"; "They laugh at the elders"; and, "They don't help the elders without being asked." This loss of respect was linked both to the loss of traditional economic roles, in which the young learned from elders, and to an increase in alcohol abuse among the young. In turn, elders' influence waned as they found it difficult to prevent the young from drinking.

With regard to relations among members of the community as a whole, many women mentioned increasing gossip, increasing tensions, and less co-operation and sharing. Two women connected these changes to the increase in alcohol consumption: "People got along a long time ago but not today, because of the drinking"; "If you start helping people who have been drinking they won't leave you alone". The comments of a few other women revealed that relationships were becoming increasingly commercialized as opposed to being based upon reciprocity and mutual need. One now had to pay for favours such as rides into town or the fetching of water and groceries: "Nobody does anything for free; ... even for water I have to pay ten dollars or they'd want the gas; ...even to go to the store I would have to pay".

It was the issue of drinking, however, and the problems associated with alcohol abuse, that permeated almost every conversation. Drinking was identified by women as being responsible for an increase in marital conflict, the breaking up of homes, and numerous fatal accidents. Perhaps the most poignant response to a question about changes within the community came from the young woman who said that "more people were dying in accidents because of alcohol". She had lost three cousins and an aunt in alcohol-related accidents. Nine different alcohol-related accidental deaths after the opening of the road and one alcohol-related suicide were mentioned during the interviews. The impact of these deaths extended far beyond the immediate families involved because, as another woman stated, "not everyone drinks, but because everyone is related, everyone is affected".

Women employed a variety of strategies to deal with the isolating effects of the social changes they were experiencing. For example, many were taking special care to maintain social ties, especially within the extended family. There were several instances of sisters having chosen to live in very close proximity to each other, and many examples of constant visiting and assistance with child care on a short-term basis. Women organized birthday parties to which all family members were invited and they drove around the community with their children to share birthday cake with others. Female cousins and sisters travelled with each other to social functions outside Little Buffalo. Extended family groups would travel into town together to do laundry or shop for groceries, or would go together into the bush for summer camp or berry picking.

Women were concerned about alcohol abuse and spent much time talking to young people about it in order to discourage them from drinking. A few mothers took their children to AADAC (Alberta Alcohol and Drug Abuse Commission) meetings held during the summer of 1988 in order to influence them not to drink, and many took their children to Bible camps for the same reason.

Women also developed ways to deal with husbands who drank and/or were abusive. These included talking to their husbands when they were sober, asking other relatives to talk to their husbands, leaving husbands temporarily, leaving them permanently, fighting back, and drinking with them. Most women who left their husbands, or who needed advice or someone to whom to talk, went to other female relatives for support. Significantly, several of the larger family groupings had one woman to whom several different female relatives usually turned.

When I began this research, I did not expect to find this focus upon alcohol abuse. I assumed that women would speak of the loss of their productive roles in the same way that men spoke of their loss of hunting and trapping. The court affidavits prepared for the 1982 court action by male elders (albeit with input from women) focussed upon the loss of hunting and trapping and the scaring away of game as the most significant change in the community. This was also true in my 1987 interviews with men, although those men also referred to some of the issues discussed by women in 1987 and 1988. Most women, however, in interviews and discussions in 1987 and 1988 identified alcohol abuse as the key change in the community after the late 1970s.

At first, this difference between men's and women's perceptions appeared inconsistent with modes of production analysis, with its emphasis upon productive roles, as found in Marxist theory. As Hartsock (1985: 237) points out, though, Marxists often use the term *production* in a way that obscures women's reproductive work. She argues that if Marxist frameworks are to be truly Marxist, they have to take into account what people do. If what women do revolves around reproductive as well as productive activities, these reproductive activities have to have as central a position in modes analysis as productive roles do.

Women's reproductive work in Lubicon society involves not only the bearing and raising of children, but also the building and maintenance of social ties that in the past, had helped to ensure co-operative relations of production. They had built and maintained these ties through the reciprocal exchange of goods and services, social activities, and the transmission of cultural skills and values such as sharing and respect for the elders. Women and the rest of Lubicon society relied heavily upon these ties.

Alcohol abuse directly affected women's reproductive roles, both biological and social. Alcohol abuse was associated with: the increase in marital discord, wife abuse, and family breakdown; children being on the loose and/or neglected; young people dying in accidents; a decline in community co-operation and sharing; and the elders' loss of authority. It was because women defined themselves "relationally" that the process of rapid social change was such a negative and stressful one for them.

Changing Political Structures: Separation of Public and Private Spheres

Innumerable changes also took place in political structures during the time when the Lubicon mounted a massive campaign for the settlement of their land claims.[4] This struggle involved community members in a whole range of non-traditional political activities. Most of the women interviewed had actively supported the land claim. Many had participated in meetings over the years, several had attended court hearings in Calgary and Edmonton in the early 1980s, and many went to the 1987 Buffy Sainte Marie concert held in Calgary in solidarity with the Lubicon. Others had participated in rallies and protests connected to the Lubicon boycott of the 1988 Winter Olympic Games in Calgary, and one female elder visited support groups in Europe. Women also allowed anthropologists and media to interview them and participated in the making of videos and films. When the Lubicon set up roadblocks at Little Buffalo for a week in October 1988 in order to assert jurisdiction over their traditional lands, many women spent hours at the main blockade, while others prepared food for the numerous supporters who came to Little Buffalo.

In order to undertake their land-claim struggle, the Lubicon Lake Cree created new structures, such as the Cree Development Board, which dramatically increased the scale of decision making within the community. According to the chief, the board was set up to provide representation for all members of the community, including those not counted as status Indians by the Department of Indian Affairs and Northern Development. The board incorporated the elected band council and the chief. The chief explained that because family groups were traditionally represented by senior male hunters, representatives to the Cree Development Board were the male heads of families. Therefore, women were not directly represented in structures outside the extended family. Women had always played, and continue to play, an important part in decision making in the context of the extended family, and so they did have a voice. Although not organized as a group, they expressed their views at community meetings and within their families. This is evident in an analysis of some of the concrete provisions the band sought in the land-claim negotiations. In addition to the demands for economic development funds to enable band members to re-establish ties to the land, obtain vocational training, and create jobs, the community sought a range of youth recreational facilities, a laundromat, and a combination child care and seniors' nursing home. All these concerns are directly connected to women's reproductive roles.[5] The need for a child-care facility reflected the fact that increasing numbers of women were seeking paid work outside the home or were training to do so and the fact that productive and reproductive roles were no longer compatible. The fact that the day care would be combined with a nursing home for the elders demonstrated a commitment to respect and care for the elders within the community, and a commitment to continue the traditional relationship between the elders and youth — a relationship of cultural transmission and guidance. Community members also hoped that recreational facilities would provide young people with constructive alternatives to drinking. In fact, stated repeatedly was the belief that with a reserve in place, the Lubicon would have a mechanism for keeping alcohol out of the community.

Leacock (1980: 9–10; 1981: 135) identifies women's role in decision making in their society as a factor related to status. In Lubicon society at the time of my interviews, traditional lines of communication, which had always allowed women's voices to be heard, did not always function. That led to some feelings of alienation and frustration. Factors interfering with communication were the loss of respect for elders, the increase in alcohol abuse among both men and women, and the increasing number of single parent families headed by women.

Changing Religious Structures: Mechanisms for Re-Knitting Social Ties

Traditional religious or spiritual roles and relationships also changed as Lubicon society shifted from one mode of production to another. The Lubicon Lake Cree had already been exposed to alternate religious traditions on a sporadic basis through contact with missionaries in the interwar years. Exposure increased in the 1940s when some children were sent away to residential schools, and in the 1950s and 1960s after the Baptist-run school and two churches were built in Little Buffalo. However, as long as the Lubicon were connected to the land through hunting, trapping, and gathering, they retained their own traditional beliefs; their religious rituals connected to healing, midwifery and hunting; and the tea dance ceremony, in which women played an important role. The death of a key spiritual leader in the 1970s, easier access via road to a range of medical services in Peace River, and the rupture of Lubicon ties to the land after the late 1970s, combined to produce a number of changes. Among these were a decline in the number of tea dances held, the end of midwifery, a decline in the practice of traditional healing and the rituals connected to hunting, and an increasing lack of awareness of traditional spiritual knowledge among women under age thirty.

Spirituality was still important in women's lives, though. Many women in the community, especially those who had experienced personal losses and who were keenly worried about their children and grandchildren, found support and strength in prayer, attendance at church, the annual pilgrimage to Lac Ste. Anne, and/or participation in Bible camps.

Of significance was the fact that growing numbers of women (twenty-two in 1988) were participating in Pentecostal Bible camps. Women usually attended with other family members, including husbands. Women said that they went because they liked the music, because they liked to see people, and because they wanted to learn more about the Bible and how to act. Another woman, when asked if she drew strength from the Bible camps, replied, "Yes, I could not have gotten through the time after _____'s death without it." This is not an uncommon response, according to some of the literature on pentecostal movements: "Behavioral patterns in the new Church are based on the same norms of reciprocity and mutual aid inherent in the relations among kin and fictive kin ... Pentecostalism flourishes where `traditional supports have been eroded without provision of ... resources for individuals to cope independently with life crises'" (Glazier 1980: 2).

CONCLUSION

The imposed and intense exploitation of the oil and gas frontier on traditional Lubicon lands in the late 1970s ruptured Lubicon ties to their land and transformed their traditional hunting, trapping, and gathering mode of production into one based on transfer payments and wage labour. This transformation brought about many inter-related changes in economic, social, political, and religious roles and relationships among the Lubicon. These changes were often negative and stressful for Lubicon Lake Cree women. They undermined the bases upon which generally egalitarian gender relations had existed in the past, and they adversely affected women's reproductive roles, both biological and social.

Recognizing the centrality of women's reproductive roles and the social values associated with these proved to be crucial in enabling modes of production analysis to account not only for Lubicon women's experiences of change, but also their perceptions and their responses. Their responses to rapid social change evolved within the context of a vision of the future based on a settlement of the land claim. A settlement, they believed, would enable the whole community — women and men, young and old — to re-establish its connection to the land, even if on a different basis than in the past. This connection would provide the Lubicon Lake Cree with the capacity to control the direction of future change and to ground change in tradition, especially the values related to social relationships. However, a just settlement of the land claim still had not been attained. Because of women's significant role in social reproduction, it is their testimony that speaks directly to the difficulty of maintaining the traditional values and the social fabric of Lubicon Lake Cree society when ties to the land have been ruptured and a way of life destroyed. At issue is how long women will be able to do so without a just settlement of the land claim.

POSTSCRIPT 1996

Multi-national resource companies continue to exploit the oil and gas frontier. During the summer of 1994, against the expressed wishes of the Lubicon community, the Unocal corporation built a sour gas plant about three kilometres from the proposed reserve boundary. To make matters worse, since 1988, when the Alberta government gave Daishowa Inc. a license to harvest trees in an area that covers almost the entire traditional territory, the Lubicon have had to fend off clear-cutting of their lands. The Lubicon Settlement Commission of Review, an independent and non-partisan body, reported in March 1993 that the federal and provincial Conservative governments had not negotiated in good faith for a land-claim settlement. Current negotiations by the federal Liberal government are being stalled by the Government of Alberta and the reserve has still not been created. In the early 1990s, the federal government attempted to undermine the land claim by creating a new band (the Woodland Cree Band), which some Lubicon members have joined. Suspicions about provincial attempts to split the community arose in 1993 when members of one family group attempted to join the Woodland Cree, and again more recently during current negotiations when the same family tried to create yet another new band.

These moves to undermine the political settlement and to divide the Lubicon have added immeasurably to the stress, strain, frustration, and exhaustion under which community members live. Because of their important position in maintaining social relations within the community, Lubicon women continue to bear the brunt of social dislocation. Some remain involved with the Pentecostal movement, while others have reaffirmed and strengthened their participation in traditional spiritual ceremonies. Lubicon women have attempted to counteract the impact of social dislocation in other ways, too. One example is the creation of the Lubicon Lake Nation Women's Circle in 1992. Their goals were to strengthen community ties and to support the land-claim struggle. As of the fall of 1995, however, the Circle is inactive.[6]

NOTES

1. This chapter is a slightly revised version of a paper originally published under the title "Exploitation of the Oil and Gas Frontier: Impact on Lubicon Lake Cree Women" in Christine Miller and Patricia Chuchryk (eds.), *Women of the First Nations: Power, Wisdom and Strength*, Winnipeg: University of Manitoba Press, 1996. Reprinted under permission kindly granted by University of Manitoba Press.
2. This paper is based upon: interviews carried out with thirty-eight Lubicon Lake Cree women during the summers of 1987 and 1988 and one week in the fall of 1988; documentary research; informal site visits between 1988 and 1994; and telephone conversations with Lubicon women during the 1990s.
3. Details about the history of Lubicon Lake Cree society are available elsewhere (Brown 1990; Lubicon Lake Cree Nation, 1989).
4. Details of the land-claim struggle are to be found in Richardson (1989), Lubicon Lake Cree Nation (1989b), and Goddard (1991).
5. The Lubicon Lake Cree Nation's negotiating demands are analysed in Lubicon Lake Cree Nation (1989a).
6. For more information, see Hill (1994).

REFERENCES

Bodden, Kenneth
1982   *Statement of Kenneth Bodden in Ominayak et al. v. Norcen Energy Resources Limited*, 15 September 1982, in the Court of Queen's Bench of Alberta Judicial District of Calgary.
Brody, Hugh
1981   *Maps and Dreams: Indians and the British Columbia Frontier*. Vancouver: Douglas and McIntyre.
_____
1987   *Living Arctic: Hunters in the Canadian North*. Vancouver: Douglas and McIntyre.
Brown, Rosemary
1990   "Rupture of the Ties that Bind: Lubicon Lake Cree Women and their Society". Calgary, Alta.: Master's thesis, The University of Calgary.
Caulfield, Mina Davis
1981   "Equality, Sex and Mode of Production". In *Social Inequality: Comparative and Developmental Approaches*, ed. Gerald D. Berreman. New York: Academic Press.
Factum of Appellants.
1982   *Ominayak v. Norcen et al.*, Alberta.
Glazier, Stephen D.
1980   *Perspectives on Pentecostalism: Case Studies from the Caribbean and Latin America*. Washington, D.C.: University Press of America.
Goddard, John
1991   *Last Stand of the Lubicon Cree*. Vancouver: Douglas and McIntyre.
Hartsock, Nancy
1983   *Money, Sex and Power: Toward a Feminist Historical Materialism*. Boston: The Northeastern Series in Feminist Theory.
Hill, Dawn
1994   "Spirit of Resistance of the Lubicon Lake Cree". Hamilton, Ont.: PhD dissertation. McMaster University.

Leacock, Eleanor
1980   "Montagnais Women and the Jesuit Program for Colonization," In Mona Etienne and Eleanor Leacock (eds.) *Women and Colonization: Anthropological Perspectives*. New York: Praeger Publishers.

1981   *Myths of Male Dominance: Collected Articles on Women Cross-Culturally*. New York: Monthly Review Press.
Lubicon Lake Cree Nation.
1989a   *Analysis of Federal Government's January 24, 1989, "take-it-or-leave-it offer"*.

1989b   Band Prepared History.
Ominayak, Bernard.
1987   Interview with the author.
Richardson, Boyce (ed.)
1989   "Wrestling with the Canadian System: A Decade of Lubicon Frustration." *Drumbeat: Anger and Renewal in Indian Country*. Toronto: Summerhill Press and Assembly of First Nations.
Rosaldo, Michelle Zimbalist and Louise Lamphere (eds.)
1974   "Introduction" in *Women, Culture, and Society*. Stanford, Calif.: Stanford University Press.
Ryan, Joan
1986   Some Lubicon Lake Cree Statistics, 1980-1986. Unpublished.
Sacks, Karen
1974   "Engels Revisited: Women, the Organization of Production, and Private Property." In Michelle Zimbalist Rosaldo and Louise Lamphere (eds.), *Women, Culture and Society*. Stanford, Calif.: Stanford University Press.
Sanday, Peggy R.
1974   "Female Status in the Public Domain." In Michelle Zimbalist Rosaldo and Louise Lamphere (eds.), *Women, Culture and Society*. Stanford, Calif.: Stanford University Press.

CHAPTER 8

ENVIRONMENTAL GEO-POLITICS AND THE NEW WORLD ORDER:
CREE EMPOWERMENT, LA GRANDE BALEINE, AND HYDRO-QUÉBEC [1]

J. Rick Ponting and Gladys L. Symons

INTRODUCTION

Territorial conflict is hardly a new phenomenon, but it has taken on some innovative dimensions in this era of the new world order. This paper focuses on a case of intense, high-stakes environmental conflict between an indigenous population and a modern bureaucracy — namely the Cree people of northern Québec and the state-owned Hydro-Québec corporation. The development at issue is a set of hydroelectric megaprojects on the Grande Baleine (Great Whale) and Nottaway, Broadback and Rupert Rivers, which collectively are known as the Grande Baleine, or James Bay II project.[2] This conflict over a $10 billion (US) project designed to generate hydroelectric power for export and domestic use, was carried onto the international political stage in Europe, North America and elsewhere by the Cree Indians, who fear irreparable damage to their lands and way of life. (*Editor's Note:* In 1994, in advance of the 1995 Québec referendum on sovereignty, the Crees did achieve the postponement, and perhaps the cancellation of the project.)

The question we ask is the following: "How did the protagonists in the conflict present their respective vested interests in forums outside Canada and what tactics did they use to procure support from other stakeholders and bystanders on the scene?" We draw upon two sociological approaches not usually coupled, namely the "social constructionist" or "claims-making" perspective on social problems, and the "frame alignment" perspective on the mobilization of participants in social movements. By linking these two schools of thought, we hope to provide a framework for understanding the internationalization of both environmental and aboriginal conflicts in the new world order.

The "New World Order"

In this paper we define the new world order as a system of international social stratification characterized by:

1. a heightened importance of international economic relations (including extreme mobility of capital and global competition for markets, investment capital and jobs);

2. the predominance of multinational corporations, with their sustaining neo-conservative ideology, over national states (with an accompanying fiscal crisis of the state);
3. increased international awareness of events in distant lands, due to global mass media and other information-sharing technology;
4. paradoxically, simultaneous tendencies toward the sharing of sovereignty among previously independent political actors, the de-centralization of power in response to resurgent ethnic nationalism, and centralization of power in supra-national and extra-national bodies such as the European Community, the United Nations, and the World Bank; and
5. the emergence of grassroots resistance movements, sophisticated in their social and material technology and aided by an internationally visible mass media in their efforts to achieve the increased internationalization of politics.

We shall return to this definition in the discussion of our findings.

Sociological Perspectives on Eco-Conflicts

The reader will recall from Chapter One that a basic premise of the social constructionist perspective (Spector and Kitsuse, 1987) is that social issues are *created* by social actors using strategically crafted discourse. By appealing to prevailing societal values, social actors attempt to impose a particular meaning on the situation and try to make that definition of the situation prevail. As Spector and Kitsuse (1987:72) note, it is important to explain the definitional process: "It is definitions that are socially processed. In this sense, we can say that definitions have careers." The campaign of the James Bay Crees to block the Grande Baleine project can be seen as the kind of activity which the social constructionist perspective calls "claims-making".

Couched in a vocabulary of discomfort (e.g., claims to being victimized) crafted to resonate with the *values* held by a target population, claims-making can take many forms. Of particular importance to this chapter is the fact that values are a resource, and choices of values on which to base a claim and forums in which to present a claim are strategic ones. Also of particular importance is the fact that claims-making is fundamentally an *interactive* process between contestants or between claimants and their targets.

The reader will also recall from Chapter One that in the "frame alignment" approach to social movements (Snow et al, 1986) a "frame" is an interpretative scheme which enables individuals to perceive, identify and label objects and events (Goffman, 1974). It is a set of categories through which we perceive and give meaning to the world. Frames organize experience and provide guides for action. For our purposes, frame alignment is the process whereby the discourse used by spokespersons for a claims-maker links the claims-maker's interpretive orientations (frames) with the interpretive orientations of recipients of the claims-making message. Some set of interests, values and beliefs of the target are made to fit with the activities, goals and ideology of the claims-maker(s).

The various types of frame alignment processes include frame amplification, frame extension and frame transformation. Frame amplification can itself be of two types: *value amplification* (idealizing a basic value in order to inspire collective action) or *belief amplification* (e.g. stereotypes, beliefs about blame, beliefs about the necessity and propriety of "standing up to be counted"). Frame *extension* extends the boundaries of the framework to encompass interests that are tangential to the claims-makers but important to the recipients of the message. Like value amplification, this involves identifying significant values and interests, and showing how support for the claim is consistent with them. Finally, *frame transformation* involves redefining (at least part of) one's perspective. For instance, what was previously seen as unfortunate but tolerable is redefined as inexcusable, unjust or immoral. Attribution of blame is shifted from the victims to some external actors or system. Frame transformation can be limited to one domain or can constitute a total conversion experience.

The Data Base

The data on which this paper is based are drawn from a number of sources. The content is the discourse used outside Canada in public speeches, press releases, advertisements, pamphlets, documents, "fact sheets" and submissions (to regulatory hearings, for example) by the Crees on one hand and Hydro-Québec and the Québec government on the other. This information was used to persuade foreign audiences and stakeholders of the correctness of each protagonist's definition of the situation.

The bulk of the data was supplied by Hydro-Québec, the Québec Ministry of Energy and Resources and the Grand Council of the Crees. Some pieces of information, for example the controversial advertisement the Crees placed in *The New York Times*, were procured by newspaper clippings. While we have no way of gauging the selection bias in the data, the documents do include those claims made in some of the most significant international forums. Moreover, a strategy document provided by the Crees was consistent with the findings of our content analysis. Finally, a two-hour telephone interview was conducted with one of the principal Cree strategists and an hour visit was made to the Montréal offices of Hydro-Québec to meet two employees from the Communications and Public Relations Department and discuss documents provided by the company.

OVERVIEW OF GLOBAL ECO-POLITICS, CREE-STYLE

With funding from compensation moneys from the James Bay and Northern Québec Agreement,[3] the Crees began a highly effective, international, political, strategic campaign in the spring of 1989. One of the key architects is the Director of Federal Relations at the Ottawa office of the Grand Council of the Crees of Quebec (GCCQ). An anthropologist and advisor to Cree politicians responsible for making the general strategy decisions, he is part of a larger team working part-time on political strategy and operations. Team members include another staff member, two secretaries, three elected Cree politicians, several lawyers and the chief of one of the affected bands. (The latter is not employed by the GCCQ.)

Targets outside Canada for the Cree strategy include Australia, Brazil, France, Germany, Greenland, Italy, the Netherlands, Norway, Spain, the United Kingdom, the United States and the Vatican. In the U.S., activity was staged in forums such as the New York Supreme Court; prominent universities like Columbia, Dartmouth,[4] and Vassar; state legislatures, senates and regulatory agencies in Maine, Vermont, New York and Massachusetts; television; international conferences; and "town hall" meetings.

The Crees' allies include the formidable environmental movement and numerous support groups for aboriginal peoples, or specifically for the Crees, in Europe and the U.S.A. An example is Survival International (U.K.). The environmental movement allies include such organizations as Greenpeace International, Probe International, the National Audubon society, the Sierra Club, Solidarity Foundation (New York City), Orange County Environmentalists, PROTECT (a New York state movement opposed to high voltage energy transmission), Natural Resources Defence Council, National Wildlife Federation (Washington, D.C.), International Rivers Network, and Global Response. Moreover, the Crees enjoyed non-governmental observer status at the United Nations' Economic and Social Council. The United Nations' International Working Group on Indigenous Peoples also provided a forum for Cree views.

Cree strategy included making and distributing films;[5] letter-writing and picture-drawing campaigns by Cree children to governors of the New England states and certain Canadian politicians; distributing briefing materials to the American press; and lobbying American legislators,[6] Members of the European Parliament's Delegation to Canada (following the Oka and Kahnawake crises), other M.E.P.s at the Barcelona Olympics and Mme Mitterand (wife of the then-President of France and herself the president of a French civil rights organization). In addition, a Cree and Inuit crew paddled a specially constructed twenty-five foot long canoe/kayak (The Odeyak) along the canals of Amsterdam, in Barcelona harbour near a replica of the Santa Maria during the 1992 Summer Olympics, and down the Hudson River in New York state to Times Square. These journeys, along with a protest demonstration at the opening of the opulent Canadian embassy in Washington, D.C., were the closest the Crees came to engaging in the Greenpeace tactic of "stunting".

The Crees' European objective was to raise public awareness both of the project's impact on the Crees and of the "European connections" to the project.[7] Conversely, the objective in the United States was to cancel the contracts of American utilities to import power from Hydro-Québec. These contrast with the Crees' Québec objective to encourage Québecers to urge greater democratic control over a "secretive" Hydro-Québec corporation, while at the same time attempting to stop the project through the Canadian courts and federal environmental impact assessment procedures.

THE SOCIAL CONSTRUCTION OF REALITY: CLAIMS-MAKING BY THE CREES

Allied with many interest groups against Hydro-Québec, the Crees sought to control the definition of the situation through sophisticated appeals to a wide range of values, beliefs, moral obligations, insecurities and/or fears of their respective target populations around the world. Using the frame alignment techniques of value amplification, belief amplification and frame extension, the Crees portrayed themselves as an environmentally responsible, spiritual people, victims of exploitation, human rights abuses and cultural genocide. They explained how these injustices were perpetrated by a socially and environmentally irresponsible, conspiratorial, secretive, selfish, state-owned corporate giant intent on constructing an unnecessary and environmentally catastrophic project, despite the fact that better alternatives exist. For analytic purposes we have reconstructed the arguments around three major themes, namely the environment, the peoples and the moral order. We examine each in turn.

The Environment

The Crees are concerned that the James Bay II project will alter the natural environment and destroy their traditional way of life. Taking advantage of the importance of environmental issues in general, the Crees amplified the value of the natural environment. This was the most common framing technique the Crees used as they sought to control the definition of the situation. Almost every document cited the environmental damage caused by James Bay I and the potential of James Bay II for the same. Engaged in a battle of symbolic manipulation, the Crees defined the environment as a "remote and beautiful wilderness", rich in plants and animals, one of the last great wild areas on earth and a valuable part of the global heritage. Cree texts called upon the value inherent in rare phenomena, such as eagles and freshwater seals in northern Québec, and described the dangers the project carried for them. Cree strategy documents advised that appeals be tailored to values held by particular audiences. For instance, the eagle is an effective symbol for Americans and seals are well known to conjure up sympathy in western culture.

Throughout the Cree texts, catastrophic adjectives and examples describe the existing and potential environmental damage — "an ecological catastrophe on a scale with ... the Amazon", "profound destruction", "massive deforestation", "horrendous effects", "Rupert Bay will become the toilet bowl of James Bay". Similar hyperbole described the threat to the Cree way of life in phrases such as "it will shatter the culture of Cree Indians", "will deliver a crippling blow to the [Cree] way of life" and "a virtual death warrant".

As Hydro-Québec promoted its claims of hydro power as a relatively clean source of power, the Crees frequently referred to release of "greenhouse" gases and mercury from the flooded lands poisoning the waters. References to damages appealed to the populist value of "experience" (e.g., from the James Bay I project), in contrast to the theorizing and speculation of "ivory tower" academics and others.

Framing their claims in symbols that resonate well with cultural values of target audiences, the Crees emphasized to Americans the destruction that a state-owned corporation such as Hydro-Québec could wreak. The presentation to the New York Bar Association notes "State-owned Hydro-Québec would destroy James Bay just as surely as the Soviets destroyed the Aral Sea". American democratic processes (under which, it was claimed, such a project would not be allowed to occur) are contrasted with the secrecy and privilege of Hydro-Québec as a state-owned corporation.

The Peoples

Almost every document claims that the Cree way of life and the very survival of the people is endangered by the potential environmental damage of James Bay II. This amplifies the value of the Cree culture. This is done by linking it to other values such as antiquity and sophistication/complexity, when, for example, it is asserted that the Cree people have been "strong and vibrant for thousands of years", and have "a highly stable, organized, complex — and delicate

— way of life". To emphasize the threat, the Crees depict themselves as the exploited minority and describe Hydro-Québec as the exploiter. The Crees used comparisons with the Third World and buttressed the argument by describing the devastating effects of colonialism on Native communities (e.g., "lowest life expectancy, highest infant mortality rate, the highest suicide rate").

Shifting the focus from the Cree people to the American people, the Crees appealed to the nationalistic American political value of independence (self-suf-ficiency or non-vulnerability) by warning of the unreliability of Hydro-Québec as a supplier, the "unstable" political situation in Québec and the dangers of depending on foreign sources of energy. Finally, calling upon the value of ratio-nality and linking it with consumers' guilt, the Crees defined the project as senseless. The devastation of James Bay II for the Cree was contrasted with the comparatively insignificant benefits associated with convenience for consumers in the south. For example, in the submission to the International Water Tribunal, a newspaper editorial cartoon reproduced from an Ottawa newspaper shows an Indian elder sitting beside a river (presumably The Great Whale) and large dam and telling a young child "Then the beaver with two faces from the south brought the great whale to our land so that the bald eagle could open garage doors automatically all over New York City."

The Crees also played to American economic values, such as full employ-ment, economic viability, rationality, and cost-benefit desirability. Americans were told that the project is not economically feasible, that it is not needed due to the existence of better alternatives, and that stopping it would not only save money for New Yorkers, but would also create additional jobs in the U.S. and Canada.

The Moral Order

Claims-making is rooted in society's moral order, and alluding to moral oblig-ations is an effective value amplification technique. Addressing American audi-ences, the Crees underscored Americans' moral obligation to practice good stewardship over natural and cultural resources: "New Yorkers [are] ... as con-cerned about the issue of endangered Native cultures as they are about endan-gered species".

Inciting guilt in American audiences by reminding them that America had destroyed Native cultures and "90% of its wilderness lands", the Crees high-lighted the present opportunity to make amends. This is an example of belief amplification (Snow, 1986) — accentuating beliefs about the efficacy of collec-tive action and the importance of "standing up to be counted". Amplifying Americans' belief in their political efficacy, advertisements in bold print in *Sports Illustrated* stated "You can stop James Bay II" and a full page advertise-ment in *The New York Times* declared, "Governor Cuomo can still save the day and you can help him ... the keys to the project lie here in the U.S." Given the negative attitudes concerning American electoral politics at the time, belief amplification of their political efficacy was an astute strategy.

The moral order involves responsibility, and the Crees exploited stereotypes (a form of belief amplification) to make their point. In contrast to Hydro-Québec as the great despoiler, the Crees portrayed themselves as a responsible people who, as caretakers of the land and its animals, live in harmony with nature. This stereotypic image of a responsible, idyllic harmony with Mother Earth triggers nostalgia for a simpler life of an earlier time. Phrases such as "an ages old balance with nature", "a self-regulating society in balance with the environment ... existing in a non-exploitative relationship with all life", and the Crees' "natural, legal and spiritual obligations to manage and protect the environment" capture the flavour of the appeal.

Negative stereotyping of size capitalized on Western civilization's ambivalence about this issue. Hydro-Québec is depicted as the irresponsible giant determined to act regardless of the damage to the Crees or others. Phrases were used such as "the giant Canadian utility, Hydro-Québec, already one of the largest in the world", "the Cree people standing up to the industrial might of Québec" and "the dictatorial planning strategies of Hydro-Québec". The "David and Goliath" motif was repeatedly used to manufacture sympathy for the underdog, while Shakespearean quotations before the International Water Tribunal added another form of "sophistication" to the campaign: "O! It is excellent to have a giant's strength, but it is tyrannous to use it like a giant".

Invoking the moral order, Cree strategy documents identify human rights violations as a campaign theme — a good example of frame extension. Here, what civil rights proponents might see as primarily an environmental or economic issue is moulded by claims- makers to fit into a human rights framework as well. The tactic was to question Canada's image as a champion of human rights. The New York City Government Committee on Environmental Protection was told, "There are those of you, perhaps, who believe that Canadian laws will protect against the abuse of human rights ... these processes however, cannot be trusted". An Australian audience was told that "Canada breaks treaties with impunity".

From there it is a small step to the Crees' allegations of racism on the part of Canada and Québec. Injecting new power into the symbol, the Crees coined the term "environmental racism". This provides another illustration of frame extension, whereby the boundaries of the issue are extended to encompass other interests important to the audience, but sometimes tangential to the claims-makers' main goals.

OVERVIEW OF GLOBAL ECO-POLITICS, HYDRO-QUÉBEC STYLE

As a matter of bureaucratic policy, Hydro-Québec publishes a number of documents in which reference to the James Bay Project is made (e.g. annual reports, *Hydro-Québec's Environment Policy* (1987)). Beginning in the spring of 1989, when the Crees launched their international campaign, Hydro-Québec used this organizational tool to respond, both directly and indirectly to claims made by opponents of the project. A document entitled "James Bay: Development, Environment and the Native Peoples of Québec" (September 1989) was distributed to some 20,000 clients in Vermont. In June of 1992, "Fact Sheets" were prepared and distributed throughout Hydro-Québec's network at home and abroad, particularly in the New England States, where American contracts are pivotal for future development. Articles with titles such as "The myth of the fragile north", "The environment at James Bay: a comprehensive ecological approach", and "James Bay: an unprecedented environmental assessment program" appeared in *Forces*, a publication financially supported by Hydro-

Québec. A series entitled "Complexe Grande Baleine" is now into its fifth bulletin updating the project, and a video entitled " The Grande-Baleine Project" has also been produced.

The speaking campaign outside Québec has been organized mainly for the New England States, but presentations have also been made to the United Nations conference on the environment and development at Rio de Janeiro (June 1992) and to other forums. The Chairman of the Board and Chief Executive Officer of Hydro-Québec addressed a number of audiences outside Canada, such as the Johns Hopkins School of Advanced International Studies in Washington (April 1991), the Fixed Income Analysts Society of New York (June, 1991), the German-Canadian Business Club of Cologne in Germany (November 1991), the Canadian Society of New York (December, 1991), the Americas Society and the Association of the Bar of the City of New York (January 1992), and the Association for a Better New York (February 1992).

Not alone in its defence of the James Bay II project, Hydro- Québec has enjoyed the support of its single share-holder, the Québec government. Between the Fall of 1990 and Autumn of 1992, the Quebec Minister of Energy and Resources travelled to the United States seven times to address the Power Planning Committee in Boston (October, 1990), the Great Lakes Conference of Public Utilities Commissioners in West Virginia (July, 1991), the New York State Sub-Committee on Energy and Environment, (Albany, 1991), the Center for Science and International Affairs at Harvard, (April, 1992), *The Boston Globe* (May 1992), the Power Planning Committee in Boston (June, 1992) and the New England Canada Business Council in Boston (September, 1992).

In mid-1991, Hydro-Québec opened a European bureau and created the post "Vice-president Europe". The company also sent its executive vice-president for Québec markets to Brussels to counter what it called a "smear campaign" against the Great Whale hydro-electric project. (Canadian Press, 1991: B3) Finally, in the autumn of 1992, a committee involving business leaders, government people, Hydro-Québec representatives and academic consultants was struck in an attempt to better market Hydro-Québec's image both at home and abroad.

THE SOCIAL CONSTRUCTION OF REALITY: CLAIMS-MAKING AND COUNTER ACTIVITY BY HYDRO-QUÉBEC

The Hydro-Québec position was, of course, articulated before the Cree claims-making began. One important characteristic of modern societies is an "imperative" for development, and pushing back frontiers (of geography, knowledge, space, science, etc.) is part of the value of progress. Modern societies need both tools and energy to drive the motor of economic and technological development. For Québec, Hydro-Québec is the tool and hydroelectricity is the energy source. Science has demonstrated that hydroelectric power is the cheapest, cleanest most reliable source of energy, and it is Hydro-Québec's duty to produce it for its customers at the least possible cost. The site of this production is La Grande Baleine. In a nutshell, then, this is the position Hydro-Québec presented to the public of Québec when the project was conceived.

As we noted above, however, definitions have careers, and claims-making is an interactive process. Hence, it is not surprising to find that Hydro-Québec's definition of the situation evolved through time in response to the Crees and other specific target populations. Along with the value of progress, we hear talk about sustainable development. To the discourse about serving clients in the south and exporting hydroelectricity to the U.S. is added the benefits of development for the northern Native populations. Finally, corporate responsibility takes on a new dimension as Hydro-Québec assumes the stewardship for development of Québec lands "for all of Quebec's people". Hydro-Québec's interpretation of the themes "the environment", "the peoples" and "the moral order" is elaborated below.

The Environment: "Hydro-Québec: A Proud Tradition of Environmental Protection"

The main thrust of Hydro-Québec's discourse on the environment focuses on sustainable development, energy conservation, and the use of the cleanest energy source possible, namely hydroelectric power. Stressing the value of the natural environment and its preservation, Hydro-Québec goes to great lengths to emphasize its energy conservation program. It repeatedly emphasizes that a balance must be struck between economic development and environmental protection, thus amplifying the value of moderation. Legitimating sources such as the Brundtland Report, *Scientific American*, and a study by Harvard's Energy and Environmental Policy Center are invoked, with reference to their conclusions that hydroelectric power is the best energy source available for sustainable development.

Using the well-known tactic that the best defence is a good offence, Hydro-Québec claims that not only will the James Bay II project not significantly affect the environment in a negative fashion, but the development will have positive effects in years to come. Hydro-Québec is committed not only to protecting the environment, but also to enhancing it. For example, "some 9 million trees were planted" in connection with the James Bay I project. Of course, changes to the environmental balance will be made by these hydroelectric undertakings, but Hydro-Québec assures its audiences that they have the scientific expertise to correct any negative consequences that might occur. Indeed, follow-up studies to James Bay I "indicate that the fauna has adapted well to the changes in its environment". Caribou use the roads and frozen reservoirs to move and find food, and the herd population is estimated to have risen from 200,000 to 750,000 since work began at James Bay. Meanwhile, less than 1% of the total number of breeding pairs of wildfowl in Québec have been displaced by the creation of reservoirs at La Grande. The implication, of course, is that similar minimal effects can be expected from James Bay II.

"Investing in the environment" is the title of a small pamphlet introducing Hydro-Québec's program for environment enhancement. Through this initiative, the company provides funding for undertakings that have at least one of the following objectives: "clean-up, protection, accessibility, improvement, enhancement and conservation of natural resources, as well as waste recovery and recycling; or protection, restoration and enhancement of natural and historical heritage sites; or environmental awareness projects (courses, educational projects, contests, hands- on experiments, etc.)".

Modern bureaucracies, Hydro-Québec included, draw their legitimacy from a system of legal-rational domination (Weber, 1947) where rationality and "truth" based on scientific knowledge comprise the buttressing ideology for the system. So, while Crees lay claims to the populist value of "experience" in an attempt to discredit "ivory tower academics", Hydro-Québec makes a direct and confident invocation of the value of modern scientific knowledge. "James Bay: Looking at facts rather than symbols" is the title of the advertisement placed in the New York Times (October 24, 1991) in response to the controversial advertisement by the Crees. In place of the Crees' emotional appeals, Hydro-Québec invokes the cool rationality of scientific truth. A document (May 1991) sent to the media and distributed throughout Hydro-Québec's network in the New England states is entitled "Future hydro development in Northern Québec: A rational and balanced choice". In large bold letters in the *New York Times* advertisement is the admonition "Let's talk sensibly". Hydroelectricity is portrayed as the rational choice when compared to other options such as fossil fuels or nuclear power.

The experience of the Crees is countered with knowledge gained through over 15 years of scientific study — experience gained from James Bay I (La Grande). "Hydro-Québec has been conducting environmental assessment studies for more than 15 years now. Approval of our development projects is contingent on such impact studies". Hydro-Québec's "bio-physical knowledge of the territory" is constantly expanding, and studies are being conducted on "12 specific environmental issues including climate, groundwater table, mercury, wildlife habitats, wildlife resources, estuarine environments, forest dynamics, regional economy and social values and way of life of the populations concerned."

Finally, belief amplification is used to stress the necessity of the Grande Baleine project. It is repeatedly emphasized that in the end, when all methods of energy conservation have been employed, when all types of energy sources have been evaluated, when all that is possible has been done for the Native population and for the environment, Québec will still need the James Bay II project.

The Peoples: "Hydro-Québec: A Progressive Partnership with Native Peoples"

To counter Cree opposition to the Grande Baleine project, Hydro-Québec has undertaken a frame transformation manoeuvre. While the Crees criticize the project, Hydro-Québec's discourse depicts them as partners in the development. It is often pointed out that both the Cree and Inuit are members of four of the five boards mandated to review the environmental impacts of the projects. Moreover, in a frame transformation gambit designed both to neutralize Cree stereotyping of Hydro-Québec as exploiter, and to counter allegations of modern colonialism, Hydro-Québec asserts that Indians in Quebec are treated better than in any other province, or in any other place in North America, for that matter. For example, the James Bay and Northern Québec Agreement, "unlike any other of its kind in North America, including the 1971 *Alaska Native Claims Settlement Act*, ensured the continuation of the hunting and trapping economy of the Native communities in Northern Quebec... [and] provides the 17,000 Crees and Inuit of Quebec a degree of autonomy and self-government unequalled elsewhere on the continent".

Hydro-Québec stresses the ways in which Native peoples are assisted in the preservation of their traditional life-styles, including the hunting, fishing and trapping way of life, their language and culture, control of education (the Cree School Board), control of health and social services, and control over the government of their lands. Not only are traditional lifestyles respected, but the Crees enjoy the benefits of modern development. "Traditional and modern economics thrive side by side", the advertisement reads. This amplification of the value of "pluralistic tolerance" is coupled with an invocation of the value of "noblesse oblige". Documents explain how, thanks to the James Bay Agreement, the Cree and Inuit now have access to instruments of modern development "necessary to develop and diversify their economy", such as Air Creebec, Air Inuit, Cree Construction and Cree Energy, enterprises "all owned and operated by Native authorities set up by the 1975 agreement". Moreover, Hydro-Québec promises that the Grande Baleine project will "maintain and improve the already existing mechanisms for hiring Native personnel and for awarding contracts to Native companies".

In contrast to Cree descriptions of the devastation of colonialism in terms of infant mortality rates, suicide and low life expectancy, Hydro-Québec documents and advertisements state that "infant mortality among the Cree dropped by half between the mid-1970s and the mid-1980s, and life expectancy increased from between 40 and 50 to about 70, comparable with other Canadians". Moreover, the Native population has grown by 3.5% per year, twice the rate for the rest of Québec.

With respect to the peoples involved, Hydro-Québec draws upon the value of universalism by stressing its concern not only for the Crees and Inuit of Northern Québec, not only for non-aboriginal Québecers in the south of the province, but more generally for all peoples of North America. "By building some generating facilities a few years before they are required to meet Québec's internal demand, Hydro-Québec can export valuable power that is environmentally sounder than any generating alternative available to Québec's neighbors. In this manner, it will contribute to a better environment for all in North America".

The Moral Order

As a public utility,[8] Hydro-Québec has certain important duties and responsibilities for the society it serves. In striving to depict itself as a good corporate citizen, the company magnifies such values as altruism, responsiveness, openness and responsibility. Its rhetoric asserts that, as a tool of development of a modern government, the company accepts and exercises its responsibility to protect the environment. It takes seriously its duty to provide a clean and cheap energy product to its clients and it respects its obligation to sustain a modern lifestyle through development. Hydro-Québec describes its open communication process,[9] and declares its commitment to the concerns of the Native Peoples. "In response to these [Native peoples'] concerns, the utility plans to adopt various measures to mitigate the impacts of the Grande Baleine Project and wishes to involve the Native communities in both the development and implementation of these measures. The object of these measures will be to integrate the project as harmoniously as possible with the environment."

Corporate responsibility towards the environment is emphasized by pointing out that Hydro-Québec "has had a comprehensive environmental policy in place for over 20 years, implemented by more than 200 environmental researchers, engineers and support staff, plus as many consultants". Moreover, it is often noted that Hydro-Québec spends heavily on environmental mitigation and remedial measures. Two percent of the total budget of phase I of James Bay — some $250 million — was spent on environmental concerns. Furthermore, Hydro-Québec will participate in five environmental review procedures established by the federal and provincial governments before construction of James Bay II begins.

Whereas the Crees stereotype Hydro-Québec as the violator of human rights, Hydro-Québec attacks their opponents (never specifically naming the Crees) for manipulating, distorting and ignoring the facts. In short, opponents of Grande Baleine are accused of the immoral behaviour of telling lies. Declares the Chairman of Hydro-Québec, "In our battles over future energy choices, I lack the dramatic gestures used by our opponents. Even though they are factually flawed — and sometimes bald-faced lies — the activists' stories certainly capture the imagination more than the facts and figures used by utility officials and energy experts". "The first victim of war is truth", a New York audience is told. "Well, we're in a public relations war with certain opponents of hydro power developments in Northern Québec. Some of you may know from past wars with activist groups that their attacks can be vicious and undeserved. I won't stoop to such gestures".

Furthermore, opponents of Grande Baleine are accused of being irresponsible: all they do is criticize. Hydro-Québec's Chairman explains to his American audience that, together, they face difficult choices in planning their energy future. "This group and others like it must lead the way in making those choices. The activists have the luxury of standing off at the side and being against everything". On the other hand, Hydro-Québec, as a good corporate citizen, along with similar companies represented in his audience "don't have that luxury. We in this room have to meet payrolls. We in this room have to make transactions, transfer funds, transmit information, manufacture products, distribute products, manage buildings". Calling upon the value of progress and development, he dramatically declares, "In the post-industrial age, all of these activities — and others essential to our prosperity — have one thing in common. They require that the lights must go on, that the machinery must keep running, that the computer must never be subject to a blackout. In other words, they require absolute reliability in energy supply". One can draw the conclusion that this will be assured with the construction of James Bay II.

DISCUSSION

Several features of the new world order take on particular relevance for relations between indigenous colonized minorities and the state which administers them. In the new world order, heightened international economic interdependency creates new points of vulnerability for political regimes, their state-controlled companies and the transnational corporations upon which they have come to depend.[10] In the Canadian case, lobby groups' effectiveness is enhanced by the federal character of the political system in this country, which provides, by definition, more avenues to decision-makers. In this new world order, the Crees can attack Hydro-Québec through additional points of access and leverage — namely its international financiers and its foreign markets. We are not surprised, therefore, to hear the Chairman of the Board and Chief Executive Officer of Hydro-Québec present his claim before the German-Canadian Business Club of Cologne, Germany, underscoring Hydro-Québec's "long history of co-operation with partners elsewhere in the world, including Europe and the Far East". Moreover, the prominence of transnational corporations in the new world order makes it easier for resistance groups to use certain antagonistic rhetoric in pressing their claims, such as xenophobic appeals and the use of a "David and Goliath" motif in the definition of a conflict situation.

Global mass media coverage and information-sharing technologies are an important characteristic of the new world order. These can have a dual effect on indigenous minorities. Such international distribution of information can create issue saturation (Downs, 1972), which could work against indigenous peoples if the public becomes desensitized to aboriginal issues. The international distribution of information, however, also expands the structure of claims-making opportunities by providing new potential allies and new arguments gleaned from similar cases abroad. For instance, Canada's hypocrisy with respect to its international human rights rhetoric is portrayed by describing the country's domestic practices pertaining to the Crees. Moreover, the Crees found allies abroad in American interest groups, in moral entrepreneurs like environmentalists, and in communities with similar interests such as indigenous peoples in Brazil. Indeed, global information sharing through modern technologies facilitates the creation of highly sophisticated transnational pressure groups skilled at manufacturing and projecting their definition of the situation.[11] Mass media tools, of course, are also available to the state and its corporations, and Communications and Public Relations departments have grown in both size and importance in modern bureaucracies. Hydro-Québec, for example describes the conflict in question as a "public relations war".

In the new world order, fiscal crises coupled with anti-statist neo-conservative ideology and competition for investment capital usually mean that state budgets give low priority to economic and social development programs for indigenous peoples. This configuration augments the pool of indigenous grievances. At the same time, the state's fiscal crisis also constricts employment opportunities for non-aboriginals. Hence, the conflict between indigenous peoples and the larger society is intensified. The former derive their cultural or economic sustenance from the land, and the latter (e.g., the working classes, state entrepreneurs and elected politicians from the larger society) depend upon natural resource extraction and regard the land as one of the last frontiers of economic opportunity. Such a situation is ripe for claims-making discourse alleging victimization of aboriginal peoples. Moreover, belief amplification built around the exploitation of negative stereotypes of the opponent can be expected here. Hydro-Québec's claims to include the Crees and Inuit as beneficiaries of the Grande Baleine complex is an attempt to counter claims of exploitation.

Finally, global trends to power sharing and decentralization make it easier for grassroots indigenous resistance movements to mobilize support by amplifying values of self-determination. Appeals to supra-national bodies such as United Nations agencies supporting self-determination are used to legitimize indigenous minority claims.

CONCLUSION

The carefully crafted discourse of colonized minorities can be highly consequential for the actions and decisions of policy-makers involved in megaprojects with large-scale environmental impacts. In this chapter we have demonstrated the complementarity of the social constructionist and frame alignment approaches for examining social issues such as the conflict over the Grande Baleine complex. Of particular importance was our finding that claims-making discourse, when projected into international public forums, can off-set the power differentials between indigenous minorities and powerful actors in the new world order. Hydro-Québec planners, state legislators and regulators in the U.S.A., for example, have come to lend a close ear to the Crees' definition of the situation.

In our approach, however, there are two missing links which suggest directions for future research. First, we have not examined how the messages projected influence opinion in the mass public and among opinion leaders. To what extent are messages received as they are sent? What is the impact on the audience, for example, of two opposing claims-makers cloaking themselves in the same values? Secondly, we know little about the filtering process for public opinion data. How do gate-keepers interpret such information before passing it on to decision-makers? This latter step in the process remains as important and almost as neglected today, as it was when Blumer (1948) first suggested it as a topic for research. Answers to the questions put forward here would be instructive to both observers and the actors involved in the complex interdependencies of the new world order.

NOTES

[1] Paper presented at the international conference "Geopolitics of the Environment and the New World Order: Limits, Conflicts, Insecurity?", Chantilly, France, January 6–9, 1993, sponsored by SORISTEC (CNRS, France), Groupe de Prospective du ministère de l'Environnement (France) ICSE and the research committee "Environment and Society" of the International Sociological Association. We wish to think the following individuals, without whose help this chapter would not have been possible: Brian Craik of the Grand Council of the Crees; Isabelle Lord and Robin Philpot, Hydro-Québec; research assistant Glenda Wall (Calgary); and librarian Francine Lanouette (ENAP, Montréal).

[2] For a brief overview of the project and an assessment of the financial cost of abandoning it (estimated at $544 million in 1992 dollars), see Bernard, Genest-Laplant, et Laplante Green (1992).

[3] The James Bay and Northern Québec Agreement is a modern treaty signed in 1975 in a context of threatened Cree court action and the hydro-electric development already in progress.

[4] In mid-December, 1992, Dartmouth announced its intention to sell all $6.8 million of its Hydro-Québec bonds, due to student pressure. The Vice-President, however, issued a statement that the college did not take a moral stand on any of the utility's development projects (Canadian Press, 1992).

[5] The films, entitled "The Land of Our Children" and "The Great Whale River", were televised in the U.S. northeast and into Québec from there.

[6] This lobbying was also undertaken by Canadian federal member of Parliament Ethel Blondin, who is an aboriginal person.

[7] The Crees contend that the European connection involved both financing and plans by a prominent European car manufacturer to produce a model which would use a hydrogen-based fuel produced by Hydro-Québec. Furthermore, the Crees allege, aluminum and magnesium companies who are large customers of Hydro-Québec produce their product for export to Europe.

[8] Hydro-Québec is not simply a public utility. Nationalized by the Québec government in the early 1960s, the company is a symbol of Francophone Québec and of
the modernization of Québec society. As a thoroughly French-speaking organization, it was one of the first large Québec companies to offer career opportunities
for Francophones at all levels of the organization.

[9] "Bulletin 5" on the Grande Baleine complex explains the three-step communication process: general information on the Grande Baleine project; feedback / information on the development of the complex; and consultation on the choice of
certain components of the project.

[10] This argument is a variation on the "multiple cracks" thesis in Canadian and
American domestic politics (Grotzins, 1967; Schultz, 1980).

[11] See McCarthy and Zald (1972) on the professional social movement leader and
Barry (1992) on the International Fund for Animal Welfare as one such transnational pressure group operating in the environmental field (e.g., the Canadian
seal hunt).

REFERENCES

Barry, Don
1992   "The campaign against the seal hunt: Boycotting Canadian fish". Atlantic
       Canada Studies Conference IX, Memorial University, St. John's, New-
       foundland.
Bernard, Jean-Thomas, Eric Genest-Laplant et Benoit Laplante Green
1992   "Le coût d'abandonner le projet Grande-Baleine". *Canadian Public Policy —
       Analyse de Politiques*, XVIII (2): 153–165.
Blumer, Herbert
1948   "Public opinion and public opinion polling", *American Sociological Review*,
       XIII. Reprinted in H. Blumer, *Symbolic Interactionism: Perspective and Method*.
       Englewood Cliffs, N.J.: Prentice-Hall.
Canadian Press
1991   "Que. utility to counter 'smears'", *Globe and Mail*, August 9, B3.

1992   "Dartmouth bails out of Hydro", *The Gazette* (Montreal), December 19, A1.
Downs, Anthony
1972   "Up and down with ecology: The issue- attention cycle", *The Public Interest*,
       XXVIII: 38–50.
Goffman, Erving
1974   *Frame Analysis: An Essay on the Organization of Experience*. Cambridge, Mass:
       Harvard University Press.
Grodzins, Morton
1967   "The federal system", in A. Wildavsky (ed.), *American Federalism in Perspec-
       tive*. Boston: Little Brown. Cited in Richard J. Schultz, *Federalism, Bureaucracy
       and Public Policy*. Montréal: McGill-Queen's University Press, 1980.
McCarthy, John D. and Mayer N. Zald
1972   "Resource mobilization and social movements: A partial theory", *American
       Journal of Sociology*, Vol. 82: 1212–1241.
Schultz, Richard J.
1980   *Federalism, Bureaucracy, and Public Policy*. Montreal: McGill-Queen's University
       Press.

Snow, David A. et al.
1986   "Frame alignment processes, micromobilization, and movement participa-
       tion", *American Sociological Review*, Vol. 51: 464–481.
Spector, Malcolm and John I. Kitsuse
1987   *Constructing Social Problems.* Hawthorne, New York.: Walter de Gruyter.
Turner, Ralph
1969   "The public perception of protest", *American Sociological Review*, XXXIV:
       815–831.
Weber, Max.
1947   *The Theory of Social and Economic Organization.* New York: Free Press.

CHAPTER 9

URBAN INDIANS: REFLECTIONS ON PARTICIPATION OF FIRST NATION INDIVIDUALS IN THE INSTITUTIONS OF THE LARGER SOCIETY

George D. Calliou[1]

INTRODUCTION

The main purpose of this chapter is to increase the reader's understanding of the participation, or lack of participation, of First Nation individuals in the urban institutions of Canadian society. Special emphasis will be devoted to participation in two institutions which are pivotal to the future of First Nation people: the economy and post-secondary education. The discussion will take us, necessarily, into a wide-ranging consideration of numerous facilitative or inhibiting factors. These include: *cultural* factors such as individuals' values, personal philosophy, spirituality, and world view; *social psychological* factors like attitudes and self-esteem; *structural* factors like systemic racism; historical factors such as the Treaties and residential schools; and such *community dynamics* as empowerment, mechanisms of informal social control, and coping strategies. Although not all aboriginal persons are status Indians or members of a First Nation, the terms "Indian", "First Nation person", and "aboriginal person" will be used interchangeably throughout, because many of their experiences in the institutions of the larger society are basically similar.

Academic authors are inclined to introduce their work with a declaration of biases and a demonstration of the intellectual roots of their work in the academic literature. In a somewhat similar fashion, I begin with a discussion of my own identity, philosophy, and mentors, even though this chapter is not primarily about me.

Identity and Philosophy

I am a Treaty 8 Cree Indian from the Sucker Creek reserve in northern Alberta, and proud of it. Here, we have a point of incongruence between First Nation people and the larger Canadian society. While the Treaties are a very important component of the identity of most Treaty Indians, too many people in the larger society are rather dismissive of the Treaties, for they regard the Treaties as relics of the past that have little relevance for contemporary society.[2] Whereas Treaty Indians view the Treaties as living, sacred agreements between two nations, Canadian society and its government bureaucrats continuously violate the spirit and intent of the Treaties.[3] Notable, from the standpoint of our interest in the participation of First Nation people in the institutions of urban society, is the federal government's refusal to recognize the portability of Treaty rights. That is to say, the participation of First Nation people in institutional life in urban Canada is rendered very difficult both by the federal government's refusal to extend various programs, such as housing assistance, to those First Nation individuals living off-reserve in the cities and towns of Canada, and by a sense of betrayal felt by First Nation persons. That sense of betrayal is easily understood by the functionalist school of sociology (e.g., Gouldner, 1960) which regards *the norm of reciprocity*[4] as vital to a smoothly functioning society. Urban Treaty Indians, whose ancestors welcomed the Europeans and agreed only to *share* the land with them, find no reciprocity in the aforementioned denial of benefits to those First Nation individuals who can find employment opportunities only off-reserve. The implicit right to sustainable development that informed our ancestors' signing of the Treaties is scarcely honoured on-reserves and is honoured even less off-reserve. As exchange theory (e.g., Blau, 1964) in sociology would predict, the resultant *mistrust* fostered in the minds of many First Nation individuals has seriously undermined the relationship between those individuals and the larger society.

The philosophy which I have learned from the respected Elders and healers, from motivational speakers, and from mentors like Ralph Steinhauer, Willie Littlechild, my grandmother, and my mother, is rooted in the traditional Indian values of generosity of spirit and non-judgementalism. "Lift the other up and the other will lift you up" said one, while another influential notion in my life has been the maxim "Treat everyone like royalty until they prove themselves otherwise. If they do not treat you with respect, then pray for them". These are very positive philosophies that leave little or no room for negativism. Admittedly, as I shall illustrate later in this chapter, the racism of the larger society sometimes tests that positive orientation as I pursue my personal commitment to bridge-building and mutual co-existence with the larger society.

Vision of the Future

Who we are today has a lot to do with both our sense of the past and our vision of the future. Indeed, if our sense of the past is not connected with our sense of who we are today, then it becomes difficult to envision what we want to become. That vision, that sense of purpose in life, that sense of what I want to see the nation, the community, the family, and myself as an individual be, certainly is a very important element of who I am today, for having such a sense of purpose bolsters my self-esteem and self-confidence to meet the challenges of relating to my own culture and to the larger society. Conversely, as the Christian *Bible* says, when people have no vision, they shall perish (Proverbs XXIX: v. 18).[5] The vision which sustains me, personally, is of myself as a bridge-builder — an educator and communicator who creates understanding between peoples. Everything in my career reflects that underlying commitment to inter-group education and communication.

Language

Language, as a major vehicle for that communication, is not just a neutral instrument. Rather, it shapes our very conceptualization of phenomena, such that some phenomena are not translatable into another language and some languages have no word for certain phenomena found in other cultures. Language also has somewhat of a paradoxical nature. On the one hand, it is a key element of aboriginal identity for many aboriginal persons, especially when we are expressing through it our spirituality, our relationship with the land, our understanding of the Treaties, or other aspects of our culture. On the other hand, language poses inherent difficulties for effective communication. Indeed, many non-aboriginal people fail to recognize that although English is an official language, it is, nevertheless, a foreign language in this country; it is not native to this land. Yet, we aboriginal people are forced to speak the foreign language of the English to convey a lot of our spirituality, our thoughts, our essence. Unfortunately, it is not adequate to the task. So, if people want to understand us and the things in which we take pride, they should learn our respective languages. I am proud of my Cree language and heritage.

Kinship and Elders

For First Nation people, whether in the city or on-reserve, family and kinship are extremely important, not only as a source of obligation,[6] but also as a source of the values or touchstones which shape our identity and guide us as we relate to the larger society. For instance, for me, the values which were ingrained in me by my mother and grandmother survived the residential school experience and remain strong to his day. In addition, my grandmother meant so much to me that when she passed away I made several vows to myself, including one that I would devote my life to playing a role in creating a better understanding between people, generally, and particularly between Indian and non-Indian people.

The potential importance of the Elders for urban Indians cannot be overstated. Historically, on the prairies when a camp moved from one location to another, people would be sent ahead to mark a trail so the camp could follow. From time to time they would put marking sticks, sometimes a stick with a feather on it, to indicate that this would be a good place to camp. The route to the camp was marked with guide posts along the way and those who followed would look for the guiding sticks. To me, it is the same in modern life. *We need the Elders to provide us with the guiding principles and to interpret for us how the traditional principles are to be translated in the contemporary urban context.* So, I try to seek out people who can leave guide posts for me and others. I am certainly not the one leaving those guide posts; it's other people who are committed to their community, to their family, to their province, and to their nation.

Maintaining Aboriginality in the City: Relation to the Land and Community

There is a well-developed sociological literature on ethnic identity retention (e.g., Breton et al., 1990). While First Nation peoples are not "mere" ethnic groups — we are, after all, the First Nations and we do have aboriginal rights not enjoyed by immigrant ethnic groups — I do recognize that some of the same principles and phenomena involved in ethnic identity retention have a parallel in the phenomenon of aboriginal people's retention of their aboriginality in an urban setting. However, my treatment of the topic here will involve me speaking from the heart, rather than playing by the more confining rules of the academic game and the academic literature, because it is important that non-Native people also develop the subjective understanding that the famous sociologist Max Weber called *verstehen*. In doing so, I shall allow myself to become more personal than elsewhere in this chapter.

Our relationship to the Creator and the land is a key component of the identity of many of us as First Nation people, although many urban First Nation individuals have grown up in the city and because of artificial barriers imposed by government (e.g., the English language, the former practice of a woman losing Indian status upon marrying a non-Indian) do not know their origins or even how to pursue their origins. Some of us who have moved from rural or remote reserves to live or work in urban areas are not conscious of any compelling feelings to make a periodic pilgrimage back to our home reserve in order to preserve our aboriginality in the city. For instance, I believe that if I have the self-confidence, the self-esteem, the sense of purpose mentioned above, then I am at home wherever I am. I have no qualms about living in the city, although I choose to live in the country because the spirit rests easier out in the country near nature than it does in the artificial environment which the city is. However, my relationship with the land is that I am at home wherever I am within what Indian people call "Turtle Island"; in my language, my relationship to the land is not restricted to my home reserve, because the reserve boundaries are not of our making. If I remain true to my vision, which includes avoiding behaviours that are harmful to the environment, then I do not lose my affinity for the land even though I work in the city.

Yet, many urban Indians have a strong desire to get out of the city. While it is rooted mainly in a strong, ingrained relationship with the land, it is also rooted in the need to stay in touch with the family, the community leaders, the Elders, those who have gone before, and the ceremonies. For me, this is central to maintaining my aboriginality in the city. The support of the Elders, for instance, is absolutely crucial for healing and for enhancing and maintaining my strength as an Indian person who has a strong spirit with strong spiritual foundations. I am also fortunate in that my involvement in various organizations enables me to stay in touch with First Nations' community leaders from across Alberta and Canada.

The unfortunate reality is that funerals provide the occasion for many of us to go back home; we need to pay respect to the family and to the departed one. An happier way of staying connected, though, is by attending pow-wows and ceremonies. Again, it is through the Elders who know those ceremonies that we are able to maintain or enhance the aboriginality that is our essence, for our aboriginality is not to be found in external trappings, but rather in our heart and spirit. That's where our culture, our spirituality, is. The urban Indian who has that spiritual strength, which in turn creates self-esteem and self-confidence, can better withstand the remarks of those who would denigrate him as an "apple" (red on the outside, white on the inside) on account of his choice to work in the mainstream of the larger society.

The Residential School and Early Encounters with Racism

At the age of seven I entered the Indian Residential School at Joussard. That's when I became an Indian. Prior to that, no one ever told me I was an Indian. I was just an happy-go-lucky kid living in an environment of love and care and generosity. Then, one day, it was time to go to the residential school where we were labelled "Indians" by the Roman Catholic staff and administrators. One of my most vivid recollections was of the first day, when all the boys were lined up and the boy at the front of the line would go in the door, the nuns would close the door, and he would come out a bit later looking very different in his haircut and clothing. When my turn came I realized that inside there was a bathtub, which I had never seen before. In there was white murky water, liquid lye soap with water, in which they bathed the "savage Indians". This white, murky water was very symbolic in that they tried to wash our browness away and make us white; that was the intent of the residential school — to assimilate and to integrate. Then they cut my hair, washed my hair, then they washed it in kerosene because "all Indians had lice." Each boy went through that kind of ordeal. They still do that to cattle today and that is how I felt they were treating us. I also remember that the first term there I was unable to speak English; that was difficult for a lot of us. We were forbidden to speak Cree, but they were very hypocritical in that most of the nuns were French and, while they forbade us to speak Cree, when they spoke to one another it was always in their own language.

I was fortunate, in that my mother worked at the residential school. So, in contrast to many other children, the experience was not as traumatic for me. Also, my home community was only seven miles away, so we were able to walk home most weekends, or they would come and get us by wagon in summer or sleigh in winter. Eventually, they would transport us home in the back of a pickup truck and later in a school bus.

Although we did derive some academic benefits from the residential school, plus the ability to speak English, the experience was a very negative one which for many First Nation individuals has exerted its influence not just on the students, but even on subsequent generations who did not attend those schools. We were told in the schools that we are an inferior people, of the devil, so to speak. Also, I can distinctly remember one nun saying to us that if we did not behave, if we did not speak the English language, if we did not go to church, the Germans would come and dig a big hole in the playground and line us up by that hole and shoot us in the back of the head, one by one, and then cover us up. So, it was rule by fear in which they modelled a lot of racist attitudes toward other cultures.

Although my experience was not as traumatic as that of those who suffered physical or sexual abuse at the hands of the priests or nuns, I, too, suffered from the loss of our connection with our home community, for when we finished residential school we no longer fit into our home community. For instance, we could not hunt and some of us had lost our language. Yet, we did not fit into the world of the larger society, either, because they rejected us. The whole experience was almost like time-warp: the safe cocoon before residential school was one time realm; residential school was another time realm; refinding ourselves as to who we are is yet another time realm, and so on. For some, those time realms are disconnected, such that their sense of the past, of who they were, is not connected with who they are today. For those people, deciding what to be in the future becomes very difficult. When that sense of purpose becomes difficult, the temptations of alcohol, drugs and other forms of negative behavior come into prominence in one's mind set and in one's life.

When I first went to the white school after grade 11 in the residential school, I began to understand why some of our people would not leave the reserve. I saw the RCMP beat the living daylights out of an old Indian man who happened to be drunk and sitting on a bench on the sidewalk in a small town. They used their nightsticks and their long flashlight on his head, for no apparent reason at all. Then I began to understand what discrimination and racism were all about and those negative things became prominent in my thinking. The cocoon of protection of our own isolated community was no longer there. It was taken away by experience and by education.

Name calling is another form of racism which First Nation people encounter upon leaving the security of the reserve. One such incident had a profound effect upon me:

> One day, as an eighteen or nineteen-year old I was walking to school in a northwestern Alberta town. On the way was an elementary school that I easily could have walked around. However, often I took the short cut through their playground. There were several instances where I would be right in the middle of the playground and the recess bell would ring and all those white "little savages" would come running out of the school and several little boys would come whooping it up as in Hollywood movies, and yelling out "dirty Indian" and "drunken Indian", and so on. I felt like wringing their ruddy little necks, but I would walk on. That happened three times. When it happened the fourth time, I decided to sit on the ground and ask them to join me. Of course, they immediately stepped back when they were confronted. I could almost see in their face the stricken look of "What have we done to ourselves?" I wanted to ask them, in a quiet way, such questions as "Why do you think I'm a drunken Indian?" One little boy stepped closer and I asked him, "Why do you believe I'm a drunken Indian, or lazy Indian?" His response was "My mom told me so". So, I started chatting with him and the other little guys came closer. They were sitting around me on the ground and I was asking them "Why do you think Indians are drunks?" and so on. Their response was "My mom tells me so"; "My dad tells me so"; "my grandmother", "my grandfather", "the books that I read", "The teachers in my school say those things". I got up from the discussion with those kids and later on gave a lot of thought to it and I came to realize that these little guys do not understand what they are saying; they're just parroting what others have taught them. They're just parroting the ignorance of their peers and Elders. As a result of this, I later changed my attitude towards white people, in general. I realized that most of the people who probably said negative things to Native people were saying them out of complete ignorance. Nevertheless, it is difficult to get over those feelings of hatred towards those people who call you down, because it affects your whole persona, your whole spirit, and your self-esteem and self-confidence. It still leaves a bitter taste in my mouth.

Education exposed all the negatives of the world, more than the positives. We began to see how we were treated. We began to see a lot of the disinformation being taught in the homes and schools, and the outright lies and myths about the reality of Indians as perpetuated by government, schools, and even academic journals and books from kindergarten up to the Ph. D. level. Those things still exist today, unfortunately.

EDUCATION: EMPOWERMENT AND OBSTACLES

Introduction

Regardless of how hospitable or inhospitable post-secondary educational institutions might be to First Nations students, it is an inescapable truth that only post-secondary institutions can provide many of the forms of education and training which First Nation individuals and governments need to thrive in the contemporary era.[7] Such institutions are pivotal to our ability to come out from under the yoke of colonialism. Therefore, a consideration of the ways in which those institutions facilitate or inhibit the academic success of First Nation students is important.

Let us begin by setting the context in which the following discussion occurs. As Eber Hampton, president of the Saskatchewan Indian Federated College, and Steve Wolfson (1993) have written, universities' (and probably other post-secondary institutions') orientations toward First Nation students can fall into any of four types. They are assimilation, accommodation, integration, and independence. The *assimilative* approach welcomes First Nation students, but implicitly requires them to change, to bear the full burden of fitting into the univerity or college on terms set by the university or college. "Leave your culture at the door" is the unspoken motto of these institutions. Most are like this. Other universities adopt the *integrative* approach, wherein the First Nation students are expected to fit into the system, but the university provides help to them in doing so. That help might take such forms as the university paying for special counsellors and tutors, special workshops, a special gathering place on campus, special awards and recognition of the accomplishments of First Nation students, and involvement of local Elders with the First Nation students. An *accommodative* approach goes significantly farther by offering some degree of autonomy, as in the case of the First Nations House of Learning at The University of British Columbia or the Saskatchewan Indian Federated College's affiliation with The University of Regina. This type of institution is able to go much farther than the integrative type in meeting the needs of First Nation students in ways that are culturally appropriate to them. Finally, there is the *independence* model, in which the institution is fully autonomous and its structures, policies, practices, and to a certain extent, curriculum are predicated upon First Nations' cultures.

Most of the discussion in this section pertains to institutions that operate in the assimilative or integrative mode.

Empowerment

There are many ways in which, to one degree or another, First Nation students are empowered to succeed in their post-secondary studies. The very existence of a Native students' centre, such as the one in which I am involved, is one such way. I have been told by Native students "If you guys [The Native Centre] didn't exist, I would have quit a long time ago. I would not put up with the crap that I put up with in class — what professors say and what students say about Native people. But because I know that you guys exist, I struggle along". Thus, in providing moral support, a place to ventilate frustration and anger, a place where First Nation students can relax and be themselves, and a place for sharing experiences and for socialization into the Native student culture, such Native centres facilitate the adjustment of First Nation students to post-secondary academic life.

Another form of empowerment of students occurs when a Native students' centre or a Native club supports and encourages Native students in challenging the system itself to become more conducive to their learning or to eliminate cultural biases, ethnocentrism, and outright racism. An example would be in asking a professor to provide forms of assessment other than the multiple choice exam format — a format which usually provides a very poor indication of the nature and amount of learning gained by students raised in a First Nation culture. The very fact that students approach their own professors to discuss these things is empowering. At the Native students' centre with which I am affiliated, when necessary we help students write letters to their professors or even go with them to their professors, if they so desire, for even the most assertive students sometimes are intimidated by the title "professor". That is something that is passed down culturally, because we have been told by the Department of Indian Affairs and by missionaries that we "must listen to authority". The professor is just such an authority figure.[8]

A third way in which First Nation students are empowered is through receiving help in articulating and clarifying their own goals and in strengthening their commitment to those goals. Those goals might be academic in nature or they might involve cultural discovery / development or personal growth. This can be particularly empowering when it is peer-based — aboriginal students helping aboriginal students. In my job I try to challenge Native students to be the best that they can be, to excel academically, rather than contenting themselves with a mere passing grade. As I point out to them, First Nation communities do not need mediocre First Nation lawyers, or teachers, or engineers, etc.; we need the best lawyers, teachers, engineers, etc. that we can get.

Often, when asked why they are attending university or college, First Nation students will reply: "I want to help my people". Part of the goal articulation function mentioned above involves getting the students to think that answer through more fully, as an Elder once challenged me to do, so as to make the goal more specific. A student who has specificity and clarity in his / her goals is a student who is empowered to get the most out of his / her post-secondary education. The student who has been challenged to look twenty years ahead to envisage the kind of community in which (s)he wishes to be living, is better able to be focused in his / her post-secondary studies — better able to decide what needs to be done today to achieve that goal.

A fourth way in which Native post-secondary students are empowered is to have their spirituality and cultural awareness enhanced. For instance, a lot of students who come to university really have never experienced their own traditions, especially traditional aboriginal spirituality. By protocol, we ask the Elders in the local area to help us to help Native students by providing an opportunity for them to attend pipe ceremonies and go to sweat lodges. For a lot of our students this is the first time they have ever experienced that. For the first time in their lives, they really anchor down, really connect to their own culture and to their own community. That's a very empowering, very motivating, and very emotional time in students' lives. They have a better sense of purpose, a better sense of what they want and where they want to be once we provide that cultural and spiritual facilitation.

Obstacles to Native Students' Post-Secondary Learning

There once was a giraffe which expressed to the world that all elephants are welcome at its house, anytime, just as most universities, colleges and corporations tend to express a similar welcome to the aboriginal community, people with disabilities, women, and visible minorities.[9] One day the elephant comes and knocks on the door of the giraffe. The giraffe opens the door to his opulent house and says to the elephant: "Welcome! Finally you've come to my house. Do come in". The elephant begins to enter but gets stuck in the doorway, because the doorway is made for giraffes, narrow and tall. So, the giraffe says, "Oh, why don't you go around to the back of the house. My basement is on the ground level. I'll chip away my basement so you can fit in and come into my house". The elephant walks around the huge house and by the time he gets to the back he hears the chinking of the cement where the giraffe is making a hole so the elephant can come in through the basement. Finally, the elephant enters the basement and the giraffe says, "Welcome! Make yourself at home." Just as he finishes saying those words, the doorbell rings upstairs. He tells the elephant, "I'll just go check who that is. Make yourself at home". The giraffe then goes up the stairs and does not come down. The elephant stands on his legs and shuffles from one side to the other and then says, "I'm getting tired waiting for the giraffe". The elephant sees a bedroom in the corner of the basement and thinks, "Well, he did say that I should make myself at home, so maybe I'll go lay down". However, in trying to enter the bedroom he once again finds that he cannot fit through a doorway, as the door is narrow and tall for giraffes. The elephant notices a grease pail in the corner of the basement and proceeds to grease himself, in the hope that he'll be able to slide into the bedroom to take a rest. He gets in a little bit further, but still cannot get through, so backs away. Getting tired, the elephant leans against the wall of the basement and the wall starts caving in, because it is not made for the weight of an elephant. Finally, after standing around for a long time, the elephant says "I'd better go check to see what's keeping the giraffe. I'll go upstairs". So, the elephant starts climbing the stairs and the stairs start giving away because they are not made for the weight of the elephant. The elephant and the giraffe never do get together again.

Post-secondary educational institutions are like the giraffe and its house. They and other corporate structures who say "welcome" to aboriginal students, international students, women, visible minorities, and handicapped people, *have not changed the structure of their organizations. Nor have they changed their mind sets, their policies, their operating practices, their teaching styles, etc. to truly welcome those of us who are different from that system.* In Hampton's and Wolfson's framework, they are more in an assimilative mode ("Leave your culture at the door") than an accommodative mode.

One of the practices of universities which is particularly inhospitable, and sometimes devastating, to First Nations students is the **multiple-choice format of tests and exams.** There are quite a few students who do well in short essay questions but poorly in multiple choice because there are cultural factors associated with the multiple choice format. For instance, the linearity of the format is at odds with the circularity of most First Nation cultures. Secondly, English is a foreign language to many of us. The assumption that the student understands all of the nuances of the vocabulary is often invalid. Thirdly, the First Nation student might bring a different interpretive scheme to the assigned reading material, such that (s)he derives a different message from that material than the instructor derives when reading that same material from the instructor's cultural perspective. Further, the intricate manipulation of the language (e.g., some combination of a negative or even double negative, an "all of the above" option, an "all except 'b' above" option, and the fact that the truth or falsehood of an option might revolve around one word or one prefix or even one letter) comes across to some First Nation students as trickery, even when not intended as such by the composer of the question. Such "trickery" is in marked contrast to aboriginal cultures which stress straightforward communication. Having been conditioned to find such "trickery" in multiple choice questions, some First Nation students look for it when it is not present, such that they misinterpret the question.

The **attitudes** which First Nation students encounter on campus, among both faculty and students, are another obstacle to the successful participation of aboriginal students in post-secondary institutions. As such, they are a powerful motivator for First Nations to establish their own post-secondary institutions, as per Hampton's and Wolfson's independence model. Promises of confidentiality that I have extended to students who have confided in me, plus my own personal philosophy of not dwelling on the negative, keep me from dwelling here on the ethnocentrism, prejudice, and racism which First Nation students encounter on campus. However, a few examples are cited below to substantiate my point and to demonstrate that the hallowed halls of higher learning are by no means immune to these malignancies. All of the examples occurred during the mid-1990s at my own or other Canadian universities:

- Item #1: Professor lists religions of the world and puts "savages" (implying North American Indian religions) at the bottom.
- Item #2: A mass on campus where the Catholic priest refers to Indians as "savages" pursuing "heathen" religion.
- Item #3: A collage of student papers was to be made into a book. Aboriginal students felt that their contribution was not appreciated and they were not given the opportunity to follow proper protocol concerning information that should be kept confidential or almost confidential. They opted out of the project and as a result were unduly sanctioned.
- Item #4: Aboriginal students, in quoting Elders as an authority, are asked to provide footnotes from academic sources.
- Item # 5: Obscene, anti-Native, graffiti written on an interior wall of the Native students' centre.
- Item # 6: Note left on the windshield of a car dangling a dream catcher and sweet grass from the rear-view mirror: "I'll kick your (expletive deleted) wagon-burning ass the next time you park so close to my car."

When such ethnocentrism or outright racism occurs in the classroom or elsewhere in the institution, it can have the effect of infuriating aboriginal students and totally destroying their ability to concentrate, not only during that class period, but sometimes for some time to come. Often they will become focused on managing their anger and trying to formulate an appropriate reply and will miss what follows in the remainder of the class period.

Academics have labelled certain behaviours of our community as "**norms**". From this perspective, several academic interpretations will be used to identify further obstacles to the success of aboriginal students in mainstream post-secondary institutions. One, identified by Ross (1992: 38–39), is the norm that *the time must be right* before undertaking a task. This is partly a cultural emphasis on excellence, but in large part the notion that "the time must be right" refers to the completion of the proper preparation for the task, including spiritual preparation. Thus, if a First Nation student has been unable to complete all the required readings for a test, or has been unable to "digest" them to her satisfaction, she might well choose not to take the test. There is no shame in not going forward under those circumstances. However, that might result in a failing grade in the course. Ironically, though, some of our people have come to believe that to prepare or plan is what the white society does — that it is non-Indian — and they reject planning for that reason. Even some who do not believe that allow their behaviour to be guided by that because of a fear of being ostracized by those who do believe it! Such a norm, obviously, is inimical to educational progress.

Another important norm is the norm of *egalitarianism* (Ross, 1992: 39). In many Native communities this is enforced when informal sanctions are imposed against those who, in the mind of the community members, are trying to make themselves "better than" the rest of the community. Some have referred to this as "the crab pot syndrome", by which they are referring to the tendency of crabs in a pot to pull down into the pot any crab that seeks to climb out. This crab pot syndrome is a very conservative ethic that results in social control being exerted against those who aspire to upward mobility. For instance, such a person might be labelled an "apple" by his reference group in his home community. This derogatory term, with its implication that the upwardly mobile person is a traitor to his/her people, can be very hurtful to its target. Anticipation of such loss of social support, or even of outright ostracism, causes some aboriginal students not to achieve to their full potential in their studies.

A third norm relates to the very high value placed upon the (extended) *family* in Native cultures. Obligations (e.g., baby-sitting) to extended family members in the city can also interfere with post-secondary schooling by placing the student in a situation of unbearable role conflict. Such conflict is often resolved in favour of the extended family.

Another rather sensitive matter should also be mentioned. That is, the **residential schools' legacy** sometimes rears its ugly head under the stress of exams and papers as students experience traumatic and academically disruptive flashbacks to abusive incidents. Non-Native counsellors are not usually sensitive to the cultural subtleties which must be involved if counselling is to help such individuals. At these times, a more culturally rooted support system (i.e., a ceremony) might be more appropriate.

There is also a **clash of values** between aboriginal cultures and the larger society on the matter of *individualism versus collectivism*. For many generations our people have been told that we should be doing things not for our own personal benefit, but for the benefit of our community. Yet, post-secondary education is primarily about personal development and self-actualization — the indulgence and sculpting of personal interests and personal potential. Our culture also instills modesty: we should not brag and, as noted above, we should not strive to make ourselves stand out above others in the collectivity.

Thus, despite the norm of excellence discussed above, it becomes difficult for academic advisers to persuade First Nation students to be the best that they can be as individuals, for there is sometimes confusion among those students as to what those norms and values really mean in a contemporary context. The Elders can be very helpful in clearing up that confusion. As an Elder once told me, "A long time ago, when our people decided to climb a mountain they climbed right to the top. They didn't stop part way to look back and say 'I wonder if I should keep going'." What he was implying, and what we need to hear more often from our community, is that it is okay to excel in the "white man's world", that it is okay to excel in the academic world, and not just by being the best academic or the best technical person, but by being the best human being that you can be. That is a very empowering message. We also need to empower our people to learn that we must adapt to any environment because that is what we were, historically. That was our essence: we had to adapt to our environment. No matter how harsh it was, we survived, and we survived with pride. And we need to survive today, in this kind of environment, with pride, and with our cultural, spiritual, and traditional integrity intact.

Other obstacles to aboriginal students feeling at home on the post-secondary campuses of Canada include: alienating curricula designed with no aboriginal input; faculty performance evaluation criteria which emphasize research to the detriment of teaching, thereby leading instructors to shy away from the more labour-intensive teaching and assessment techniques that many aboriginal (and other) students need; the use of out-dated books which no longer reflect the true reality of aboriginal communities and cultures and which therefore result in the perpetuation of myths under the protection of academic freedom; and the fact that most post-secondary institutions employ very, very few aboriginal people, especially on faculty.

Less detrimental than a generation ago is the size and corresponding impersonality of post-secondary institutions, for many aboriginal students are the second generation in their family to have received a post-secondary education. Some are graduate students who are well accustomed to universities. Similarly, culture shock among students is less of a problem than formerly. Indeed, the tables have turned on this matter, as an increasing number of aboriginal students who were not raised in the aboriginal culture are experiencing the temporarily disruption of cognitive re-organization as they encounter their aboriginal culture for the first time.

In concluding this discussion of participation in educational institutions, it should be noted that there have been many positive developments. For instance, my experience has been that once faculty members are confronted with their ethnocentrism or with the need for alternative assessment modes for aboriginal students, they tend to be very co-operative. Secondly, Native student centres at various universities are putting their initial growing pains behind them and are becoming much more spiritual places than they used to be. As such, they are becoming not just a "comfort zone", but an empowering institution within the larger institution. They are becoming a place where First Nation students derive solace, respite, and strength from each other and from the Elders.[10] Thus, a third development is not surprising — namely, that the number of university graduates has grown enormously over the last two decades. For instance, at the university with which I am affiliated we regularly have about two dozen aboriginal students receive an academic degree (graduate or undergraduate) each year. It is also significant that First Nation graduates now come from more diverse disciplinary backgrounds, rather than mainly the faculties of education and social work which predominated among graduates as recently as a decade ago. Finally, this blossoming of First Nation talent is taking us closer to the day when Hampton's and Wolfson's independence model, the model of autonomous post-secondary institutions of First Nation learning, will come to fruition in provinces across Canada.

PARTICIPATION IN OTHER SOCIETAL INSTITUTIONS

Introduction

Positive developments are by no means restricted to the realm of post-secondary education. I have had the good fortune to witness first-hand such developments in the economy, in municipal politics, and in policing during my many years in Calgary. Notwithstanding that city's reputation as a haven for "rednecks", the fact remains that there and elsewhere the institutions of the larger society are slowly coming to grips with the new realities that define Canada around the turn of the millennium. Prominent among those new realities is the emergence of aboriginal people into the mainstream of the larger society. While I am not inclined to civic boosterism, I'd be remiss if I did not acknowledge the significant strides — sometimes of a path-breaking nature — that have been taken in Calgary, for they can be instructive. I hasten to add, though, that much remains to be done to facilitate the successful participation of First Nation individuals in the institutions of Calgary and other cities.

Among Calgary's "firsts" are: its creation of a committee within its Chamber of Commerce to promote the expansion of business opportunities for aboriginal people and the Chamber's appointment of a Treaty Indian to its board of directors; Calgary's appointment of a Treaty Indian to its Police Commission; Calgary's incorporation of a Treaty Indian as an instructor in its training program for rank and file police officers; Calgary's creation of an aboriginal affairs advisory committee to the civic government; Calgary's incorporation of Indians in a featured role in its annual festival (The Calgary Stampede); and the creation of aboriginal development and liaison units in some of the commercial corporations in the city's dominant industry. Some of the gains from these initiatives are very concrete, others are by no means quantifiable, and yet others are transitory or elusive or overshadowed by negative phenomena elsewhere in the organization. An anecdote illustrates the second type:

> The president of the Calgary Chamber of Commerce was hosting a visiting senior executive from an international company. As they were walking downtown they came across two Indian people who were drunk on the street. The attitude of the visitor was, "Isn't this disgusting. Why don't they (Indians) do something about this"? The response of the Chamber of Commerce president was, "No, just a minute. It's not just 'they'. We have a role here, too. We need to provide employment and business opportunities so that this kind of thing doesn't occur. We personally need to take some initiative to create an environment of success for any member of our communities so that they can pursue the benefits that we have". The president relayed that experience to me later and admitted that if he had not had the experience of meeting with, and being educated by, the Indian member of the Chamber's board, his response would have been "Yes, isn't that disgusting."

Unfortunately, other anecdotes are less encouraging, as we shall see below.

Obstacles to Participation

The saga of the elephant and the giraffe is relevant to institutions other than post-secondary education. The extension of a welcome to aboriginal people (and other minorities), accompanied by a failure to carry such official policy through to actual effective implementation by modifying related policies, structures, attitudes, and practices, is commonplace. Consider the following example from the corporate sector, as told to me:

> Managers in a firm received a two-day orientation on Native issues, including family relationships. Later, a Native person approached a manager who had participated in that orientation session and asked for some time off to attend the funeral of his grandmother. In sympathy, the manager, of course, granted the request. The Native person returned at his own time rather than at the time allotted by the corporate policies. The manager was not pleased and the Native person did not explain why he took a longer leave than company policy allowed, perhaps because within his own community people take for granted that the longer time is needed. Aboriginal people often feel that people who care about us should know these things.
>
> After a fairly short time interval, this person again went to the same manager and said, "I'd like to ask for some time off; my grandmother passed away". The manager granted the leave. Some time after the Native person had returned to work, he again approached the same manager with the same request: "I'd like to take some time off. My grandmother passed away. I'd like to go to the funeral". The manager replied, "No way! You only have two grandmothers!" because in the Euro-canadian interpretation "grandparents" are the mothers' mother and father, and the fathers' mother and father. Therefore, one can have only two grandmothers. The Native person left anyway, because the grandmother was more important than the job. He did not return to the job.
>
> Now, the manager had attended the workshop that clearly outlined that in the traditional aboriginal society there are many grandmothers and many grandfathers. However, the policy manual was not changed and the manager's attitude seems to have been only partially changed. The result was that the Native person lost the job, the manager judged him to be a liar, and the stereotype of Native people as unreliable was reinforced.

The **attitudes and world views** of both Native people and non-Native people can also impede the participation of Native people in the institutions of the larger society. On the Native side, the bias against individuals who are upwardly mobile, as noted in the education section above, also applies in other institutional spheres. Closely related to that is the categorical world view that is often expressed among Native people as "You're either with us or you're against us". That is, a social dichotomy, based on distrust and a confrontational strategy for socio-political reform, has emerged in some First Nations communities such that participation in the institutions of the larger society is interpreted as an act of disloyalty to one's people ("selling out"). Even among the less radical, there is often a skepticism about the motives of one who becomes involved with the institutions of the larger society. The suspicion is that such an individual is mainly concerned with personal aggrandizement or with money.

Another problematic attitude is the "Why try?" mindset. This way of thinking, captured in the notion "I've tried, so why should I try it again?", is found among both Native people and non-Native individuals. As Ponting and Wanner (1983) observed in a study of Black Canadians, when such a defeatist attitude permeates a group which is the target of discrimination, the systemic discrimination becomes very difficult to eradicate. That is because it is not only the attitudes and behaviours of Euro-canadians which must be transformed, but also those of the members of the disadvantaged group.

Among non-Native people, there is often a stigma attached both to any Native person who is hired or promoted under an employment equity program, and to the manager responsible for that personnel decision. That stigma can be manifested in practices of social exclusion wherein the individual so hired or promoted is not allowed to fully participate in formal or informal decision-making and informal social interaction. Closely related to this is the widespread *attitude that the only form that equality should take is uniformity or "same-ness"*, as illustrated in such comments as "If we do this for Indians, we'll have to do it for Germans, and Jews, and one-legged males, and ..." *This attitude fails to recognize that true equality can be achieved only when equity considerations are taken into account.* That is, persons in different situations must be treated differently, according to their special needs and strengths, if the ideal of equality is to be achieved at a more meaningful level than hollow rhetoric. So-called "special status" for severely disadvantaged groups, like First Nation people, is a necessary part of true equality.

Another problematic attitude held by non-Native people, especially in the business community, is the notion that opening opportunities to aboriginal firms and individuals is basically just another form of "welfare". Such thinking fails to recognize that it often makes good business sense to provide local economic development for aboriginal communities. The welfare mentality is sometimes accompanied by an attitude which might be colloquially summarized as "Prove it to me. Prove to me that Native people are reliable in this organization". If no Native people have ever worked in that corporation, the proof is rather difficult to assemble! A related attitude is captured in the business slogan "Success breeds success". Both of these attitudes can become a *self-fulfilling prophecy*. That is, Native people will not succeed in that organization because the opportunity is not opened to us, because the "failure" of one is generalized to the larger set of Native employees and Native applicants, or because people fail to recognize the success which does exist within their midst. Conversely, the strength in some organizations is that they quickly eliminate such obstructionists and put in place people who will act before the evidence is provided, who believe that it is good business to do those things, and, thus, do not need prior evidence. Indeed, they create the evidence by doing whatever they can to provide an environment for success for Native people who come into the organization.

Widespread *ethnocentrism* among Euro-canadians also impedes the institutional participation of First Nation individuals. Euro-canadians tend to display a "Do-it-our-way; leave-your-culture-at-the-door" attitude of cultural superiority and tend to be antagonistic toward aboriginal efforts at institutional pluralism. That is, aboriginal people's efforts to create parallel institutions, such as an aboriginal justice system or a First Nations university, tend to be opposed as separatist or, again, as "special status".[11] We even encountered that attitude in creating the Calgary Indian Friendship Centre, which, in many respects, is a bridging institution rather than a parallel institution. For the most part, the Euro-canadian society has not gone over to understand the First Nation population. Five hundred years of contending with that have left my people very distrustful of whites. An optimistic sign, though, is that the corporate world is gradually shifting to a managerial style that is more consistent with aboriginal culture. Reference here is to the increasing popularity of the more egalitarian, less hierarchical managerial styles that have characterized aboriginal social organization for generations. I submit that Euro-canadian ethnocentrism is breaking down, although perhaps without much awareness on the part of Euro-canadian managers of just how ethnocentric they had become. The emergence of books like Murphy's *The Genius of Sitting Bull: Thirteen Heroic Strategies for Today's Business Leaders* might mean that the larger society is beginning to become more open to learning from aboriginal people. Regardless, in re-inventing the corporation for the twenty-first century, the larger society's corporations and other institutions are going to have to take aboriginal people into account, as clients and as employees, in their organizational structures, policies, reward systems, etc. In addition, the aboriginal people and communities will become effective and efficient institutional and business partners.

Language is an important barrier to successful participation. The inability of the larger society to receive Native people, even occasionally, in the Native people' own language was identified above as a source of frustration to Native peoples. Sometimes First Nation people and the bureaucracies of the larger society simply operate in different universes of discourse, to the detriment of First Nation people's effective participation in them.[12] For instance, when it comes to complaints against the police, the term "excessive use of force" has a narrow, technical meaning within the bureaucracy for adjudicating complaints against police. A First Nation individual might complain about being "roughed up" by the police or "beaten up" by the police. In a formal complaint, that is translated into "excessive use of force", which activates various definitional criteria that must be met before the allegation is considered to be upheld as a *bona fide* case of "excessive use of force". When the complainant is asked to explain his complaint, he might merely say "Well, I got beaten up". As the investigator seeks to deconstruct the incident by asking various questions about the specifics of it, the complainant, whose recollection of the incident is in more holistic terms, can come to feel that his integrity is being questioned, that he is not being accorded proper respect, and that he is being victimized again. This interpretation might be particularly likely if he is from one of the First Nations cultures in which asking many questions is considered to be rude. The fact that he is not articulate in English and the conversion of his experience into "legalese" contribute to an outcome wherein the English language, in effect, operates as a shield to protect and vindicate the perpetrator.

Racism and stereotyping, however, are still commonplace in Canadian society. In my business career I have encountered racism in the field (e.g., in restaurants, hotels, and car rental agencies) and, more importantly for our interest in participation in societal institutions, in corporate headquarters. I hasten to add that some corporations have inspired leaders who lead by example in the respect shown to the aboriginal community and in efforts to open opportunity structures to aboriginal people. Often, however, that orientation is not shared widely enough within the organization. In addition, some corporations' commitment to employment equity is highly suspect, such that their employment equity efforts appear to be grounded more in compelled compliance with federal regulations than in conviction. In my capacity as Director of Native Affairs for a large oil company, I also had the experience of having First Nation people from other companies come to me to share their experiences with racism in the workplace. Two examples illustrate how offensive, demeaning, and disheartening such racism can be:

ITEM #1: A meeting was called to discuss strategy on how to pursue development in a particular area and the socio-economic and environmental impact
of that development. In the area were several trap lines held by Métis and
Indian people; so, the potential impact on Native people was substantial. An
aboriginal member of the professional staff and two non-aboriginal colleagues who worked with him on a regular basis were to attend this meeting
in the corporate board room, along with the project manager who was an
engineer from elsewhere in the organization. However, the aboriginal staff
member had prior commitments which would cause him to be about ten minutes late for the meeting. The project manager did not know the other participants in the meeting; he had only a list of names of those who would be
attending. When the aboriginal staff member walked into the room after his
other commitment, the project manager abruptly stopped the meeting and
gruffly said, "Are you in the right building?" The aboriginal staff member's
colleagues quickly informed the project manager that the person was, indeed,
in the right building, was, indeed, in the right room, was, indeed, in the right
meeting, and was, indeed, in the right corporation addressing issues important to the corporation.

ITEM #2: A corporation voluntarily undertook to provide a program for
Native people where they would offer First Nation secretaries or reception-
ists, chosen by their bands, three or four months of experiential learning in a
corporate setting to enhance their skills. The appropriate location within the
corporation was sought, the appropriate supervisor was sought, and a Native
person from the Native affairs office in the company was asked to assist in this
selection. One of the persons being considered as a supervisor of these
"interns" was considered a top performer. The Native affairs representative
had never met her. From the corporate perspective, her behaviour and comments were positive, but in "reading between the lines" of her comments and
in reading her body language, the tone of her voice, and the things left unspoken, the Native affairs representative became uncomfortable with her as a
supervisor of the Native interns. These concerns were expressed to the personnel officers, but the Native affairs representative was out-voted because of
this person's reputation as a "top notch" supervisor.

   When one of the interns was assigned to that supervisor, the supervisor's
behaviour toward her became deplorable. She would literally wait at the door
looking at her watch until the Indian intern came in, whether the intern was
five minutes early or five minutes late. The supervisor would then leave the
door and white people would walk in late after the intern, and that was never
noted. The supervisor scrutinized the intern relentlessly. She would stand
behind the intern and literally look over her shoulder on a regular basis. She
also timed the intern's coffee breaks. Thus, the supervisor appeared to be
operating on the basis of stereotypes of Indians as late and unreliable.

   Of course, such behaviour, reminiscent of that of the nuns in the residential schools, infuriated the intern. Not surprisingly, her performance suffered.
The Native affairs representative tried to intervene but the intern decided
that this was not the experience for which she had come, and returned to her
reserve.

   Stereotypes also afflict the thinking of police officers whom I encounter in
the training sessions which I deliver to the police department. The stereotype of
Native people as alcoholics is perhaps the most prevalent.

   A **value conflict** between Native people and non-Native people also affects
the ability of Native people to integrate into the institutions of the larger society.
Of particular relevance in the natural resource extraction industries is the clash

between Native values of living in harmony with the natural environment and Euro-canadian values of conquering or exploiting the environment. That reluctance to do harm to the environment will sometimes cause a Native employee not to live up to the expectations of his or her corporate employer. However, the employer, perhaps consciously or unconsciously operating under the biblical notion in the Book of Genesis that God gave dominion over the land and the animals to human beings, is more likely to interpret such behaviour as laziness or lack of reliability than as a response to the ethical dilemma that it is for the Native employee. Interestingly, though, I observe a certain convergence of values among some of the most "successful" (in Euro-canadian terms) business people and aboriginal cultures, in terms of such important matters as spirituality, giving to the community, and care of Mother Earth. The irony is that it is only some five percent of the business community who have reached that elite status, and the other ninety-five percent who seek to emulate them seem to largely overlook those value positions as they reach in harmful ways for the "brass ring".

The **assimilative and restrictive policies of DIAND** (the Department of Indian Affairs and Northern Development) should not be overlooked as an obstacle to successful participation. Here I refer, in particular, to the Department's refusal to provide the same benefits to off-reserve First Nation individuals as it provides on-reserve. Most people, Native or non-Native, coming to the city for the first time find cities alienating in their seeming inhumanity and in the insularity and competitiveness of their residents. That alienation impedes participation in urban institutions and DIAND's withholding of benefits merely exacerbates the problem for First Nation migrants. Similarly, DIAND's policy pertaining to the funding of post-secondary education has created waiting lists of First Nation individuals who seek funding to attend a post-secondary institution. I submit that it would be difficult to find a more short-sighted policy than one, like this one, which denies educational opportunities to the highly motivated and capable members of a disadvantaged population.

Coping Strategies

From all of the above it is evident that the participation of First Nation persons in the institutions of the larger society is often a very difficult matter, sometimes for both the First Nation persons and the personnel of the institution in question. A few comments are in order on the strategies employed by First Nation individuals in coping with the trials and tribulations associated with participating in those institutions.

Coping strategies can be divided roughly into those which are dysfunctional to empowerment and pursuit of opportunity, and those which are functional for empowerment and opportunity. Most of the former are well known, such as escapism through the abuse of alcohol, drugs, or other substances that dull the pain, the indignation, the exasperation, and the despondency.[13] Such substance abuse might be seen as the internalization of frustration, which inevitably increases internal tension. If no positive outlet is found, internalization can culminate in withdrawal from the situation (e.g., quitting a job) or in a downward spiral of substance abuse and dysfunctional social relations. Role models who provide examples of more constructive ways of dealing with the challenges of participation are of vital importance in combatting dysfunctional coping.

Key among those role models are the Elders of the person's home community, as I have experienced personally. They have taught me to avoid lashing out in ways that are very hurtful to me. In addition, they have been invaluable in helping me to build a degree of self-confidence and self-worth that give one the "thick skin" which is sometimes necessary when dealing with non-Native people. As noted earlier, Elders also provide spiritual anchorage, interpretations of traditional cultural norms, and spiritual nourishment that can be invaluable in sustaining the individual in the face of adversity in the institutions of the larger society. Somewhat similar functions are served, formally and informally, by Native Advisers hired by corporations. Indeed, First Nation employees sometimes reach outside the boundaries of their own corporation to seek the counsel of a Native Adviser in another corporation or institution.

CONCLUSION

Boldt's (1993) vision of justice for First Nation peoples is defined in terms of our ability to survive in Canadian society with our aboriginal culture in a healthy condition such that it can adapt to modern times. He calls for First Nation individuals to participate more fully in the mainstream, urban economy (Boldt, 1993: 237). This chapter has focused on two institutions that are of vital importance for the attainment of any such justice. Our gaze was fixed upon obstacles that stand in the way of that justice. I conclude by emphasizing and developing four points from the text above.

First, if an healthy, mutual co-existence between First Nation peoples and the larger Canadian society is to be attained, Canadian society must fundamentally re-invent some of its core institutions. Mere tinkering will not suffice. Good intentions will not suffice. The saga of the giraffe and the elephant must come to an end with a much different resolution than in the fable. Decision-makers in the institutions of Canadian society must wake up, for enlightened self-interest dictates that aboriginal people must be taken into account, as employees, and as markets or clients or politicized foes. It is ironic that the major chartered banks in this country, long considered a bastion of conservatism, have awakened to that enlightened self-interest. Also ironic is the fact that academia, ostensibly a hot-bed of radicalism, vision, and creativity, is largely oblivious to the need to better accommodate aboriginal people.

That takes us to our next point. Aboriginal people do have things to teach to the larger society and its institutions, such as universities and colleges, law enforcement, justice, and commercial corporations. That, however, requires that the persons in positions of power and control in those institutions help to create, *and disseminate within the organizational culture*, an environment for aboriginal people to be successful. Institutional change must not be confined to the hearts of a few good people. It must permeate the organization, including its structures, its implemented policies, its operating procedures, and its reward system.

Thirdly, resistance to justice for aboriginal people must be overcome. A new social contract must be developed and it must address the fundamentals of how First Nation people are to be incorporated into Canadian society. Strident calls for uniformity in the name of equality must be denounced for what they are: assimilationist and inherently dishonest, whether that is recognized by their proponents or not. Aboriginal people have finely tuned receptors for detecting assimilation in any guise. As long as those assimilationistic undertones remain, the trust that is necessary for healthy, smoothly functioning inter-group relations will be elusive. As long as that trust is elusive, the healing of First Nation people will not be complete. As long as trust is elusive, First Nation people will find that the appeal of what Hampton and Wolfson called the independence model will be substantial and there will continue to exist a contingent within the aboriginal community for whom withdrawal is more appealing than working within the system of the larger society.

Finally, let us not overlook aboriginal youth. Our guiding vision must be one that opens opportunity structures for them. The negative impact of the residential schools, which was transmitted multi-generationally to even the grandchildren of the residential school students, has been described as "paradise lost"; we must open the structures of opportunity to allow for paradise to be regained by aboriginal youth. By that I refer not to some former, ostensibly idyllic way of life, but to a condition of pride in one's culture, one's people, and oneself — a condition where role models of aboriginal success are to be found throughout one's home society and among the institutions of the larger Canadian society.

NOTES

[1] Editor's Note: The author has granted the editor licence to add certain sociological perspectives to this chapter and to reference in conformity with the style used elsewhere in this book.

[2] Ponting (1988:66–72) found in his 1986 national survey of non-aboriginal people in Canada that Canadians are evenly split on the issue of Treaties. Forty percent agreed and forty percent disagreed with the statement: "Treaties with Indians are historical documents that have little relevance to modern times". (Another 11% were neutral and 8% fell in the "Don't know; No answer" category.)

[3] In promoting his government's infamous and highly assimilation-oriented 1969 white paper, then Prime Minister Pierre Trudeau said: "It is inconceivable, I think, that in a given society one section of the society have a treaty with the other section of the society. We must all be equal under the law and we must not sign treaties among ourselves. . . ."

[4] The norm of reciprocity is a norm which obliges us to return benefits to those from whom we have previously received benefits. Gouldner (1960) and others have observed that, to the best of our knowledge, it is found in all cultures.

[5] The reference is to the King James Version of the *Bible*. Ironically, the very people (missionaries) who are some of the most devoted adherents to the *Bible* were responsible for First Nation people almost losing our vision as First Nations.

[6] Isajiw (1990:36) points out that ethnic identity has a moral component that involves a sense of obligation to the ethnic group. Among First Nation people, that sense of obligation is very strong, especially in the form of obligation to extended family.

[7] That First Nation cultures can provide many insights and practices that would enhance the functioning of those post-secondary institutions is also certainly true, as is the point that First Nations need to develop their own post-secondary institutions, but these two arguments will not be developed in this chapter.

[8] Of course, some non-aboriginal students hold a similar deference towards authority.

[9] This story is taken from an account by Roosevelt Thomas, founder of the American Institute for Diversity.

[10] Increasingly, Native student centres are also becoming a place where non-aboriginal students are expressing their hunger for knowledge about aboriginal people as provided by aboriginal people.

[11] In Ponting's 1986 national survey of non-aboriginal people, he found strong and consistent antagonism to special status for Native people. See Chapter Six in this volume and Ponting (1987: 5, 55–60).

[12] See Ponting (1986: 93, 102) for related examples. Maynard (1988: 320–321) provides many additional references in the discourse analysis literature on language in institutional settings.

[13] Obviously, Native people have no monopoly on such dysfunctional behaviours.

REFERENCES

Blau, Peter
1964 *Exchange and Power in Social Life.* New York: John Wiley & Sons.
Boldt, Menno
1993 *Surviving as Indians.* Toronto: University of Toronto Press.
Breton, Raymond et al.
1990 *Ethnic Identity and Equality: Varieties of Experience in a Canadian City.* Toronto: University of Toronto Press.
Hampton, Eber and Steve Wolfson
1993 "A Vision of First Nations Controlled University Education in Canada: The Saskatchewan Indian Federated College Model and Beyond". Brief presented to The Royal Commission on Aboriginal Peoples' National Round Table on Education, Ottawa: July 6–8.
Gouldner, Alvin
1960 "The Norm of Reciprocity", *American Sociological Review* XXV: 161–178.
Isajiw, Wsevolod
1990 "Ethnic Identity Retention", pp. 34–91 in Raymond Breton et al., *Ethnic Identity and Equality: Varieties of Experience in a Canadian City.* Toronto: University of Toronto Press.
Maynard, Douglas W.
1988 "Language, Interaction, and Social Problems", *Social Problems*, XXXIII, 4: 311–334.
Murphy, Emmett C. (with Michael Snell)
1993 *The Genius of Sitting Bull: 13 Heroic Strategies for Today's Business Leaders.* Englewood Cliffs, N.J.: Prentice-Hall.
Ponting, J. Rick and Richard A. Wanner
1983 "Blacks in Calgary: A Social and Attitudinal Profile", *Canadian Ethnic Studies*, XV, 2 (1983): 57–76.
Ponting, J. Rick
1986 *Arduous Journey: Canadian Indians and Decolonization.* Toronto: McClelland & Stewart.

1987 *Profiles of Public Opinion on Canadian Native People and Native Issues/Module 2: Special Status and Self-Government.* Calgary: University of Calgary Research Unit For Public Policy Studies (Research Report 87-02).

1988 *Profiles of Public Opinion on Canadian Native People and Native Issues/Module 5: Land, Land Claims, and Treaties.* Calgary: University of Calgary Research Unit For Public Policy Studies (Research Report 88-02).

Ross, Rupert
1992 *Dancing With a Ghost: Exploring Indian Reality.* Markham, Ont.: Octopus Publishing.

FURTHER READING

Breton, Raymond and Gail Grant Aikian
1984 *The Dynamics of Government Programs for Urban Indians in The Prairie Provinces.* Montreal: Institute for Research on Public Policy.

Reeves, William J. and James S. Frideres
1981 "Government Policy and Indian Urbanization: The Alberta Case," *Canadian Public Policy* VII, 4: 584–595.

Culture and Community

CHAPTER *10*

FIRST NATION CULTURES AND COMMUNITIES
EDITOR'S INTRODUCTION TO PART *3*

J. Rick Ponting

INTRODUCTION

Chapters Three (History: 1970–96) and Five (Introduction to Part 2) dealt with various aspects of First Nation cultures. Chapter Three discussed the commodification of aboriginal culture. The government's policy of cultural genocide was also discussed there, while Chapter Five considered the residential school as a vehicle for that policy. Boldt's thesis of cultural crisis, with its emphasis on the culture of poverty and the culture of dependence, was discussed at length in Chapter Five and a critique of it was offered. Special attention was devoted there to the multifacetted cultural revival that is occurring among First Nations.

This chapter and Part 3 of the book will not cover that same ground. This chapter begins with a cursory overview of the great cultural diversity which exists among First Nation peoples in their diverse physical environments. Next, the web of institutional interdependencies (e.g., how economy, family, and religion are intertwined) in the traditional hunting, fishing, trapping, and gathering economy is emphasized and illustrated briefly.

The second main section of this chapter dwells on the centrality of language for the preservation of First Nation cultures. It presents quantitative data, from the 1991 Aboriginal Population Survey (APS), which show the demographically very precarious existence of numerous First Nation languages, especially off-reserve. From the same survey, other data will show language-use patterns across a number of institutional spheres.

The section thereafter outlines the value conflicts which exist between First Nation cultures and the culture of more technological societies such as the capitalistic society which dominates North America.

The fourth section addresses the issue of acculturation and the associated issues of cultural insecurity and authenticity. It advocates a conceptualization of acculturation that allows for the acquisition of some traits of another culture without necessarily losing part of one's original culture in the process (the "150% person" thesis). The section then shifts to a consideration of the spiritual revival among First Nations.

The final part of this chapter deals with First Nation communities. Drawing from the sociological and social anthropological literature, it addresses such phenomena as First Nation families, social stratification, social control, politics,

247

and cleavages. A sociological conceptualization of leadership will serve to introduce Crowfoot's account of the role of First Nation chiefs.

TRADITIONAL FIRST NATION CULTURES AND THE WEB OF INSTITUTIONAL INTERDEPENDENCIES

The vastly different geographical and ecological settings in which First Nations lived naturally produced highly varied cultures. Six major cultural areas have been identified: the Algonkian, Iroquoian, Mackenzie River, Plains, Interior Plateau, and Pacific Coast. While this is not the place for an anthropological exposé, a cursory review of each culture is in order to set the context.

The Iroquoian culture, with its agriculture-based economy, and the Pacific Coast culture, with its reliance on the salmon and other fruits of the sea, were sedentary, while the others were mainly migratory. The Plains peoples were noted for their economy based on the buffalo and their use of the horse, "travois", and "tipis". In contrast, the Pacific coastal peoples were noted for their use of cedar dugout canoes, cedar plank houses, cedar bark clothing, and highly developed artistry with cedar (e.g., totem poles) and other materials. They traded extensively with both other coastal peoples and interior peoples. Birch bark canoes were an hallmark of the southern Algonkians, as were snowshoes and toboggans. The Iroquois were noted for their bark longhouses and their highly developed political systems, including The Great Law of Peace, a constitutional document of one hundred and seventeen clauses after which the constitution of the United States of America is said to be modelled (see Maclaine and Baxendale, 1990: 100–121). The Mackenzie River culture was a hunting (e.g., caribou and moose), fishing, trapping and gathering migratory culture, although log homes were sometimes used. The Plateau culture of British Columbia and Yukon was similar in many respects, but its economy also included the catching of migrating salmon through the use of dip nets and wicker cage traps and its western peoples adopted aspects of the social organization of the Pacific Coast peoples.[1]

From the above, it is apparent that the land is pivotal in most First Nation traditional cultures. "The land", however, encompasses not only earth, but also the waters, the heavens, and all living and "non-living"[2] entities in nature. The land is also viewed as the source and sustainer of life. As Chief Harold Turner told the Royal Commission on Aboriginal Peoples:

> Our responsibilities to Mother Earth are the foundation of our spirituality, culture, and traditions.

(RCAP, 1996b: 117)

Furthermore, in First Nation cultures, the biblical notion that people have dominion over the land is heresy; rather, people are subject to the land's dominion.

Dale Auger's chapter in this section richly illustrates First Nation cultures' close connection to the land. Rupert Ross also captures the close ties to the land and the tight integration of what in the larger society are differentiated institutional spheres. Says Ross (1992: 140):

> Each family off on its own in the bush occupied at one and the same time what we would call its workplace, its home, its recreation centre, its school, its

nursery, its library, its shopping centre and, most critically, its place of worship. … By contrast, we lead very compartmentalized lives.

Thus, different institutional spheres were highly interdependent. A person's role in the economy was inseparable from his/her role in the family; spirituality permeated daily life; education came at the side of a family member and was also spiritually imbued. Perhaps this tight cultural-institutional integration is brought into boldest relief with the introduction of stressors which disrupt one institution, such as the hunting economy. The relocation of a community from one ecosystem to another is an example of a stressor having a multi-institutional dysfunctional impact. The final report of the Royal Commission on Aboriginal Peoples discussed this at length (RCAP, 1996a: 411–520.) Rosemary Brown's (1990: 92–103, 112, 120–143) account of the impact of oil exploration among the Lubicons of Northern Alberta provides a concrete illustration of tight institutional linkage.

Brown points out that the arrival of a flurry of oil exploration traffic and activity (e.g., the drilling of over four hundred wells within a fifteen-mile radius of their community between 1979 and 1986) drove away the moose, the mainstay of the Lubicon diet, and other fur-bearing animals and small game. Social relationships that had been based on a hunting and trapping economy fell into disarray. As social assistance payments replaced hunting as the main form of sustenance, the men lost their role as provider for their families and sank into frustrated alienation and depression. The men lived in the community for most of the year, rather than working in the bush, and the family came under obvious pressure. Substance abuse became a common mode of coping with boredom and despair, and marital conflict and spousal abuse emerged. In addition, extended family ties weakened, for the glue provided by sharing the gains of the moose hunt dissolved when hunting was replaced by shopping for pre-packaged foods. As Brown described in Chapter Seven of the present volume, the roles of women underwent dramatic change, some of it in a less egalitarian direction. In addition, religious ceremonies attendant upon the catching, preparing, and consumption of the animals fell into disuse; respect for elders diminished; and, with the decline in traditional rituals and knowledge, participation in the religious structures of the larger society increased. Gossip and tension increased, while co-operation and sharing diminished. New political structures emerged in response to negotiations with government and the Lubicon action in the courts.

LANGUAGE

In Canada there are about fifty different First Nation languages which can be classified into ten major linguistic groups.[3] Many First Nation languages are endangered, for the number of speakers is dwindling to alarmingly low levels. For instance, 1991 census data (Statistics Canada, 1993: Appx. 4) reveal over half of all First Nation languages in Canada to be spoken by fewer than five hundred adults (persons aged 15 and over). Examples of some of the most precarious languages, with the number of adult speakers in parentheses, are: Sarcee (110), Tahltan (130), and Tutchone (185) from the Athapaskan family of languages; Haisla (160), Heiltsuk (190) from the Wakashan family; Bella Coola (135), Lilooet (90), Sechelt (115), and Squamish (120) from the Salishan family; Maliseet (430) from the Algonkian family; and Haida (170). Indeed, among persons covered by the 1991 census, only two languages exhibited real strength in numbers. They are Cree, spoken by 59,335 adults and by 12,655 children aged 5–14, and Ojibwa, spoken by 23,600 adults and 3,445 school-aged children.[4]

A truism among linguists is that different languages are not merely equivalent ways of expressing the same reality. For instance, unlike the English language, some languages do not differentiate between the genders or between past, present, and future tenses. Some languages, like French, ascribe a gender to seemingly inanimate objects, like a table. Some concepts simply cannot be translated from one language into another, for a language embodies and structures our way of thinking and of perceiving the world. Thus, the death of a language is of major concern, for *when a language is lost a world-view is lost with it*. Furthermore, transmission of the indigenous culture to succeeding generations is severely handicapped by the loss of the language. Simply put, some aspects of the broader culture of a First Nation die when its language dies. As the Royal Commission on Aboriginal Peoples stated:

> For Aboriginal people, the threat that their languages could disappear is more than the prospect that they will have to acquire new instruments for communicating their daily needs and building a sense of community. It is a threat that their distinctive world view, the wisdom of their ancestors, and their ways of being human could be lost as well.

(RCAP, 1996c: 602–603)

Only a small number of aboriginal people speaks an aboriginal language, due to a rupturing of language transmission from older to younger generations in the aftermath of the residential schools (RCAP, 1996c: 603–607). Data from the 1991 census and Aboriginal Population Survey show that only about 165,000 First Nation individuals have an aboriginal mother tongue and only 70% of that number have an aboriginal language as the language most often spoken at home. Clearly, linguistic assimilation is rampant.[5]

The data also convey, loudly and clearly, the message that First Nation reserves are an incubator for First Nation languages, while the off-reserve environment poses major threats to First Nation languages. This is shown in Table 1. Let us first examine First Nation children. On-reserve First Nation children are almost five times more likely than off-reserve First Nation children to speak an aboriginal language at home, and are six times more likely to speak it at school. Whereas over one-third of on-reserve children speak an aboriginal language and another one-fifth understand it but do not speak it, among off-reserve First Nation children only about one in twelve speaks an aboriginal language and the combined total of those who speak or understand an aboriginal language is only about one-fifth.

Among First Nation adults, over half residing on-reserve speak an aboriginal language, whereas only one-fifth of First Nation adults living off-reserve have that ability. Those adults living on-reserve are roughly three times more likely to speak an aboriginal language—whether at home, at school, at work, or elsewhere—than are off-reserve First Nation adults. Over half the off-reserve First Nation adults never spoke an aboriginal language, whereas the same is true for only one-quarter of on-reserve adults.

For the total First Nation population aged five and over, about 30% speak an aboriginal language and another 15% understand it, but do not speak it. Another 5% formerly could speak an aboriginal language, but no longer can,

TABLE 1 Aboriginal Language Use, By Age and Residence, 1991

	Children (5-14)					Adults (15+)					TOTAL On- and Off-Reserve	
	On-Reserve Freq.	On-Reserve Percent	Off-Reserve Freq.	Off-Reserve Percent	Children Total	On-Reserve Freq.	On-Reserve Percent	Off-Reserve Freq.	Off-Reserve Percent	Adult Total	Freq.	Percent
A. Speak aboriginal language	17945	36.3	6095	8.2	24035	66720	56.7	43045	20.3	109765	133800	29.5
B. Venue in which spoken												
Home	17325	35.0	5690	7.7	23015	64615	54.9	36160	17.1	100775	123790	27.3
School	15145	30.6	3665	4.9	18810	8755	7.4	4185	2.0	12940	31750	7.0
Work						21750	18.5	9885	4.7	31635	31635	7.0
Other Places	15970	32.3	4685	6.3	20655	63405	53.9	37945	17.9	101350	122005	26.9
C. Understand, but not speak	9585	19.4	9090	12.3	18675	16865	14.3	34165	16.1	51030	69705	15.4
D. Did speak, but no longer	3450	7.0	2585	3.5	6035	5445	4.6	13140	6.2	18585	24620	5.4
E. Never spoke	18460	37.3	56385	76.0	74845	28585	24.3	121625	57.4	150210	225055	49.7
TOTAL: A+C+D+E	49440	100.0	74155	100.0	123595	117615	100.0	211975	100.0	329590	453180	100.0
Ratio: A / E	0.97		0.11		0.32	2.33		0.35		0.73	0.59	

Note: Eighty-seven percent of on-reserve adult respondents who never spoke an aboriginal language reported that they would like to learn one. For off-reserve adult respondents the corresponding figure is 74%. Ninety-two percent of on-reserve adult respondents who have lost their ability to speak an aboriginal language that they once spoke reported that they would like to relearn it. For off-reserve adult respondents the corresponding figure is 88%.
Source: Statcan Cat. No. 89-533, Table 2.3 & 3.3, pp. 20, 26, and 32 (for adults) and pp. 70, 76, and 82 (for children).

while the remaining half of the First Nation population never could speak an aboriginal language. Interest in learning or re-learning the aboriginal language is high among First Nation adults who do not speak it, especially among those living on-reserve.

The above rather unsurprising pattern of greater aboriginal language use on reserve also applies to consumption of aboriginal language media, such as newspapers radio, television, and videos (Statistics Canada, 1993: Table 2.3). Similarly, of those First Nation adults who had used the services of an health, social, or legal professional in the two years prior to the 1991 Aboriginal Population Survey, on-reserve residents were far more likely than off-reserve residents to have received service in an aboriginal language (44% vs 12%, respectively, for a combined total of 31%). On-reserve adults (65%) were also more likely to participate in traditional aboriginal activities, although such participation by off-reserve First Nation adults was reasonably high at 45%. The total for the off- and on-reserve populations together was 52%.

First Nation elders, teachers, and other leaders are well aware of the gravity of the linguistic situation and are taking steps to preserve aboriginal languages. These include such measures as language instruction programmes, aboriginal media programming, and the recording of the elders' stories, songs, and accounts of history in the Native language. It remains to be seen whether this form of cultural revitalization is keeping pace with the death rate among the First Nation senior citizens who are the repository of the language.

VALUE CONFLICTS BETWEEN FIRST NATIONS AND THE LARGER CANADIAN SOCIETY

Sociologists attach considerable importance to the lack of congruence or isomorphism between First Nations' civilizations and western European civilizations. That cultural incongruence is to be found in such fundamental realms as epistemology (ways of knowing) and conceptions of causation, of the cosmos, of the land, of time, and of spirituality.

Table 2, adapted slightly from Sikora's (1994) excerpting of Mander (1991), captures much of the breadth and depth of the incongruence between aboriginal societies and more technologically oriented societies. As part of his coming to grips with living with a Carrier First Nation in the British Columbia interior plateau, Sikora (1994) emphasized some additional differences in the focus of the larger society and the focus of First Nation societies, respectively. Among those differences are the following, where the larger society is described first:

  i. a focus on "scientism" (secondary and tertiary data, information and ideas provided by "experts" and "representatives") as opposed to responsibly investigating primary sources on an individual basis;
 ii. a focus on specialization as opposed to generalization;
iii. a focus on "control" rather than adaptation;
 iv. a focus on life (coupled with a corresponding generalized fear of mortality) rather than existence (which accepts death as part of the natural order and the nature of humankind);
  v. a focus on "relativism" rather than a collective "moral set" which reflects a spiritual base and context; and
 vi. a focus upon "ritualistic" as opposed to authentic behaviour.

TABLE 2 Mander's Differences Between Technological and Aboriginal Peoples

Technological Peoples	Aboriginal Peoples
Economics	
Concept of private property a basic value: includes resources, land, ability to buy and sell, and inheritance. Some state ownership. Corporate ownership predominates.	No private ownership of resources such as land, water, minerals, or plant life. No concept of selling land. No inheritance.
Goods produced mostly for sale, not for personal use.	Goods produced for use value.
Surplus production, profit motive essential.	Subsistence goals: no profit motive, little surplus production.
Economic growth required, especially in capitalist societies, hence need for increased production, increased use of resources, expansion of production and market territories.	Steady-state economics: no concept of economic growth.
Currency system — abstract value.	Barter system — concrete value.
Competition (in capitalist countries), production for private gain. Reward according to task/wages.	Cooperative, collective production.
Average workday, 8–12 hours.	Average workday 3–5 hours.
Nature viewed as "resource."	Nature viewed as "being"; humans seen as part of nature.
Politics and Power	
Hierarchical political forms.	Mostly non-hierarchical: "chiefs" have no coercive power.
Decisions generally made by executive power, majority rule, or dictatorship.	Decisions usually based on consensual process involving whole tribe.
Spectrum from representative democracy to autocratic rule.	Direct participatory democracy; rare examples of autocracy.
Operative political modes are communist, socialist, monarchist, capitalist, or fascist.	Recognizable operative political modes are anarchist, communist, or theocratic.
Centralization: most power concentrated in central authorities.	Decentralization: power resides mainly in community, among people. (Some exceptions include Incas and Aztecs.)
Laws are codified, written. Adversarial process. Anthropocentrism forms basis of law. Criminal cases judged by strangers (in U.S., western Europe, Soviet Union). No taboo.	Laws transmitted orally. No adversarial process. Laws interpreted for individual cases. "Natural law" used as basis. Criminal cases settled by groups of peers known to "criminal." Taboo.
Concept of "state."	Identity as "nation."
Socio-cultural Arrangements and Demographics	
Large-scale societies; most societies have high population density.	Small-scale societies, all people acquainted; low population density.
Lineage mostly patrilineal.	Lineage mostly matrilineal, with some variation; family property rights run through female.

TABLE 2 *(continued)*

Technological Peoples	Aboriginal Peoples
Nuclear two- or one-parent families; also "singles."	Extended families: generations, sometimes many families, live together.
Revere the young.	Revere the old.
History written in books, portrayed in television docudramas.	History transmitted in oral tradition, carried through memory.

Relation to environment

Living beyond nature's limits encouraged; natural terrain not considered a limitation; conquest of nature a celebrated value; alteration of nature desirable; anti-harmony; resources exploited.	Living within natural ecosystem encouraged; harmony with nature the norm; only mild alterations of nature for immediate needs: food, clothing, shelter; no permanent damage.
High-impact technology created to change environment. Mass-scale development: one-to-millions ratio in weaponry and other technologies.	Low-impact technology; one-to-one ratio even in weaponry.
Humans viewed as superior life form; Earth viewed as "dead."	Entire world viewed as alive: plants, animals, people, rocks. Humans not superior, but equal part of web of life. Reciprocal relationship with non-human life.

Religion and Philosophy

Separation of spirituality from rest of life in most Western cultures; church and state separated; materialism is dominant philosophy in Western countries.	Spirituality integrated with all aspects of daily life.
Either monotheistic concept of single, male god, or atheistic.	Polytheistic concepts based on nature, male and female forces, animism.
Futuristic/linear concept of time; de-emphasis of past.	Integration of past and present.
The dead are regarded as gone.	The dead are regarded as present.
Individuals gain most information from media, schools, authority figures outside their immediate community or experience.	Individuals gain information from personal experiences.
Time measured by machines; schedules dictate when to do things.	Time measured by awareness according to observance of nature; time to do something is when time is right.
Saving and acquiring.	Sharing and giving.

(Source: Mander, 1991, 215-219. Copyright 1991 G. Mander. Reprinted with permission of Sierra Club Books.)

Non-Native lawyer Rupert Ross (1992) explores various ways in which differences such as those above result in clashes in the daily operation of the criminal justice system. Ponting's and Kiely's chapter in this volume illustrated the operation of what Ross calls the "ethic of non-interference". Another example would be the clash between the fatalism of many aboriginal cultures and the concept of deterrence in the larger society's criminal justice system (Ross, 1992:

50–65). As Ross explains, the fatalism and seeming apathy of many First Nation individuals is rooted in a conviction that much of what happens in the world (including among the fish, birds, plants, animals, insects, rocks, etc., in addition to among the people) is determined by the actions of spirits, rather than by the exercise of human free will. Hence, deterrence, which is to say the imposition of penalties in an attempt to shape the behaviour of offenders and potential offenders, makes little sense. Rather, many First Nation individuals believe that humans should pay significant attention to the appeasement of the spirits, for ignoring them is an invitation to disaster. It is at their own peril that humans attempt to force the spirits to change. Similarly, Ross submits that the extraordinary capacity for forgiveness and the low levels of blame and rancour against even serious offenders are a reflection of the belief that outside forces (the spirits) are operative.

> The re-establishment of harmony, health, and good fortune on the physical plane depended upon re-establishing as quickly as possible a harmonious relationship with the inhabitants of the spiritual one.
>
> (Ross, 1992: 57–8)

Such beliefs can also go a long way toward explaining the paucity of violent political reactions from First Nation people in the face of government obstinacy in making the fundamental structural changes necessary to lift the colonial yoke from First Nations.

Ross identifies various other norms which are prominent in many First Nation cultures. Among them are some variants of the norm of non-interference. For instance, there are widely held cultural proscriptions against offering advice (even when it is requested), criticism, or praise (Ross, 1992: 13–16). Especially important is the norm that one must not cause another to lose face. That is, no one should feel "put down", ignored, or "bettered" by anyone else and no one should act as though (s)he is superior to anyone else (p. 23–24). This norm is linked to the high value that is placed on equality, and as Crowfoot's chapter observes in conjunction with what he calls "the crab-pot syndrome", that egalitarianism sometimes militates against individual self-improvement.

Another common norm in First Nation cultures is that emotions, such as grief and anger, not be shown (Ross, 1992: 28–31). Sometimes that leads to the use of very indirect referents for tragic events, such as a reference to "that morning with the fog and the car" as a way of alluding to a fatal car accident. A corollary of this norm is that the name of a deceased person, such as a victim of an accident or of violence, not be mentioned for many months after the death. Hence, some of the means for dealing with bereavement that are recommended by grief counsellors in the dominant society could be quite inappropriate in some First Nation cultures. Similarly, where counselling for victims of sexual abuse or family violence is based on models assuming the need to speak openly about the abuse, a clash with the norms of First Nation cultures could occur. Knowing this helps us to better understand the importance of the culturally sensitive approaches to healing advocated by Dion Stout's chapter in this volume and by the Royal Commission on Aboriginal Peoples (RCAP, 1996c: 209–215). As the Commission notes:

> Often, the ideas, and practices of the dominant culture — in health and social services and in all fields — simply fail to connect with Aboriginal feelings, Aboriginal experience and Aboriginal good sense. Better connections come

from within. In fact, as several speakers told us, it is often the most distressed and alienated Aboriginal people who find the greatest healing power in the reaffirmation (or rediscovery) of their cultures and spirituality. ... [As one intervenor said:] "I want the rest of the country to recognize that there is more than one way to heal. Social workers and medical people have to realize the validity of our ways. Your way is not always the right way".[6]

(RCAP, 1996c: 209–210)

Another intervenor[7] suggested that educational and health initiatives that are not based on First Nation culture are "just another form of assimilation" (RCAP, 1996c: 210). By extension, the Commission also noted that Métis people and Inuit strongly object to the imposition of treatment programs designed for or by First Nations.

In part, the norm against emotional indulgence is rooted in a broader norm prohibiting the burdening of others. Ross (1992: 33–39) discusses how this and other norms might well be rooted in the survival needs of the group in traditional times. Consider, for instance, the norm that a task should not be attempted until a thorough mental preparation for it has been completed and there is a clear likelihood of success. In short, the time must be right. Ross suggests that this norm might have its origins in the fact that traditionally there would often be no second, third, or subsequent chances, for resources were simply too scarce to permit much in the way of practice. Similarly, the time must be right for embarking upon subsistence activities like hunting, trapping, and berry picking. One would not trap until the time of year when pelts are at their fullest and one would not pick berries or wild rice until they had ripened optimally.

> Successful activity, then, required waiting until all of the physical variables promised optimum opportunity, all the preparatory thought promised optimum performance and, just as importantly, all the preparatory spiritual dedication promised optimal co-operation from the spirit world.

(Ross, 1992: 39)

Such value clashes as those adumbrated by Ross, Sikora, Mander, and numerous anthropologists help us to understand such phenomena as First Nations' determination to resist assimilation, the difficulty which some First Nation individuals have in functioning within the culturally imbued institutions of the larger society, the alienation which they feel from that larger society, and their desire to establish parallel institutions (e.g., day care centres, criminal justice systems, schools, universities, healing lodges) which will operate under aboriginal precepts and assumptions.

ACCULTURATION AND SPIRITUAL REVIVAL

Acculturation and Authenticity

A strong sense of **cultural insecurity** among First Nation individuals is one legacy of the policy of cultural genocide which the federal government pursued for most of the twentieth century. In this insecurity there is a parallel with the feelings of many French Québécois. First Nation individuals' sense of cultural vulnerability has been heightened by many factors, including urban migration and alienation from the land in which the traditional culture is rooted; the passing of many of the elders who are bearers of the traditional culture; and traditional languages, songs, dances, and ceremonies falling into disuse after being suppressed by the colonizers. Additional factors contributing to that sense of cultural insecurity are the alienation of First Nation youths from the elders and the traditionalists as those youths have been seduced by the music and materialism of the larger Canadian society; and the culture of dependence and of poverty that has come to characterize large sectors of many First Nation communities.

In his chapter on leadership of First Nation communities, Crowfoot refers to the sense of cultural insecurity, and the associated high value placed upon traditionalism, as factors which make a chief's job difficult. However, acculturation is inevitable, to some degree. It is also desirable, to a certain extent, for without acculturation there could be no enduring adaptation to the drastically changed social environment which First Nations now face. Just as First Nations in the seventeenth century and later adopted some aspects of the material and non-material culture of the Europeans, so must adoption occur in contemporary times. The culture of the larger society has much to offer by way of improvements in health and safety, efficiency (e.g., the snowmobile used on the trapline), comfort and convenience, communications, acquisition of knowledge, etc. Those features of the larger society's culture can be exploited by First Nations without necessarily sacrificing the fundamental values of First Nations' traditional cultures. Indeed, some features of the larger society's culture can be put at the service of the protection of the traditional culture, as demonstrated in various world wide web sites. Furthermore, cultural transfer is not a "zero-sum game". That is, there are many material and non-material traits which individuals can add to their cultural repertoire without having to relinquish traits from the culture into which they were first socialized. In short, individuals can become bicultural — "150% persons", so to speak (McPhee, 1968).

To recapitulate, culture is both material and non-material in its manifestation, but is neither static nor of a "zero-sum" nature. Traits can be appropriated from another culture and used in a variety of adaptive ways, including subversively against the hegemonic forces of the larger culture itself. Furthermore, reciprocal influence is possible, which is to say that through contact with non-Native people in various institutions, First Nation individuals can promulgate aspects of First Nation cultures. This happened historically as First Nations helped Europeans adapt to the harsh Canadian environment, and is happening in contemporary times in such realms as the pharmaceutical industry, the management of renewable resources, and as Calliou noted in Chapter Nine, business management practices. At a more abstract level, the high value which aboriginal cultures place upon spirituality, holism, living in harmony with the natural environment, participatory decision-making, and restitution and healing in instances of interpersonal strife, are all tenets of aboriginal cultures which the larger Canadian society is gradually coming to accept more.

In light of the potential for such reciprocality of influence, it is unfortunate that, in First Nation communities, negative sanctions are sometimes brought to bear against those who would be the bridges between the two cultures. As Calliou and Crowfoot point out, such persons' **authenticity** as Indians is often called into question by members of their First Nation community. They sometimes become what sociologist Robert Park (1928), in his classic article, called "the marginal man". Park was referring to a person (male or female) who has a foot in both social worlds but is fully accepted in neither. Such a position of marginality is an highly stressful one, for as Auger has observed, the marginal person tends to be judged according to the standards of both cultures.

The forces of cultural homogenization in the contemporary world are formidable. For instance, the advertising arms of multinational corporate behemoths operate with the accumulated sophistication of experimental social psychology, survey research, and focus group methodologies, and often with budgets that would stupefy a grassroots community social activist. The world wide web offers a veritable explosion of enticing information, most of which is in the English language. Satellite technology, especially as applied to television, has enabled Hollywood's depiction of middle class American culture to penetrate even the most remote of Canadian First Nation communities. On the basis of his experience with First Nations, Ross (1992: 118) suggests: "The major formative influence in many homes has now become satellite television". Lamenting the lack of in-home control over channel selection in many northern remote communities,[8] Ross attributes much aboriginal youth rebellion against parents to "the overwhelming impact of television" (p. 121). He adds:

> Those Indian children (and there are thousands) who spend their pre-school years parked all day in front of a television set are learning, quite simply, to be us.

(Ross, 1992: 123)

Nevertheless, a First Nation cultural revival is clearly under way, as discussed in the Editor's introduction to Part 2 of this volume. Chapter Thirteen, by Auger, fleshes out the notion of cultural revival by conveying the rich flavour of the bush culture which, he hopes, bush Crees will embrace when they regain control over their educational system. Central to that culture, and to many other First Nation cultures, are the notions of learning not only from the elders, but also from a variety of sources in nature; the salience of the spiritual; and the importance of the traditional First Nation language as not just a means for learning, but as a carrier of a world view and philosophy.

Spiritual Revival

It is important to recognize that most First Nation traditional cultures were profoundly spiritual before the arrival of the Europeans and that even when First Nation religion was being suppressed, in many communities it continued to flourish underground.[9] Some individuals adhered to both Christianity and their Native religion.

In some respects, the revitalization of Native spirituality is not highly visible to a non-Native outsider such as I, or even Friesen (1997), for among many First Nation people it is considered quite inappropriate to talk about or write about spirituality. Dale Auger, for instance, expressed to the editor considerable hesitation about making the public revelations that he has made about Cree spirituality in his chapter in this section. He has concluded, however, that the time is right to speak publicly about such things as the spirit rings and the crossing of knowledge, in part because he sees the spiritual revival as being both very widespread and of vital importance. Russell Willier (Mehkwasskwan) came to a similar conclusion in agreeing to the writing of a book about his activities as a Cree medicine man (Young et al., 1989). Others, however, fear that revealing spiritual knowledge can destroy its sacredness or twist the meaning of teachings (Spence, 1995; RCAP, 1996c: 597).

The spiritual revival is taking many forms among First Nation peoples. The Sacred Assembly, held in Ottawa in December 1995 and organized under the auspices of Elijah Harper, M.P., is one manifestation of the spiritual revival at the national level.[10] Another is the effectiveness of spiritual leaders in ending the armed confrontation at Gustafsen Lake, B.C. in 1995, after the failure of secular leaders like Ovide Mercredi. At the microlevel, evidence of the spiritual revival among First Nation peoples is to be found in individuals returning to the ways of the elders, in the now common use of sweat lodges and sacred sweetgrass in purification ceremonies, and in the use of traditional healers.

The repatriation of sacred bundles and artifacts from museums around the world is another form which the revival of indigenous spirituality is taking. The Royal Commission on Aboriginal Peoples has pointed out that their return to the rightful owners is often essential to the spiritual health of First Nation communities, and that repatriation can be a deeply spiritual and powerful experience (RCAP, 1996c: 588, 592). Similarly, a renewed interest in sacred sites attests to the spiritual revival. Unfortunately, though, First Nation people's access to some of those sites is restricted by government policy (e.g., in national parks).

Art has long been an important vehicle for the expression of aboriginal spirituality and continues as such today, as illustrated by the cover art for this volume. The great popularity of aboriginal art with non-Natives facilitates this artistic blossoming.

Certain developments, foreseen by Native prophets, have come to pass and have provided a focal point for discussion of traditional spirituality in First Nation communities throughout North America. Perhaps the most noteworthy example is the birth of a white buffalo, which is said by elders to be the fulfillment of a sacred prophecy and to signal a new age of global spirituality, unification of the races, a major change in the fate of First Nation peoples, and a return to the power of the people and the old ways.[11] Its appearance caused great excitement among many First Nation individuals.

Waldram (1997) points to another manifestation of the resurgence of indigenous spiritualism — namely, the movement demanding that the prison system accommodate Native religious ceremonies and beliefs. For many inmates that spiritualism fills an inner void or otherwise helps them to get more in touch with themselves. Similarly, at an aboriginal gang "summit" held in Winnipeg in 1997, elders steeped in First Nation spiritualism were made available to the gang members.

From this spiritual revival we should expect much healing and empowering of First Nation individuals and communities. It is truly a source for optimism about the future of First Nations.

COMMUNITY

Family: A Pivotal Institution in Distress

The First Nation family is an institution in distress. As the Royal Commission on Aboriginal Peoples has noted, the First Nation family traditionally stood between the individual and the larger society. It played an interpretive or mediating role. Hence, its disruption is highly consequential:

If an Aboriginal person has been socialized in a situation where the family is the all-encompassing mediator between the individual and the social, economic, and political spheres of the larger society, and that family is subsequently lost or disrupted, then the individual has lost not just one support, but also the principal agency that helps him or her make sense of the world.

(RCAP, 1996c: 18)

The First Nation family has also been at the centre of an historical struggle between colonial governments and First Nation parents. Government was intent on eradicating First Nation languages, cultures, and world views, while parents sought to carry out their sacred responsibility to preserve their culture.

Dion Stout reports that 24% of on-reserve First Nation families and 30% of off-reserve First Nation families are led by a single parent. Indeed, the stresses on the First Nation family, as an institution, have been enormous. In addition to single parenthood, they include not only the colonialism, poverty and racism of the larger society, but also multiple bereavements, overcrowded housing, migration out of closely-knit communities (RCAP, 1996c: 18–20), scarcity of affordable and culturally appropriate child care arrangements in urban areas (RCAP, 1996d: 87), and the so-called "scoop of the sixties". In that "scoop", which peaked in the 1970s, provincial social workers apprehended many First Nation children in allegedly dysfunctional families, removed them from their communities, and placed them in non-Native foster or adoptive homes, often with disastrous results for the children. Fortunately, contemporary practice draws much more constructively on the extended family, on other resources in First Nation communities, and on Native foster and adoptive parents.

Perhaps the most significant stressors for the family are the residential school and its aftermath. For some students the residential school experience was traumatic; in such cases, we should not be surprised if post-traumatic stress syndrome emerges, with all its attendant family disruption. Yet, even among those for whom the residential school was not traumatic, the contradictions between what was taught at home and what was taught at school, and between what was taught at school and what was modelled by some staff there, could be profoundly unsettling. Furthermore, the loss of culture and the poor role models of parenting and nurturing left many residential school students poorly equipped for the demands of parenting later in life. Similarly, the distrust and blockages to emotional bonding which the residential school engendered left an indeterminate number of former residential school students with an inability to sustain intimate relationships. Related to that is the abdication of responsibility by some parents, such as absent fathers who do not support their children financially.[12] Unfortunately, many of these traits were then role-modelled to the next generation of children, such that the residential school has had a multi-generational negative legacy.

Dion Stout's chapter in this section addresses the family violence that is a product of the above stresses and of the substance abuse through which some First Nation individuals attempt to cope with those stresses. Dion Stout submits that a chronic state of family violence exists today in First Nation and other aboriginal communities. The elimination of family violence and of its structural causes must be seen as the number one development priority for aboriginal peoples, she asserts. Radical approaches are necessary if peace is to be restored to aboriginal families and if the family is to take its place at the core of the renewal process for aboriginal communities. In her chapter she advocates a multifaceted form of development in which self-responsibility, mutual aid within the community, and moral responsibility are pivotal. Her more recent thinking on the issue emphasizes women's agency (proactivity) in bringing about change and women's participation in community power structures as a way of achieving such agency.[13]

First Nation families are by no means exempt from inter-generational conflict. Of particular note is the conflict between youths and their parents. That is particularly likely to appear as youths, in a transitional stage of acculturation which leaves them confused about their identity, are pulled in two opposite directions (RCAP, 1996d: 88). Such strains will be familiar to readers who come from immigrant families, but in the First Nation situation the tension is exacerbated by the colonial legacy, by the highly constricted opportunity structure, and by prevailing societal stereotypes. Not surprisingly, the response of some First Nation youths, like that of some immigrant youths, has been to form youth gangs, as noted above. These have emerged both on some reserves and in urban areas (e.g., LaPrairie, 1996: 67). For instance, at time of writing, Winnipeg police estimated that there were 1,800 aboriginal gang members in Winnipeg.[14]

As Dion Stout's chapter notes, the extended family, an hallmark of First Nation communities, is both an asset and a liability. The liability is in the diffuse obligations which one has to members of the extended family (e.g., expectations of nepotism in politics, as described in Crowfoot's chapter in this section). Conversely, the asset is the vital support which is available to extended family members, such as in the form of a place to stay, assistance with child care, monetary loans, etc.

The extended family functions in a manner similar to the "social safety net" of the larger society. Its restoration to health is pivotal to the success of other healing efforts within First Nations.

Social Stratification

It is now widely recognized that in First Nation communities, social class is an important form of differentiation and basis of conflict. Boldt (1993: 124–127) has made the point forcefully. He sees a chasm in First Nation reserve communities between a small politico-administrative-business class — often highly educated, land-holding, and largely assimilated — and a large, uneducated, unassimilated, unpropertied, largely unemployed lower class. Wotherspoon and Satzewich (1993: 50–74) generally concur, although they refer to the total aboriginal population and divide it into a larger number of classes.

At the top of Satzewich's and Wotherspoon's class stratification hierarchy is the **bourgeoisie**, likely "no more than 1 percent of the total aboriginal population". Its members have risen to prominence largely as a result of the control that they exercise over commercial firms that emerge out of land claim settlements. Of course, few First Nations have such settlements. Second is the petite bourgeoisie, which can be broken into the old and the new. The **old petite bourgeoisie** consists of independent commodity producers like commercial fishers, trappers, or farmers, and the owners of small restaurants, garages, grocery stores, taxis, school buses, etc. The **new petite bourgeoisie** consists of those who hold professional, managerial or administrative positions, usually in the public sector. In contrast, the **proletariat** is a working class whose members sell their labour in paid employment. The blue collar "fraction" of the proletariat is found in the primary, processing, fabricating, and construction sectors, while the white collar "fraction" is found in clerical, sales, and lower tier service occupations. The majority of aboriginal people who are in the paid labour force and who have jobs occupy [these] working class positions. The **reserve army of labour** comprises the unemployed who are seeking work. These are people who can be brought into the production process when the cyclical fluctuations of the capitalist system require their labour. Aboriginal people are over-represented in this class. Particularly over-represented here are First Nation youth, when compared to either older aboriginal people or non-Native youth. The **lumpenproletariat** consists of the permanent welfare recipients and urban skid-row residents. Wotherspoon and Satzewich offer a very useful discussion of the formation of these classes and address the issue of class conflict, which they see as a growing phenomenon in First Nation communities.

The preoccupation with allocative fairness, to which Crowfoot refers in his chapter, can be seen as one expression of social class tensions and interfamilial tensions. Indeed, in the Ojibwa community studied by Lithman, a basic function of the main unit of political organization — "the bunch" — is to ensure that no sector of the community "is constantly 'on the short end of the stick' or receiving disproportionate favours" (Lithman, 1984: 137, 148). Lithman (1984: 149) identifies the most prominent feature of the political system of the reserve he studied as the prevention of accumulation of financial and political capital.

An important aspect of social stratification on reserves is the land tenure system. Boldt (1993: 123–124) maintains:

> In "advanced" bands/tribes, it is mainly through privatized landholdings that most families of the ruling class have achieved and maintain their status. They have translated their landholdings into political-administrative power and they are using their political-administrative powers to protect and enhance their landholdings.

The "privatized landholdings" to which Boldt refers is the system of *certificates of possession* ("CPs"). While not formally a deed to property, a CP does entitle the holder to pass reserve lands on to relatives in a will. Thus, inequality is institutionalized and Boldt (1993: 125–127) is concerned that what he sees as a two class system of stratification could endure for many generations and attain a caste-like rigidity, especially in the absence of an on-reserve taxation system to redistribute income from land ownership and entrepreneurial activities. With the elite class controlling the political agenda, he asserts, lower class interests get neglected. Those elite interests tend to be power-oriented (related to expanding jurisdiction), rather than problem-oriented (related to high unemployment; excessive rates of family disintegration; alcohol and substance abuse; and extraordinary levels of violence, suicide, and incarceration).

Social Control

Reserve life is replete with gossip, as is social life in any small community. One function performed by the rumour mill, and by the factions or "bunches" described below, is social control. For example, even visiting on-reserve is subjected to close scrutiny by neighbours and is imbued with great political significance at election time. Yet, even this informal social control could be experiencing an erosion of its potency, if Carsten's (1991: 164–165) observations of an Okanagan First Nation community are indicative of a wider trend.

Sociologists and anthropologists attach great importance to the fact that traditional mechanisms of social control in many First Nation communities have lost much of their effectiveness. At the extreme, this means that the bonds of the family have been shattered, traditional codes of moral conduct have broken down and once strict taboos are disregarded, respect for the elders is negligible, role models are scarce, spirituality and respect for human life are numbed, and norms of forgiveness prevail over norms of accountability (Shkilnyk, 1985: 46–49).

LaPrairie, in trying to account for the over-representation of aboriginal[15] people in the criminal justice system, does not focus on such extremes of community pathology. Nevertheless, she sees some of the same factors as being among a wider array of explanatory variables:

> The argument put forward here is that a *decline in interdependency* in aboriginal communities has come about as the result of historical processes (which have reproduced mainstream social structure without accompanying institutional development), as well as cultural dislocation and the decline of informal mechanisms of social control. The end result is socially stratified communities where limited resources and resource distribution create large groups of disadvantaged people, a growing youth sub-culture with few legitimate outlets or opportunities, decontextualized exposure to the mass media, and the lack of cultural and social resources to assist in identity formation which support pro-social values. It is, however, misleading and incorrect to assume that all aboriginal communities in Canada are exposed to the same contingencies and limitations. …
>
> (LaPrairie, 1996: 63; italics not in original)

The decline in interdependency contributes to a decline in the power of what might be called "reintegrative shaming", whereby initial expressions of disapproval are followed by forgiveness and acceptance back into the group. In a community with a high degree of interdependency among members, such shaming reduces re-offending because of the offender's desire to avoid bringing shame upon him/herself and upon those individuals who are important to him/her.

In seeking to explain youth gangs, LaPrairie (1996: 65) not only draws upon the above factors, but also upon members' experience of a "disruptive, neglectful and often physically abusive childhood". In the same vein, Shkilnyk (1985: 32) writes:

> The children who repeatedly get into trouble say that no one cares about them. They pass from childhood to adolescence without guidance and without love. Gone are the elaborate rituals of puberty and transition that were practiced on the old reserve. To substitute for the family, the children of heavy drinkers organize themselves into gangs. … [W]here children belonging to alcoholic families have neither emotional nor physical security, the only sense of belonging comes from membership in a gang.

She adds that some children respond to their powerlessness to change things by using violence and vandalism as a means to an end, where the end is to get out of the community, even if that requires being formally taken into the criminal justice system.

The rage that has built up inside some First Nation youths is often directed inward at members of their own family or community, or even at themselves through suicide attempts. The same is true of adults. The demographic chapter in this volume depicted the appallingly high suicide rates in the First Nation population. Correctional Service of Canada data for adult offenders in 1995 show that, compared to the non-aboriginal offender population, aboriginal offenders are over-represented in certain categories of violent crime — namely, manslaughter, assault causing injury, and to a slight extent, sexual assault (LaPrairie, 1996: 51–53). Data for 1995 show the top five offences for aboriginal offenders were assault causing injury, robbery, second degree murder, manslaughter, and sexual assault (LaPrairie, 1996: 39–40). LaPrairie also reports Canadian Centre for Justice Statistics data showing that aboriginal people make up over one-sixth of Canada's homicide victims, but aboriginal people comprise only about 3% of Canada's population. Aboriginal sex offenders comprise 17% of all sex offenders in federal institutions, and 28% of all aboriginal offenders are sex offenders. Aboriginal women admitted to federal institutions are more than twice as likely as their non-aboriginal counterparts to be incarcerated for crimes of violence. Comack's (1993) study of women at the Portage Correctional Institution in Manitoba found aboriginal women to have had more abusive relationships than their non-aboriginal counterparts.

Not all First Nation communities are experiencing major problems of social control. For those that are, it is easy and appropriate to identify factors outside the community which are the major causes of the breakdown of social control. To the list identified above we could add the intrusion of the economy of the larger society and the relocation of communities. Commenting on the tendency for community relocation to undermine traditional authorities, the Royal Commission stated:

> When traditional authority is undermined, the potential for community co-operation and reciprocity is broken, sometimes irreparably. This leads to further deterioration of mores and traditions, codes of behaviour, ethics, and value systems.

(RCAP, 1996a: 502–504)

Nevertheless, it is clear that *responsibility* for ameliorating the situation must be borne, in the first instance, by the community members themselves, for if they do not take up that responsibility it is unlikely that lasting change will occur. Crowfoot's chapter, however, points out that one of the legacies of the colonial regime is a reluctance by First Nation individuals to take on responsibility. That reluctance is reinforced by the norm of non-interference and the associated high value placed upon respecting the autonomy of others.

In concluding this discussion of social control, it is important to note the strong social control still exerted by women in many matriarchal First Nation cultures. Spence (1995: 120) captures this well:

> The power of women has … been eroded, but not entirely. Traditionally, women have the status to put men in positions of executive power and remove them if they were not acceptable. The men will ask for their wisdom. The power of traditional women was never more obvious to the astonished eyes of the world as it was in the events that unfolded at Oka in the summer of 1990. We saw the Clan mother, with a few choice words, command the AK-47-toting Mohawk soldier to turn on his heels and back off from the invading army.

The Royal Commission (RCAP, 1996d: 83) notes that aboriginal women are often both the mainstay of the family unit and the catalyst for social change. As guardians of the values, cultures, and traditions of their peoples, First Nation women are increasingly stepping forward into political roles to help re-establish in their communities a social order which is more respectful of the traditional role and status of First Nation women. For instance, that a woman runs for political office as counsellor is probably quite unremarkable in most First Nation communities. By the early 1990s, about 10% of elected chiefs were women.

On-Reserve Politics

In the literature, one of the few studies to be found on the role of First Nation women is Fiske's (1990) study of the political mobilization of women in a Carrier community in central British Columbia. On most reserves, politics tend to be of the so-called "brokerage" variety, whereby political influence is gained by individuals acting as intermediaries or power brokers between their community and state funding agencies. When the Carrier women studied by Fiske found that their interests in providing for family needs were not being recognized in the political process, they adopted a brokerage strategy. Organized as the Native Mothers' guild, they obtained funds from a number of government departments for projects like a laundromat and a crafts centre. These funds were not controlled by chief and council and through this independent power base the women were able to establish with the men they employed the kind of client-patron relationship which is common on reserves. The women subsequently elected one of their own as chief and successfully thwarted male resistance to their competitive assertiveness. In the end, though, women's collective, feminist interests were superseded by bitter inter-familial factionalism and patronage politics re-emerged along the traditional factional lines of cleavage.

Lithman (1984: 125, 133) uses the analogy of a funnel to describe brokerage politics on reserve. That is, a very large proportion of the common resources which enter most on-reserve communities comes through chief and council and is distributed by them. The entitlement ideology, described in Crowfoot's chapter, is rooted in the belief that the larger Canadian society has shirked its obligations to First Nations. This ideology further holds that each band member is entitled to his/her share of the scarce resources that enter the community. Thus, for many, "politicking" becomes an essential part of making a living. It can determine who gets a high position on the waiting list for band housing, who gets the contract for garbage collection or water delivery, who gets hired on a band housing construction team, who gets the white collar administrative position, and on some reserves, who gets fired from such positions. Although in many bands the tendency is to develop universalistic allocative criteria in an attempt to buffer politicians and administrators from such political pressures, Lithman's (1984: 136) discussion of the allocation of band housing shows that those criteria are sometimes applied according to a particularistic logic such that the whole process is not as straightforward as an outsider might think. Nepotism is still widespread, *allegations* of nepotism are even more widespread, and as Crowfoot reports, even when nepotism is not practiced, the expectation is that it soon will be. "It's our turn" (to benefit) is a widely held sentiment in many reserve communities and is a reflection of a strongly held egalitarian ideology.

Community cleavages can also fuel on-reserve politics. Among the many potential bases of cleavage within reserve communities are geography, religion and religious denomination, education and social class, traditionalism vs modernism, "progressivism" vs conservatism, Bill C-31 status, and especially family and clan. While sometimes these cleavages are cross-cutting (cancel each other), often they are reinforcing. For instance, the boundaries of clan, class, geography, and religion might all coincide, such that clans stand apart from each other on all three dimensions. To take an hypothetical example, the Bear clan might be primarily employed Anglicans who live on the west side of the reserve where most of the community facilities are located, while Wolf clan members might be primarily Catholics who live on social assistance across the river on the east side of the reserve. The generalized sense of distrust which Crowfoot's chapter identifies as a feature of some communities, is understandable in the context of such reinforcing cleavages and the federal government's colonial practice of favouritism and divide and conquer tactics.

Carsten's (1991: 157–165) anthropological study of an Okanagan First Nation describes community life there as shaped by "rampant factionalism". He stresses the "overwhelming importance" of ideology in factions and describes factions as "large aggregations whose members insist that they share certain specific common ideological commitments and interests". These ideologies, he says, "are always shaped and maintained by opposition to the principles of other factions or to the status quo" (Carstens, 1991: 158). As with the "bunches" studied by Lithman, the lines of cleavage between factions in the community studied by Carstens are constantly shifting.

Bunches serve as nodes in political information networks. Also, it is important to remember that in most reserve communities, as in most small towns, everyone knows everyone else. Given that fact, and the fact that many community members have much free time, the "rumour mill" is an extremely important institution on-reserve. Furthermore, the stakes in community politics are high (e.g., access to jobs in a community with a high level of unemployment), the issues are close to home, and they directly affect people whom one knows well. Thus, it should be of little surprise that First Nation politics have a reputation for being fought with great intensity.

Paradoxically, reserve politics can also be extremely subtle. Lithman (1984: 150) provides an instructive example. He describes a five hour visit which he and a local candidate made to one of the informal leaders of a faction ("bunch") on reserve. Despite an absence of any conversation explicitly about local politics, the candidate saw the meeting as having come close to reaching some kind of a political agreement, by virtue of the fact that the meeting: was timed to occur close to the election, was lengthy, lacked definite disagreement on any particular topic, and revealed an agreement on the performance of some federal cabinet ministers. Similarly, constituents bring pressure to bear upon chief and council through various subtle actions which lack any explicitly acknowledged political content but are pregnant with implicit political messages. An example would be the denial of small favours. This weighs heavily in a small community which is based, to a large degree, upon the exchange of precisely such favours (Lithman, 1984: 158).

Leadership

Leadership is by no means a single quality. Different situations call for quite different leadership skills — a fact which members of traditional First Nation societies understood well. Regrettably, the colonial regime in Canada largely destroyed the traditional leadership system (Boldt, 1993: 121), such that today perhaps the most pressing need in First Nation communities, other than healing, is for skilled and dedicated leadership. That is not to say that such leaders are totally lacking; rather, such leadership is needed in many institutional spheres in any given community. While some communities are virtually devoid of constructive, visionary leadership, others have it but in only some institutional spheres. In this part of the chapter I briefly outline this sociologist's conception of the leadership skills most needed in First Nation communities.

The *sine qua non* of good leadership is positive role modelling. In First Nation communities, with their sense of generalized distrust that Crowfoot describes, positive role modelling is particularly important in order to enhance trust. That is so because trust is a currency in social exchange that "makes things happen" just as much as money "makes things happen" in economic exchange.

A good leader also achieves optimal deployment of the human resources that come under his/her command or influence. This requires recognition of individuals' talents or aptitudes and a knack for organizing a division of labour in such a way as to enable those talents and aptitudes to flourish.

Achieving an expansion of structures of opportunity is a leadership outcome that is particularly needed in First Nation communities. That requires skill at procuring resources and, for sustained effectiveness, impartiality (rather than nepotism or excessive patronage) in the allocation of those resources. Related to this is the good stewardship of existing resources, which to the extent it is achieved, enhances the trust[16] and confidence of the "constituents".

A good leader is also one who prepares her people for the future through goal-setting, environmental scanning, and explanation. That is to say, leadership involves being a visionary, an alert analyst, and a teacher. The teaching involves explaining constraints, possibilities, causes, and consequences.

The ability to mobilize followers is crucial, for no leader, no matter how gifted, can single-handedly make a large "difference" over a sustained period of time. Furthermore, as a change agent a leader will be more successful if he leaves his people with a meaningful sense of ownership of the changes achieved or sought. Mobilization skills include the provision of gratifications to followers for their participation (thereby increasing morale) and the manipulation of symbols to achieve among followers a positive collective identity, a commitment to the collectivity, and feelings of obligation to the collectivity (Turner and Killian, 1987: 325–346).

Notwithstanding the importance of trust, a good leader in a First Nation must also be willing to subject him/herself to rigorous accountability for performance and for use of resources.

Finally, it is vitally important that First Nation leaders be able to instill hope in their followers. That hope will come from leaders demonstrating that "things don't have to be as they are" — that fatalistic resignation is not necessary because change is possible through human action. This can be a considerable challenge in the context of a culture which emphasizes the influence of the spirit world in shaping daily events. Hence, leaders might meet with the most responsive reception among traditionalists if they emphasize how their plan of action restores or enhances harmony with the spirit world. Whatever means is used, the instilling of hope is crucial if the leader is to evoke good **followership** from community members.

In concluding this section, a few words on followership are in order. "Followership" is a term which Crowfoot's chapter tends to eschew, perhaps because of egalitarian values held by him and his community. Nevertheless, followership is of equal importance to leadership. Good followership involves such traits as a willingness to trust, becoming engaged rather than being aloof or apathetic, suspending cynicism, keeping informed, expressing appreciation and support, offering constructive criticism and avoiding pettiness and rumour mongering, and seizing opportunity when it is presented. Regrettably, because of the colonial legacy, inertia, escapism, and other reasons, these traits are in short supply in many First Nation communities.

CONCLUSION

Many First Nation communities are troubled places and much attention has been devoted to that in this chapter. So, too, are many non-Native communities. It would be very unfortunate if an impression of social pathology were to be the only message that readers take from this chapter, for there is much that is positive in First Nation cultures and communities. I conclude by pulling together here various strands of that positive side of First Nation community and cultural life.

One of the most important developments in First Nation communities over the last quarter of the twentieth century was that the communities took control of education. This has resulted in more culturally appropriate curricula, much higher rates of high school graduation, and the successful launching of post-secondary education careers by many thousands of First Nation students. In academic year 1993–94, for instance, an estimated 7,150 First Nation students between the ages of 17 and 34 were enrolled in full-time university studies. This represented an enrollment rate of 3.7%, while the rate for all Canadians was 6.6%.[17] A large proportion of these and other post-secondary students will carve out fulfilling careers such that they will serve as role models of success for others in their community. They also represent a significant increase in the depth of the pool of human talent which First Nations, as small populations, very much need if they are to capitalize upon whatever opportunity exists in the federal government's policies of devolution and *Indian Act* revision.

The radicalization of youth is another positive sign in First Nation communities. Whether we like it or not, experience suggests that radicalization will be a catalyst for change, especially if it turns violent. It is easy for a non-Native academic, such as I, to make such a seemingly glib statement when I do not have to live the consequences of any such violence. Yet, the sad fact is that the government's dismissal of the Royal Commission report invites violence and violence has proven to be one of the few tactics that can command public attention and muster political will among non-Native politicians. Even if violence does not occur, though, the radicalization of First Nation youth will produce competition for leadership which will lead to some circulation of elites and a more assertive stance toward the federal, and perhaps provincial, government.

Another point of light in many First Nation communities is a re-discovered agency on the part of women. That is, First Nation women in communities across Canada are organizing to resist violence and paternalism and to assertively pursue their and their families' needs. The Royal Commission (1996d: 96) described aboriginal women as having a vital role in facilitating healing in families and communities and its researchers wrote-up case studies (e.g., Descant et al.) which demonstrate how such leadership can be carried out in practice and even extended to the men of the community.

The spread and successes of healing circles is another extremely positive development in First Nation communities. While they are no panacea and can offer no "quick fixes", healing circles and other forms of healing are gradually lifting an oppressive weight from the spirit of First Nation individuals and communities. They are addressing head-on the causes and manifestations of the dysfunctionality that has tormented families and communities. In the 1990s, more so than at any prior period since the inception of the residential schools and the imposition of the welfare state, we are seeing the chain of inter-generational transmission of dysfunctionality being broken.

In addition, much hope can be taken from the restoration — albeit ever so gradual — of part of the First Nation land base and from the cultural revival that is occurring in First Nation communities. An integral part of that revival is the rescue and reinvigoration of aboriginal languages in the schools and over the airwaves. The spiritual component of the cultural revival is central and, sources tell me, is gaining considerable momentum at the grassroots level. It is aided by the emergence of the elders from the era of cultural banishment created by the culturally imperialistic and genocidal propaganda of the residential schools. The cultural revival is also being aided by the flourishing of First Nation artists and by powerful new technology such as the world wide web.

Finally, while no one would deny that the onus for creating change rests with First Nation people themselves, outside First Nation communities there are also some grounds for hope. The keen interest of the international community in First Nation affairs in Canada is a case in point. I close this chapter, though, on a note far-removed from that plane of international politics — namely the receptivity of non-Native Canadian students to the message of First Nation leaders. As one who is quite familiar with non-Native public opinion on aboriginal matters, I have been amazed at the extremely positive reception which aboriginal spirituality has received from my non-Native students. For instance, I expected the message of Dale Auger's chapter in this section to be dismissed with derisive labels of "superstition" by a majority of students. Instead, the predominant reaction of students has been one of captivated approval, identification, and eagerness to learn more. The same is true of students' reactions to visits to my class by Dale Auger and by another contributor to this volume, George Calliou. If such reactions are the norm among other readers, that might be an indication that one strand in the new relationships that are to emerge between First Nation peoples and non-Natives could be cultural-spiritual in nature. This might not be far-fetched, given the cultural-spiritual void experienced by many non-Natives in our secularized, materialistic, and environmentally reckless industrial society. In any such cultural-spiritual rapprochement, even if it be with only a small portion of the larger Canadian society, First Nations will be proceeding from a position of inherent and increasing strength.

NOTES

[1] This summary is from Indian Affairs Branch (1970). For a more detailed treatment, see Morrison and Wilson (1995) and Friesen (1997) and the sources they cite.

[2] While a rock would be viewed as inanimate in western cultures, in some aboriginal cultures it would be regarded as a living entity with a spirit.

[3] Any given language might have both a formal and a more colloquial variant. The linguistic families, with examples of languages belonging to them, are: the **Algonkian** family (Abenaki, Blackfoot, Cree, Delaware, Maliseet, Mi'kmaq, Montagnais-Naskapi, Ojibwa, Saulteaux), the **Athapaskan** family (Beaver, Carrier [Wet'suwet'en], Chipewyan, Dogrib, Kutchin, Sarcee, Sekani, Slavey), the **Salishan** family (Bella Coola, Comox, Okanagan, Shuswap), the **Tsimshian** family (Coast Tsimshian, Gitksan, Nisga'a), the **Iroquoian** family (Seneca, Cayuga, Mohawk), the **Wakashan** family (Kwakiutl, Nitinat, Nootka), the **Siouan** family (Dakota, Lakota, Nakota), and the **Haida, Kutenai, and Tlingit** languages which belong to no other linguistic group. Source: RCAP (1996c: 605).

[4] The Iroquoian language might rank next to Cree and Ojibwa in prevalence, but it is not possible to state with certainty because Iroquoian language peoples, including some large First Nations like Kahnawake and Six Nations, were particularly heavily represented among non-participants in the 1991 census. The remaining languages rounding out the top ten First Nation languages are listed below with 1991 census data on the number of adult speakers, the number of school-aged children speakers, and the total of those two shown in parentheses: **Montagnais-Naskapi** (5005 + 1725 = **6730**); **Micmac** (4705 + 970 = **5675**); **Slavey** (3455 + 730 = **4185**); **Blackfoot** (3605 + 390 = **3995**); **Dakota** (2785 + 610 = **3395**); **Chipewyan** (1970 + 255 = **2225**); and **Dogrib** (1495 + 520 = **2015**). By way of comparison, it is noteworthy that the Inuktitut language was spoken by 14960 adult Inuit persons and by 6025 Inuit school-aged children in the 1991 census, which made it the third most common aboriginal language (20985 speakers) in the census. All language data in this chapter refer only to persons who both speak the language and reported aboriginal identity in the census.

[5] Special tabulations done for RCAP (1996c: 608) reveal that only 29% of Registered Indian children in the 5–14 year old age range can speak an aboriginal language while the figure is 75% among Registered Indians in the age 55 and older group.

[6] Sherry Lawson, Chippewas of Rama First Nation, Orillia, Ontario, 93-05-13.

[7] Jeanette Costello, Terrace, B. C., 93-05-25.

[8] He is referring to the situation in which the television signal comes from the satellite to the community dish and the person who operates the dish selects the program that everyone in the community must watch, if they watch at all.

[9] For an overview of aboriginal spirituality, see RCAP (1996a: 628–631).

[10] Addressing the Assembly, Harper said: "…. These injustices have led to a loss of dignity and pride. We have seen social chaos in our communities, substance abuse, domestic violence, suicides, sexual abuse and poverty. We have also seen frustration in resolving these issues. Confrontations are developing, people are blocking roads. This has led to two tragic deaths in recent years, as a result of these escalating frustrations. It has become more apparent that these things need to be resolved, that the political process has failed us. I believe something is missing, which is the spiritual element. Thus came the idea of the Sacred Assembly, to bring spiritual leaders together and to bring understanding amongst our communities and the whole country". (Source: "Canadians Drawn to Sacred Assembly", Peaceweb News, http://www.ottawa.net/~peaceweb/pnsacred.html)

11 Source: "Birth of White Buffalo a 'Modern Day Miracle'" at http://www.bossnt.
   com/1295/bufintro.html   Posting might have lapsed.
12 Indeed, some First Nation administrations refuse to co-operate in enforcing child
   support orders (RCAP, 1996d: 86).
13 Personal communication with the author.
14 CBC Radio news, 97-04-04.
15 Data sources used in this section do not differentiate between First Nation, Métis,
   and Inuit.
16 Trust can be seen as the opposite of accountability.
17 The gap seems to be closing, although 1995–96 data show a drop in First Nation
   university enrollment to 6,636 students. See Departmental Statistics Section (1996:
   43) for details. The age range of 17–34 years captures only about 80% of First
   Nation university students, but about 95% of all Canadian university students.

REFERENCES

Boldt, Menno
1993   *Surviving as Indians*. Toronto: University of Toronto Press.
Brown, Rosemary
1990   *Rupture of the Ties That Bind: Lubicon Lake Cree Women and Their Society*. M.A.
       Thesis, The University of Calgary.
Carstens, Peter
1991   *The Queen's People*. Toronto: University of Toronto Press.
Comack, Elizabeth
1993   *Women Offenders' Experiences with Physical and Sexual Abuse*. Winnipeg,
       University of Manitoba, cited in Carol LaPrairie, *Examining Aboriginal
       Corrections in Canada*. Ottawa: Supply and Services Canada.
Departmental Statistics Section
1996   *Basic Departmental Data, 1995*. Ottawa: Department of Indian Affairs &
       Northern Development.
Descant, Danielle et al.
1993   *Violence and Healing: Data on Family Violence and Healing Among the Innuat of
       Uashat mak Mani-Utenam*. Pre-publication report to the Royal Commission on
       Aboriginal Peoples.
Fiske, Jo-Anne
1990   "Native Women in Reserve Politics: Strategies and Struggles", pp. 131–146 in
       Roxana Ng, Gillian Walker, and Jacob Muller (eds.), *Community Organization
       and the Canadian State*. Toronto: Garamond Press.
Friesen, John W.
1997   *Rediscovering the First Nations of Canada*. Calgary, Alta.: Detselig Enterprises.
Indian Affairs Branch
1970   *Linguistic and Cultural Affiliations of Canadian Indian Bands*. Ottawa:
       Department of Indian Affairs and Northern Development.
LaPrairie, Carol
1996   *Examining Aboriginal Corrections in Canada*. Ottawa: Supply and Services Canada.
Lithman, Yngve Georg
1984   *The Community Apart*. Winnipeg: University of Manitoba Press.
Maclaine, Craig and Michael Baxendale
1990   *This Land is Our Land: The Mohawk Revolt at Oka*. Montréal and Toronto:
       Optimum Publishing.

Mander, Jerry
1991   *In The Absence Of The Sacred: The Failure of Technology and the Survival of the Indian Nations.* San Francisco: Sierra Books Club.
McPhee, Malcolm
1968   "The 150% Man, a Product of Blackfeet Acculturation", *American Anthropologist* LXX: 1096–1107.
Morrison, Bruce R. and C. R. Wilson (eds.)
1995   *Native Peoples: The Canadian Experience.* Toronto: McClelland & Stewart.
Park, Robert
1928   "Human Migration and the Marginal Man", *American Journal of Sociology,* XXXIII, 6: 881-893.
Ross, Rupert
1992   *Dancing with a Ghost: Exploring Indian Reality.* Markham, Ont.: Octopus.

1996   *Returning to the Teachings: Exploring Aboriginal Justice.* Toronto: Penguin.
Royal Commission on Aboriginal Peoples (RCAP)
1996a   *Final Report of The Royal Commission on Aboriginal Peoples; Vol. 1: Looking Forward, Looking Back.* Ottawa: Ministry of Supply and Services Canada.

1996b   *Final Report of The Royal Commission on Aboriginal Peoples; Vol. 2: Reconstructing the Relationship.* Ottawa: Ministry of Supply and Services Canada.

1996c   *Final Report of The Royal Commission on Aboriginal Peoples; Vol. 3: Gathering Strength.* Ottawa: Ministry of Supply and Services Canada.

1996d   *Final Report of The Royal Commission on Aboriginal Peoples; Vol. 4: Perspectives and Realities.* Ottawa: Ministry of Supply and Services Canada.
Shkilnyk, Anastasia
1985   *A Poison Stronger Than Love.* New Haven, Conn.: Yale University Press.
Sikora, M. Stefan
1994   *Chants of a Lifetime: Explorations in Native Philosophy.* Ph.D. Dissertation. The University of Calgary.
Spence, Doreen
1995   "Aboriginal Women and Religion", pp. 117–124 in Morny Joy and Eva K. Neumaier-Dargyay (eds.), *Gender, Genre, and Religion.* Calgary, Alta. and Waterloo, Ont.: Calgary Institute for the Humanities and Wilfrid Laurier University Press.
Statistics Canada
1993   *Language, Tradition, Health, Lifestyle, and Social Issues: 1991 Aboriginal Peoples Survey.* Cat. # 89-533. Ottawa: Minister of Industry, Science and Technology.
Turner, Ralph and Lewis Killian
1987   *Collective Behaviour.* Englewood Cliffs, N.J.: Prentice-Hall.
Waldram,, James B.
1997   *The Way of the Pipe: Aboriginal Spirituality and Symbolic Healing in Canadian Prisons.* Peterborough, Ont.: Broadview Press.
Wotherspoon, Terry and Vic Satzewich
1993   *First Nations: Race, Class, and Gender Relations.* Scarborough, Ont.: Nelson.
Young, David, Grant Ingram, and Lise Swartz
1989   *Cry of the Eagle: Encounters with a Cree Healer.* Toronto: University of Toronto Press.

CHAPTER *11*

STOPPING FAMILY VIOLENCE: ABORIGINAL COMMUNITIES ENSPIRITED[1]

Madeleine Dion Stout with the assistance of Catherine R. Bruyere

FAMILY VIOLENCE: THE MISSING PEACE

The aboriginal concept of family involves more than the nuclear family which is dominant in mainstream Canadian society. Aboriginal families incorporate and embrace extended family members as well. Grandparents, aunts, uncles, cousins, and increasingly non-blood relations, all come under the rubric of the aboriginal family. Traditionally, a healthy aboriginal family was all encompassing.

The Royal Commission on Aboriginal Peoples facilitated public discussion of a wide range of social problems, among which few are as debilitating as family violence. From all accounts, family violence is a complex, multifaceted and widespread social problem in many aboriginal communities.

The relationship between aboriginal peoples and violence is bitter and long. It is the number one development problem for aboriginal peoples today. It plays an important role because it blocks Aboriginals' complete well-being. Full stop.

Thus, it is urgent to write about the relations, processes and conditions by which the total integrity of aboriginal peoples has been violated. Judging from aboriginal people's testimony to the Royal Commission, a **chronic state of violence** exists. Poor housing, high unemployment, high suicide rates and family violence relegate aboriginal people to the margins of society. In the end, poverty visited upon individuals, communities and nations translates into unmet human needs and generates pathologies like alienation, forced migration, and more violence.

The problem of family violence must be seen in context. This requires understanding how the overriding structural forms of violence fuse with physical violence. More weight should not be given to the former, for doing so would make the human impact of personal violence appear insignificant and small. In addition, others caution against the justification of family violence as a natural outcome of the chronic state of violence. Instead, they treat violence as a spectrum. For them, peaceable solutions to family violence will be brought about only when personal and structural violence are opposed in tandem.

Numerous heartbreaking stories from the First Nations, Métis and Inuit people alike, indicate that most aboriginal peoples have not been, and are not now, at peace. As the family bears the brunt of an unredeemed past and present, a special challenge of helping them find peace emerges. A future must be charted which is not a mere repetition of that against which they have already toiled heavily.

Knowing the general status of aboriginal families is the first step toward coming to terms with family violence. For instance, we know many aboriginal families have lost their ability to act as mediating structures. Further, because they are in the midst of existing problems, they are no longer able to provide their members safe refuge from life's stresses. Being under siege, they do not have the energy and confidence for renewal. All of this occurs because the sacredness of the aboriginal family has given way to escalating and destructive violence.

The fact that the aboriginal family has been weakened to the extent that it now poses a barrier to human development and stands in dire need of healing is a terrible twist of irony that most aboriginal persons of an earlier era would have thought impossible. However, *a remedial course where peace is commonplace will unfold within this chapter*. We shall show that more radical and critical approaches to controlling and ending family violence are required. In the process, we consider the words and stories of victims, victors, and kindred spirits, for in these stories lie directions for the future.

To come to terms with family violence, it is important to get a sense of the "big picture", the larger context. We begin that task by introducing some of the major issues aboriginal people raised with the Royal Commission on Aboriginal Peoples and by including some essential background facts to those issues. Seeing the issues through the same lens and filter as aboriginal people is vital, for it is aboriginal people who have the capacity to change the situation. It is also important to note that there is a strong connection between the features of family violence and the ingredients for a successful strategy for combatting it.

Women Disclose and Oppose the Problem

In an earlier RCAP report, *Focusing the Dialogue*, aboriginal women raised family violence as an issue of great import. Almost in the same breath, they voiced strong angst about their place in male-dominated governing systems. However, even before this Commission came into existence, aboriginal women were protesting against the effects of violence in all its forms. For instance, in 1991, the Native Women's Association of Canada recommended that a task force on family violence in aboriginal communities be set up by the federal government. Other women's organizations, such as L'Association des Femmes Autochtones du Québec also took up the cause as a major concern of the members of the Association. In 1989 the Ontario Native Women's Association produced a landmark document called *Breaking Free*. It showed the alarming extent of violence within aboriginal communities and highlighted the pressing need for the issue to be addressed. Inuit women also bravely broke the silence about child sexual abuse in their communities. In the face of almost daily pain and in a desperate call to action, Métis women, too, went public about domestic terrorism.[2]

Not all aboriginal women are able to participate in open, hard-hitting protests. In many ways, larger movements are too far removed from the ordinary women to be of direct benefit to them. There are also more practical reasons why most women are unable to take part in broader forms of protest. They lack the necessary resources, time, and transportation. Often, possessive partners keep them close to home and work, thereby isolating them. In addition, cultural and language barriers prohibit their involvement, as do child-bearing and nurturing responsibilities. The chronic burden of disease and family violence itself also keeps them in the margins. Together, these factors help to drive women's resistance underground. However, they still resist through daily acts of defiance, anonymously, in isolation and often, in the privacy of their own homes. Other aboriginal women take advantage of their own human agency and through dance, gossip and art they make it possible to move beyond the limits of family violence.

Some aboriginal women faced with daily abuse fight back; others snap under the pressure. Pushed to the wall, they respond with violence, and wind up in prison, as The Native Women's Association of Canada (NWAC) pointed out at RCAP's public hearings (Toronto, 92-06-26: 51).

Aboriginal women and children bear the burden of the social discord occurring in aboriginal communities. Those women are caught in a never-ending struggle to take back the space that has traditionally been theirs in the family and community. They are struggling to restore the social balance therein.

Numbers and Stories Show The Need for Change

For many children, family violence is a fact of life. First-hand experiences with abuse, alcoholism and violence are so great that few children grow up unscathed (Rogers, 1990: 105). This speaks volumes about **the danger of normalizing high-risk behaviour in aboriginal communities.** It also helps to explain how family violence can span generations. In the case of inner city aboriginal people, breaking the cycle means changing childhood conditions but it also requires promoting social and economic changes for the adults who survive these conditions (La Prairie and Steinke, 1994: vi). These options pose a special challenge for the Inuit who, with the highest birth rate of any Canadian population, face grinding poverty, poor housing, family violence and high unemployment and drop-out rates from school (Canadian Panel on Violence Against Women [CPVAW], 1993: 101–142). Even though exact numbers are not available on the incidence of family violence among the Métis, it is argued that they suffer as much from it as their cultural relatives on reserves (Larocque, 1994).

While most aboriginal people migrate to urban centres in their quest for employment, many aboriginal women and children are forced into urban areas in a desperate flight from the violence they are experiencing in their homes.

The issue of gender received a great deal of attention during the Commission's hearings. The remarks of the Program Director of the Women's Resource Centre of Hay River NWT bear witness to the hidden costs of family violence, particularly as it affects women:

> Spousal assault is an immense and usually hidden problem. The cost begins to occur long before, regardless of whether or not a woman goes to the shelter. It is hidden in lost productivity if the woman works outside the home. It is hidden in medical costs. It is important to realize that women do not seek medical attention for injuries inflicted by their spouses, unless they absolutely have to. [Usually] the doctor misses the fact that the injury is due to spousal assault.

RCAP Public Hearings, Hay River, NWT, 93-06-17: 110

A Lethbridge, Alberta study of sixty-one women located through Native agencies hints at the prevalence of the problem. The researchers found that 91% of the respondents reported having personal experience with family violence. While these women identify psychological and verbal abuse as the most common, (ranging from blaming at 88%, to swearing at 82%) a significant number had also been subjected to slapping (77%), hitting (64%), and punching (54%). Sixteen percent reported being touched against their will and being forced into sex with partners (Wierzba et al., 1991: 136).

Consider the following findings from empirical studies of violence against women:

- In a study by the Ontario Native Women's Association eight out of ten aboriginal women had personally experienced violence. Of these women, 87% had been injured physically and 57% had been sexually abused.
- In a study in the London (Ontario) area, 71% of the urban sample and 48% of the reserve sample of Oneida women had experienced assault at the hands of current or past partners.
- In some northern aboriginal communities, an estimated 75% to 90% of the women are battered.
- In a Northwest Territories survey, 80% of girls and 50% under 8 years old were sexually abused

(CPVAW, 1993: 156).

Of course, family violence often goes beyond battery, with devastating consequences as one speaker pointed out. Catherine Brooks, Executive Director of Anduhyaun, stated:

Twenty-four per cent of the respondents to our questionnaire indicated that they know of deaths as a result of aboriginal family violence. And 54 per cent of the respondents suggested that they know of cases where a woman who sustained injuries which required medical treatment as a result of family violence did not seek medical attention out of fear and shame.

RCAP Public Hearings, Toronto, 92-06-26

Statistics Canada's Aboriginal Population Survey found that 44% of on-reserve adult respondents identified family violence as an important problem in their community and 29% see sexual abuse as an important problem in their community. On-reserve respondents regarding these as not a problem amounted to only 27% for family violence and 34% for sexual abuse. To put these in context, consider that the number of on-reserve residents citing unemployment, alcohol abuse, suicide, and rape as an important problem in their community was 78%, 73%, 34%, and 16%, respectively (Statistics Canada, 1993: Table 4.3).

Family violence does not occur in a social vacuum. In her presentation to RCAP, Donna Sears, from the Atenlos Women's Group, showed how racism intersects with sexism to create multiple burdens for aboriginal women:

The portrayal of the squaw is one of the degrading, more despised and most dehumanizing anywhere in the world. The squaw is the female counterpart of the Indian male savage and, as such, she has no human face. She is lustful, immoral, unfeeling and dirty. It is this grotesque dehumanization that has rendered all native women and girls vulnerable to gross physical, psychological and sexual violence.

I believe there is a direct relationship between these horrible racist, sexist stereotypes and violence against native women and girls.

I believe, for example, that Helen Betty Osborne was murdered in 1972 by four young men because these youths grew up with twisted notions of Indian girls as squaws. Racist and sexist stereotypes not only hurt aboriginal women and their sense of self-esteem, but actually encourage abuse, both by aboriginal men and others. Our family violence programs attempt to help both victims and offenders to see beyond the stereotypes.

RCAP Public Hearings, London, Ont., 93-05-12

Understanding Family Violence in Context

Aboriginal peoples have told many stories about how structural or systemic violence in the form of colonialism, racism, economic disenfranchisement, and cultural and spiritual invasion, has embossed itself on the psyche of aboriginal peoples. *Aboriginal people have been shaped by this violence* and unfortunately, in the process, have become its heirs. Aboriginal people are now *starting to turn this violence inward*, as they strike out at their own in growing incidents of brown-upon-brown violence. Roy Fabian, a Dene from Hay River, N.W.T. spoke about this sad development at the RCAP Public Hearings (93-06-17):

When you are talking about oppression, there is a process that goes on. [First] there is a process that demeans us, that belittles us and makes us believe that we are not worthy, and the oppressed begin to develop what they call cultural self-shame and cultural self-hate, which results in a lot of frustration and a lot of anger. At the same time this is going on, because our ways as Native people are put down, ... we begin to adopt our oppressors' values and, in a way, we become oppressors [of] ourselves. ... Because of the resulting self-hate and self-shame we begin to start hurting our own people [and ourselves].

When you talk about things like addiction and family abuse, elder abuse, sexual abuse, jealousy, gossip, suicide and all the different forms of abuses we seem to be experiencing, it's all based on [the original] violence. Its all a form of [internalized] violence. . . .

Communal violence[3], where one segment of the population attempts to limit the rights of others, is born of **structural violence** but, it feeds upon the political, ethnic, economic and spiritual differences now inherent in many aboriginal communities. Where once aboriginal societies were markedly homogeneous, bound by custom and tradition, many have now been organized into competing clans, classes, reserves and other interest groups. Regrettably, untethered political disagreements can spill over into physical violence, as the RCAP Public Hearings in Kelowna, B.C. (93-06-17) were told. Other incidents where ethnicity has been factored into the communal violence equation have been disclosed. While ethnic pride is important to the survival of aboriginal communities, ethnic nationalism can build its own tyranny. In its extreme form, it can result in **ethnic cleansing**, previously unknown in aboriginal communities. This is a dangerous and worrisome development about which all aboriginal peoples should be concerned.

Aboriginal self-government has emerged as a rallying point for many aboriginal groups. While it holds great promise for local control, many aboriginal people voice ambivalent feelings about it. Most aboriginal people want self-government because they see it as half of the solution to their under-development problems. (The other half is a return to traditionalism.) Many others view the advent of self-government with trepidation because they have seen the **excesses of the aboriginal political elite and** have suffered from their **exclusionary practices**.

Aboriginal leaders can impose their own forms of structural and communal violence. While aboriginal leaders strive to personify themselves as the vanguard of reserve communities and the stewards of their development, the common aboriginal person can experience certain struggles in the thrust toward participatory development[4], not the least of which are the inadequacies of aboriginal leadership.

The fact that the State has often condoned structural violence through its own racist policies and practices is not lost on many people. Harold Orton, for example, described one of the legacies of the Oka/Kahnawake incident as follows:

> Our people got stoned going down the highway just trying to get to safety. ... The government is pushing and pushing and pushing us, and they don't realize that there is a breaking point and that breaking point comes in the form of violence. And we can't have that.
>
> Harold Orton, RCAP Public Hearings, Orillia, Ont., 93-05-13

Encounters with racism cause grief, but the joint blow of religion and violence is even more injurious. Frequently aboriginal people have experienced the betrayal of trusted religious leaders. Organized religion has fallen out of favour for this reason and because it has inflicted its own forms of violence on the people. Organized religions and churches have, in many cases, continued to act as centres of power and control in aboriginal communities. We cannot turn a blind eye to the fact that they can act as a locus of community abuse. As Falk (1988) notes, religions can set back thinking and action on social issues like family violence. One report that was submitted to the Commission supported this argument:

> Christian churches, particularly the Roman Catholic Church (which has played a dominant role in most Dene communities), are patriarchal in structure. The churches reinforce a subservient role for women and the traditional Dene belief in life-long marriage arrangements. Aboriginal women participating in a Yellowknife focus group explained that women brought up in convents or hostels were taught to respect the institution of marriage, accept abuse and look for a better day tomorrow. ...
>
> Churches and residential school have had a role in promoting silence about sexual abuse and sexual assault, whether it occurred in school or elsewhere. As one woman said, in the old days there was little discussion about sexual abuse because people were taught in the mission that anything sexual was dirty. The effects of this silence are still being felt today.
>
> [C]hurches are condoning family violence and abuse by their silence on the issue, and the absence of any programs to prevent or address it. It is significant that [victims] seldom seek help from a priest or pastor after a violent or abusive incident.
>
> (Chambers et al., 1993: 3)

High Risk Stages and Conditions

The evidence presented strongly suggests that more effort and resources should be devoted to reducing, controlling or eliminating the critical times and conditions in an aboriginal person's life when she or he is most vulnerable to family violence. This is a major departure from past thinking. Earlier there was a tendency to see all aboriginal peoples as victims of social problems from birth until death. Sadly, this can be the case for some, but not all aboriginal people are equally at risk to problems of family violence at all times. Our programs must be cognizant of that, but must also avoid favouring one high risk group over another. To favour one such group over another would be to fall into the trap of contributing to the "imbalance and abuse of power [which] is at the core of family violence" (Chambers et al., 1993: 53).

Aboriginal people have urged instead, that we cast the net widely and that we use the right size of net. Pulling in people for healing is not a mere happening. It has to be a just, inclusive and sustainable process. The net needs to pull in those who are suffering through high risk stages and conditions. Those high risk stages for family violence include the time before birth, childhood, youth, motherhood and old age. From testimony quoted to this point, it is evident that certain economic, social, physical, mental, and sexual differences predispose individuals to being caught in the nightmare of family violence.

Being young in aboriginal communities can mean being at high risk for being a victim *or* perpetrator of family violence. There is a paradox in some aboriginal communities, such that youth are indulged but that very indulgence opens the door to alien values which cause **a profound shift in social relationships**. One form that this takes is that youth come to focus on self-fulfillment, rather than on community co-operation,[5] and are often left to make their own way in life. Disregard for traditional systems and learning paths, coupled with individual isolation, has led many of them to solitary pursuit of their cultural roots and identity.[6] This can result in youth taking new knowledge as their own, with little regard for potential hazards. Faulty interpretations and connections in this rediscovery can be misleading. Where cultural teachings are not well thought out in their given context, dangerous self-denial of vulnerability can take place.

For aboriginal youth to avoid that vulnerability and fully benefit from exploring the traditional path, they need the gentle and supportive guidance of good leaders — people with whom they can identify and in whom they have confidence as protectors, teachers or mentors.[7] When they are completely at sea, young people develop unhappy relationships with their families, children and spouses along with a lack of personal direction and development. Very often, this discontent ends in family violence. This is often rooted in a home-grown cynicism.

All of us have heard aboriginal leaders affirm that: "Our children are our future". While this is a positive assertion, the stark realities in many aboriginal communities can diminish this statement to mere rhetoric. Aboriginal youth want aboriginal leaders to move beyond platitudes and back-up their statements with tangible demonstrations of their beliefs.

Homeless spirits plague aboriginal youth. Much has been written about their hunger for culture, identity and future. Unfortunately, many begin life's journey as "throw away" children with wasted lives, having no value in the context of human society (Gore, 1992: 162) and, as elder Harriet Arcand pointed out, wind up in prison.

> I have been to the Correctional Centre in Prince Albert twice and I am sure a lot of you people know the majority of kids in the place are Natives. . . . And

it really hurt my feelings to think that so many people don't care what happens to their children. When they are out of the house, they are on their own. Nobody tries to find out what is going on. They just do as they please and they get into trouble. And who is there to stand by them? They send them out to the correctional centres and when they come out they rebel to these things. They don't think they should be in that place but they are in that place because nobody seems to care what happens to them.

RCAP Public Hearings, North Battleford, Sask., 92-10-29: 192

In another presentation, Joyce Courchene, of the Indigenous Women's Collective in Winnipeg, provided insight into how abuse of power, gender discrimination, and exclusion contribute to the "feminization" of **poverty** in aboriginal communities. She and Grace Meconse relate poverty to vulnerability to abuse.

There is abuse in our communities. Women are laid-off from work if they speak about their rights or talk about sexual harassment in the workplace. We have to live in those communities. We have families to support. A large portion of our women are the supporting member of the family. We need our jobs. So we will not ... speak [out].

And many times, in our communities and our aboriginal organizations, aboriginal women are not hired. Non-aboriginal women are hired for positions that we both qualify for. If we speak [out] publicly, we are threatened over the telephone. ... Our president in the Indigenous Women's Collective had threatening telephone calls. There's all kinds of ways of trying to silence us. We asked for an in-camera hearing for the women from the Province of Manitoba within the Royal Commission. It fell on deaf ears. We asked for funding so we could bring our women to come out and make presentations in these hearings. It fell on deaf ears.

RCAP Public Hearings, Winnipeg, 93-06-03: 76

I attempted to gain employment with a Tribal Council, and I travelled a distance for my interview. [In] my meeting with a Chief, who had called me for the interview, he attempted to rape me. This is two years ago. I am 51 years old, and I know of cases of younger women who have been extremely abused in similar ways.

Grace Meconse, Vice-President, Native Mediation Inc.,
RCAP Public Hearings, Winnipeg, 92-04-22: 388

Much of the testimony and briefs presented to the Royal Commission refers to aboriginal women and children as a vulnerable unit within the aboriginal community. The rates of **single parent Indian (and Inuit) families** are at an all time high (Canadian Institute of Child Health, 1994: 138). Thirty percent of all Indian families living off-reserve are headed by a single parent, while 24% of Indian families living on-reserve are lone parents. Single parent families are disproportionately low income and, as noted above, a lack of financial resources can leave one vulnerable to other forms of abuse. Consider the following testimony:

Single mothers are subjected to all avenues of abuses by landlords in order to give favours if rent is not paid on time. Substance abuse is high in these low rental areas. Younger generations are exposed constantly to these abuses. CMHC has made it known that there will be no allocation of subsidized rental units in the lower mainland.

Ben Stewart, RCAP Public Hearings, Terrace, BC, 93-05-25: 74

Substance abuse is a serious predisposing condition for family violence in aboriginal communities (Dumont-Smith and Sioui-Labelle, 1993). However, as Chambers et al. (1993) found, while violence often occurs in proportion to substance abuse, one can exist without the other. To paraphrase one observer, where alcohol is combined with a poor view of women and pornography, "volatile conditions emerge". Similarly, when gambling replaces alcoholism, child neglect increases.

In the same vein, Rosemary Brown, drawing upon her research among the Lubicon, decried the extensive destruction that alcoholism can wreak on the aboriginal family structure and community. She testified:

> Women's focus upon alcohol abuse as a key change in their society reflected the fact that, while alcohol abuse was a symptom of the dislocation experienced as a result of the disjunction between their socialized roles and their capacity to perform these roles, it had also caused many of the increasing social strains and problems experienced by Lubicon Lake Cree women as wives, as mothers and as Elders. It was associated with the increase in marital discord, [with] wife abuse and family breakups, [and with] the fact that children were on the loose and/or neglected, that children had died in accidents, that community co-operation and sharing had decreased, and that the Elders were no longer listened to.

> R. Brown, Committee Against Racism,
> RCAP Public Hearings, Calgary, 93-05-26: 158

The conditions under which single mothers live, and their chosen lifestyle, can lead to the abuse of the not-yet-born. Chambers et al. (1993) note professional care providers' growing concern about **Fetal Alcohol Syndrome (FAS)** and people suffering **Fetal Alcohol Effects (FAE)**. Yet, in their NWT study, they found few resources for diagnosing FAE and no special programs for those who are so diagnosed. We also need basic data on fetal alcohol syndrome. The absence of such data prevents effective planning and service development. Lorraine Stick told the Commission:

> We don't have a good data base in the Yukon or elsewhere — we are not even monitoring those 88 diagnosed in 1985 by Dr. Asante in any kind of organized or co-ordinated way. We need to at least know who those are, but we are not using this information, never mind knowing anything about those not yet diagnosed. We have a critical lack of information on people with FAE. ... We are developing random and unco-ordinated plans and not following up or demanding accountability, i.e., treatment centres that advertise as being able to treat people with FAS/FAE. What kind of treatment are they getting? What happens to them? What are the criteria for success? Nor do we follow-up on people as they move between programs, i.e. a transfer from an early childhood centre to public school. They need access to other support services such as physio and occupational therapy, family support, et cetera.

> Lorraine Stick, RCAP Public Hearings, Whitehorse, 92-11-18: 150

People suffering from Fetal Alcohol Syndrome or other Fetal Alcohol Effects sometimes are rendered vulnerable by mental impairment, for one of the consequences of FAS is a diminished ability to distinguish right from wrong.

> We need to emphasize the poor judgment and the inability to predict consequences or to learn from events. We also need education about the multiple [correlates] of FAS/FAE, including physical and sexual abuse and attachment

issues. Children who are affected by FAS/FAE are very vulnerable to be physically abused and sexually abused.... Currently we believe many adults with
FAS/FAE are either on the street or in jail.

> Lorraine Stick, RCAP Public Hearings, Whitehorse, 92-11-18: 148

Family violence affects aboriginal children profoundly. Its costs, in terms of
both human suffering and dollars, are staggering:

> Our children are vastly affected by family violence even when they are not the
> direct victims. The cost to our children is hidden in their inability to be atten-
> tive in school, in feelings of insecurity and low-esteem, and in acting-out
> behaviour which may manifest itself in many ways, such as vandalism, self-
> abuse, bullying and often these children suffer in silence.

> Sharon Caudron, Program Director,
> Women's Resource Centre of Hay River
> RCAP Public Hearings, Hay River, NWT, 93-06-17: 110

I have seen some of the children from abused homes and some of their scars
are very, very deep, so that when they become adults they will have serious
psychiatric problems. There is not much we can do once the damage is done
for some of these children, especially when one lives in an isolated area; there
are no professions there and certainly even fewer that speak the Native language to support these children, to understand what has happened to them,
and to work through their problems.

> Heather Clements, RCAP Public Hearings, Toronto, Ont., 92-11-03: 180

Old age is another time of vulnerability to family violence. Some elderly
aboriginal people suffer the indignity of neglect and abuse at the hands of those
closest to them. This extremely sad development in the very communities that
claim to hold the elderly in such high regard, is incomprehensible until one considers how many have devalued their traditional commitment to others.

Elder abuse can take the form of financial exploitation and repression
(Dumont-Smith and Labelle, 1992), but it can also involve coerced activities like
baby-sitting, rape, physical, emotional and verbal abuse (Zellerer, 1993: 10).
Angela Jones laments the manipulation of elders when she states:

> There is a lot of Elder abuse. ... A lot of times some of your relatives will
> manipulate you. You sign your farm over to them, and they promise to do this
> and that for your but, after the transfer is done, you don't even see them any
> more. A non-Indian looks forward to retiring from their farm and selling it
> and taking that long-awaited trip they always wanted to take, but for a lot of
> us Natives that doesn't happen.

> Angela Jones, British Columbia Native Women's Society
> RCAP Public Hearings, Prince George, B.C., 93-06-17

Homosexuality can also be a factor in communal or family violence in aboriginal communities. As yet, it is not well tolerated or openly discussed in most
communities. This intolerance makes the lives of many two-spirited aboriginal
people very difficult as one presenter testified:

> The other young brother — and this is a realistic life experience that I had a
> couple of weeks ago when I was in Vancouver — this other young brother
> who is 25 years old and has AIDS now. He too was abused, raped and sepa-

rated from his family when he was three-years old. He had witnessed seven murders when he was a child, in his youth. He has had this virus now eight years, since he was 18 years old. I have asked him, besides a wish for life, what would he like? His response, "My mother."

Ken Ward, RCAP Public Hearings, Edmonton, Alta., 92-06-11: 129

Abuse against **mentally or physically disabled** people is another problem, especially in the form of incest and sexual abuse. Said Judi Johnny at the RCAP Public Hearings in Whitehorse (92-11-18: 488):

So I would just like to say that it would be our pleasure to work with you, as far as aboriginal people with disabilities, because we are less recognized and the most violated against by both races, both sexes, and both communities. We are raped by disabled men; we are raped by disabled women; we are raped by aboriginal women; we are raped by aboriginal men; we are raped by white women; we are raped by white men, and believe you me we have been raped by our medical attendants, doctors, nurses, occupational therapists — you name it, we've had it. We know what it is like to be down low, but for God's sake you don't have to keep us there either.

Other intervenors before RCAP alluded to the psychological, social, and economic stresses arising from the fact that aboriginal cultures are going through a period of rapid transition. Not surprisingly, mental health problems have become of increasing concern to health professionals in aboriginal communities.

Many Fingers' study highlights how the aboriginal **extended family** can be both an asset and a liability. She found that extended families are accessed for support by 57% of all respondents, with men (67%) accessing family support more frequently than women (47%). This notwithstanding, she also found that in tribal communities, extended families often act as a stressor, especially for women.

There is evidence of **growing social stratification** in aboriginal communities — the emergence of a class of "haves" and a class of "have nots" — for even though a community as a whole is poor, not everyone in the community will be poor (Lithman, 1984: 124). The gap between the rich and poor on-reserve often stems from discriminatory economic development policies and practices which are pro-elite, pro-rich, and anti-tradition. Today, chiefs and councils are entrusted with a great deal of power. They often determine who gets housing, who is offered employment, and who is included and who excluded from the community's economic and social order. The concentration of such power in the hands of the few can be a breeding ground for nepotism and patronage (Shkilnyk, 1985: 106). Such charges are often directed at the chief and council by ordinary community members. There is a widespread belief that these individuals may dispense favours in the form of houses and jobs and that all too often, the only people to benefit from their influence is their next-of-kin.

Aboriginal leaders recognize that elders hold a special and honoured status within the aboriginal community. Leaders, therefore, often strike alliances with elders in order to benefit from their spiritual guidance and wisdom or because they know this group has the credibility and ability to keep peaceful discussions going as political agendas get done. Generally, community members tolerate and support the fact that elders are accepting larger roles in guiding community change around issues like family violence while at the same time exerting extraordinary power and influence on the decision makers.

Some community members, however, find elder-political alliances more troublesome, for it is not unknown for some aboriginal leaders to use elders, aboriginal traditions or culture, for more self-serving personal or political reasons. While elders can play a critical role in bringing popular opinions forward into power domains, *bringing a "spiritual" process into political decision-making can silence people who do not dare to challenge it because they fear the repercussions of doing so.* Many aboriginal people feel deceived by the aboriginal leadership and by elders alike, when they are denied access to the decision arena by the political **abuse of spirituality**.

Spiritual abuse is beginning to surface as a topical issue in aboriginal communities. More people are re-attributing their living problems to the abuse of "medicine". Despite this, there remains a great deal of reticence among most aboriginal people to talk about it. This contrasts sharply with the dogmatic criticism that the Churches have received on such issues as the residential school syndrome. The task of dealing with spiritual abuse is complex and one must consider the role "medicine" plays in aboriginal development. Because many aboriginal communities are undergoing a revival expressed primarily through spiritual and cultural recovery, they can be especially vulnerable to such abuse. Greater dialogue and research is needed in this area.

Elders hold a position of honour within the aboriginal community. Despite this, in the hearings and in the research, it was evident that elders are not immune from exercising their own forms of abuse. Because of the status of elders and their "spiritual" or "medicine" powers, people are terrified whenever they have to confront an elder who is transgressing taboos like touching children inappropriately in a sweat lodge ceremony (Martens et al., 1988: 117). Also some "so-called" traditional healers have used their positions of respect and trust in the aboriginal community to take advantage of the pain and suffering of their own people.

Dogmatic criticism of community leaders and community authorities is generally not well received by them. While it might not be popular to attribute a community's dysfunction to its leaders, the fact remains that many aboriginal people took advantage of the hearings to speak out about how some leaders have pursued their own interests ahead of the collective interests of their constituents.

Situating communal violence in the context of aboriginal self-government means aboriginal leaders will have to move beyond their tendency to attribute all the social ills of aboriginal communities to external forces. They will have to examine how their own behaviours, attitudes and biases contribute to the structural violence inherent in many aboriginal communities. Aboriginal leaders should note that true self-government can only be achieved when, "each centre of power is carefully balanced against all others..." (Martens et al., 1988: 117) and "... a dynamic balance between the needs of the individual and the needs of the community, between freedom and order, between passions and principles" has been delineated, respected and maintained (Gore, 1992: 171).

STRUGGLE AND RESISTANCE: THE MISSING PIECE

The extent to which **the aboriginal family has become the new arena of struggle and resistance** has little recognition. Yet, the struggle is obvious when we consider what families are experiencing.

First, aboriginal families have become increasingly insular. Sharing and assistance, even from elders, have become restricted to family groupings and are often contingent on cash payments.[8] Higher rates of teenage pregnancies, single mothers dependent upon the welfare system, and detached partners have skewed family structures. These trends indicate that rather than breaking up, families are not even forming. Little wonder single-parent families lack the support systems of strong family networks.

Admittedly, aboriginal families are in constant struggle. Whether it is because they have limited financial means, have fewer opportunities to take part in beleaguered community affairs, or have adopted oppressive value systems,[9] **aboriginal families are in a dangerous slide to total disintegration**. However, taking an eagle's eye view of the situation, one can see how aboriginal peoples have turned this danger into an opportunity for resistance.

By glorifying the past, aboriginal people have driven home the point that aboriginal families traditionally worked in a co-operative and communal manner. This provided people with meaningful roles and encouraged close relationships between parents and offspring. They said healthy families came about because each individual was personally committed to this end. However, aboriginal intervenors before the Commission also bared their souls about family violence and the immense suffering it has caused. On both counts their memories cannot be erased. To do so would be to undermine their resistance to the problem.

There is an urgent need to deepen the understanding of aboriginal family violence and to heighten people's ability to respond to its devastating impact. Probing the nature and origin of family violence will help increase knowledge of the relationship between healthy aboriginal families, sustained human development, and strong aboriginal nations. Furthermore, healthy aboriginal families are a source of community wealth and individual self-determination. In various ways, though, family violence serves as an impediment to aboriginal development and self-determination. These are outlined in Box 1.

The tenacity and ingenuity of spirit with which aboriginal peoples have resisted repression and exploitation is legendary. Even with words, they express a twofold experience: they defy the oppressive effects of dominant forces as they affirm their own social reality. Whether words have taken the form of songs, dreams, prayers, or prophecies, they play a key role in inspiring the people to move toward greater self-sufficiency, self-reliance, healing and one-ness with others.

Integrating Men Into Family Violence Initiatives

There is alarming evidence of the unwillingness of aboriginal male leaders to acknowledge or respond to the issue of family violence. By failing to protect the rights of aboriginal women, the aboriginal male leaders have not only put the safety and well-being of aboriginal women at risk, but have implicitly condoned this type of violence. At the Commission's Winnipeg public hearings Marilyn Fontaine of the Aboriginal Women's Unity Coalition quoted from the findings of the Manitoba Aboriginal Justice Inquiry in her presentation to RCAP:

> Most chiefs and council members are male and often exhibit bias in favour of the male partner in a domestic abuse situation. This can effectively chase the woman from her home and community.

BOX 1 Family Violence as an Impediment to Aboriginal Development

Family violence interferes with aboriginal development in several ways, because it:

1. undermines the high esteem aboriginal peoples bestow upon the family as the bastion of human life and relations;
2. diminishes the social integration of family members;
3. jeopardizes the sharing of responsibilities aimed at improving aboriginal social well-being;
4. contributes to aboriginal social instability and social disintegration;
5. affects the ability of the individual and community to cope with the on-going impact of structural and cultural change;
6. threatens aboriginal community democracy, productivity and values; and
7. crowds individual and public agendas, putting a stress on limited aboriginal development resources.

The unwillingness of chiefs and councils to address the plight of women and children suffering abuse at the hand of husbands and fathers is quite alarming. We are concerned enough about it to state that we believe that the failure of aboriginal government leaders to deal at all with the problem of domestic abuse is unconscionable. We believe that there is heavy responsibility on aboriginal leaders to recognize the significance of the problem within their own communities. They must begin to recognize, as well, how much their silence and failure to act actually contribute to the problem...

(92-04-23: 110)

Several witnesses before the Commission stated that male leaders have criticized aboriginal women for speaking out against family violence and accused them of undermining the drive for self-government.

A number of testimonials at the hearings dealt with the need to integrate men into the war against family violence. Intervenors said this is necessary for four reasons. First, this arrangement would encourage change in the unequal relations between aboriginal men and women. Secondly, it has become evident that aboriginal men, as well as aboriginal women, have high victimization rates when it comes to family violence. Two recent studies show this to be the case. In inner cities (LaPrairie and Steinke, 1994) and in childhood, more males are generally exposed to spousal and severe child abuse while females are subjected to child sexual abuse. Similarly, professionals working in the North say aboriginal men have suffered more child sexual abuse than previously believed and they have been as devastated by this as women have been (Chambers et al., 1993).

Many of the male leaders within aboriginal communities are very unhealthy; this makes for unhealthy communities.

Lillian George, RCAP Public Hearings,
Prince George, B.C., 93-05-31: 226

The third reason why men have to be part of family violence prevention rests with their dual experience. Raising sensitivities and creating a collective consciousness ensures an informed viewpoint of men as both perpetrators and victims of family violence. All told, this is critical to achieving long-lasting resolution of aboriginal family violence. Several witnesses spoke about male victimization and its relation to male-initiated violence.

> I think that when a man abuses there is a problem there that he was a victim before he was an abuser. I think we need to look at issues that are going to deal with this man not just as an offender, but also as a victim.
>
> Christine Hoffman, Chairman,
> North Central Alberta Crisis Intervention Association
> RCAP Public Hearings, Lac La Biche, Alta., 92--6-09: 195

Finally, men must be involved in family violence activities because, in keeping with the aboriginal view of the interrelatedness of all elements within aboriginal society, men play an integral part in human development. Jim Penton told the Royal Commission:

> I think there needs to be a tremendous stress on education which enhances the pride and abilities of our youth. A good deal is said … about the plight of aboriginal women. I don't want to disparage those remarks in any way, … but my own experience is that the group within our society which is suffering the most is aboriginal men. It is largely our men, both Indian and Métis, who are in the prisons and penitentiaries of this country.
>
> Part of that arises out of the fact that the pride of our people has been killed in many individuals. Our young men have suffered a psychological castration complex for the last one hundred years, and it is time that this was stopped so that our young men can turn to positive pursuits by way of education, so that we can break the cycle of criminality and imprisonment, so that we can break the cycle of the mistreatment of women and children in our communities — and it happens all over, again a result colonialism. It is only through positive education controlled by our own peoples that that can take place.
>
> RCAP Public Hearings, Lethbridge, Alta., 93-05-25: 121

Integrating men into family violence activities poses many challenges. Programs aimed at male perpetrators of family violence must be closely tied to sound aboriginal concepts of justice and punishment. Because tribal concepts of justice are often conciliatory rather than adversarial, and are grounded in restitutive principles rather than retribution, mainstream approaches to jailing abusers might not be viable or acceptable options in many aboriginal communities.

Of utmost importance is that when we make changes we not lose sight of women's real, well-grounded fears of abusive men. Some women would have serious reservations about involving men in family violence initiatives, for they simply have no faith in men's intentions and potential to change for the better. As Sharon McIvor states:

> The development of programs, services, and policies for handling domestic violence has been placed in the hands of men. Has it resulted in a reduction in this kind of violence? Is a woman or a child safe in their own home in an aboriginal community? The statistics show this is not the case. As one woman said, people are killing each other in our communities. Do they want to govern that? Men rarely speak of family violence. Men rarely speak of incest. Men rarely speak of gang rape and what they are doing about it.
>
> RCAP Public Hearings, Toronto, 92-06-26: 51

Drawing Upon Traditional Strengths

Numerous witnesses before the Royal Commission spoke of the need for elders to assume a co-active role in the fight against family violence and in the strengthening of aboriginal families. While some people express concern about elders who use or abuse their authority or standing within the community, the vast majority of aboriginal people believe in their legitimacy and potential to make a difference in aboriginal life. However, rather than merely being asked to say an opening and closing prayer, elders should be more fully utilized, such as in teaching parenting skills and teaching in the schools and daycare centre, even if they don't have formal credentials recognized in some certificate or diploma.[10]

In her study, Many Fingers (1994) found that all of the male tribal respondents gave positive feedback on the utilization of elders for family stress, [while] female respondents were much less likely to do so. The researcher attributes the lower rate of female participation in traditional counselling to "lack of exposure to elders and counsellors". Interestingly, 75% of urban respondents, male and female, provided positive feedback on working with elders (Many Fingers, 1994: 55). In the main, elders appear to be an invaluable source of inspiration for better living formulas.

Although it is not the only spiritual symbol at work in aboriginal communities, the Medicine Wheel[11] is one of the most popular. Its appeal lies in its ability to reflect aboriginal ideology and thought. An holistic approach is also inherent in the Medicine Wheel: an individual must be personally involved and morally committed to strive toward the inner and outward balance depicted in natural and supernatural laws. Because the healing circle is based on the concept of the medicine wheel, it seems to win universal favour among all aboriginal groups. Healing circles have been adopted as a preventative, supportive and rehabilitative measure in dealing with family violence. Several witnesses spoke to the Commission about these circles and their healing effects:

> Many people in the different communities who have used the Healing Circle process have become very effective in their helping role. Many of us who are in that healing process have worked to empower ourselves and others and, by doing so, we have become effective agents of positive changes within the Native community.

> Peggy Bird, Chippewas of Sarnia Healing Circle
> RCAP Public Hearings, Sarnia, Ont., 93-05-10: 226

> The ultimate goal for the S.A.T.S. [Sexual Abuse Treatment Services] program is family unification. This program was developed by Aboriginal people for Aboriginal people and services to be provided by Aboriginal therapists. We have incorporated traditional and contemporary healing methods. For example, sweats, smudging, healing/talking circles, ceremonial rights, versus art and play therapy, psychodrama, gestalt and psychotherapy. Our traditional healing methods were very effective before European contact. It they worked then, why can't they work now?

> Lillian George, RCAP Public Hearings,
> Prince George, B.C., 93-05-31: 22

Self-help groups are now beginning to emerge and [are] sharing their knowledge of traditional medicine, because modern medicine does not heal the whole body. It is necessary to relearn and reappropriate knowledge of traditional medicine. . . .

Danielle Descent, RCAP Public Hearings,
Mani-Utenam-t, Qué., 92-11-20: 82

Aboriginal healing priorities and strategies include the development of healing lodges or healing centres. It is not surprising that aboriginal people see these as places where people unite and gain the self-esteem, pride and empowerment they need so badly. Another intervenor adds her voice on the merits of healing places:

> The community healing aspect talks about healing our people. We are talking about one global treatment centre but also dealing with all the different areas that people need. One area may be in dealing with the cultural aspect of our people, maybe the Stoney Creek elders healing camp ... where they can bring people back into their culture after treating them for their addictions. We might have another tribal area where they would focus on sexual abuse, but all these areas need to be touched. [Our approach needs to be] holistic in another sense, not just in the policy of giving us funds but also [it] deals with the spirit, soul, and body of a person. That is the holistic treatment that our people ... want in order for a person to be adequately healed.

Lynda Prince, Northern Native Family Services, Carrier Sekani Tribal Council
RCAP Public Hearings, Stoney Creek, B.C., 92-06-18:370

Another pointed out that healing can have ripple effects beyond the individual to the children, the family, peers, and beyond,[12] and yet others stressed the holistic approach in terms of the focus being placed on the whole family:

> We have to concentrate on the healing of the whole family, not just one individual. We have to heal the whole family. In the area of abuse, the victim and the offender must be healed and all the family members that are affected by this one situation of abuse. For that, we need money to train our own people to do the healing, to train our own people to do the counselling.

Rosa Wright, Native Women's Association for NWT
RCAP Public Hearings, Fort Simpson, NWT, 92-05-26: 50

The credibility and authenticity of some healers is now a subject of aboriginal debate. As aboriginal communities revive traditional organizational and service models such as healing lodges and centres, it will be incumbent upon them to enact codes of conduct, regulations and standards of surveillance to ensure that the rights of their citizens are not infringed and that their clients are not placed in harm's way. Lillian Sanderson of the Aboriginal Women's Council in Saskatoon, posed a possible solution for regulating the activities of those who would identify themselves as "healers" as follows:

> We have also come across many self-proclaimed healers who have abused or exploited traditional spirituality in their own aboriginal people.
>   No, it is gift that you are given. For controlling the spiritual malpractice, I guess it would be through all the Elders in each community. They would know the ones who are abusing the sweat lodge and abusing the medicines. It would be up to all the different Elders in all the different communities and provinces, both in Canada and in the States, to have a list of qualified

healers and non-qualified healers, and that list could be distributed throughout each reserve.

RCAP Public Hearings, Saskatoon, Sask., 93-05-13

Helping the Helpers

Family violence initiatives have provided aboriginal communities with the
opportunity to explore different formulas and mechanisms for increasing the
involvement of their own as helpers. Often, the employment of community
members is the preferred approach because local helpers are perceived as culturally sensitive and knowledgeable about community circumstances.
However, the fact that some of these workers, themselves, might have either
come from an abusive family environment or might be currently involved in an
abusive relationship, as some witnesses reported, should not be ignored.
Intervenors argued for helping the helpers:

> I believe there is a great need for healing and support services for the aborig-
> inal healers in the community. I have worked with a number of them. For
> some of them, I have actually acted as their counsellors. Counsellors, as well,
> most of them are working on their own healing issues. They are isolated. They
> are under immense social pressure within the communities to often not report
> violence and to follow through on the legal route. A lot of that pressure is
> coming from extended families.

Sarah Calaher, RCAP Public Hearings,
Yellowknife, NWT, 92-12-07

> Community care givers may need help too along with support and under-
> standing. There is a belief that helpers should live a perfect life themselves
> before they are able to help others. Excessive judgement and a lack of trust
> and faith in each other's abilities makes helping difficult. Lack of personal
> responsibility in a situation arises from non-traditional approaches such as
> blaming and victimization.

Carol Croxon, Director, Ojibway Family Resource Centre,
RCAP Public Hearings, North Bay, Ont., 93-05-10: 124

These workers need support so they can deal with their personal issues and
so that they do not bring dysfunctional attitudes or practices into the work setting where they might pose a further risk to their clients. Aboriginal organizations should establish employee assistance programs so that these workers can
begin their own healing journey.

> You have to remember that although these men are violent and abusive, they
> are also victims themselves and they need someone to listen and to under-
> stand as well.

Kula Ellison, Aboriginal Women's Council of Saskatchewan
Saskatoon Area Women's Local, RCAP Public Hearings,
Saskatoon, 92-10-28: 139

The Benefits of Using Culturally Acceptable
Institutions and Symbols

The aboriginal community is undergoing a traditional, cultural, and spiritual
renewal. Healing circles, sweat lodges, and elders are becoming institutional

cornerstones in prisons, alcohol and drug treatment centres, and educational centres. Today, almost every aboriginal gathering includes some form of spirituality. Authentic traditionalism is no longer the exclusive domain of a select few and must not be allowed to become so.

It is important, though, to establish who the traditionalists are. Obviously, they include elders, traditional healers, and participants in ceremonial sundances, sweat lodges, and pipe ceremonies. These are individuals for whom spirituality has become the major resource for reconnecting to "self" and humanity. Elders often mediate this experience.

Aboriginal peoples see elders as living treasures. As Harold Cardinal (1977: 29) says: "To find the models we need, the first place to look is within ourselves. We have to go back to our elders…". Elders are the "soul" of the aboriginal experience. Their wisdom is seen as coming from deep within their being and it reaches into the past to link contemporary aboriginal peoples with their ancestors and their traditions.

In today's aboriginal community, elders are not necessarily old; rather they are individuals who are seen to have many gifts. Aboriginal people look to elders as oral historians, teachers, cultural workers, ecologists, environmentalists, and healers. While the wisdom of elders is now enjoying recognition worldwide, it is the practical and extraordinary sensitivity they show to the intricacies of the natural world which garners them the admiration of their aboriginal and non-aboriginal followers.

It is easy to see why aboriginal people see elders as valuable community members. Elders help to *validate and affirm* aboriginal society in all its aspects. Allocating communal rights and responsibilities to individuals with the full expectation that these will be exercised in due course and with due respect to others is a well developed notion of what elders do.

Aboriginal cultures dictate that healing not stop or begin with the personal acquisition of coping skills. With the aboriginal community, there is a powerful obligation of **mutual aid** — an obligation for community members to reach beyond their own personal pain to help one another. As Peggy Bird noted in her presentation to RCAP (Sarnia, Ont., 93-05-10), "many of the social problems occurring within our communities can be greatly reduced if we make a systematic effort to help our people heal their personal pain". Aboriginal peoples consider personal awareness of such obligations to be in keeping with tradition and the "Indian" way of life. In formulating family violence policies and intervention programs, it is important that we remain cognizant of the emphasis that aboriginal peoples place on concepts of mutual-aid and mutual support.

The inclusion of culture and tradition in aboriginal healing practices has made it much easier for aboriginal people to seek out healing. Aboriginal people have come to see healing as a celebration of survival and triumph over one's human condition. Healing is now being viewed as a life-long process that helps people cope with the harmful effects of *both* structural and personal violence. Furthermore, aboriginal people are now talking in terms of the healing of whole families, communities, and nations.

Balance, peace, and harmony are central to aboriginal belief systems and the maintenance of personal and community well-being. Failure to live in balance and in harmony can cause an individual to become unwell in spirit and body. Failure to live in balance and harmony can also kill the spirit of whole communities and nations. For the restoration of harmony, peace and balance, though, the individual or community or nation must be free from the tyranny of violence.

Moving to the Soul of the Aboriginal Community

A major reorientation of people's **social responsibilities for self and community** is needed not just in aboriginal communities, but also in Canada as a whole. However, self-responsibility is often opposed when family violence is explored from within, for such exploration exposes the secrets of "self" to those outside.

Many people have a tendency to dissociate themselves from their moral obligations to "self" or community. In the same way, many consider the "spirit" to be an abstraction. However, aboriginal people deal comfortably with the concept of "spirit". They apply it to human relations in the way Dion Stout articulates in her research paper, "The Ethical Dimensions of Participatory Development in Reserve Communities". She advocates a multifacetted form of development in which self, community, and moral responsibility are pivotal. It includes the following elements:

1. discovery of the centrality of *self*, especially individual ability or "medicine";
2. the transition of individual power to *family* through values, attitudes, behaviour and institutions;
3. extending the family to the broader *community* and developing *agency* to connect with more diverse groups of people;
4. challenging the existing imbalances between the cultural/structural divide of all peoples of the *world*; and
5. re-creating *self* in solidarity with those who are, those who have been, and those who are yet to be.

Despite the fact that many do not live out the concept of **self-responsibility**, the role which it can play in eradicating family violence should not be underestimated. Because aboriginal societies value *self*-responsibility (the taking of responsibility onto oneself), the concept of self-responsibility has enormous potential for extending the safety net to the aboriginal victims of family violence. Aboriginal peoples find the concept more congruent with their traditions which recognized and valued *self*-responsibility, as well as the responsibility of "self" to the family and community.

In an aboriginal view of the world, the individual is urged to accept responsibility for his/her own actions while extending *self*-responsibility to the immediate family, next-of-kin, to the reserve community, and to the rest of the world. There exists also an obligation for other parts of the collective to support the individual and each other. In other words, the morality and the duty and obligation found in community, are at once the domain of the individual and the collective. In this system, "each individual is intensely aware of his accountability for the welfare of others, to which he must attend, albeit in his own way and according to dictates of his own conscience. There is no State, or any omnipotent, generous Deity on which to thrust the satisfaction of human needs — or to blame for hardships" (Barsh, 1986: 185). *Thus, healing does not stop or begin with good coping abilities. It also includes the presence of powerful obligations among community members to help each other.* Aboriginal people consider personal awareness of such obligations to be crucial to sustaining life. Therefore, it is of vital importance to align policies and programs as closely as possible with existing relationships.

It is very clear that "we" rather than "me" was the traditional concept among aboriginal peoples.[13] Otherwise stated, *traditional aboriginal societies mea-*

sure the personal worth of individuals on their ability to contribute to the broad goals of the family and community. Not living by this code renders individual achievement meaningless and can also lead to the spiritual bankruptcy of the individual.

An aboriginal world view also focuses on the concept of "medicine". This view recognizes the power of each and every person. It also suggests that power is not given or taken away and that every individual is empowered by his or her unique talents and capabilities or "medicine".[14] Empowerment comes from within.

As in other areas, so too in combatting domestic terrorism, aboriginal people have relied heavily on simple human measures. These can be as basic as "letting go and letting God", or seizing every small advantage to shift power. A telephone call for help will do this for them, as will participation in a healing circle. Rightly or wrongly, aboriginal people are also calling for more safe houses and healing centres, rather than safe neighbourhoods or communities. For the most part, though, aboriginal people are improvising with low-cost, non-technological ways of dealing with family violence, often in and through formal organizations. Central to their actions are the values to which they cling.

In traditional aboriginal societies the concept of *self*-responsibility acted as a means of social control. Commenting on the value changes affecting many aboriginal communities, the author (Many Fingers, 1994: 33) of a Treaty 7 study writes:

> It's an absence of values. Before the values were so strong, so stringent that to step over those boundaries would mean severe, maybe, ostracization or the family would do something. Because the values were so strong then, individuals would have to think quite hard before they did something. Because they had so much strength and spirited value that such thoughts never entered their mind. But now there are so many things that are eroding our culture.

One respondent in the Treaty 7 study (Many Fingers, 1994: 36) illustrated how this concept has been replaced in some communities with more self-serving values.

Elizabeth Penashue, speaking to the Royal Commission in Sheshatshiu, Labrador, attributed aboriginal people's lost values to the influences exerted by outside social forces and government policies. There were other testimonies which suggest that traditional values such as loving, caring and sharing in aboriginal communities have little chance of survival once family violence rears its ugly head.

Many presenters suggested that social conditions like family violence can only be addressed effectively when women have the opportunity to fully participate in community power structures. This argument is evident below:

> Unless aboriginal women are guaranteed the right to share equally with men the powers to develop the forms of self-government and the instruments required for dealing with poverty, conjugal violence, incest, the consequences of unemployment, the exclusion of C-31 women and their children from their communities, there will be no significant improvement in living and social conditions. Since women are the main care givers for the children, the ailing, the disabled, and the very old, the organization of educational, health and other social and community services can only be successful where women share in the powers of planning and carrying out those services.

Madeleine Parent, RCAP Public Hearings, Montréal, 93-05-27: 240

Sadly, for many aboriginal women, violence often defines the difference between their potential and actual self-actualization. Rix Rogers testified to the scope of this lost human potential:

> [The] final thing that really had an impact on me was the tremendous poten-
> tial for the role of aboriginal women. My own conclusion that I made to the
> Minister was that if there's going to be a restoration of full richness of abo-
> riginal culture, it's probably going to be through the women; somehow or
> other that has to be supported.

> Rix Rogers, Institute for the Prevention of Child Abuse,
> RCAP Public Hearings, Toronto, 93-06-03: 87

For aboriginal peoples, **healing** is a celebration of survival and it is the ability to cope with one's human condition. It is a lifetime process that reduces the
harmful effects of systemic and personal violence. A growing concern among
aboriginal peoples over exploitation and repression has accelerated the adoption of healing as a preventative, supportive, and rehabilitative measure.

Peace is essential for individual and collective productivity and well-being.
Aboriginal people see community disintegration as symptomatic of the need for
peace. Pearl Keenan is a well-known elder and peacemaker from Yukon. When
she appeared before the Commission she stressed that it is familiarity with traditions that is the key to peace.

Family violence can be viewed as a desperate struggle to adjust to difficult
circumstances. Having political, economic, cultural, and social **space** is of vital
importance to everyone, particularly in producing more positive adjustments.
In essence, space is freedom. Adequate space encourages free, spiritual, and
equal relations in aboriginal communities.

A long-term goal in the area of family violence is that each human be
respected as a special and indispensable creation. Out of that respect springs
hope. **Hope** is also a product of the work of numerous social service organizations for aboriginal women and their families.

CONCLUSION

Family violence is tied to the moral systems in aboriginal communities. A major
shift in thinking and actions is necessary if family violence is to be eliminated.
Old structures in this new approach are unacceptable because they stand in the
way of change just as much as old thoughts and actions do. It is also vital to recognize where ideas for change originate and to recognize that change comes
from constant struggle and resistance.

After months of meeting and talking with aboriginal people through the
Royal Commission on Aboriginal People, it is evident that they have learned
tough life lessons from "the school of broken windows". Therefore, a special
effort has been made here to give voice to their issues, struggles and triumphs
around family violence.

NOTES

[1] *Ed.'s Note:* This chapter was prepared for the Privy Council Office's Royal
Commission on Aboriginal Peoples (RCAP), July 1996. The present version is

abridged from a much longer one, entitled *Family Violence in Aboriginal Communities: The Missing Peace*, which readers are encouraged to read. Many of the footnotes in the original have been omitted here, as have many quotations from intervenors at the RCAP public hearings. Reproduced with the permission of the Minister of Public Works and Government Services Canada, 1997.

[2] For a larger discussion of silence on child sexual abuse, see Pauktuutit (1991) and for Métis women's voices on family violence see Poelzer and Poelzer (1986, Ch. 6 & 7).

[3] Korton (1990: 14) defines "communal violence" as the "violence that occurs among people who share the same national boundaries and identity".

[4] Anastasia Shkilnyk (1985: 152) quotes a forty-one year old woman who spoke of her inability to be heard in her own community or have her needs met: "The Chief talks about `my people' and `our people.' Hell, on this reserve, there are those who work steady, and those who are on welfare and drunk most of the time. We're the ones on the bottom of the heap. Why doesn't someone give us a chance?"

[5] Brodeur et al. (1991: 25-26) describe the recent emergence of a moral order among the James Bay Cree which indulges the youth with supervisory positions over older people. This new order casts aside traditional moral systems where individuals were "encouraged to view themselves as a participant in an order that stressed differences of social positioning between people — such as grandmother and granddaughter, older brother and younger brother, husband and wife — and how these differences are drawn together in orderly arrangements by people actively fulfilling their proper duties and obligations to each other".

[6] As Brodeur et al. (1991: 27) state, traditionally, knowledge was passed down from one generation to the next without formal codification and precise explanations. Lessons learned could only be demonstrated by exploratory approximation since, in the traditional learning environment, "little opportunity for the younger to challenge the knowledge of the older exists".

[7] Russel Lawrence Barsh (1986: 193) writes: "Those fit to lead are also deemed to be the foremost examples for children. Education is not entrusted to technicians, but lodged with the highest levels of public leadership, because forming young minds is at least as important and challenging as helping adults make collective decisions. Education and government are inseparable, moreover because well-educated children tend to be self-disciplined adults — and respected teachers can become influential leaders". Brodeur, La Prairie and McDonnell (1991: 57), in their study of Québec Crees, note the correlation between the erosion of traditional authority and the discontent of young Crees.

[8] Jean-Paul Brodeur et al. (1991: 36), describing Cree society, state: "...[T]here are people who live in the same communities today who have never had anything to do with each other. Individual wage labour and a weakening of the value of sharing [have] made ... relationships within the household pretty uncertain in many ways. Beyond this, relations are weaker still...".

Carol La Prairie also writes about an almost complete lack of willingness on the part of many Crees to perform tasks for one another without pay. She includes "elders speaking at schools, children bringing aged parents to clinics or looking after them at home, youth lacking interest in 'games' and wanting tournaments which involve money, selling moose or other game rather than giving it away" (Brodeur et al., 1991: 101).

[9] York (1990: 90) quotes Theresa Bull, who is a Councillor of the Louis Bull Band and Vice-Chair of the Hobbema Health Board, as follows: "When we had no

money, we had a lot of family unity. Then we had all this money and people could buy anything they wanted. It replaced the old values. If you weren't sure of the old values of the community, money brought in a value of its own. It doesn't bring happiness. It put more value on materialistic possessions. The family and the value of spirituality got lost".

[10] Edith Young, RCAP Public Hearings, Thompson, Man., 93-05-31: 43 and Lorraine McRae, RCAP Public Hearings, Orillia, Ont., 93-05-13: 5.

[11] See Bopp (1984) for a discussion of the Medicine Wheel.

[12] Cindy Sparvier, Social Worker, Joe Duquette High School, RCAP Public Hearings, Saskatoon, Sask., 92-10-27: 198.

[13] Boldt and Long (1985: 336) state "[I]n Indian tribal society, individual self-interest was inextricably intertwined with tribal interests; that is the general good and the individual good were virtually identical. Laslett's "onion skin" analogy aptly illustrates the mythical quality of individuality in traditional Indian society. To apprehend the individual in tribal Indian society, he says, we would have to peel off a succession of group-oriented and derived attitudes. The individual turns out to be metaphorical layers of group attitudes, at the bottom of which nothing remains".

[14] The James Bay Crees believe that unearthly beings transfer power to select individuals, thus enabling these beneficiaries to draw strength from a secret and sometimes insidious power base.

REFERENCES

Barsh, R.L.
1986   "The Nature and Spirit of North American Political Systems", *The American Indian Quarterly: Journal of American Indian Studies*, X, 3: 181–196.

Boldt, Menno and J. Anthony Long
1985   "Tribal Philosophies and the Canadian Charter of Rights and Freedoms," pp. 333–346 in Menno Boldt and J. Anthony Long (eds.), *The Quest for Justice: Aboriginal People and Aboriginal Rights*. Toronto: University of Toronto Press.

Bopp, Julie et al.
1984   *The Sacred Tree*. Lethbridge, Alta.: Four Worlds Development Press.

Brodeur, Jean-Paul, Carol LaPrairie, and Roger McDonnell
1991   *Justice For The Cree: Final Report*. Val d'Or, Qué.: Grand Council of the Crees (Québec)/Cree Regional Authority.

Brodribb, Somer
1984   "The Traditional Roles of Native Women in Canada and the Impact of Colonization", *The Canadian Journal of Native Studies*, IV, 1: 85–103.

Bulhan, Hussein A.
1985   *Frantz Fanon and the Psychology of Oppression*. New York: Plenum Press.

Canadian Institute of Child Health
1994   *The Health of Canada's Children. Second Edition*. Ottawa.

Cardinal, Harold
1977   *The Rebirth of Canada's Indians*. Edmonton: Hurtig.

CPVAW (Canadian Panel on Violence Against Women)
1993   *Changing the Landscape: Ending Violence–Achieving Equality*. Ottawa.

Chambers, Cynthia et al.
1993   *Damaged and Needing Help: Violence And Abuse in Aboriginal Families in Yellowknife and Lutsel K'e* (Draft Final Report). Yellowknife.

Dion Stout, Madeleine
1993   "The Ethical Dimensions of Participatory Development in Reserve Commu-
       nities." Research paper, Carleton University, Ottawa, Ontario.
Dumont-Smith, C. and P. Sioui-Labelle
1992   *National Family Violence Survey.* Ottawa: Indian and Inuit Nurses of Canada.
Falk, Richard
1988   "Satisfying Human Needs in a World of Sovereign States: Rhetoric, Reality
       and Vision," pp. 560-597 in Charles K. Wilber (ed.), *The Political Economy of
       Development and Underdevelopment.* New York: Random House.
Gore, A.
1992   *Earth in Balance: Ecology and the Human Spirit.* Boston: Houghton Mifflin.
Health Canada
1992   *Family Violence: Situation Paper.* Ottawa: Supply & Services Canada.
Korton, David C
1990   *Getting to the 21st Century: Voluntary Action and the Global Agenda.* Connecticut:
       Kumarin Press.
La Prairie, Carol and Bruce Steinke
1994   *Seen But Not Heard: Native People in the Inner City.* Ottawa: Department of
       Justice.

———
1994   *Seen But Not Heard: Native People in the Inner City, Report 2: City-by-City
       Differences–The Inner City and the Criminal Justice System.* Ottawa: Department
       of Justice.
LaRocque, Emma
1994   "Violence in Aboriginal Communities" in Royal Commission on Aboriginal
       Peoples, *The Path To Healing.* Ottawa.
Lithman, Yngve G.
1984   *The Community Apart: A Case Study of a Canadian Indian Reserve Community.*
       Winnipeg: University of Manitoba Press.
Many Fingers, Brenda
1994   *Treaty 7 Community Study: Violence and Community Stress.* Ottawa: Royal
       Commission on Aboriginal Peoples.
Martens, Tony, Brenda Daily, and Maggie Hodgson
1988   *The Spirit Weeps.* St. Albert, Alta.: Nechi Institute.
Pauktuutit,
1991   *No More Secrets: Acknowledging the Problem of Child Sexual Abuse in Inuit
       Communities,* Pauktuutit: Ottawa.
Poelzer, Dolores T. and Irene Poelzer
1986   *In Our Own Words: Northern Saskatchewan Métis Women Speak Out,* Saskatoon:
       Lindenblatt and Hamonic.
Rogers, Rix
1990   *Reaching for Solutions: the Report of the Special Advisor to the Minister of National
       Health and Welfare on Child Sexual Abuse in Canada.* Ottawa: National Clearing
       House on Family Violence, Health and Welfare Canada.
Shkilnyk, Anastasia
1985   *A Poison Stronger Than Love: The Destruction of an Ojibway Community,* New
       Haven, Conn.: Yale University Press.
Statistics Canada
1993   *Language, Tradition, Health, Lifestyle and Social Issues.* Ottawa: Ministry of
       Supply and Services Canada.

Wierzba, Joan, Betty Bastien and Elsie Bastien
1991   "Native Family Violence in Lethbridge", *Native Studies Review*, VII, 1: 143–146.
York, Geoffrey
1990   *The Dispossessed: Life and Death in Native Canada*. London: Vintage U.K.
Zellerer, Evelyn
1993   *Violence Against Aboriginal Women*. Ottawa: Royal Commission on Aboriginal Peoples.

CHAPTER 12

LEADERSHIP IN FIRST NATION COMMUNITIES: A CHIEF'S PERSPECTIVES ON THE COLONIAL MILLSTONE

Strater Crowfoot [1]

It might well be asked why anyone even bothers, or wants, to run for chief given his actual political impotence and the ambivalence with which he is regarded.

(Carstens, 1991: 234)

[T]here is an urgent need to study the psycho-social effects of the *Indian Act*. . . .

(Carstens, 1991: 288)

INTRODUCTION

The purposes of this chapter are to identify and describe various challenges and constraints that are involved in being a leader in a First Nation community and to provide insights into the community dynamics and social psychology of reserve communities. I draw mainly upon the case of the Siksika Nation in Alberta and upon my experience as Chief there, although much of what I have to say has applicability to other leaders (e.g., elected councillors)[2] and to other First Nation communities whose leaders I have met in my work with First Nations across Canada. At certain points I shall identify similarities with community dynamics that have been described in the anthropological literature on First Nations.

Compared to other First Nations in Canada, the Siksika Nation is a large nation geographically and demographically and relatively prosperous socio-economically. Our population of about five thousand persons contains many talented people, including many holders of university degrees and post-graduate degrees. We have various successful economic development ventures on our land and a community college which offers university transfer courses. The rates of suicide and violent death among the Siksika people are low. Over the years, we have moved to the forefront nationally or provincially in various ways. Examples are our child welfare arrangements, our participation in both the *Indian Act* revision process and the federal government's lands and trust review, and our fiscal arrangements and management. Although all is by no means "milk and honey", opportunities for the Siksika people abound, in comparison to many other First Nations.

Despite all of the above, it is a massive and, at times, disheartening challenge to be the chief of this First Nation. That is largely because the legacy of the federal government's colonial regime continues to be felt to this day as a debilitating force which tears at the very social fabric of community. If the challenge of local leadership is so great in such a progressive and accomplished community as Siksika, imagine how formidable the leadership task is in First Nations where the opportunities are few and far between and social problems are much more severe and widespread. In both types of community, and those in between on the continuum, the colonial forces that operate are fundamentally the same. It is that which makes what I write below applicable well beyond the Siksika case.

I believe in being forthright. At times, this makes me appear critical of my people. In reply, I can only say that constructive criticism and community introspection do have a role to play in the needed transformation of First Nation communities. My comments are intended as a wake-up call to First Nations and are offered in a spirit of concern and hope that First Nations will focus more on what is really important.

I begin with a few comments about leadership, in general, and about the formative influences on me as a leader. I describe some aspects of my term in office and some types of leaders whom I observed across the country while I was chief. The next section deals with the colonial context and colonial legacy which First Nations encounter. The dynamics and social psychology of the leader-follower relationship are the focus of the section after that. Included there are such topics as: community expectations and the multifacetted role of the chief; trust and distrust; a leader's legitimacy and challenges to it; community members' reluctance to take on responsibility; the leader's relations with the Elders; and the role of nepotism in reserve politics. The section after that identifies various features of First Nation cultures and communities which make leadership difficult or easy. The next section describes different aspects of dealing with the Department of Indian Affairs and Northern Development (DIAND) and the concluding section discusses community Elders and my suggestions for others who would be leaders.

Sociological Approaches to Leadership [3]

The treatment of leadership in the sociological literature has tended to focus mainly on either the social psychological dynamics of very small groups or on the social movement leader, especially the charismatic leader. For instance, in the social movements literature Gusfield (1966) has distinguished between "the mobilizer" and "the articulator", where the mobilizer is involved mainly in rousing his/her people to action and the articulator is involved mainly in representing his people's needs and interests to outsiders. The "resource mobilization" school of thought (e.g., McCarthy and Zald, 1973) in social movements treats the leader as an educated, almost entrepreneurial professional who is skilled at analysis, fund-raising, management, and media manipulation and who is likely to move on to apply his/her skills as a generalist on behalf of another related social movement as circumstances change. Classical sociologist Max Weber, on the other hand, focussed on authority relations between leader and follower and upon the chemistry (e.g., sense of obligation) in the leader-follower relationship. Turner and Killian (1987: 377–378) emphasize the notion of the leader as a symbol. All of these social movement perspectives on leadership have considerable relevance to leadership in First Nation communities and to any community mobilizing for "development". Unfortunately, they are cast at a level of abstraction that does not take into account important features of the social context — in our case, colonialism — in which leaders operate. Thus, the influence of social movement perspectives is implicit in this chapter, rather than being a primary focus, for the colonial social context must be given its due consideration.

Formative Influences Shaping My Philosophy of Leadership

In my personal philosophy I tend to view leadership primarily as a *service* and the leader as a *change agent* who is always out promoting his/her vision and trying to ensure that it catches hold. The leader should be asked by the community to lead, rather than the leader seeking out elected office on his/her own initiative. For that reason, I never campaigned for the position of chief. In fact, I never considered myself a politician. I believe, from my personal convictions, that we are here for a reason, with a mission of service. In that regard, the words of the late Nathan Eldon Tanner, former Speaker of the Alberta legislature, carry much weight with me: "Service is the rent we pay for living upon this earth".

So, in some respects, I think it was the will of the Creator that I be chief of the Siksika people and I was prepared to serve for as long as the people would vote for me. To be honest, though, I must say that I would probably not be willing to give as much of myself again if the people asked me to run again. It is too much to ask of one's family, especially if you feel that your sacrifices on behalf of the tribe are not appreciated by the tribe. In addition, it is a big financial sacrifice. When I first took office I took almost a 60% cut in pay to be chief and had to do outside teaching and consulting to meet my financial commitments.

I believe that a leader should provide vision, direction, and stability. A true leader should lead by example and exude positiveness, confidence, enthusiasm, energy, and openness. These are the best ways that I know to instill hope and to empower people, both of which are absolutely crucial for achieving change.

A true leader must also be willing to take on responsibility.[4] This I learned from the example of my great-great-grandfather, the legendary Crowfoot who was a signatory to Treaty Seven on behalf of the Blackfoot people. He is clearly one of the pivotal formative influences on my life. I look at what he had to endure and the responsibilities that he bore, such as whether to join Poundmaker's rebellion against white encroachment. His example instilled in me a great sense of responsibility toward coming back to the reserve to help out my tribe and a sense of obligation to self-improvement. He was a doer. When something had to be done, he didn't hesitate; he went in and did it. That was my approach, too. Rather than waiting until all the facts are in, I move and then I adjust later as required.

My parents and grandmother were also important formative influences on me. I enjoyed helping my grandmother and it is from my experience with her that my respect for the Elders comes. She was the epitome of a real Blackfoot person. She was kind, understanding, and told us traditional stories of Napi and of our family when my father was young. From her I developed a pride in who I am. My mother taught me to do my best and to be conscientious. My father was a wealthy farmer and a councillor. I went around with him and from him I learned what hard work could bring. At university I started to develop that work ethic myself. I also spent time in non-Native foster homes in Cardston (Alberta), Vancouver, and after my parents separated, in Edmonton. I was well treated in those homes and my foster parents not only helped form my personal beliefs and my relation to the Creator, but also helped me a lot in learning to deal with white society.

Two other institutions have had a major formative influence on me. One was the non-Native schools that I attended, especially high school in Edmonton. I found it very useful being exposed to their perspective. I learned a lot there and experienced important developments in my own identity. Especially important were some teachers and peers, under whose influence I developed a strong determination to rise to the occasion when faced with opposition or with somebody who said that something is not possible. The other major institutional influence on my entire attitude toward life, including leadership, was the Church. The Church urges us to be compassionate and genuine, and to give honest service. It has set my moral beliefs and my character, including the belief that a good leader must be a moral leader who is not engaged in cheating, stealing, lying, womanizing, or drinking. This is particularly important in the First Nation context, where there have been too many examples of leaders becoming corrupt while in office. Although such corruption might be no more prevalent than among non-Native politicians, on the reserve the corruption is more visible because it is so close and everyone knows everyone else. The chief who does not lead by good moral example creates among the people a cynicism or generalized distrust that makes it very, very difficult for those who follow in his/her path.

My Term in Office

This section aims both to ground the subsequent discussion of leadership in the kind of concrete reality which a chief must face and to show examples of my leadership philosophy in practice. In considering my remarks below, it is worth bearing in mind that I initially took office during a period of transition from old-style community politics to new-style political leadership. I regard myself as one example of the new style.

In the first three or four years alone, I brought in over twenty-five million dollars to the Siksika Nation. (I lost track after that.) It is an interesting comment on the social dynamics of reserve life, though, that because such "fund-raising" takes a leader away from the reserve a lot, it can generate criticism. Some of my council members once accused me of travelling too much and said: "We're not going to pay for your travel. Pay your own way. Your travel is of no value to us or the tribe." I pointed out that the tribe had spent twenty-two thousand dollars on my travel over the last ten months and had received $1.2 million in benefits. The response was silence and then the motion for the tribe to pay for me to go on the trip in question was passed unanimously.

I think that opposition to a chief's travelling is rooted in short-sightedness and in ignorance both of the benefits it brings to the tribe and of the costs (jet lag, fatigue, time away from family) that the chief bears in travelling. The opposition is also rooted in jealousy and in the myth that chiefs like to travel and be out enjoying "the good life" (good hotels and good meals). Although, some leaders have regarded trips as an opportunity for a big drunk, the times are changing and such behaviour is less likely to be found today. In fact, some leaders, like the chief and council of the Dene Tha First Nation in Alberta, now take a personal oath that they will not consume alcohol or engage in behaviour that will bring their office into ill repute.[5] Unfortunately, some persons holding the cynical view have failed to recognize that the times are changing; their views are stuck in the earlier era.

Partly for that reason, I tried to have a very transparent style of leadership. If people had a question, I'd answer it. If I could not deal with something, I'd explain why. If people wanted to see my travel expenses, or the books, or the audit, or the budget, we showed them. Such openness establishes credibility and helps to counter both distrust and the negative image of Indian leaders as corrupt, "skimming off the top", or being there mainly to look out for their own interests. A chief must let the people know what is going on.

There is another sense in which openness is important — namely, openness to the ideas of others on the "team". For instance, on more than one occasion my secretary literally whispered a suggestion in my ear during a council meeting and we went on to adopt it. Sometimes I'd say to her, "Don't tell me; tell them!" and have her share her ideas with the whole council. Secretaries have their ear to the ground and can help the management team stay in touch with the "grass roots".

During my term of office I tried to move Siksika to a position that I would consider to be at or near the forefront nationally in many areas, such as policing and justice, child welfare, economic development, self-government negotiations, finance, property, taxation, and restructuring of tribal government to reflect our needs and priorities rather than merely mirroring DIAND's organization. My approach was to have many irons in the fire at the same time — to be involved on as many program and policy fronts as possible in order to see what was going on and to be part of the process and influence it, rather than having the changes imposed on Siksika. The self-government negotiations with the federal government are a good example of that: I preferred to have us in there developing the models of self-government that could be adopted by the federal government, rather than having them impose on us some model that did not fit our circumstances.

I strongly believe that we do not have time on our side. I cannot emphasize this enough. We need to make substantial changes and to make them very abruptly — *a paradigm shift*. So, my approach to leadership was very proactive; I tried to make the federal government react to us. My philosophy is: do it and do it and do it and do it! We have to get past all the very good excuses that exist for not being accomplishers. We have to accept responsibility like the warriors and hunters of old and become the maker of our own destiny. Furthermore, we have to push the government with relentless determination. I tried to let them know that we were always going to be there pushing proactively, aggressively, constantly, insistently.

I also tried both to seize opportunities that presented themselves and to be a precedent setter. Taking up the federal government's offer under the so-called "Alternative Funding Arrangements"[6] would be one example of seizing opportunity, while developing our bilateral relationship in an accord which we signed with the provincial government is an example of setting a precedent. Most First

Nations shy away from dealing with provincial governments due to a fear that it will jeopardize their treaty relationship with the federal government. I believe, though, that we must deal with the modern day Canadian reality which includes powerful provincial governments which we should not ignore as potential partners.

On the economic development front, we established an oil and gas pilot project that is designed to help First Nations to develop the skills to take over control of oil and gas administration and field operations (land, environmental protection, etc.); a project potentially worth millions of dollars is now in place. Still in the economic development area, I have a special sense of satisfaction over the building of a mall and commercial centre on our reserve. We encountered much DIAND red tape on that initiative, but I gave the Minister a deadline and their red tape quickly disappeared. This project signalled to the surrounding community and to the Siksika people that we had entered a new era — that we had taken the first steps to self-sufficiency and to providing services to ourselves, rather than relying on adjacent outsiders.

This kind of symbolic statement is a very important part of what First Nation leadership is all about. For instance, in the area of public administration, the building of our tribal administration complex to replace the portable trailers and run-down old buildings in which our offices had previously been located, signalled to our people that our tribal government is a real government worthy of respect and being taken seriously. Other examples during my term of office included such things as road signs and road construction, changing our name from "Blackfoot Band" to "Siksika Nation", and changing existing co-operative arrangements with neighbouring communities. More specifically, we convinced the provincial government that our community should be recognized on road and distance signs on the Trans-Canada highway. We told the federal government that they were no longer to refer to us by their colonial name of "Blackfoot Band" and we removed a colonial element (our reserve number) from our coat of arms. Internally, when some of our tribal staff members delayed construction of new roads, I personally intervened and assumed the role of project co-ordinator to ensure action. We also asserted ourselves by changing a water and sewage agreement with a neighbouring non-Native town. That was the first time that we had ever told them what they could and could not do and what they would have to pay to us.

Through the above I was attempting to convey to the Siksika community and to outsiders that we are a people with a viable, responsible government that can accomplish much when we set our minds to it. I wanted to convey the image of a nation on the move — determined, business-like, sensible, understanding, fair, not afraid to deal with issues — rather than a community of social outcasts and derelicts. I wanted to affirm the self-worth of the Siksika people. First Nation people have lost contact with "the real people"[7] we were and should be; we were raised to be what others thought we were. An important part of a chief's job is to help to change that through instilling pride in the people.

Another strategy I followed as chief was to try to expand our powers and areas of jurisdiction. Rather than that being a power trip, as some (e.g., Boldt, 1993) would contend, we were trying to control the agenda, control the policy, and control the dollars so that we could offer better services and design better programs to meet the needs of the local people here. We'd rather have that than have things be designed by some bureaucrats in Ottawa who have never been on a reserve and have no knowledge of us and our needs. We do not want them designing our future. To seize the initiative, though, sometimes required a certain boldness. For instance, one time we built a new building to house a government function when we had not even had the jurisdictional authority for that function transferred to us yet.

I also tried to involve the youth and Elders of Siksika — our future and present leaders. I created the position of "Youth Chief" and had that person attend meetings and gain first-hand exposure to what it is like to be chief. Similarly, we gave formal recognition to the office of traditional chief. I made Elders a priority and incorporated them in such key areas as our self-government initiative. We spent over one million dollars per year on our one hundred and thirty senior citizens, in the form of subsidies, personal and home care, two tribal vehicles, an Elders' Lodge, an Elders' department and Elders' liason, an Elders' committee, and an Elders' retreat. We also established cultural programs in which the Elders played a large role.

Throughout my term in office I tried to maintain a sense of humour. Doing so was both a natural part of my personality and a conscious strategy to relax people and help make them happy doing their work. My leadership style involved looking for funny issues and funny circumstances among the serious ones. Who says work has to be serious?

In concluding this section, it is worth mentioning that during my first two terms in office I brought in a team of outside consultants for a very special task. These consultants were Native Americans who had been my professors in university. They held holistic Indian values that I appreciated. I thought that it would be good to identify who we — chief and council — were, what personalities and personal styles we had, what kind of management styles, etc. to make the team work and to put people in portfolios where they would function best. This proved very useful, which is why I did it again with a different council.

The above illustrates the challenges and issues that cross the desk of a First Nation leader at the reserve level. Indications of my own leadership style and preferences, ranging from simple humour and persistence to the more technocratic techniques, are found throughout that discussion. I turn now to a brief consideration of leadership styles which I encountered elsewhere.

Other Leadership Styles

During my time in office I met, worked with, or heard about many other chiefs from across Alberta and Canada. They differ in style from the sophisticated, dynamic politico to the self-interested to the dictator to the quiet statesperson. The "sophisticated dynamic politico", for instance, is a person who possesses: a vision of the greater good of his people; strong oratorical skills; keen political insight; and an understanding of people (inside and outside one's own community), of government, and of bureaucrats and politicians. This type of leader tries to fit what he/she wants with other people's agenda. Conversely, the "self-interested" chiefs have no vision or purpose other than to help themselves and their families. They want the chieftainship for the power or wealth that they think the position can bring them. Their nations go nowhere. Some of these chiefs become virtual dictators who, it seems, do whatever they can to stay in power. Although I've never seen it first-hand, I am told that some abolish the elective system of government or pay for votes (e.g., with cigarettes, alcohol, or cans of Lysol) if they retain the elective system, while others destroy or lose ballots. Conversely, the "quiet statesperson" type of leader is one who commands respect by his/her actions and integrity. This type of leader might lack strong oratorical skills and is unlikely to engage in rhetorical bombast, but there will likely be much substance to what he/she says.

Given the diversity of First Nations in Canada, it is not surprising that there is such diversity in leadership styles. In my opinion, though, the crucial factor which distinguishes among these leaders is their motives. Is the leader there for his people or for himself? If the latter, there can be no lasting respect, because it is not deserved.

THE COLONIAL CONTEXT OF FIRST NATION LEADERSHIP

> "...[A]ll complaints and criticisms of the system tend to be levelled at the soft part — the councillors and particularly the chief — rather than at the system itself. One of the many effects of the reserve system is to divert people's anger and resentment away from the real source of power in Ottawa..."

> (Carstens, 1991: 255)

As the title of this chapter implies, leadership of First Nations cannot be understood without an appreciation of the colonial history of governments' policy toward, and administration of, First Nations. That colonial history has left a legacy in Indian communities and in the federal government in contemporary times. It is a millstone around the neck of Indian leaders.

While this is not the place for an history lesson, a few salient historical points should be highlighted. First is the *assimilationist* thrust which characterized government policy. That assimilationist orientation led to such sociological atrocities as the demolition of First Nations' structures for decision-making and for community integration. Assimilation was also the main purpose of the residential schools and taints some First Nation individuals' orientation toward education to this day. The residential schools themselves were a *traumatic* experience for many who attended and for their communities. Those schools left many of their students with a poor self-concept, a lack of self-confidence, and few skills in the areas of constructively critical analysis and responsible decision-making. Indeed, the colonial system took responsibility for decision-making out of the hands of First Nation people. Our people were left in a state of impoverishment and disempowerment. Government betrayal and government's use of divide and conquer tactics against us shaped our view of the trustworthiness of the federal government. Over and above the foregoing, there is the paternalistic *Indian Act* and the inherently paternalistic fiduciary (trustee-like) obligations which define the federal government's orientation toward First Nations.

The above are not features which contribute to community vibrancy and development. Instead, they are more likely to produce alienation, withdrawal, and, paradoxically, the simultaneous holding of a dependency mentality and a generalized distrust and cynicism toward authority. A further irony is that in resisting change out of a fear that change will jeopardize the fiduciary obligations of the Crown, many of our people today are seeking to preserve precisely what our ancestors sought to avoid — namely, what is tantamount to a dependency on the state. These circumstances do not make for an enviable working environment for any leader, much less for a First Nation leader confronting widespread dire need among constituents and a corresponding dire need for change.

Another part of the colonial legacy is that there are *inherent contradictions* built into the role of chief. In addition to acting as a spokesperson for the tribe, the chief must act almost as an agent of the federal government (DIAND), at least insofar as finances are concerned. The chief and council are accountable first to the federal government for how we spend money and deliver programs. If a program is overspent or DIAND's advice is unheeded, DIAND can adjust how much money it gives us the next year, although that is less likely to happen nowadays than was the case earlier. In addition, the chief and council are a recognized legal entity only because of the government's *Indian Act* and the federal government has to ensure that we adhere to other federal laws pertaining to Indians, of which there are many.[8] The chief is caught in the middle, for the government and the people of the tribe want different things. For the most part, the agenda of the people and the agenda of the government cannot meet. Remember, part of the role of DIAND is *containment* — containment of the demands of the First Nation people to what is acceptable to the bureaucrats' political masters. The needs of First Nations are growing exponentially and neither the First Nations nor the federal government have enough money to meet those demands. So, often the needs and demands of the tribe put them on a collision course with the federal government which sees those needs as too expensive. Alternatively, they might be seen as setting a precedent with which the government is not comfortable for whatever reason (e.g., cost, implications for Québec sovereignty, implications for federal-provincial relations or for third parties). Either way, the chief and council are caught in the middle. If the chief adopts a collaborative, compromising orientation toward DIAND in an attempt to maximize the benefits that are available to the tribe, he/she is seen as a "sellout". On the other hand, if the chief is unyielding in pressing the tribe's demands, he/she is seen by the government as a "hardliner". I am beginning to think that being labelled a "hardliner" is not such a bad thing, though, for it is often "the squeaky wheel that gets the grease" as DIAND's regional office tries to quietly appease such bands with discretionary funds.[9] Finally, despite the fact that the government could treat the *Indian Act* more flexibly to accommodate First Nations' needs and demands, that is rarely done. As a result of that inflexibility and of fiscal tightfistedness, the chief is left "taking the heat" from the people.

DYNAMICS AND SOCIAL PSYCHOLOGY OF THE RELATIONSHIP BETWEEN THE CHIEF AND THE TRIBE

Community Expectations

> Chiefs are expected to express the wishes of all band members from the point of view of their traditional "Indianness"... — an expectation which could, in fact, never be realized.
>
> (Carstens, 1991: 233)

What are the expectations attached to the role of chief? That is, what do the people of the tribe expect of a leader? The answer is complex and reflects the multifacetted role of the chief. On the one hand, the people have lofty ideals. They want the chief to be a visionary and a role model and spiritual leader of exemplary character. They want him/her to be a skillful orator who is a formidable spokesperson and negotiator for the tribe. At times, they expect the chief to be an accomplished corporate executive, especially with regard to tribal businesses and economic development, yet at other times they want the chief to be the wise and sensitive counsellor on personal matters. At yet other times, when they over-estimate the power and authority that the chief holds, they regard him as practically a king or a head of state.

Paradoxically, the chief is also expected to be a servant and a father figure who takes care of his "children's" every need. That colonial, dependent mind-set comes through when individual tribal members come to chief and council and ask for such things as medicine, a new water softener, a clothes washer or dryer, or even a vehicle. Some expect the chief and council to wait on them hand and foot, to do everything for them and deal with all their problems, including even domestic, religious, and financial problems. In that respect, the role of chief and council goes far beyond mere governance; it is as if chief and council have merely taken over the role of the paternalistic Indian agent. However, as a bureaucrat appointed from outside, the Indian agent never had to face the "You're not good anymore; I'm not going to vote for you anymore" reply that chief and council sometimes get when they decline someone's request for assistance. I believe that the potential for such personal attacks (non-physical) is far greater in First Nation politics than in other politics, simply because of the *broad scope* of the expectations placed on First Nation politicians.

What the people actually do, as compared to what they say they want in a leader, can actually be quite inconsistent. For instance, some people will say they want an educated leader, but later say that the educated person has followed the white man's ways and lost touch with his/her people. Another example involves jobs. The people say they want the chief to provide jobs and economic development for the tribe, but when those jobs are created some of those same people fail to show up at work. They do not do their part. That reinforces the "unreliable Indian" stereotype, which makes it very difficult for the chief to attract other job-creating investors to the reserve. They perceive tribal members as not being committed — as unable or unwilling to follow through.

One role in which some chiefs can maintain broad support is the role of protector of the culture. Tribal members are looking for security in culture and language. Unfortunately, that was not my strong suit. As a symbol of that cultural security, I fell short. I do not speak the language and am too fair in my skin complexion. Furthermore, some of my ideals came to be considered too "non-Blackfoot". These things eventually caught up to me in electoral politics.

The chief is seen as a lot of different things to different people at different times, such that at any given time the chief is not sure what role people are expecting him/her to play. In trying to play all those roles, the chief cannot please everyone. As the First Nation baby boomers and their offspring become more of a force in First Nation politics, the leadership challenge will become significantly greater, for the young people are looking for a new type of leader — a new warrior, a new hunter. That style, however, will clash with the containment function of DIAND. The results of that clash will be interesting.

Trust and Distrust

One need not be a sociologist to appreciate how absolutely fundamental the element of trust is to any human relationship, be it interpersonal or international or something in-between. Unfortunately, on reserves trust is scarce and elusive. In its place we find not some suspension of judgement, but a *generalized distrust*. If trust is like a lubricant in the political machinery, distrust is like sand in the gears. Distrust is a major problem in First Nation government and politics. In large part, its roots can be traced historically to the government's colonial approach to First Nations.

One need not look far to find answers to the question of how, after the signing of the treaties, government came to be distrusted by First Nations. The government's violation of the treaties, its abrogation of its fiduciary responsibilities, its use of divide and conquer tactics, its duplicity surrounding the 1969 White Paper, its unfulfilled promises, its assimilationist agenda and proposals to wipe out reserves and treaties, are all part of the repertoire of government behaviours that First Nations have experienced. All such behaviours leave First Nations people very wary of the government.

The fact that chiefs and councils exist in their present form as a result of the *Indian Act* associates them with the federal government in the mind of many of their tribal members. Hence, to a certain degree, we have guilt by association. To the extent that chief and council are viewed as agents of the federal government, the problem is exacerbated. The problem of distrust is also made worse by the fact that some chiefs and councillors have, unquestionably, abused their powers. Some have stolen from the tribal funds, cheated in elections, travelled excessively and lavishly on tribal business, or otherwise exhibited low moral standards such that tribal members conclude that the First Nation politicians are out to exploit the tribe and achieve self-aggrandizement.

With the federal government perceived by tribal members as being basically at odds with tribal interests, the chief's relations with the federal government become crucial in establishing trust with tribal members. Tribal members' fear that the chief will "sell them out" to the federal government in exchange for some short term benefit for the tribe or for the chief personally. One form of this is the fear that some action or proposal by the chief will jeopardize the tribe's treaty rights or its special legal relationship with the federal government. The basic *cultural and economic insecurity* of First Nations produces in tribal members a great reluctance to embark on any course of action which might let the federal government "off the hook" (diminish its fiduciary or treaty obligations to First Nations) or which might move the tribe closer to what is seen as the white man's aspirations for Indian government. As a result, actions of the chief which are designed to lessen the dependence on the federal government easily arouse suspicions of a "sell-out". In the local rumour mill tribal members come to speculate on what personal gains the government must be offering to the chief for him/her to be advocating such a plan of action that jeopardizes the fiduciary or treaty relationship.

Experience has led large numbers of First Nation individuals to be cynical toward their elected leaders. This is a big problem on reserves, as far too many First Nation individuals merely sit back and complain, rather than coming forward with alternatives to the courses of action chosen by chief and council. Cynicism breeds distrust and is a corrosive force, not a constructive force. I believe that there is much truth in the adage that skeptics do not create, doubters do not achieve, and cynics do not contribute. Cynicism is a frame of mind; on reserve, it is often part of a *colonial mentality*.

Jealousy, envy, and individual or family pride are also sources of distrust of First Nation leaders. Let us consider the family dimension here. First Nations individuals have been so disempowered under the colonial regime that most have little or no experience with exercising the power of an officeholder. Therefore, the tendency is to assume that officeholders will abuse power or use it in their or their family's own selfish interests rather than in the tribe's collective interests. Accordingly, the tendency is to want one's own son or brother or aunt to be chief. Furthermore, when one's relatives are in power there is also a greater sense of efficacy, of feeling that the person in political office will listen and act upon one's needs. ("You're my brother. I voted for you. I need your help now. So, help me".) However, if that relative loses the election, that family will often refuse to trust the victor. They expect that in a time of shortage, if the leader must alienate someone by denying a request for assistance, that leader is most likely to choose to alienate the person who is not a member of the family.

Distrust also characterizes relations with other First Nations in Canada, although not with those in the United States. Historical rivalries and competition for scarce government funds are at the root of much of this distrust. Even though chief and councils of two or more First Nations might agree to co-operate, deep down among the tribal members and bureaucrats the distrust exists. Bureaucrats question whether their tribe is getting enough back for what it is contributing to the co-operative relationship, including whether the other First Nation is being sufficiently forthright when one's own tribe is "showing all its cards". Such distrust can undermine confidence in the leader's judgement.

Legitimacy and Legitimacy Challenges

> In theory, the chief stands at the apex of the band. But such a position is impossible to maintain, and he has to face constant criticism for his inevitable failure to create a little utopia in the white man's space. Band members, moreover, are constantly involved in a process of re-evaluating their positions. ... Thus, if chiefs often fail to be re-elected, the answer lies not in personal inadequacies, but rather in the sociological and ideological positions they occupy in the community.
>
> (Carstens, 1991: 235)

As used here, the term "legitimacy" refers to the degree of consistency which constituents perceive to exist between the values they hold and the values which they believe the leader (or candidate for political office) holds, as inferred from the leader's (or candidate's) behaviour and personal characteristics. Legitimacy is a precious commodity for any leader. Its erosion calls into question the very continuance of the relationship between the leader and those who are led, as Pierre Trudeau, Brian Mulroney, and others have found. In First Nation communities, the chief is highly vulnerable to legitimacy challenges, even when the chief assiduously avoids getting involved in corrupt practices.

The case of the decline in the legitimacy attributed to me as chief by members of my tribe is an instructive example in the discourse of community-level First Nation politics and in the *fragility of legitimacy* in First Nation communities.

I believe that I started my term as chief with a high degree of legitimacy broadly spread throughout the tribe. My credibility was probably strengthened by a number of factors, including my past record as tribal economic development officer, my level of formal education, my reputation as a "doer", my reputation as a fair individual who is not nepotistic, and my ancestry as a descendant of the famous Blackfoot chief Crowfoot. I articulated a vision in which people could believe, and then I tried to share that vision with them. The tribe trusted me. Nevertheless, by the end of eight years in office I was being attacked vigorously in the tribal rumour mill, where I was accused of corruption and of not being a real Blackfoot.

One foundation of the legitimacy of a First Nation chief is that he/she is viewed as an authentic Indian. Authenticity is greatest when the leader is like the people being led, in terms of education, employment, skin colour, and ability to speak the mother tongue language. To be different in a significant way is to be not a part of the people. When that social distance creeps into the relationship, we know that the relationship is in danger. For instance, if the leader is highly educated he/she might come to be labelled by many as an elitist.

Legitimacy can be called into question by a variety of other simple, but remarkably effective, tactics (c.f. Carstens, 1991: 210). One is to criticize the leader's family members in such a way as to implicitly question the leader's ability to represent the community. This is done by questioning how "typical" of other community members he/she is. For instance, a leader's mother or wife might be subjected to the criticism: "She's not from here" or "She's white or Métis." Alternatively, the individual's bond to the community — and ostensibly his/her ability to lead, serve, and represent the community — can be denigrated with the slur: "He's from the city" or "He's been off the reserve too long." Age ("He's too young" or "He's too old") has been invoked as a basis for opposing a candidate, as has a past reputation for excessive imbibing. Even the location of a person's residence on the reserve can become a basis for attacking his/her legitimacy as a candidate, as in the dismissive remark: "He's from the West End". Lithman (1984: 139) found a similar geo-political cleavage in the Manitoba Ojibway community of "Maple River" (Fort Alexander) which he studied in the early 1970s, as did Carstens (1991: 220) in the Okanagan First Nation which he studied historically.

Lithman (1984: 149–150) also found a subtlety to the way in which politics is practiced in "Maple River". I have experienced that subtlety in my community, too, although it is difficult to know whether it was used merely to signal opposition or to challenge the very legitimacy of my chieftainship. Refraining from using the title "Chief" when addressing the chief is one such subtle way of showing that you do not honour him/her, as is ignoring the chief or looking away when the chief smiles. Rather less subtle is the fabrication of vicious rumours about the chief.

Reluctance to Make Decisions to Take on Responsibility

One characteristic feature of a colonial regime is its paternalism and lack of opportunity for the colonized people to take on meaningful responsibility for their own affairs. In addition, self-doubt and a dependency mindset are prominent in the thought patterns of colonized people. Together, these obviously have enormous implications for self-government.

It is very difficult to embrace change when you are in a really poor situation and hold the very negative view that anything you do might jeopardize what little you already have. This is a widespread way of thinking in some treaty communities: there is a reluctance to do anything that might jeopardize the treaty and its meaning and a reluctance to do anything that might "let the government off the hook". Persons who think like that would rather let the government continue doing what it has been doing than move into self-government negotiations. They see the signing of a self-government agreement as potentially the first step in violating the treaty — in absolving the government of its treaty and fiduciary responsibilities. Understandably, such persons want to see the treaty fulfilled first and only then move to self-government negotiations. That preference, I believe, is rooted not only in a lack of trust for the federal government, but also in some degree of ignorance and in a fear that we are not yet ready for self-government.

In some respects we are our own enemy. The biggest weights holding us down are our lack of faith in ourselves, our perceptions of government and of business, and our lack of willingness or courage to take the steps to move ahead. Too often our people are content to wait with hands out for the government to drop off a few crumbs, rather than going out and developing our talents and abilities and being "the true people" that we should be. We should not be worrying about giving up a few crumbs when we can earn a full meal through our own efforts.

We need a more aggressive attitude, like the warriors and hunters of days gone by. Where are all our modern-day warriors and hunters? We need a *paradigm shift* in how we view our treaties, ourselves, and our position in Canada. If our forefathers saw us today, with so many of us on welfare, they would ask: "Where is the resolve of our people to say `Yes, we have these social problems, but we can overcome them'?" We need an attitude change about our culture and who we are, to focus on what we have to do, rather than on what should be done for us.

I have seen a lot of opportunities lost by First Nations being indecisive. Their people hope that the situation will go away or will resolve itself. Many First Nations are unable to reach a consensus among their members on the specifics of what they want from the government, for instance, with self-government arrangements. It is my belief that those First Nations which cannot or do not make a deal with the federal government place themselves at the mercy of those who do and at the mercy of the government's good will (to the degree that government's conscience is spurred). The government has all the "cards": time is on its side; it can change the rules as the game goes on; it has the money; etc. All that First Nations have is the treaties (and not all First Nations have a treaty) and the ability to embarass Canada internationally on the issue of First Nations' poverty in the midst of Canadian affluence.

Too often First Nations just talk, talk, talk, but back away from taking a position at the negotiating table to identify what our responsibilities will be as we move toward self-sufficiency. Unfortunately, a lot of chiefs and councils are afraid to make the hard decisions (e.g., on user fees) that are necessary, but that go against the will of the people. A large part of the resistance to such change comes from the older people who were exposed to the Indian agent and the federal government telling them "We have to do it for you". They were led to believe that they were not good enough, not quite ready, not sufficiently educated, not capable, etc. That is the big, subconscious myth in our minds, for they eventually believed what they were told.

Fortunately, though, First Nations' reluctance to make decisions is changing now as more First Nations are proactively taking control of their own destiny and weighing the costs of action against the costs of inaction. They are willing to take some risk, which is how our people were in the past. In those days there were no guarantees, no sure things. Our ancestors had to adapt or they would not survive. The same could happen to us.

A Leader's Relations With The Elders

I believe that the Elders are crucial to the future of First Nation communities. I hold the true Elders in high regard and I genuinely listened to what they had to say. A good chief must be able to relate well to the Elders (among others), particularly in obtaining knowledge and insight from them. The chief must let them know that they have a voice in decision making and that their input is welcomed and valued. To fail to pay adequate homage to the Elders can result in them turning against the chief.

It is also important to note that some members of First Nation communities claim Elder status and demand respect simply because of having reached some particular age, even though they might have wasted decades of their earlier life through drinking. That bothers me greatly, for a true Elder would never push his/her claims to Elder status upon the community. Also, a true Elder knows that being an Elder is much more than singing and drumming and speaking the language. A true Elder, one who has the community's interests at heart rather than seeking self-aggrandizement, does not boast and is very humble and pure. True Elders have no animosity, hatred, envy, or jealousy in them. Unfortunately, there are very few of them around.

I was once asked by a non-Native what a chief expects to get when he consults the Elders — political intelligence, cultural insight, generic wisdom, the right decision, or something else? I pointed out that the chief cannot go to an Elder and say: "I've got a problem. What should I do?" The chief would not get a direct answer. In fact, to expect any direct problem-solving by the Elders would be wrong. Instead, the Elders are there mainly to be supportive; when a chief approaches an Elder (s)he is looking to share the burden, to have the Elder lighten the burden of responsibility associated with holding office. It always helped for me to have the Elders listen to me. So, the chief will merely discuss the situation with the Elder and try to discern the interpretation that should be put on the stories or words of wisdom that the Elder shares. The Elder will not always give the response that the chief wants or that will help resolve the chief's problem. Nevertheless, the chief must show respect and be open to whatever the Elder has to offer.

Nepotism in Reserve Politics

In an earlier era the clan played an important role in many, perhaps most, First Nation cultures, as the different minor chiefs from the different families would get together and select a head chief. From those cultural roots the family has emerged today as a pivotal unit in reserve politics, as anthropologists such as Carstens (1991) and Lithman (1984) attest. However, when I agreed to let my name stand as a nominee for chief, I was not fully aware of how central the family is in reserve politics where we now have the people as a whole voting for the head chief ("the chief") and for the minor chiefs (the council members). I thought the voters simply selected the person whom they felt was best for the job. I was unaware of how prevalent nepotism[10] is in the thinking and behaviour of some families. However, as chief I quickly learned to look for hidden nepotistic motives, for councillors would frequently put some family issue on the agenda under some other guise.

To understand the political role of the family, one must understand both the rather impoverished socio-economic circumstances of most reserve residents and the meaning or significance of the chieftainship in the mind of many of the voters, especially as that meaning is captured in the phrase "It's our turn". By "impoverished socio-economic circumstances" I am referring to the relatively low levels of income, wealth, prestige, power, and hope which characterize most reserve residents, and to the relatively scarce opportunities for increasing them. This gives rise to what Covey et al. (1994) call a "scarcity mentality", which is a mindset in which people have a short-term vision of what is possible and fail to see the big picture; therefore, they adopt a win-lose (rather than a win-win) orientation and seek short-term victories, even though that might be to their disadvantage in the long term. By "the meaning and significance of the chieftainship" I am referring above to the notion that the chief is in office to represent the family and to help his/her supporters, most of whom are his/her family and friends. Thus, with regard to the representational dimension, it is very much a source of honour and prestige to the family to have a family member elected as chief. With regard to the helping dimension, the reader should remember that the collegiality of chief and council tends to be overlooked by voters. The chief is thereby erroneously perceived to have control over the distribution of scarce resources and over the allocation of other positions that also allocate scarce resources. When that view is combined with the "scarcity mentality", the tendency is to expect nepotistic behaviour from the chief.[11]

After the election where I was defeated, one voter said: "The Crowfoots are no longer in charge; it's my family's turn." He seemed to be implying that now that his family is in power, he could do what he wants. That is, he seemed to think that his family's occupation of the top elected office in the tribe would remove some constraint that previously operated on him. As noted earlier, trust plays a role here: it is easier to trust a family member than someone from outside the family. Also important, though, is the perception on the part of the elector that a chief who is a family member can be *controlled* more easily than a chief who is not a family member. This perception arises because the elector knows that there is a whole set of diffuse obligations to the extended family that the needy constituent can invoke in pressing a claim for assistance upon the relative who is chief. For instance, if the relative who is chief does not "deliver the goods", he/she will have to answer to the family as to why the relative was denied assistance. For the chief to fail to come to the aid of a relative would cause a rift in the family. The voter who spoke to me after the election knows that voting support is largely circumscribed by family boundaries and that most chiefs, when faced with the choice of making enemies of family members or of non-supporters, will likely opt to offend the non-supporters (those outside the family).

Nepotism in reserve politics takes on a life of its own, with its own *sustaining discourse*. In certain families — friends and foes alike — the expectation of nepotism is always present. Whether the leader does or does not practice nepotism, there remains the perception that s/he could, might, or probably will at some time. The leader can never escape that and can only hope to minimize expectations of nepotism through developing a "track record". However, over that time the leader's family may turn against him/her ("You're not doing this for us; so, I'm not going to support you"), while those who are not family say "You're going to do it [practise nepotism] sometime, maybe; so, we're not going to support you". The leader is definitely caught in the middle between these two orientations.

The chief always has to be aware of the friendship and extended kinship connections among tribal members and between tribal members and certain issues. In my experience, what certain (by no means all) councillors are promoting in council is very often based on benefitting family or friends (or self). In contrast to the less personalized politics of the larger society, they do not see anything wrong with that. In fact, they have a legitimating discourse that might be called "the tale of woe". This takes the form: "He's suffering. He's just starting out. We've got to help him because nobody else will". I have heard this many times. It is a discourse that is reserved for advocacy on behalf of relatives and close friends.

What are the consequences of nepotism? It is difficult to see a positive side to nepotism, in contrast to the positive side that some analysts have identified for the practice of patronage in the larger Canadian polity (e.g., Simpson, 1993). On the negative side, the practice of nepotism can *distort the opportunity structures* on reserve and empower some who are not the best available person for the job. For instance, on some reserves where nepotism is blatant, the entire tribal administration is of one family. Surely, no family has a monopoly on administrative aptitudes. On some other reserves, where nepotism is confined to one sector of tribal administration, one family might come to dominate only a certain department. However, one other consequence of nepotism that is found on most reserves is a sense of skepticism that tarnishes the leader-follower relationship and weakens the moral fibre of the community. That is, the practice of *nepotism undermines the public service ethic* upon which I believe the healthiest form of leadership is based. Nepotism engenders skepticism and distrust, which are divisive forces within a community and serve as a drag on community development. Nepotism reinforces not only non-Natives' stereotypes about First Nations' alleged incompetence, but also the entitlement and dependency mindsets held by many First Nation individuals themselves. In short, I believe nepotism to be *inimical to the sociological vitality* of First Nation communities.

Features of First Nation Cultures and Communities That Facilitate or Hinder Leadership

Many Canadians tend to regard First Nations and our governments as being essentially like non-Native municipalities and their governments. Although this is true in some limited respects, there are numerous features of First Nation cultures and communities which depart markedly from the situation of non-Native municipalities and affect the leadership of First Nation communities. The above-described distrust and emphasis on the family in First Nation politics are just two such features. Other specific differences are examined in this section.

At a more general level, though, it should be noted at the outset that there is greater opportunity to exercise leadership in First Nation politics than in non-Native politics at the municipal or provincial level.[12] In part, that is because First Nation politics are set against the very vivid backdrop of the tribal history and culture and the thinking that we are a sovereign nation. Whereas a provincial or municipal leader's goals are usually very narrow in scope (e.g., economic development), the goals of the chief of a First Nation extend much more widely into the social, psychological, and spiritual-moral realms and the issues addressed have their roots in sovereignty. In addition, most First Nation chiefs deal more directly with their constituents, and in a more "hands-on" manner, than do most non-Native politicians.

One of the more specific differences lies in the lesser value placed upon individualism in First Nation communities. While a non-Native municipality and a First Nation community might both have a strong sense of community, in the non-Native community that is mitigated by a sense of individualism. Conversely, in the First Nation community the sense of community is reinforced by a group consciousness of kind, a sense of shared fate, and a sense of being a beleaguered minority collectivity. This more *collectivist orientation* and the sense of closeness or solidarity which accompanies it facilitate leadership by making it relatively easy to rally the people politically for some purposes. On the other side of the coin, these values and sentiments also make life difficult for the leader because they also facilitate the mobilization of opposition to the leader.[13] Also, the rationale that something is "for the benefit of the tribe" is a little too conveniently available; some have exploited that discourse to the maximum for their own personal benefit.

The leaders of many small non-Native communities face resistance to change among their members. In First Nation communities, the fact that *traditionalism* is highly valued in and of itself while development needs are extremely acute, leaves the leader in a dilemma which is much more acute than among non-Native politicians. That is, the value placed upon traditionalism in First Nation communities is a drag on the need for "modernization" (adaptation). The leader must constantly balance the two, even when elected on a platform of sweeping change.

Related to this is the *clash of cultures* that is commonplace in First Nation communities but comparatively rare in non-Native communities. This is a major problem which is particularly likely to surface in business dealings with the non-Native corporate world. One example is the low level of importance which many First Nation people attach to time frames and deadlines.[14] Another is the corporate world's slowness to recognize that at the time of a death or a funeral, commercial and administrative activity will shut down for a while on reserve. Sometimes the chief will be caught in the middle of such a cultural clash, in that the non-Native corporations which the chief is trying to recruit to do business with or on the reserve will point to such time conflicts as obstacles interfering with, or even precluding, the commercial relationship. While it is obvious to the chief that both sides must adapt, such a conclusion is often by no means obvious to the others involved.

The *concept "un-Indian"* is another feature of First Nations' culture that makes the chief's role difficult. It has no counterpart in most non-Native communities, but becomes salient in First Nation communities due to the widespread fear of assimilation among tribal members. To criticize a leader, or the leader's proposal, or even the leader's advanced education, as "un-Indian" or as "the white man's way" is a very effective and frequently used political weapon, for our people sometimes shun and fear what they do not have. The criticism is full of irony, though. That is, I am convinced that many of those who use this discourse have themselves lost sight of the true precepts of First Nation cultures. Also, there is irony in the fact that the "un-Indian" label is used negatively against a person, because, hypothetically, it could equally logically be used to compliment the person for breaking through and putting the lie to the negative stereotypes of "the Indian". In fact, I maintain that the authentic First Nation way is the way of adapting to challenge and pursuing excellence. In contrast, the reserve culture becomes very accepting of mediocrity and very prone to rejecting even some of the best of what the larger non-Native culture has to offer, such as advanced education and the value placed on personal initiative. So, in reserve politics, authenticity-as-Indian comes to be defined in other ways and many persons, including leaders, who have demonstrated an ability to function productively in the "white man's world" encounter marginality and even ostracism from First Nation people on reserve. Fortunately, this is slowly changing.

A further irony is that in other quarters on reserve there is a growing lack of respect for experience and for the Elders. Otherwise stated, the culture of some First Nation communities contains *contradictory strains* such that both traditionalism and modernism are denigrated. This exacerbates, rather than alleviates, the cross-pressures felt by the chief who is trying to balance traditionalism and modernism. It can lead the chief to conclude "I'm damned if I do and damned if I don't".

Reference was made above to the "entitlement" mindset that is common among First Nation people. This orientation is probably justified, both in light of First Nations' generosity in relinquishing land to the European settlers and in light of the colonial regime's betrayal of treaties and other promises. However, the fact that it is justified does not make it any more productive or any less of a millstone around the neck of First Nation leaders. For instance, part of the entitlement way of thinking is to regard it as unfair if one group on reserve has more of something. This way of thinking often exhibits its most intense expression on the issue of housing — one of the major issues in reserve politics. Regardless of one's level of wealth or poverty, the reserve resident who has an entitlement mindset views himself as having an equal right to the benefit of housing provided by the tribe. Thus, reserve politics come to involve a much greater *preoccupation with allocative fairness* than do politics in most non-Native municipalities. This is the most difficult part of the job of chief. The community's preoccupation with allocative fairness leaves the leaders having to balance the needs and wants of different sectors of the community, probably to a much greater extent than is true for most non-Native politicians in communities of similar size. The concept of need as a driving force behind the conferral of benefits on reserve, if not subordinated to notions of rights or entitlement, is certainly compromised significantly in First Nation politics.

Another factor which has colonial roots but which is now internalized into the way of thinking of First Nation people, is the *negativism and pettiness* which are commonplace on reserve. The negativism includes the aforementioned distrust, lack of self-confidence, petty jealousies, cynicism (fault-finding) and skepticism. This factor is exacerbated by the fact that most First Nation communities are small communities in which there is a very active rumour mill, especially among that fairly large proportion of the people who have much spare time available. Thus, the situation is structurally conducive (Smelser, 1963) to intense rumour activity. In such a situation, it is easier to point critical or blaming fingers than to take responsibility for one's own situation. So, for instance, it is easier to level accusations of "un-Indianness" at the person who leaves the reserve to pursue an higher education than it is to acquire an advanced education one's self. Yet, it is precisely the skills and talents of such highly educated individuals that are so desperately needed to open the opportunity structures for others on reserves and to empower First Nations in our dealings with outside governments and corporations.

The colonial system is the root cause beneath two other factors which greatly hinder the chief in his/her job and which have no direct counterpart in non-Native communities. Those are the "Indian agent mindset" and the breakdown of traditional forms of social control. The Indian agent mindset refers to the abdication of initiative and responsibility to others. When the Indian agent was on reserve, paternalistically executing the fiduciary responsibility, he took care of the people and told them what they were allowed to do and what they could not do. To some extent, DIAND still does tell First Nations what we should and should not do and what we cannot do. After decades of the Indian agent system and with the social safety net in place, it is now very difficult to break the *mindset of abdicated-responsibility* for looking after oneself. There is the thinking that "the government will take care of us because we're Indian". That is, there is a certain *sense of security* which comes from the monthly welfare cheques provided by government. It is a formidable challenge for a First Nation leader to instill in his/her people the hope and confidence that things will be better in the direction in which he/she is leading — to replace the sense of security which for decades has been provided by government welfare payments. Having sacrificed so much already, how many of our people are willing to face the short-term insecurity and make the sacrifices that are necessary to achieve self-reliance? When people are preoccupied with their economic survival, as many First Nation people are, it is very difficult to broaden their horizons to get them to think about other issues beyond food and shelter.

So, the sense of security that the government welfare cheque and fiduciary responsibility provide is a major obstacle — one of our biggest stumbling blocks — to change on reserves. Yet, **we must take responsibility** and get the government out of its interfering ways in our lives. We have a right and duty to take responsibility for our own directions and actions, and then to accept the consequences. We can be like the Indians of old; we can go out there and face the unknown, face all the elements and adversity, and survive. It's in our genes to do so; let's find it! We need to have our modern-day hunters and warriors go out there to face the challenges and bring back what they can, especially in terms of education and employment. Instead, too often we have people engaging in escapist behaviour, such as substance abuse and bingo[15] addiction, which have become serious social problems in many First Nation communities.

Any social system must have some degree of social control; otherwise, anarchy would prevail. The *breakdown of traditional forms of social control* within First Nation communities refers to such phenomena as the diminished influence of the Elders, the loss of spirituality, the breakdown of the socialization function in which the values and culture are passed on from parents to children, and the loss of traditional dispute resolution mechanisms. Traditionally, social control served to maintain order, protect from danger, and ensure collective effort toward shared goals. In contemporary times that is not happening to the extent needed. In part, this is because many of our present day seniors have themselves been affected by the residential school and/or alcohol. Also, the First Nation family has experienced much breakdown; how can a parent transmit the culture to the child if the parent is absent? Indeed, how can today's parents transmit to their children what the parents do not have?

In the absence of traditional forms of social control, or adaptations of them, the job of chief and council becomes exceedingly difficult, as they must cope with the social problems associated with escapism, withdrawal, displaced aggression, and loss of a sense of purpose in individuals' lives. A case of theft from our tribe by a tribal employee provides one illustration both of the difficulties faced by community leaders in this regard and of another kind of problem. We talked "tough" and fired the guilty party. When he lost his job, the perpetrator and his large family went on welfare, which made it impossible for the tribe to collect any restitution. To have formally prosecuted him and sent him to jail would have hurt his family and would have created political and personal animosity that would have lasted for years. People on-reserve do not forget things like that; they will hold a grudge for many years. That seems to be part of a *generalized grievance mindset*. It extends well beyond the grievances against the Government of Canada; it operates even within the local community against other tribal members. Individuals harbour their pent-up anger against "the system" and displace it onto the local community. Perhaps some of us have not yet grieved properly for the great losses which we suffered. Perhaps we have not gone through the full grieving cycle. Perhaps some in our communities are suffering post-traumatic stress syndrome. Call it what you will, this situation of grudge-bearing, a generalized sense of grievance, and the breakdown of traditional forms of social control obviously poses especially difficult challenges for the justice system of a First Nation government.

Cleavages within a First Nation pose difficult challenges to First Nation leaders. Examples are geographic cleavages even within small communities (the north side versus the south side of a river dissecting the reserve), family cleavages (clans), religious cleavages (Protestant versus Catholic, Christian versus traditionalist), and educational and social class cleavages. Sometimes these cleavages reinforce each other, such as when a clan tends to be geographically concentrated and primarily of one particular religious persuasion. Also problematic is the fact that the revival of traditional First Nation religion has led to invidious distinctions being made on reserve, whereby some practitioners of traditionalist religion contend that a person cannot really be an Indian unless he/she practices traditionalist religion. That exclusionary orientation, it seems to me, violates the essence of First Nation religions.

Suicide and accidental death have an enormously devastating impact on both the community and the immediate family of the victim. In fact, some First Nation communities are in a state of almost perpetual mourning. A suicide in the community causes much soul-searching by the family and by the chief and council. Suicide provokes the politicians to ask: "Why are our programs not being effective?"; "Do our actions not inspire hope?" Family members and politicians alike experience acute anxiety that the suicide might be part of a pact or otherwise be the start of a suicide epidemic. Where they diverge, though, is in the victim's family's tendency to blame chief and council for the death, on the grounds that chief and council allegedly did not do enough and did not provide help when it was requested. In addition, the chief is expected to comfort and support the aggrieved family members. Furthermore, any local First Nation politician who does not attend the victim's funeral will not be quickly forgiven. Adding to the toll taken on the community is the fact that during the period of mourning the wheels of tribal administration turn more slowly.

One final difference between First Nation leadership challenges and those faced by non-Native leaders is that the *mandate* conferred upon First Nation elected officials is at once conditional or tenuous and two-tracked. Although both First Nation and non-Native elected officials may be granted a so-called "honeymoon" period in office, in First Nation communities the mandate is more readily revoked, for it comprises both a spoken and an unspoken component. The chief who lives up to her campaign promises might, nevertheless, find her mandate revoked if she comes to be seen as "un-Indian", if she fails to live up to the full breadth of the unspoken obligations (e.g., as economic provider, spiritual advisor, interpersonal relations counsellor, defender of the treaty, etc.) that are attached to the role, or if she violates the previously described contradictory expectations concerning nepotism. For the non-Native elected official the mandate is much more narrowly interpreted.

RELATIONS WITH THE DEPARTMENT OF INDIAN AFFAIRS AND NORTHERN DEVELOPMENT (DIAND)

Dealing with DIAND can be an extremely frustrating activity for a chief. Elsewhere in this chapter I alluded to some of the reasons for that, such as the containment role of DIAND and the imposition of DIAND's agenda. Here I shall touch briefly on other facets of the relationship. Although my tone will be mainly critical, it is only fair to point out that in DIAND there are some very good individuals who are hamstrung by government policies, by the *Indian Act*, and sometimes by an unwillingness to change on the part of some First Nations. DIAND's job is not an easy one (Ponting, 1986: 106) and the intense criticism which it receives for its mistakes can lead individual bureaucrats within the Department to pull back and keep a low profile, rather than becoming innovators and risk-takers.

In its relations with First Nations, though, DIAND operates on the basis of who the favourites are and on the principle that "the squeaky wheel gets the grease". The "squeaky wheel gets the grease" approach is an inherently unsound operating philosophy, for it rewards fiscal mismanagement and punishes fiscal responsibility. Thus, regional DIAND officials are more likely to dispense their discretionary funds to an aggressive, protesting, table-thumping, over-spending chief than to a First Nation, like those in Treaty 7, which they have categorized as business-like. DIAND plays a game of "fiscal hide-and-seek" with First Nations. DIAND officials know how much money is available and for what, but they do not tell us exactly; chiefs are supposed to play the game and chase after the money through lobbying and putting forth proposals. If we catch them, we get the money, if it is available. Furthermore, when DIAND does set aside funds for new initiatives, those funds are bound up with terribly restrictive conditions and are inadequate; usually the amount is just sufficient to ensure failure of the venture, although that is not necessarily their intention.

Thus, a now long-retired DIAND employee once suggested to me that the role of DIAND is like that of a pharmacist whose job is to dispense medicine to the ailing patient, but not enough to cure the patient, for that would put the pharmacist out of a job. Were it not for the fact that DIAND is now confronted with much more highly educated First Nation leaders, many more of its officials would be mainly just going through the motions in some ritualistic manner in their dealings with First Nations.

Games-playing is a long-standing practice of bureaucrats (Bardach, 1977) and DIAND bureaucrats are no exception. In addition to the game of "fiscal hide and seek" described above, DIAND officials sometimes engage in what might be called the "make me" game, which is a variant of the "squeaky wheel gets the grease" game. That is, departmental officials would sometimes urge me, as chief, to put political pressure on them! An instance of this occurred early in my first term in conjunction with our efforts to get DIAND's approval for a certain project on our land. A bureaucrat said to me: "Chief, you didn't put enough pressure on me politically". Implicit in his remarks was the notion "Why should I hurry?" I replied: "Okay, I'll take care of that." Within a day I had the Regional Director-General (the most senior official in the region) come in and the first comment she made in the meeting with us was "Chief, how much money do you want?" I learned from that experience that DIAND officials are not always there for First Nations' interests; they will play games with us and use the money they control to buy us off or to get their own purposes accomplished, to make friends, or do other things. Of course, money has a certain power attached to it and DIAND officials are not averse to using that power.

Obstructionism is not unknown among DIAND bureaucrats. The Siksika Nation encountered this on one of our economic development priorities — the construction of a commercial mall. I am convinced that one DIAND bureaucrat simply did not like us and actively sought to obstruct us in our efforts to get the land re-designated for that use. It took us almost one and one-half years to get DIAND's approval for that.

Another source of frustration in my relations with DIAND was DIAND's extreme caution in exercising its fiduciary obligations. That resulted in us constantly having to seek DIAND's approval concerning certain decisions regarding finances, lands, and development, even though it was our own land that was involved. It is very galling to lack direct control over our own lives, to have the *Indian Act* hanging over us all the time with DIAND ensuring that we are in compliance with what they say we have to do. They often force things on us and it does not matter what we say; they have their own agenda and they are not always forthright in telling us what it is.

Underlying many of First Nations' problems with DIAND has been the fact that, on the part of some of the bureaucrats' political masters, until recently there has been no political will to earnestly tackle First Nation issues. There was some political will created by the "Oka crisis" in 1990, but it dissipated after the defeat of the Charlottetown Accord in 1992. Governments also have to try to keep non-Natives happy and in the present fiscal climate the political will for constructively and decisively dealing with First Nations' problems has been replaced in many quarters with an attitude that First Nations are "getting too much for nothing". However discreetly and covertly pursued, the federal government does have an agenda for First Nations and its underlying goal, many observers believe, is to maximize the assimilation of First Nation people while minimizing expenditures on First Nation people. The means for achieving that objective seem to be to allow conditions on reserves to be so bad that people are compelled to leave. Thus, DIAND's forecasts that the population balance will soon tip, such that a majority of First Nation individuals will live off-reserve by early in the twenty-first century, could become a self-fulfilling prophecy. If it does come about, it will produce a new set of challenges for First Nation leaders and will create a need for additional leadership skills.

Nevertheless, I believe that the government is changing in a positive direction. Consider, for instance, a public statement by Hon. Ron Irwin, Minister of Indian Affairs in 1996. At the opening of a First Nation high school, he said: "We destroyed almost seven generations of parenting. That's a terrible thing for any civilization to have to admit".[16] However, whether such politicians of good will can bring their cabinet colleagues along with them is another matter entirely. So, too, is the question of whether bureaucrats of good will can overcome institutionalized bureaucratic forces which seem to have a life or momentum of their own which is independent of the will of decision-makers.

CONCLUSION

This has been a very personal account of my leadership among the Siksika and of the constraints imposed by the colonial legacy. Yet, the situation which I have described has important parallels with what academic researchers have found in other communities and my experience assures me that most of what I have written above has applicability well beyond the Siksika Nation. I identify below a few lessons that I have learned from that experience.

My experience as chief has taught me the importance of strategic planning — of seeing "the big picture" holistically and acting decisively on that. (By "big picture" I mean the inter-relationships among different policy fields.) It is imperative to develop a vision to channel one's daily energies, for without such a long-term goal it is entirely too easy to get lost in the day-to-day mundane trivia. Yet, I also learned the importance of not going too far too quickly — that is, the importance of not pushing the cutting edge too aggressively without ascertaining what the people's needs, thoughts, and fears are. Only if the leader demonstrates such empathy toward, and understanding of, the people being led will those people "buy into" the vision that the leader is promoting. To achieve that, it is imperative that channels of communication be opened, which is why we at Siksika established a radio station and community newspapers and revised the structure of the administration to allow for community input into the planning and direction of tribal programs.

Governments and their bureaucrats also have long-term objectives and hidden agendas. I learned that it is important to understand the government's agenda and to be cognizant of the constraints (e.g., limited budget, demands made by other First Nations) faced by any given government bureaucrat. Yet, I also learned that it is possible for First Nation leaders to be bold, which I would define in terms of aggressively taking calculated risks with innovative measures or programs. It is possible to be bold in dealings with DIAND and with one's own constituents, although boldness is more difficult in the latter case due to constituents' distrust, instant criticism, and low level of understanding of First Nation affairs.

I also came to appreciate that transparency is crucial. A chief must let the people know exactly what (s)he is doing and thinking. This is one of the most important rules of leadership in First Nation communities, because the negative image of First Nation leaders must be countered.

One of my main messages in this chapter has been that time is not on our side and that First Nations therefore desperately need to have our "lost warriors" come forward to take responsibility, as in the days of old. We must put behind us the excuses and escapism of the colonial era. Now is a time of both opportunity and risk. It is a time — perhaps the most pivotal era since the signing of the treaties — when our actions or inaction will have lasting effects. Our numbers are expanding dramatically, while at the same time government is capping and rearranging and refinancing the Indian agenda. If we wait to take action, it will be too late. We must choose our leaders wisely, we must be clear and decisive about what we want, and our leaders must make wise choices. Then we must take action to implement the vision.

Another main message is that we need a paradigm shift in our thinking, away from the cynical, defensive, dependent, entitlement mindset that has been inculcated in us under the colonial *Indian Act* regime, and toward a more trusting, assertively proactive, persevering, visionary, affirming, meritocratic, and inclusive orientation. We must summon the courage to take calculated risks in adapting to our changing environment, for our survival depends upon that adaptability, just as it did in our ancestors' time. In our interpersonal relations we must learn to forgive and forget — to set aside petty jealousies and grudges based on actions or slights done years earlier. We must take from what is good in the non-Native cultures and refrain from disparaging those of our First Nation brothers and sisters who seek to better themselves, whether it be through education or business. We must also firmly reject what is undesirable in non-Native cultures, such as vote buying and personal aggrandizement. If we do not make these shifts in our thinking and in our actions, it will matter little what kind of leadership we have, for our present orientations not only undermine our leaders, but also tear at the very fabric of our culture and our community.

If First Nations do not experience a drastic shift in leadership *and* followership, in the direction outlined above, our very future as First Nations will be jeopardized. We cannot survive another one hundred years in our present mode of existence. Indeed, I predict that as First Nations are pushed toward self-sufficiency over the next twenty-five years, those which do not rise to the challenge will be assimilated into some generic melting pot where their rights as First Nation people will be lost because their community has succumbed to the debilitating influences discussed above. That is perhaps the ultimate paradox: that by clinging too strongly and defensively to the past in an effort to preserve what is Indian, we run the risk of jeopardizing our ability to assert our Indianness in a modern context.

Fortunately, governments and First Nations realize that the solutions lie within the First Nations themselves and that the government's role is to provide support. First Nations are taking responsibility for our own destiny and are stepping forward to assert that it is our time and it is only right that we make our own decisions.

NOTES

[1] Editor's Note: Strater Crowfoot served as elected chief of the Siksika Nation from January 1, 1988, to December 31, 1995. During that eight years he won four elec-

tions but was defeated in the election of December 1995. The Siksika (Blackfoot) Nation's territory is located about one hour's drive east of Calgary, Alberta.

[2] Carstens (1991: 233) points out that in some First Nations, such as the one he studied, community members' expectations of the chief differ greatly from their expectations of councillors.

[3] *Editor's Note:* See Royal Commission on Aboriginal Peoples (1996: 130–134) for a discussion of traditional forms of leadership among aboriginal peoples.

[4] Later in this chapter, as part of the discussion of followership, I return to the topic of willingness to take on responsibility.

[5] The Alkalai Lake First Nation, which experienced great success in overcoming a widespread substance abuse problem in the community, has served as an important role model for many other communities and their leaders.

[6] Alternative Funding Arrangements (A.F.A.) involved new arrangements both for the federal government's allocation of funding to First Nations and for First Nations' accounting for those funds. The stated intention was to allow First Nations greater autonomy in how they spent moneys received from the federal government.

[7] This phrase is translated from Blackfoot.

[8] Besides the *Indian Act,* some examples of the many federal statutes which DIAND administers are: *The Indian Oil and Gas Act, the B.C. Indian Reserves Mineral Resources Act; the St. Peters Indian Reserve Act, and The Northwest Territories Act.*

[9] Lithman (1984:164–165) discusses problems associated with the collaborative strategy and the challenging strategy, respectively.

[10] *The Concise Oxford Dictionary of Current English* (1964) defines "nepotism" as "undue favour from holder of patronage to relatives".

[11] The same expectations can be applied to council as a whole if one's relatives control the largest block of votes on council.

[12] Non-Native politics in Québec would be an exception to this generalization.

[13] In many First Nation cultures, mobilization of opposition to the leader is also facilitated by the tradition of defecting to a new leader if one is not satisfied with the present leader. In part, this is because entire clans or families can shift loyalties at once.

[14] See Ross (1992) on the notion, found in many First Nation cultures, that the time must be right.

[15] Gambling has always been a part of Indian life. However, in contemporary times balance has been lost as bingo has become too dominant. For some people it has become an obsession, such that their families are suffering (e.g., child neglect in the form of leaving one's children unattended at the shopping mall on reserve while going to Calgary to play bingo). The problem of child neglect on the part of gamblers is by no means confined to First Nations, as Canadian Press (1996) attests.

[16] CBC Radio news, August 28, 1996.

REFERENCES

Bardach, Eugene
1977   *The Implementation Game: What Happens After a Bill Becomes Law.* Massachusetts Institute of Technology.
Boldt, Menno
1994   *Surviving as Indians.* Toronto: University of Toronto Press.

Canadian Press
1996   "Casino Bans Gamblers Who Abandon Their Kids", *Calgary Herald*. August
         8: A3.
Carstens, Peter
1991   *The Queen's People: A Study of Hegemony, Coercion, and Accommodation Among
         the Okanagan of Canada*. Toronto: University of Toronto Press.
Covey, Stephen R. et al.
1994   *First Things First: To Live, To Love, To Learn, To Leave a Legacy*. New York: Simon
         and Shuster.
Gusfield, Joseph
1966   "Functional Areas of Leadership in Social Movements", *Sociological Quarterly*.
         VII (Summer): 137–56.
Lithman, Yngve Georg
1984   *The Community Apart: A Case Study of a Canadian Indian Reserve Community*.
         Winnipeg: University of Manitoba Press.
McCarthy, John D. and Mayer N. Zald
1973   *The Trend of Social Movements in America: Professionalization and Resource
         Mobilization*. Morristown, N.J.: General Learning.
Ponting, J. Rick (ed.)
1986   *Arduous Journey: Canadian Indians and Decolonization*. Toronto:
         McClelland & Stewart / Oxford University Press.
Ross, Rupert
1992   *Dancing With a Ghost*. Markham: Octopus Publishing.
Royal Commission on Aboriginal Peoples
1996   *Final Report of the Royal Commission on Aboriginal Peoples; Vol. 2: Restructuring
         the Relationship*. Ottawa: Minister of Supply and Services Canada.
Simpson, Jeffrey
1993   *Faultlines: Struggling for a Canadian Vision*. Toronto: HarperCollins.
Smelser, Neil
1963   *Theory of Collective Behavior*. New York: The Free Press.
Turner, Ralph and Lewis Killian
1987   *Collective Behavior*. Third Edition. Englewood Cliffs, N.J.: Prentice Hall.
Weber, Max
1947   *The Theory of Social and Economic Organization*. A.M. Henderson and Talcott
         Parsons (trans.), Talcott Parsons (ed.). New York: Oxford University Press.

CHAPTER 13

EMPOWERMENT THROUGH FIRST NATION CONTROL OF EDUCATION: A SAKAW CREE PHILOSOPHY OF EDUCATION[1]

Dale F. Auger

INTRODUCTION

At this time, in many First Nation communities there is a questioning of exist-ing schools as effective educational systems. Many factors have affected the school's role in Native communities. Primary among these factors is that there has been a long history of little or no community control. Generally speaking, as this country called Canada was forming, we the Native people ended up with our lives in the hands of foreign societies or governments. Schooling was no exception; for centuries, governments and the churches sanctioned by them have structured our education. The imposed educational systems have restricted our ability to educate our children according to our own philosophy and traditions.

> I remember the words of the Old Ones, "Wunska, wunska!" they would say. "Wake up, wake up from your sleep!" I remember pulling the blankets from over my head, my eyes open. I see the Old Ones in the corner of our hand-made home. I see the spruce bows above and below. Our home had been made days before; I remember helping build it. I remember first picking the spot and how there was nothing there but the open Land. I remember how I watched and learned how my people, the Sakaw Cree, roamed the bushland of the north.
>
> I awake to see my grandfather preparing to skin the beaver; in the middle of our home there is a Fire. On the Fire there is a pot of tea. I hear the language of my people, the Sakaw Cree, being spoken. Giving acknowledgement to the beaver spirit, my grandfather takes the feet of the beaver, binds them tightly and hangs them from the branched ceiling. "Listen!" my grandfather says to me. "Utee-peeyepi." "Come and sit with me," he calls. "It is time for your teachings; come and learn." With excitement I rush to his side, my teacher. He begins his lesson to me about the beaver. He talks about the beaver as though we are brothers; he is careful when handling him. There is a long standing respect between these two beings, my grandfather and the beaver. He tells me the beaver was the one who helped us to understand the Land, the Soil, the Trees. Because, he says, the Water was once everywhere and it was the beaver that introduced us to this land. I listen and learn the ways of my people, where the Land and all beings — the two-legged, four-legged and winged

ones, the Trees, the Land — are all sources of knowledge; where knowledge among all these beings is willingly shared; where walls of a building, words written into countless numbers of textbooks, and paper-certified teachers are no longer the limits of an educational system. I affirm my birthright to be educated as a Sakaw Cree and to ensure that my children and my children's children for generations to come will have the means to do so as well.

It is no longer acceptable for someone to make decisions from another part of the Land, towards the future of my children as well as the other children in my community. We in our community must assume total responsibility for the control of our educational systems and we must define our own visions of education in our own communities. Only then can a school become a more relevant place for students in each particular community situation.

As Native visionaries begin the processes of creating Native educational systems, a diversity of models will emerge. These models might incorporate common elements, such as the inclusion of Elders as "teachers", the use of the Native language as the language of instruction, and the use of curricula which have been constructed from a Native point of view. Beyond inclusion of elements such as these, however, Native educational systems will embody a philosophical context which is uniquely Native. Those who truly wish to implement Native educational systems and not merely replace Canadian systems with Native teachers and Native curricula must give serious consideration to what is a Native philosophy of education.

I view this chapter as an exploration of what might be involved in identifying a Native philosophy of education. What I describe results from my being Sakaw ("northern" or "bush") Cree. My purpose in writing is to present aspects of a Sakaw Cree philosophy of education, in the hope that the identification of such a philosophy will provide a means for establishing a solid foundation from which a genuine Sakaw Cree educational system can arise, and to inspire other First Nations to undertake a corresponding process.

In this chapter I speak in my own voice. I have been actively involved in the knowledge I am relating here, for the knowledge was inside me. One Native professor described this research orientation by contrasting it with "academic writing":

> In academic writing, the rule is that authors do not identify their voices. They speak from a pedestal of knowledge. The individual speaking is not a central part of that knowledge, nor is he or she actively involved in the knowledge he or she has produced. The knowledge is outside of the self... In my culture [Mohawk], not speaking from the "me" is a violation. The only true knowledge that I can have is that which is learned from what I have experienced.

(Monture-Okanee, 1992: 126–127)

My methodology did include some elements which resembled some of the western sense of research. For instance, I conducted interviews with Elders and analyzed Elders' documents. However, I have also journeyed into my inner being to honour inner and spiritual realities, for as Cajete (1994: 20), a Tewa Indian from New Mexico, states:

> It is the affective elements — the subjective experience and observations, the communal relationships, the artistic and mythical dimensions, the ritual and ceremony, the sacred ecology, the psychological and spiritual orientations —

that have characterized and formed Indigenous education since time immemorial. These dimensions and their inherent meanings are not readily quantifiable, observable, or easily verbalized, and as a result, have been given little credence in mainstream approaches to education and research.

SAKAW CREE PHILOSOPHY AND KNOWLEDGE

With some hesitation, I approach the task of putting into words general commentary on Sakaw Cree philosophy and knowledge. I feel reluctant to expose the ways of my people's minds. The reason is that, in the past, knowledge was taken from us, from our Elders, and used in the wrong way to further control our destiny. We have always wished to be free to totally control our own future. In spite of these fears, I feel the timing is right to write about these ideas. It seems the western view of knowledge is in a state of break down or at least is being seriously re-evaluated in light of the social and environmental chaos around us today. We, the Cree, are not alone in our search to rediscover new and whole knowledge.

It is my belief that answers cannot be found in the middle of the problem. My feelings are that I must go back before the time when a process was disrupted. I must backtrack and gather information on how my people looked at knowledge before the western ways disrupted the natural flow of my people's way of life. How is it possible to go back that far? Much has changed over the years; many different philosophies have invaded the minds of my peoples. What has not changed is the way we access and view knowledge. Even though we might appear to have changed on the surface, inside our old ways are still with us. Our philosophy still occupies the centre of our core. It is from this core that our future will take shape.

I remember the words of many of the Old Ones. "Go inside," they would say. "Go and talk to your spirit, your soul." If the Old Ones have been saying these words for countless generations, words which talk about going inside the "Core", then shouldn't we be taking steps to at least try to understand the meaning of the Core?

Exploring the Core

A little boy stares out the window of the cabin. His eyes focus on something downward. The grandmother asks him from the other side of the room, what does he look at. The boy replies that his two little friends are calling him to come out and play. The grandmother tells the boy to tell his friends that he can't go out because he is not well. She says, "Tell them to forgive you for not going. Tell them you will feed them." The grandmother walks to the window and on the ground two chickadees hop up and down. The boy runs to the door with food for his friends and calls to them to eat.

Short stories like the above illustrate a primary aspect of Sakaw Cree worldview: that all beings, whether they be two-legged (human), winged, or four-legged, are encouraged to communicate with each other. The boy was encouraged to recognize and communicate with the winged ones. The winged ones were encouraged by the boy when they took the food from him. The boy did not openly talk to the winged ones; messages were sent in other ways.

Generally speaking, communication without words is deemed to be possible, not just between two-leggeds but among all beings.

The meaning of "beings" is difficult to discuss in the English language. In the Cree language, for example, when stories refer to the weather or Trees, it is as though they live. The story might say "The Tree being talked to the weather being; together they talked". The language is expressing a fact of the Cree world, that these entities do indeed live. Cree language and philosophy are complementary. There is no consideration of fantasy in the fact that Trees, Animals and humans "talk", or communicate with one another. There are no barriers (such as the concept of "fantasy") which prevent humans from experiencing knowledge from other sources, or beings, in addition to human beings.

> This tree they call the Birch is such a powerful being, like the mother. I look to her as a mother of the tree beings. She is a giver of life, new and old, always giving. When you look at her she looks as though she has a dress on, a white dress. Her bark is white like the buckskin dress she wears. The branches look like fringes; they move so nicely when the wind blows. The spring is one of my best times with her; this is when she gives milk. Fresh clean milk, Sap, they call it. When I was a child I would put my head at her feet looking upward. My mouth opened, I would catch the drops she offered me. The Old Ones make tea with this pure mother's water; they say it gives them new knowledge. I work with this great tree being; we work together, we help each other. When I take her bark I ask her and tell her over and over again how grateful I am. I tell her I will not harm her being. In return I feed her and pray for her. We treat each other well. It is "likeweareone".

There is so much to be told about the relationship humans have with other beings, the Tree beings, for example. Humans have relied on them from the beginning of time. It is a relationship that has never faltered. Each, until now, has been fairly loyal to the other. One such loyal relationship is that of one whom I have come to know as the "Birch Woman".

> When I drove up to her log house facing the small lake, I was greeted by a group of small children. She lived in the larger cabin with the one side blocked off, her private place. Her daughters and granddaughters surrounded her in each of their own homes. The oldest daughter is the one who cares for her on a daily basis, tending to her every need. The daughter calls her mother "Mom" or "My Mom". Everyone in the camp and the surrounding area respects her mother greatly.
>
> I had known the old lady and her daughter for some time and they were glad to see me. They had word that I was coming and that I was wishing to learn the ways of the Birch. They also knew that when someone came for such knowledge, there was an unwritten and unspoken law. That law was that it was done in the right way, the giving and respecting way, the way of the Creator. For the last several months I had collected clothes, pots and pans to be given as gifts. It is the Sakaw Cree way that you first give tobacco and cloth print as recognition to the Creator and the knowledge they share. To the old lady I gave a second batch of tobacco for her own use. I was told that she loved peppermint candy. In between the candy and tobacco I also offered money. I offered this to her and humbly asked her if she could teach me the way of the Creator and the way of the Birch.
>
> She accepted the offerings and with a prayer offered them to the Creator on my behalf. Her own personal offerings went under her pillow almost immediately. To the older daughter, I offered the clothes for the children and

money for herself. Everyone at that point was very happy and all was proper; all offerings had been accepted.

I had come there to learn and she was my teacher, and in that way it was plain and simple. I had not even settled in when she called one of the younger boys, about eight years old. She handed him a small axe and instructed him as to where I was to start my learning. I followed this young man through the bush, thinking to myself, "I'm going to learn from this young man".

As we walked I noticed just how sure-footed he was. He had done this many times before. He stopped several times, tilting his head upward, listening, saying nothing, and then continuing on. At this point I had really no idea just what I was to be working on first. In the Indian way one asks few questions and learns first from observing what is all around. In the Indian way there are no short cuts to learning the right way. Learning is done with all senses first.

Once more he stopped and once again his head turned, looking upward. At that point I had allowed myself to open all my senses, to feel the unspoken learning. What I got had to do with something between the Trees and the weather. I knew what kind of Trees these were: they were Spruce and I was going to start with picking their roots. This young man did not start his teaching just yet; he sat down next to the tree and waited. I sat next to him and said nothing. Then in a soft voice he said to me in Cree, "Not yet; it's too windy."

Without realizing it, I was already learning, learning without voice. I could feel the tree talking to me, telling me, "Grandson, you must wait for our relative the wind to quit blowing. You must ask him to help you just like you must ask me of the tree beings".

Just then the young man pulled out a small pouch with tobacco in it. He took some in his hand and began offering it to the wind and the spruce tree. No sooner had we done this when the wind stopped and the big spruce tree was still. The young man proceeded to tell me that if we had started looking for the roots prior to doing this, they would not be there. First, we had not yet acknowledged the tree or the wind; secondly, the roots are like the fingers of a human. When a human is standing in the wind and the wind is threatening to blow him down, what does he do? He hangs on. Trees are alive and they react the same way. So, if you are looking for them closest to the surface they are nowhere to be found. They are underground, hanging on; otherwise, the tree will fall over. Everything is related; everything works together. So, to get at the roots you must check with the tree being and to work with the tree you must also talk to the wind; it is that simple.

Not until after all this unspoken communication had occurred did we eventually begin to dig. At that point all senses are working together; so, locating their whereabouts was easy for the young man. He peeled off the top layer of moss and there they lay. I watched this young man as he worked with the roots. His hands were so sure, almost gentle. Soon I, too, was working with this great part of the tree being, the roots.

All that afternoon we worked with the Tree beings, collecting their roots. Each time I would start I found myself checking and almost openly talking to the wind. Such is the power of unspoken communication, learning without spoken words; that young man put me in the presence of a real teacher.

Later that day I had gotten so many roots that each arm was full with these rings of roots. On my fingers were smaller ones; a good day it was!

When I returned back to the cabin, the old lady was pleased to see that I had learned the way of the roots. She had a bucket of Water beside her and took some of them to put into the Water. She then handed me a small knife which was not very sharp. She reached in the bucket and handed me one root, then took one for herself. "These roots are like rivers; each has a bend in it like the river. When splitting them in half you must get over the knots in order to have them long to sew with." She explained that they would be used for the sewing of the baskets we were to make. "We must make them soft so they can be like thread"; she spoke no English and her words in Cree were few. That does not mean that she was not communicating; she spoke to me in an unspoken language, as it is so often with our Elders.

When we were done we had piles of small, wrapped root threads. The daughter had prepared a basin of warm Water and several natural dyes. The roots were then dyed many colours. I felt good at this point; the learning felt good. I could not help thinking how this was my way of learning. I felt at home in this classroom; the language was my way.

The next morning I was told that I would be going out with a man who had been taught by the old lady to get birch bark. His name was Muniaw and he knew all there was to know about the way of the Birch. We drove about an hour. When we got to the place I was shocked to see piles of destroyed birch Trees. There must have been some kind of government program that cleared land, acres and acres of destroyed lands. I looked at Muniaw and asked him why had they done this destructive thing; he smiled and said nothing. Muniaw had come to accept the ways of the whiteman; after all, he was one of these people. "Muniaw" in Cree means "Whiteman" or "white person". He was a whiteman who had been adopted at a young age by the Indian people. As far as he was concerned, the Cree were his people and that was final.

We left the truck and walked to the other side of the mass destruction. On the other side were the most beautiful, large, pure white birch. To find such large Trees of this nature was rare; birch are very sensitive tree beings and do not just grow anywhere.

Muniaw walked up to the largest tree and placed tobacco at her roots. With his large hands he held the tree, feeling the surface and looking upwards. Like the young man the day before, communication between other beings needed to happen. The day before, it was with the wind. Today it was with another being, that of the sun. The sun, the giver of light, worked with the birch and that was what Muniaw was addressing.

The lesson the sun gave was this. If I tried to take the birch without acknowledging her being, the birch could not be taken without scarring her surface. Without the sun the bark simply cannot be taken. It was the same with humans, it was told to me. Say a human is walking in the hot sun; he will start to get hot and tired. He begins to recognize the sun as the cause of his own rising heat. What does he do? He takes off some of his clothing. Just like the birch tree. When humans are forced to take off their clothes when it's cold, they resist. So, too, does the birch. Two beings react the same way to the higher being, the sun. So I waited for the sun to communicate with the tree being. Then, when the tree being said it was O.K., I learned to take the birch bark. That is the way, the way of all beings. Today my respect for the sun is greater than it has ever been. Learning of the sun, the birch, and of even myself as a human helped me understand better the power of "whole Knowledge". Working relationships with all other beings, that is what this learning was about.

Now roots and bark had been gathered and prepared for the creating process. One more entity had to be acknowledged and that was the saskatoon willow. At this point I had already learned the pathways to communicating; so, talking to this tree being had become more familiar.

In the Birch Woman's cabin once more we sat, ready to start the creative process. In her bag she pulled out a small bundle, opened it and spread it out on the table. These items were taken care of like her special little helpers: red willow pegs, natural string, measurement sticks, all the natural tools to create.

Over the next several days I learned the many meanings of creation. Human being, the initiator, and the different tree beings working hand in hand. The "crossing of knowledge" I like to call it, where many beings working together, cross each other's path, sharing and learning each other's knowledge. I could feel the crossing of knowledge working through my fingers as I created the basket. The making of the basket and its result is not what this was all about. It was something greater: the pleasurable feeling you get when you can see the spiritual beings working together as one. Oh, how I felt so pure as one who creates.

For the next several days I could feel the Spirit Beings with me, so clearly. In my dreams they appeared talking as though they were human themselves. When I looked at the old lady after that I no longer had the need to be spoken to, or told how to. I was just a being that had gotten on that path, the pathway that so many of our ancestors had travelled — a path that requires no previous knowledge, just the willingness to accept that there are other beings on this great mother, the earth. They are here, they are around us, as sure as I am the smallest of beings on this great Island.

Sources of Knowledge: Elders

Our Elders have been a source of knowledge in our community as long as we can remember. They have been our source of knowledge by helping us to be aware of our roots. As the most prominent part of our traditional education, they are themselves the roots of our culture. The role of Elders is like that of the roots of a tree. They hold the tree stable; when the wind blows, it is the roots that hold the tree intact. Roots are the foundation.

Just as there are many roots forming the foundation of one tree, so are there many Elders, each one distinct in his or her own right and with his or her own knowledge, forming the foundation of Sakaw Cree traditional education. Through lifelong experience, our Elders are our knowledge-carriers; through their wisdom and spiritual insights, they are our knowledge definers. They have always been there to help those who have wandered, those who wish to find their way back, as is described in this next story.

> I sat in his cabin. I sipped on his tea. I shared his muskrat tail. He is one of my grandfathers. He is from the people of the beaver. His whiteman's name is Old Man Beaver. His cabin is small and it faces the lake. His wife has since passed on. He is a calm man; he likes his cigarettes rolled very round and thick. "Come with me", I ask him one day. "I'll drive you to the store." He agrees. He walks to the corner of his cabin, dragging his old worn out moccasins on the floor. He then grabs his belongings and we walk towards my new vehicle.
>
> He thinks nothing of the world from which I come. Yet, he is aware that I come from a different world — a world where a man's own philosophy is not as important.
>
> He knows that we were born brothers and we once shared the same pond. For some reason I left and was forced to swim elsewhere. He tries not to lose perspective of that.
>
> Old Man Beaver taught me a lesson that day — a lesson of what is important for now and for the future. A young university student driving an old traditional professor to the store. In some ways I want him to see that I am successful in the whiteman's world. He knows that I want him to recognize that. He does not speak. We proceed. He stares straight ahead and says nothing.

One mile down the road he begins his lesson to me. He reaches for his small bag of tobacco and paper and begins to roll himself a big round cigarette. Once it is in his mouth he pulls out a wooden match. I observe him from the corner of my eye. He knows that I observe him. I say nothing.

So, here we are driving down the road in a brand new 1988 Dodge Caravan, complete with all the trimmings of luxury. My personal canoe. I am proud of this vehicle because in the whiteman's world you are supposed to be proud of material things — things that shine and show well.

He reaches forward with his wooden match and goes directly to my dashboard. He strikes very firmly across it with his match. He lights his cigarette. I am stunned. He has threatened me. He has sent shock waves down my spine. In my mind I scurry like a chipmunk who senses danger. Outwardly, I don't react. I couldn't react because he waits for me to react. I say nothing. We drive on.

In the whiteman's world where I come from his act can easily be viewed as savagely disrespectful, uneducated, unsophisticated. However, there is another world with which I am very much losing contact. This is his signal to me. This man of the beaver gave me a signal: Don't ever lose contact with our world. Don't let shiny objects burn your eyes, because once your eyes are gone you can no longer see beneath the Water.

We got his tobacco and we went back to his cabin by the lake. We smoked. We talked.

The eight hours it took for me to return to my city home were long. The scar that showed itself so clearly on the dash board of my new van is still there. So, too, is the thought of my grandfather, the Beaver.

Elders like Grandfather Beaver continue to share their philosophical thoughts on the importance of staying true to one's roots. Our Elders are essential sources of knowledge for Sakaw Cree. It is critical to incorporate them as teachers, as knowledge-carriers, into a Sakaw Cree system of education.

Sources of Knowledge: Animals

In the larger Canadian society learning takes place in institutions, such as schools, colleges, and universities. In these institutions, learning is done primarily in classrooms. In the Native society, learning is not confined to classrooms. Elders believe that learning takes place in the whole of life: Life and all that lives are viewed as the true teachers on this earth. Included among these teachers are the Animals, better known to us as the four-legged beings.

Indian people have lived off the Land for many generations. They have come to know the Land and all that moves on it. For instance, when a family experienced a shortage of meat, the first thing they would do would be to look to the sky. They would do this because the sky can predict where the moose will be a day from then. If the sky shows a warm spell, the hunter knows the moose will be coming down from the hills to where the snow is shallow. A moose knows that if the snow begins to melt, the top part will eventually freeze, forming a hard crust. To a moose, this crust is about as bad as the bugs they get in the spring. If he were to stay in the hills where it is deep, he would surely fall prey to wolves. A moose cannot run in this type of snow because whenever he takes a step he breaks through the crust. The problem comes when he lifts his foot out again. The front of his feet scrape against the crust causing his hair to eventually wear away. (This would be like a man banging his knuckles one hundred times against a table.) Down below, where the snow is much shallower, he can move more easily.

This is one example of knowledge derived from observation of animal behaviour. In the past, understanding the behaviour of Animals meant feeding your family or not. Knowledge from Animals goes beyond the surface level of observing animal behaviour, though.

Animals teach us about the many worlds that exist around us. They have no barriers, no limits. They have the ability to cross back and forth to each other's world, four-legged talking to the winged ones, the winged ones talking to the two-legged ones. No limits, no lines. The next story provides an example of how easy it can be for all beings to cross into each other's world.

A young boy looks to become a man. For the first time he must provide for a family of his own. The young man must go to the grandfathers of his community. He approaches the grandfathers and says, "I must go fishing to provide for my family for the first time. I have never been on the lake alone before. I am asking for your guidance so that I will have a strong spirit and will have a strong mind." The grandfather turns to the young man. "If you wish to catch many fish you must call on the spirit of the MAGWA, the loon. The MAGWA is the one who understands the Fish Spirits. It is he who has come to understand how they swim. It is also he who has total understanding of where they swim. It is also he who has total respect of the Fish Spirit."

In order for this young man to succeed, he is asked by the grandfathers to call on the loon. That night he goes to the lake's edge and begins to call the loon. Across the lake the loon replies and swims towards the young man. The loon calls, "What is it that you ask of me and the loon spirit?"

"I ask that you give me the knowledge to understand the Fish Spirits. I need the wisdom to be able to capture the Fish Spirits. I am a young man with a young family and they depend on me." The loon turns towards the lake and says, "Yes, I will help you because you have come to me in the right way. I will go to the Spirits of the Fish below and tell them that you need them to help you provide for your family." The loon dives and the young man waits.

Before long the loon reappears on the surface of the Water. "Young man, the Fish Spirits have said that it is okay that you take them for your needs. They also said to take only what you need; do not be greedy."

The young man asks the loon where he must go to capture the fish. The loon replies, "At the mouth of the river you will see a tree that has been cut by our brother the beaver. Beside that tree they will wait."

The young man was so happy he turned to the loon again and said, "Loon spirit, what must I do to repay you for your good deed?"

"You need not repay me, young man," the loon said. "Repay only the Fish Spirits. When you get your first drum, make a song about the fish beneath. When you make that song, tell the Fish Spirits how grateful you are that they provide for your family."

"This I will do," said the young man. At the next feast, the young man sang his new song in honour of the Fish Spirits.

Stories such as these look to the Animals and Birds as a source of knowledge. The people looked to the Animals and Birds for answers on how they could feed their families. Animals had a firm place in the circle of beings; all were connected; all were one. This connectedness formed the foundation of education.

Learning about and acknowledging that there is order and respect in the relationships among all beings is part of the educational process. The language of "natural relationship" includes proper respect given to other beings, as the following story illustrates.

I remember as clear as there is day. I was just a boy when I again witnessed the respect our people had for the four-legged ones. In this case it was a big, older bull moose. A funny kind of respect, I remember thinking at the time. The moose pulling the hunter deeper and deeper into other worlds, worlds that only could have been travelled by a people who understood the meaning of all other beings, beings that acknowledged each other and depended on each other. It is not the taking that was the challenge but the asking for the right to take. Imagine man, the two-legged, asking the four-legged for the right to capture his being. Many times the right is not given and in some cases the right must be earned.

Skids, the people called him; a big man about six foot six or so. He was, I should think, in the prime of his life; fit as a fiddle. He had grown up in a family of boys or young men, where each day brought with it always new ways for the hunt. His father was known by the people as the "bear man" because it was said that one time many years ago he had problems with the other worlds. The talking and the asking for the right to take had not been learned yet at the time. His father, still young at the time, had killed a moose and had left it only to return to see a grizzly claiming it. He attempted to chase the big bear away only to find himself being torn apart. The bear ripped through half his face, leaving him scarred for life. He had a little dog at the time that taunted the bear away for him. Skids laughs at this next part. I guess the bear was leaving his father as he lay on the ground. As the bear was leaving, his father got up, picked up a big stick, and with the biggest swing he hit the bear square on the head as he walked away. The bear barely felt it, of course, and once again continued his assault on his father. Once again the small dog kept biting the bear in the back foot, luring him away. Skid's father's life was spared by the bear.

Skids talked about the lessons learned that day by his young father at the time. First, he said, perhaps his father did not ask in the right way for the right to take the four-legged, the moose he had killed. Perhaps the bear, who is the protector anyway, was asked to step in and restore order. Bears are protectors of the spirit world, you see. His father resisted the law of the being world by hitting the bear, only to find himself harmed even more. Skids talks a lot about his father, who has since passed on to the spirit world himself. His father bore the scars of the bear, reminding him for the rest of his life of the power that all beings possess.

This man, Skids, was taught the ways of all other beings early in life. He was on a hunt himself one time. He had shot a moose, but the moose refused to die, just refused to stop. It ran and ran, taking him further and further into the hills. The snow and the wind beings began to help the moose being by falling and blowing as hard as they could. Skids soon lost the trail in the wind and the snow. He turned back to his camp where I was waiting. We both sat in silence, each of us aware of the need to have that moose. Then in through the space in the top of our tent flew the hunter's friend, the wiskeyjack. He perched on the side of the poles looking down at us. His eyes spoke to us, almost as if to say, "Can't get him, eh? What's the matter with you, two-leggeds, don't you ever learn? You've got to ask first. Ask the moose being, like you should". Skids kept his head down, then looked up only to see the wiskeyjack fly way. I heard him; I knew what he meant, but I said nothing. Skids turned to his medicine pouch, opened it and pulled out a small willow fungus. He took a stone near the Fire and placed it on top. He lit the fungus and began to pray; together we prayed.

Soon the weather began to let up and Skids decided to return in pursuit of the moose. This time I followed a distance behind. What I saw was amazing. That wiskeyjack was leading Skids into the hills without tracks to follow. Soon the wiskeyjack stopped; it was as though he was calling to the raven to help from that point on. One raven came; then there were two, then many. They took him straight to where the moose was lying. He had given his life to Skids. The ravens watched above, almost as though they were supervising in honour of the moose being. Skids turned the moose over and with his knife he lifted the head and took above the top lip a small piece of bare skin. He later told me that the cleanest part of the moose was this part, and in honour of the moose being, it must be given back. He took this part and offered it to the tree beings in order that this moose spirit might still walk high as the Trees. He placed it on the tree branch with a prayer. Why this part, I asked. Because before this moose eats anything, he cleans it first with this part of his top lip. It is as though he wipes it clean first before he eats. The moose is a clean animal, you see, one of the cleanest. Sure enough, when you look close to a moose you see that there is no hair on the small area above his top lip. That is what it is for.

As all this was going on, the ravens watched above together with the wiskeyjack who had joined them. Skids opened the moose up; with his hand he scooped a hand full of blood. He drank it. This one is for me, he said. This is what I had offered to do in honour of the moose being. Skids offered me to drink and so I did.

What was so amazing was that as soon as we drank and offered there to the moose being, the ravens and wiskeyjack flew away all together. What was all this about, I thought through the years. Was this really direct communication with other beings? Yes, it was; I witnessed it. I felt it even as a young boy. Skids neglected to ask the moose for its being to feed the family. The moose resisted, making it hard for Skids. The snow and the wind beings helped the moose by making it impassable for Skids. Only when the wiskeyjack gave him a second chance to take the right way, did everything go right.

There are many worlds that form layers in understanding all other beings. Many times they are as clear as day and other times one has to call for them. Calling them might be in the form of prayer. Prayer is recognized by all beings as the channel for communication. If one being fails to recognize it, all other beings can refuse to cooperate and might eventually work against that being. That is why every event is started with a prayer: to recognize all beings, no matter how big or small.

Skids learned what was to be learned from his father's encounter with the bear spirit. Once on his own, he continuously tested this unspoken spiritual law. Time and time again, though, he was reminded of the fact that he, as the two-legged, is not superior to all other beings. Without recognition of all beings in the right way, life can be difficult. In all this crossing of knowledge between all other beings, I watch and learn. This is how it is done; this is our way, the way of learning from all beings.

Sources of Knowledge: Land

The Land has always found a firm place in the language of our people. Like the Elders and the Animals, the Land holds equal to all. Even in today's words, people will still refer to the Land and the people as one — "PEOPLE OF THE LAND". The Land is everything to the Native people.

Each group of people has a way of speaking of the Land; *it is the central core of their existence*. In their prayers, the Land is mentioned to the highest of honour. In the songs, ever so sacred, Sakaw Cree sing to the Land, "We are ever grateful that you take care of us; we are ever so grateful that you provide for us; pity us for we are small". The Land was, and still is, ever so sacred to the Sakaw Cree people.

So prominent to our people was the Land's voice that even our clothing spoke of the Land. Although ever so decorative, the designs' true intent was never to be overlooked. The designs spoke of where a people lived on the Land. For example, if a people lived by the Water, then their designs would speak of all that existed around and in the water: the Fish, the Flowers, each spoke about their place on the Land. Or if a people lived near the mountains, then it was the mountains that were represented in the designs. The people showed respect for the Land by carrying these designs on their clothing. Wherever the people went, they carried constant representation of their Land with them. The designs were a language that spoke of where the people lived and how they moved.

The Land also offers to the people very special and sacred places. The people help the Land speak by protecting and honouring these sacred places. For example, a place by a certain lake could carry spiritual significance, so a song or design might have been given to honour that place. In many cases, the particular place might have been an area which had helped the people to survive, a place where the fish came to shore, for example. That place might then have been honoured each year with a feast. The Land was, and still is, ever so sacred to our people, the people of the Land, Sakaw Cree.

When a man walks the Land from one end of his territory to the next he comes to understand its every move. This understanding does not stop at the level of physical environment.

When his children need Fish in their diet, he goes to the Water and asks if it will be all right to move on its surface. This may be done the night before. The hunter might take a small gift to the Water, maybe a handful of Fire ashes. The Water likes ashes because when they are spread across the surface, it leaves the images of smiling, happy faces. Quiet time with each other; that is what is needed — acknowledgement.

The next morning the Water would grant the hunter his request by giving calm days for as many days the hunter would take Fire ashes. To have the Water not working with you can mean windy, rough waters.

The hunter asks the Water for a moose to feed his family. The Water can make a deal with any being. He might ask the mosquitoes to bring the moose into its depths. In many ways these deals that are made are much the same kind of deals that any human makes, providing, of course that it is done in a respectful manner. When one goes and asks for help from another, the unspoken deal might be that he has to return some day, a deal is in order. When you go to the Water and ask, you give.

What does the Water have to give to the flies to bring this huge beast to its shores? Let's ask.

Little mosquitoes, this spring you called to me to help you with your eggs. You were afraid at the time that the Water wasn't bringing you enough nourishment to help you grow. That was done. Do you remember this time? The mosquito replies, "I have grown well and strong, thank you Water." The Water and the mosquito have come to an understanding. They must work together.

That night when the hunter has taken his ashes once again to the Water as an offering, the Water tells him in the smiling faces the deal he has made with the mosquito. Tomorrow at this time the moose will be directed to the depths of the Water. The hunter the next day waits and, sure enough, gets his reward.

The seasons are tied so closely to the Land that they are almost one. Everything goes by the seasons. We all know that moose run to the Water to escape the mosquitoes and flies in the mid-summer. But did we have any idea that somewhere someone was making a deal about something? The Land has these powers. Only the Land can make such deals with higher powers such as seasons. We as humans know this. That is why we have this close relationship with the Land. We talk about the Land being an important source of knowledge and before we know it the Water and mosquito enter. There comes that circularity of Life again: every thing relates to each other.

The binding force of these relationships is the Land, referred to as "THE MOTHER" to all beings that walk her ground. She is the one that plants the seeds of wisdom and respect for all and each. To speak about the Land is to speak about the interconnectedness within the natural world. However, it is more than this. It goes beyond the surface level of ecology. All beings are related, connected; they are one. Humans are the brothers and sisters to the Animals, the Trees, and all that is part of our Mother Earth.

Sources of Knowledge: Spiritual Messengers

There has never been any question in the minds of the Sakaw Cree of the past and of today as to who is the higher power. It is "the Creator". Sakaw Cree people of today might live differently than those of centuries past, but this basic belief remains the same. Today, as before, when a person needs help or seeks knowledge, he or she goes to a "medicine man", the Creator's messenger.

These messengers bring direct knowledge and teachings from the Creator to all beings. These messengers are chosen not only by the Creator, but by the Elders of that community as well. These chosen ones are a gift to the people from the Creator. They are born into power and knowledge. When they are brought into this world, their learning begins from birth until the time they return back to the spirit world. The Elders take this chosen child and begin his lifelong teaching. The teachings will be based on the understanding of the higher power, the Creator. This student will grow to be a teacher and a messenger as soon as possible. The people await his new and fresh knowledge.

The spiritual philosophy he gathers from the Creator and the Elders will be re-taught to others when it is time. In the time that this teacher is teaching the philosophy of the Creator, he or she can at no time think of himself or herself as "the power". Messengers do not control the basic teachings. So, they might say something like, "Creator, I am small, I am helpless. Please help these people, they ask of you". The teacher must not be the one who controls knowledge; instead, the teacher is one of the providers of knowledge.

The spiritual teacher has a heavy responsibility in his teachings to the people. Sometimes the people go to these spiritual teachers on a daily basis for small problems. Often it is just to sit and listen and learn. It must be kept in mind that a spiritual teacher is not the only teacher in the community; there are many. Each teacher has his or her own distinct chosen "profession", shall we say. There is the hunter, the tree person, the medicine root person and the list goes on and on. What is unique about the spiritual teacher is that most of the other teachers seek the knowledge he carries with him.

When problems are too great for the spiritual teacher, he can call on the help of the Creator directly. This may be done in many ways, one of which is the sweat lodge. The sweat lodge is a small, dome-like "school house". The lessons include how to take better care of the body and the spirit or the soul. Lodges like these are common in native communities even today. They remain as the most active teaching centres.

> A sweatlodge is made from willows that are interwoven to create a half-moon, dome-like structure. It traditionally was covered with animal hide, but today canvas is used. Before the willows are cut, the ground must be given tobacco. This is what must be done: an offering to the willow tree, the Land, Water and Stone spirits.
>
> The ground is taken and made into a mound where the pipe or the spiritual powers will sit. Again an offering is given to the Stones and to the Fire for heating them. Everything is acknowledged, everything has a place.
>
> The messenger conducts the lodge. He calls on the spirits. Whatever kind of teaching spirit is needed is called. Within the lodge, teaching is done in many ways. There are the oral teachings, the spiritual healing, and the physical healing (the body). Learning and healing merge into one process. The spiritual messenger makes it possible for all people to have access to spiritual knowledge through the sweatlodge.

The spiritual world is still the main source of knowledge for Sakaw Cree. There are many sources of knowledge in the worlds of the spirit that have not been used for a long time. The return of the spiritual world to the Indian community can mean a return not only to an old but also a new philosophy.

The law that followed after Canada made treaties with Indian nations, called the *Indian Act*, outlawed First Nations' spirituality and attempted to put an end to our way of thinking and the way we gather knowledge. Taking our way of thinking and replacing it with another does not always work, especially when it is done by force, as in this case. The language of the Cree was spiritual language. It contained secrets of how to enter the spiritually philosophical thought. Outlawing all aspects of these processes left a people looking for the messengers, their spiritual teachers.

THE CROSSING OF KNOWLEDGE

Knowledge comes from many sources. As I have described in the previous section, a Sakaw Cree worldview acknowledges the Elders, the Animals, the Land and the Spiritual dimension as primary sources of knowledge. These sources do not exist in isolation of each other but are deeply intertwined, or interrelated. To "educate" a child using these sources of knowledge involves a process that interweaves, or interrelates, the child in among all these sources. Such an educational system is not foreign to the child, for the child comes into our world already able to tap into these sources of knowledge. The newborn has engaged and continues to engage in a process of "crossing knowledge" with all beings. In times past, the affirmation and support of this process formed the basis of Sakaw Cree education. To provide a truly Sakaw Cree education today, this process which is natural to the child, must once again be nurtured.

In order to explain how this process occurs naturally and how it can be nurtured throughout a child's lifetime, I must first discuss the concept of "beings", that we are all equal and are of one creation, without lines or barriers, free.

Within this discussion I shall look at the idea of "spirit rings" and what it means to acknowledge and use them (versus what happens to children when their "schooling" denies them).

Following from my examination of the concepts of "beings" and "spirit rings", I shall discuss the notions of "new knowledge", "old knowledge", the "crossing of knowledge", which results from the free communication among beings, and the "sharing of knowledge", where all beings teach each other as was intended by the Creator. These ideas form the foundation of a Sakaw Cree philosophy of education.

Beings and Spirit Rings

The concept of "being" involves viewing reality as multi-dimensional. Rose Auger, a Cree Elder, states,

> It [a being] is a spirit that is in a different plane than this Earth plane. It can be an ancestor who at one time was here. Or it can be the spirit of an eagle or even the spirit of the moon. The real spirit in the moon is who we address as "Grandmother". And then we have other beings like Thunder Beings. They exist in the spiritual plane. We can't physically see them, but we know they are there and we have our connection to the Thunder Beings and know what they look like spiritually. So that's what beings are. There's beings below the earth. There's beings in the mountains. ... There's all kinds of beings and Indian people know this. And it's all been passed down from generation to generation of the knowledge of these beings and powers that they carry.

(Rose Auger, 1995)

Acknowledging planes or dimensions other than just the physical one opens doors to different kinds of communication. Elder Rose Auger states,

> When you have a human being then you have a body, a face and a person you know is here; you can comprehend that. But people who have lost connection to the Great Mystery, they don't have what we have. They've created a body; us, we have our visions, our connections. So our connection to the Creator allows us to relate to other Beings, the Moon, Animals, etc. And we can relate to that spirit.

(Rose Auger, 1995)

Understanding how communication among all beings is possible requires an understanding of the notion of "spirit rings".

The Creator gave all beings the same right to this planet; this was made clear in the natural law, a law that has been passed down for generations in our traditional teachings. The Creator gave all beings the tools to reach out and communicate with each other, a kind of invisible code, a code with which all beings are born. This code I shall call "spirit rings". These rings are needed to communicate and interact with each other. It works like this. If one being is reaching out, the other will read and also reach out in a language, a spiritual language.

Imagine yourself standing on a very crowded sidewalk, at a bus stop, for example. Your eyes are focussed forward. You need not turn around and count all the people around you to know that you are in the company of many human beings. You can "feel" their presence, their existence. Though you might attribute this feeling to your senses of sound or even smell, I suggest that it is more than this. It is that you are "tuned in" to the human "being", that you have an awareness of the human form of being that goes beyond the five physical senses.

Acknowledging other beings and their existence can be of a similar nature. As I sit in the middle of a beautiful, natural area, I feel the presence of many beings, the tree beings, for example. I *feel* their presence; I acknowledge their existence. By extending into my own spirit rings I can be "tuned in" to the spirit rings of other forms of being. Perhaps a short story will provide a clearer vision of how these rings might look and respond.

> I remember walking along a quiet, little pond when I was a lot younger, just a boy. This was a frog pond. I can remember because of the sounds that came from it. Frogs in the spring — there is no sound like it. As I got closer to the edge I could see large dark spots in the still Water, almost greyish black. The closer I got I could see more and more of them. I had seen the likes of these before but had never investigated them until that time. I entered the Water to my knees and leaned over to get a closer look. What I saw was little black eyes staring back up at me. They were eggs, frog eggs. I could see the eggs inside but I wondered what was that stuff around it. I reached in with my bare hand and attempted to scoop them up. I couldn't. They kept sliding through my fingers, like slippery coating or film around the egg. Why was it there? To protect the egg? From what or whom? Maybe it was there to help the eggs grow? Maybe it was food? I left the eggs as I found them. Somehow my interest had been satisfied.

Spirit rings, then, are like a coat or film around each being. They are a means of communication among beings; they are the key to accessing knowledge from many sources.

Portrayals of humans who can communicate with Animals are not unknown in our contemporary Canadian culture. There was the "Grizzly Adams" television series, for example. Characters like these are depicted as "special" or as having extraordinary abilities. However, to our people, nurturing this openness to other forms of beings, including animal beings, was a very core part of our educational system.

Ceremonies were given to us by the Creator so that different beings might be present in one fixed area. The sweatlodge is a place where beings come together and communicate as equal beings. In this context, as a human, you are no more than a participant in a congregation of beings, including the willow being, the Stone, the Fire, the Water, and so on. Then with the presence of the bear spirit being or the eagle spirit being, a powerful gathering force takes place in the sweatlodge. You are giving up your human self to be able to unite with all other spirits that are there; you are opening yourself up to merge with a congregation of beings. Through your prayers you humbly acknowledge that you are only a small part of this union of beings. By shifting from your physical being into your spiritual self, into your spirit rings, you are able to openly communicate with other beings.

Sometimes when you come out of a powerful sweatlodge, when your body has been put up as an offering and your mind has been put to rest and your spirit has travelled freely, and you lie down on the ground with your arms and legs sprawled out and look up at the Trees, you feel so good that you can see again the same rings around every being that is surrounding you. What was experienced in the sweatlodge in a spiritual state continues to be manifest in the physical state. You can see the spirit rings of the winged ones as they fly by and you can see the spirit rings radiating power that the tree beings carry. These are the ways that the Creator has given to us, the Sakaw Cree. As long as there are Trees on this great Land and as long as the winged ones continue to fly and the four-leggeds continue to roam, we, the Sakaw Cree, will continue to respect and acknowledge the existence of all beings and keep open the paths to communication which are made possible through spirit rings.

The whole time we have been talking through this journey, without realizing it, we have been checking ourselves to see if this is reality as we know it or if it is some kind of spiritual path we allowed ourselves to enter. Again, without realizing it, we were actually walking down a spirit path of some kind, just the same kind that little children talking to animal beings do, doubt-free or questioning-free paths. We, the Sakaw Cree, know this as the spirit walk.

As we know it, no one being can take a walk like what I have been describing without having these spirit rings around his/her being. Like the frog eggs and the questions I had back then, these rings are the key to what path walks are all about. Perhaps they are the test that the Creator has given all of us, a test that we need as beings to help us get over this thing westerners know as reality. The word "faith" might be used, but I think the phenomenon is something bigger than this human label. Faith can restrict; the word can restrict humans to one area, one belief, religion or god. To our people this cannot be the case, because spirit walks are too prevalent in our every day lives and in the teachings of the Elders.

We do not see this all lumped under the name of religion. It, the Elders believe, is the way we can open and close access to any world we choose, and with this unique gift of entering and exiting worlds comes greater knowledge. All of a sudden we are not dealing with just one world or one reality; we are dealing with many, as many as we feel we can handle. The more one can handle, the more knowledge one obtains. For example, if I were to live in the world with one path, one definition of reality limited to one plane of existence, I could very likely exhaust myself on that one path by the time I reach elder-hood. We all know what Canadian society thinks of people who are old and tired. They are put in a place where their usefulness is not important. In our culture, however, our Old Ones continue their spirit walks throughout their lives, constantly bringing forth new knowledge.

By allowing ourselves to accept spirit rings, we also accept that we can take a spirit walk when needed or when called. In the end, knowledge is moved from being to being. To understand this movement of knowledge among beings, we shall begin with how a child brings new knowledge into this world.

New Knowledge

Understanding knowledge in the purest sense is very important to our people, especially in recognizing that Knowledge is sent directly from the Creator through a child. Elder Rose Auger states,

> In our own traditional way we view a child as a spirit, an entity that comes from the spirit world and brings its own duty and its own identity and its own knowledge from the spirit world. It's new knowledge. The spirit of the child has an endless amount of new knowledge and senses. When he comes into the world he develops those senses to what are his gifts.

(Rose Auger, 1995)

This new knowledge of the child is accessible to Elders, as is illustrated in the following story. The images in this story were and are still quite common in any Native community today. Because of the changing times, however, such an occurrence might be less open than it has been in the past.

> This is her first child. Her growing child within is preparing to enter the world. She is visiting the Old Ones once more. She feels it is time to learn more about her growing child. This is the way it is done with the Old Ones. You visit them; you learn from them. Before long she is entering their home. With a sudden burst of energy she is greeted by two of the community's older women. To them this is a special time, not only because of the child's physical being but because of the new knowledge this child carries with it. "Come sit, young granddaughter, sit here", says one of the kohkoms; the other gets her tea. The attention is welcomed gratefully by the young mother. She sits in the same place she sat the last time she was there, her back rested, hand to the side. She is comfortable. Already the mood changes, breathing slows down. All three are in tune with each other, silence.
>
> Then, with her eyes closed, one of the kohkoms lifts her hands upward above her head with continuous prayer. She then moves them slowly, still in prayer, downward, resting them on the young mother's belly. Still in prayer she begins her communication, her hands still both pressed softly.
>
> Soon the tenseness turns to relaxation. Talking becomes open and then everyone talks. "He is a happy child, he smiles a lot", says the kohkom. "He needs you to eat more Fish, maybe those fish eggs you ate not long ago; he likes those. He talked of the winged ones, yellow ones, little yellow winged ones. These are the Spirit beings he talks to the most."
>
> The kohkom goes on to say that because this child has the gift of talking to other spiritual beings like the winged ones, he shall be given the name of YELLOW WINGED ONES, a powerful name. "In the spirit world the yellow winged ones are highly respected for their good luck and honesty," says the Kohkom. Because of this name, this child will have the power to work with people who have hard times in their lives. In this name-giving to the child all people recognize the power that comes with it.
>
> "Granddaughter, they say you are healthy; your child is healthy. Prepare." With that the grandmother ends her prayer with a song, hands still on the belly of the young mother. Before walking home the mother talks with the kohkoms once more over tea.

Because of the changing times this sort of communication among Creator, child and Elder does not go on quite so openly. However, because generations have communicated this way, it simply does not disappear altogether. What happens is that different approaches are taken, leaving the basic understanding still intact.

The newborn child, then, is a source of knowledge from the Creator. Elder Rose Auger states,

> When children are born into this world their new knowledge is endless. Because they have that connection, a powerful connection with whatever, and they [the Elders] can learn from this spirit of the child. This spirit has not been interfered with; his spirit is strong.

(Rose Auger, 1995)

The Elders recognize the newborn's purity of knowledge, that this knowledge is endless, and that the newborn is connected powerfully, without interference, pure.

As such, newborns arrive with an intact process of accessing knowledge from other beings. This is possible because the unborn child has been in an unbounded, free state of being. I call upon the dandelion being to explain this further.

> When spring moves towards summer, many great changes occur on the earth. Birds return, then settle on the Land; Trees reach upward with their changing colours. Not far behind, Animals move, looking for each and their own kind. Amongst these many changes one being comes to mind, that of the dandelion. Growing dandelion works its way up to the open air; then it settles in with the brightest of yellows; dandelion yellow, they call it. But as it moves towards summer something changes, the colour of yellow disappears. What replaces it is a unique, circular, ball-like thing. This ball looks like it is made up of many little arms, branches. Soon the whole landscape is filled with so many of these white circular images. When you get up close to them, they seem so perfect in their creation; they are one. But then, the Wind being blows and blows, and soon ones turn to millions of free, new beings flying through the air. Free.

To describe the free state of a child's whole knowledge, I think I could find no better comparison: free like the dandelion seeds in the air; there are no lines or restrictions. The child's new and whole knowledge is pure and free. Like the dandelion, the Creator gives the seed, then growth, only to have the new seed blow in the wind, free, a time to communicate with others. As the new seed blows from the white ball, it is set free to discover all other beings. So, too, does the Creator give the gift of whole knowledge to the child.

Into the care of the Elders, the child is sent out into the world. Birth. This child has a firm understanding of what it takes to communicate with all other beings. This communication might not come in the same form as what we as "mature adults" recognize; nevertheless, it is still there. The newborn's motor skills are not yet developed; the spoken language is also not yet present. What is there is this deeper understanding of communication, a set path, a path that was learned in the unborn stage. This we call the "chosen path". As in the story above, the Creator had given the child yet unborn a name which reflected what his chosen path might be. All three parties accept these words that give the name, "yellow winged ones". By the Creator giving this name, much of this child's future will depend on how well the channels are left open. That is where the Elders come into play, like the kohkom who put her hands on the belly of the young mother; she is assuming her role. She, like many Elders, is like the path openers. They work to guide all the young to their respective chosen paths.

Without the work of the Elders, it would be easy for anyone to forget his or her chosen path. Unfortunately, this is what is happening to our chosen young today: they have little or no path openers in their lives. Then, too, some choose not to use such channels even if they be placed directly in front, as in the gifted child or the name. I can see that the physical task the Elders have, keeping paths open, is a bit overwhelming for them. With the language diminishing, the new Elders know less and less about the overall value of keeping paths open. On one hand this might seem hopeless, but on the other there is this new-found strength in keeping communication lines open and free. When you have had this way of thought in your past for thousands of years, it is so deep in the blood of your veins, you do not even know it. Only when we sit down with our Elders or our Old Ones do we see and understand. It is still there, clear as a blue day.

Old Knowledge: The Education of the Child

The context in which the Elders strive to keep paths open is one that results from generations of accumulation of knowledge which is based on the natural laws of the Creator. This context, or system of "Old Knowledge", is founded on ideas that have been discussed above. That is to say, the Old Ones believe that when a child comes into this world he brings with him many sources of knowledge. These sources are often called gifts from the Creator. A newborn child, then, does not come into this world blank or empty. On the contrary, the newborn is whole and full of knowledge. He or she also has the ability to communicate with other beings. All beings cross each other's paths, free moving. There are no lines or barriers. This is what a newborn child might "see" even before his eyes are opened. As a child, or two-legged being, the first thing that is done is to recognize all other beings. The Tree, Water, Fire and everything else is seen as equal. The Old Ones believe that all beings communicate with each other even before physical birth takes place. In any case, all beings are quite familiar with one another already. Before the child can even see or speak a language, he or she is communicating.

This unique ability, or gift, continues as the child grows. Even before a child has spoken the first word, much communication has gone on already. What the spoken word does is merely open the line of communication with other two-legged beings. When the doors to this unique world are opened to others, that is where the Elders come in. Elders are masters of opening and closing the doors to other beings. They have been recognized as the true masters of teaching the knowledge of all other beings. Because they have a lifetime of knowledge, they can tap into all forms of knowledge. Theirs is the domain of "old knowledge". Within this domain, the process of recognizing and nurturing new knowledge was in place; deeply hidden in some communities today, it still is.

The uniting of old and new knowledge, then, traditionally formed the basis of a child's education. The Elders see the child progress; when the time is right they decide how the child should proceed. The child and the Elders begin a life-long bond together.

Elders do not attempt to discourage the way a child looks at or communicates knowledge. They encourage it; they broaden this knowledge. This is the time that we know as teaching, as expanding the sources of knowledge, as "school".

In the teaching or expansion of knowledge by the Elder, there is a reinforcing of the child's awareness of all the beings. The Old Ones take recognition of the child's spiritual companions, all the spiritual equals with which this child works. They assist the child to work within this spiritual realm. For example, a child might be given the spirit of the bear. So from that point on, the bear spirit becomes one of the main focuses of that child's existence. That child will learn from the bear and will call on the bear as a working partner. That child will think like a bear and can contribute to the community in doing so.

As the Elders nurture the child, there are checking points. For each child, what kind of knowledge shows up more than others, what the Creator has given, is noted. For example, the child might have a strong sense of working with his or her hands. Or he or she might have a deep interest in the Water source.

Once these predominant kinds of knowledge become more and more evident, the Elders designate a specialist for the child. The child will be in the company of this specialist for years to come. The child might become a physical healer, so that he or she is best put in the company of a physical healer, one who works with the hands. In another case, the child might be sent to a plant healer, one who works with plants, if that child has been given the gift to understand the plants (where they can be found and how to use them). Other examples include the child who is given the gift of animal communicator or the child who, as a water communicator, understands the Water, the Fish and all that moves beneath. A final example is the child who has been noted to be a tree communicator. To understand the tree means to understand the roots. Soon the roots become a source of knowledge in themselves. Doors open when you discover the way to communicate with beings within beings.

Through his or her relationship with the Elders and then with a specialist, the child's original ability to communicate in the many, many different worlds is greatly expanded. In the process, the child comes to understand that there are sources of knowledge within; she learns to access the knowledge she has brought with her into this world. Old and New unite.

The Elders also learn from the child and her knowledge. They re-acquaint themselves with the child's "whole knowledge". The Elders admire the child for her boundary-less sense of knowledge. The child is respected for her New or Whole knowledge.

Another way of looking at accessing knowledge is through the imagery of an eagle. An eagle in flight soars through the air until he focuses on his next meal and swoops down and skims the surface of the Water. When he breaks the surface of the Water with his claws, he pulls out a fish, taking only what he needs. The Water closes again. Like the eagle, a young mind accesses the knowledge it needs without having learned any particular accessing skills because it is a natural process; the sources of knowledge from other worlds have not been blocked. The doors to other worlds open and close just as the surface of the Water opens and closes to the eagle as he gathers his food.

Let me give an example. When my four-year-old son was first exposed to his guardian spirit, he was more than willing to push it to its limits. His guardian is the hawk and his words to me were, "I ride my spirit; we ride over the Trees. Dad, can you ride with us? We go so fast." Indeed, the knowledge to which my son has access is limitless.

In the Sakaw Cree worldview, there are many worlds and children have direct access to them. To venture into these other worlds, as children do, is to experience the core knowledge of my Cree people. Elders support and facilitate this process.

Crossing Knowledge

The creating of a sweatlodge provides a means for understanding the concept of "crossing knowledge". To make a sweatlodge, willows are twisted to cross each other, creating a dome-like structure.

> When the willow tree is approached, a small amount of tobacco is given to its being as a sign of acknowledgement and respect. When each tree is taken, thought and prayer are given to all beings with which the person works. One tree might be given to the winged ones; another might be for the four-legged. Thought and recognition are given. These Trees are taken to a place that is clean and free of any pain or bad thoughts. Tobacco is again given to the

Land, the mother, for her recognition. A sweatlodge will be built. When the poles are placed in the ground, each pole represents some kind of being. Then the willow is bent to meet another being from the opposite side. As this goes on, what begins to happen is a crossing of other beings. Willows representing beings cross to touch and support each other, leaving a tight circular structure. A sweatlodge is born. The sweatlodge is where beings meet to talk with each other.

The willows are the Spirit Beings that connect us to all the universe; so their crossing becomes a place where there are no boundaries, there are no set rules of thought. The sweatlodge can be a place where humans can cross over to the many different worlds, a crossing place of knowledge.

The crossing of knowledge happens like the willow Trees crossing to make a sweatlodge. Old knowledge meets new and together they form whole knowledge. Other processes for combining old and new knowledge include the vision pit, or vision quest, as people like to call it today, and the daily practice of lighting smudge and praying. These are all tools for crossing over, for connecting with our spirit rings.

All beings, including human, have the ability to cross over to seek and gather each others' knowledge. Earlier this was called "communicating freely with other beings". Among all beings, the winged ones (Birds), the four-legged (moose, deer, etc.), the Trees, Water and so on, none is more prominent than the next and there is the recognition and respect of each other. From this comes talking or communicating in a language known only in the spirit world. Trees talk to Birds, and so on, all made possible by this "spirit talk". Elder Rose Auger states,

> When you are of that path and you live by natural laws of the Creator, you can feel a lot of times you need to go here for some reason. That's spirit talk and it comes and goes anytime. But you, the human being, have to be in a clean state; you have to love yourself and take care of yourself. You don't do anything which is abusive to yourself. And you have to be like a channel that is free of anger, jealousy, selfishness — these are things that inhibit so many people.

> (Rose Auger, 1995)

Young children, unlike adults, live in clean states naturally. Spirit talk, communicating with other beings, comes much easier for them. Here is an example of how this talking might occur.

My son, Sohkes, who is four, said to me as we talked about our return to our first home by the lake, "That bear is still around the cabin, Dad; he's looking for food". "Are you scared?" I asked him. "No", he replied, "because that is Neepin's [his sister's] spirit and he knows that we're his friend, and you know what Neepin always feeds him in that same spot, you know that place right by the Water. That's why I'm not afraid and you know what else? My spirit is the hawk and I could fly; Hawks and bears are good friends, that's right, eh Dad?"

There is still the checking point that a child needs to refine his free thought, but basically his path is clear when communicating with other beings. It is this open freedom to which I am referring when I talk about open path. There is no doubt in the mind of the bear, nor is there in my son. The hawk? Well, his voice is waiting to speak.

It is this kind of language that has carried our people for thousands of years on the Land. Sharing, speaking to each and to all other beings. It is a way that we need to affirm to our children and our teachers. It is a way that has not left us, a way that is still with us.

Old and new knowledge must continue to work with each other; paths must stay open. Open paths are like the sweat lodge when the willow branches cross: something powerful happens. Open paths allow for communication among all beings, which affirms the sharing of knowledge.

Sharing Knowledge

Years ago, our traditional world was based on sharing, not only in terms of the essentials of survival, but more importantly, with regard to knowledge. *Knowledge was the main commodity in the traditional world of our people.* The Creator's beings from all worlds shared with each other. This was done in many different forms. For example, among the two-legged (humans), when death approached, the one who was about to leave this earth passed on old knowledge to one of the next generation through special ceremonies. I myself have gained knowledge in this way.

Sometimes the Creator gives certain powers to one special being so that it might be carried and passed on to other beings, shared. The owl is one such being, who might have been chosen to teach the two-legged the meaning of sharing and connectedness.

Whoo-hoo, the owl, the owl call, such a distinctive call, a call that speaks a language like no other language of the being world. The owl is a communicator that can be understood by all beings and is so well respected in the being world that when he sits on his tree he commands respect. What is it about this owl, this winged-one being, that carries such wisdom and deep knowledge but sends fear into all beings, misunderstood fear, this powerful winged-one being?

This winged-one, the owl, is the carrier of all information directly from the spiritual world. He is not just restricted to what is "bad information" as many might think. He can be and is also a carrier of what is good and pure information. When he sits on his tree, his eyes are fixed in one position, leaving only his head to move with such authority, giving the impression he is not fully in this physical world. I am told that he is not only in this physical world but is equally present in the other world, spirit world, being world. He is a great representative of both worlds and has equal respect and authority in those two worlds.

What is it that gives this winged-one being such authority in these two complex worlds? The Creator gave this being this authority not only by giving him the wisdom, knowledge, and farsightedness to walk in those two worlds, but also gave him the physical appearance which represents what we know as spirit rings, visible in the appearance of his eyes. The eyes represent the beings, each separate in their own right, distinctive. Separate, side by side but located in one fixed area, the head. The owl's head.

What is even more unique about this being's eyes is a striking ring around them, a circular ring around each eye. The rings around each eye do not close but are joined. These rings around the eyes join together to form one; this is the crossing point. Crossing knowledge. Beings crossing, uniting independently but free to form one.

This is the power the Creator has given this wise being, this winged-one we know as the owl — a sign and reminder to all other beings, including humans. This is the Creator's way of reminding us of this connectedness that he wishes all beings to have. It is his wish for all to work together as one but still stay independent. This is the message he left on the eyes of the owl for all to be reminded. His word is marked on the head of the messenger, the owl.

Our people have always had a deep fear of the owl. The reason might be that the owl was given the right to carry many messages. As humans we only remember the owl when he brings messages that are "bad". Since the coming of the European we adopted the idea that bad is evil, the devil. Traditionally our people looked at something tragic that happened as "meant to be". That is the way of the Creator, the Creator's will.

We learned from the owl and the owl was grateful to let us use his name in one of our dances, "the owl dance", which is still used today in high regard across this land by many nations. The owl dance represents unity, connectedness, wholeness, sharing of knowledge. This owl dance is one of the highest of dances because it brings two human beings together to connect as one. Two distinctive human beings come together as one man and woman — two of Creator's gifts together as one. This dance requires both man and woman to physically touch and dance as one. However, this name, the owl dance, was not given because of the physical nature itself but something more.

Like the rings around the owl's eyes, the two humans are brought together in unity to share spiritual knowledge. Two spiritual rings come together as one. This again is what I have called "crossing of knowledge". We, as Indian people, are born with the gift to recognize each other's spiritual rings. We are born to feel when another being is reaching out and wishing to cross knowledge. This is what the owl dance represents. This dance you can still see today. It is a dance that requires that your body and spirit be whole before entering into it. This is the way of the owl when we see him sitting high on the tree taking care of not only the physical Land but the spiritual as well. He sits there representing himself and the Creator as one. The owl, the old wise owl.

There are many other examples of how the sharing of knowledge happens among all beings. The crossing of knowledge is a process that can occur among all beings, but the sharing aspect adds the dimension of intent and responsibility. Especially for the human being, sharing implies a willingness, a choice, to work towards uniting old and new knowledge, knowledge from multi-dimensional sources, from among all beings.

THIS JOURNEY'S END IS A BEGINNING: SUMMARY AND CONCLUSIONS

The coming of the Europeans to North America disrupted and altered the way of life of First Nation peoples, which made it difficult for us to maintain our long-standing processes for having old and new knowledge come together as one. The newcomers, over the years, worked to separate our spiritual connections, replacing our ways with their own structured system, which we know as schools. When our traditional children entered these schools they were taught a different way, a way that has not been good for us as a people nor for the maintenance of our spiritual connectedness.

We are truly at a disadvantage when entering the school systems as they are structured today. We enter into these structured systems having been encouraged by our families and the Elders to maintain our birthright, our spiritualness. However, in the schools we are taught to not rely on our spiritual knowledge, our spirit rings, or to communicate with other spiritual beings. We are taught not to communicate or connect with all other beings. Instead, we are taught that we are individuals who need to rely on one primary individual, the classroom teacher, for our knowledge.

We are at a disadvantage when having to learn a foreign language, the English language, a language that speaks of the human individual as the superior being. Talking to other beings or following our spiritual dreams is classified as myth or fiction, not truth. *Emphasis on humans as only body and mind diminishes humans as also spirit*, and spiritual rings become fantasy, non-existent, and therefore deemed not important. The structure of Canadian schooling tells us that spirit is separate from teaching and learning. Even knowledge is considered separate, something out there to be poured into the minds of the children by the all-knowing classroom teacher. We are told the Tree, the Birds, the Animals are separate from us and function at their own levels of existence without crossing over into ours.

We as a people who have been functioning for thousands and thousands of years on this Land have been forced by law to turn against our own ways, our spiritual ways. What is in schools today is truly not our way of thinking and it is truly not the way that the Creator had intended for us to be. It is not our way to disregard all other beings. Without a system that supports the use of our spirit rings which the Creator has given us at birth, we are clearly at a disadvantage. Without spirit rings we become floating, spiritless beings, alone. We float in time and space without truly connecting with other beings.

All said, that does not mean that we cannot learn these new ways, since they are here to stay. We will and do learn the Euro-Canadian ways, but in learning them we should not give away our spiritualness, the Creator's gift to us. I believe we can learn the foreigners' ways and still hang on to our own spiritual knowledge. We can be true to this crossing of knowledge old and new, as true as an owl flies, reminding us that this is the way of the Creator. The Creator gave us these gifts; surely, the intention was that we hang on to them.

We, the Sakaw Cree, are a unique people and we have a way of thinking that differs from that of the Euro-Canadians. We are connected, yet free — free to access traditional knowledge, old and new, as we wish.

The educational systems that will emerge as true Sakaw Cree educational systems must support the continuation of processes which acknowledge and affirm the spiritual connectedness of all that exists. These systems will honor the interrelatedness of all beings and encourage the crossing of knowledge among all beings. Sources of knowledge will be not just books or classroom teachers but the Elders, the Animals, the Land, and the Spiritual realm through which all sources of knowledge are interconnected, in which old and new knowledge unite, and by which we become who we as humans, as Sakaw Cree, are intended to be.

NOTES

[1] *Editor's Note:* Various words (e.g., the Land, Water, Fire, Animals, Birds, Fish, Soil, Spirit Beings) which are common nouns in the English language and culture, in this chapter usually begin with an uppercase letter, as proper nouns (especially when used in the plural). This convention is adopted as a rough means of cap-

turing in translation the respect in which these parts of creation are held in the author's Cree language and culture.The editor asks the reader's indulgence for any inconsistencies in the application of these difficult-to-articulate stylistic rules. No disrespect is intended to reader, author, or creatures.

REFERENCES

Cajete, Gregory
1994   *Looking to the Mountain*. Durango, Colo.: Kivaki Press.
Monture-Okanee, Patricia
1992   "Ka-Nin-Geh-Heh-Gah-E-Sa-Nonh-Ya-Gah", *Canadian Journal of Women's Literature* VI: 119–123.

FURTHER READING

Battiste, Marie and Jean Barman
1995   *First Nations Education in Canada: The Circle Unfolds*. Vancouver, B.C.: University of British Columbia Press.
Hanna, Darwin and Mamie Henry (comps. and eds.)
1995   *Our Tellings*. Vancouver, B.C.: University of British Columbia Press.
Joseph, Gene (comp.)
1992   *Sharing the Knowledge: A First Nations Resource Guide*. Vancouver, B.C.: University of British Columbia Press.
O'Meara, Sylvia and Douglas A. West (eds.)
1996   *From Our Eyes: Learning from Indigenous Peoples*. Toronto: Garamond Press.

PART 4

Self-Determination

CHAPTER *14*

SELF-DETERMINATION
EDITOR'S INTRODUCTION TO PART 4:

J. Rick Ponting

THE MEANING OF "SELF-DETERMINATION"

The term "self-determination" is open to a wide variety of meanings and can be used to refer to individuals or collectivities. At its root it refers to a degree of autonomy that enables individuals or collectivities to shape their own economic, social, cultural, and political destiny. By virtue of the interdependencies that inhere in social organization, no individuals or peoples exercise absolute self-determination; self-determination is necessarily a relative term. However, the *Indian Act*, with its imposition of colonial policies and practices involving the systematic subordination of a category of people defined in law, is the antithesis of self-determination.

The Royal Commission on Aboriginal Peoples (1996b: 178–184) concluded that the right of self-determination is vested in aboriginal *nations*, rather than small, local communities. The Commission defines an aboriginal nation as "a sizeable body of Aboriginal people with a shared sense of national identity that constitutes the predominant population in a certain territory or collection of territories." The Commission adds (181): "In our view, an Aboriginal nation cannot be identified in a mechanical fashion by reference to a detailed set of objective criteria". Hence, the Commission is vague on just how many aboriginal nations presently exist in Canada; it says that there are between sixty and eighty historically based aboriginal nations in Canada, as compared to approximately one thousand local aboriginal communities.

The Commission (1996b: 175) is careful to distinguish between self-government and self-determination. Taking a narrower approach than that identified in the first paragraph of this chapter, the Commission defines self-determination in purely political terms as the right of an aboriginal nation to choose how it will be governed. Self-government, in contrast, "is one natural outcome of the exercise of the right of self-determination and refers to the right of peoples to exercise political autonomy. Self-determination refers to the collective power of choice; self-government is one possible result of that choice".

Just as the daily existence of individuals is multifacetted, so, too, is self-determination. Political leaders deal with this inherent complexity of self-determination through the use of "condensation symbols" (Jhappan, 1990: 21),[1] like the terms "aboriginal rights", "sovereignty", and "self-government", which gloss over differences of interpretation and thereby facilitate the mobilization of support. Institutions of international law and diplomacy, such as the United Nations, deal with the complexity of self-determination by constructing elaborate codes such as the charter of The United Nations and the draft Declaration of the Rights of Indigenous Peoples. The latter contains a lengthy preamble and over forty articles which specify rights which the international community proposes be recognized for indigenous peoples. In effect, it also specifies the meaning of the term "self-determination", and the particulars of its implementation, as it would apply in international law to indigenous people. In the unlikely event that it be adopted in anything like its present form, the Declaration will recognize such indigenous rights as the right to an indigenous identity; the right of indigenous peoples not to be forcibly relocated from their lands; the right to establish and control their educational systems and institutions in their own language; the right to maintain and strengthen their distinctive spiritual and material relationship with the lands, waters and other resources and to uphold their responsibilities to future generations in this regard; the right to self-government in matters relating to their internal and local affairs; the collective right to determine the responsibilities of individuals to their communities; and the right to special measures to control, develop, and protect their sciences, technologies, and cultural manifestations, including human and other genetic resources, medicines, and performing arts.

The draft Declaration is a codification of *a new morality* for colonial societies. It serves as a set of ideals, only some of which will be enshrined in the legislation of some member states of the United Nations. Regrettably, the world is replete with examples of statements of lofty principles which are embossed in the statute books of states but which are never implemented. There is good reason to believe that in Canada such will be the fate of many of the articles of the final version of the Declaration of the Rights of Indigenous Peoples.

The Dene Declaration of 1975 (reprinted in Ponting and Gibbins, 1980: 351–352) and the 1981 Declaration of First Nations (reprinted in Boldt, 1993: 323–324) are examples of domestic manifestos which deal with self-determination. The latter is noteworthy for its emphasis upon the Creator, including its reference to the Creator as having given First Nations "the right to govern ourselves and the right to self-determination". Both declarations are noteworthy for their lack of separatist orientation. The Dene Declaration is very explicit on this point: "What we seek, then, is independence and self-determination within the country of Canada". Those First Nation leaders who espouse an interpretation of "self-determination" as separation are rare exceptions. Even the James Bay Crees' interventions at the United Nations on the issue of the Declaration of the Rights of Indigenous Peoples have been couched in terms which eschew separation and emphasize the Crees' desire to be able to choose to remain part of Canada if Québec were to separate. According to Ted Moses, Cree Ambassador to The United Nations (where the Crees are the only North American aboriginal people to have standing as a non-governmental organization), the Crees have always recognized that, internationally, self-determination does not mean withdrawing from any state (Platiel, 1996).

ABORIGINAL RIGHTS

An Aboriginal Conception of Aboriginal Rights

Aboriginal conceptions of aboriginal rights and of aboriginal government tend to place much emphasis upon **spirituality** and the role of the Creator. For instance, aboriginal elders stress the obligation to perform spiritual ceremonies as part of the responsibilities which accompany aboriginal rights. Iroquois leader and academic Oren Lyons (1984: passim) has written about the fact that for many First Nation people, self-government is profoundly spiritual and is intimately tied to First Nations' relation to the Creator, to the land, and to the living creatures on the land:

> The primary law of Indian government is spiritual law. Spirituality is the highest form of politics, and our spirituality is directly involved in government. ... We native people understand that all living things are one large extended family. ... Central to [our] responsibility is a recognition and respect for the equality of all the elements of life on this land.
>
> We believe it is equal because we are a spiritual people. ... We are the spiritual centre and always have been. ... We must hold on to what we have because we have "the natural law". ... When a government develops laws to rule people, it must develop those laws in accordance with the natural law; otherwise the laws will fail.

Viewed as granted by the Creator, aboriginal rights are seen by aboriginal people both as part of natural law and as inalienable. Because of the holism of most aboriginal world views and the interdependence of all spheres of life, aboriginal rights tend to be viewed by aboriginal people as very broad in their scope — as extending far beyond land rights. This is reflected in the Draft Declaration of the Rights of Indigenous Peoples.

A Sociological Conception of Aboriginal Rights

In sociology's so-called "social constructionist" school of thought (Spector and Kitsuse, 1977), rights are socio-political-legal constructions with a foundation in the moral order of a society. That is, they are **social products**, not divinely ordained: rights can be granted and rights can be rescinded in the legal code of a society, as we have seen, for instance, with the rights of organized labour and rights to health care in some provinces of twentieth century Canada. As Little Bear (1986: 243) has written, the norms or decision rules which the courts issue as the basis for judging future cases "are not necessarily `cast in stone', for they may be modified or superseded by competing norms that emerge as circumstances, paradigms, and moral standards change".

The recognition or "granting" of a right is usually promoted by moral entrepreneurs and/or victims who make moral claims which are legitimated in terms of, or appeal to, fundamental values in the society. That is, they seek to persuasively define a situation in a particular way and to have that definition become widely accepted (normative) in the society. In so doing, they use the values of the society as a resource, and the choice of values to which they appeal is a strategic one. Aboriginal rights, from this perspective, can be seen as legally recognized entitlements which acknowledge the special status of the original occupants of a territory. They are rooted in moral conceptions of fairness and of just compensation for the society's earlier failure to grant moral validity to claims of prior occupancy.

Like many other claims, aboriginal rights are contested by counter-claimants such as resource exploitation companies, British Columbia fishers and loggers, provincial governments, ideologues such as certain members of The Reform Party of Canada, and backlash movements such as B.C. Fire and its counterparts in Manitoba and Ontario. The exercise of some aboriginal rights can lead to a clash of competing economic interests. Those clashes, in turn, can give rise to non-aboriginal counter claimants' attempts to curtail aboriginal economic rights.

Before concluding this discussion of a social constructionist approach to aboriginal rights, two disparate points should be made. First, the fact that one views aboriginal rights from a social constructionist perspective with its "claims-making" vocabulary is not a comment on the moral validity of the claim to aboriginal rights. That is, the perspective can be used to yield insights into both claims with which we sympathize and claims which we oppose. Secondly, the social constructionist model, with its emphasis on the response-counterresponse interactive process between contestants, alerts us to the fact that rights are inherently political and therefore aboriginal rights that are recognized today could succumb to shifting political or judicial tides such that they are rendered hollow or extinct just a few years later.

A Constitutional Conception of Aboriginal Rights[2]

Aboriginal rights were not recognized by the Government of Canada until 1973 when three judges of the Supreme Court of Canada, writing in the famous Calder (Nisga'a land claim) case, asserted that aboriginal rights do, indeed, exist. This minority ruling by the intellectual peers of then Prime Minister (and constitutional lawyer) Pierre Trudeau led to the reversal of his government's extinguishment policy found in the 1969 white paper. Since then, the limits of aboriginal rights have been **contested terrain** as aboriginal rights have been processed in the courts, bureaucracies, and political backrooms of the Canadian state and in the mass media. After the adoption of *The Constitution Act, 1982,* successive attempts to come to a political resolution of the conflict failed at either the level of the political elite (the constitutional conferences of 1983 through 1987) or the grassroots (defeat of the Charlottetown Accord in the national referendum of 1992). Thus, the courts of Canada have become an important venue for defining aboriginal rights in law.

The Constitution Act, 1982 (Sec. 35.1) recognizes and affirms existing aboriginal rights. Whereas the First Ministers explicitly sought to limit those rights by the inclusion of the word "existing", the Supreme Court of Canada has taken an expansive interpretation that directly contravenes the intentions of the First Ministers. However, in contrast to the aboriginal view of aboriginal rights as inalienable and as not capable of being superseded by the laws of mere human beings, the state regularly requires aboriginal people to relinquish one aboriginal right — namely, aboriginal title to land — as part of comprehensive land claim settlements. Furthermore, the state does not automatically recognize the existence of aboriginal title. Instead, the Supreme Court of Canada has specified a test whereby four criteria must be met before aboriginal title to a certain territory will be legally recognized.[3] The Supreme Court of Canada has ruled that even a provincial government can override aboriginal rights if it has a "valid legislative objective" in so doing and meets certain other tests.[4]

As noted in Chapter Two, the Supreme Court of Canada has ruled that, in its dealings with First Nations, the state must act both to preserve the honour of the Crown and to respect the Crown's fiduciary obligations to First Nations. With regard to treaty rights, the Court has ruled not only that the treaties must be interpreted in a flexible manner that takes into account changes in technology and practice and resolves ambiguities in favour of the First Nations, but also that the treaties are "sui generis", which is to say that they cannot be subsumed under either existing contract law or existing international law.[5]

Notwithstanding the above, some lower court decisions and some Supreme Court of Canada decisions have gone against aboriginal people. Even some decisions widely assessed as favourable to First Nations, are also open to very negative interpretations, as Boldt's (1993: 32–39) scathing critique of the Supreme Court of Canada's ruling in the Sparrow case attests. To the extent that First Nations continue to be frustrated in achieving recognition and implementation of aboriginal rights within Canada, we can expect the international arena to become more important than in the past as an arena for pressing claims concerning aboriginal rights. If adopted, the United Nations' Declaration of the Rights of Indigenous People will assist in this effort.

SOVEREIGNTY

Some Cautionary Notes

Some First Nation leaders have sought to legitimate their claim to an inherent aboriginal right to self-government in terms of the notion of sovereignty. Boldt and Long suggest caution here.[6] They submit that the history of sovereignty is the history of competing claims to the legitimate exercise of authority, as different doctrines of sovereignty have been used to justify particular power arrangements and social arrangements. Theories of sovereignty were constructed to legitimate the Crown, to eliminate the Crown, to justify the power of the state and to assert the power of the people. Furthermore, the concept of sovereignty is inherently hierarchical: the sovereign holds authority over the people. In many traditional aboriginal world views that element of hierarchical authority is absent, for First Nations traditionally invested their customs and traditions, not their chiefs or elders, with the authority to guide their behaviour. There was no dichotomy between the rulers and the ruled. Hence, for some First Nations to adopt European, "democratic", hierarchical forms of government would be to violate a fundamental First Nation value of egalitarianism. In some First Nation communities it might relegate members of the community to the periphery of decision-making and create an Indian political-administrative elite with a vested interest in maintaining the externally imposed authority structure, the authors suggest.

Boldt (1993: 136) suggests that First Nations need to ask themselves whether sovereignty is a necessary condition for the survival and well-being of Indians *as Indians*. He believes that it is not, and to make his case points to the experience of the people of the Jewish diaspora. The Jewish people have retained their collective cultural identity, which is based on a codified set of beliefs and principles, despite being subjected to enormous social and geographical disruption as a result of slavery, persecution, the Holocaust, and dispersal "into virtually all cultures of the world" where they have lived thousands of years without the protection of national boundaries or political sovereignty. Boldt (1993: 185) observes:

> Throughout this experience they have preserved the continuity of their traditional fundamental philosophies and principles. Jews started as a tribal peo-

ple with a spiritually defined cultural identity that was based on a covenant between themselves and the Creator. This covenant has been a "constant" in maintaining their sense of cultural identity and their will to survive as Jews. It has stood as a barrier between them and assimilation into other cultures.

In Boldt's view, then First Nation leaders should reconsider their demands for a province-like "third order" of government.

The Assertion of Sovereignty

In the United States, the Supreme Court long ago (*Cherokee Nation vs Georgia*, 1831) ruled that Amerindians are "domestic dependent nations" whose inherent self-governing rights derive from their original occupancy of the land and are largely unaffected by treaty or trading acts. Thus, Amerindian Nations retain a degree of sovereignty which, in contemporary times, is reflected in such phenomena as the existence of tribal courts and the existence of gambling casinos on reservations. To a degree, the "nation-to-nation" relationship which Canadian First Nations seek with the Canadian federal state is a reality in Native Americans' relations with the American federal state.

On occasion, First Nations in Canada have sought to unilaterally assert sovereignty. Examples include the issuing of passports on which Mohawk diplomats travel around the world; the eviction of the RCMP and provincial court by the Innu of Davis Inlet (Labrador); and the White Bear (Saskatchewan) First Nation's opening of a casino that did not have regulatory approval from the provincial government. That casino was raided and closed by the RCMP.

Claims to sovereignty that are ignored or violated by other relevant governments are tantamount to political posturing. First Nation strategists usually do not know in advance, though, whether the relevant government will turn a blind eye or will enforce its own jurisdiction. Hence, there is considerable risk to this strategy, which is probably why First Nations often do not follow through on their rhetoric with action to unilaterally assert sovereignty. However, since the "Oka crisis", governments have been anxious to avoid provoking another confrontation that could escalate to Oka-like proportions with attendant political, financial,[7] and humanitarian costs. In turn, that increases slightly the bargaining power of First Nations. That is, the events at Oka/Kanehsatake and Kahnawake in 1990 created leverage or manoeuvering room for an expansion of the boundaries of First Nation sovereignty.

FIGURE 14.1 A Model of First Nations' Fluctuating Sovereignty

The model in Figure 14.1 depicts First Nations' sovereignty as being in a constant state of flux, as indicated by the shifting boundaries of the sovereignty box. That is, it expands and contracts in response to a number of factors which themselves are variable. For instance, the memory of the Oka crisis operates to increase the first factor in the model — the political will of non-Native politicians to concretely demonstrate some respect for First Nations' sovereignty. However, subsequent images in the media of armed and masked First Nation warriors diminish support for First Nations in the mass public and thereby diminish the non-Native politicians' political will. Supreme Court decisions sometimes affirm First Nations' sovereignty, but sometimes curtail it, and these two contrasting stances can be taken in rapid succession. The third factor in the model, First Nation assertiveness, can be influenced by such other factors as leadership competition and perceived vulnerability of the non-Native political regime (e.g., times of constitutional crisis, political uncertainty, or international scrutiny). The fourth and final factor is identified as the perceived availability of opportunities for using alternative means of accomplishing First Nations' goals. For instance, Assembly of First Nations Grand Chief Ovide Mercredi's promised campaign of non-violent direct action, in combination with the spiritual revival and emphasis on personal healing of the late 1990s, could have shifted attention away from sovereigntist "solutions" toward other more individualistic or incorporative[8] solutions, had it ever lifted off the launching pad. Any such shifts in attention away from sovereignty, if they were to persist for a number of years, could contribute to First Nations' sovereignty contracting.

Before leaving the model, a few additional comments are in order. First, the two-headed arrows portray both the movement in the jurisdictional (non-territorial) boundaries of First Nation sovereignty and the mutuality of causation between First Nation sovereignty and the four factors on the periphery. For instance, the degree of First Nation assertiveness can influence (positively or negatively!) the extent of First Nation sovereignty, but the extent of First Nation sovereignty can also influence the degree of First Nation assertiveness. Secondly, the four factors on the periphery can themselves be causally related to their adjacent factors, their opposite factors, and to factors (e.g., leadership competition) which are extraneous to the model. Hence, what appears on the surface to be a simple model is actually fairly complex.

Recognition and The Inherent Right to Self-Government

In the Charlottetown constitutional accord of 1992, the Government of Canada and the provincial governments recognized First Nations' long-sought inherent right to self-government.[9] That recognition has no legal standing, though, because the political accord was not ratified in the 1992 national referendum. Subsequently, the federal government issued a policy statement recognizing the inherent right to self-government. That 1995 statement[10] asserted the federal government's willingness to recognize the inherent right of self-government as an existing right within section 35 of *The Constitution Act, 1982*, but limited that right in various ways such that it would be tantamount to a delegated right rather than a sovereign right. For instance, the relevant provincial or territorial government would have a veto over those parts of any First Nation's self-government agreement which affect provincial or territorial jurisdiction or interests. In addition, the Canadian *Charter of Rights and Freedoms* and the *Criminal Code* of Canada would be imposed, and "laws of overriding federal and provincial importance" would prevail over aboriginal laws. Furthermore, federal funding for self-government would be achieved through the reallocation of existing resources.

Not surprisingly, the federal policy statement was denounced by First Nation leaders.[11] The Assembly of First Nations called it "demeaning and paternalistic" and "even more regressive than any of our worst fears". AFN dismissed the policy as falling short of the standard set by the Charlottetown Accord and reasserted that the right to self-government is given by The Creator, rather than delegated by any other government. A scathing analysis by The Chiefs of Ontario found the policy's focus on local government powers to be highly offensive and criticized the imposition of the *Charter of Rights and Freedoms* as the imposition of external cultural standards which do not protect collective rights in First Nation communities. The Chiefs' assessment was that the policy was both an extension of historic attempts to rob First Nations of their sovereignty and an attempt by the federal government to rid itself of its fiduciary obligations to First Nations. Similarly, the leader of the Congress of Aboriginal Peoples called the policy a "wholesale off-loading" of federal responsibilities onto provincial governments. The Minister of Aboriginal Affairs in the Government of British Columbia expressed a similar fear.

Clearly, the federal policy statement failed to meet First Nation leaders' aspirations for recognition of First Nations' inherent right to self-government, based on unextinguished aboriginal sovereignty. Those aspirations should be understood not only as being based on strategic considerations (namely, how best to protect and enhance any aboriginal right to self-government), but also as being based on other considerations. That is, the constitutional recognition of an inherent right to self-government, and the subsequent conduct of relations between First Nations and the Canadian federal state on a "nation-to-nation" basis, would yield important social psychological, spiritual, and political benefits for First Nation individuals. Formal constitutional recognition of a people and of the fact that it is "special" in some way bolsters the self-esteem of members of that collectivity. Recognition fosters group pride and affirms a sense of individual and collective self-worth. For First Nation peoples it would combat the inferiority complex which the residential schools instilled in students. To use an aboriginal concept, it would make the circle whole again.

Significantly, the Royal Commission on Aboriginal Peoples (1996b: 202–213) concluded that the inherent right to self-government is implicitly recognized by the *Constitution Act, 1982*, and recommended that the federal government renew its relationship with First Nations on a nation-to-nation basis. However, it also recommended (RCAP, 1996b: 236) that the right of self-government be recognized as vested in aboriginal nations, rather than in small, local, aboriginal communities.

The quest for constitutional entrenchment of an inherent right to self-government can be seen from a sociological perspective as an example of the **status-striving** that is common among subordinated groups. Success could yield a political payoff, in terms of support from constituents, for the aboriginal political leaders who achieve it. In the interim, though, to the extent that a focus on such sovereignty issues diverts time and energy away from the amelioration of the daily life problems of the grassroots constituents, the political leaders might be trying the patience of those constituents.

In concluding this discussion of sovereignty, we must not overlook the fact that, in essence, the sovereigntist aspirations of First Nation leaders are not uniformly shared by their constituents. In particular, some First Nation women's organizations have expressed the desire that the *Canadian Charter of Rights and Freedoms* protect them from the possible excesses of First Nation governments. As we saw above, though, other First Nation organizations have denounced the application of the *Charter* to First Nation governments as the imposition of external cultural standards, and by implication, a violation of First Nation sovereignty.

COMPREHENSIVE CLAIMS AGREEMENTS AND THE COOLICAN REPORT (1985)

Background

Comprehensive land claim agreements are an important means for some First Nations to increase their level of self-determination. In many respects, these agreements are the treaties of the contemporary era: they usually cover large tracts of land over which aboriginal title had never been ceded and they are recognized as treaties in *The Constitution Act, 1982*. However, they differ from the numbered treaties and the treaties of peace and friendship in that they provide for a degree of nation-building (Salisbury, 1986) by the aboriginal signatories. Examples involving First Nations include the James Bay and Northern Québec Agreement of 1975 (the first of the modern era), the Cree-Naskapi (Northeastern Québec) Agreement of 1978, the Yukon Umbrella Final Agreement of 1990, and the Nisga'a Agreement-in-Principle (AIP) of 1996. Examples where the Inuit have been the main signatories are the Inuvialuit Final Agreement (1984) in the western Arctic and the eastern Arctic (Tungavik Federation of Nunavut) settlement which led to the creation of Nunavut.

From a sociological perspective, the treaties and comprehensive claims agreements can be viewed as **structures of accommodation** (Grimshaw, 1970), as per Grimshaw's theory outlined in Chapter One. Let us consider northern Canada as an illustration of this point. The old accommodation consisted of the imposition of colonial territorial governments and band councils, both of which had very limited powers. The aboriginal peoples were left with a tiny land base over which they had few rights that were recognized in the legal system imposed by the dominant Euro-Canadian society. Mining and other resource-extraction companies were given substantial property rights and the Crown exacted a share of their profits through royalties and taxes. Over time, some devolution of administrative powers and, in the case of the territorial governments, legislative powers was accorded by the federal government to these subordinate governments. However, with the political awakening of aboriginal peoples after the 1969 white paper, the injection of new perspectives from the "Red power" and "Black power" movements in the U.S.A., and a crack in the legal ramparts provided by the minority opinion in the Supreme Court of Canada's 1973 ruling on the Nisga'a aboriginal rights case (see below), among other factors, aboriginal peoples in the north were emboldened to seek a new relationship with Canada. Out of that came several comprehensive land claims and eventually agreement on new accommodations in the form of claims settlements. Grimshaw's theory leads us to expect that those accommodations, to the extent that they avoid real power-sharing, will also be temporary, regardless of the federal government's quest for finality.

The negotiation of comprehensive claims agreements is a long and tedious process that became bogged down in the mid-1980s. As a result, the federal government appointed a task force chaired by Murray Coolican to recommend ways of expediting negotiations in productive ways which would yield agreements acceptable to the aboriginal peoples and non-Native governments. As Fleras and Elliott (1992: 230–231) note, Coolican's 1985 report stands with the Penner report on Indian self-government (see below) as a crucial document in shifting government thinking and policy on aboriginal self-government to a position much more compatible with that of aboriginal leaders. That is not to say, though, that the federal government adopted all of Coolican's recommendations. Nor did government wholeheartedly implement some of the recommendations which it professed to have adopted. This section of the chapter identifies some highlights of the Coolican recommendations and illustrates and assesses the federal government's response through a consideration of relevant provisions of two comprehensive claims settlements reached in the 1990s: the Yukon Umbrella Agreement and the Nisga'a Agreement-in-Principle (AIP).

Coolican's Recommendations and Assessment of their Implementation

The Coolican task force, perhaps recognizing the inherent instability of structures of accommodation, urged the federal government to recognize that finality can never be achieved in land claim agreements. Therefore, it urged, the government should be flexible and willing to re-open the agreements for renegotiation after fifty years, one hundred years, or even later. Just as the rights of non-aboriginal Canadians expand and constrict with changes in aspirations, circumstances, and ideological climate, one could argue that aboriginal Canadians should not be faced with the ossification of their rights in a land claim settlement. Such flexibility, what might be called a "sunshine clause", would offer the important benefit of making aboriginal communities less likely to resist ratifying what their leaders had negotiated with the government. Such resistance had already necessitated the renegotiation of one agreement in the early 1980s.

The provisions of comprehensive claims agreements negotiated since Coolican reported ignore both the above recommendation and another key recommendation which the government professes to have adopted — namely, that the government not require the extinguishment of aboriginal title. The extinguishment of aboriginal title to vast tracts of land falling under the James Bay and Northern Québec Agreement was a major reason why First Nations objected to that Agreement. A "bottom line" assessment reveals that federal practice pertaining to aboriginal land title remains virtually unchanged. Although aboriginal title to small tracts of land is retained by the First Nations, for most of the claimed land it is relinquished. For instance, Section 2.5.1.1 of the Yukon Umbrella Final Agreement of 1990 states:

> ... each Yukon First Nation and all persons who are eligible to be Yukon Indian People ... cede, release and surrender to Her Majesty the Queen in Right of Canada, all their aboriginal claims, rights, titles, and interests, in and to: (a) Non-Settlement Land ...; (b) the Mines and Minerals within all Settlement Land; and (c) Fee Simple Settlement Land ...

Coolican also recommended that the government not attempt to impose a standard model for settlements. Again, the necessity of flexibility was emphasized, so that the important sociological, cultural, and economic differences among First Nations could be respected. This recommendation has been implemented. For instance, within the Yukon settlement alone, in addition to the Umbrella Agreement-in-Principle and Umbrella Final Agreement which cover all of the First Nation signatories to the Yukon settlement, there are to be separate self-government agreements, separate claims agreements, separate financing agreements, and separate implementation agreements for each of fourteen Yukon First Nations or Councils. Nevertheless, there are commonalities across various comprehensive claims agreements inside and outside Yukon. In part this occurs because good ideas developed for one agreement are adopted or adapted for inclusion in another agreement (diffusion of social technology), and in part because there are similarities in negotiating demands by the parties to the respective agreements.

That the federal government should be willing to broaden the scope of claims negotiations to include self-government plus more economic and cultural matters was another of Coolican's recommendations. For the government to come to the negotiating table with a commitment to abandoning assimilationist objectives and to **power-sharing** with First Nations would be pivotal to establishing the trust necessary for creating a new social contract with First Nations. Although the James Bay and Northern Québec Agreement certainly contained economic development provisions designed to give the Crees the choice of participating in either the modern or the traditional economy (e.g., a guaranteed income system for Cree hunters and trappers), essentially Coolican was calling for economic development to receive even more emphasis. Ending First Nation economic dependency has, indeed, been a common goal of government and First Nation negotiators and the 1996 Nisga'a AIP, for instance, contains elaborate provisions for the economic development of the Nisga'a. A few of them are contained in Chapter Three (Box 5) of this volume. The government also implemented Coolican's recommendation that self-government and culture be part of the land claim negotiations. For instance, the Nisga'a AIP contains a sixteen-page chapter on Nisga'a government (plus additional related chapters such as those on taxation and the administration of justice) and a five-page chapter (plus many pages of appendix) on cultural artifacts and heritage.[12] Thus, the holistic approach recommended by Coolican is very much in evidence, with the notable exception of spirituality, which is largely left in the private domain or included only by implication (e.g., in the provisions for protecting Nisga'a culture and the provisions for regulating aboriginal healers).

The power-sharing recommended by Coolican can be institutionalized in many forms, such as co-management of resources, participation on regulatory boards, and the sharing of the right to pass legislation. The Nisga'a AIP establishes a committee to manage wildlife within the designated area. It has equal representation from the Nisga'a and the Government of British Columbia, but its terms of reference call for it to provide the provincial Minister with advice and recommendations, rather than it being empowered to make the decisions itself. However, the areas in which it can provide advice and recommendations are very important (e.g., setting the total allowable harvest levels for designated species and establishing which species are designated) and the Minister is required to provide written reasons for decisions which reject or are at variance with recommendations made by the committee. In the realm of environmental impact assessment for projects on Nisga'a Lands, the Nisga'a Central Government may make laws, but those laws are subordinated to any relevant federal or provincial laws of general application. In addition, the Nisga'a AIP recognizes the Nisga'a Central Government's right to have standing before federal or provincial environmental assessment bodies for projects which are located off Nisga'a Lands but may reasonably be expected to have adverse environmental effects on residents on Nisga'a Lands. Such recognition as a stakeholder is commensurate with the recognition of other stakeholders, but in no way should be confused with sharing in the decision-making. Indeed, while the Nisga'a AIP explicitly allows for the Nisga'a Central Government to nominate (not appoint) a member of a federal or provincial environmental assessment body, that right of nomination is explicitly denied where the body is a decision-making body (such as the National Energy Board).

Thus, the power-sharing involved in modern comprehensive land claim settlements can be very limited. Admittedly, those agreements do embody major gains in power sharing over the almost non-existent provisions for power-sharing in the numbered treaties. However, if we were to take our reference point as the James Bay and Northern Québec Agreement instead, a systematic comparison would have to conclude that First Nations' gains in power-sharing have been of modest proportions. Power holders usually do not yield power easily.

Coolican recommended that aboriginal claimants be permitted to retain some sub-surface mineral rights in order to achieve a reduction in the size of the compensation payments made to the claimants for past infringement of aboriginal rights. The Nisga'a AIP stipulates that the Nisga'a Government will own all mineral resources on or under Nisga'a Lands, but British Columbia will own all mineral resources on or under another category of lands (not to exceed 250 hectares in total) over which the Nisga'a will hold fee simple interests.

Coolican called for the government to approach the bargaining table with the political will to achieve a just settlement of land claims, rather than adopting a negotiating stance which would make it inevitable that claimants would resort to litigation. That is, rather than a "winner takes all" approach which might involve hollow pyrrhic victories for the government in the courts, Coolican sought a new, negotiated social contract that would replace dependency with mutual development. As Fleras and Elliott note, Coolican's desired approach would entail a **new distributional ethic** governed by a philosophy of power sharing and revenue sharing. In the harsh fiscal realities of the late 1980s and the 1990s, such an ethic was rarely in sight and First Nations sometimes felt compelled to resort to costly litigation (e.g., in the Gitksan-Wet'suwet'en case, the background to which is described in Sterritt [1989]).

SELF-GOVERNMENT

Elements and Forms

Self-government among First Nations will take many different forms. Some First Nation governments will be almost province-like in their powers, while others will be much more modest. At an abstract level, though, certain component elements will be held in common by most First Nation governments. These are summarized in Gibbins and Ponting (1986a: 177–181) as: (1) political institutions; (2) territorial base; (3) control over membership; (4) fiscal support from the federal government; (5) a division of powers between First Nation, federal, and provincial governments; and (6) an external reach. (See also RCAP, 1996b: 245–280.)

The political institutions will be democratic and representative in character and will be accountable to the First Nation electorate. They will incorporate features of traditional aboriginal political institutions (e.g., representation of clans). The territorial base will usually be the reserves. However, with difficulty and imagination some off-reserve institutions of governance can be devised, as in the "community of interest model" identified by RCAP (1996b: 273–280). Separate school boards and self-governing professional associations provide two practical examples of this model (Reeves, 1986).

Control over membership is a form of boundary maintenance. It refers to the First Nation's right to determine who is and who is not a member of that First Nation. With the 1985 amendments to the *Indian Act*, the federal government conceded that right, but retained the right to determine who will have status as a Registered Indian with its attendant rights and privileges.

Adequate fiscal support will be an absolute necessity for First Nation governments and the Royal Commission devoted considerable attention (RCAP, 1996b: 280–310) to principles and sources of such funding. Among the types of funding which the Commission discussed are own-source funding (e.g, user fees, resource royalties, gaming, aboriginal corporations), transfers from other governments, entitlements from treaties and land claims, and borrowing. Clearly, an adequate land and resource base will be vital to the economic self-reliance of most First Nation governments.

It is a truism that self-government without adequate fiscal resources would be a trap, not an opportunity. For instance, fiscal support will be needed to bring infrastructure up to standard before First Nations assume control of it, to train staff in the new managerial, administrative, and policy-making skills that will be required, and to meet the operating and capital needs of First Nations. However, the federal government will undoubtedly persist in its present stance of insisting that First Nation governments work toward greater self-sufficiency. One consequence of that is that as part of the division of powers, First Nations governments will be given taxation powers over their own members. This very fact will undermine support for self-government among First Nation individuals who currently enjoy tax exemptions by virtue of living and/or working on-reserve. Cockerill's and Gibbins' chapter in this Part of the book addresses this delicate issue of taxation in more detail.

The division of powers will be highly variable from one First Nation government to another. The Penner Report (Penner, 1983: 63) asserted that "self-government would mean that virtually the entire range of law-making, policy, program delivery, law enforcement, and adjudication powers would be available to an Indian First Nation government within its territory". Penner's statement would cover a very broad range of jurisdictional responsibilities which presently fall under either federal, provincial, or joint jurisdiction. For instance, some leaders have demanded jurisdiction over land, water, air, wildlife and renewable and non-renewable natural resources, environmental protection, economic development, all levels of education, social development, culture and communications, health and welfare, justice and enforcement of First Nation laws, marriage, citizenship and immigration, First Nation elections and constitutions, revenue, treaty-making, and local and private matters. Although there is little that is omit-ted from this list, the federal government offers considerably less under its 1995 policy on the inherent right to self-government. Boldt (1993: 138) also advocates a minimalist model as a starting point. That is, he calls for First Nations to ini-tially take on only such powers as are essential for the survival and well-being of Indians as Indians, so that First Nations can build up their organizational capacity. Other sociologists (e.g., Kallen, 1982: 88–92 and Ponting, 1991: 437) and the Royal Commission (1996b: 326–353) also emphasize the importance of build-ing organizational capacity. The Royal Commission also distinguishes between "core" and "peripheral" areas of jurisdiction[13] and suggests (1996b: 217) that an aboriginal government could proceed at its own pace by gradually occupying various jurisdictional areas within the core as need and circumstance dictate.

Let us briefly consider two realms of jurisdictional responsibility — immi-gration and air. To some it might seem unreasonable that First Nations would seek control over these two fields. However, consider the following: (1) the inter-national border which divides Canada and the U.S.A. is a creation which non-aboriginals have imposed upon aboriginal peoples in total disregard for the fact that it divides extended families; and (2) the Innu of Labrador, lacking control over the airspace above their land, are powerless to prevent the many thousands of N.A.T.O. jet fighter training flights that thunder over traditional Innu hunt-ing territory at treetop level. Thus, there are practical, albeit not necessarily read-ily apparent, reasons why many of the powers listed are sought by First Nations. Box 1 reports on two important areas of jurisdictional responsibility — one which has already been assumed by most First Nations and one which could spring to the forefront as a result of the work of the Royal Commission.

The Commission recommended that the creation of aboriginal justice sys-tems be included on the agenda of current negotiations (e.g., for comprehensive land claims) and that governments consider re-opening existing treaties and agreements to address justice issues, if the aboriginal parties so desire (RCAP, 1996: 312). The creation of a pan-Canadian aboriginal appeal body for criminal justice cases was also recommended for consideration (RCAP, 1996: 313). *Inter alia*, the Commissioners recommended that, in the allocation of financial resources, the federal, provincial, and territorial governments give greater pri-ority to providing a secure financial base for the development and implemen-tation of aboriginal justice systems.

The sixth and final dimension of First Nation governments is external reach. This could pertain to any or all of the following: jurisdiction over non-members on the First Nation land base; jurisdiction over members off that land base; co-management of, or a participatory role in decision-making concerning, matters that directly impinge on the First Nation territorial base from the surrounding province or territory (e.g., migrating fish stocks); and international affairs. The federal government seems intent on avoiding negotiating self-government pro-visions that involve external reach of the last type. External reach of the third type will be very limited and will occur only with the consent of the province or territory involved. Federal government preferences notwithstanding, though, we should bear in mind that some First Nations or First Nation orga-nizations already have a considerable international reach. For instance, the Mohawks have an informal embassy in The Hague, the James Bay Cree have official status as a non-governmental organization at The United Nations, the Roman Catholic Pope made a special visit to an aboriginal community in the

---

BOX 1 First Nation Jurisdictional Authority in Education and Justice

Education

The "Indian control of Indian education" policy adopted by the federal government in 1974 is one limited manifestation of self-government. It involves First Nations taking delegated jurisdiction of an area (education) that, under *The Constitution Act, 1867*, is a provincial responsibility among non-Indians, but a federal responsibility among Indians. The policy provides for First Nations to establish their own school board, select and be the employer of the staff, and add to the standard provincial/territorial curriculum as appropriate. Although slow to take-off, the policy has largely been successful and is a major contributor to the dramatic decline in the drop-out/push-out rate from about 85% in the early 1970s to about 25% in the mid-1990s, as noted in Chapter Four. The number of band-operated schools has risen from 64 in the 1976/77 school year to 429 in the 1995/96 school year.

Justice

The Royal Commission on Aboriginal Peoples attached such high priority to justice issues that it released the justice volume of its final report many months ahead of the remainder of the report. In that volume (RCAP, 1996: 310–311) the Commission, whose members included former Supreme Court of Canada Justice Madame Bertha Wilson, concluded that the aboriginal right to self-government is recognized and affirmed in Sec. 35 of *The Constitution Act, 1982* and that that right "encompasses the right of Aboriginal nations to establish and administer their own systems of justice, including the power to make laws within the Aboriginal nation's territory". The Commissioners also concluded that *The Canadian Charter of Rights and Freedoms*, including Sec. 33 (which permits governments to suspend the operation of certain protections normally available under the *Charter*), applies to aboriginal nations' governments and their justice systems.

Northwest Territories, the European Parliament has had direct (unmediated) contacts with Mohawks and other First Nations in Canada, and various First Nations have engaged in lobbying abroad before private and governmental organizations. In the future, the potential for the conflict between First Nations and the Government of Canada to be waged in foreign diplomatic circles is large. Some of the same issues which arose concerning the participation of the Québec government in La Francophonie will also emerge with First Nations and the Québec issue will always figure in the federal government's orientation toward the external reach of First Nation governments.

Concerning the different generic forms which aboriginal self-government could take, the Royal Commission (1996b: 245–280) identifies three — the nation, the public government, and the community of interest models — and Boisvert (1985) identifies over one dozen. This he accomplishes by identifying and cross-classifying three main aspects of self-government: type of *authority* held by the government (law-making vs. administrative vs. none[14]); type of *participation* in the government (reserved exclusively for aboriginal peoples vs by all residents of the territory), and *scale* (national vs regional vs local) of the government.[15] Examples of types which are likely to be most common include:

- local aboriginal governments on-reserve
  - law-making authority, exclusively aboriginal participation, local in scale, based on one or more reserves of one First Nation

- regional public governments
  - law-making authority, public participation (not restricted to aboriginal people), regional in scale. For aboriginal people to be interested in this model, aboriginals would likely have to form a demographic majority in the region. Example: Nunavut.
- regional (or treaty area) aboriginal governments
  - law-making authority, exclusively aboriginal participation, regional in scale. Example: the proposed Nisga'a Central Government
- national aboriginal special purpose bodies
  - administrative authority, exclusively aboriginal participation in representation and clientele, national in scale. Hypothetical example: a national aboriginal parole board
- regional aboriginal special purpose bodies
  - administrative authority, exclusively aboriginal participation, regional in scale. Example: most of the regional institutions established under the James Bay and Northern Québec Agreement
- local corporate government off-reserve
  - law-making authority, exclusively aboriginal participation, local in scale, not based on-reserve. Hypothetical example: an aboriginal school board in a metropolitan area with a large aboriginal population
- band council government on-reserve
  - primarily administrative authority, exclusively aboriginal participation, local in scale

It is possible that some aboriginal governments which start with an exclusively aboriginal clientele might, if successful or for reasons of achieving economies of scale, contract to provide services to certain non-aboriginal clientele. However, interesting issues of democracy arise when an aboriginal government serves a clientele that includes non-aboriginals. As Boisvert (1985: 35) notes, and the Royal Commission endorses, democratic principles of representation would suggest that if people are covered by the laws and programs of a government, they should have the right to a voice in that government. Says the Commission (1996: 252–253):

> Different rights and responsibilities may apply to citizens and non-citizens on Aboriginal lands. For example, cultural rights or rights to carry on certain economic activities on the nation's lands, may differ for citizens and non-Aboriginal residents on those lands. However, all residents, regardless of citizenship, should have some means of participating in the decision making of Aboriginal governments.

Yet, in the larger Canadian society the vote is not granted to those who are not citizens, even though they are covered by the laws. Hence, whether a given First Nation government will be open to elected representation by non-Natives probably depends upon the demographic balance of power in the constituency. Clearly, the "bottom line" consideration is that the First Nation government be used to further the self-determination of the First Nation people — to replace non-Native decision-makers with First Nation decision-makers who are sensitive to First Nation values.

The Penner Report (1983)

As noted above, the sweeping report of the Special Parliamentary Committee on Indian Self-Government (Keith Penner, M.P., Chair) was crucial both in contributing momentum to First Nations' drive for self-government and in legitimating a new paradigm for the federal government's approach to First Nation affairs. Also, large parts of that paradigm were adopted in the recommendations of the Royal Commission. A few of the highlights of the Penner committee's seminal document are identified below.

First and foremost, the Committee recommended that the federal government establish a new relationship with First Nations, that an essential element of that relationship be recognition of Indian self-government, and that that recognition be entrenched in the constitution of Canada. First Nation governments "would form a distinct order of government in Canada, with their jurisdiction defined". Secondly, lacking faith in the Indian Affairs side of the Department of Indian Affairs and Northern Development, the Committee recommended that DIAND's programs relating to First Nation people be phased out over five years as First Nation governments come to exercise more control over their own affairs. Thirdly, the Committee called for the creation of a Ministry of State for Indian First Nations Relations, which would manage and co-ordinate the federal government's relations with First Nation governments. It would be linked to the Privy Council Office to give it "clout" within government.

The *Indian Act* should not be amended as a route to self-government, the Committee stated. Instead, the committee recommended the government pass an Indian First Nations Recognition Act which, among other things, would establish criteria to be met by any First Nation government wishing to be recognized as self-governing. One important criterion listed was a system of accountability of the First Nation government to its constituents.

Penner's committee also recognized the importance of the federal government providing an adequate land and resource base and settling outstanding claims against it. Substantial economic development and correction of serious infrastructure deficiencies were seen as foundational for successful self-government. Funding to First Nations through direct grants, rather than conditional ("strings attached") grants-in-aid was also favoured by the Committee. Full title to, and control over, Indian lands, waters, and resources would also be transferred from the Crown to the First Nations, under the Committee's proposals.

In the area of comprehensive land claims, the Committee recommended that the federal government no longer require the extinguishment of aboriginal title to the land and that the federal government abandon the position that some aboriginal rights have been superseded by law.

On the basis of a major research project on the fiduciary (trustee-like) obligations of the government toward First Nations, the Committee also recommended that the fiduciary relationship be renewed and enhanced.

The Penner Report contributed in a major way to the elevation of the expectations of First Nation leaders, mainly in the substance of its recommendations but even through its inclusion on the Committee of an ex-officio member from The Assembly of First Nations and Liaison members from The Native Women's Association of Canada and The Native Council of Canada. The fact that the Committee's report was released during the period of constitutional negotiations to define aboriginal rights in the constitution was also important in raising expectations. However, the report was seen as radical and the Committee members did not have much political influence over their parliamentary colleagues (e.g., committee member Warren Allmand had already been removed from Cabinet) and the government's response over the short-term contained more rhetoric than substance. Then, less than a year after the report's release, the government changed. Over the longer term, though, and in conjunction with other inputs and events (e.g., the Coolican report, the impasse at the 1987 constitutional conference on aboriginal rights, Supreme Court rulings, Elijah Harper's torpedoing of the Meech Lake Accord, and the Oka incident), the government's position shifted dramatically in the direction of many of the Penner Committee's recommendations. Once dismissed or given mere lip-service because of being too radical, much of the Penner report has become received wisdom.

The popularity of the Penner report does not immunize it against criticism. For instance, the Cockerill and Gibbins chapter in this volume criticizes the Penner committee for insufficiently thinking through the implications of its recommendation that "the primary relationship of the Indian people involved with the federal government would be through those [First Nation] governments" (Penner, 1983: 56). This raises fundamental issues of citizenship which Cockerill and Gibbins examine.

Nunavut: A Portent [16]

Many readers are aware of the plan to split the Northwest Territories into two jurisdictions, the eastern portion of which will be called "Nunavut" and might some day become a province. The creation of Nunavut Territory comes partly in response to a negotiated settlement of a comprehensive land claim filed by the Inuit of the eastern Arctic and partly in response to the signing of a political accord. In its description of the future Government of Nunavut, Légaré's chapter in this section provides a detailed account of the inner workings, structure, and challenges of an aboriginal government of the "public government" type cited by the Royal Commission. Technically, a chapter on the Inuit has no place in a book on First Nations, for the situations of the two peoples differ in many important respects. However, their situations and the issues their governments will face, are not totally dissimilar, especially in light of the Royal Commission's recommendation that the inherent right to self-government be implemented at the level of the nation (e.g., the Haida nation, the Mohawk nation) rather than at the level of the community. Before elaborating on the relevance of the Nunavut case for First Nations, it is important that a clear picture of their differences be painted.

First, the opportunity structures of the Inuit have been limited more by geographic isolation than by legislation, for the *Indian Act* does not apply to the Inuit. Similarly, the Inuit were not covered by treaties prior to their recent land claim settlement, with the result that the identity and social psychology of the people does not revolve, even in part, around grievances associated with treaty implementation. Nor do they have any counterpart to the Bill C-31 problems experienced by Indian women and communities. Fourthly, the twenty-seven Inuit communities of Nunavut are dispersed over a vast geographic area that has no parallel among the First Nation communities that comprise a nation. Furthermore, that territorial base of the Inuit is of enormous strategic significance (Canada's Arctic sovereignty and jurisdiction over the Northwest Passage) to Canada, unlike virtually all of the Indian reserves of southern Canada. This strategic significance is empowering for the Inuit because it creates political leverage for them. Another difference pertaining to the territory is that the Inuit cannot control the influx of people to their lands, whereas First Nations can invoke the trespass provisions of the *Indian Act* to control population influx. Hence, the Inuit, but not First Nations, face the prospect of someday losing their electoral majority. Finally, the vastly different ecological setting of the Arctic, compared to southern Canadian reserves, has produced some noteworthy cultural differences, among which is a pronounced tendency for the Inuit to be pragmatic rather than ideologically dogmatic. Similarly, nationalism as a contemporary ideology is less characteristic of the Inuit than of First Nations.

Notwithstanding those differences, the Nunavut case is worth examining in detail, as Légaré does. For instance, he discusses some of the same problems as are identified below under the rubric "Problems with Self-Government". Allocation of employment opportunities to different communities served by the government is another problem shared by First Nation governments and the future government of Nunavut, as is the staffing and training of the public administration itself. Devising formal arrangements to enable the political voice of women to be heard is yet another problem shared by the Nunavut Government and some First Nation governments. Légaré discusses the two-member constituency solution that has been proposed to resolve that problem in Nunavut. The list of similarities goes on to include such matters as the challenge of translating lofty principles into implementable solutions, co-management, official languages, relations with the federal government, building a fiscal base, provisions for the transitional period, aspirations for external diplomatic reach, etc. In short, the Inuit are taking the lead with one form of self-government and their experience can be instructive for First Nations.

Problems with Self-government

For non-Native academics to refrain from discussing problems that could be associated with aboriginal self-government might be "politically correct" in some circles, but such silence would also be tantamount to a neo-paternalism. It is highly unlikely that the fact of academics pointing out problems is going to significantly detour progress toward self-government. On the other hand, pointing out in advance problems that can be anticipated enables practitioners to take preventative or mitigative measures.

Life will not be idyllic for First Nation governments. Various authors,[17] including Légaré and Cockerill and Gibbins in this volume, address the substantial problems which aboriginal governments already face or will face.

A common concern among academics is rooted in issues of social class. Boldt (1993: 143), for instance, emphasizes the need to guard against replacing racial oppression by class oppression. First Nation governments could include authoritarian regimes in which ruling elites are empowered, but not grass-roots constituents. Gibbins and Ponting (1986: 188) write: "As opportunity structures are opened, those who are already advantaged will be disproportionately able to partake".

The small size of First Nation populations poses several problems. First, any small population, First Nation or otherwise, offers a shallow pool of human talent. It is also possible that First Nation government will absorb much of the available skilled human resources of a First Nation, such that a healthy private sector might not be able to develop in that First Nation. Thirdly, small size creates ineconomies of scale wherein the per unit cost of delivering services is very high, if those services are provided at all. For instance, whereas a major metropolitan school board can afford to hire specialists to deal with severely learning disabled students and has enough such learning disabled students to be able to occupy those specialists, a small First Nation school board might have only one such student and a small revenue base. Hence, it would be prohibitively expensive to hire the specialist to deal with that one student, whereas the big city school board can spread that specialists' salary over several students (or several dozen!). It might cost the First Nation school board forty thousand dollars per student to hire the specialist, but the big city school board might pay the same salary but it would work out to only about six thousand dollars (or less) per student to hire the specialist. Similar principles apply to the provision of infrastructure and other services. (These are among the reasons why the Royal Commission recommended that the inherent aboriginal right to self-government apply at the level of the nation rather than the community.)

Small populations tend to be much less diverse than large populations. However, diversity produces cross-cutting cleavages which tend to neutralize conflict by producing cross-pressures and divided loyalties. With diversity at low levels in small First Nation communities, conflict could be more readily manifested than in large communities, with the result that the conflict-regulating mechanisms within the community might be put to severe test.

The so-called "tyranny of the majority" is another problem associated with the relatively high degree of homogeneity in the population of small political units. Cockerill and Gibbins cite dramatic examples of this problem among First Nations as part of their impassioned argument in favour of requiring First Nation governments to be constrained by having *The Canadian Charter of Rights and Freedoms* apply to them.

Other problems associated with small size include the weak bargaining power of small units and the fact that the burden of government is not spread widely (Gibbins and Ponting, 1986a: 219).

Political scientists are particularly interested in intergovernmental relationships. Cockerill and Gibbins note that in the Canadian federal system there is a large number of inter-governmental meetings that must be attended and many inter-governmental relations must be nurtured or otherwise maintained. Such work is very labour intensive and requires highly skilled, highly educated workers. Figure 14.2 (from Gibbins and Ponting, 1986b) captures some of that complexity and density of First Nation governments' relationships with other governments, other organizations, and their own constituents.

In Figure 14.2 it is worth noting that not only does each plane of the cube make demands upon the First Nation government as it seeks to sustain a relationship with actors from each plane. In addition, the First Nation government leaders will want to keep track of *relations between other actors* in its political environment, as represented by the dark edges (e.g., provincial government's interaction with "supra-level" aboriginal organizations) and by the logically possible linkages across the "void" to the opposite side of the cube (e.g., provincial government with other local First Nation governments).

Legitimacy is extremely important to governments. Indeed, the Royal Commission (1996b: 163–165) identifies legitimacy as one of three basic attributes that a government must have to be effective. When legitimacy is present, the constituents of a First Nation government will trust the incumbents. When legitimacy is lost, alienation sets in and sometimes voluntary compliance is withdrawn. There are two especially important aspects of legitimacy. First, the

FIGURE 14.2 The Faces and Interfaces of First Nations Government

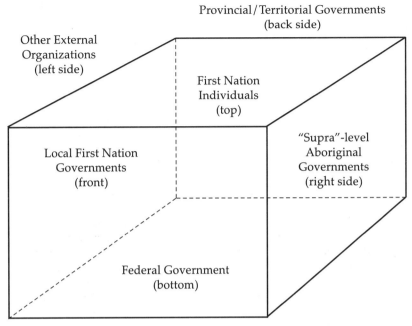

Source: Gibbins and Ponting (1986b).

constituents of a First Nation government must see themselves reflected in the symbolic output of the state. If they do not, legitimacy is withdrawn and alienation rises (Breton, 1986: 31). Secondly, First Nation governments must "deliver the goods", symbolically and materially, to their constituents. They must make people's daily lives better than they had been under DIAND. This is, in part, the issue of re-distribution of wealth which Cockerill and Gibbins raise as fundamental to First Nation government. If constituents develop unrealistically high expectations on the retention/redistribution of wealth issue or on any other issue, or if the latent tensions between traditionalists and modernists erupt, or if the First Nation government is co-opted by the larger state, a major crisis of legitimacy could arise.

The Cockerill and Gibbins chapter raises various other thorny points, such as the dilemma over taxation. The taxation issue is also taken up in Courchene and Powell (1992). Cockerill and Gibbins also raise the issue of the franchise (vote) and in so doing revive an old question: At what price does the vote come? A further irony in their piece is their assertion that self-government will necessarily require the transfer of some authority from First Nation local governments to "supra-level" First Nation or aboriginal governments. Having fought so strenuously to become empowered, First Nations will apparently have to relinquish some of their powers to a "supra-level" (e.g., Pan First Nation) aboriginal organization. Finally, the Cockerill and Gibbins chapter is also useful in keeping before us two issues that are never far from the surface in First Nation affairs — implications for Québec and for the dominant liberal philosophy in Canada.

Accountability

A major issue in the mind of a variety of interested parties is the issue of accountability of First Nation governments. Ensuring First Nation governments' accountability to the First Nation membership is an important part of the mandate of federal participants in the comprehensive claim and self-government negotiations. In part this is important because accountability is an important feature of democracy. In part, though, accountability looms large in federal government priorities because the federal government can only escape its fiduciary obligations to First Nations if First Nation governments hold control and have mechanisms of accountability in place.

The basic purpose of this brief section is to demonstrate that building mechanisms of accountability is not "rocket science"; there is no unfathomable mystique. Rather, mechanisms of accountability abound. In this section they will be illustrated.[18]

Requirements for financial auditing by an independent auditor are an obvious mechanism of accountability, as is a set of administrative policies which clearly define expenditure regulations (e.g., travel expense claim regulations; regulations governing the use of competitive bids for government contracts). Electoral spending and campaign contribution limits guard against undue influence of special interests over elected politicians. However, accountability can take many non-financial forms, as shown below.

Providing information is inherent in many forms of accountability. The classic case is the granting to citizens various rights covering access to government information and the granting of protection in law to "whistle-blowers". In tandem with access-to-information legislation, many governments have a code of ethics and a separate set of conflict of interest guidelines for elected officials and public servants in the bureaucracy.

Statutory guarantees of due process being followed are another form of accountability. The very existence of appeal mechanisms and of the phenomenon of judicial review (whereby the judiciary can overrule the executive branch of government when a law is unconstitutional) enhance accountability of the executive branch of government.

Formal consultative processes and requirements for social and environmental impact assessments of development projects also increase accountability.

The requirement that legislative sessions be held in public (rather than *in camera*) and the very existence of an electoral system of choosing leaders enable constituents to hold leaders accountable. The right to petition government and the right to recall a legislator are populist mechanisms of accountability.

Conducting evaluation research and making the results publicly available is one means of holding bureaucrats accountable for how they spend government money.

The requirement that lobbyists be registered in a public register and that they make a public record of every contact with a politician or senior executive in the government bureaucracy is also helpful in building confidence in government integrity.

In the final analysis, though, if the constituents are not engaged in the political process and are not practicing good followership, and if there is no independent mass media, then even elaborate provisions for accountability will probably be rendered meaningless.

Impact

The impact of First Nation government will depend upon a variety of factors, some of which pertain to the amount of money and other resources made available to First Nations. Other factors predisposing First Nation governments toward success are: the economic development potential and on-reserve tax base of the community; the adequacy of the preparation for, and the gradualness of, the transfer of responsibilities to the First Nation; and the leadership *and followership* skills of the people of the First Nation.

Holding all of that constant, the question remains as to what the impact of self-government will be. Elsewhere (Ponting, 1986), I conducted a speculative analysis which addressed precisely that question. The vehicle for that analysis was the concept of *community social vitality* which was elaborated from its original use by Matthews in studying the Newfoundland outport resettlement programme. Community social vitality encompasses a wide spectrum of activities that contribute to the sociological health of a community. The analytic approach used was to assess the probable impact of self-government on each separate dimension of community social vitality.

By my assessment, self-government will have a very positive impact on institutions of socialization (especially the schools, as has already been demonstrated under the "Indian control of Indian education" policy), but will probably have its greatest impact in the realm of meaning-conferring activities. In particular, the symbolic output of First Nation governments will likely instill in their citizens a sense of pride, positive identity, and restored or strengthened dignity. Boundary maintenance is a third dimension of community social vitality that is likely to be strengthened under self-government, especially to the extent that the institutional completeness[19] of First Nation communities increases under self-government.

Assessing the impact of self-government on some other dimensions of community social vitality is more problematic. Crowfoot's chapter in Part 3 attests to the fact that First Nation leaders cannot take their legitimacy for granted. Furthermore, if a First Nation government fails to meet the reasonable expectations of its constituency, the consequence might be the withdrawal of legitimacy by those constituents — a very serious development. Similarly, conflict regulation and resolution mechanisms will be put to a severe test under self-government with the withdrawal of some long-standing conflict-mediating structures and external scapegoats (DIAND and RCMP). Finally, leadership and organization are important aspects of community social vitality. First Nation governments likely will be able to reclaim some of the leadership potential that, under the colonial regime, had been lost to their constituents' alienation, incarceration, escapist behaviour, migration, and conformity to traditional sex-role prescriptions.

Notwithstanding all of the problems identified earlier in this chapter, the conclusion of my speculative analysis is that First Nation governments have the potential to have a profound and positive sociological impact on the people being governed. One must bear in mind, though, that not all First Nation governments will be successful, just as not all non-Native governments are successful.

SUMMARY

This chapter has provided a general overview of and introduction to the topic of self-determination among First Nation peoples. We saw that the term "self-determination" refers to a variety of phenomena and that codifications such as the United Nations' Draft Declaration of the Rights of Indigenous Peoples provide useful specification.

The existence of aboriginal rights provides one basis for claims to the right to self-determination. We contrasted an aboriginal conception of aboriginal rights, with its emphasis upon holism and spirituality, with a sociological conception rooted in the social constructionist school of thought. Then we examined a legal-constitutional view of aboriginal rights and the paradox of the Court recognizing the existence of aboriginal rights but allowing their extinguishment.

Sovereignty has been a major demand of First Nation leaders; in Boldt's view mistakenly so. He identified several reasons for caution on the part of First Nation leaders, including the prospect of sovereignty, with its inherently hierarchical nature, marginalizing some of the grassroots band members.

The risks involved in the unilateral assertion of sovereignty were addressed next. Sovereignty was conceptualized as a phenomenon in a state of flux and a model was developed to show the stresses and strains which impact on the concept.

The federal government's offer to recognize the inherent right to self-government was subjected to scrutiny next and found to be largely window-dressing that does not yield the "nation-to-nation" relationship with the federal state that many aboriginal leaders seek. Sociological reasons (e.g., compensatory status striving) for the pursuit of the inherent right were identified.

Two seminal reports of the 1980s received considerable attention in this chapter. The Coolican Report on comprehensive claims agreements was introduced with a brief discussion of the nature of comprehensive claims and identification of examples. Coolican's main recommendations were identified and their implementation assessed. Similarly, various recommendations of the Penner report on First Nation self-government were identified. Taken together, these two reports were important in legitimating a new discourse of power sharing in the First Nations' claims-making. Some important recommendations from both reports were ignored by government, just as the federal government is largely ignoring the comprehensive report of the Royal Commission on Aboriginal People.

The discussion of self-government, per se, identified the six main elements that most First Nation governments will have. Emphasis was placed on the division of powers between federal, provincial, and First Nation governments. Education and justice were singled out for special attention. The fact that First Nation government will take a variety of forms was illustrated with several forms from Boisvert's model in which the main dimensions were authority, exclusivity of participation, and scale. Numerous serious problems of self-government were identified from the existing literature and many of them will be addressed in the Cockerill and Gibbins chapter in this Part of the book. The model of community social vitality was identified as forming the basis for a sociological assessment of the probable impact of self-government.

NOTES

[1] Condensation symbols, as used here, are terms which "are malleable, allow for a multiplicity of definitions, tend to induce emotional responses and to provoke value judgements, and their imprecision gives the appearance of commonality

while masking significant differences in interpretation between various users" (Jhappan, 1990: 21).

2 For a more comprehensive but "plain language" discussion of constitutional aspects of aboriginal rights in Canada, see RCAP (1996b: 184–234).

3 In the Baker Lake case of 1985, the Supreme Court ruled that four criteria must be met for the Court to recognize the validity of aboriginal title (Dickason, 1992: 353). The aboriginal claimants must prove that: (1) they and their ancestors lived in organized societies; (2) they occupied the specific territory over which they are claiming aboriginal title; (3) their occupation of the territory was exclusive; and (4) their occupation was in effect when England claimed sovereignty over the region. These are not easy conditions to meet. The Royal Commission's interpretation (1996b: 201) is that in subsequent decisions the Supreme Court distanced itself from another aspect of the Baker Lake decision — namely, that an aboriginal right is automatically extinguished to the extent that it is inconsistent with a statute.

4 According to the Supreme Court of Canada's ruling in the famous Sparrow case, other criteria which must be met for a government's extinguishment of, or encroachment upon, aboriginal rights to be constitutionally valid are: (1) the restriction of the aboriginal right must be such as to minimize the interference with the daily lives of the people; (2) the honour of the Crown must not be compromised; and (3) the fiduciary duty of the Crown must be upheld.

5 These rulings are in the Simon case of 1985 and the 1990 decisions in the Sioui and Sparrow cases.

6 The passage summarized here is from a pre-publication draft of Boldt and Long (1984).

7 Newspaper accounts of the total cost of the "Oka crisis" vary widely. However, it is clear that it cost hundreds of millions of dollars.

8 "Incorporative" solutions are those which have as their goal the maximization of First Nations' participation in the existing institutions of the larger society. In contrast, self-government based on aboriginal sovereignty is an institutionally pluralist solution in that it involves First Nations establishing government institutions that are roughly "parallel" to (albeit philosophically and operationally perhaps quite different from) those of the larger society.

9 See my web page for a detailed, "plain language" compilation of provisions of the Charlottetown accord as they pertained to First Nations. At time of writing the address was http://www.ucalgary.ca/~ponting

10 The August 1995 policy statement was posted on the DIAND website and is available as Catalogue # R32-155/3-1995 (ISB-662-61954-4).

11 Aboriginal commentary here on the federal policy statement is taken from Alexandra Macqueen's column entitled "National Aboriginal Organizations Reject New Federal Self-Government Policy" in the September 1995 issue of *The First Perspective On-line Newspaper*.

12 The areas of legislative jurisdiction and authority of Nisga'a government are listed as: culture and language; social services; health services; education (preschool to grade 12); post-secondary education; child and family services; adoption; child custody; solemnization of marriages; employment; Nisga'a lands and assets; public order, peace, and safety; gambling and gaming; intoxicants; traffic and transportation; public works, buildings, and other structures; wills and estates; and matters pursuant to other chapters of the final agreement, including administration of justice, taxation, lands and resources, environmental assessment and protection, fisheries, wildlife, and sub-surface resources.

¹³ The Commission (1996b: 215) describes the core of aboriginal jurisdiction as including all matters that: (i) are of vital concern to the life and welfare of a particular aboriginal people, its culture, and identity; (ii) do not have a major impact on adjacent jurisdictions; and (iii) are not otherwise the object of transcendent federal or provincial concern. The periphery makes up the remainder of the sphere of inherent aboriginal jurisdiction.

¹⁴ The case of no authority would be the case of the First Nation organization with mere advisory or lobbying powers.

¹⁵ Boisvert uses the rather unhelpful term "dimensions" to refer to what is here called "scale".

¹⁶ Portent: omen, significant sign; prodigy, marvellous thing (*The Concise Oxford Dictionary*, 1964)

¹⁷ Ponting and Gibbins (1984), Gibbins and Ponting (1986a, 1986b), Boldt (1993), and Ponting (1995) all discuss problems surrounding aboriginal self-government.

¹⁸ The original source for some of the mechanisms of accountability listed here has been lost. Some derive from the author's general familiarity with the public policy literature. Some are perhaps taken from a Siksika Nation draft report to RCAP prepared under the supervision of political scientist Andrew Bear Robe.

¹⁹ "Institutional completeness" refers to the ability to have one's needs met while staying within the confines of the ethnic group.

REFERENCES

Boisvert, David A.
1985   *Forms of Aboriginal Self-Government*. Kingston, Ont.: Institute of Intergovernmental Relations, Queen's University.

Boldt, Menno
1993   *Surviving as Indians. The Challenge of Self-government*. Toronto: University of Toronto Press.

Boldt, Menno and J. Anthony Long
1984   "Tribal Traditions and European-Western Political Ideologies: The Dilemma of Canada's Native Indians", *Canadian Journal of Political Science*, XVII, 3: 537–553.

Breton, Raymond
1986   "Multiculturalism and Canadian Nation-Building", pp. 27–66 in Alan Cairns and Cynthia Williams (eds.), *The Politics of Gender, Ethnicity and Language in Canada*. Volume 34, Research Reports of the Royal Commission on the Economic Union and Development Prospects for Canada. Toronto: University of Toronto Press.

Coolican, Murray et al.
1985   *Living Treaties, Lasting Agreements — Report of the Task Force to Review Comprehensive Claims Policy*. Ottawa: Department of Indian Affairs and Northern Development.

Courchene, Thomas J. and Lisa M. Powell
1992   *A First Nations Province*. Kingston, Ont.: Queen's University Institute of Intergovernmental Relations.

Dickason, Olive P.
1992   *Canada's First Nations: A History of Founding Peoples from Earliest Times*. Toronto: McClelland and Stewart.

Fleras, Augie and Jean Leonard Elliott
1992   *The Nations Within: Aboriginal-State Relations in Canada, the United States, and New Zealand.* Toronto: Oxford University Press.

Gibbins, Roger and J. Rick Ponting
1986a "An Assessment of the Probable Impact of Aboriginal Self-Government in Canada", pp. 171–245 in Alan Cairns and Cynthia Williams (eds.), *The Politics of Gender, Ethnicity and Language in Canada.* Volume 34, Research Reports of the Royal Commission on the Economic Union and Development Prospects for Canada. Toronto: University of Toronto Press.

_____
1986b "Faces and Interfaces of Indian Self-government", *The Canadian Journal of Native Studies*, VI, 1: 43–62.

Grimshaw, Allen D.
1970   "Interpreting Collective Violence: An Argument for the Importance of Social Structure", *Annals of the American Academy of Political and Social Science*, Vol. 391: 9–20.

Jhappan, Radha
1990   "Indian Symbolic Politics: The Double-Edged Sword of Publicity", *Canadian Ethnic Studies*, xxii, 3: 19–39.

Kallen, Evelyn
1982   *Ethnicity and Human Rights in Canada.* Toronto: Gage Publishing.

Little Bear, Leroy
1986   "Aboriginal Rights and the Canadian 'Grundnorm'", pp. 243–259 in J. Rick Ponting (ed.), *Arduous Journey: Canadian Indians and Decolonization.* Toronto: McClelland and Stewart/Oxford University Press.

Lyons, Oren
1984   "Spirituality, Equality, and Natural Law", pp. 5–13 in Leroy Little Bear, Menno Boldt, and J. Anthony long (eds.), *Pathways to Self- Determination: Canadian Indians and the Canadian State.* Toronto: University of Toronto Press.

Penner, Keith et al.
1983   *Report of the Special Parliamentary Committee on Indian Self-Government.* Ottawa: Supply and Services Canada.

Platiel, Rudy
1996   "Canada Tells UN Natives Have Right to Choose Future: Grand Chief Sees Statement as Sign Crees Have Right to Stay in Canada if Quebec Leaves", *Globe and Mail*, Nov. 2: A3.

Ponting, J. Rick
1986   "The Impact of Self-Government on Indian Communities", pp. 359–368 in J. Rick Ponting (ed.), *Arduous Journey: Canadian Indians and Decolonization.* Toronto: McClelland and Stewart / Oxford University Press.

_____
1991   "Crisis and Response: Challenges of the 1990s in Alberta Indian Affairs", pp. 89–104 in J.S. Frideres and R. Gibbins (eds.) *Alberta into the 21st Century.* Calgary, Alta.: The University of Calgary Faculty of Social Sciences.

1995   "On Reserve Casino Gambling: Musings of a Nervous Sociologist", pp. 57–68 in Colin S. Campbell (ed.), *Gambling in Canada: The Bottom Line.* Burnaby, B.C: Simon Fraser University.

Ponting, J. Rick and Roger Gibbins
1980   *Out of Irrelevance: A Socio-political Introduction to Indian affairs in Canada.* Scarborough, Ont.: Butterworth.

1984 "Thorns in the Bed of Roses: A Socio-political View of the Problems of Indian Government", pp. 122–135 in Leroy Little Bear, Menno Boldt, and J. Anthony Long (eds.), *Pathways to Self-Determination: Canadian Indians and the Canadian State*. Toronto: University of Toronto Press.

Reeves, William J.
1986 "Native Societies: The Professions as a Model of Self-Determination for Urban Natives", pp. 342–358 in J. Rick Ponting (ed.) *Arduous Journey: Canadian Indians and Decolonization*. Toronto: McClelland & Stewart.

RCAP (Royal Commission on Aboriginal Peoples)
1996 *Bridging the Cultural Divide: A Report on Aboriginal People and Criminal Justice in Canada*. Ottawa: Canada Communication Group.

1996b *Final Report of the Royal Commission on Aboriginal Peoples; Vol. 2: Restructuring the Relationship*. Ottawa: Minister of Supply and Services Canada.

Salisbury, Richard
1986 *A Homeland for the Cree: Regional Development in James Bay, 1971–1981*. Montreal: McGill-Queen's University Press.

Spector, Malcolm and John I. Kitsuse
1977 *Constructing Social Problems*. Don Mills, Ont.: Benjamin/Cummings Publishing.

Sterritt, Neil J.
1989 "Unflinching Resistance to an Implacable Invader", pp. 267–294 in Boyce Richardson (ed.), *Drumbeat: Anger and Renewal in Indian Country*. Toronto: Assembly of First Nations and Summerhill Press.

CHAPTER 15

RELUCTANT CITIZENS?
FIRST NATIONS IN THE
CANADIAN FEDERAL STATE

Jodi Cockerill and Roger Gibbins

INTRODUCTION

Over the past decade, the principle of aboriginal self-government has come to receive broad support not only within aboriginal communities but across the Canadian political system.[1] The consensual nature of this support, however, should not lead us to conclude that the *implementation* of self-government will be easily achieved. The integration of self-governing aboriginal communities into existing federal institutions raises various practical problems. Moreover, it reveals a deeply rooted value conflict between the principles implicit in aboriginal self-government and those embedded in liberal-democratic institutions.

First Nation people maintain that past problems must be remedied, and similar problems avoided in the future. For their part, non-Natives are likely to defend liberal-democratic beliefs deeply embedded in the Canadian political culture, and to defend those beliefs even where they may compromise aboriginal values and traditions. The resolution of this conflict promises to be one of the most difficult political and intellectual problems that Canadians will face in the coming decade.

How, then, do we contend with these difficult issues? Our strategy will be to address in turn topics arranged in a fashion analogous to the layers of an onion. The first or outermost layer concerns pragmatic problems relating to intergovernmental relations. The second draws us into more complex, theoretical ground as we discuss the broader concepts of federalism within which intergovernmental relations are embedded. Assuming that self-governing communities must be integrated into federal structures, we turn next to a discussion of the franchise and taxation, two issues that head us toward the substantive core of the relationship between aboriginal peoples and the Canadian state. This core is to be found in the fourth and last layer, the discussion of the application of the *Charter of Rights and Freedoms* to self-governing First Nations. The *Charter* brings our theoretical concerns into their sharpest focus. Although the same concerns are to be found in the issues of taxation, the franchise, federalism, and intergovernmental relations, the possible antagonism between aboriginal and liberal-democratic principles is most evident in the contemporary *Charter* debate.

Our central question is critical: how might Canada incorporate a new form of citizenship, one violating neither aboriginal nor liberal-democratic principles, and thus facilitate the integration of self-governing aboriginal communities within Canadian institutions? The notion of *citizenship* permeates the discussion to follow. The specific issues such as taxation or the *Charter* raise the same question in different ways: is there a concept of citizenship rich enough, or complex enough, to capture both liberal-democratic and aboriginal values? How much accommodation is possible, and where are the points of accommodation? Finally, who should do the accommodating?

Before exploring this question of citizenship, we must note the limitations of our analysis. First, we shall not debate the desirability of aboriginal self-government. In our view, this debate is over, and the more contested terrain relates to questions of implementation. Second, we shall not address those models of self-government that place aboriginal communities outside Canada's federal institutions. While we acknowledge the proponents of truly autonomous self-government, we shall address only the more probable scenario that places self-governing communities *within* existing liberal-democratic institutions. Third, we shall confine our discussion mainly to First Nations with an established land base. Given the current emphasis on the territorial foundation for self-government, territorially based First Nation people will be the first to confront the dilemmas raised in this chapter. Although the sociological conditions of other groups, including Métis without a land base[2] and most aboriginal peoples living in urban centres, are often dire, these groups without a land base are unlikely to achieve broadly ranging self-government soon. Thus, we shall deal primarily with First Nations possessing an established territorial base; the more difficult cases of the Métis and urban aboriginal communities will be discussed only in passing.[3]

First Nation people in Canada have much in common. First, there are land bases in reserves of varying, and sometimes hotly contested, sizes. Second, in many cases there are treaties, which are legally binding claims on the federal government. Third, at no point did First Nation people express explicit consent to be governed by Canadian institutions. Yet, for all the similarities, First Nation people are very diverse; indeed, the label "Indian" is really only a legal categorization. In terms of culture, and politics, First Nation people's languages and traditions vary widely. Significantly, more than a third live outside the reserves. Each of these factors — First Nation people's land claims, treaties, diversity and mobility — promises to complicate the political journey ahead.

First Nation leaders insist, though, that the journey must be undertaken if First Nation people are to endure. "We have before us," writes Michael Mitchell, former Grand Chief of the Mohawk Council of Akwesasne, "a glorious purpose":

> ... that is, to replace these many frustrations and difficulties caused by the arrogance and indifference of the nations that surround us, with a consensual system of government that responds to our deepest needs, springs from the most profound wisdom of our past and our elders, and holds out for us the restoration of harmony, honour and truth in our daily affairs.

> (Mitchell, 1989: 133)

Members of the First Nations, we are told, seek a revival from their torpor of dependency, a restoration of dignity and self-sufficiency. To this end, the existential ties joining individuals to their social and political institutions, and to the Creator must be repaired and rendered visible.[4] According to this view, First

Nations must exercise jurisdictional autonomy in areas of education, justice, political organization, and economic development to restore traditional forms of government. What autonomy might mean to an individual community, however, is by no means certain. The Royal Commission on Aboriginal Peoples maintained that it "lies with each group to determine the character and timing of any moves to enhance its own autonomy" (RCAP, 1992: 41). In the context of our discussion, *the critical issues are the means and extent to which this autonomy can be exercised within Canada's liberal-democratic institutions.*

The discussion to come reaches beyond technical problems of institutional design to explore fundamental and recurrent cultural debates. First Nations spokespeople insist that in finally acknowledging Canada's rightful "third order" of government, non-aboriginals must rethink not only existing institutions but also the beliefs animating those institutions. This imperative has been stressed by the First Nations since the early politicization of their communities. For example, former Alberta leader Harold Cardinal (1977: 9) wondered why an Indian who suggests simply that he wants to remain an Indian is perceived as un-Canadian. Cardinal asked that non-Aboriginals modify their understanding of citizenship, so that aboriginal people might come to enjoy both their Canadian and Indian identities. Similarly, he and others insist that the larger society revise its conceptions of individual freedom and collective rights so that political manifestations of the "Indian way" might flourish in the midst of a liberal-democratic environment.

Clearly, leaders of the First Nations advocate significant changes to the existing political landscape. For their part, non-aboriginal politicians must address First Nations' proposals cautiously, for the admission of this third order of government to the federal state has significant implications for Canadians' strongly affirmed liberal-democratic values. The scope for compromise is not unlimited. When does reconciliation of conflicting values give way to unreflective relativism? What are the consequences for social order, and when do the traditional symbols of Canadian citizenship wane in significance?

INTERGOVERNMENTAL RELATIONS

The existing system of government in Canada incorporates an array of intergovernmental relations that shapes everything from the process of constitutional amendment to the delivery of social services. If self-government is to become a reality, First Nation governments must be worked into existing intergovernmental structures. This cannot be done, however, at the level of individual communities. Simply put, some six hundred self-governing First Nations, or even 10% of that number, could not be worked into the full array of existing intergovernmental structures. Integration will require a "senior" First Nation government endowed with the authority both to bargain with other governments and to enforce intergovernmental agreements within its own constituent communities. This will require the transfer of power from individual communities to larger aboriginal governments. Without such a transfer of power, effective participation in "executive federalism" (the general term applied to the conduct of intergovernmental relations) would be difficult if not impossible. The present system works because participants speak with the power of governments behind them; if deals are made, participants know that all parties have the capacity to deliver. A situation in which the First Nation representative in intergovernmental negotiations could not deliver, in which he or she could only *recommend* to one hundred or more self-governing communities, would not work.

Although the same dilemma can be identified for the literally hundreds of ministerial and bureaucratic federal-provincial and interprovincial conferences held every year, the problem is best illustrated by the First Ministers' Conference. If First Nations are to be represented in forums such as the First Ministers' Conference, if they are to be included in such mechanisms as the constitution's amending formula, they will have to speak through a *single government*. One cannot imagine a situation in which individual communities or even provincial associations could be effectively represented at First Ministers' Conferences. There would have to be a single First Nation *governmental* representative to speak for a constituency much more diverse than that faced by any provincial premier.[5] Like the Prime Minister and the Premiers, he or she would have to be able to deliver on intergovernmental agreements; the representative could not go back to the local communities to consult, nor could those communities hold the power to block decisions.

The intergovernmental negotiations leading up to the 1992 Charlottetown constitutional accord illustrate the problems of having a non-governmental representative for First Nations. Throughout the negotiations, the Grand Chief of the Assembly of First Nations (AFN), Ovide Mercredi, was a powerful and effective advocate for his people, and the final agreement provided wide-ranging recognition for the concerns and aspirations of First Nations (Delacourt, 1994). In the referendum that followed, however, the support of First Nation people for the agreement that Mercredi had helped create was half-hearted at best. Many did not vote, and those who did vote were far from united in their support of the accord. Should the constitutional debate be re-opened, Mercredi's inability in the past to deliver his own constituents in the referendum campaign will badly damage his credibility, or that of his successor.

It is tempting, of course, to suggest that these institutional problems should be left to First Nations as details to be worked out once the principle of self-government is constitutionally entrenched. Unfortunately, the matter is not so simple. Given that First Nation governments must mesh with federal institutional structures, Canadian and provincial governments are necessarily involved. This in turn raises a larger issue. While it can be argued that First Nations are not obliged to adjust either their governments or the values upon which they rest to existing intergovernmental structures, it also can be argued that some accommodation is essential if First Nation governments wish to provide their residents with an optimum level of public services. Certainly the smaller communities, and probably even the larger ones, will not be able to deliver a full range of autonomous services.

The concern about intergovernmental relations is not restricted to pragmatic institutional issues; it also involves a basic feature of Canadian citizenship. A narrow focus on intergovernmental relations could lead us to assume that individual residents of First Nation communities will relate to the provincial and federal governments *exclusively through their First Nation governments*. Yet, if this were to be the case, it would be a very truncated form of Canadian citizenship. Federal theory presumes both indirect, intergovernmental linkages and direct, electoral linkages between citizens and their national government. Therefore, if we think of self-governing First Nations as existing within the Canadian federal system, we must explore a broader conception of citizenship than that which is assumed in a discussion of intergovernmental relations.

THE REQUIREMENTS OF FEDERALISM

The recent transition from the theory of aboriginal self-government to its implementation has revealed *a fundamental contradiction* in some of the First Nation rhetoric. The contradiction has extensive implications for Canadian institutions, as it stems from the assertions both that aboriginal self-government is compatible with Canadian federalism and that the foundational principles of Canadian federalism embedded in the constitution should not apply to First Nation people.

Although some First Nations have asserted their status as independent nations,[6] most have sought the creation of a third order of government within Canada. For example, former National Chief of the AFN, David Ahenakew, insisted that Canadians must not interpret First Nations' words, "no matter how strongly spoken, to mean that we are separatists — seeking to divide Canada and assert the status of foreign nations". Rather, "[w]e are committed to strengthening and building Canada — not to dismantling it" (quoted in Asch, 1984: 35). First Nation leaders insist that a third order of government might speedily be established if only federal and provincial governments would summon the political will to vacate areas rightfully belonging to aboriginal jurisdiction. In both structure and principle, Canadian federalism is said to lend itself to the inclusion of First Nation governments. Elijah Harper (in Cassidy, 1991: 166) asks:

> If the Canadian government can incorporate the fundamental laws of common law of Great Britain, then what is more Canadian than to embrace and incorporate the laws, customs, and traditional democracies of aboriginal people in this country?

"The real issue," he concludes, "is about power and control".

Yet, is "power and control" the sole issue? Some Canadians might retort that the real issue, apart from money, is the degree to which the autonomy implied by "sovereign" First Nations is compatible with the limited autonomy enjoyed by provinces, the residents of which are still national citizens. Indeed, the strong interpretation of self-determination suggests that First Nation people should negotiate their future relationship with Canada on a *nation-to-nation basis, which all but precludes First Nation individuals' Canadian citizenship except as a loose affiliation with Canadian authorities mediated by First Nation governments*. Although the rejection of Canadian citizenship is not necessarily a consensual position, it often appears to have been embraced tacitly by First Nations, even as officially, it is dismissed. For example, when then National Chief of the AFN, Georges Erasmus (in Cassidy, 1991: 173), insisted that "Canada will operate on a nation-to-nation basis with Indigenous First Nations", he also stressed that "... we are not talking about separate nation-states". For Erasmus to profess, on a continuing basis, equal commitment to dichotomous positions is contradictory. On practical issues of implementation, we should expect First Nation leaders to fall either to one side or the other of a substantial breach.[7]

The breach itself marks the distinction between a federal and a *con*federal relationship. Federalism requires not only areas of shared jurisdiction, but also individual linkages between citizens and their national government. Although the existing federal system might prove sufficiently flexible to accommodate First Nation governments, the flexibility of existing arrangements is not limitless. *Certain institutions are permanent features of Canada's federal composition, and to "opt out" of these institutions would amount to opting out of the federation itself.* Thus, if First Nation people are, indeed, committed to maintaining ties with the larger federation, they must accept the requirement for certain linkages between First Nation individuals and non-aboriginal governments. For example, and as we suggest below, the *Charter of Rights and Freedoms*, no less than the federal courts that interpret it, necessarily must apply to First Nation people.[8] A federal model for the relationship between First Nations and the broader political community also presumes that First Nation people will retain electoral ties with the provincial and national governments, a connection that raises the closely related issue of taxation.

THE FRANCHISE AND TAXATION

We submit that, if Canadian citizenship is to be maintained, the residents of self-governing First Nations must retain the federal and provincial franchise. This point, however, is not as self-evident as it might seem. For example, it was not fully recognized in the Penner Report, which stated that "legislative authority would ... be with Indian governments, and the primary relationship of the Indian people involved with the federal government would be through those governments" (Penner, 1983: 56). One could infer from this that First Nation people would not need the franchise, that they would speak to Canadian governments *through their own governments*, through the instruments of executive federalism rather than the federal or provincial ballot. Yet, were this to be the case, there would be a serious risk that non-Aboriginals would come to see First Nation people as existing outside the Canadian community, as non-citizens. This, in turn, would harden opposition to fiscal transfers from federal or provincial taxpayers to First Nations. Such transfers might come to be seen as more similar to foreign aid than to a financial responsibility based on shared citizenship. *It also could restrict access to off-reserve public services for residents of self-governing First Nations.*

The franchise implies other, less commonly acknowledged entanglements. Taxation, for instance, is the "price" of the vote in democracies; citizens are obliged to support expenditures approved by elected governments. Thus, the retention of the federal and provincial franchise implies that residents of self-governing First Nations will be subject to both federal and provincial taxation in addition to the new taxes that will have to be imposed by First Nation governments themselves.[9] Admittedly, it has been argued that First Nation people should have a tax-exempt status based on the claim that taxes already have been paid in perpetuity by the surrender of aboriginal title. Yet, it is not certain that this argument can be sustained in the political arena. First, residents of self-governing communities would continue to receive benefits from both federal and provincial programs; national defence, old-age pensions, employment insurance, and provincial highways are but a few examples. Secondly, is it not likely that federal and provincial governments will insist on the power to tax non-aboriginal residents of First Nation communities? Are these same governments likely to tolerate the use of such communities as tax havens for individual and corporate entities?[10] Finally, although existing tax exemptions might meet with manageable levels of public or governmental resistance as long as Canadians see aboriginal peoples to be relatively impoverished, political support for tax exemptions would be difficult to maintain if self-government brings economic success.

The discussion of taxation raises a related implementation problem that may introduce strain not only between First Nations and other governments, but also among First Nations themselves. We refer here to one of the central political problems in democratic states — the redistribution of income. With self-government, First Nation governments will face this issue on two fronts: the redistribution of income *within and among* First Nation communities. Although substantive problems arise in both cases, it is only the second front — the redistribution of wealth among communities — which will concern us here. Redistribution within specific communities can be left to those communities to address, as it does not raise federal concerns.

At present, there are various mechanisms for the redistribution of wealth among Canadian provinces. The symbolic centrepieces of these are the equalization formula and the transfers it generates from the national treasury to "have-not" provincial governments. Although we could envisage the extension of this mechanism to First Nations, two important problems remain. First, equalization payments are made from the national treasury; thus, access to equalization payments implies the exposure of First Nations to federal taxation. (Individual taxpayers in the net recipient province of Newfoundland, for example, contribute to the equalization payments that Newfoundland receives by paying their federal income tax.) Second, it is not clear that the existing formula would provide anything close to equalization of fiscal revenues of First Nations, as the income range among them is far greater than that among provinces. While equalization payments could help "level up" income, they would not redistribute it from the relatively small handful of resource-rich communities. It is quite likely that Canadian governments will insist on some "leveling down," some redistribution of wealth among First Nations, as a condition for equalization payments.[11] Given the much greater variance in community wealth among First Nations, the redistributive problem is much greater for First Nations than it is for the Canadian provinces.

It might be best to leave the redistribution of income to First Nations. Funds could be transferred from the government of Canada to First Nation governments *in general*, and the distribution of such funds among communities could be managed by First Nation people rather than through existing mechanisms such as the equalization formula. This approach is envisaged in a proposal by the Federation of Saskatchewan Indians for a Canada-Saskatchewan Indian Resources Fund, "a pool of revenues to be created by statutory formula governing the Indian sharing with Canada of revenues and resources which would be controlled, managed, administered and distributed on the basis of policies established by the Chiefs of Saskatchewan" (Sanderson, 1981: 34). Even in this case, however, the distributive mechanism would have to be *governmental* in character. The allocation of federal funds could not be carried out by a body such as the Assembly of First Nations, from which dissenting individual communities could withdraw. Any redistributive mechanism would require the force of law, the power to allocate the federal funds, and the ability to withstand the inevitable internal criticism over any such allocation. At very least, what would be required is a province-wide First Nation government with the power to enforce its decisions within its constituent communities. *Self-government, in other words, will entail not simply an increase in power for individual communities; it also will mean the transfer of a significant part of that power to a larger First Nation government.* Not only must individual First Nations consider what powers would continue to be lodged with the Canadian and provincial governments, they also must determine what powers should be relinquished to larger First Nation governments that, like the governments of Canada, would lie beyond their direct control. This matter is of particular importance both for wealthier communities, who well might fear the redistributive power of this larger aboriginal government, and for poorer communities, who well might depend upon those same redistributive powers.

In summary, the related issues of franchise and taxation are important in trying to fit aboriginal self-government into the context of Canadian citizenship. There is, though, scope for considerable flexibility and accommodation in both issues. The primary concern with respect to the franchise is that First Nation people retain their vote in federal and provincial elections; whether they choose to *exercise* that vote is of secondary concern. For its part, taxation is seldom a straightforward matter; Canadian tax law is riddled with special circumstances and exceptions. Thus, in these areas, accommodation of both aboriginal self-government and conventional Canadian citizenship might well be possible. It is not certain, however, that such a felicitous arrangement is possible with the *Charter*.

THE CANADIAN CHARTER OF RIGHTS AND FREEDOMS

First Nations' Objections

For Canadians living outside Québec, the *Charter* has become the pre-eminent symbol of Canadian citizenship. Indeed, its sections define what that citizenship means. Yet from the *Charter's* inception, First Nations have contested its applicability to First Nation governments. In a 1981 brief to the subcommittee on Indian Women and the *Indian Act*, the AFN submitted:

> As Indian people we cannot afford to have individual rights override collective rights.... we could not accept the *Charter of Rights* as it is written because that would be contrary to our own system of existence and government.

> (AFN, 1981, cited in Boldt and Long, 1985a: 171)

Despite the provision of section 25 that *Charter* protections "shall not be construed so as to abrogate or derogate from any aboriginal, treaty or other rights or freedoms that pertain to the aboriginal peoples of Canada", the AFN perceived several debilitating effects of the *Charter's* application.

First, it saw certain sections of the *Charter* as posing practical obstacles for emerging First Nation governments. Where First Nations might hope to reinstall traditional governing institutions, or where they might seek to introduce long-term residency requirements for the franchise in First Nation elections, the *Charter's* guarantee of democratic rights would be contravened.[12] A second practical obstacle is the usurpation of the special legal status enjoyed by First Nation people. First Nation organizations have long been wary of the Canadian government's efforts to erode members' legal status. Cases brought by Native women in the 1970s against discriminatory sections of the *Indian Act* appeared to threaten the *Indian Act's* independence from the *Bill of Rights*. Although the Supreme Court eventually decided that the *Act* was indeed an independent piece of legislation, many observers saw it to be a close call.[13] At that time, the National Indian Brotherhood (NIB) insisted that the offending parts of the *Indian Act* should be revised on their own rather than held to be in conflict with the *Bill of Rights*. Because the NIB wished to protect Indians' status as *a group apart* from other Canadians, it insisted that legislation respecting *individual* rights should not extend to status Indians. The parallel with the *Charter* is clear. Despite the presence of section 25, the AFN has been reluctant to submit matters of hard-won jurisdiction to the capricious eye of the Supreme Court. The *Charter's* "centralizing effect" threatens Indian autonomy in a way similar to its threat to provincial jurisdiction (Boldt and Long, 1985a: 171).

Practical issues aside, the *Charter* is held to present a symbolic affront to traditional principles. As the AFN reminds us, provincial legislators find encroachments upon their authority irritating, but the *Charter's* philosophical language is at least consistent with their own. Provincial governments accept liberal principles. First Nations, on the other hand, come from an entirely different tradition, one that did not conceive of individual rights in the Western European sense. Thus, by the *Charter's* application to First Nation governments, one of the fundamental aims of self-determination, the maintenance and revitalization of traditional values, would be subverted. Where leaders might seek to imbue members with traditional conceptions of existence, they would be bound by incongruent notions. Under the *Charter*, First Nation citizenship would seem perpetually subordinate to Canadian beliefs. Insistence upon the *Charter's* application would mark yet another attempt to assimilate aboriginal peoples, to deny the ultimate validity of traditional beliefs.[14]

Clearly, the *Charter* is contested terrain as Canadians try to determine the implications of aboriginal self-government for citizenship. Notwithstanding the arguments offered by the AFN, we submit that the *Charter* must apply to all Canadians, including First Nation people. For practical, political and philosophical reasons, institutional recognition of group rights must not exclude certain governments from *Charter* accountability. In the first place, the mobility of First Nation people poses a weighty practical problem. Is it conceivable that an individual could claim *Charter* protection outside her First Nation community, yet not when she is at home? Conversely, would a non-aboriginal Canadian residing in such a community be excluded from his *Charter* rights? Individuals from First Nations could face legal difficulties in traveling back and forth across hastily erected "international borders" dividing their communities from Canada. Second, if we accept our assertion that the *Charter of Rights and Freedoms* has become the practical and symbolic affirmation of Canadian citizenship, its rejection by First Nation leadership is telling. *If First Nation leaders take seriously their commitment to remain within Canada, is it unreasonable to maintain that the Charter* should apply within the jurisdiction of their governments, just as it applies within the provinces?

We also must discuss political and philosophical justifications. Some would argue that "the national interest" dictates the *Charter's* uniform application, and still others that First Nation people will *need* the *Charter's* protections. In our view, each argument merits consideration, as each attests to the impossibility of an easy resolution. Yet, we must move beyond political considerations to examine the debate's conflicting philosophical assumptions. At this point, we reach not only the most central and problematic layer of our discussion of citizenship, but also a fitting justification for the *Charter's* uniform application to all Canadians.

The National Interest

Menno Boldt (1993: 67–78) has critically identified the "national interest" as the "overwhelming and permanent force in Canadian policy development" in the areas concerning First Nation people. Though it is loosely defined, the "national interest" undoubtedly has helped to shape policy from the *Indian Act* through a variety of assimilationist policies to provincial and federal governments' stalling on proposals for self-government. In the past, any major constitutional or legislative change concerning First Nation people has not been considered separately from its anticipated impact upon the rest of the nation.

What relevance might the "national interest" have for the question of the *Charter's* application to First Nation governments? The most obvious speculation concerns Québec. If it were determined that, for cultural reasons, the *Charter* should *not* apply to First Nation governments, Québec nationalists might read into that decision an invitation for Québec to opt out of the centralizing *Charter.*[15] Undoubtedly, the parallel between First Nations' and Québecois constitutional aspirations unnerves Canadian nationalists. From a national unity perspective, the prospect that First Nations, and perhaps even an entire province, might abandon their constitutional orbits around the *Charter* precludes even a consideration of the AFN's proposals. What is more, public opinion would appear to support Canadian nationalists. Most Canadians voted against the Charlottetown Accord in 1992 and, in so doing, they appear to have rejected special constitutional status for any group. Despite various attempts to convince Canadians of their nation's bi-, tri-, or multi-cultural heritage, Canadians outside Québec have demonstrated an abiding attachment to the fetchingly simple principle of equal treatment among individuals. If the exemption of First Nation governments from the *Charter* is seen to subvert that principle, most Canadians might be expected to disapprove and resist.

Concern for both national unity and public opinion undoubtedly must play a role in policy formation. On the other hand, these should not serve as the sole basis for aboriginal policy. Too often, an appeal to the national interest has been an appeal to expediency rather than fair treatment; this observation holds particularly in cases concerning identifiable minority populations. Any talk of the national interest refers to a "Canadian interest" in which First Nation people historically have been politically and numerically marginal actors. As Boldt has indicated, it should be acknowledged that reflection of First Nations' interests in the broader "national interest" has been achieved only by fortunate coincidence.

It appears that, in the long run, exclusive preoccupation with the national interest makes for poor politics. Certainly, it seems to have alienated First Nation leaders. In 1990, for example, Elijah Harper was unmoved by threats that the failure of the Meech Lake accord would amount to a national political disaster. Similarly, Grand Chief of Québec's Crees, Matthew Coone-Come, displayed little anxiety over the prospects for national unity, *per se*, in the months preceding the 1995 Québec sovereignty referendum. Instead, he seemed intent on exploiting the rifts among Québecois and Canadians outside Québec to benefit the Cree. That First Nation leaders show little affection for the country in which they have found themselves should not surprise us; their conspicuous indifference has been paralleled historically by successive Canadian governments' indifference to the well-being of First Nation people.

Thus, while we do not deny the relevance of the national interest, we do not affirm its paramountcy as a justification in itself. In the case of the *Charter's* uniform application, a more substantial justification is required and, indeed, one exists. We move now to a distinctively liberal defense of the *Charter*. It is conceivable that members of self-governing First Nations might actually need the *Charter*, perhaps even more than other Canadians do.

Concerns for Individual Rights Violations

A principle of liberalism holds that if a state violates an individual's rights, the aggrieved party is entitled to a third-party appeal. In Canada, we have legal channels by which we can petition courts and a written document by which we know the rules and limitations to which all levels of government are subject. So it would be for First Nations. If First Nations residents were to retain their *Charter* rights, they would enjoy the same protections against their governments as other Canadians enjoy from theirs. First Nation residents could petition their national government for redress of *Charter* violations incurred at the local level.

There is reason to expect that violations would occur. First Nations can expect their fair share of crooks and thieves in government, as we all can. Yet the nature of First Nation communities poses an additional danger; extensive kinship ties coupled with small community size have encouraged nepotism and corruption. Harold Cardinal himself encountered corruption during his brief career as the Alberta Regional Director-General of the Indian/Inuit Affairs Programme. Some Alberta chiefs, Cardinal concluded, were "village tyrants". Such developments are not surprising; indeed, it has been the experience of many Third World nations. If we have learned anything from the general experience of decolonization, it is that the surrender of political control to indigenous populations by no means ensures fair treatment of individuals. Where the good intentions of leaders are questionable, the *Charter* of Rights could serve to check possible abuses.

There is a further danger to individual liberty. Culturally, socially, and economically, First Nations are quite homogeneous, and just such communities pose the greatest threat to the individual and minority rights protected in the *Charter*. As James Madison argued at the founding of the American constitution, "tyranny of the majority" is most likely to be checked by large, heterogeneous societies in which a plurality of conflicting goals prevents the clear articulation of a "majority will." Traditionally, the majority will has been well-articulated in First Nations, even dangerously so. By way of an extreme illustration, we note a personal anecdote related by Mohawk Grand Chief, Mike Mitchell (1989: 111) who reported approvingly that a Mohawk has voted only once in a Canadian election, in the 1950s. When community members discovered his treachery, they felt "betrayed and incensed by his action". The offender's house was promptly burned down, and he was forced off the reserve. In Mitchell's own account, it appears that the community's authorities were involved in the incident.

Most Canadians would argue that the *Charter* offers a welcome protection when the policy agenda includes torching people's houses. In light of the preceding example, we might consider an additional cause for concern: by the fact of bitter past relations with the federal government and indeed, with Canada generally, many First Nations seem to have closed ranks against "outsiders". They sometimes have required strict conformity in the opinions of their members. As a lonely advocate of the White Paper, William Wuttunee, former Chief of the National Indian Council, felt the consequences of his opinions; he was banned in 1970 from presenting his views at several reserves in Saskatchewan. In the wake of this controversy, Wuttunee (1971: 10) warned that "[p]resent-day Indian leaders acutely dislike anyone who will stand up to them", and "they are very anxious to maintain their exclusive power over the Indian people". Indeed, in many states, such luxuries as freedom of speech and expression are considered to be politically extravagant. Given the visible rift between First Nation leaders' ennobling rhetoric and the often dire realities of reserve life, some communities conceivably would promote cultural traditions at the expense of individual freedom. Thus, we must not ignore the potential of First Nations to compromise individual rights; neither should we over-emphasize it, though.

That Indian governments are increasingly responsible for daily matters of state also might bode ill for individual freedom. The potential danger to individual rights could go beyond the decision of self-governing communities to undertake special measures to prevent assimilation and to revive beleaguered traditional cultures; it could also emerge from the routine transactions of bureaucratic politics. As a general rule, First Nation people shun bureaucratic red tape. Historically, First Nations faced considerable frustration with Indian Affairs, which seemed erratically to dispense or withhold aid. More recently, prolonged land claims negotiations, court battles, and constitutional conferences have only intensified leaders' distaste for big government. Yet, as First Nation individuals continue to assume bureaucratic roles in their own administrations, they may find themselves offering the same excuses and incurring the same delays.[16] Moreover, some First Nation bureaucrats could be insensitive, partial and arbitrary, and could use cultural values and the "Indian way" as a cover for incompetence and corruption.

There is, of course, another side to this issue. Objections to self-government made on behalf of individual liberty are valid only if we accept certain individualistic assumptions. Where we assert that neutrality of government, bureaucratic organizations, and judicial institutions easily could be compromised, Harold Cardinal would retort that the problem exists only if First Nations seek neutrality. Where some Canadians argue that state protection of culture is an *illiberal* goal, a First Nation leader might shrug his shoulders and remark that finally, some have caught on. In short, *a liberal defense of the Charter's* uniform application addresses a conception of humans and society that is fundamentally incompatible with First Nations' traditional conceptions. Thus, we cannot fully understand First Nations' objections to the *Charter* without examining the philosophical assumptions underlying those objections. It is to these assumptions, to the philosophical core of our discussion of citizenship, that we now turn.

Philosophical Assumptions: Liberalism vs Traditional Aboriginal Thought

For both philosophical and practical reason, according to liberal theory, the individual should be the basic unit of political society[17] — a single, irreducible self that maintains "a unity through time, despite all physiological, psychological, intellectual and environmental changes" (Schwartz, 1986: 41). Moreover, the individual is the simplest unit capable of possessing rights. While there can be no disagreement as to who is entitled to the rights of a single individual, there can be marked confusion in determining the status of members of a group. Indeed, it has been so in Canada. Note, for example, the legal contortions Canadian governments have undergone in determining who is and is not "Indian". Setting aside even the troublesome question of who is Métis and what rights are held by Métis, the legal status of "full-blooded" Indians must still be determined. As noted by contemporary liberal commentator Bryan Schwartz (1986: 42), the "initial determination is, in many cases, going to be highly arbitrary". Some who have felt close ties to their community and have practiced its traditions have been excluded from Indian status by existing rules of membership prescribed either by bands themselves, or by the *Indian Act* and Bill C-31. Others have retained their legal Indian status, yet very little personal identification with the community. The problems, however, do not end with the determination of membership. Liberals submit that to ascertain special rights for a group, the state must endow the group *as a whole* with certain attributes. It first must determine First Nation people's general, definitive characteristics, and then deal with individuals simply as members of the group. "The inaccuracy and imprecision that comes from applying group generalizations to individuals," objects Schwartz (1986: 43), "is at the heart of the criticism of the worst forms of discrimination".

As a being capable of determining his or her ends in life, an individual within the context of liberal theory should be free, as far as possible, to choose those ends. The assumption that members must be coerced by the state to adopt the practices of their group offends liberal principles. For liberals, then, the *Charter* issue is one of philosophical principle: as human beings and as free agents, First Nation people should have their *Charter* rights whether they wish them or not. Not only do the rights articulated in the *Charter* guarantee individuals' fundamental equality before the law, they also are legal protections of humans' defining characteristic — our ability to choose among different ways of life. As it turns out, this argument is difficult for First Nations to accept.

Although acceptance of the *Charter* varies among First Nations, many aboriginal leaders and academics agree that its emphasis upon individual rights at the expense of community "poses yet another serious threat to the cultural identity of native Indians in Canada" (Boldt and Long, 1985a: 165). At best, the *Charter* lacks relevance for traditional conceptions of society. At worst, its application to First Nation governments would frustrate attempts to articulate essential beliefs and principles. Ultimately, it may subvert the cultural identity of First Nations. The argument merits further inquiry, as it is difficult for many Canadians to acknowledge.

Defenders of traditional cultures remind us that liberal individualism is not in our chromosomes. Rather, it is a particular view of human nature, and one many aboriginals find offensive. Cardinal (1977: 155), for example, chastens his fellow Indians for being "... brainwashed into believing that an individual could survive on his own, be self-sufficient, without reference to anything or anyone else". In support, Long and Chiste (1994: 96–98) note that although traditional mythologies encourage autonomy in fulfillment of obligations, they are incapable of envisaging individuals apart from the context of the "harmonious whole". Noted anthropologist Diamond Jenness (1963: 167) observed in 1930 that, whether they were Mi'kmaq, Algonquin or Haida, Indians did not "picture any great chasm separating mankind from the rest of creation". Nature and society defined the roles assumed by persons; a human was satisfied only through cheerful fulfillment of the responsibilities conferred upon her by external sources. In such a society, "individual rights" such as those found in the *Charter* would have been not only unwelcome: they were conceptually impossible. Their fit with traditional First Nation societies would be as misplaced as it would have been two thousand years ago in the Athenian polis.

Given their conception of themselves, traditional First Nation people did not require impartial laws to govern behaviour. Rather, they relied wholly upon "customary authority" representing the "sacred and ultimate wisdom" of past generations. Custom, according to Menno Boldt and J. Anthony Long (1985b: 338), was the Creator's "sacred blueprint" for the tribe's survival. An individual's breach of custom not only jeopardized the tribe, it marked a revolt against oneself and Nature. Through members' common observance of custom, traditional communities maintained order without resorting to institutional enforcement. An interplay of deeply held religious beliefs and guidance from others checked individual eccentricities. In cases of extreme anti-social behaviour, offenders were banished from the group, a measure that effectively destroyed their existence as social beings.

When First Nation leaders explain their cultures' traditional beliefs, they often are accused of "utopianism" or of sentimentalizing the past. Certainly, some have succumbed to such tendencies. However, the importance of tribal customs must not be dismissed out of hand. While hierarchical institutions were not necessary in traditional tribal societies, it does not follow that First Nation people were naturally "good". And nowhere in Boldt and Long's presentation of custom is it suggested that, before contact with Europeans, First Nation people required no constraints upon their behaviour. Instead, the constraints were informal rather than formal, so informal that individuals likely would not have experienced them as constraints at all. Traditional aboriginal communities were of the sort that British philosopher Peter Laslett has labeled "the face to face" society. "It is like a family," Laslett (1963: 159) submits,

> an enormously large family, a whole kin living together...but it is not a family. It has an infinitely longer continuous history, with no break at the generations: its purposes are ever so much wider; they are, in fact, the totality of purposes.

For many thousands of years, tribal societies in North America existed successfully without rights guaranteeing a sphere of inviolable autonomy. And for many thousands of years, not only did members not perceive their *lack* of rights, they did not perceive rights at all.[18]

"So we lived life differently," said Georges Erasmus (in Cassidy, 1991: 24), but, "because we lived this way for tens of thousands of years, is that to mean we lost our sovereignty, because we had a different vision of why human beings are alive?" Erasmus' question is critical. Although referring to the notion of sovereignty generally, he has identified a pressing, central frustration of First Nations. If First Nation people are truly seen to be Canadians, then why should their traditional self-conception continually be rejected in favour of the dominant liberal one? And if, by being Canadians, they are compelled to set aside the ultimate worth of their beliefs, why should they *wish* to be Canadian? At present, of course, they have no choice. The *Charter* of Rights applies equally to citizens throughout the country, including First Nation individuals. Despite its commitment to the "inherent right to self-government", the ill-fated Charlottetown accord clearly stipulated that the *Charter* would "apply immediately to governments of aboriginal peoples". Our concern, though, is not whether the *Charter* does apply; rather, the question is whether it should apply.

Certainly in terms of superior political strength, Canadians could impose *Charter* protection upon First Nations. Yet such an imposition is not legitimate without meaningful justifications. Non-Aboriginals must seek to convince not only themselves, but also First Nations, of the legitimacy of existing arrangements. Both in its practical application to First Nation governments and in its symbolic worth to First Nation people, the *Charter* must be seen to be relevant.

TOWARD A RESOLUTION?

We have seen that First Nations are unlikely to be persuaded by concerns for the national interest, for federalism's requirements, or for liberal principles with respect to the *Charter's* application to their communities. Yet, First Nation people and other Canadians will both concede that we all must co-exist somehow. With the aim of co-existence in mind, we suggest the adoption of certain guiding principles. We first assert the obvious: despite cultural differences, we all are humans sharing certain traits and experiences. Secondly, we should search for a solution that suits the present context of First Nation people rather than that of a pristine traditional culture. Thirdly, we should observe a commitment to fairness rather than to pure expediency. Finally, we should consider the impact upon social order. We believe that the *Charter's* application to First Nation governments can be justified. Yet contrary to many liberal observers, we submit that adherence strictly to liberal argumentation does not suffice.

There are a number of persuasive arguments for the *Charter's* application. First, it is far from certain that the general First Nation population would reject its *Charter* rights. First Nation women's organizations, in particular, have expressed concern that women's rights would be endangered by First Nation governments. In 1930, Diamond Jenness (1963: 52) contended that in every tribe, women's "lives were full of drudgery at all times and their status very inferior". According to recent testimony, Indian women's status has improved only slightly. In their 1994 report to the Royal Commission on Aboriginal Peoples, members of the Native Women's Association of Canada expressed concern about models of self-government being considered in their communities; they were not certain their rights would be adequately protected by local governments thought to be "sexist" and "elitist" (see RCAP, 1994: 23–24). For these reasons, Indian women's organizations consistently challenged the NIB and later, its AFN counterpart by recommending that the *Charter*, or at very least an Indian Bill of Rights, apply to First Nation governments.

A second significant factor is the large aboriginal population living outside the territorial boundaries of First Nations. Although many non-status and urban-dwelling status Indians suffer the sociological ills faced by aboriginal people generally, they are unlikely to see far-reaching implementation of self-government in urban areas soon. And certainly, the *Charter* will continue to apply to urban aboriginal people living beyond the territorial range of self-governing communities. Yet, the Royal Commission's 1992 report on urban Indians has indicated that this population also seeks to retain its cultural heritage. One of the report's participants declared that "We don't leave our identity at the edge of the city" (RCAP, 1992: 3). First Nation leaders stressing only the territorial dimension of self-determination implicitly threaten to restrict Indian cultural identity to its territorial base. Exemption of First Nation governments from the *Charter* would serve to deepen the legal/political rift between the residents of self-governing communities and their urban cousins. Yet, urban dwellers could play an important role in reminding community-based leaders that without the will to survive as a people, no amount of territory or political recognition will ensure the survival of a cultural identity. Would not the cultural survival of First Nation people be better served by emphasizing the on- and off-reserve populations' commonality through the application, to all, of a document which certainly will apply to half?

Thirdly, First Nations might wish to reconsider their symbolic rejection of Canadian citizenship from the standpoint of political and social order. Political stability in self-governing communities is vulnerable, especially in those communities which unilaterally have asserted their sovereignty. For example, in 1986 Ponting (1986: 177) concluded in a case study of Kahnawake Mohawks that their experience in self-government had been exemplary, and indeed, that it offered "development lessons and models" for other bands' consideration. Recall not only the Kahnawake of 1990, but also the "neighbouring" Mohawk community of Kanehsatake (adjacent to Oka) of the mid-1990s; "lawlessness" and "bitter factionalism" were said to prevail in an area where Québec police were reluctant to intervene. Mohawk traditionalists claim they were overwhelmed by opportunists, quick to exploit the area's uncertain authority for personal aggrandizement (Makin, 1994). Although the situation at Oka/Kanehsatake and Kahnawake should be construed as much Canada's making as the militants' own, it points to a social dissolution to which all communities, at least potentially, are prone. From the standpoint of order, the advantages of retaining an unambiguously federal relationship with Canada might outweigh the costs.

Fourthly, Laslett (1963: 163) has written that the continued survival of face-to-face society is precarious: "… it is liable to complete breakdown when the correspondents no longer share enough knowledge of each other's experience, a breakdown which can only be repaired by the renewal of shared situations". At first glance, Laslett's statement seems like a classic argument favouring self-determination. However, given the context in which First Nation communities presently find themselves, First Nation traditions are unlikely to survive in a pristine state. Already, contemporary First Nations' communities have incorporated some elements of western political beliefs and structures.[19] Although First Nation people may not have perceived their individual rights before the arrival of Europeans, we can be sure they perceive them now. Traditions aside, how many of us personally would reject a document guaranteeing our right to act more or less as we please? Conceivably, if a First Nation government were to reject the *Charter's* application, individual members would resent their lack of rights. True, aboriginal charters could be drafted, but some "rights talk" similar to the Canadian *Charter's* language probably would have to be included. Where Canadians in Edmonton and Bonnyville possess rights against their governments, the residents of Hobbema are likely to want similar protection as a final appeal. We submit that if First Nation governments are to retain the allegiance of their members, the language of rights must enter the picture at some point. We suggest, for practical reasons concerning equality and uniformity, and for symbolic reasons concerning citizenship, that the point at which individual rights should enter the picture is in the Canadian *Charter's* application to First Nation governments.

We turn now to the philosophical assumptions involved in the *Charter* debate. Already, we have seen that in their conceptions of human beings, First Nation leaders and liberal democrats seem to be opposed. For the former, "individuality" is not a relevant base upon which to build political institutions. For the latter, individuality is everything; any obligation conferred upon the individual by an external source is construed as an imposition, as coercion. In the liberal context, the rights and freedoms of individuals must be protected even at the risk of group interests and values, including cultural survival. Which view is correct?

Certainly, liberal individualists could gain from a meaningful consideration of traditional First Nation beliefs. If, by its emphasis upon personal autonomy, the liberal argument seems indifferent to the particular circumstances of aboriginal claims, it is because it must be. The theoretical implications of Western liberal political theory preclude consideration of a meaningful continuity *between* individuals. Where humans are conceived as autonomous subjects freely choosing or refusing to follow certain life plans, the "associations" we form can only be voluntary. In this world view, our history and culture in no way constitute our understanding of ourselves. At best, individuals can experience only sentimental ties with others. Cultural and historical communities can be only voluntary associations to which autonomous selves subscribe.[20]

Does liberal theory fit with the evidence, with actual human experience? We can only offer some suggestions at this point. What of the social dimensions of poverty and abuse that have afflicted various First Nation communities? Are we to attribute that poverty and abuse entirely to individual band members' freely chosen pursuit of an impoverished and abusive life plan? The experience of Indians attending residential schools earlier in this century also attests to culture's centrality to our conception of self. Former students describe a sense of radical disorientation and permanent loss as they were stripped of their languages and traditional beliefs. From much of the evidence within First Nation communities, it would appear that liberal theory's autonomous self who defines and pursues her own ends does not live anywhere in the real world.

Yet does it necessarily follow that we are defined wholly by our social context? Turning once again to experience on reserves, it appears that this portrayal of behaviour also is incomplete. Certainly, there has been violence and alcoholism on reserves, but there has also been recovery. Examples have been set, lives have been turned around, individuals have achieved sufficient distance from their social environment to reflect upon living habits, and to change those habits. In spite of our contextual existence, it appears as though humans are capable of a significant measure of choice.

The problem has preoccupied theorists for centuries; it would be a feat, indeed, if we were to arrive at a definitive answer in this chapter. Yet, by attending to the evidence, we find that the individual's lot includes both choice and context. Perhaps only a mutual acknowledgment of both *features* of individual identity can provide a genuine accommodation of aboriginal beliefs and liberal tenets.

It is our belief that heightened clarity in philosophical matters might yield a fuller conception of citizenship. In the *Charter* debate, Canadians, including aboriginal peoples, have been offered an opportunity to apply this conception in practice. First Nation people have valuable political and cultural traditions that could come to sustain a healthy cultural identity where they do not already. Thus, existing Canadian governments' political commitment to First Nations' enhanced autonomy seems philosophically justified. So too, though, does constitutional affirmation of equality among *individuals*, insofar as that equality is based upon a justifiable assumption of an equal capacity for free decision. Seen in this light, the *Charter* is a legitimate symbol of Canadians' commitment to the possibility of free choice. For our part, we are convinced that this possibility holds equally for First Nation people and for other Canadians. It is our hope that First Nation leaders will be convinced as well.

NOTES

[1] In the months preceding the drafting of the constitutional accord at Charlottetown in 1992, an unprecedented number of Canadians favoured not only self-government, but even constitutional recognition of First Nations' cultural distinctiveness. In a poll conducted by Gallup on January 6, 1992, 47% of adult Canadians responded affirmatively to the proposition that aboriginal communities should exercise powers similar to provincial powers. ("More Favour than Oppose Native Self-Government Concept", *Gallup Report*, Monday, January 6, 1992.) More striking still were the polling results March 26, 1992: 59% of adult Canadians approved of the proposal to designate First Nation people as a constitutionally "distinct society". ("Majority Supports designating Natives as 'Distinct Society'", *Gallup Report*, March 26, 1992).

[2] The Métis settlements in Alberta are closely analogous to the First Nations discussed here.

[3] The unique situations which prevail in the northern territories will not be addressed in the present analysis, as it is difficult to encompass their idiosyncratic features into a more general analysis.

[4] See for example, Cardinal (1977).

[5] One could imagine that in some forums there would have to be a single Aboriginal representative who could speak with authority not only for First Nations but also for the Métis and Inuit.

[6] Various Mohawk leaders, for example, have rejected unequivocally their Canadian citizenship. Grand Chief Michael Mitchell (1989: 135) wrote, "I am a citizen of Haudenosaunee; and if anyone says I am also a Canadian citizen, the most I can agree is that we have certain benefits in Canada, by treaty, the same benefits as we have in the United States".

[7] The conceptual confusion also has been noted by Thomas Flanagan (1985). The problem, Flanagan suggests, stems directly from First Nation leaders' self-interpretive terminology. The concept of "nation" historically has been wedded to the concept of "sovereignty"; thus, it is meaningless to speak of a nation without "implying a vision of self-government, either past, present, or future". Symbolism incompatible with the Canadian political order, he adds, "will inevitably tend to produce institutional disarray, for accepted symbols form the matrix of ideas in which public policy is made". The problems inherent in the attempt to accom-

modate several hundred nations within a federal state provide an example of Flanagan's observation.

[8] *Editor's Note:* After this chapter was written, the Royal Commission on Aboriginal Peoples released its final report, in which it recommended (Vol. 2, pp. 230–234) that the *Charter of Rights and Freedoms* apply to First Nation governments, but that in relation to core areas of aboriginal jurisdiction, they have the right to opt out of it by means of Sec. 33 (the "notwithstanding" clause). The Commission emphasized both that Sec. 35.4 of the *Constitution Act, 1982* provides an "unshakeable guarantee" of the equality of the sexes in the enjoyment of aboriginal and treaty rights and that Sec. 25 probably will have the effect of shielding only certain actions of aboriginal governments from *Charter* scrutiny.

[9] Self-government, whether modelled after Canadian municipalities or not, implies that First Nation governments will raise at least part of their revenue by taxing their residents. This aspect of First Nation government has understandably received much less attention than has been received by the increased power and control that self-government would bring.

[10] Here the Federation of Saskatchewan Indians (n.d.) has suggested, to the contrary, that only Indian governments should be able to tax non-Indians living and working on a reserve and non-Indian corporations located on a reserve.

[11] The equalization formula is based on revenues derived from close to thirty provincial tax sources. Thus, policy makers would determine which of these sources fall within the powers of First Nation governments; then, First Nation governments would be under pressure to impose those taxes falling within their domain.

[12] See Frank Cassidy and Robert L. Bish (1989), Chapters 3 and 4 on citizenship and policy-making, respectively.

[13] For an engaging first-hand discussion of the Laval and Bedard cases in the early 1970s, see Cardinal (1977: 107–115).

[14] J. Anthony Long and Katherine Beaty Chiste (1994) have made this point in a very useful article. According to them, the "generic individualism that underlies Western liberalism is, in its basic form, a homocentric philosophy, producing a concept of society composed of discreet persons...." (96). Such a conception of man and society, they submit, is "radically different" from the traditional belief systems of First Nation people. Consequently, the *Charter*, the underlying principles of which are largely alien to First Nation populations, should not apply to First Nation governments. For a complementary discussion, see Menno Boldt (1993).

[15] For a discussion of the centralizing effects of the *Charter*, see Knopff and Morton (1992: 73ff).

[16] Boldt has expressed concern for the increasing bureaucratization of First Nations. See Boldt (1993: 80–81).

[17] There is much debate among Western liberals as to the details of liberal theory. Our intent, however, will be limited to presenting only those aspects of liberalism that are fundamental to the theory. The primacy of the individual as the basic political and philosophical unit of society is both central to liberal theory and unique to the Western European tradition. See Long and Chiste (1994: 98). For an explanation of the basic philosophical tenets of liberalism, see Ball and Dagger (1995: 51–92).

[18] We are using the term "rights" here in the sense of its philosophical origins in Western liberal thought. Long and Chiste (1994) have indicated that "individual

entitlements" indeed existed in traditional Indian societies. They also have suggested (p. 97), though, that this conception of rights is the "logical outgrowth of
a belief in the interrelatedness of all life and the necessity of harmony between
parts". We are convinced that a conception of rights based outside the individual
is no conception of rights at all. At very least, the designation of two very different perceptions of existence by a single term invites confusion. At worst, it threatens to undermine that term's original significance.

[19] Long's and Chiste's (1994: 111, 112) contribution contains a comparative analysis
of traditional and contemporary beliefs among Canada's Plains Indian tribes.
They submit that a "polar opposition" between the cultures and governing
processes of traditional indigenous societies and Western ones no longer exists.
Rather, contemporary First Nation communities have been required to modify
their traditional orientations.

[20] For a thorough critique of the sort of self that is assumed by modern liberal theorists, see Michael Sandel (1982).

REFERENCES

Asch, Michael
1984 *Home and Native Land: Aboriginal Rights and the Canadian Constitution.*
Toronto: Methuen.
Ball, Terence and Richard Dagger
1995 *Political Ideologies and the Democratic Ideal*, 2nd ed. (New York: HarperCollins
Publishers.
Boldt, Menno
1993 *Surviving as Indians: The Challenge of Self-Government.* Toronto: University of
Toronto Press.
Boldt, Menno and J. Anthony Long
1985a "Tribal Philosophies and the *Canadian Charter of Rights and Freedoms*", PP.
165–179 in Menno Boldt and J. Anthony Long (eds.), *The Quest for Justice:
Aboriginal People and Aboriginal Rights.* Toronto: University of Toronto Press.

1985b "Tribal Traditions and European-Western Political Ideologies: The Dilemma
of Canada's Native Indians", pp. 333–346 in Menno Boldt and J. Anthony
Long (eds.), *The Quest for Justice: Aboriginal People and Aboriginal Rights.*
Toronto: University of Toronto Press.
Cardinal, Harold
1977 *The Rebirth of Canada's Indians.* Edmonton: Hurtig Publishers.
Cassidy, Frank (ed.)
1991 *Aboriginal Self-Determination.* Lantzville, B.C.: Oolichan Books.
Cassidy, Frank and Robert L. Bish
1989 *Indian Government: Its Meaning in Practice.* Halifax: Institute for Research on
Public Policy.
Delacourt, Susan
1994 *United We Fall: In Search of a New Canada.* Toronto: Penguin Books.
Federation of Saskatchewan Indians
n.d.   "Revenue and Resource Sharing and Indian Economic Development".
Flanagan, Thomas
1985 "The Sovereignty and Nationhood of Canadian Indians: A Comment on
Boldt and Long", *Canadian Journal of Political Science*, XVIII:2, 371–374.

Jenness, Diamond
1963   *Indians of Canada*, 6th edition, (Ottawa: Roger Duhamel, F.R.S.C.).

Knopff, Rainer and F. L. Morton
1992   *Charter Politics*. Scarborough, Ont.: Nelson Canada.

Laslett, Peter
1963   "The Face-to-Face Society", in P. Laslett, ed., *Philosophy, Politics and Society*. Oxford: Basil Blackwell.

Long, J. Anthony and Katherine Beaty Chiste
1994   "Indian Governments and the Canadian *Charter* of Rights and Freedoms", *American Indian Culture and Research Journal*, 18:2.

Makin, Kirk
1994   "When gangs ride herd: Lawlessness the issue in Oka of today", *The Globe and Mail*, October 27, A1.

Mitchell, Michael
1989   "Akwesasne: An Unbroken Assertion of Sovereignty", pp. 105–136 in Boyce Richardson (ed.), *Drum Beat: Anger and Renewal in Indian Country*. Toronto: Summerhill Press.

Penner, Keith, M.P. (Chairman)
1983   *Report of the Special Committee on Indian Self-Government*. Ottawa: Supply and Services Canada.

Ponting, J. Rick
1986   "Institution-Building in an Indian Community: A Case Study of Kahnawake (Caughnawaga)", pp. 151–178 in J. Rick Ponting (ed.), *Arduous Journey: Canadian Indians and Decolonization*. Toronto: McClelland and Stewart.

Royal Commission on Aboriginal Peoples (RCAP)
1992   *Aboriginal Peoples in Urban Centres*. Ottawa: Supply and Services Canada.

_____
1993   *Partners in Confederation*. Ottawa: Supply and Services Canada.

_____
1994   *Toward Reconciliation: Overview of the Fourth Round*. Ottawa: Supply and Services Canada.

Sanderson, Chief Sol
1981   "Submission to the Parliamentary Task Force on Federal-Provincial Fiscal Arrangements", Ottawa, May 12.

Schwartz, Bryan
1986   *First Principles, Second Thoughts: Aboriginal Peoples, Constitutional Reform and Canadian Statecraft*. Montreal: The Institute for Research on Public Policy.

Sandel, Michael
1982   *Liberalism and the Limits of Justice*. Cambridge: Cambridge University Press.

Wuttunee, William I. C.
1971   *Ruffled Feathers: Indians in Canadian Society*, Calgary: Bell Books.

CHAPTER 16

THE GOVERNMENT OF NUNAVUT (1999): A PROSPECTIVE ANALYSIS

André Légaré [1]

The forthcoming creation of the government of Nunavut[2] Territory (1999) is the result of nearly twenty years of arduous negotiations led by the Inuit Tapirisat of Canada (ITC) and the Tungavik Federation of Nunavut (TFN) opposite the federal and Northwest Territories (NWT) governments. The reasons which encouraged the Inuit, during the 1970s, to reclaim their own territory revolved principally around three facts: they constitute a culturally homogenous majority in central and eastern NWT; they had no treaty with the federal government to clarify their aboriginal rights; and the seat of NWT administrative and political power is geographically far-removed in Yellowknife. With the coming establishment of their own government, the Inuit of NWT are convinced that they will be able to better protect their culture and that they will be better off politically and socio-economically.

According to the federal statute (Bill C-132) creating Nunavut, passed by Parliament on June 10, 1993, the Nunavut Territory government will be officially installed on April 1, 1999. It will be the newest member of the Canadian federation. Although Nunavut Territory will be administered by a public and non-ethnic government, the Inuit majority in the central and eastern Arctic will render the Nunavut Territory government *de facto* Inuit. It will probably better respond to the needs and interests of the Inuit than the present NWT government.

The formation of Nunavut Territory will necessitate the division of NWT. However, there is nothing unique about that, for the borders of NWT have been altered several times down through history in order to create Manitoba (1870), Yukon (1898), and Saskatchewan and Alberta (1905). In addition, the area of the territory shrank when the borders of Manitoba, Québec, and Ontario expanded northward. As Hamelin (1982: 251) has observed: "The history of the NWT is, above all, one of modifications of space, especially in the sense of the shrinking or stripping of its territory". Thus, we should not be surprised at the forthcoming division of the NWT to form two new territories (see Map 1) — the Western Territory,[3] of which the population of 33,335 persons is composed of a non-aboriginal majority, and in the east, the Nunavut Territory of 20,466 persons composed of an Inuit majority (87%).

Geographically, at 2,121,102 square kilometres (20% of Canada), Nunavut Territory will be the largest jurisdiction in the federation. In addition to the bulk of the Canadian Arctic archipelago, Nunavut will encompass the islands of Hudson Bay, James Bay, and Ungava Bay. In fact, the outline of Nunavut's bor-

MAP 1 Nunavut Territory (1999)

Source: Adapted from NIC, 1994b: i.

ders corresponds largely to the area of traditional use and occupation of the Arctic by the Inuit of NWT (c.f., Freeman, 1976).

The Nunavummiut[4] are grouped into 27 widely dispersed communities. Generally, these communities are small (average population is 800 people), except for the regional administrative centres of Cambridge Bay (population 1,800), Rankin Inlet (2,400) and Iqaluit (3,600).

This chapter first provides a brief account of the events which led to the idea of the division of NWT and the approval of the political accord on Nunavut. The chapter also highlights the role of various actors implicated in the implementation of the Nunavut territorial government. However, the principal objective is to perform a prospective analysis of the financing and legislative and administrative structures of the future government of Nunavut. We shall lay out the political structure which the Government of Nunavut will inherit at its inauguration on April 1, 1999. Finally, we shall examine the substantial political issues which surround the creation of the Nunavut government. In order to attain these objectives, the chapter draws largely on various works, press releases, and reports, especially the report entitled *Footprints in New Snow / L'empreinte de nos pas sur la neige fraîche* (NIC / CEN, 1995a), already disseminated by the Nunavut Implementation Commission, which commission is charged with providing advice on matters pertaining to setting up the Nunavut government.

The Issue of the Division of NWT

In an earlier article (Légaré, 1993a), I traced and analysed the stages which led to the signing of the accord on the land claims of the Inuit of Nunavut (DIAND, 1993). Before getting to the heart of the matter in the present chapter, it is appropriate to review here the principal events which led to the settlement of the Inuit claims. I shall emphasize the obstacles which TFN had to surmount before finalizing a political accord on Nunavut.

In February 1976, Inuit Tapirisat of Canada, which represents all Canadian Inuit, proposed the creation of the Government of Nunavut within the framework of the federal government's comprehensive land claims policy (DIAND, 1973). In its document entitled "Nunavut: A Proposal for the Settlement of Inuit Land Claims in the NWT" (ITC, 1976), ITC called for the formation of a new government which would cover central and eastern parts of the NWT:

> The fundamental idea is to create a territory where the great majority of the inhabitants will be Inuit. In itself, this territory and its institutions would better reflect the values and views of the Inuit than does the present NWT. (ITC, 1976: 15)

This demand was reiterated in the subsequent versions of the document as published in 1977 and 1979. Nevertheless, the federal government, already occupied with the separatist inclinations of the Québec government, was scarcely interested in creating another political entity of which the population would be largely culturally distinct from the anglophone majority of Canada.

Paradoxically, it was the political initiatives of the Government of the NWT (GNWT) during the 1980s, which forced Ottawa to negotiate the division of the Territories and to create Nunavut. Following the election of November 1979, the Legislative Assembly of the NWT was, for the first time, composed of an elected aboriginal majority.[5] The latter launched a Special Committee on Unity in order to guage the opinion of the residents of NWT on the idea of the creation of Nunavut. In its report presented in October 1980 (GNWT, 1980), the committee indicated that there was no consensus in the NWT population on the issue of the preservation of the geographical integrity of the NWT. Taking the [recommendations of the] report into account, the legislators voted in favour of the division of the NWT by a vote of sixteen to one[6], but in March 1981 the Legislative Assembly ordered a Territories-wide plebiscite in order to settle the issue of division.

The plebiscite of April 14, 1982, demonstrated that a majority (56%) of the NWT population endorsed the idea of division into two new political entities — in the west, the Western Territory, and Nunavut in the east. In the region of Nunavut itself, the level of approval was even higher at 69%.

The federal government, which until that time had been reticent about the idea of Nunavut, recognized the legitimacy of the plebiscite. Its Minister of Indian and Northern Affairs, John Munro, announced that the federal government would abide by the decision of the residents and Legislative Assembly of the NWT. However, Ottawa set three preconditions on division. They were: (1) the prior settlement of the Inuit land claims; (2) the establishment of a boundary which would separate the east and west of the Territories and would be approved by the residents of NWT; and (3) the reaching of a political accord defining the basic structural arrangements of the Government of Nunavut Territory.

The Land Claim Agreement

The task of arriving at an agreement with Ottawa on the Inuit land claims was placed in the hands of the Tungavik Federation of Nunavut (TFN).[7] In April 1990, after ten years of often intense negotiations (cf. Légaré, 1993b and Fenge et al., 1989), the representatives of TFN and of the federal government initialled an Agreement-in-Principle on the Inuit land claims (DIAND, 1991). Article 4 of that agreement recommended the creation of Nunavut and proposed a distinctive process of negotiation in order to ratify an accord on the political demands of the Inuit:

> Consistent with their long-standing positions, the Government of Canada, the Territorial Government, and the Tungavik Federation of Nunavut support in principle the creation of Nunavut Territory. . . . The Territorial Government and TFN undertake to develop, within six months of the Final Agreement, a process for giving effect to Section 4.1.1. . . . [T]he process shall include a territory-wide plebiscite on a boundary for division. . . .

> (DIAND, 1991, Art. 4.1.1 and 4.1.2).

The Final Agreement on the NWT Inuit land claims was signed several months later (December 1991) by the same actors. The document also reiterated the need to create a new territory in the central and eastern Canadian Arctic:[8]

> The Government of Canada will recommend to Parliament, as a government measure, legislation to establish, within a specified time period, a new Nunavut Territory with its own Legislative Assembly and public government, separate from the Government of the remainder of the Northwest Territories.

> (DIAND, 1993, chapt. 4.1.1)

Imbroglio[9] on the Frontier

Before a political accord on the creation of Nunavut could be concluded, there still remained the thorny question of the border for dividing the NWT. The Constitutional Alliance (CA), created in July of 1982 with a membership comprising aboriginal representatives and members of the Legislative Assembly of NWT, had, as one of its main tasks, the finding of a consensus among the diverse aboriginal factions on the question of the border between Nunavut and the western Territory.[10] However, after five years of negotiations, the members of the CA were not able to reach a consensus. The ticklish question of the use of lands by the Inuit and the Dené in the regions of Contwoyo Lake and the Thelon Game Sanctuary complicated the CA's task of finding a compromise border (cf. Légaré, 1993a: 44–47). Therefore, the Alliance was disbanded in July of 1987 with the border question still unresolved.

Pressured by the approach of the signing of the Final Agreement on Inuit land claims and impatient to arrive at a solution to the border issue, the leaders of TFN and the GNWT wrote to Canadian Prime Minister Brian Mulroney. By means of that letter they urged the federal authorities to find a solution to the border dispute and to enter into negotiations on a political accord. In fact, the letter of January 20, 1990, stipulated clearly (threatened) that there could be no Inuit approval of the Final Agreement on land claims if there were no parallel agreement on the Inuit political claims:

Inuit leaders believe strongly that the ratification of the Nunavut land claims by Inuit is likely only if there is a commitment to the creation of a Nunavut Territory and Government. In response to these considerations, we are proposing that Canada agree to introduce legislation to Parliament creating a Nunavut Territory on or before the time the Nunavut land claims ratification legislation is expected to be introduced.

(GNWT, FTN, 1990)

Responding to the pressure of the TFN and the GNWT and desirous of de-escalating the border impasse in order to open the way for the signing of a land agreement and a political accord with the Inuit, in April 1990 the federal government named former Commissioner of the NWT, John Parker, to act as mediator to settle the border question in advance of the dividing of the NWT. After multiple consultations with the Inuit and Dené representatives, in April 1991 Parker recommended a compromise border.

In a plebiscite on May 4, 1992, Parker's border was approved by 54% of the residents of NWT.

The Nunavut Political Accord

The signing of The Nunavut Final Land Claims Agreement in December 1991, coupled with the approval, in May of 1992, of the "Parker boundary line", opened the possibility of fulfilling the last condition established by the federal government at the beginning of the 1980s — the conclusion of a political agreement.

Chapter 4 of the Agreement-in-Principle and of the Nunavut Final Land Claims Agreement envisaged, over the short term, the creation of a negotiation process between TFN and the federal and territorial governments aimed at the creation of Nunavut Territory. The representatives of the TFN and of the governments entered into discussions on this subject beginning in April 1992. After six months of negotiations, they concluded a political accord on Nunavut (Canada, GNWT, TFN, 1992). That accord was signed on October 30, 1992, five days before the crucial vote by the Inuit on the Nunavut Final Land Claims Agreement.[11]

The political accord comprises five chapters and various articles. Table 1 highlights its principal features. Overall, this accord obliges Ottawa to support the creation of Nunavut Territory once the accord on the Inuit land claims in Nunavut is approved by the Parliament of Canada.[12] In addition, the accord envisages the creation of a commission [The Nunavut Implementation Commission] to provide advice to all parties on the details of the design of the political structure of the future government of Nunavut.

The political accord became the foundation of federal Bill C-132 (Canada, 1993), which is essentially modelled on the *NWT Act*. Thus, Nunavut Territory will get similar powers to those of the present NWT. Finally, on June 10, 1993, Bill C-132 was passed by Parliament — the same day as the Bill (C-133) respecting the Final Agreement on Inuit land claims in Nunavut. Bill C-132, *the Nunavut Act*, sets April 1, 1999,[13] for the inauguration of the Nunavut government.

The Nunavut Implementation Commission (NIC)

In the six months following the adoption of the *Nunavut Act*, a commission called "The Nunavut Implementation Commission" [in French, La Commission

TABLE 1 Summary of the Content of the Political Accord on Nunavut

1. The bill on Nunavut will go before Parliament at the same time as the bill on Nunavut land claims.
2. Nunavut Territory will come into legal existence on April 1, 1999.
3. The political powers of Nunavut will be the same as those presently held by the GNWT.
4. The structure of the Nunavut Legislative Assembly will be similar to that of the NWT.
5. The laws of NWT will all apply in Nunavut until such time as they are modified or abrogated by the Nunavut legislature.
6. A ten-member commission will have the task of designing the political structures of the Nunavut government.
7. Ottawa will pay the costs associated with the creation and operation of Nunavut Territory.
8. In Nunavut, education will be a priority; projects for the training of Inuit within the public service of Nunavut will be given priority.

Sources: Canada, GNWT, TFN (1992).

d'établissement du Nunavut (CEN)] was mounted. According to *Bill C-132*, the objective of the Commission was to formulate recommendations with the federal government, among others, on such matters as the site of the capital of Nunavut, administrative structures of the government, and operating procedures for the Nunavut Legislative Assembly. However, the decisions on implementing the Commission's recommendations are solely in Ottawa's hands (Canada, 1993: art. 58).

In December 1993, the ten members of the Commission were named by Ottawa from lists submitted by the federal government, GNWT, and Nunavut Tunngavik Inc. Each of these parties placed three members on the commission, while the chairman, John Amagoalik, was chosen by consensus.[14] The commissioners are supported in their work by about twenty bureaucrats. The operating costs of the Commission, which runs until July 1999, are about three million dollars per year. These sums are paid by the federal government.

In contrast to Nunavut Tunngavik Inc. (NTI)[15], which is an ethnic institution concerned exclusively with the interests of the Inuit of Nunavut, the Nunavut Implementation Commission is a public institution which is to be responsive to the interests of all of the residents of Nunavut. Tables 2 and 3 permit us to distinguish clearly the functions of each of these bodies.

During their first meeting, in January 1994 at Iqaluit, the commissioners established five permanent committees to help them with their task.[16] They concentrated on the conducting of preliminary research to produce a first draft working paper on the elaboration and operation of the Government of Nunavut (NIC, 1994a). The document establishes the general themes for discussion among the people of Nunavut. Thus, the Commission focussed efforts around the administrative structure of Nunavut, the composition of Nunavut's legislative assembly, the training of future civil servants, and the process for selecting the capital.

Equipped with its first discussion paper, the Commission undertook a consultation tour throughout all twenty-seven communities of Nunavut beginning in September 1994. These consultations took diverse forms. The commissioners met members of local councils and members of the Inuit associations (e.g., Nunavut Tunngavik, Inc.). They participated also in open-line radio shows and held public meetings in each of the communities. About 2600 persons attended

TABLE 2 The Nunavut Implementation Commission

Created	December 15, 1993
Pursuant to	*The Nunavut Act* (Bill C-132)
Composed of	ten commissioners, most of whom are Inuit
Objective	To formulate recommendations on the political structures of the future public government of Nunavut
Accountable to	federal government
Represents	all citizens (Inuit and non-Inuit) of Nunavut
Costs	$3 million per year, borne by Ottawa
Sunset	The Commission will cease to operate three months after the inauguration of Nunavut on July 1, 1999

these meetings. The public meetings attracted principally the Inuit and were conducted, for the most part, in the Inuktitut language. Between September 1994 and January 1995, the NIC convened sixty-two meetings with municipal leaders and community members and organized three radio phone-in shows. The process culminated in a conference which was held at Iqaluit on January 22–23, 1995. It attracted nearly one hundred delegates from all regions of Nunavut.

The consultations with the citizens as well as the negotiations with the leaders and representatives of the federal, territorial, and local governments led to the publication of the Commission's first report entitled *Footprints in New Snow* (NIC, 1995a). In this 100-page report divided into fourteen chapters and about twenty appendices, the NIC makes one hundred and four recommendations aimed at defining the political structures of the Government of Nunavut. This report, which, let us remember, constitutes the basis of the present chapter, was tabled in May 1995 around the time of certain federal and territorial actions aimed at co-ordinating activities preparatory to the establishment of the Government of Nunavut.[17] The report gathered ideas revealed by the Commission in various working papers and ideas garnered from the Nunavut population during the consultative meetings. With considerable lucidity, it envisaged a model of the probable operations of the future Government of Nunavut.

TABLE 3 Nunavut Tunngavik Inc.

Created	March 23, 1993
Pursuant to	*An Act on Land Claims* (Bill C-133)
Composed of	eight elected members
Objective	manage the land claims agreement
Accountable to	the Inuit of Nunavut
Represents	the 17,500 Inuit of Nunavut
Costs	$15 million per year, drawn from the funds directed to the Inuit under the Agreement
Sunset	ITN is a permanent institution

The Government of Nunavut

According to Bill C-132 [*The Nunavut Act*], Nunavut Territory will have a public, responsible government in which legislative authority will be exercised by the elected members of the Assembly. Nunavut Territory will be equipped with the same public institutions as NWT: a Commissioner, an Executive Council (Cabinet), a Legislative Assembly, a public service, and various boards. The powers of the Government of Nunavut will be similar to the present powers of GNWT[18] (Canada, 1993: Part I).

In addition, the laws in effect in NWT will apply to the future Nunavut Territory from April 1, 1999, onward. Thus, there will not be a legislative vacuum during the period following the establishment of Nunavut (Canada, 1993: Sec. 29). However, the first session of the Nunavut Legislative Assembly could eventually be called upon to modify or repeal certain laws of NWT which might seem incongruous in Nunavut. By way of example, the *Act Pertaining to Indian Reserves* would be useless in Nunavut; it would also be appropriate to revise the *Official Languages Act of NWT*,[19] for it mentions several Amerindian languages which are not spoken in Nunavut.

The establishment of the Nunavut Territory government will put into the hands of the Inuit the powers that they do not already hold under the land claims Final Agreement. These powers are principally of a socio-economic nature: language, culture, health, social services, sustainable development, finances, etc. The NIC believes that these powers will protect Inuit culture from excessive acculturation, in a manner somewhat akin to the case of the powers of the Government of Québec and french culture:

> The Government of Nunavut will undertake to protect and preserve the distinct society which has existed in Nunavut for thousands of years.
>
> (NIC, 1994b: 1)

Finally, the coat of arms and the flag of Nunavat ought to convey the unique and distinct character of the people and wildlife of the Arctic. Thus, it would be of no surprise if this flag bears an Inuk, an inukshuk, or a polar bear. For the NIC, it is important that the emblems reflect the cultural and ecological richness of Nunavut.

The Structure of the Nunavut Legislative Assembly

The election of a first Legislative Assembly will take place in February 1999. The Assembly should hold its first working session in April 1999. This Assembly will be elected for a maximum period of five years by all the Nunavummiut.[20] The Assembly would hold its first working session by August 1999.

As in NWT, the Nunavut Legislative Assembly will function on the basis of the principle of consensus. Thus, there will not be any political parties in Nunavut;[21] all members of the Legislative Assembly would sit as independents. In this unique variant of the British parliamentary system, the policy decisions are made by a majority of the legislators and all would have the right to freely express divergent views (cf. White, 1991). Bills would generally be put forward by Cabinet and would have to garner the support of the majority of the independent legislators [to become law]. For example, in a Nunavut Legislative Assembly of twenty-three members, it would be necessary to have at least twelve members voting in favour of a bill for it to pass. Bearing in mind the fact that such a bill would enjoy unanimity within a seven-person Cabinet [Executive Council], it would be necessary to bring only five additional members of the Assembly "on-side" for the bill to become law. In such a context, the opinions of several members are often ignored. A member who is not a member of Cabinet and who tables a bill would have little chance of seeing his/her bill adopted, for (s)he would have a difficult time winning over at least eleven colleagues. Succinctly stated, the Nunavut parliamentary system, based on the principle of consensus, would give an important weight to [the Territorial] Cabinet, for there would be no parties and therefore no party discipline.

The electoral map of Nunavut would include eleven electoral districts. However, according to NIC, an assembly of only about a dozen members would not adequately reflect the opinions and interests of the population. Moreover, with so few legislators, it would be difficult to form a suitable Executive Council [Cabinet]. To address this problem, the Commission, in a document published in September 1994 (NIC, 1994c), suggested the election of two members — a man and a woman — in each electoral district. The Legislative Assembly thereby would have twenty-two members and also would become the first parliament in the world to guarantee an equal representation of male and female members. As such, it could have been a model for democratic peoples everywhere, [had it not been defeated in a 1997 referendum — Ed.].

However, the suggestion of creating dual-member constituencies does not yet enjoy unanimous support in Nunavut. The federal government support is, at best, lukewarm, while the GNWT does not support it, for that larger number of legislators would create additional administrative costs for the assembly — an assembly which would have as many members as the legislative assembly of Prince Edward Island (pop. 130,000) but which would represent only about 28,000 persons in 1999.

The Premier of Nunavut would be elected by the total electorate of Nunavut, as a twenty-third member of the Assembly. He would select and control a Cabinet of six ministers who would be chosen from among the elected members of the Assembly. As elsewhere in Canada, the Cabinet would be responsible to the Legislative Assembly.[22]

The highest dignitary of the Nunavut Assembly will be a Commissioner who will represent the Queen and will be appointed by the federal Cabinet. As in NWT, the Commissioner's function will be essentially ceremonial. As with the provincial lieutenants governor, he is expected to comply with the decisions of the Legislative Assembly.

In order to ensure a smooth transition, an Interim Commissioner will be named about two years before the installation of Nunavut[23] (NIC, 1995a: 20). The Interim Commissioner would have the requisite authority, under *The Nunavut Act* (Sec. 71), to make binding commitments on behalf of the future Government of Nunavut in the following areas: (1) recruitment of personnel for the future ministries; (2) entry into agreement with the federal government on the financing of the future Government of Nunavut; (3) entry into agreement concerning the division of the assets and liabilities of NWT; (4) intergovernmental agreements with GNWT on certain programmes and services which could be jointly provided by both governments (GNWT and Nunavut) in the future.

Thus, the Interim Commissioner would have important powers. He or she would be one of the principal architects of the Government of Nunavut. He or she would be named by the federal cabinet[24] and would have to abide by written instructions issued by the federal Minister of Indian Affairs and Northern Development. However, the other actors involved in the formation of Nunavut Territory — NIC, NTI, and GNWT — would be consulted in advance on matters dealing with any such written instructions which the Interim Commissioner might receive. In the exercise of his/her authority, the Interim Commissioner would also have to consult those sitting members of the NWT Assembly who come from the Nunavut region and the presidents of NTI and NIC (NIC, 1995a: 87–89).

To assist him/her in the job, the Interim Commissioner would have an office in Yellowknife and another in Ottawa. However, his/her main office would be located at Iqaluit. The Interim Commissioner would cease his/her duties with the appointment of the first permanent Commissioner, at the time of the establishment of the Government of Nunavut.

The Administrative Structure of Nunavut

The future Government of Nunavut will have only ten ministries and eight agencies (see Figure 1). all of which would begin functioning on April 1, 1999. Thus, the administrative structure of Nunavut would be less complex than that of the present GNWT.[25] For instance, there will be no Board of Health; the delivery of programs will be done directly under the auspices of the Nunavut Ministry of Health and Social Services. Education will be administered by a single pan-territorial council and not, as is the case presently in the NWT, by regional councils (NIC, 1995a: 40).

Certain other bodies would operate under a co-management regime due to the shared political jurisdiction of the GNWT and the Government of Nunavut. Notable examples are the NWT Power Corporation and the NWT Workers' Compensation Board (NIC, 1995a: 40).

In addition to being a more streamlined administration, offering programmes and services similar to those of NWT, Nunavut Territory, in order to affirm its legitimacy and to distinguish itself from the present administration of NWT, will likely fashion itself into a decentralized government that is closer to the Inuit people, as much by its policies as by the geographical presence of its institutions, as it asserts its presence throughout the vast territory over which its very small population is dispersed.

Decentralization

For NIC, it is clear that the Government of Nunavut ought to be decentralized (NIC, 1995a: 25). The decentralization envisaged by the Commission actually would be a means of assuring that the new jobs created by the administration of Nunavut would be distributed throughout the territory, in order to benefit the greatest number of communities. In fact, it would involve further decentralizing administrative positions from the capital to the regional centres.

Thus, it might be that the headquarters of certain ministries will be grouped into three thematic areas. The administrative offices of these three respective thematic sectors could each be located in a different region of Nunavut. The three broad areas are the "public domain", comprising health, education, and [social] services; (2) "lands and resources", comprising natural resources,

FIGURE 1 Nunavut Proposed Departmental Structure

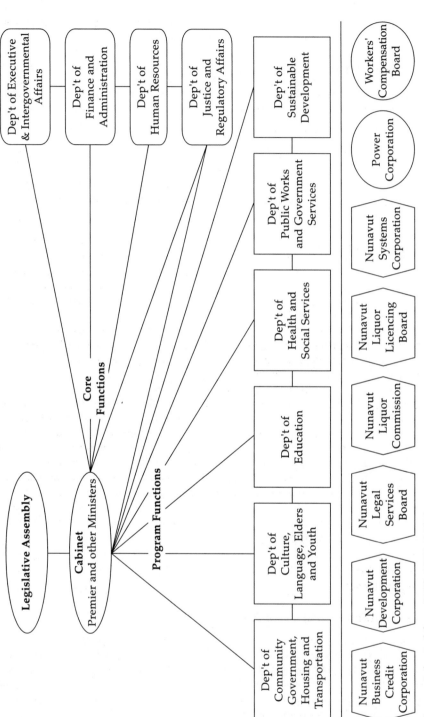

Source: Adapted from NIC, 1995: A10.2

energy, and economic development; and (3) "services", comprising housing and transportation (Nunavut, 1994a: 7)

Regional Administration in Nunavut

The distribution of Nunavut government services will be based on three administrative regions with which the Nunavummiut are already familiar. These are:

- Baffin, with a population of 11,500 distributed in 14 communities over 900,000 square kilometres. It's capital is Iqaluit.
- Keewatin, with a population of 5,500 distributed in 7 communities over 550,000 square kilometres. It's capital is Rankin Inlet.
- Kitikmeot, with a population of 4,500 distributed in 6 communities over 650,000 square kilometres. It's capital is Cambridge Bay.[26]

These regions were created in 1982 by GNWT in order to facilitate the delivery of its programs and services. The proportion of the territorial public servants who will work in each of these respective regions should reflect their respective demographic weights in relation to the overall population of Nunavut (NIC, 1995a: 24). Thus, half would be concentrated in the Baffin region, while the Kitikmeot and Keewatin regions would each likely get a quarter of the government employees.

During the 1980s, regional councils were created at the initiative of certain communities' mayors. Essentially, these councils which, at the outset, sought to become regulatory powers, lacked efficacy, for they generated much talk but little action. GNWT accorded them only consultative powers.

In Nunavut, there will not be regional councils. The Commission recommended earlier that regional summits be adopted. Thus, in each of the regions of Nunavut, several summits could be held each year. During those summits, the mayors of the communities would meet with the members of the Nunavut Legislative Assembly in order to express their concerns and expectations concerning government policy. Said John Amagoalik:

> There's agreement between the NIC and NTI that regional councils, I think in the mind of most people, have outlived their usefulness.

> (Nunavut, 1994b: 3)

In fact, the Commission recommended (NIC, 1995a: 79) that policy responsibilities in Nunavut be concentrated solely in the hands of the Legislative Assembly and the local municipal councils. There would be no legislative body at the regional level.

Local Administration in Nunavut

Since the municipal councils represent the order of government closest to the citizens, it would be appropriate that the leaders of Nunavut return important administrative [and service delivery] powers to the communities. Without specifying the scope, the Commission recommended that the municipal councils receive powers and responsibilities in the fields of education, health, social services, justice, and housing (NIC, 1995a: 24).

Employment with the Government of Nunavut

Presently in the Nunavut region there are five hundred GNWT public servants, of whom half are Inuit. With the establishment of the Government of Nunavut, the Commission expects that 50% of the employees of the future public service of Nunavut will be Inuit:

> The Commission recommends that ... the new Nunavut Government, at its inception, be at least as representative of the Inuit share of the Nunavut population as is the public sector of Nunavut today.

(NIC, 1995a: 47)

However, over the longer term (not later than the year 2021), the NIC would like the Inuit to attain a level of employment in the Nunavut public service that is proportionate to their percentage in the population, which is about 80% (NIC, 1995a: 47). This idea of a representative number of Inuit in the Nunavut public service is also prescribed in the Inuit land claims agreement (DIAND, 1993: Art. 23.2.1).

A study recently ordered by the NIC and conducted by the consulting firm Price Waterhouse estimates that Nunavut would get about six hundred new public servants in 1999 (NIC, 1995a: A6.1-A6.12 [sic: A16.1-A16.12]). Those would be added to the five hundred positions already in existence in the Nunavut region. The public service of the future Government of Nunavut would thus amount to eleven hundred employees. It is anticipated that about 450 of them would be located in the capital (Iqaluit), but more than half (650) would be out in the region. In addition, to this number one must add about 150 municipal public servants and nearly one hundred federal employees who would also be working in Nunavut Territory. In fact, the bureaucratic class in Nunavut would represent about 10% of the jobs held by the active population in 1999. If one adds the whole gamut of jobs tied to the public sector (doctors, social workers, nurses, teachers, municipal workers, etc.), this percentage would exceed 30% or 3600 jobs (NIC, 1995a: A6.1-A6.12). Thus, in 1999, about 30% of the jobs in Nunavut would be financed directly or indirectly by its government. This will likely make the public sector the principal employer in Nunavut.[27]

In order to help fill the future positions in the Nunavut public service, the Commission suggests, first, a resort to the public service work force already in existence in the region, then a turning to training programmes for administrative employment, the content of which we shall examine in the next section.

The political institutions which operate presently in the Nunavut region are those of GNWT and those of Nunavut Tunngavik Inc. The Commission hopes that certain of some two hundred jobs, for the most part held by Inuit, in the co-management boards and in the central office of NTI, would turn out to be a launching pad for those who would eventually decide to follow their career in the Nunavut public service. The Commission also hopes that the majority of the five hundred civil servants in the administrative structure of NWT who already live in Nunavut would eventually be transferred to similar functions with new units of the Government of Nunavut. In fact, the Commission recommends that at least 50% of the persons called upon to hold positions in the administration of the future government of Nunavut have prior work experience in the operations of the federal, territorial and municipal public service in the Nunavut region (NIC, 1995a: 44). Therefore, one could deduce that all of the two hundred and seventy-five Inuit presently employed by NWT will be employed by the Government of Nunavut.

The Inuit civil servants of NWT occupy mainly non-specialist or semi-specialist positions: fewer than 10% of the management positions in the NWT administration in the Nunavut region (about ten jobs) are held by Inuit persons. The Commission would indeed rectify this lacuna by means of programmes of specialization offered to the Inuit employees of NWT. The objective would be to ensure that about 50% of the managerial positions in the future public service of Nunavut (about one hundred jobs) would be filled by the Inuit from the outset on April 1, 1999 (NIC, 1995a: 44).

In summary, in recruiting personnel from political institutions already in existence in Nunavut, the objective of NIC is to avoid too large an influx of non-Inuit from southern Canada. For the Commission, it is essential that the public administration reflect the ethnic composition of the population of Nunavut in the same measure as the legislature will (NIC, 1995a: 45). The Territory of Nunavut ought not to attract too large a number of non-Inuit bureaucrats who are not familiar with Inuit society. In effect, such a scenario would risk setting in motion both a diminution in the proportion of the Nunavut population which is Inuit[28] and the creation of a certain lack of understanding between the citizens of Nunavut and the non-Inuit employees in the public sector:

> The Nunavut government will not meet the expectation of the public if we're importing great numbers of civil servants from Yellowknife or southern Canada.

> (Nunavut Forum, 1991a: 7)

A civil servant in Nunavut ought to know the needs of the Nunavummiut and ought to possess a minimal familiarity with the culture and language of his/her principal clientele — the Inuit (NIC, 1995a: 47).

In order to encourage the employment of the greatest possible number of Nunavummiut in the public service of the future government of Nunavut and to avoid the influx of non-Inuit from the South, the NIC ought to make up for certain lacunae in the present population of Nunavut. These include: (1) a lack of geographical mobility of the Inuit; (2) ignorance of Inuktitut by nearly 35% of the Nunavummiut; and (3) educational deficiencies on the part of some Nunavummiut. The solution to these problems lies, in essence, in appropriate educational programmes.

Training of Future Employees of the Nunavut Civil Service

To reach the level of 50% Inuit representation in the public service of the future Government of Nunavut, there is an urgent need for about three hundred Inuit to be trained so as to be ready to take the reins of administrative affairs on April 1, 1999. However, this task could prove to be difficult, for qualified Inuit candidates to fill the jobs in the bureaucracy are rare. The majority of northern residents who are college or university graduates are non-Inuit. In fact, in Nunavut, only about one dozen Inuit persons, in a population of 17,500 persons, hold a university degree, while less than 2% of the Inuit have completed their secondary school studies (Bell, 1992: 21).

The governments of Canada and NWT, along with the Inuit institution NTI, are the principal actors sharing responsibility for education and the training of the administrative labour force. Over the last few years, various educational projects were launched by these parties (NIC, 1995a: A15.1–A15.19). These programmes try, in part, to improve the skill level of Inuit youth and of other Inuit who are already employed by local, federal, and territorial administrations in Nunavut.

The Nunavut Implementation Commission is planning on a transitional period (1995-99) for attaining the objective of five hundred and fifty Inuit public servants ready to take on the task of managing the administration of Nunavut. The NIC is also counting on a second phase of transition (1999-2021) for increasing to 80% the proportion of public servants who are Inuit. The Commission believes it to be important that the bureaucracy of the future government of Nunavut eventually become predominantly Inuit, in order that the residents of Nunavut feel at ease with their new institutions and develop a feeling of ownership toward Nunavut Territory (NIC, 1995a: 44). In light of numerous programmes designed to familiarize the Inuit with the public sector, it would seem that the NIC has every chance of seeing the targets of 50% and 80% Inuit staffing of the public service of Nunavut being achieved.

Financing the Government of Nunavut

The financing of Nunavut could emerge as a more complex problem than that of training Inuit public servants. According to the Price Waterhouse study (NIC, 1995a: A16.1–A16.12), the cost of bringing Nunavut onto the Canadian political scene could exceed 280 million dollars. These costs are tied mainly to new infrastructure for Nunavut's capital — Iqaluit — and to moving costs for office personnel. In addition, it will likely cost about six hundred million dollars annually to administer Nunavut Territory. Pursuant to the political accord on Nunavut, Ottawa has already undertaken to finance that budget:

> Canada, following consultation with the other parties hereto, shall establish the financial arrangements for the Government of Nunavut …, such financial arrangements may be analogous to those which presently exist for the GNWT.

> (NIC, 1995a: A5.3)

Presently, 80% of the revenues of GNWT, for which the total annual budget for 1994 was $1.2 billion, come from the federal government. In its study, Price Waterhouse estimated that about 95% of the annual budget of the Government of Nunavut would be dependent on revenues from Ottawa. In fact, although a Territory has the same powers of taxation as a province, its population base is much smaller and is not sufficient for supporting its expenses:

> … the ratio of strictly local revenues to total government expenses falls far short of the needs of the territories.

> (Hamelin, 1982: 260)

In addition, a territory cannot impose development taxes or royalties on non-renewable resources because it does not hold title to the lands.

[Some might suggest that] the key to fiscal autonomy for Nunavut could lie in the transfer of Crown title over public lands and in the exploitation of non-renewable resources with which they are endowed. However, the profit which would be gained from such an initiative would be relatively meagre due to the distance from markets, the difficulties in extracting resources, and the shipping problems associated with the greatly foreshortened shipping season caused by the annual freeze-up. At best, the royalties derived from the mining and energy sectors would amount to only a minimal portion of the annual budget of Nunavut:

> Based on the level of royalties collected at this time, it is estimated that this could bring in ten to twelve million dollars annually.
>
> (Nunavut Forum, 1991b: 9)

Thus, even if Nunavut Territory eventually holds title to all its resources, that would bring, at most, ten to fourteen million dollars per year into the Nunavut treasury. These gains would be well short of the expenditures (six hundred million dollars per year) which would be incurred by the administration of the Government of Nunavut.

Thus, to depend solely upon the exploitation of non-renewable resources to finance Nunavut would not be sufficient and, in our opinion, would not be a wise decision, for the exploitation of underground resources relegates Nunavut to an unstable, boom and bust economy. The history of Yukon, with its boom and bust cycles since 1898, is not reassuring (Robertson, 1985: 44).

The compensation payments ($1.15 billion over fourteen years) which the Inuit will receive as a result of the Final Agreement on their land claims are solely for the 17,870 persons identified as beneficiaries under that Agreement. Those moneys will serve, notably, to pay the cost of the programme of subsidies for Nunavummiut hunters and trappers, to finance the costs of the co-management structures envisaged in the Agreement, and to pay the administrative costs of NTI. In short, the compensation payments will in no way contribute to the budget of the public government of Nunavut.

Thus, at first glance, the sources of internal financing of Nunavut seem to be meagre, which portends, over the long term, a large contribution from the federal government in the annual budget of Nunavut. To summarize, the absence of a solid economic base, difficult access to the territory, its geographic isolation, and its small population will likely condemn Nunavut to dependency on the Canadian government for its economic survival. However, this situation ought not to endanger the political authority of Nunavut:[29]

> Ottawa-Nunavut financial arrangements should promote Nunavut self-sufficiency.
>
> (NIC, 1995a: 15)

Finally, the present transitional period ought to settle the question of the division of assets (e.g., government buildings) and liabilities (e.g., salaries of state employees) between the Interim Commissioner of Nunavut and the GNWT. In order to settle this issue harmoniously, the division of assets and liabilities ought to be carried out, to the extent possible, according to geography (NIC, 1995a: 83). Thus, assets and liabilities situated in Nunavut ought to belong to Nunavut and those located in NWT ought to belong to NWT. In short, this issue has every chance of being resolved before April 1, 1999.

The Government of Nunavut and Its Political Strategy

The Nunavut Implementation Commission has emphasized five major political themes which issue from the formation of the Government of Nunavut (NIC, 1994a; 1995a). These are: (i) the choice of the capital; (ii) linguistic policy; (iii) relations between the institutions of the Government of Nunavut and the co-managed organizations issuing from the land claims Final Agreement; (iv) the dilemma surrounding the existence of the Government of Nunavut and Inuit self-government; and (v) relations between the Government of Nunavut, the Government of Canada, and the circumpolar world.

(i) The Choice of The Capital   According to the *Nunavut Act* (Sec. 58), one of the tasks of NIC is to recommend a site for the capital of Nunavut. However, it is up to the Governor-in-Council (the federal Cabinet) to officially designate the chosen community. With that designation, that community will likely see its prestige increase considerably and its economy grow.

As early as the beginning of the work of the Commission, the regional centres of Cambridge Bay, Iqaluit, and Rankin Inlet expressed their interest in becoming the capital of Nunavut Territory.[30] In order to select the ideal site for the future capital of Nunavut, the Commission relied primarily on four criteria: (1) infrastructure, services, and facilities already in place; (2) potential or pre-existing air and marine transport linkages; (3) geographical location of the community in relation to Nunavut Territory as a whole; and (4) the climate.

In its report on the choice of the capital, tabled in September 1995 (NIC, 1995b), the NIC said that Iqaluit best fit the above four criteria. Leaders of the other communities in the running — Cambridge Bay and Rankin Inlet — actively opposed the conclusions of the report. They demanded that the then Minister of Indian and Northern Affairs, Ron Irwin, intervene in the case. In order to settle the ever-escalating polemic on the issue of the capital, on September 25, 1995, Irwin convened a special meeting comprising representatives of NIC, NTI, and the communities in the running. It was decided to settle the issue by a public plebiscite to be held throughout the twenty-seven communities of Nunavut on December 11, 1995. The Minister indicated that he would recommend to the federal Cabinet that the community that gets 50% plus one of the votes would be designated the capital.

Early in the campaign, Cambridge Bay withdrew its candidacy. The leaders of the community said that the geographic isolation of Cambridge Bay, its meagre population, and its paucity of infrastructure reduced considerably its chances of winning a Nunavut-wide plebiscite where the majority of the population is located in the regions of Baffin and Keewatin.

In the plebiscite, 79% of the 12,382 electors of Nunavut turned out at the polls. Iqaluit received the support of 5,869 voters, while Rankin Inlet was favoured by 3,876 voters. Thus, Iqaluit carried the vote with about 60% supporting it. This result is explained by the larger number of voters (6,499) in the Baffin region and their high participation rate (88%), as well as by the low participation rate (70%) of voters in the Keewatin and Kitikmeot regions. Ninety-eight percent of the residents of Iqaluit turned out to the polls, but only 64% did so at Cambridge Bay and 72% at Rankin Inlet.

By the time of [original] publication of this chapter, the federal Cabinet ought to have already designated Iqaluit as the capital of the future Nunavut Territory. Thereafter, the responsibilities of the regional centre of Baffin, heretofore held by Iqaluit, would likely begin to be delegated to the community of Igloolik (NIC, 1995b).

(ii) Linguistic Policy in Nunavut   In the present NWT, bureaucrats who administer programmes and services for the Nunavummiut are not obliged to speak the language of the majority of the citizens of Nunavut — Inuktitut.

The cultural survival of the Inuit involves a flowering of their language. Today, nearly 25% of the Inuit of Nunavut have English as the language most often spoken at home and work. English is the language which permits one to communicate with the administration of NWT. As protector of Inuit culture in the central and eastern Arctic, the Government of Nunavut has the firm intention of changing this situation and returning to Inuktitut the importance which it merits in Nunavut Territory:

> We can give the language of a majority of our people (Inuktitut) a role in the workplace that it could never have in an undivided NWT.

> (*Nunavut Newsletter*, 1992: 26)

Although there will likely be three official languages in Nunavut (English, French, and Inuktitut), the main language of work in the administration of Nunavut will likely be Inuktitut (NIC, 1995a: 14). It will be used in all realms of government activity. The strategy here is one of improving the health of the Inuit language. Thus, the Commission wishes to have the whole corpus of laws of NWT translated into Inuktitut before Nunavut is officially born. The NIC also favours a standardization of the spoken and written forms of the Inuit language,[31] in order to facilitate its spread (NIC, 1995a: 65). However, owing to the complex task of finding a compromise Inuktitut dialect, this will accrue to the benefit of the Inuktitut dialect spoken in the Baffin region and the syllabic writing, through which a majority of Inuit of Nunavut express themselves.

In summary, there is no doubt that the Government of Nunavut will reinforce the role of Inuktitut in the Canadian Arctic. By way of example, the first session of the Legislative Assembly will likely debate a languages bill, perhaps somewhat similar to Québec's law governing the use of French on signs and in public places, which would privilege the use of Inuktitut throughout Nunavut Territory.

(iii) The Linkages Between the Administrative Structures of the Government of Nunavut and The Co-Management Structures Issuing From the Land Claims Final Agreement   It becomes important, in order to avoid political imbroglio in Nunavut, to develop a close co-ordination between the structures, programmes, and services of the Government of Nunavut, on the one hand, and, on the other hand, the structures, programmes, and services which originate from the Nunavut land claim Final Agreement. Further to the constitutional protection enjoyed by the land claim Final Agreement, and because of its pertinence to the majority of the Nunavummiut, the Nunavut government institutions and ministries must bear in mind the various sections of the land claim Final Agreement in their decision-making:

> ... the field of competence of the territorial government must not abrogate, harm, or impinge upon the rights which flow from the Final Agreement.

> (DIAND, 1993: sec. 2.10.2).

Ministries of the Government of Nunavut, in particular, those pertaining to sustainable development, are obliged to work alongside the five co-management boards created by the Land Claim Agreement. (See Table 4.) As I emphasized earlier, the co-managed structures have as their principal function the management of economic development and the protection of the Arctic ecosystem throughout Nunavut Territory. The majority of the members of these insti-

TABLE 4 Co-management Boards Under the Land Claim Agreement

Name: **Nunavut Wildlife Management Board**
Date of Activation: January 1995
Function: This body supervises and regulates the exploitation of wildlife while assuring that principles of conservation are respected. It determines quotas for the capture of certain animal species.

Name: **Nunavut Environmental Impact Commission**
Date of Activation: January 1995
Function: This body examines economic development projects in Nunavut and determines if there are going to be any adverse impacts on the arctic eco-system. Drawing upon environmental impact studies, this Commission has the power to block any project.

Name: **Nunavut Management Commission**
Date of Activation: January 1995
Function: This Commission administers and plans land use in Nunavut. It assures that land development conforms with environmental and land use zoning regulations.

Name: **Surface Rights Board**
Date of Activation: January 1994
Function: This tribunal adjudicates legal disputes arising out of ecological damages caused by a developer. It determines the damages awarded to the Inuit.

Name: **Nunavut Waters Office**
Date of Activation: January 1995
Function: The Office has responsibility for issuing permits for the use of potable water and for garbage disposal in the waters of Nunavut.

Source: Légaré (1993b: 134)

tutions are Inuit residents of Nunavut named jointly by Nunavut Tunngavik Inc. and by the federal government. The decisions of these institutions prevail over any regulations which are put forward by the Government of Nunavut and which do not comply with the directives of the land claim Agreement:

> The provisions of the Agreement prevail over incompatible provisions in federal, territorial, or local law.

> (DIAND, 1993, sec. 2.12.2)

In fact, only [the federal] Cabinet can abrogate a regulation issued by one of these co-management boards if Cabinet considers that a directive runs contrary to one of the sections of the Agreement (DIAND, 1993: sec. 5.3).

Nevertheless, the Agreement foresaw that it would be necessary to have a symbiotic collaboration between the co-management boards and the ministries of the Government of Nunavut. Thus, the Minister whose ministry would have an interest in a decision of a particular co-managed institution would most likely be briefed on that decision before it would be made public. He could express his opinion and ask that the decision be altered. If, on the other hand, he rejects the decision of the co-managed body, he would likely inform the Executive Council of that and the Council could lodge an objection with the federal Cabinet in an attempt to get Cabinet to over-rule the decision of the co-managed body (DIAND, 1993: sec. 5.3).

Thus, to avoid political tensions that are so often fruitless, and delays in decisions which would affect the Nunavummiut, it would be to the advantage of both types of organization to assure an harmonious relationship. The Government of Nunavut will have to accommodate itself to the five co-management bodies by ensuring that its laws and regulations are not incompatible with the provisions of the Final Agreement on Land Claims (NIC, 1995: 32).

> Amagoalik said ... "we're going to have to work closely with institutions like the Nunavut Wildlife Management Board to make sure that the kind of regime we put together meshes with their plans".
>
> (Nunavut, 1994: 3)

It would be difficult for the co-management bodies, as much on the political level as the juridical, to ignore the territorial ministries on issues pertinent to the management of lands and the protection of the arctic ecosystems. In fact, the Final Agreement on land claims clearly envisaged that the expertise of the territorial government would be added to that of the joint management boards in decision-making (DIAND, 1993: sec. 5.3).

Thus, the challenge for the NIC and the NTI consists in arriving at the elaboration of a protocol which would establish clearly the structural linkages between the ministries and the co-management boards, before the establishment of Nunavut Territory. Such an initiative would permit the avoidance of superfluous and unfortunate political conflicts. One must remember that these two different types of structure emerged from the same process of negotiation and seek the same central objective — namely, the return to the Inuit of the majority of the levers of power over social, economic, and cultural life in Nunavut.

(iv) The Territorial Government of Nunavut and Inuit Self-Government   There is a divergence of opinion as to the respective interpretations of the federal government and the Nunavut Implementation Commission on the issue of the public government of Nunavut and the right of the Inuit of NWT to self-government.

For Ottawa, the establishment of the territorial government of Nunavut responds to traditional demands of Inuit organizations (ITC, TFN) in the matter of political autonomy. Through their demographic majority, the Inuit of Nunavut are assured of *de facto* control over government. Furthermore, the federal government will dispense a considerable sum of money in the name of Canadian taxpayers for the creation and administration of the Government of Nunavut. Thus, Ottawa is not interested in investing additional sums on the still ill-defined subject of Inuit self-government in Nunavut. It prefers to put off this issue until such time as pigs can fly(!)

However, for NIC and NTI, the formation of the territorial government of Nunavut has nothing to do with Inuit self-government and does not extinguish this right that they consider to be inherent. Without defining precisely what form this inherent right would take in the present context of a Nunavut with an Inuit majority, NIC (1995a: 73) affirms that it is nevertheless necessary to distinguish between Nunavut as public, non-ethnic administration and the right of the Inuit people to dispose of it and to create an ethnic (aboriginal) government:

For the time being, NIC and NTI figure that the problem of Inuit political autonomy in Nunavut is not acute, for the Inuit form the majority of the population of Nunavut. They are, therefore, assured of a strong representation in the Legislative Assembly of Nunavut, while the policy of NIC in matters of employment ought to assure them a substantial weight in the administration of the

Government of Nunavut. Thus, Nunavut will likely respond to the expectations and interests of the Inuit for as long as they are a demographic majority.

However, what would happen if the non-Inuit one day became the majority in Nunavut? Few scholars involved in Northern research have ventured to respond to this important question, undoubtedly because of the improbability of such a scenario. The geographical isolation of Nunavut, its high cost of living, the paucity of housing, and its arctic climate all render quite unlikely any influx of massive numbers of non-Inuit into the region. In fact, only the development of large-scale energy and mining deposits, which would entail the introduction of several thousand southern workers over a long period, would be able to alter the demographic balance in Nunavut in favour of the non-Inuit.

However, the high costs of such an undertaking in the Arctic render improbable the scenario of large-scale exploitation of energy or mining deposits.[32] Yet, that has not prevented NIC from trying to solve the issue. The consultation hearings held with the Nunavut population permit us to draw two conclusions on the hypothesis of the Inuit becoming a minority. The first suggests that NTI would become the government of the Inuit, such that there would be two parallel governments in Nunavut. The second consists in creating a senate, composed entirely of Inuit, which would have the right of veto over all regulations and laws adopted by the Legislative Assembly (NIC, 1995a: A9.7). These solutions have scarcely been elaborated by NIC for, as was emphasized above, it is more than likely that the Inuit will never have to seriously debate this issue.

(v) Relations Between the Government of Nunavut, the Government of Canada, and the Northern Circumpolar World   The formation of the Government of Nunavut will permit the Inuit of NWT to rearrange their relation with Ottawa and to obtain a new political contract which will confer on Nunavut Territory, like the provinces, a certain political "clout" with Ottawa.

> The intergovernmental relationship between the Nunavut Territorial Government and the Government of Canada should respect conventions and practices that have evolved, and are evolving, to reinforce the political autonomy of Nunavut.

> (Nunavut, 1994c: 12)

Like the present Yukon and NWT, Nunavut will be able to participate in various intergovernmental conferences. That will allow the Nunavummiut to get their concerns onto the agenda of intergovernmental debates:

> The NIC recommends that the Government of Nunavut participate in federal/provincial/territorial and provincial/territorial inter-governmental activities, on the same footing as other territorial governments, and that the Nunavut Government be supplied with the policy-making and administrative capacity to participate effectively.

> (NIC, 1995a: 73)

A government representing the 17,500 Inuit of NWT would, without doubt, be an excellent spokesperson for the Inuit cause in Canada. Thus, when Canada would come to negotiate international agreements, which could be highly consequential for the interests of Inuit Canadians, Nunavut would have its say. For example, without consulting the Government of Nunavut in advance, it would

be very politically awkward for the Canadian government to sign some international accord limiting the hunting and fishing rights of the Inuit.

In addition, we must bear in mind that the Inuit are a people who live under
the sovereignty of several countries — namely, Denmark, Canada, the U.S.A.,
and Russia. Thus, it is not surprising to see the Inuit of Nunavut seeking to
maintain close ties with their fellow Inuit living in Greenland, Alaska, Chukotka
(Siberia), or elsewhere in Canada.

> The Nunavut Government should seek to pursue common interests with re-
> gional governments in the Beaufort Sea [Inuvialuit], Nunavik, and Labrador.

> (NIC, 1995a: 77)

The Commission also wishes that the Government of Nunavut be able to freely
negotiate with their northern partners certain agreements pertaining to the ecology, the economy, and the culture of the circumpolar region:

> Nunavut will be a government operating within the circumpolar world and
> it should be equipped with the ability to develop relations, consistent with
> Canada's overall foreign policies, with other parts of the circumpolar world.

> (NIC, 1995a: A7.3)

Finally, international contacts from which Nunavut would benefit would
reinforce the weight of the Inuit Circumpolar Conference (ICC).[33] Thus,
Nunavut would become, along with Greenland, the head of the political spear
of the ICC and at the United Nations would be able to serve as a model of self-
determination for the other Inuit groups:

> The creation of Nunavut will give added incentive to create strong regional
> governments within the Beaufort Sea and Northern Quebec (Nunavik)
> regions of arctic Canada.

> (NIC, 1995: 6)

CONCLUSION

The creation of the Nunavut territory and government is a golden opportunity
for the Inuit of the NWT to create political institutions grounded in the unique-
ness of their society. However, Nunavut will not be a panacea for all the socio-
economic problems of Inuit society; at best, it will permit the Inuit to take their
social, economic, and political destiny into their own hands so as to better meet
the challenges of tomorrow.

For the federal government, the establishment of Nunavut Territory is the
test of the will of the political leaders to use the flexibility which Canadian federalism offers for accommodating the political aspirations of aboriginal peoples.
According to some of those who have been involved from the federal government's side (Molloy, 1994: 9–11), Canada's engagement in working toward the
creation of Nunavut is concrete expression of Canada's willingness to truly
share its legislative and administrative powers with its aboriginal citizens.
However, to explain the birth of Nunavut one must go well beyond the simple
magnanimity of the federal government.

In entering into negotiations on the demands of the Inuit of the NWT,
Ottawa sought to prove the good faith of its aboriginal land claim policies

(DIAND, 1987a; DIAND, 1987b), in order both to score points in the chess game of public relations in the media and to substantiate its credibility in the eyes of the international community:

> The creation of a new territory in Canada's Arctic with a solid Inuit majority and political rights for all its residents will be a powerful signal to the world that Canadians have the will and the ways to reconcile aboriginal self-determination with parliamentary democracy.

> (Nunavut Forum, 1991f: 7).

In addition, the establishment of Nunavut will reinforce Canadian sovereignty in the North. This thesis is clearly established in Article 15 of the Final Agreement on the Nunavut land claim:

> Canada's sovereignty over the waters of the Arctic archipelago is supported by Inuit use and occupancy.

> (DIAND, 1993: Art. 15.1.1)

The stakes here are important, for the Americans have never accepted Canadian claims to the waters separating the arctic islands. There can be no doubt that the creation of Nunavut is going to reinforce Canadian claims [to sovereignty] over the Northwest Passage, for the political leaders of the Nunavut government will act to protect the interests of their population. They will oppose any compromise of the territorial integrity of Nunavut:

> Trans-Arctic shipping must now take into account a new player, the Inuit people.

> (Purich, 1992: 152).

Canada, therefore, has several reasons, above and beyond magnanimity, to justify its support for the formation of Nunavut Territory.

The portrayal here of the future governmental structures of Nunavut has demonstrated that there can be no doubt that the Nunavut Implementation Commission wishes to establish a structurally innovative and unique government. However, the implementation of certain of these initiatives, such as the extensive decentralization of governmental administrative structures or the establishment of dual-representative electoral districts, would likely increase the set-up and operating costs of Nunavut. In these times of fiscal restraint, that is hardly likely to please the principal supplier of funds, the federal government. Thus, certain recommendations set out by the Nunavut Implementation Commission in the document *Footprints in New Snow* will, perhaps, not be implemented. However, only through an analysis conducted after the establishment of Nunavut Territory will we know for sure.

During the present transitional period, the Commission will pursue its work in order to fine-tune some of the recommendations which it has put forward. In 1996 the commission will make a second tour of the communities and will gather the reactions of the Nunavummiut to the publication of its first comprehensive report on the structure of Nunavut's government (NIC, 1995a). Having, for a second time, taken the pulse of opinion of the citizens of Nunavut and Inuit leaders, the Commission will publish a second [comprehensive] report in the Spring of 1997. It will deal with various points which were not explored in the first report, notably: (i) the future of the administration of justice; (ii) the sectors which will be privileged for economic development in Nunavut; and (iii) the role of the information highway.

Originally introduced onto the political stage in February 1976 with the tabling of the document *Nunavut: Proposed Settlement of Inuit Land Claims* (ITC, 1976), the idea of creating the Government of Nunavut is a political event which spans three decades. The construction of this unique political entity can be compared, by analogy, to that of an inukshuk: the Final Agreement on the land claims of the Inuit of Nunavut has installed the legs of the inukshuk, the Nunavut Implementation Commission added the body, the interim commissioner will attach the arms. The head will be set in place with the establishment of the Nunavut territorial government on April 1, 1999.

NOTES

[1] Reprinted with permission from *Études / Inuit / Studies* XX, 1 (1996): 7–43. Translated from the French and edited by J. Rick Ponting.

[2] "Nunavut" is an Inuktitut word for which the English translation is "Our Land".

[3] The residents of the western NWT eventually will decide, by means of a plebiscite, on the new name for the western part of NWT. It is probable that the name chosen will be "Denendeh".

[4] "Nunavummiut" is an Inuktitut word which refers to the Inuit and non-Inuit residents of Nunavut.

[5] In fact, out of a total of twenty-two legislators, eighteen were aboriginals, including eight Inuit, six Denés, and four Métis.

[6] Two abstained while three were absent from the legislature at the time of the vote.

[7] At the beginning of the 1980s, the Inuit of Nunavik [Northern Québec] and Labrador found that The Inuit Tapirisat of Canada (ITC) devoted too much time to the cause of the NWT Inuit and did not dwell sufficiently on the problems of other regions of the Great Canadian North. Therefore, in May 1981 ITC decided to create The Tunngavik Federation of Nunavut, a body dedicated solely to the interests of the Inuit of Nunavut.

[8] Over and above its support for the creation of the Nunavut government, the final agreement contains three other broad provisions pertaining to the Inuit: (1) land ownership rights over a surface area of 355,981 square kilometres, including mineral rights over 37,992 square kilometres; (2) financial compensation of 1.15 billion dollars spread over fourteen years; and (3) the creation of certain jointly administered public institutions with a dual mandate of economic development and environmental protection. However, in exchange for particular rights stipulated in the Agreement, the Inuit of Nunavut relinquished their aboriginal rights over the lands of the central and eastern Arctic.

[9] Imbroglio: "confused heap; complicated situation" (*The Concise Oxford Dictionary of Current English*, Fifth Edition, Oxford: Oxford University Press, 1964).

[10] The Constitutional Alliance also had as one of its objectives the formulation of a preliminary proposal for the political structures of each of the future Territories (cf. GNWT, 1987).

[11] In the referendum held November 3–5, 1992, 69% of the Inuit said "yes" to the land claim agreement. This largely favourable vote can be attributed, in part, to the signing, a few days earlier, of the political accord guaranteeing the arrival of Nunavut.

428 PART 4 SELF-DETERMINATION

[12] The establishment of a new territorially based political entity in the Canadian North did not require the prior approval of the provinces. Indeed, the Territories are under the sole jurisdiction of the federal government.

[13] The law which created Nunavut Territory is not itself protected by the constitution of Canada. It is a federal law which can be modified unilaterally by the Parliament of Canada. However, this scenario is quite unlikely, for it would seriously compromise the relations between the federal government and the Inuit people. Conversely, the Inuit Land Claims Agreement, which is considered a treaty under Section 35 of the *Constitution Act, 1982*, enjoys constitutional protection. Let us not forget, though, that Chapter 4 of this Agreement prescribes the birth of Nunavut Territory. Consequently, one might wonder if the existence of Nunavut Territory would also be protected by the Canadian constitution, after all. However, this hypothesis would have to be confirmed in the courts.

[14] Nine of the ten members of NIC are Inuit, including eight who are permanent residents of Nunavut.

[15] NTI succeeded TFN in March, 1993. NTI manages the Final Agreement on Inuit Land Claims in Nunavut. One of its most notable tasks is to administer the co-management institutions born out of the land claim agreement.

[16] These committees and their responsibilities are: (a) Capital Committee, which advises the Commission on the location of the capital; (b) Committee on Governmental Activities, which determines the principles and objectives which will guide the creation of Nunavut governmental structures; (c) Human Resources Committee, which determines the training and education needs of the future public sector workers in Nunavut; (d) Communications Committee, which informs members of the public and solicits their opinions; and (e) Committee on Internal Direction, which supervises the direction of the Commission and of its personnel. Source: NIC (1994b:4).

[17] There were three governmental bodies involved in the division of NWT: (a) the Special Joint Committee on Division, comprising eight members of the NWT Legislative Assembly; (b) the Review Committee on Division, comprising twenty-seven deputy ministers and regional directors of NWT; and (c) The Nunavut Secretariat, comprising six federal bureaucrats under the direction of DIAND. Source: NIC (1995a).

[18] The GNWT holds powers similar to those of the provincial governments, except that GNWT does not hold rights to Crown lands. Those rights are held by the federal government.

[19] However, this law could be modified only with the approval of the Parliament of Canada (Canada, 1993: Sec. 38).

[20] A voter must have taken up residency in Nunavut at least one year before the date of the elections and must be at least eighteen years old.

[21] The Inuit have always expressed their disagreement with the implementation of party politics in NWT. They perceive this system, which is practiced throughout the rest of Canada, as divisive. They favour an approach where everyone can express his/her opinions without partisan constraints.

[22] In Nunavut, there would be about ten ministries. Therefore, it remains to be seen if certain ministers will hold two or three portfolios.

[23] The person who sits as Interim Commissioner will not necessarily eventually be named Commissioner of Nunavut.

[24] Before appointing the Interim Commissioner, the Minister would have to consult GNWT and NIC concerning his/her choice.

[25] In 1994, NWT had seventeen ministries and more than one hundred agencies.

[26] Source: NIC (1994b: 8).

[27] In 1995, the public sector in Nunavut already represented nearly 25% of the jobs.

[28] The coming of five hundred public servants who are not residents of Nunavut, along with their families, would likely involve the arrival of about two thousand additional persons in Nunavut.

[29] Newfoundland relies on Ottawa for more than 50% of its budget, but no one denies its political weight in the Canadian confederation.

[30] The community which will be designated as the capital would be highly unlikely to remain a regional centre. The objective of this policy is to better spread jobs, which will flow from the administration of Nunavut, throughout the territory.

[31] In Nunavut, Inuktitut is spoken in six different dialects and is written in two different forms (c.f. Dorais, 1976).

[32] Presently, there are only three active mines in Nunavut: Lupin, Nanisivik, and Polaris. They produce zinc, silver, and lead. Altogether, these mines employ only about one hundred workers, most of whom are non-Inuit.

[33] Founded in Barrow, Alaska in 1977, the Inuit Circumpolar Conference has as its objective the publicizing and defence of the rights and interests of the one hundred thousand Inuit of the northern circumpolar region on the international scene.

REFERENCES

Bell, Jim
1992   "Training for Nunavut: many questions, few answers", *Nunatsiaq News*, Special Publication, 25 Sept.: 2, 21.

1994   "The NIC — Designing a whole new Government", *Nunavut*, 20 May: 20, 25.

1995a   "NIC Recommends translation of Nunavut laws", *Nunatsiaq News*, 19 May: 17.

1995b   "Highlights of the NIC's first report", *Nunatsiaq News*, 12 May: 2.

Canada, House of Commons (34th, 3rd Session)
1993   *Bill C-132 Statutes of Canada, Chapter 28: An Act to Establish a Territory to Be Known as Nunavut and Provide for Its Government and to Amend Certain Acts in Consequence Thereof*. Ottawa: Queen's Printer.

1993   *Bill C-133 Statutes of Canada: An Act Respecting An Agreement Between The Inuit of the Nunavut Settlement Area and her Majesty the Queen in Right of Canada*. Ottawa: Queen's Printer.

Canada, GNWT, TFN (Government of Canada, Government of the Northwest Territories, and Tunngavik Federation of Nunavut).
1992   *Nunavut Political Accord*. Ottawa.

DIAND / MAINC (Dept. of Indian Affairs & Northern Development)
1973   *Indian Affairs Policy Statement*. Ottawa: Supply and Services Canada.

1982   *Le MAINC, les autochtones, le Nord: Tour d'horizon*. Ottawa: Approvisionnement et Services.

1987a   *Comprehensive Land Claims Policy*. Ottawa: Supply & Services Canada.

1987b *L'autonomie gouvernementale des autochtones.* Ottawa: Approvisionnment et Services.

1991 *Agreement-in-Principle Between the Inuit of the Nunavut Settlement Area and Her Majesty the Queen in Right of Canada.* Ottawa: Supply and Services Canada.

1993 *Agreement Between the Inuit of the Nunavut Settlement Area and Her Majesty the Queen in Right of Canada.* Ottawa: Supply and Services Canada.

Dorais, Louis-Jacques
1976 "La langue des Inuit", *North/Nord,* 23 (1): 25–29.

Fenge, Terry *et al.*
1989 *Nunavut: Political choice and manifest destiny.* Ottawa: Canadian Arctic Resources Committee.

Freeman, Milton M. R. (ed.)
1976 *Inuit Land Use and Occupancy Project.* 3 vols., Ottawa: DIAND, Milton Freeman Research Ltd.

Gregoire, Lisa
1995 "NIC chief glad it will soon be all over", *Nunavut,* 1 Dec.: 7.

GNWT (Government of the Northwest Territories)
1980 *Special Committee on Unity.* Yellowknife.

1987 *Boundary and Constitutional Agreement for the Implementation of Division of the Northwest Territories.* Iqaluit: Constitutional Alliance.

1991 *Statistics Quarterly.* Yellowknife, Bureau of Statistics.

GNWT, TFN (Government of the Northwest Territories, Tunngavik Federation of Nunavut)
1990 *Letter to the Prime Minister of Canada, Rt. Hon. Brian Mulroney, 20 January 1990.* Yellowknife.

Hamelin, Louis-Edmond
1982 "Originalité culturelle et régionalisation politique: Le projet Nunavut de Territoires-du-Nord-Ouest (Canada)", *Recherches Amérindiennes au Québec,* 12(4): 251–262.

ITC (Inuit Tapirisat of Canada)
1976 *Nunavut, réglement proposé des revendications territoriales des Inuit.* Ottawa.

1977 *Speaking for the First Citizens of the Canadian Arctic.* Ottawa.

1979 *Political development in Nunavut.* Ottawa.

Légaré, André
1993a "Le projet Nunavut: bilan des revendications des Inuit des Territoires-du-Nord-Ouest", *Etudes/Inuit/Studies,* 17(2): 29–62.

1993b *Processus et progrès du projet Nunavut (1976–1993): revendications territoriales et autonomie gouvernementale des Inuit des Territoires-du-Nord-Ouest.* Mémoire de maîtrise, Québec: Université Laval.

Molloy, Tom
1993 "Negotiating the Nunavut Agreement: A View from the Government's Side", *Northern Perspectives,* XXI, 3: 9–11.

NIC/CEN (Nunavut Implementation Commission/Commission d'établissement du Nunavut)
1994a *Document de travail sur l'élaboration des principes régissant la conception et le fonctionnement du gouvernement du Nunavut.* Iqaluit.

1994b *The Nunavut Implementation Commission.* Iqaluit.

1994c *Circonscriptions binominales et égalité des sexes,* Iqaluit.

1995a *Footprints in New Snow /L'empreinte de nos pas dans la neige fraîche.* Iqaluit.

1995b *Le choix de la capitale: rapport supplémentaire de la Commission d'établissement du Nunavut.* Iqaluit.
Nunavut
1994a "The NIC: The Story So Far", *Nunavut,* 2 Dec.: 7.

1994b "A Talk With the NIC's Chief Commissioner", *Nunavut,* 2 Dec.: 3–5

1994c "What Kind of Government NTG Will Be", *Nunavut,* 2 Dec.: 12.
Nunavut Forum
1991a "Advantages for Inuit Firms and Individuals", *Nunavut Forum,* I, 6: 6–7.

1991b "Economic Diversity Focus of Negotiation", *Nunavut Forum,* I, 6: 9.

1991c "Inuktitut in Nunavut: Giving Our Language the Place it Deserves", *Nunavut Forum,* I, 5: 16.

1991d "Money and Training Are Biggest Challenges for Nunavut", *Nunavut Forum,* I, 5: 15.

1991e "Constitutional Development: Nunavut a Model of Aboriginal Self-Government", *Nunavut Forum,* I, 5: 9.

1991f "Nunavut Workshop 'Gets on with the job': Building a new Territory is the Aim of TFN and Government", *Nunavut Forum,* I, 5: 7–8.
Nunavut Newsletter
1992 "Nunavut and the West", *Nunavut Newsletter,* XI, 2: 26.
Phillips, Todd
1995 "NIC Gets Moving On Key Issues in Nunavut", *Nunatsiaq News,* 9 June: 15.
Purich, Donald
1992 *The Inuit and Their Land: The Story of Nunavut.* Toronto: James Lorimer.
Robertson, Gordon
1985 *Northern Provinces: A Mistaken Goal.* Montréal: Institute for Research on Public Policy.
White, Graham
1991 "Westminister in the Arctic: The Adaptation of British Parliamentarism in the Northwest Territories", *Canadian Journal of Political Science,* XIV, 3: 499–523.

PART 5

Conclusion

CHAPTER 17

"GETTING ON WITH LIFE"

J. Rick Ponting

Student's Question: Why can't Indians put the past behind and "get on with life"?

This question, which is probably widely held in the Canadian population, probably exasperates and infuriates most First Nation people. A similar reaction likely would be evoked by the remark: "My ancestors came here from Europe, didn't speak English, were poor and subjected to discrimination, but worked hard and eventually fit in. Why can't Indians do the same?" The questions bespeak not only low levels of knowledge about First Nation people, but also an ethnocentric bias of a culture that places little value upon history.

For the sociologist, the answers to the questions are multifacetted. While a non-Native sociologist such as the author cannot presume to speak for First Nation people, he or she can speak to the issue from a sociological perspective. Indeed, addressing such questions that are found in the discourse of everyday life among the members of the mass public just might be one of the more valuable contributions which sociologists can make to progress on aboriginal issues. The results of the 1992 Charlottetown Accord referendum demonstrate that, regardless of how enlightened elites are in framing the issues, progressive social change can be blocked by a mass public whose resistance is based on myths and on such ignorance and perceptions of inequity as are found in the questions above.

Let us tackle those questions now. We begin with a comment on the importance of history in most aboriginal cultures and then turn to a consideration of the comparability of the situation of First Nation people with that of European immigrants. The bulk of the discussion, though, deals with the resources, opportunity structure, and obstacles (social psychological, spiritual, cultural, and structural) which confront First Nation people.

THE IMPORTANCE OF HISTORY IN ABORIGINAL CULTURES

First Nation cultures place major emphasis upon history. This is evident to any non-Native who has ever attended a meeting or negotiating session involving First Nation representatives: a history lesson for the non-Natives present is mandatory. The importance of history is also manifested in the exhaustive attention which the final report of the Royal Commission on Aboriginal Peoples devotes to it. Hence, the injustices of the past are indelibly imprinted in First

Nations' collective consciousness and many, perhaps most, First Nation individuals cannot ignore the past. In part, this is because of the fact that in most aboriginal cultures the past, present and future blend together. In contrast to the English language, some aboriginal languages do not even differentiate between past, present, and future verb tenses. Furthermore, aboriginal cultures set forth an obligation to the ancestors for the individual not to forget the past.

To achieve that sense of wholeness which must be the foundation for any lasting individual or community transformation, First Nation individuals need to be acquainted with First Nation culture, which, in turn, cannot be divorced from history. Thus, the extremely ethnocentric admonition to First Nation people to "get a life" must imply the retrieval of relevant parts of aboriginal culture and, as such, is incompatible with the admonition to "put the past behind you".

COMPARISON WITH EUROPEAN IMMIGRANTS

Although, on the surface, the situation of European immigrants to Canada might appear to exhibit similarities with the situation of First Nation people, the similarities are merely superficial and are far outweighed by the numerous and profound differences.

One of the most important of those differences lies in the nexus of the First Nations' loss of land, subsistence, language, and religion. In contrast to late nineteenth-century immigrants, who were given grants of (aboriginals') land to homestead under the *Dominion Lands Act* (1872), most First Nations lost all but a small fraction of their land and with it the source of their subsistence. That loss of connection with the land also constituted a *spiritual wounding or disconnection*, for the relationship with the land and its creatures and spirits is pivotal in most aboriginal religions. Hence, the disconnection from the land destroyed many of the most important *stable anchorages* of the First Nation peoples. Furthermore, consider the situation of immigrants arriving in Canada during the last third of the twentieth century. They were the recipients of government largesse and an official policy and ideology of multiculturalism and heritage language preservation. In contrast, First Nation people were subjected to government efforts at forced assimilation, as government consciously tried to sever indigenous people's traditional spiritual connection to the past, present, future, and Creator. This left many First Nation people alienated from their culture and therefore, from their ability to define themselves. Whereas government dismantled the very foundations — language, religion, family, and economy — upon which First Nations' social systems were built, the institutional completeness and norms of mutual aid in many ethnic enclave communities offer much support to more recent European immigrants.

For First Nation people, interaction with Canadian society is not an adventure that, if unsuccessful, can be reversed or abandoned by a retreat to a homeland, friends and relatives, and a traditional way of life.[1] Nor has the relationship between First Nation people and the larger Canadian society been primarily about expansion of opportunities. Rather, First Nation people experienced formal, legal segregation on reserves that usually offered very limited structures of opportunity.

The institutional experiences of First Nations and immigrants also have been widely divergent. With the notable exception of Japanese Canadians, French habitants, and a small number of Italians and Ukrainians, immigrants to Canada have not faced the degradation and trauma of total institutions such as the residential schools to which many First Nation persons were subjected in their formative years. Nor have immigrants come up against the bureaucratic might of a colonial, paternalistic, manipulative, and at times unaccountable Department of Indian Affairs implementing a federal statute like the *Indian Act* which relegated them to a legal status akin to wards of the state. As discussed earlier, the *Indian Act* is a control-oriented statute that pervades Registered Indians' daily lives and at various times has legally censured First Nations' cultures. Apart from the *War Measures Act*, it has no counterpart in immigrants' experience.

Cultural congruence refers to a similarity in two or more peoples' values, beliefs, language, and ways of perceiving the world. The relatively high degree of congruence of most European cultures with the dominant cultures of Canada stands in marked contrast with the pronounced incongruence between most First Nations' cultures and the dominant cultures of Canada (e.g., with regard to time, co-operation, holism, etc.), as portrayed in Chapter Ten of this volume. This incongruence is particularly noteworthy with the political, economic, and legal culture. Unlike most of Canada's twentieth-century immigrants, who were part of a capitalist economy prior to living in Canada, First Nation people had no experience with the political and legal systems or the capitalist economy prior to contact. Ross (1993) identifies numerous ways in which the dominant Canadian culture and many aboriginal cultures clash in the criminal justice system, usually to the detriment of aboriginal persons. As noted, even the central concept of deterrence, which is at the root of the sentencing phenomenon in Canadian courts, totally eluded some of Ross' informants until he explained it to them (Ross, 1993: 64). Mr. Justice Cawsey (1991), in his inquiry report, identified numerous other value conflicts between aboriginal and non-aboriginal criminal justice systems, as noted in Chapter 6.

Most European immigrants have another advantage over aboriginal Canadians. That is, most are white and, with the exception of some central and southern Europeans, most have not been subjected to *racism* or to such *debilitating stereotyping* as First Nation people have faced. Recall that initially First Nation people were regarded by the European settlers as pagans and as virtually sub-human. Even today, stereotypes of First Nation people are commonplace. The importance of this in the employment market is difficult to overstate.

Yet, the stereotyping and other injustices experienced by Native people extend well beyond the economic sector, as the stories of victims Donald Marshall Jr., Helen Betty Osborne, J.J. Harper, Shelley Napope, and numerous others attest.[2] For instance, Boldt (1993) vigorously denounces the injustice of Supreme Court of Canada decisions involving First Nations, such as in the famous Sparrow case. He points out how the courts allow the dominant society's conception of "*the national interest*" to regularly override First Nations' interests, despite the class and ethnic biases of the notion of "the national interest".

SCARCITY OF RESOURCES

For many First Nations, the *loss of the means of subsistence* and the subsequent entanglement in the tentacles of the welfare state was the precursor of a dramatic slide into the grips of poverty. (This was facilitated by the fiduciary, or trustee-like, relationship which the state has had with First Nation people.)

Escaping that poverty is a task of Herculean proportions which requires resources which are in short supply in most First Nation communities. Also militating against such escape is the alienating school experience which contributed significantly to the high push-out/drop-out rate in the schools.

Another resource which is in short supply in some First Nation communities is *positive role models*. Note the further contrast with immigrants here, as most immigrants have a repertoire of cultural heroes and role models available to them in their ethnic culture. As discussed in our coverage of residential schools, First Nation individuals who attended those schools had scant opportunity to observe role models of skillful parenting or positive aboriginal role models in the history curriculum. Furthermore, parents' responses to the family disruption caused by the residential schools' wedge-driving were sometimes quite dysfunctional. The absence of positive parenting — whether among residential school attendees, their children, or their children's children — affects one's self-concept and one's goal formulation, among other things. Thus, it directly influences one's ability to overcome adversity.

Time is another resource. For First Nation people to overcome the problems and injustices of the past, healing must first occur (Ponting, 1991; Mercredi and Turpel, 1993; Royal Commission, 1996c). Though commonplace now, both the public identification of the horrors of the residential school experience and the recognition of the need for healing are relatively recent phenomena and the resources for developing healing programs and healing lodges have only recently started to become available. Furthermore, the *healing itself requires time*. Hence, it is not realistic to expect much progress to have been made yet in this regard, and we can expect to have with us for some time to come those who react dysfunctionally to the psychological and spiritual wounds which they acquired in the residential schools and the aftermath of the residential schools.

OPPORTUNITY STRUCTURE

It is clear from this book that the structure of opportunities faced by First Nation people is severely *truncated*. This fact is manifested in many First Nation communities' geographic isolation from markets, in the chartered banks' past reluctance to loan money for economic development on reserves, in widespread health problems, in racism, and in the larger society's denial of First Nations' rights, especially the rights of urban First Nation individuals. Added to this is the political marginalization of First Nations since the defeat of the Charlottetown Accord in 1992. Because opportunity is a major focus of this book, it is not elaborated here.

OBSTACLES

Social Psychological Obstacles

The important role of the *residential school experience,* and its aftermath, is evident at numerous points in this book and rears its head again here. The residential school was a sweepingly destructive experiment in brainwashing. Among their students, the residential schools left a legacy of low self-esteem, shame over First Nations' cultures, inability to sustain intimate relationships, and poorly developed critical thinking skills and problem-solving skills. Singly or together, these are a significant handicap to First Nation persons seeking to "get on with life".

Perhaps equally important is the *colonial mentality* instilled by the *Indian Act* and its administrators, the Department of Indian Affairs and Northern Development (and its predecessors). That mindset, which regards First Nation people as helpless or incompetent, has been adopted by some First Nation people themselves through the subtle processes of informal socialization. Clearly, it is at odds with the value of self-reliance (initiative) which lies behind the question of "why Indians can't just get on with life".

Also operating at the social psychological level are the phenomena of *distrust and hopelessness*. Trust is a crucial factor in any social relationship. Regrettably, it is often in short supply not only in First Nations' relations with governments, but even within and among First Nations themselves. Such a paucity of trust is a corrosive influence, when what is really needed is trusting collaboration. However, government behaviours viewed by First Nations as continuing oppression[3] undermine that trust and, in so doing, diminish the hope which is vital (Turner and Killian, 1987: 247) to the mobilization of both collective social movements and smaller scale community development initiatives.[4]

Cultural Obstacles

In addressing cultural obstacles to the transformation of First Nation individuals and communities one must be careful to avoid blaming the victim. However, to neglect to mention First Nation cultural features which stand in the way of transformation would be to give an account which is incomplete in important respects. To include such features is not necessarily tantamount to blaming First Nation people, though, for there is an onus on Canadian society, as an enlightened, modern, multicultural democracy, to respect minority cultures. Even with regard to such cultural phenomena as "the crab pot syndrome" (Chapters Nine and Twelve), which appear to be "self-imposed" by First Nation individuals on other First Nation individuals, it is incumbent upon the larger Canadian society to bear in mind the dynamics of cultural insecurity. In a colonial context, that *cultural insecurity* can produce such clinging to First Nation culture as we observe in "the crab pot syndrome", even where the culture to which one is clinging is, in part, a culture of poverty and dependence.

The cultural incongruence between First Nation cultures and the cultures of the larger Canadian society has already been discussed and will not be elaborated here. Instead, we turn first to Boldt's emphasis on *deculturation and the loss of survival skills* in First Nation cultures.

Boldt (1993: 174–175) suggests that "many of First Nations' traditional social systems, normative patterns, and practices of surviving and living have disappeared as a result of government repression", and others have become irrelevant. This has left a cultural vacuum which has not been filled by new functional forms, he contends. To the extent that his assessment is accurate, the result is that the means of maintaining social order in many First Nation communities are greatly weakened and violence breaks out against those with the least power — children, women, and the elderly. For victims traumatized by such violence, "putting the past behind" and "getting a life" are particularly difficult. For them, as for victims of the residential school and its aftermath, the difficulty is exacerbated both by the paucity of healing resources and by *norms in aboriginal culture which frown on expressing emotions and burdening others* (Ross, 1992: 33). Hence, in a therapeutic relationship with an elder or other counsellor, breaking the cultural code of silence is an uphill struggle. Because of that and because of a lack of confidence in the justice system and an awareness of the power of informal sanctions in small communities, many victims of family violence, sexual abuse, or the residential schools are unable to come to grips with their victimization and move beyond it.

Boldt regards culture as a blueprint for adapting and surviving in the world, but sees government policies of forced assimilation and the colonial administration of Indian affairs as having derailed that adaptation. His remarks are worth quoting at length:

> The lengthy experience of individual and collective economic dependence has profoundly influenced the Indians' cultural adaptation to their world. Instead of adapting their traditional cultures to an industrializing world, Indian communities have been forced to adapt their cultures to a dependent form of surviving and living. By force of circumstances, their cultures, their social and normative systems, have become designs for surviving on government grants and social assistance rather than by their own productivity. In consequence, their identity and self-concept have been significantly formed within a framework of structural, social and psychological dependence.

> (Boldt, 1993: 173)

An *identity as a dependent, powerless victim* breeds a sense of hopelessness, apathy, and alienation. Furthermore, as Boldt notes, these are atomizing or *individuating* responses; they are inimical to the formation of a collective will for community betterment. Those feelings also work against the taking of individual initiative to "get on with life".

The *loss of Native languages* is another factor impeding positive adaptation to the larger society. A language is not merely some set of neutral symbols, interchangeable with some other set. Rather, language embodies a culture, a way of viewing the world and capturing reality, and a set of power relations. Take gender, for instance. As noted, some languages do not differentiate between male and female. Where gender does not exist as a concept, it cannot be used as a basis of organizing to contend for power. Some concepts in one language are simply not translatable into a certain other language, and others (e.g., the English concept "government") are only roughly translatable, lose subtle nuance in the translation, or can be translated only through the telling of a story.

When a First Nation loses its language as a lingua franca (working language of daily life), the members of that First Nation must relate to the larger society literally on the terms of the larger society. Also, a bilingual person can have a different personality in the different languages and being required to use the language of the dominant society can stifle part of the bilingual person's personality. In like manner, because language is also "a window on the soul" and in that sense is a carrier of a people's identity, its loss diminishes a people and alienates them from themselves and from what would have been a source of an inner strength had it survived. Finally, *language is also a power resource* (Richardson et al., 1993: 10–18). Consider, for example, First Nation persons whose education ended in, say, elementary school. They are unlikely to have a broad vocabulary in the dominant society's language. Thus, in relating to the dominant society they will be handicapped in their ability to discern the subtlety of the dominant society's legitimating discourses and defend against them,[5] and perhaps in other ways, such as in their ability to conceptualize complex causal relations which impinge on them and in their ability to mount an argument which is persuasive to the dominant society.

Ross (1993) identifies various cultural patterns which militate against "getting a life". One is the *fatalistic, spiritualistic world view* which characterizes many First Nation cultures and another is the equally prevalent norms of *egalitarianism*. The fatalistic, spiritualistic philosophy of life regards events in the world as happening not through some scientifically identifiable chain of causes and effects, but through the operation of the will of spirits. The spirit world includes not only the spirits of the ancestors, the Creator, and the Trickster, but also the spirits of the birds, animals, trees, rocks, etc. Hence, when misfortune befalls a First Nation individual who holds these cultural views, there is a cultural inclination to merely accept the misfortune as the will of the spirits, rather than to challenge the spirits by trying to take one's fate into one's own hands.

Norms of egalitarianism sometimes bring censure upon the individual who tries to "better" him/herself. That is, (s)he who seeks to improve his lot in life will sometimes face informal social sanctions arising out of community members' belief that he probably thinks that he is better than those he seeks to leave behind. Some have described this as "the crab pot syndrome" in reference to the tendency of crabs to pull back into the pot any crab which seeks to climb out. This norm of egalitarianism, or more correctly, its enforcement, runs counter to the very individualized initiative and striving that is the basis of the "get on with life" admonition.

Structural and Other Obstacles

Our discussion of opportunity structures and of comparisons with European immigrants identified certain structural obstacles to First Nation people "getting on with life". Included there were such obstacles as the *Indian Act*, the Department of Indian Affairs bureaucracy, the dependency-inducing social welfare system, an alienating school curriculum, and the inherently paternalistic fiduciary relationship that exists, in law, between First Nation people and the federal state. To this list we can add the relatively high degree of *economic, geographic, and social isolation* which characterizes most First Nation people's existence in Canadian society. For instance, the extremely high rate of unemployment on most reserves is explained, in part, by discriminatory employment practices in the larger society and in part by the fact that the First Nation population constitutes a reserve army of cheap labour that, despite affirmative action (employment equity) programmes, is often the last hired and the first fired ("downsized").

The *criminal "justice" system* of the larger society is another important structural source of First Nation people's difficulties in "getting on with life". Canada's policing, court, and prison system can be described in various ways, but rarely can these institutions be said to make a positive contribution to the offender's adjustment to society. Natives, as we observed, are highly overrepresented in that system.

Leadership deficiencies in some First Nation communities are another obstacle to the kind of community development that enables First Nation individuals to "get on with life". The colonial Indian Affairs administration undermined traditional forms of aboriginal leadership and placed band chiefs and councils in the untenable structural position of being accountable as much to the Department of Indian Affairs as to the First Nation electorate. In such a position, chiefs and council tend to lose credibility with their constituents. In addition, the leaders of some First Nation communities have lost touch with the needs of their constituents. Boldt (1993: 124–126) accuses them of being a self-serving, nepotistic, power-oriented, assimilated, sometimes tyrannical, virtually closed, elite class of landholders, politicians, bureaucrats, and a few entrepreneurs. They are, he rhetorically asserts, separated by a chasm from the vast majority of their constituents — a large lower class of destitute, dependent, and powerless people. The elite class, he contends, controls the political agenda and is more interested in issues which affect their own power, status, and privileges (e.g., expansion of jurisdiction) than in the problems afflicting the lower class. Furthermore, the redistribution of wealth, entitlements, and opportunity in this bifurcated class system is neither equitable nor done according to need, Boldt (1993: 127) contends. Instead, these scarce goods are appropriated by the elite whose behaviour, evidence suggests, is no longer regulated by First Nation philosophy, values, and communal customs. To the extent that this is true, the structural obstacles in the path of First Nation individuals "getting on with life" within their own community are formidable.

Finally, *physical and mental health problems* constitute another major obstacle for some First Nation individuals. One consequence of the astronomically high rates of suicide and accidental death among First Nations, especially in light of the existence of the extended family kinship system and the small size of First Nation communities (such that everyone knows everyone else), is that First Nation individuals are often engulfed in grief. Recall that many First Nation cultures have a proscription against the expression of that grief, such that it must be bottled up inside the individual. Imagine the state of mind of an hypothetical thirty-four-year-old on-reserve individual who experiences the loss of a son to suicide, the loss of a young niece in a house fire six months later, the loss of a neighbour in a drowning the next year, the loss of a close cousin and a distant cousin the next month in a car crash, the birth of a grandson with foetal alcohol syndrome that same month, the diagnosis of a parent with diabetes eight months later, the spouse's loss of a job immediately thereafter, and, in the next band council election the defeat of the uncle upon whom the family was counting to get the family a band-owned house. Such a litany of tragedy and loss would be mild compared to that endured in some First Nation communities over a similar time span. Under the circumstances, it is not surprising that some individuals resort to *escapist behaviours* such as bingo, the abuse of alcohol, or the abuse of prescription drugs such as Tylenol 3 (with codeine) and benzodiazepines (Valium-derivatives), as is common in some First Nation communities (Clarkson and Collins, 1994a–e).[6]

CONCLUSION

In light of all of the above, the question "Why can't Indians put the past behind and get on with life" emerges as an highly insensitive one. We are well advised to "walk a mile in the moccasins" of First Nation people before leaping to the conclusion that First Nation individuals' successful adaptation to Canadian society is merely a question of "putting mind over matter" or of developing individual initiative. Canada has unfinished business with First Nations and until such time as there is a just resolution of that unfinished business, the more appropriate questions might be "How on earth are so many First Nation individuals able to overcome the past and cope so well in Canadian society?" and "Why are there so many First Nation success stories in business, education, and the arts?"

NOTES

1 This statement is by no means intended to minimize the hardship and trauma faced by perhaps most refugees and by some other immigrants to Canada.

2 Cordon (1996) reports on the sentencing of John Martin Crawford in a case which received little publicity outside Saskatchewan. He murdered three Native women (Shelley Napope, Eva Taysup, and Calinda Waterhen) whom he picked up in Saskatoon's skid-row bars in 1992, after killing a Native woman in Lethbridge, Alberta, in 1981. Testimony at his trial reported that he also raped Shelley Napope and has raped and beaten other Native women. Commenting on Crawford's actions, Native Studies instructor Janice Acoose said that abuse and violence of aboriginal women will continue as long as they are seen as objects and not as people (Cordon, 1996).

3 Examples abound. Among them are the federal government's renewed resort to "divide and conquer" tactics (such as in the creation of the Woodland Cree band out of the Lubicon band), continuation and intensification of N.A.T.O.'s highly disruptive low-level training flights over Innu lands in Labrador, government foot-dragging on numerous land claims, police harassment, and government insistence on the extinguishment of aboriginal title in comprehensive land claims settlements. For specifics on some of these, see Goddard (1991) and Richardson (1989).

4 On the issue of hope, Boldt (1993) criticizes as false hope the notion that land claims settlements will enable First Nations to return to traditional ways. First Nations persons who hold those hopes will, obviously, not be inclined to "put the past behind" and "get on with life" in the larger Canadian cultural mode.

5 The campaign which the James Bay Crees waged against Hydro-Québec on the James Bay II project is an example of a First Nation's skillful manipulation of the dominant society's language(s) in just such a power struggle. There, language was pivotal. See the chapter by Ponting and Symons in this book.

6 Personal communication, E. N. Blachford, M.D., June 11, 1996. On the topic of widespread and severe abuse of Tylenol 3 and other narcotics and the extremely debilitating consequences thereof for community social vitality, see the award-winning investigative journalism on this topic by Clarkson and Collins (1994b).

REFERENCES

Boldt, Menno
1993   *Surviving as Indians: The Challenge of Self-Government.* Toronto: University of Toronto Press.
Cawsey, Hon. Mr. Justice Robert A.
1991   *Justice on Trial: Report of the Task Force on the Criminal Justice System and Its Impact on the Indian and Métis People of Alberta.* Edmonton: Queen's Printer.

Clarkson, Michael and Ron Collins
1994a "Death by Prescription: A *Herald* Special Report", *Calgary Herald*, June 25: A1.

1994b "Death Valley: At Eden Valley, Ninety Percent of the Adults Abuse Prescription Drugs, Say Doctors and Social Workers", *Calgary Herald*, June 25: A9

1994c "Scamming Widespread: Scheming to Get Prescriptions is Part of The Game", *Calgary Herald*, June 25: A10.

1994d "Propoxyphene a `Killer'", *Calgary Herald*, June 25: A11.

1994e "Drugs Offered Escape", *Calgary Herald*, June 25: A12.
Cordon, Sandra
1996 "Killer of Three Given Life: Natives Still Skeptical About Justice", *Calgary Herald*, June 1: A3.
Goddard, John
1991 *Last Stand of the Lubicon Cree*. Vancouver: Douglas and McIntyre.
Mercredi, Ovide and Mary Ellen Turpel
1993 *In the Rapids: Navigating the Future of First Nations*. Toronto: Viking Penguin Books.
Ponting, J. Rick
1991 "Crisis and Response: Challenges of the 1990s in Alberta Indian Affairs", pp. 89–104 in James S. Frideres and Roger Gibbins (eds.), *Alberta into the Twenty-First Century*. Calgary, Alta.: The University of Calgary Faculty of Social Sciences.
Richardson, Boyce (ed.)
1989 *Drumbeat: Anger and Renewal in Indian Country*. Ottawa: Assembly of First Nations and Summerhill Press.
Richardson, Mary, Joan Sherman and Michael Gismondi
1993 *Winning Back the Words: Confronting Experts in an Environmental Public Hearing*. Toronto: Garamond Press.
Ross, Rupert
1993 *Dancing With a Ghost: Exploring Indian Reality*. Markham, Ont.: Octopus.
Royal Commission on Aboriginal People
1996c *Final Report of the Royal Commission on Aboriginal People; Vol. 3: Gathering Strength*. Ottawa: Minister of Supply and Services Canada.
Turner, Ralph and Lewis M. Killian
1987 *Collective Behaviour*. Englewood Cliffs, N.J.: Prentice-Hall.

CHAPTER 18

GETTING A HANDLE ON RECOMMENDATIONS OF THE ROYAL COMMISSION ON ABORIGINAL PEOPLES[1]

J. Rick Ponting

INTRODUCTION

The Final Report of the Royal Commission on Aboriginal Peoples (RCAP) is a weighty tome comprising five volumes which amount to 3536 pages. If we include the 135 page special report (entitled *Choosing Life*) on suicide issued in 1995 and the 315 page special report (entitled *Bridging the Cultural Divide*) on criminal justice issued in 1996, the total increases to 3986 pages. Those seven volumes contain four hundred and seventy recommendations which consume one hundred and twenty-two pages. Many of those recommendations will never be implemented. Nevertheless, it is useful to give the Commission's corpus more than a cursory examination here, for the recommendations embody a set of ideals and implementation actions that together constitute a profound paradigm shift in aboriginal affairs in Canada. In addressing head-on the major problems and dysfunctions that were identified in earlier chapters of this book, the Commission's recommendations also provide some much-needed hope to those who might otherwise despair. Furthermore, the work of the Commission is an investment of over fifty million dollars in Canada's future by a talented staff and an illustrious panel of commissioners. Their work envisages a new era involving major reconstructive surgery to many parts of Canadian society such that "justice" and "equality" would not be merely hollow slogans, and instead would be living realities for First Nation and other aboriginal peoples.

The commissioners were:

- Hon. René Dussault (Co-Chair), Justice of the Québec Court of Appeal, former academic, and former deputy minister of Justice (Government of Québec)
- Georges Erasmus, (Co-Chair), former National Chief of the Assembly of First Nations
- Paul Chartrand, Métis lawyer in Department of Native Studies, University of Manitoba
- Hon. Bertha Wilson, first woman appointed to the Supreme Court of Canada
- Mary Sillett, founding member and former president of Pauktuutit, the Inuit Women's Association of Canada; and former Vice-President of Inuit Tapirisat of Canada

- Viola Robinson, Nova Scotia Micmac and former President of the Native Council of Canada
- Peter Meekison, political scientist (constitutional studies) at University of Alberta and former deputy minister of Federal and Intergovernmental Affairs (Government of Alberta).

The Commission was established in August 1991 with a mandate to make a sweeping examination of virtually the full scope of the past and present situation and relationships of the aboriginal peoples of Canada — the Indian, Inuit, and Métis peoples — and to propose solutions rooted in domestic and international experience.[2] It issued its Final Report on November 21, 1996.

This chapter focuses on those of RCAP's recommendations which pertain to First Nations and ignores recommendations which pertain only to the Métis or Inuit populations. Even within the First Nations area, coverage is necessarily highly selective. Selectivity is also exercised through the exclusion of most recommendations that pertain to interim (transitional) measures.

There are many ways in which this compilation could have been organized, for there are many ways of dividing up the world. The categories used here are the following: (a) Priorities; (b) Constitutional Changes; (c) New Structures and Organizations; (d) Legislative Changes; (e) Recognition; (f) Principles of a New Morality; (g) Other Policies; (h) Reallocation of Resources; (i) Strategies; (j) New Inclusiveness: Standing and Representation; (k) Other Recommendations. These are not always mutually exclusive categories. For instance, a constitutional change could create a new structure, such as the aboriginal parliament. In addition, although the reallocation of resources has been identified as a separate category that is particularly suited for capturing recommendations which call for increased funding, the reallocation of resources is implicit in probably most of the recommendations.

Commentary in this chapter is kept to a minimum. One type of comment that is included, though, is that which relates the Commission's recommendations to major foci of other chapters in this book.

Before we plunge into the substance of the recommendations, a few words on style are in order. First, for ease of flow, editorial licence has been taken with the phraseology of recommendations, such that readers are urged to consult the Commission's own phraseology if precision is needed. Numbers in parentheses are provided for purposes of referring back to the original report. Those references refer to page numbers in Volume 5 of the Final Report, where all of the recommendations, except those from the *Bridging the Cultural Divide* and *Choosing Life* volumes, are compiled by the Commission. Those few recommendations taken from *Bridging the Cultural Divide* and from *Choosing Life* are denoted by BCD and CL, respectively. Secondly, references here to "provincial governments" usually include the territorial governments and references to "governments" and "other governments" encompass the federal, provincial, and territorial governments. Hence, a recommendation that "aboriginal, municipal, and other governments should do ..." would be calling for action by aboriginal, municipal, federal, provincial, and territorial governments. Finally, although our concern is with First Nations, the more encompassing phraseology is retained in recommendations that refer to "Aboriginal people", "Aboriginal governments", "Aboriginal communities", and "Aboriginal organizations" and the Commission's conventions for capitalization of "Aboriginal" as an adjective will be respected.

SOME ASSESSMENT CRITERIA

Limitations of space preclude an assessment of the Commission's recommendations here. That is left to the reader. However, it is useful to identify some of the numerous criteria which could be evoked to evaluate the recommendations. For instance, to what extent do the recommendations open opportunity structures and provide for real empowerment of aboriginal people? To what extent do the recommendations provide for an increased and meaningful decision-making role for aboriginal people? Would implementation of the recommendations create a reservoir of hope and trust among aboriginal people? Do the recommendations adequately address aboriginal people's other social psychological needs, such as the need for recognition, respect, and healing? Are the recommendations fair to third parties? Do the recommendations adequately take into account the need to institutionalize new structures, processes, and expectations so as to give durability to changes that are achieved and prevent "backsliding" by Native and non-Native organizations and individuals? Conversely, do the recommendations create excessive bureaucracy? Are the Commission's priorities sociologically sound, in terms of what we know about the presence and strength of various causal forces that have shaped aboriginal affairs to date? In aboriginal affairs are there any contradictions that have gone unrecognized in the Commission's work, such that they might undermine the attainment of the ends desired by the Commission? Do the recommendations give sufficient attention to equity issues, as between the sexes, social classes, on- and off-reserve residents, and aboriginal people of different legal status? Is the "nations" model the best one for organizing aboriginal government and delivery of services and is it compatible with the "community of interests" model advocated for urban areas? Do the recommendations give adequate attention to enhancing community social vitality and building up the expressive, organizational, and instrumental capacity of aboriginal communities? Readers could probably expand this list considerably.

RECOMMENDATIONS

Priorities

Identifying the precise priorities of the Royal Commission from its compendium of recommendations is a challenge. No time-line is provided for most recommendations and the Commission eschewed the approach of classifying the recommendations in terms of what should be accomplished by the end of year one, year two, etc. That is only realistic. Nevertheless, at various points the Commission did flag some items as priorities and did specify a time frame within which action should be launched or completed. These are reported below, in the recognition that the assault which the Commissioners recommended was envisaged as proceeding on various fronts simultaneously.

   The early release of the reports on suicide (1995) and criminal justice (February 1996) is indicative of the extremely high priority which Commissioners placed on these two very debilitating situations. Concerning suicide prevention, the commissioners wrote:

> Suicide and self-injury in Aboriginal communities together constitute a problem with effects so damaging to community life, a message of public policy

failure so compelling, that the Royal Commission on Aboriginal Peoples has decided to recommend immediate measures to combat it. ... Commissioners believe it is a matter of utmost urgency that the people and government of Canada, Aboriginal and non-Aboriginal alike, join in a concerted effort to bring high rates of suicide and self-injury to a rapid end.

(CL, 88–89)[3]

In the realm of criminal justice, the Commission recommended that certain actions be taken within one year of the release of its *Bridging the Cultural Divide* report. These included a joint meeting of the various bars, law societies and lawyers' associations (*BCD*, 315) and a "high-powered" meeting of federal and provincial ministers of justice, attorneys-general, solicitors-general, ministers of correctional services, and ministers responsible for Aboriginal affairs, to address the issues and recommendations in *Bridging the Cultural Divide* (*BCD*, 314). Of course, representatives of Aboriginal peoples and national Aboriginal organizations were to be invited.

The appropriation of funds from Parliament is obviously another very high priority of the Commission. A strategy of sweeping change was proposed and very little of it could be accomplished without "an immediate and major infusion of resources" (56). The Commissioners wrote:

> [W]e strongly recommend that, to give effect to our recommendations, governments increase their annual spending over the first five years of the strategy, so that by year five, expenditures are between $1.5 and $2 billion more than they are today. Governments will then need to sustain that level of additional expenditure for a number of years. (56)

The Commission also urged that a meeting of First Ministers and leaders of the national Aboriginal organizations be held within six months of the release of the RCAP Final Report to review its principal recommendations and begin consultations on such matters as the drafting of a new royal proclamation (see below) and a Canada-wide framework agreement (251–252) on funding Aboriginal government.

In order to send "a clear signal that the Government of Canada not only intends to reform its fundamental relationship with Aboriginal peoples but is taking the first practical steps to do so" (173), action within a year of publication of the RCAP report was urged on re-structuring federal institutions. As noted later in this chapter, this includes initiatives to abolish the Department of Indian Affairs and Northern Development, replace it with two new departments, create a Cabinet committee on Aboriginal affairs, and create an elected Aboriginal parliament with enumeration of Aboriginal voters to occur during the federal election of 1997.

The Commission's recommendations in the area of housing and water and sewage system infrastructure (see "Reallocation of Resources" below) were designated for immediate action so that within five years acute threats to health would be eliminated (71).

Various measures were also proposed to provide interim relief while other matters, such as land claims, are under negotiation or development (181). For instance, the Commission recommended that governments hold in trust any revenues from royalties or taxation of resource developments on lands that are the subject of claims. Presumably, such action was to be undertaken immediately. Similarly, interim measures were proposed in the realm of economic development (186ff).

Finally, two educational thrusts were singled out for high priority. Specifically, in light of the precarious demographic state of many Aboriginal languages, as observed in Chapter Ten of this book, the Commissioners recommended that Aboriginal language education be assigned priority in Aboriginal, provincial, and territorial education systems (220). They also recommended that the International Aboriginal Peoples' University (see "New Structures and Organizations" below) be established by the year 2000 (229).

These measures alone would not consume the entire increased budget which the Commission recommended be appropriated. Accordingly, other measures, such as consultations, research, land claim negotiations, and development of a proposed youth strategy (68), were envisaged as being implemented concurrently with these, but no priority was explicitly designated for, or among, them. In other cases, financial appropriations are designated as beginning in year five, which by default suggests that these areas have lower priority. Examples would be early childhood initiatives and restructuring off-reserve Aboriginal health care (69).

Constitutional Changes

Most of the solutions advocated by RCAP are not at the constitutional level. One important exception is the recommendation that the federal government prepare a royal proclamation for the consideration of the Queen (150). It would supplement the *Royal Proclamation* of 1763 that is part of the *Constitution Act, 1982*. The new royal proclamation would set out fundamental principles to govern (i) the nation-to-nation relationship between the Crown and Aboriginal treaty nations and (ii) the treaty-making, treaty implementation, and treaty renewal processes. The Minister of Indian Affairs has publicly stated his indifference to such a royal proclamation, for he and the Commission (131) see it as merely a symbolic gesture. However, it is highly unlikely that First Nations would attach so little importance to such a royal proclamation and the courts could well side with the First Nations on this.

The Commission also called for representatives of Aboriginal peoples to be included in the planning and preparation for future constitutional conferences (255) but, significantly, stopped short of calling for Aboriginal participation in all constitutional conferences themselves, despite leanings in favour of such a move as expressed in the body of the Final Report (132). RCAP recommended several items for the constitutional reform agenda, such as the granting of veto power to Aboriginal people on changes to those parts of the constitution which explicitly mention Indians or Aboriginal people, the recognition of the inherent right of self-government, treaty-making and implementation, and certain other matters (255).

The proposal for the creation of an Aboriginal parliament (173) as a first step toward creating a House of First Peoples as the third chamber of the Parliament of Canada, would require constitutional amendment, but not necessarily unanimous consent of the provinces (129).

The Commission stopped short of recommending that the fiduciary responsibility of governments to Aboriginal peoples be entrenched in the constitution (131). Peculiarly, while the Commission argued (131) that an Aboriginal Lands and Treaties Tribunal (see below) should receive the protection of constitutional entrenchment and that the constitution should be amended to state a commitment to the principle of making equalization payments extend to Aboriginal governments (132), it did not formally recommend that. The same is true of extending to Aboriginal governments the principle of intergovernmental immunity from taxation (132).

New Structures and Organizations

A wide variety of new structures and organizations is proposed by the Commission. Most conspicuous among them is the aforementioned creation of an **Aboriginal parliament** whose main function would be to provide advice to the House of Commons and the Senate on legislation and constitutional matters relating to Aboriginal peoples (173). The Aboriginal parliament would be strictly advisory; it would have no law-making powers, no expenditure powers, and no power to delay or veto legislation passed by the Commons or Senate. *As with any other new structure, it is impossible to know in advance whether, if created at all, it would be created exactly as recommended by RCAP and whether, over time, its function might evolve such that it becomes more or less powerful.*

A second major structural change proposed is the **abolition of the federal Department of Indian Affairs and Northern Development** and its replacement by two new departments: a **Department of Aboriginal Relations** and a **Department of Indian and Inuit Services** (172). The new position of Minister of Aboriginal Relations would be a senior portfolio in Cabinet, while the new position of Minister of Indian and Inuit Services would be more junior (172).

Within the Department of Aboriginal Relations there would be a new **Crown Treaty Office** (152). An **Aboriginal Lands and Treaties Tribunal** also would be created to replace the Indian Claims Commission (153, 183). The Tribunal would be empowered to ensure good-faith negotiations, order interim relief, and decide appeals regarding funding of treaty processes at the treaty commissions (see below) level (153). The Tribunal would also handle the settlement of specific (not comprehensive) claims and the treaty-making, implementation, and renewal processes (182). **Treaty commissions** would be established by the Aboriginal nations and other governments (152). These would be permanent, independent, neutral bodies given the task of facilitating and overseeing treaty negotiations. Included among their powers would be the power to provide binding or non-binding arbitration (when requested by the disputing parties), conduct research, provide remedies for abuse of process, and others (153).

The Commission also recommended the creation of a new and permanent cabinet *committee* **on Aboriginal relations** (172). Such a move would raise the status of Aboriginal issues from their traditionally low level among bureaucrats and politicians in Ottawa, and would provide important access to Cabinet for Aboriginal leaders.

To implement its proposed Canada-wide suicide prevention offensive, the Commission proposed the creation of a **National Forum on the Prevention of Suicide Among Aboriginal People** and a small accompanying secretariat (*CL,* p. 93–94).

A very important part of the nation-building effort envisaged by the Commission is the creation of **Aboriginal justice systems**. The Commission recommended that governments include the creation of Aboriginal justice systems on the agenda of current negotiations on land claims, treaty-making, and self-government and consider re-opening existing treaties and agreements to address justice issues if the Aboriginal parties so desire (*BCD*, 312). These Aboriginal justice systems will include such institutions as peace-keeping organizations, courts, sentencing circles in some nations, and if the Commission's recommendation (*BCD*, 313) is followed, appeal bodies. The Commission also recommended the creation (by legislation) of an Aboriginal Justice Council to facilitate the development of Aboriginal justice systems (*BCD*, 315).

The creation of an **Aboriginal Peoples' International University (APIU)**, with a Canada-wide research and development capacity in Aboriginal economic development (197, 228), was an important recommendation. This university would be Aboriginally-controlled and would have the capacity to function in all provinces and territories. Among other things, its mandate would be to promote traditional knowledge, to pursue applied research in support of Aboriginal self-government, to serve as an **electronic information clearinghouse**, and to house statistical data bases. This could be a controversial recommendation, for to the extent that the APIU succeeds in drawing Aboriginal students and Aboriginal faculty away from other Canadian universities, the opportunities for Aboriginal and non-Aboriginal students and faculty to learn from each other will be diminished.

Concerning those other Canadian universities, the Commission recommended the creation of such new structures as **Aboriginal student unions** (226) and **Aboriginal residential colleges** to serve as the focal point for the academic, residential, social, and cultural lives of Aboriginal students on campus and to promote Aboriginal scholarship (227). The establishment of **other post-secondary educational institutions controlled by Aboriginal people** was also recommended (227). Such "indigenization" measures could be effective in countering the stigma which in some Aboriginal communities is attached to advanced formal education. As Crowfoot's chapter noted, in First Nation youths' peer groups, formal education is sometimes denigrated as being the "white way".

At the level of elementary and secondary education, RCAP recommended both the establishment of **Aboriginally-governed schools** affiliated with school districts (if requested by Aboriginal people) and the creation of **Aboriginal advisory committees to school boards** (221).

The creation of a federally endowed **Aboriginal Languages Foundation** was also recommended for purposes of supporting Aboriginal initiatives in the conservation, revitalization, and documentation of Aboriginal languages (234). The Commission also recommended the creation of an **Aboriginal Arts Council**, with an annual budget equivalent to 5% of the Canada Council budget, to foster the revitalization and development of Aboriginal arts and literature (236).

To facilitate the development of Aboriginal government, RCAP recommended that the federal government and Aboriginal organizations co-operate to create an **Aboriginal government transition centre** (167). This organization, which would be funded by the federal government for a maximum of ten years and would operate under a predominantly Aboriginal board, would assist in developing and sharing expertise in leadership, negotiating skills, social animation, citizenship codes, citizen participation, constitution and institution-building, nation-rebuilding, etc. (167–168).

To enhance business development, the Commission recommended that governments assist in the formation of **Aboriginal venture capital corporations** by extending tax credits to investors in such corporations (201). Another recommendation called for the establishment of **a national Aboriginal development bank**, staffed and controlled by Aboriginal people (202). It would not only provide equity and loan financing to large-scale Aboriginal business projects, but would also offer development bonds to raise capital from private individuals and corporations.

Turning from economic development to personal development, the Commission recommended the creation of a system of **healing centres** (for out-patient services) and **healing lodges** (to provide residential services), both under Aboriginal control (210) so as to make the services offered culturally appropriate. It also recommended that **youth centres** be established on reserves and in communities where there is a significant Aboriginal population. The establishment of **Aboriginal youth camps** was also recommended. Their purposes would include offering cultural activities that link youth with elders and providing positive social interaction between Aboriginal youth of different nations and between Aboriginal and non-Aboriginal youth (238–239).

In response to the housing crisis, one of the Commission's recommendations was for the creation of an Aboriginal version of the **Habitat for Humanity** co-operative housing program (239).

For the urban population, the Commission advocated organization around the notion of a "**community of interest**". It recommended that governments foster community-building, including, "where appropriate", governance initiatives from "communities of interest". Out of those governance initiatives will come many local structures.

The Commission also recommended the creation of an **Aboriginal Peoples Review Commission** that is independent of government, reports to Parliament, and is headed by an Aboriginal Chief Commissioner. The Chief Commissioner would, in some respects, be like the Commissioner of Official Languages. The mandate of this commission would include monitoring progress being made in honouring governments' commitments and in implementing the recommendations of RCAP (252).

In addition to the creation of these new structures, the Commission recommended major changes be made by some existing institutions to accommodate Aboriginal needs and priorities. In line with Calliou's parable of the giraffe and the elephant and his account of the difficulties which Native students face at mainstream post-secondary education institutions, the Commission advanced a long list of accommodations that they recommend such institutions make in order to increase the participation, retention, and graduation rates of Aboriginal students (226). The Commission called for such changes as cross-cultural sensitivity training for faculty and staff, active recruitment of Aboriginal students and faculty members, Aboriginal content and perspectives in course offerings across disciplines, and the offering of Aboriginal studies as part of the institution's regular program offerings (226). Other realms were also singled out as needing organizational accommodation. They include: health and social services (215, 249); government employment policies in the North, so as to accommodate the demands of traditional economic activities (246); and mass media organizations, in staffing and coverage (254).

Clearly, the above-listed new structures and these organizational accommodations recommended by the Commission would involve a substantial reshaping of the organizational landscape of Canada.

Legislative Changes

To establish some of the above structures and accomplish various goals identified by the Commission, it would be necessary to introduce new legislation or amend some existing statutes. Once the policy decisions are taken, some such legislative undertakings would be essentially "housework" or enabling legislation. One example would be the passage of a statute to repeal the *Department of Indian Affairs and Northern Development Act* and create the Department of Aboriginal Relations and the Department of Indian and Inuit Services. Other examples would be legislation to create the national Aboriginal development bank and the Aboriginal Peoples Review Commission. Slightly less routine would be amendments to the *Canada Water Act* to provide for guaranteed Aboriginal representation on existing inter-jurisdictional water management boards and to establish federal/provincial/Aboriginal arrangements where none currently exist (193).

Important new legislation would include **companion treaty legislation** to the proposed royal proclamation (150). This companion legislation would affirm liberal rules of interpretation for historical treaties and declare the commitment of Canada "to the implementation *and renewal*[4] of each treaty in accordance with the spirit and intent of the treaty and the relationship embodied in it". Significantly, this legislation would also commit the Government of Canada to making treaty with treaty First Nations "whose treaty does not purport to address issues of lands and resources" and with Aboriginal nations that do not yet have a treaty with the Crown (150–151).

An **Aboriginal Nations Recognition and Government Act** is another one of the centrepieces of the Commission's proposals. It would establish the process whereby the Government of Canada "can recognize the accession of an Aboriginal group or groups to nation status and its assumption of authority as an Aboriginal government to exercise its inherent self-governing jurisdiction" (165). The Act would also establish criteria for the recognition of Aboriginal nations; RCAP suggested the six criteria (165–166) listed in Box 1 later in this chapter.

Also part of the legislative package to implement the RCAP recommendations would be a federal law to create the **Aboriginal parliament** (173).

Another recommendation called for governments to review legislation to ensure that it provides Aboriginal organizations and communities with access to urgent remedies to prevent or arrest damage to significant **heritage sites** that are threatened by human actions or natural processes (232). A related recommendation urged governments to review legislation affecting historical and **sacred sites** and the conservation and display of **cultural artefacts** to ensure that a set of criteria identified by the Commission (232) is met. Federal government review of its legislation on the **protection of intellectual property** was also recommended so as "to ensure that Aboriginal interests and perspectives, in particular collective interests, are adequately protected" (233).

The Commission also recommended that Canada give some greater substance to its obligations to Canadian Aboriginal people under **international law**. Specifically, it recommended that the federal government enact legislation which would (i) affirm the obligations it has assumed toward Aboriginal people under international human rights instruments to which Canada is a signatory and (ii) give Aboriginal people access to a remedy in Canadian courts for breach of those commitments under international law (174).

At the level of Aboriginal nations, one of the most consequential recommendations for legislation is that which calls upon Aboriginal nations to develop their own **charters of rights** to supplement the protections in the Canadian *Charter of Rights and Freedoms* (*BCD*, 312). Also at the level of Aboriginal nations, the Commission sees one part of the solution to the First Nation housing crisis as involving First Nation governments assuming jurisdiction over **housing** at the earliest opportunity. That would enable them not only to enact clear laws regarding housing tenure but also to pursue authority to adjust other programs (such as redirecting social assistance) so as to marshal more resources for housing (218).

One of the most noteworthy legislative amendments recommended by the Commission is an amendment to the *Canadian Human Rights Act* to authorize the Canadian Human Rights Commission to hold inquiries into the relocation of Aboriginal communities and to make it a violation of the *Act* if a relocation does not conform to a set of criteria established by RCAP (144–145).

A recommendation that the Government of Canada explicitly recognize in federal legislation the **special status of Aboriginal language broadcasting** would presumably require an amendment to the *Broadcast Act* (234). The recommendation that the Canadian Radio-Television and Telecommunications Commission include in licence conditions for public and commercial broadcasters (in regions with significant Aboriginal population concentrations) requirements for fair representation and distribution of Aboriginal programming (235), could possibly be accomplished without legislative amendment.

Other proposed amendments would be in the area of **family law**, including at the provincial and territorial level. The intentions behind these amendments would include resolving anomalies in the application of family law to Aboriginal people, filling current gaps, putting in place mechanisms for the transition to Aboriginal control of family matters under self-government, and others (208).

Certain amendments to the *Income Tax Act* were implicit in the Commission's recommendations. For instance, the Commission proposed that tax incentives be established to encourage private and corporate support for the development of Aboriginal media content (236) and for Aboriginal venture capital corporations (201).

With regard to Aboriginal people in the North, the Commission also saw a need to amend **employment insurance** legislation and **social assistance** legislation to take into account specific differences in employment patterns, high costs of living, and other factors characterizing the North.

The Commission also recommends that legislation (presumably amendments to provincial school acts) be passed to guarantee Aboriginal representation on **school boards** where Aboriginal population numbers so warrant (221).

Recognition

Sociologically, recognition is extremely important to colonized or otherwise subordinated people. Recognition offers not only social status and symbolic gains, but also eligibility for a share of scarce resources.[5] Recognition can re-define not only a situation (e.g., recognition of a need, grievance, or right), but also the public discourse which surrounds that situation and the mandates of organizations which are potentially or actually involved with that situation. At the social psychological level, formal recognition can provide a sense of valida-tion and acknowledgement of the worth of a people, of the individuals who comprise that collectivity, and of their historical contributions to the larger soci-ety. Recognition can alleviate alienation and instill a sense of belonging in, and commitment to, a larger collectivity. Thus, recognition is of vital importance not only to the healing and restoration of the dignity of individuals who have been stigmatized, traumatized, or otherwise denigrated through stereotypes, racism, humour, abuse, or neglect; recognition is also important to the healing and restoration of the honour of the larger society. In short, recognition is not mere tokenism; recognition can be empowering. The Royal Commission demon-strated an appreciation of these multiple functions of recognition.

The very creation of RCAP, with its sweeping mandate, was a form of recog-nition. Also, the very fact that recommendations are made by RCAP to address any given situation, is a form of recognition. For instance, the recommendation that the Government of Canada commit to publishing a multi-volume general history of Aboriginal peoples of Canada (142) validates Aboriginal assertions that Aboriginal history and civilization have been ignored or denigrated by the larger society. There are, though, numerous recommendations which explicitly call for one or another form of recognition or acknowledgement. It is to them that we now turn.

Among the most important such recommendations are those which call for all governments in Canada to recognize that **Aboriginal peoples are nations** vested with the right of self-determination (155) and that the **right of Aboriginal self-government is an inherent right** which is recognized and affirmed in the *Constitution Act, 1982* (Sec. 35.1) and arises out of

> the sovereign and independent status of Aboriginal peoples and nations before and at the time of European contact, and from the fact that Aboriginal peoples were in possession of their own territories, political systems and cus-tomary laws at that time (158).

Implementation of this recommendation would grant the recognition that was denied in the First Ministers' and Aboriginal Leaders' Constitutional Conferences of the 1980s and in the defeat of the Charlottetown Accord. Also very important, symbolically, is the recommendation that the federal govern-ment recognize Aboriginal people in Canada as enjoying a unique form of **dual citizenship** as citizens of an Aboriginal nation and citizens of Canada, and that the Canadian passports of Aboriginal citizens explicitly recognize that dual cit-izenship (161). Related to the inherent right to self-government is the recom-mendation that governments recognize that Section 35 of the *Constitution Act, 1982* provides the basis for a **third order of government** (Aboriginal govern-ment) within Canada (162).

Concerning that third order of government, the Commission's report on Aboriginal people and the criminal justice system, entitled *Bridging the Cultural Divide ("BCD")*, recommended that governments recognize the right of Aboriginal nations to establish and administer their own systems of justice pur-suant to their inherent right of self-government (*BCD*, 312). Particularly noteworthy is the fact that such recognition would include recognition of Aboriginal governments' power to make criminal laws for application within their territory (*BCD*, 312).

Of particular importance also is the fact that the Crown's **fiduciary obligation** to First Nations is not only repeatedly reaffirmed by RCAP (e.g., 162, where it is described as "a fundamental feature of the constitution of Canada", 175, 184), but extended to other Aboriginal peoples. For instance, one recommendation calls for the federal government to "acknowledge a fiduciary responsibility to support Aboriginal nations and their communities in restoring Aboriginal families to a state of health and wholeness" (206).

Traditional knowledge of indigenous people is often denigrated by ethnocentric scientists and academics of the larger society. In recent years more open-mindedness has begun to appear in those quarters and RCAP's recommendations display a respect that was lacking in an earlier era when traditional Aboriginal knowledge was often dismissed as superstition. Thus, the Commission calls for Aboriginal and other governments to "acknowledge the common understanding of the determinants of health found in Aboriginal traditions and health sciences ..." (209). Similar respect was urged in a recommendation pertaining to post-secondary educational institutions and associations involved in regulating and licensing health and social services professionals (214). The Commission also urged the federal government to recognize the contribution of Aboriginal traditional knowledge to environmental stewardship, to support its development (245), and to support the development of institutes that gather and research traditional knowledge and apply it to contemporary issues (247).

The recommendation that the federal and First Nation governments undertake to meet the need of First Nation people for adequate housing within ten years (217) is an affirmation of the housing crisis and associated grievances that have long prevailed in First Nation communities. It is also fundamental to the restoration of dignity and of health.

The recognition that would flow from the **Aboriginal Nations Recognition and Government Act** (165) would flow to specific Aboriginal nations, rather than to Aboriginal people in general. On the surface, this might be reminiscent of the provisions of the *Indian Act* whereby a band could receive the dubious recognition of having reached "an advanced stage of development". Such a concern is probably unwarranted, though, when viewed in the larger context of the whole set of RCAP recommendations. However, the recommendation does place the federal government in a gatekeeping role, albeit one that is similar to the gatekeeping involved in granting recognition to foreign regimes.

The **granting of rights and recognition of jurisdiction** are other ways in which recognition can be bestowed with tangible consequences. The RCAP recommendations contain numerous examples of these. For instance, the Commission recommended that governments enact legislation to establish a process for recognizing Aboriginal people as having ownership rights and at least shared jurisdiction over cultural sites, archaeological resources, religious and spiritual objects, and sacred sites located within their traditional territories (194).

Another recommendation calls for Aboriginal and other governments to promptly acknowledge that child welfare is a core area of Aboriginal self-government (206) and yet another calls for governments to acknowledge the validity of Aboriginal customary law in areas of family law, such as marriage, divorce, child custody and adoption (208). As transitional economic development measures, RCAP recommended that the provinces: (i) give Aboriginal people the **right of first refusal** on unallocated Crown timber and on water rights for hydroelectric developments, where those resources are situated close to reserves or Aboriginal communities (188); (ii) require resource extraction companies, as part of their operating licence, to develop land use plans to protect traditional Aboriginal harvesting areas and sacred sites (189) and to **provide significant economic benefits** to Aboriginal communities (197); and (iii) require Crown corporations developing hydroelectric power sites, as part of their licence, to develop socio-economic agreements (covering training, employment, business contracts, joint ventures, equity partnerships) with the affected Aboriginal communities (192–193).

The recommendation for recognition of Aboriginally-controlled **schools** under the jurisdiction of Aboriginal community-of-interest governments (221) is particularly noteworthy, not only because it would likely increase access to funding for such schools, but because it is also implicitly a symbolic validation (statement of respect for) Aboriginal culture itself. The recommendation (226) that post-secondary education institutions recognize Aboriginal languages on a basis equal to other modern languages (e.g., for fulfilling students' entrance requirements or second language proficiency requirements) is also a statement of respect and a concrete measure to facilitate Aboriginal students' academic progress. The commission also recommended that Aboriginal governments declare their Aboriginal language an official language in their territory (234). Such an action, where implemented, will not only be a source of pride, but will probably also assist in practical ways in keeping the Aboriginal language alive.

Aboriginal **print and broadcast media** have been subjected to highly politicized funding procedures. RCAP recommends that governments, including Aboriginal governments, recognize the critical role of independent Aboriginal media in the pursuit of Aboriginal self-determination and that they, therefore, support freedom of expression through dedicated funding *at arm's length* from political bodies (235).

The Commission's mandate made explicit reference to the role of **Elders**. The Commission recommended that Aboriginal and other governments "acknowledge the essential role of Elders and the traditional knowledge that they have to contribute in rebuilding Aboriginal nations ... self-determination ... and well-being" (237). In support of the Elders and other traditionalists, the Commission recommended that governments recognize Aboriginal people's right of access to public lands for the purpose of gathering traditional herbs, plants, and medicines, where that right is not incompatible with existing land use (238). With regard to urban areas, the Commission urged Aboriginal and other governments to launch programs to promote Aboriginal culture in urban communities, including means to increase access to Aboriginal Elders.

Finally, at the largely symbolic level, the Commission recommended that a national First Peoples Day be declared (254), that greater use be made of Aboriginal place names, languages, ceremonies, etc. (254), that Aboriginal Veterans be recognized and honoured in various ways (147), and that the federal government ensure that the history and present circumstances of Aboriginal peoples are communicated to immigrants and persons acquiring Canadian citizenship (254).

These numerous measures, if implemented, would not only buttress Aboriginal government and culture, but would also significantly increase non-Natives' awareness of Aboriginal people as full-fledged members of the Canadian polity.

Principles of a New Morality

Ideas are among the most important forces contributing to social change. One type of idea is a set of principles and criteria, embodying certain values and priorities, assembled to guide the formulation of policy in a particular area.[6] Often, the same values will also have influenced the defining of the policy problem itself. These sets of guiding principles can be highly abstract, or very concrete, or both. The Royal Commission enunciated numerous value-based principles and criteria which, taken together, constitute a new morality or new ethic in First Nation affairs in Canada. This section illustrates the most important of them.

At the most abstract level, the Commission recommended that governments and national Aboriginal organizations commit themselves to building a renewed relationship based on **justice and fairness** — in particular, on the principles of mutual recognition, mutual respect, sharing, and mutual responsibility (141). The historical treaties should be implemented from the perspective of both justice and **reconciliation**, the Commission urged (148). Of equally fundamental significance is the recommendation that governments renounce, as factually, legally, and morally wrong, the concepts of "terra nullius"[7] and "the doctrine of discovery"[8], by which Aboriginal lands were usurped and "sovereignty" abrogated (141).

A pivotal recommendation calls for the **expansion of the land base** of Aboriginal governments (175, 184). This is an essential condition for any effective reform and was a provision of the defeated Charlottetown Accord. Equally pivotal are the criteria recommended to govern whether or not Canada recognizes an Aboriginal people as a nation (165–166). These are so important as to warrant being listed in their entirety in Box 1. With regard to the citizenship code mentioned there, it is significant that the Commission adopted the principle that citizenship should not be contingent upon the applicant possessing a certain minimum "blood quantum" of Aboriginal ancestry (161). That is, *citizenship criteria should reflect Aboriginal nations as political and cultural entities, rather than as racial groups.*

In a similar vein to the Charlottetown Accord, the Commission recommended principles according to which the *spirit and intent* **of the historical treaties**, rather than merely the written record, be implemented as part of the renewal of the Crown's relationship with the treaty First Nations (148-149). Included in these principles are such maxims as "The Crown is in a trust-like and non-adversarial fiduciary relationship with the treaty nations" and "treaty nations did not intend to consent to the blanket extinguishment of their Aboriginal rights and title [to land] by entering into the treaty relationship". With regard to new treaties, the Commission recommended that a process for making new treaties replace the existing comprehensive claims policy and that the new process be based on such principles as **availability** to the "Indian, Inuit and Métis nations" and to treaty nations that are parties to peace and friendship treaties "that did not purport to address land and resource issues" (149). Of particular note is the principle that the blanket **extinguishment of Aboriginal land**

BOX 1 Criteria for Granting Recognition to an Aboriginal People as a Nation

---

1. Evidence among the communities concerned of common ties of language, history, culture, and of willingness to associate, coupled with sufficient size to support the exercise of a broad, self-governing mandate;
2. Evidence of a fair and open process for obtaining the agreement of its citizens and member communities to embark on a nation-recognition process;
3. Completion of a citizenship code that is consistent with international norms of human rights and with the *Canadian Charter of Rights and Freedoms*;
4. Evidence that an impartial appeal process has been established to hear disputes about individuals' eligibility for citizenship;
5. Evidence that a fundamental law or constitution has been drawn up through wide consultation with its citizens; and
6. Evidence that all citizens of the nation were permitted, through a fair means of expressing their opinion, to ratify the proposed constitution.

Source: RCAP (1996e: 165–166)

---

rights is not an option to be considered in negotiating the new treaties (149) and the principle that, in calculating treaty land entitlements, the amount of land owing under treaty be calculated on the basis of population figures (including urban residents, Bill C-31 beneficiaries, and non-status Indians) as of the date new negotiations begin (185). Had this principle been adopted at the outset of the infamous Lubicon negotiations mentioned in Brown's chapter, the dispute might not have been as prolonged as it has been.

In contrast to the expressed desire of many treaty First Nations to deal only with the federal government, and on a nation-to-nation basis, the Commission recommended the principle of **full participation by provincial governments** in treaty-making, treaty implementation, and treaty renewal processes (180).

The Commission also recommended that not only all treaty-related processes (namely, the making, implementation, and renewal of treaties), but also all federal policy, conform to a set of general principles (175). These principles include the axioms that the Crown has a special **fiduciary obligation** to protect the interests of Aboriginal people, the Crown has an **obligation to reconcile the interests of the public with Aboriginal title** (rather than allowing the so-called "national interest" to automatically prevail), and agreements be subject to **periodic review and renewal** (as per the recommendations of the Coolican report [Coolican, 1985] and in contrast to the policy of the Reform Party of Canada discussed in Chapter Five of this book).

In accord with the policy of the Reform Party of Canada, the Commission did recommend that governments **keep the public fully informed** about the nature and scope of land negotiations (195). It further recommended that public education be a major part of treaty processes (195) and that "building public awareness and understanding should become an integral and continuing part of every endeavour and every initiative in which Aboriginal people, their organizations and governments are involved and in which non-Aboriginal governments and stakeholders have a part" (253–254).

Not surprisingly, **Aboriginal control** is a principle which surfaced at numerous points in the Commission's recommendations, including in conjunction with various economic development measures (e.g., the national Aboriginal development bank to have an Aboriginal majority on its board of directors (202)), education (219, 221, 228), cultural and historic sites (194), social assistance programs (206), and healing lodges (210), to cite just a few examples.

Another fundamental precept advocated by the Commission (207) was the **inclusion of women, youth, Elders, and persons with disabilities** in governing councils and decision-making bodies (e.g., women on justice committees and on the boards of directors of healing places, as advocated in Dion Stout's chapter in this book).

In addition to inclusiveness, **holism** is another general principle endorsed at various points by the Commission, such as in the realm of social assistance programming (206), healing (209), health and social services (211), and suicide prevention (*CL*, 91).

Principles were also adumbrated to guide various other specific actions of the federal government, such as the provision of housing (216), the provision of funding to Aboriginal governments (176), negotiations on the additional lands that are to be made available to Aboriginal governments (176–177),[9] return of expropriated lands (186), interim measures to improve Aboriginal peoples' access to resource-based economic opportunities (186–187, 189–190), the administration of federal equity contribution programs for Aboriginal economic and business development (201), respect for third party interests (179, 186), and the protection and management of Aboriginal heritage resources (194).

The Commission also established various norms or principles that it deemed should apply to Aboriginal governments. Of particular relevance to the Cockerill and Gibbins chapter in this book and to the concerns about abuse of power which Dion Stout and some First Nation women's organizations have expressed, is the fact that the Commission asserted that Aboriginal governments should be subject to the Canadian *Charter of Rights and Freedoms*, but that they should have access to the "notwithstanding" clause whereby some basic rights and freedoms could be temporarily over-ridden by Aboriginal governments (163). The recommendations that Aboriginal citizens living on their territory **pay personal income tax to their Aboriginal governments** and that the **tax effort** made by Aboriginal governments be taken into account when designing arrangements for financing Aboriginal governments (163) are also highly germane to the concerns of Cockerill and Gibbins and consistent with the federal government's proposed *Indian Act* amendments to give taxation powers to First Nation governments.[10]

The **accountability** of Aboriginal governments is a related major concern of First Nation women's organizations, grassroots activists, and the federal government. The Commission recommended four steps that Aboriginal governments take to sustain the principle of accountability (170), but otherwise gave short shrift to contemporary mechanisms[11] of accountability in favour of strategies for accountability and responsibility which "reflect and build upon Aboriginal peoples' own customs, traditions and values" (170).

Other principles recommended to Aboriginal governments pertain to such areas as resolution of disputes over citizenship rules (161), the establishment of economic institutions (196–197), and "zero tolerance" of actions that violate physical or emotional safety (207).

Among the other miscellaneous, yet important, principles recommended by the Commission are **representation for non-Aboriginal residents** of

Aboriginal territory in Aboriginal governments' decision-making (164), **employment equity** in public and private media organizations (235), and museums' and cultural organizations' adoption of **ethical guidelines pertaining to Aboriginal artefacts** (232).

Other Policies

If adopted, the principles outlined in the preceding section would be embodied in policies. Similarly, to cite two later sections of this chapter, decisions to allocate resources in certain ways and to implement strategies can also be considered to be policies. Thus, policy considerations are ubiquitous in the Commission's reports. Therefore, the present section identifies a few policies that are not captured under other rubrics in this chapter.

A long-standing complaint of First Nations has been that the government's approach to treaties and other matters (e.g., off-reserve services) has been narrowly legalistic. The Commission recommended that that "minimalist" orientation of merely fulfilling "**lawful obligations**" be reinterpreted in an interim government policy pertaining to expanding First Nations' land base, so as to take into account the government's broader fiduciary obligations to First Nations and to be consistent with Supreme Court decisions on government's obligations to Aboriginal peoples (184). While such a policy is already in place in some realms (e.g., funding health care for First Nation individuals who are not covered by the Treaty Six "medicine chest" clause), its spread into an area as important as land would be significant indeed.

Another controversial federal policy has been the federal government's preferential allotment of the allowable Pacific coast fishery catch to Aboriginal fishers. The Commission recommended a **fisheries policy** whereby Aboriginal commercial fisheries have priority over non-Aboriginal commercial and sport fishing interests (190). It further recommended that the size of the Aboriginal commercial fishing allocations be based on certain criteria, one of which is that resources are essential for building Aboriginal economies and Aboriginal people must be able to make a profit from their commercial fisheries (190). All provinces were also urged to adopt the Ontario and British Columbia policy of buying up and turning over commercial fishing quotas to Aboriginal people as partial restitution for historical inequities in commercial allocations (190).

In the realm of **education and the arts**, the Commission addressed a glaring weakness in existing teacher training when it recommended that provinces require that pre-service training leading to teacher certification include at least one component on teaching Aboriginal subject matter to Aboriginal and non-Aboriginal students. It also recommended that provinces adopt the policy of requiring teacher education programs to collaborate with Aboriginal people in developing Aboriginal-specific components of their programs (224). In addition, any organizations that provide support for the visual and performing arts should review all aspects of their programs to ensure that the criteria embodied in their policies for grants and awards are relevant to Aboriginal arts and artists, the Commission recommended (236).

Inter-governmental **fiscal relations** and responsibilities are an important area of public policy. The Commission recommended that governments and national Aboriginal organizations negotiate a **Canada-wide framework** to guide the fiscal relationship among the three orders of government (165) and that this be on the agenda of a First Ministers' and national Aboriginal leaders' "summit" to be held within six months of the release of the Commission's Final Report (252).

Reallocation of Resources

By Canadian standards, any body which recommends an additional one to two billion dollars of funding per year for over twenty years, as RCAP did (58), is recommending a massive reallocation of resources. This is not only a thorny political issue, especially in an "era of fiscal austerity", but is also the crucial factor around which the success or failure of the Commission's vision revolves. The political appeal made by the Commission and the responses of Cabinet members can be analyzed fruitfully using the claims-making model through which Ponting's and Symons' chapter analyzed the interaction between Hydro-Québec and the James Bay Cree. That is, recommendations for such large new expenditures must be supported with skillfully crafted legitimating arguments,[12] but a deficit-constrained government can be expected to resist with all the diplomacy and rhetorical skill that its "spin doctors" can muster. Such an analysis would be highly worthwhile. However, because limitations of space preclude such an analysis here, we turn now to the Commission's identification of the uses to which funding and other resources should be allocated.

The discussion below does not identify specific amounts to be spent on specific purposes. In part this is done to simplify the presentation, but the lack of numbers also reflects the fact that amounts allocated vary by year of the program and the fact that usually the Commission does not provide a breakdown as between Indian, Inuit, and Métis. Readers interested in financial specificity are referred to Volume 5 (especially Chapter 3) of the Commission's Final Report.

The Commission identified four "dimensions of social change". They are: healing, improving economic opportunity and living conditions, human resources development, and institutional development. The last is so much a part of the first three that the Commission includes its funding allocation with them.

(i) Healing   To foster a climate conducive to healing, the Commission proposes a number of measures pertaining to social services, justice, education, culture, and health care.

One measure of obvious relevance here is a recommendation calling for federal and provincial funding of both the capital and operating costs of a network of **healing lodges** (212). Another is the recommendation (CL, 93) for Aboriginal and other governments to assess gaps in the **suicide prevention** services recommended by the Commission and to allocate additional resources accordingly to reach the goals of the ten-year campaign[13] recommended by the Commission.

In various Aboriginal cultures, **justice** is almost synonymous with healing.[14] In *Bridging the Cultural Divide ("BCD")*, two recommendations deal with the reallocation of resources. One calls for governments to provide long-term funding for criminal justice initiatives undertaken by Aboriginal nations or communities (BCD, 315). The other calls for governments to conduct a complete review and audit of the current justice system so as to provide detailed figures on the cost of administering justice as it affects Aboriginal people at all stages — namely, crime prevention, policing, courts, probation, corrections, parole, and reintegration into society (BCD, 315).

Other measures pertaining to healing are discussed below under the rubric "human resources development".

(ii) Improving Economic Opportunity and Living Conditions   One of the paramount recommendations in the entire tome is that governments provide Aboriginal nations with **lands** that are sufficient in size and quality to foster Aboriginal economic self-reliance and cultural and political autonomy (175). Canada cannot escape the lands issue; it must be addressed. Related to this is the recommendation that the federal government establish a **land acquisition fund** to enable all Aboriginal peoples to purchase land on the open market under the "willing buyer, willing seller" principle (185). With regard to the negotiation of a land base for each Aboriginal nation, the Commission recommends a three-fold categorization of lands wherein each category of lands has attached to it a different set of rights with respect to governance and resource exploitation (177). Since the James Bay and Northern Québec Agreement of 1975, this has become a common approach to settling land issues.

The Commission advocates federal funding for Aboriginal negotiating parties on land issues (182) and a variety of interim measures to ensure that benefits flow to Aboriginal peoples from economic development undertaken before land negotiations are finalized (186–193). Examples of the latter are the recommendation that the federal government renegotiate existing agreements with the provinces to ensure that First Nations obtain the full beneficial interest in minerals, oil, and natural gas located on-reserve (188) and the recommendation that provincial and territorial governments increase their allocation of tourist outfitters' licences to Aboriginal people (191). While the latter is not a matter of government funding, *per se*, it does definitely put greater resources into the hands of Aboriginal individuals.

The paucity and insecurity of federal economic development funding has long been the curse of Aboriginal governments. The Commission recognized that with its recommendation that governments enter into *long-term* economic development agreements with Aboriginal nations so as to provide **multi-year funding in support of economic development**. Similarly, the Commission recommended that the federal government restore the funding of First Nation agricultural organizations (199) and that federal and provincial governments fund a **major ten-year initiative for Aboriginal employment development and training**. Addressing Boldt's (1993) criticism of **land tenure** regimes on-reserve, the Commission also recommended that band councils change patterns of land tenure and land use so that efficient, viable reserve farms or ranches can be established (199).

On the First Nation **housing** front, an important recommendation was that the federal government complement the resources supplied by First Nation people in a two-to-one ratio or in whatever ratio is necessary to ensure that First Nation housing is fully adequate in quantity and quality within ten years (217). Among the means suggested was the offering of financial incentives for private home ownership. Recommendations were also made with regard to inter-governmental co-operation to ensure that off-reserve Aboriginal housing needs are adequately met within ten years (218).

Other measures that the Commission recommended the federal government take included: government trade promotion agencies actively seeking out markets for Aboriginal goods and services abroad (199); re-directing social assistance payments to support employment and social development (205); and funding of Aboriginal child care (204).

(iii) Human Resources Development Cognizant of the importance of reaching Aboriginal people early to shape positive life experiences for them, the Commission recommended that governments support an integrated **early childhood education** funding strategy that extends early childhood education services to *all* Aboriginal children regardless of residence [and] encourages programs that foster the physical, social, intellectual and spiritual development of children, reducing distinctions between child care, prevention and education. ..." (220).

Other aspects of **education** also received considerable attention from the Commission. For instance, it recommended that Aboriginal authorities and other governments fund programs for Aboriginal youth who left secondary school before graduation, so as to enable them to resume their studies with appropriate curriculum, scheduling, and academic and social support (223). The Commission also recommended that the federal government not only continue to support the costs of post-secondary education for First Nation and Inuit students, but also make more money available to offset increased costs and the anticipated higher level of demand (225). Another recommendation called for governments to expand financial support for teacher education programs "delivered directly in communities" (224) and support to post-secondary institutions for Aboriginal teacher education programs that meet four criteria identified by the Commission (223). Finally, a reallocation of resources was implied in the recommendation that Elders be treated as professionals and compensated for their education contribution at a rate that shows respect for their expertise, unique knowledge, and skills (228).

The Commission recommended that the federal government provide funds to the national Aboriginal organizations (including women's organizations) to enable them to *prepare* a **comprehensive human resources development strategy in health and social services** according to a set of objectives identified by the Commission (212–213). A related recommendation was that governments provide the necessary funding to *implement* a co-ordinated and comprehensive human resources development strategy. While this strategy is, apparently, not confined to health and social services, part of it would involve **training ten thousand Aboriginal professionals** of various kinds (e.g., health administrators and psychologists) over a ten-year period in health and social services (213).

Separate from the last recommendation were others which called upon governments to establish funding programs, at both the individual and institutional levels, in support of **education for self-government** (230). Yet another urged professional associations and self-governing bodies in the professions to actively support the professional training of Aboriginal people in a variety of ways (e.g., mentoring, distance education, scholarships) identified by the Commission (231).

The Commission's mandate made explicit reference to Aboriginal **women.** Hence, one of the recommendations was for the federal government to provide funding to Aboriginal women's organizations, including urban-based organizations, so as to enable them to participate fully in all aspects of nation-building and the development of self-government processes and citizenship criteria (237).

Concerning the **urban** component of the Commission's mandate, Commissioners recommended that land dedicated to Aboriginal cultural and spiritual needs be set aside in urban areas (247). Another recommendation called for the federal government to be responsible for the costs of developing and operating Aboriginal self-government initiatives off a land base (247) and for the federal government to pay for social programs for off-reserve status Indians to the extent that on-reserve benefits under those programs exceed the benefits provided to other residents by the province (247–248). Significantly, the Commission did not call for the federal government to pay the full cost of social programs to off-reserve status Indians, but it did call for services to Aboriginal people in urban areas to be delivered without regard to legal or treaty status (249). It also urged that, where numbers warrant and until community-of-interest governments are established, provincial governments provide funding to off-reserve "voluntary agencies endorsed by substantial numbers of Aboriginal people resident in the areas" so that those agencies can provide child welfare services (comparable to those provided to the general population) where authorized under provincial or territorial law (207).

Other proposals related to the urban situation include the recommendation that the cost of affirmative action programs and services to address the economic and social disadvantage of urban Aboriginal people be shared by the federal and provincial governments on a basis that reflects provincial fiscal capacity (248) and the recommendation that the federal, provincial, and municipal governments fund services and programs for urban Aboriginal youth (249).

Other recommendations called for governments to enter into long-term core funding agreements with Aboriginal media organizations (236), to support Aboriginal literary, visual, and performing arts in certain specified ways (235), and to provide (federal government only) funding for a national organization to speak on behalf of Aboriginal people with disabilities (249).

Strategies

Cast in a rational planning mould, the Royal Commission found it appropriate at various points to recommend that a comprehensive strategy be developed to pursue its policy objectives. That is, it was not deemed sufficient that resources be reallocated to a problem. Instead, a plan for identifying, mobilizing, and co-ordinating the deployment of those resources was deemed necessary. That such a strategy be recommended is sometimes an indication that one or more of the magnitude, complexity (including number of governments and government departments), variability (e.g., from one locale to another), and scope of the problem are formidable — perhaps too formidable even for the Commission and its considerable resources. That being the case, it is worthwhile to flag here the problems for which the Commission recommended the development of a national, or even local, strategy.

Suicide is one such area. The recommended strategy in this crucial area is a community-based one comprising three elements: "local prevention and crisis intervention services; community development to address the most pressing local causes of suicidal hopelessness and helplessness; and the opportunity to achieve autonomy and self-determination as Aboriginal peoples" (*CL*, 90). The Commission called for a ten-year, high-priority, Canada-wide campaign, with progress to be evaluated in the fourth, seventh, and tenth years. The primary goals of the campaign would include ensuring that all Aboriginal communities have in place both a suicide crisis response capacity and the capacity to initiate a community development plan to address the underlying causes of suicide and self injury (*CL*, 90). These would involve each Aboriginal community having at least one resource person trained in suicide prevention, intervention, and postvention (grief support) techniques by 1997 and each Aboriginal community having at least one resource person trained in community development planning and methods by 1998 (*CL*, 91). In an attempt to address the clustering of suicides, the Commission also called upon governments to facilitate the creation of local and regional resource teams and support networks for immediate mobilization in case of crisis so as to provide back-up for any community that experiences an outbreak of suicide and self-injury (*CL*, 91). The Commission's proposed National Forum on the Prevention of Suicide Among Aboriginal People would serve as a facilitator for the exchange of information on suicide prevention and a "watch-dog" to ensure fulfilment of commitments to the national campaign. Significantly, the Commission also made some pointed recommendations which buttress remarks in Crowfoot's chapter in this volume. The reader will recall that Crowfoot criticized both the abuse of power by First Nation local leaders and the reticence of First Nation individuals and communities to take responsibility for their own lives. The Commission urged Aboriginal leaders to set a clear priority on stopping suicide and self-destructive behaviour by, among other things, working to change abuses of power and evasion of responsibility by Aboriginal people and by working to change other factors which contribute to suicidal feelings (*CL*, 92). Aboriginal communities were also urged to take responsibility for designing community plans, delivering and evaluating programs, sharing information, and mobilizing voluntary and public resources.

The **empowerment of Aboriginal youth** is another vital area in which the Commission recommended the development of a strategy (222–223). Of course, this is not unrelated to suicide prevention. The Commission called for an Aboriginal youth empowerment strategy to include: cultural education; acknowledgement of spiritual, ethical, and intuitive dimensions of learning; education to support critical analysis of Aboriginal experience; learning as a means of healing from the effects of trauma, abuse, and racism; academic skills development; sports and outdoor education; leadership development; and youth exchanges between Aboriginal nations, across Canada and internationally.

Other areas in which the formulation of a strategy was explicitly recommended, sometimes in considerable detail, are shown in Table 1. They include various aspects of education (222–224, 233) and early childhood education (220), human resources development in health and social services (212–213), and data collection and analysis for development (229). Various other recommendations were made for large-scale joint action to develop programmes, but none of them were called "strategies" *per se*. An example is that which called upon faculties of agriculture, forestry, and business administration in Canadian universities to collaborate with the proposed Aboriginal Peoples International University to develop a northern research program focused on the creation of employment and business opportunities through the use of the renewable resources sector, the export of traditional foods, and sustainable development (246).

New Inclusiveness: Standing and Representation

In colonial regimes, the colonized people seldom have meaningful representation in the decision-making that affects their lives. Weaver (1985) has docu-

TABLE 1 Areas Recommended for Development of Comprehensive Strategy

Strategy (and Page #)	Level	Participants
Comprehensive Campaign to Prevent Aboriginal Suicide and Self-Injury (CL, 90–94)	National, but community-driven and community-designed	Aboriginal and other governments, and Aboriginal communities
Aboriginal Youth Empowerment (222)	Aboriginally controlled schools	School staff and youth
Comprehensive Aboriginal Education (222)	School boards serving Aboriginal students	School boards, Aboriginal parents, Elders, and educators
Early Childhood Education Funding (220)	National	Federal, provincial, and territorial governments
Aboriginal Secondary School Teacher Training (223–224)	National	Governments, Aboriginal education authorities, post-secondary institutions
Access to Aboriginal Cultural Education (233)	National and local	Governments, Aboriginal Elders, artists, educators, and youth
Comprehensive Human Resources Development (212–213)	National	National Aboriginal organizations (including national Aboriginal women's organizations)
Data Collection and Analysis for Development (229)	Nations and communities	First Nation, Inuit, and Métis working group

Sources: RCAP (1995; 1996e). Page numbers shown in left column.

mented a tendency on the part of the federal government of both Canada and Australia to confer and withdraw legitimacy upon/from Aboriginal organizations as it suits the needs of the government, such that decision-making will circumvent those organizations when the government so desires.

Recognizing such tendencies, the Commissioners made several recommendations designed to confer standing upon Aboriginal people and institutionalize Aboriginal representation on decision-making bodies in government and elsewhere. One example, already noted above, is the recommendation for representatives of Aboriginal peoples to be included in the agenda setting for **future constitutional conferences** convened by the federal government (255). Another is the recommendation that the majority of commissioners appointed to a proposed **public inquiry into residential schools** and their aftermath be Aboriginal people (143). That inquiry would have the power to recommend redress[15] in the form of a public apology, compensation of communities, and funding for the treatment of affected individuals and their families. **Elders** were also recommended for inclusion in various forums, such as in the formation and implementation of policies pertaining to sacred sites, on the boards which manage those sites (238), and in the range of nation-building and institutional development activities that the Commission recommended (237–238). Other recommendations (237, 250) called for the full and fair participation of Aboriginal **women** (including urban-based groups) in a wide range of decision-making roles, such as the governing bodies of all Aboriginal health and healing institutions, in order to "enable them to participate fully in all aspects of nation building, including developing criteria for citizenship and related appeal processes". On the **urban** front, the Commission recommended that positions be designated for Aboriginal representatives on local boards and commissions responsible for services and on the boards of institutions in which Aboriginal people have a significant interest (250). Furthermore, with respect to Aboriginal polities themselves, the Commission responded to the demographic fact of a large off-reserve Aboriginal population by recommending that Aboriginal nations institute mechanisms to ensure that their urban citizens are represented in the political structures and decision-making processes of the nations (251).

In the realm of **education and the arts**, the Commission recommended that Aboriginal persons be appointed to the boards of governors of post-secondary institutions (226) and that legislation be passed to guarantee Aboriginal representation on school boards where population numbers warrant (221). Organizations that provide support for the visual and performing arts should ensure that Aboriginal people and perspectives are adequately represented on decision-making bodies, juries, advisory committees, and staff, the Commission recommended (236).

Finally, various recommendations called for Aboriginal representation in **economic development** in the natural resources sector. Some recommendations pertaining to traditional Aboriginal territories called for interim measures such as co-jurisdiction or co-management, with "relative parity of membership between Aboriginal nations and government representatives", until treaty negotiations are concluded (193). The Commission also recommended such measures as Aboriginal participation (including bearing part of the costs) in provincial forest management (187) and intervenor funding to enable Aboriginal communities to participate in the consultation process on the Aboriginal land use plans (e.g., re trap lines and sacred sites) which the Commission recommended companies in the oil, gas, and minerals sector be required to develop when they are operating on Crown lands. The proposed amendment of the *Canada Water Act* to provide for guaranteed Aboriginal representation on inter-jurisdictional water management boards (193) was noted earlier in this chapter. Similar to it is the recommendation that the federal government ensure Aboriginal representation on the Canadian commission created under the 1985 Pacific Salmon Treaty with the United States (190).

Other Recommendations

A truism in the public policy literature is that **process** is sometimes as important as policy. For instance, as noted in Chapter Six, the formal processes of the criminal and civil courtroom are foreign and alienating to many Aboriginal people. Process is also important if participants are to take "ownership" of the final decision or the policy product that issues from some government body. The Royal Commission took such considerations into account in its recommendations. For instance, the Commission recommended that the pivotally important Aboriginal Lands and Treaties Tribunal emphasize informal procedures and be directed by law "to adopt a broad and progressive interpretation of the treaties, not limiting itself to technical rules of evidence, and to take into account ...

Aboriginal customary and property law...." (183). In addition, the Commission recommended that the Tribunal's jurisdiction include both monitoring the good faith of the bargaining process as claims and treaties are being negotiated, and in the event of a breach of the duty to bargain in good faith, making binding orders on those in breach and imposing interim relief agreements (182). Such powers are far from tokenism.

Process can be highly significant outside judicial, quasi-judicial, and policy settings. **Exchange** is an example of an important process and the Commission recommended several types of exchange between Aboriginal people and other Canadians. For instance, one recommendation called for educational institutions to facilitate opportunities for Elders to share traditional knowledge with Aboriginal and non-Aboriginal students and scholars in university settings (228). A related recommendation called for boards of education and education ministries to take action to make traditional Aboriginal knowledge accessible in the education of all students, whether Aboriginal or non-Aboriginal (228). Two final examples of exchange are the recommendations for the twinning of Aboriginal governments with Canadian governments of similar size and scope of operations (169) and for non-Aboriginal corporations and governments to establish executive interchange opportunities in partnership with Aboriginal governments (230).

Feedback is a vital process in any social system. The recommended creation of a task force to promote understanding and wide public discussion of RCAP's findings and recommendations during at least the first year after release of its Final Report is one such feedback mechanism (255). More important as feedback, though, are numerical data. In formulating its funding strategy and various other recommendations, the Commission made much use of Statistics Canada's projections and data collected in censuses and in the 1991 Statistics Canada post-censal survey of the Aboriginal population ("APS"). The Commission recommended both the continuation of such post-censal surveys of the Aboriginal population and other steps that Statistics Canada should take to improve its data collection and make it more useful to Aboriginal governments (170–171). If collected, such data would be an important means for measuring the nature and amount of change that implementation of the Commission's recommendations brings to the "grass-roots" Aboriginal population.

SUMMARY

Probably never before in Canadian history has a Royal Commission recommended so many profound and sweeping changes to the structure and functioning of Canadian society. Indeed, the Commission is proposing to take Canadians back to first principles (e.g., "terra nullius") and to rebuild a relationship from there. As the Commission itself notes (1), the scale and complexity of the task are daunting. To bring this chapter to a close, it is fitting to quote the Commissioners one last time:

> Implementation will be much easier ... if the essential themes of this report are kept in view. If one theme dominates our recommendations, it is that Aboriginal peoples must have room to exercise their autonomy and structure their own solutions. The pattern of debilitating and discriminatory paternalism that has characterized federal policy for the past 150 years must end.

Aboriginal people cannot flourish if they are treated as wards, incapable of controlling their own destiny. . . .

The rebalancing of political and economic power between Aboriginal nations and other Canadian governments represents the core of the hundreds of recommendations contained in this report. Unless accompanied by a rebalancing of power, no progress can be made on other fronts without perpetuating the status quo. The essential themes that underpin our recommendations and can assure the rebuilding of Aboriginal life in Canada are as follows:

First, Aboriginal nations have to be reconstituted. . . .

Second, a process must be established for the assumption of powers by Aboriginal nations. . . .

Third, there must be a fundamental reallocation of lands and resources. . . .

Fourth, Aboriginal people need education and crucial skills for governance and economic self-reliance. . . .

Finally, economic development must be addressed if the poverty and despondency of lives defined by unemployment and welfare are to change. (1–3)

NOTES

[1] Material from the Final Report of the Royal Commission on Aboriginal Peoples is reproduced with the permission of the Minister of Public Works and Government Services Canada, 1997. Source: Privy Council Office.

[2] The full text of the Royal Commission's mandate is contained in Order-in-Council PC 1991 – 1597 and is reproduced in RCAP (1996a: 699–702).

[3] See the "Strategies" section of this chapter for a brief elaboration on some of the specific measures that the Commission recommended as part of the national strategy to combat suicide and self-injury.

[4] Emphasis not in original.

[5] The eligibility noted in the text is essentially a legitimation of some claim to a right of access to the scarce commodity. Sometimes, the conferral of recognition will result in access being granted on a priority basis (e.g., the Aboriginal fishery on the Fraser River in British Columbia).

[6] The very creation of the Royal Commission is predicated upon the notion that policy-making in the field of Aboriginal affairs should be done by systematic, rational planning, rather than by ad hoc or incrementalist means. It does not necessarily follow, though, that policy will actually be developed according to such a rational plan.

[7] The term "terra nullius" refers to the ethnocentric notion of Europeans whereby land occupied by Aboriginal inhabitants was deemed in law to be unoccupied if the Aboriginal inhabitants were deemed to be "uncivilized" or were deemed to not be putting the lands to "civilized use" (RCAP, 1996a: 695).

[8] The "doctrine of discovery" was another ethnocentric British legal principle which held that the discovery of lands considered to be "terra nullius" gave the discovering nation sovereignty over, and all right and title to, that land (RCAP, 1996a: 695). See also Little Bear (1986).

[9] Examples of principles or criteria recommended to govern the amount and quality of additional lands are: the current and projected Aboriginal population, the economic and cultural needs of that population, and the nature and extent of third-party interests. An example of a principle concerning lands to be made available by governments is that no unnecessary or arbitrary limits be placed on lands for selection (e.g., waterbeds and resource-rich areas not be ruled out).

10 The Commission also recommended that Aboriginal governments reimburse provincial governments for services which provincial governments provide to citizens of Aboriginal nations. Thus, Aboriginal people would not pay provincial taxes (164).

11 Examples of contemporary mechanisms of accountability are ombudsmen, access-to- information legislation, electoral financial contribution limits, and program evaluation.

12 For instance, the Commissioners noted that by shortly after the fifteenth year, the expenditure of such amounts will yield a net benefit which will grow every year thereafter (57). The Commission also refers to the costs (an estimated $5.8 billion for all Aboriginal people) of **forgone production** (24, 47), the burden (estimated at $1.7 billion for all Aboriginal people in 1996) of **remedial costs** (33, 47), and the **escalating cost of the status quo**, which is projected to rise from the present $7.5 billion per year for all Aboriginal people to $11 billion by the year 2016 (47–49). Co-Chair Justice René Dussault stated: "It would be a travesty of justice if concerted and effective action to rectify the results of a history of dispossession were abandoned on grounds of fiscal restraint. A great debt is owing, and Canadians cannot, in good conscience, default on it" (Feschuk, 1996). In response, Indian Affairs Minister Ron Irwin appeared to minimize the gravity and urgency of the situation when he told a CBC *Morningside* radio audience that governments frequently hear the argument that more money must be spent now in order to save money later.

13 For more on the Canada-wide anti-suicide campaign, see "Strategies" on page 465. The Commission also recommends that governments fund the National Forum on the Prevention of Suicide Among Aboriginal People, "with a reasonable contribution (in cash or in kind) from Aboriginal governments" (*CL*, 94).

14 For elaboration, see Ross (1996).

15 Another proposal called for a legislative amendment to enable the Canadian Human Rights Commission to conduct an inquiry into the relocation of Aboriginal communities and recommend (and pursue before the courts) remedies to redress the negative effects of relocations. However, there was no explicit provision in the recommendation for Aboriginal representation on the inquiry panel (145–146).

REFERENCES

Boldt, Menno
1993   *Surviving as Indians*. Toronto: University of Toronto Press.

Coolican, Murray
1985   *Living Treaties, Lasting Agreements: Report of the Task Force to Review Comprehensive Claims Policy*. Ottawa: Department of Indian Affairs and Northern Development.

Feschuk, Scott
1996   "Cost of Reforms $30-billion, Report on Aboriginals Says", *Globe and Mail*, November 22: A9.

Little Bear, Leroy
1986   "Aboriginal Rights and the Canadian `Grundnorm'", pp. 243–259 in J. Rick Ponting (ed.), *Arduous Journey: Canadian Indians and Decolonization*. Toronto: McClelland & Stewart / Oxford.

RCAP (Royal Commission on Aboriginal Peoples)
1995   *Choosing Life: Special Report on Suicide Among Aboriginal People*. Ottawa: Minister of Supply and Services Canada.

1996a   *Final Report of The Royal Commission on Aboriginal Peoples; Vol. 1: Looking Forward, Looking Back.* Ottawa: Minister of Supply and Services Canada.

1996b   *Final Report of The Royal Commission on Aboriginal Peoples; Vol. 2: Restructuring the Relationship.* Ottawa: Minister of Supply and Services Canada.

1996c   *Final Report of The Royal Commission on Aboriginal Peoples; Vol. 3: Gathering Strength.* Ottawa: Minister of Supply and Services Canada.

1996d   *Final Report of The Royal Commission on Aboriginal Peoples; Vol. 4: Perspectives and Realities.* Ottawa: Minister of Supply and Services Canada.

1996e   *Final Report of The Royal Commission on Aboriginal Peoples; Vol. 5: Renewal: A Twenty-Year Commitment.* Ottawa: Minister of Supply and Services Canada.

1996f   *Bridging the Cultural Divide: A Report on Aboriginal People and Criminal Justice in Canada.* Ottawa: Minister of Supply and Services Canada.

Ross, Rupert

1996   *Returning to the Teachings: Exploring Aboriginal Justice.* Toronto: Penguin Books.

Weaver, Sally

1985   "Political Representivity and Indigenous Minorities in Canada and Australia", pp. 113–150 in Noel Dyck (ed.), *Indigenous Peoples and the Nation State: Fourth World Politics in Canada, Australia, and Norway.* St. John's, Nfld.: Institute of Social and Economic Research, Memorial University.

Appendices

TREATY #7
WITH THE BLACKFOOT, 1877

ARTICLES of a TREATY made and concluded this twenty-second day of September, in the year of our Lord one thousand eight hundred and seventy-seven, BETWEEN Her Most Gracious Majesty the Queen of Great Britain and Ireland, by her Commissioners, the Honorable David Laird, Lieutenant-Governor and Indian Superintendent of the North-West Territories, and James Farquharson McLeod, C.M.G., Commissioner of the North-West Mounted Police, of the one part, AND the Blackfeet, Blood, Peigan, Sarcee, Stony, and other Indians, inhabitants of the territory north of the United States boundary line, east of the central range of the Rocky Mountains, and south and west of Treaties Numbers Six and Four, by their head Chiefs and minor Chiefs or Councillors, chosen as hereinafter mentioned, of the other part:

WHEREAS the Indians inhabiting the said territory, have pursuant to an appointment made by the said Commissioners, been convened at a meeting at the "Blackfoot crossing" of the Bow River, to deliberate upon certain matters of interest to Her Most Gracious Majesty, of the one part, and the said Indians of the other;

AND WHEREAS the said Indians have been informed by her Majesty's Commissioners that it is the desire of Her Majesty to open up for settlement, and such other purposes as to Her Majesty may seem meet, a tract of country, bounded and described as hereinafter mentioned, and to obtain the consent thereto of her Indian subjects inhabiting the said tract, and to make a treaty, and arrange with them, so that there may be peace and good will between them and Her Majesty, and between them and Her Majesty's other subjects; and that her Indian people may know and feel assured of what allowance they are to count upon and receive from Her Majesty's bounty and benevolence ;

AND WHEREAS the Indians of the said tract, duly convened in council, and being requested by her Majesty's Commissioners to present their head Chiefs and minor Chiefs, or Councillors, who shall be authorized, on their behalf, to conduct such negotiations and sign any treaty to be founded thereon, and to become responsible to Her Majesty for the faithful performance by their respective bands of such obligations as should be assumed by them, the said Blackfeet, Blood, Peigan and Sarcee Indians have therefore acknowledged for that purpose, the several head and minor Chiefs, and the said Stony Indians, the Chiefs and Councillors who have subscribed hereto, that thereupon in open council the said Commissioners received and acknowledged the head and minor Chiefs and the Chiefs and Councillors presented for the purpose aforesaid;

AND WHEREAS the said Commissioners have proceeded to negotiate a treaty with the said Indians; and the same has been finally agreed upon and concluded as follows, that is to say:

the Blackfeet, Blood, Peigan, Sarcee Stoney and other Indians inhabiting the district hereinafter more fully described and defined, do hereby cede, release, surrender, and yield up to the Government of Canada for Her Majesty the Queen and her successors forever, all their rights, titles and privileges whatsoever to the lands included within the following limits, that is to say:

Commencing at a point on the international boundary due south of the western extremity of the Cypress Hills; thence west along the said boundary to the central range of the Rocky Mountains, or to the boundary of the Province of British Columbia; thence north-westerly along the said boundary to a point due west of the source of the main branch of the Red Deer River; thence south-westerly and southerly following on the boundaries of the tracts ceded by the Treaties Numbered Six and Four to the place of commencement; and also all their rights, titles and privileges whatsoever, to all other lands wherever situated in the North-West Territories, or in any other portion of the Dominion of Canada:

To have and to hold the same to Her Majesty the Queen and her successors forever:

And Her Majesty the Queen hereby agrees with her said Indians, that they shall have right to pursue their vocations of hunting throughout the tract surrendered as heretofore described, subject to such regulations as may, from time to time, be made by the Government of the country, acting under the authority of Her Majesty; and saving and excepting such tracts as may be required or taken up from time to time for settlement, mining, trading or other purposes by her Government of Canada, or by any of her Majesty's subjects duly authorized therefor by the said Government.

It is also agreed between Her Majesty and her said Indians that reserves shall be assigned them of sufficient area to allow one square mile for each family of five persons, or in that proportion for larger and smaller families, and that said reserves shall be located as follows, that is to say :

First-The reserves of the Blackfeet, Blood and Sarcee bands of Indians, shall consist of a belt of land on the north side of the Bow and South Saskatchewan Rivers, of an average width of four miles along said rivers, down stream, commencing at a point on the Bow River twenty miles north-westerly of the "Blackfoot crossing" thereof, and extending to the Red Deer River at its junction with the South Saskatchewan ; also for the term of ten years, and no longer, from the date of the concluding of this treaty, when it shall cease to be a portion of said Indian reserves, as fully to all intents and purposes as if it had not at any time been included therein, and without any compensation to individual Indians for improvements, of a similar belt of land on the south side of the Bow and Saskatchewan Rivers of an average width of one mile along said rivers, down stream; commencing at the aforesaid point on the Bow River, and extending to a point one mile west of the coal seam on said river, about five miles below the said "Blackfoot crossing;" beginning again one mile east of the said coal seam and extending to the mouth of Maple Creek at its junction with the South Saskatchewan ; and beginning again at the junction of the Bow River with the latter river, and extending on both sides of the South Saskatchewan in an average width on each side thereof of one mile, along said river against the stream, to the junction of the Little Bow River with the latter river, reserving to Her Majesty, as may now or hereafter be required by her for the use of her Indian and other subjects, from all the reserves herein before described, the right to navigate the above mentioned rivers, to land and receive fuel and cargoes on the shores and banks thereof, to build bridges and establish ferries thereon, to use the fords thereof and all the trails leading thereto, and to open such other roads through the said reserves as may appear to Her Majesty's Government of Canada, necessary for the ordinary travel of her Indian and other subjects, due compensation being paid to individual Indians for improvements, when the same may be in any manner encroached upon by such roads.

Secondly-That the reserve of the Peigan band of Indians shall be on the Old Man's River, near the foot of the Porcupine Hills, at a place called "Crow's Creek."

And thirdly-The reserve of the Stony band of Indians shall be in the vicinity of Morleyville.

In view of the satisfaction of Her Majesty with the recent general good conduct of her said Indians, and in extinguishment of all their past claims, she hereby, through her Commissioners, agrees to make them a present payment of twelve dollars each in cash to each man, woman, and child of the families here represented.

Her Majesty also agreed that next year, and annually afterwards forever, she will cause to be paid to the said Indians, in cash, at suitable places and dates, of which the said Indians shall be duly notified, to each Chief, twenty-five dollars, each minor Chief or Councillor (not exceeding fifteen minor Chiefs to the Blackfeet and Blood Indians, and four to the Peigan and Sarcee bands, and five Councillors to the Stony Indian Bands) fifteen dollars, and to every other Indian of whatever age, five dollars; the same, unless there be some exceptional reason, to be paid to the heads of families for those belonging thereto.

Further, Her Majesty agrees that the sum of two thousand dollars shall hereafter every year be expended in the purchase of ammunition for distribution among the said Indians; provided that if at any future time ammunition became comparatively unnecessary for said Indians, her Government, with consent of said Indians, or any of the bands thereof, may expend the proportion due to such band otherwise for their benefit.

Further, Her Majesty agrees that each head Chief and minor Chief, and each Chief and Councillor duly recognized as such, shall, once in every three years, during the term of their office, receive a suitable suit of clothing, and each head Chief and Stony Chief, in recognition of the closing of the treaty, a suitable medal and flag, and next year, or as soon as convenient, each head Chief, and minor Chief, and Stony Chief shall receive a Winchester rifle.

Further, Her Majesty agrees to pay the salary of such teachers to instruct the children of said Indians as to her Government of Canada may seem advisable, when said Indians are settled on their reserves and shall desire teachers.

Further, Her Majesty agrees to supply each head and minor Chief, and each Stony Chief, for the use of their bands, ten axes, five handsaws, five augers, one grindstone, and the necessary files and whetstones.

And further, Her Majesty agrees that the said Indians shall be supplied as soon as convenient, after any band shall make due application therefor, with the following cattle for raising stock, that is to say: for every family of five persons, and under, two cows; for every family of more than five persons, and less than ten persons, three cows; for every family of over ten persons, four cows; and every head and minor Chief, and every Stony Chief, for the use of their bands, one bull; but if any band desire to cultivate the soil as well as raise stock, each family of such band shall receive one cow less than the above mentioned number, and in lieu thereof, when settled on their reserves and prepared to break up the soil, two hoes, one spade, one scythe, and two hay forks, and for every three families, one plough and one harrow, and for each band, enough potatoes, barley, oats, and wheat (if such seeds be suited for the locality of their reserves) to plant the land actually broken up. All the aforesaid articles to be given, once for all, for the encouragement of the practice of agriculture among the Indians.

And the undersigned Blackfeet, Blood, Peigan and Sarcee head Chiefs and minor Chiefs, and Stony Chiefs and Councillors, on their own behalf and on behalf of all other Indians inhabiting the tract within ceded do hereby solemnly promise and engage to strictly observe this treaty, and also to conduct and behave themselves as good and loyal subjects of Her Majesty the Queen. They promise and engage that they will, in all respects, obey and abide by the law, that they will maintain peace and good order between each other and between themselves and other tribes of Indians, and between themselves and others of Her Majesty's subjects, whether Indians, Half breeds or whites, now inhabiting, or hereafter to inhabit, any part of the said ceded tract; and that they will not molest the person or property of any inhabitant of such ceded tract, or the property of Her Majesty the Queen, or interfere with or trouble any person, passing or travelling through the said tract or any part thereof, and that they will assist the officers of Her Majesty in bringing to justice and punishment any Indian offending against the stipulations of this treaty, or infringing the laws in force in the country so ceded.

In witness whereof Her Majesty's said Commissioners, and the said Indian head and minor Chiefs, and Stony Chiefs and Councillors, have hereunto subscribed and set their hands, at the "Blackfoot crossing" of the Bow River, the day and year herein first above written.

(Signed) DAVID LAIRD,
Gov. of N.W.T., and Special Indian Commissioner.

SELECTED PROVISIONS OF THE CONSTITUTION ACT, 1982

PART I:
CANADIAN CHARTER OF RIGHTS AND FREEDOMS

Equality Rights

15. (1) Every individual is equal before the and under the law and has the right to the equal protection and equal benefit of the law without discrimination and, in particular, without discrimination based on race, national or ethnic origin, colour, religion, sex, age, or mental or physical disability.

   (2) Subsection (1) does not preclude any law, program or activity that has as its object the amelioration of conditions of disadvantaged individuals or groups including those that are disadvantaged because or race, national or ethnic origin, colour, religion, sex, age, or mental or physical disability.

General

25. The guarantee in this Charter of certain rights and freedoms shall not be construed so as to abrogate or derogate from any aboriginal, treaty or other rights or freedoms that pertain to the aboriginal peoples of Canada including

   (a) any rights or freedoms that have been recognized by the *Royal Proclamation* of October 7, 1763; and

   (b) any rights or freedoms that may be acquired by the aboriginal peoples of Canada by way of land claims settlement.(15)

27. This Charter shall be interpreted in a manner consistent with the preservation and enhancement of the multicultural heritage of Canadians.

28. Notwithstanding anything in this Charter, the rights and freedoms referred to in it are guaranteed equally to male and female persons.

Application of Charter

33. (1) Parliament or the legislature of a province may expressly declare in an Act of Parliament or of the legislature, as the case may be, that the Act or a provision thereof shall operate notwithstanding a provision included in section 2 or section 7 to 15 of this Charter.

(2) An Act or a provision of an Act in respect of which a declaration made under this section is in effect shall have such operation as it would have but for the provision of this Charter referred to in the declaration.

(3) A declaration made under subsection (1) shall cease to have effect five years after it comes into force or on such earlier date as may be specified in the declaration.

(4) Parliament or the legislature of a province may re-enact a declaration made under subsection (1).

(5) Subsection (3) applies in respect of re-enactment made under subsection (4).

PART II:
RIGHTS OF THE ABORIGINAL PEOPLES OF CANADA

35. (1) The existing aboriginal and treaty rights of the aboriginal peoples of Canada are hereby recognized and affirmed.

(2) In this *Act*, "aboriginal peoples of Canada" includes the Indian, Inuit, and Métis peoples of Canada.

(3) For greater certainty, in subsection (1) "treaty rights" includes rights that now exist by way of land claims agreements or may be so acquired.

(4) Notwithstanding any other provision of this *Act*, the aboriginal and treaty rights referred to in subsection (1) are guaranteed equally to male and female persons.(17)

35.1 The government of Canada and the provincial governments are committed to the principle that, before any amendment is made to Class 24 of section 91 of the *"Constitution Act, 1867"*, to section 25 of this *Act* or to this Part,

(a) a constitutional conference that includes in its agenda an item relating to the proposed amendment, composed of the Prime Minister of Canada and the first ministers of the provinces, will be convened by the Prime Minister of Canada; and

(b) the Prime Minister of Canada will invite representatives of the aboriginal peoples of Canada to participate in the discussions on that item.(18)

PART IV.1:
CONSTITUTIONAL CONFERENCES

37.1 (1) In addition to the conference convened in March 1983, at least two constitutional conferences composed of the Prime Minister of Canada and the first ministers of the provinces shall be convened by the Prime Minister of Canada, the first within three years after April 17, 1982 and the second within five years after that date.

(2) Each conference convened under subsection (1) shall have included in its agenda matters that directly affect the aboriginal peoples of Canada, and the

Prime Minister of Canada shall invite representatives of those peoples to participate in the discussions on those matters.

(3) The Prime Minister of Canada shall invite elected representatives of the governments of the Yukon Territory and the Northwest Territories to participate in the discussions on any item on the agenda of a conference convened under subsection (1) that, in the opinion of the Prime Minister, directly affects the Yukon Territory and the Northwest Territories.

(4) Nothing in this section shall be construed as to derogate from subsection 35(1).(21)

PART VII:
GENERAL

52. (1) The *Constitution of Canada* is the supreme law of Canada, and any law that is inconsistent with the provisions of the *Constitution* is, to the extent of the inconsistency, of no force or effect.

61. A reference to the *"Constitution Acts, 1867 to 1982"* shall be deemed be to include a reference to the *"Constitution Amendment Proclamation, 1983"*.

APPENDIX C

THE INDIAN ACT: SELECTED PROVISIONS AND COMMENTARY

Examples of the Powers of the Federal Cabinet*

* NOTE: The powers listed below can be wielded by an Order-in-Council, which requires the signature of only three Cabinet Members.

Sec.

18. 1 Determine whether any purpose for which lands in a reserve are used or are to be used is for the use and benefit of the band.

39.1 Refuse to approve surrender of reserve lands.

60.1 Grant a band "the right to exercise such control and management over lands in the reserve occupied by that band as the Government in Council considers desirable."

60.2 – or withdraw that right

MONEY

61.1 Determine what is/is not an expenditure of Indian moneys "for the use and benefit of the band."

69.1 Determine whether a band is fit to manage/control its revenue moneys.
      – can also revoke such an order

REGULATIONS

73.1 May make regulations for on-reserve:
      – fish and wildlife conservation
      – weed control
      – pest and disease control
      – dog control
      – pool rooms, dance halls and places of amusement
      – concerning bands borrowing money for housing or other band projects or for housing loans
      – etc.

ELECTIONS

76.1 May make orders and regulations regarding band elections (including definition of residency for purposes of determining voter eligibility)

79.a   May set aside the election of a Chief or Councillor if Minister is satisfied that corruption or violation of the *Act* occurred.

BAND MEETINGS

80   May make regulations (e.g., notice of meeting; quorum).

BY-LAWS

83.5   May make regulations regarding the exercise of by-law making powers of bands (under Section 83).

ADMINISTRATION OF JUSTICE

107   Appoint justices of the peace to deal with *Indian Act* Offences and certain *Criminal Code* offences where the crime is committed by an Indian or related to the person or property of an Indian (i.e. is on-reserve)

Examples of the Powers of the Minister (or His Designate)

DELEGATION

3(2)   Delegation of his powers to the Deputy Minister or other bureaucrats.

EXEMPTION

4(2)   Exempt any Indians from most provisions of the *Act* (except regarding
32.2   membership and lands) e.g., exemption from requirement, on prairies, of Ministerial approval for selling agriculture products to persons not band members.

CREATION OF NEW BANDS AND DIVISION OF ASSETS

17.1   Create new bands upon request (e.g. Woodland Cree) or amalgamate old bands.

17.2   Divide up reserves and band assets when a band splits.

18.2   Determining compensation to Indian individuals when band
23   expropriates land or removes an Indian from land after Indian has made
25.2   improvements to that land or been expelled from the reserve.

PRESCRIBE CONDITIONS

20.4   – e.g., as to use of land before approving allotment of a parcel of land to an Indian individual by Chief and Council

RESIDENCY ON-RESERVE

28.2   Authorize (even against Council's wishes) a person to reside on a reserve for up to one year.

MANAGEMENT OF THE ASSETS OF INDIAN BANDS AND INDIVIDUALS

34.1   Issue orders to a band to repair roads, bridges, or fences.

39.2   Call another land surrender vote if a land surrender is approved but a majority of eligible voters did not vote

39.4   – Order a secret ballot (versus customary decision-making procedures)

39.5   – Must provide government officials to be in attendance at such a meeting

:

42.5   a. Sweeping Powers over administering the will of Indians, and over the estate of Indians who die with or without a will

51.   b. Sweeping powers also over the property of 'mentally incompetent' Indians

52.   and over the property of Indian children.

EXPENDITURE

66.3   With/without band council approval, expend revenue moneys of the band for certain purposes
e.g. weed control; disease control; to provide for sanitary conditions in private or public premises on reserve

71.2   Minister may apply any reserve farm profits "in any way that he considers to be desirable to promote the progress and development of the Indians"

ELECTIONS

74.1   Call an election "whenever he deems it advisable for the good government of a band"

BY-LAWS

82.2   Disallowance of band by-laws (for any reason)

Remuneration to Chief and Council
83.1d   – Minister must approve the rate of remuneration.

EDUCATION

115.a   May make regulations regarding standards for school buildings, teachers, education, discipline, etc.

May require an Indian who becomes 16 to continue to attend school up to age 18.

STUDENT REPLY CARD

In order to improve future editions, we are seeking your comments on

FIRST NATIONS IN CANADA by J. Rick Ponting

After you have read this text, please answer the following questions and return this form via Business Reply Mail. *Your opinions matter. Thank you in advance for your feedback!*

Name of your college or university:

Major program of study:

Course title:

Were you required to buy this book?   yes ___   no _____

Did you buy this book new or used?   new _____   used ____ ($___)

Do you plan to keep or sell this book? keep _____   sell _____

Is the order of topic coverage consistent with what was taught in your course?

Are there chapters or sections of this text that were not assigned for your course? Please specify:

Were there topics covered in your course that are not included in this text? Please specify:

What did you like most about this text?

What did you like least?

If you would like to say more, we'd love to hear from you. Please write to us at the address shown on the reverse of this card.